I-CAR
PROFESSIONAL
AUTOMOTIVE
COLLISION
REPAIR

Delmar Publishers' Online Services

To access Delmar on the World Wide Web, point your browser to:

http://www.delmar.com/delmar.html

To access through Gopher: gopher://gopher.delmar.com

(Delmar Online is part of "thomson.com", an Internet site with information on more than 30 publishers of the International Thomson Publishing organization.)

For information on our products and services:

email: info @ delmar.com

or call 800-347-7707

I-CAR PROFESSIONAL AUTOMOTIVE COLLISION REPAIR

JAMES E. DUFFY

Delmar Publishers

I(T)P An International Thomson Publishing Company

Albany • Bonn • Boston • Cincinnati • Detroit • London • Madrid • Melbourne
Mexico City • New York • Pacific Grove • Paris • San Francisco • Singapore • Tokyo
Toronto • Washington

NOTICE TO THE READER

Cover design courtesy of Printup Graphic Design.

Cover photos courtesy of Audi of America and Snap-On Tools Corporation.

Delmar Staff:
Publisher: Susan Simpfenderfer
Administrative Editor: Vernon Anthony
Project Manager: Patricia Konczeski
Production Coordinator: Dianne Jensis
Art/Design Coordinator: Cheri Plasse
Marketing Manager: Lisa Reale

COPYRIGHT © 1996
By Delmar Publishers
a division of International Thomson Publishing

The ITP logo is a trademark under license

Printed in the United States of America

For more information, contact:

Delmar Publishers
3 Columbia Circle, Box 15015
Albany, New York 12212-5015

International Thomson Publishing Europe
Berkshire House 168 - 173
High Holborn
London WC1V7AA
England

Thomas Nelson Australia
102 Dodds Street
south Melbourne, 3205
Victoria, Australia

Nelson Canada
1120 Birchmount Road
Scarborough, Ontario
Canada M1K5G4

International Thomson Editores
Campos Eliseos 385, Piso 7
Col Polanco
11560 Mexico D F Mexico

International Thomson Publishing GmbH
Königswinterer Strasse 418
53227 Bonn
Germany

International Thomson Publishing Asia
221 Henderson Road
#05 - 10 Henderson Building
Singapore 0315

International Thomson Publishing - Japan
Hirakawacho Kyowa Building, 3F
2-2-1 Hirakawacho
Chiyoad-ku, Tokyo 102
Japan

3 4 5 6 7 8 9 10 X X X 01 00 99 98

Library of Congress Cataloging-in-Publication Data

Duffy, James E.
    I-CAR professional automotive collision repair / James Duffy.
       p.   cm
    Includes index.
    ISBN 0-8273-6500-4 (alk. paper)
    1. Automobiles--Bodies--Maintenance and repair. I. Inter
-Industry Conference on Auto Collision Repair.   II. Title.
TL255.D84   1995
629.26'028'8--dc20   94-48561
                                                   CIP

CONTENTS

PREFACE

Since we are a "Nation On Wheels" and accidents happen, there is a great demand for properly trained auto body technicians. By learning the material in this book, you will be on your way to a rewarding career in collision repair.

This text was written to summarize the most important aspects of collision repair technology. You will learn the challenging methods used to properly repair cars and light trucks after accidents. No longer can the untrained "sledgehammer and anvil" layperson hope to repair lightly constructed high-tech vehicles.

Since you have limited time to learn a large amount of information, every effort has been made to streamline the learning process. The sentence structure, artwork, and layout of this book are designed to maximize learning. They present more information using less words and more illustrations.

This text defines technical terms the first time they are used and highlights them in *bold italics.* Since you must learn a "whole new collision repair language," understanding technical terms is critical to your success.

Since a "picture paints a thousand words" about this technology, an abundance of carefully selected illustrations have been used. Color use throughout the book increases the educational value of the artwork. This helps the student quickly grasp the content of the educational artwork.

The text contains special "Notes!" and "Warnings!" The *Notes* give important information that will help you complete a particular procedure will less difficulty. They help prevent errors that could damage the vehicle or tools. *Warnings* should be followed for working safely to prevent injury to yourself and others.

New coverage on hand and power tools, basic measurement skills, service manuals, fasteners, materials, liquid mask, fine line masking tapes, surface evaluation, sanding, scuffing, stripping, using paint mixing sticks, paint matching, waterbase paints, computerized estimating, entrepreneurship, and many other new topics are included.

The book summarizes what it takes to become a competent, certified collision repair technician. It is designed to help you pass ASE Certification Tests and is organized around NATEF competency tasks for collision repair technology.

The text now has a good mix of all types of questions—essay, fill-the-blank, true-false, multiple choice, and ASE style. It also has a list of technical terms that must be understood fully for efficient communication. Many chapters also have activities for outside learning tasks.

James E. Duffy
"A Fellow Educator"

CREDITS

Please support all of these companies that helped make this textbook possible:

Auto Manufacturers

American Honda Motor Co., Inc.
American Isuzu Motors Inc.
Audi of America
BMW of North America
British Leyland Motors, Inc.
Chrysler Corporation
Ford Motor Company
Hyundai Motor Co.
Infinity
Jaguar Motor Cars
Mazda Motors of America, Inc.
Mercedes-Benz of North America, Inc.
Mitsubishi Motor Sales of America
Nissan Motor Corp.
Peugeot
Porsche North America, Inc.
Range Rover
Saab Cars USA, Inc.
Saturn Corporation
Subaru of America and Fugi Industries, Ltd.
Toyota Motor Sales, U.S.A, Inc.
Volkswagen of America
Volvo of America

Collision Repair Related Companies

3M Automotive Trades Div.
AC—Delco
ADP Collision Estimating Services, Inc.
Alloy Rods Co.
Allstate Insurance Co.
American Family Insurance Co.
American Welding Society
Ammco Tools
AP Parts Co.

Applied Power, Inc.
Armstrong Bros. Tool Co.
Automotive International
Badger Air Brush Co.
BASF Corporation
Bear Automotive
Bee Line Co.
Belden Corp.
Bendix
Binks Manufacturing Company
Black & Decker, Inc.
Blackhawk Collision Repair, Inc. Subsidiary of Hein-Werner® Corporation
Body Shop Business Magazine
Bonney Tools
Borg-Warner Corp.
Car-O-Liner Company
Champion Spark Plug Co.
Chief Automotive Systems, Inc.
Chilton Book Company
Dana Corp.
Data Welder Inc.
Deere & Co.
Delco-Remy Div. of GMC
Detroit Art Services, Inc.
DeVilbiss Automotive Refinishing Products, Maumee, OH
DuPont
Dorman Products
Duro-Chrome Hand Tools
The Eastwood Company
Edelmann
Edu-Tech-A Division of Commercial Service Co.
E & L Instruments
Evercoat Fibreglass Co., Inc.
Fel-Pro Inc.
Firestone Tire and Rubber Co.
Florida Dept. of Vocational Education

FMC Automotive Equipment Division
Fram Corp.
Fred V. Fowler Co, Inc.
Gates Rubber Co.
General Tire & Rubber Co.
The Goodyear Tire & Rubber Co.
Gould Inc.
Gunk Chemical Div.
Hako
Hein-Werner® Corporation
Helicoil Fastening Systems Division
Helm Inc.
Hennessy Industries, Inc.
Hopkins Manufacturing Corporation
HTP America, Inc.
Hunter Engineering Company
Ingersoll-Rand Co.
John W. Hogg
Kansas Jack, Division Of Hein-Werner® Corporation
K-D Tool
Keller Crescent Co.
Kent-Moore
Killian Corp.
Klein Tools, Inc.
Kwick-Way Mfg. Co.
Lab Safety Supply, Inc., Janesville, WI
Lisle Corp.
The L.S. Starrett Company
Lyons Metals Co.
Maaco Auto Painting & Bodyworks
Mac Tools Inc.
Maremont Corp.
Marson Corp.
Mobil Oil Corp.
Mitchell International, Inc.
Moog Automotive Inc.
Morgan Mfg., Inc.
Motorola
Munsell Color Group
Mustang Monthly Magazine
National Institute for Automotive Service Excellence
NCG Company/Spotle Distributor
Norco Industries, Inc.
Norton Co.
Oatey Bond Tite
OTC A division of SPX Corporation
Owatonna Tool Co., A division of SPX Corporation
Parker Hannifin Corp.
Pavlick
Perfect Circle Dana Corp.
Plews
Posisnip
PPG Industries, Inc.
Precision Brand Products
Proto Tool Co.

Robert Bosch Corp.
Rotary Lift/A Dover Industries Co.
Sartorius
Sealed Power Corp.—Replacement Products Group
Seelye, Inc.
Sellstrom Mfg. Co.
Shell Oil Co.
Simpson Electric Co.
Sioux Tools, Inc.
SM Arnold
Snap-on Tools Corporation
Stanley Tools New Britain Connecticut 06050
State Farm Insurance Company
Steck Manufacturing Co., Inc.
Stewart-Warner
Sunnen Product Co.
Talsol Corporation
Team Management Network
Tech-Cor, Inc.
Texaco Inc.
Thatcham
3M Automotive Trades Division
TIF Instruments, Inc.
TRW Fasteners Division, Westminster MA and
    Roseville MI
U.S. Chemicals and Plastics, Inc. Canton, Ohio
U.S. Environmental Protection Agency
Vaco
Valvoline Oil Co.
Victor Gasket Co.
Weatherhead Co.
Wedge Clamp International, Inc.

Acknowledgments

The author and Delmar Publishers would like to thank the following reviewers for the comments and suggestions they offered during the development of this project. Our gratitude is extended to:

Jack D'Armond

Arthur Balthazar
Assabet Valley Regional Vocational School

John Brosda
Northern Alberta Institute of Technology

Kurt Carlson
Cape Cod Regional Technical High School

Tom Dykstra
Portage Central High School

Bruce Gamroth
Wyoming Technical Institute

Dennis V. Green
Cumberland/Perry Vocational Technical School

Paul A. Jones

Yuma High School
Mike Jund
Scott Community College
John B. Kelly, Jr.
Southern Georgia Technical Institute
Duane G. Kimball
Shreveport-Bossier Regional Technical Institute
Kurt A. Luethy
Pickens Tech
Darrel Lee Luna
Neosho County Community College
John J. Macko
Pennsylvania College of Technology
John Marhefka
Lenape A.V.T.S.
Maurice Mires
Cass Career Center
Dan Mullins
Mid-East Ohio Vocational School District
Michael Netzinger
Hennepin Technical College
Patrick J. O'Boyle

Schuylkill County A.V.T.S.
Charles Parke
Boise State University
Jim Phillips
Hawkeye Community College
Joel T. Sabella
Trumbull County Joint Vocational School
Danna Snyder
Hewes Education Center
Norman States
York County A.V.T.S.
Philip C. Volpe
Craig Automotive Resources
Steve White
Portland Community College

Special Thanks

The author would like to thank I-CAR Tech Center for its technical-editorial supervision on this project.

For their patience and help, a very special thanks goes out to my "soul mate," Jeanette Joy Duffy, and children—Danielle, Jimmy, and Derrick.

Figures courtesy of Delmar Publishers Inc., 1992, I-CAR Unibody Collision Repair:
2–4, 2–5, 2–17, 4–23, 4–24, 5–8, 5–9, 5–24, 7–2, 7–4, 7–5, 7–19, 8–15, 9–1, 9–3, 9–4, 9–5, 9–6, 9–7, 9–12, 9–14, 9–15, 9–18, 9–19, 9–22, 9–23, 9–25, 9–26, 9–27, 9–35, 9–37, 9–38, 9–39, 9–40, 10–2, 10–4, 10–5, 10–6, 10–7, 10–8, 10–9, 10–11, 10–12, 10–13, 10–14, 10–15, 10–16, 10–17, 10–18, 10–19, 10–20, 10–22, 10–23, 10–24, 10–28, 10–29, 10–30, 11–4, 11–6, 11–7, 11–8, 11–11, 11–12A & B, 11–14, 11–15, 11–18, 12–6, 13–4, 13–5, 13–10, 13–11, 13–12, 13–13, 13–15, 13–16, 13–18, 13–21, 14–1, 14–2C, 14–5, 14–6, 14–7, 14–8, 14–9, 14–11, 14–12C, 14–13, 14–15, 14–16, 14–17, 14–19, 14–20, 14–21, 14–22, 15–2, 15–3, 15–6, 15–7, 15–8, 15–10, 15–11, 15–12, 15–20, 15–21, 15–22, 15–23, 15–25, 16–1, 16–2, 16–3, 16–8, 16–10, 16–11, 16–12, 16–14, 16–15, 16–16, 16–17, 16–18, 16–19, 16–21, 16–22, 16–23, 16–24, 16–25, 16–26, 16–27, 16–28, 16–29, 17–4, 18–27, 18–31, 20–21, 20–22, 20–23, 20–24, 20–27, 20–28, 20–29, 20–33, 20–38, 20–39, 20–43, 20–47, 20–52, 20–53, 21–52, 22–2, 22–12, 22–14, 22–31, 24–10, 25–9, 25–25, 25–26, 26–25, 26–28, 26–31, 28–18, 28–19, 28–20

Figures courtesy of Delmar Publishers Inc., 1992, Scharff, Motor Auto Body Repair 2/E:
14–2, 20–3, 20–4, 20–5, 20–6, 20–7, 20–8, 20–9, 20–10, 20–11, 20–12, 20–13, 20–14, 20–15, 20–16, 20–17, 20–18, 20–19, 21–1, 21–3, 21–4, 21–5, 21–8, 21–9, 21–38, 21–40, 21–47, 21–52, 21–62, 21–63, 21–67

Figures courtesy of Delmar Publishers Inc., 1992, Busch, Fundamentals of Dimensional Metrology:
6–5, 6–6, 6–10

FUNDAMENTALS

Body Shop

CHAPTER 1

INDUSTRY OVERVIEW, CAREERS

Objectives

After studying this chapter, you should be able to:

- Summarize the collision repair industry.

- List the related skills needed to become a good body shop employee.

- Explain the typical movement of a vehicle through a body shop.

- Summarize the major areas of repair in a body shop.

- Describe basic procedures for repairing a collision damaged vehicle.

- Know the meaning of being a true professional technician.

- Identify the setup and inner workings of a typical collision repair shop and its various personnel.

Introduction

This chapter will overview the collision repair industry. It will build the "framework of knowledge" needed to fully understand later text chapters. Its content will also help you learn the basic terminology and repair methods of this field. You will, on paper, follow damaged vehicles and shop personnel through a typical process of estimating, parts ordering, structural repair, painting, detailing, and final delivery to the customer. See Figure 1–1.

Considering we are a "nation on wheels," you have selected an excellent area of employment to study. The skills you learn will be in high demand as long as there are people driving cars and trucks.

Figure 1-1 Various construction methods and designs are used in modern cars. To be a successful auto body technician, you must be well educated and knowledgeable in various areas of automotive technology. A: This car uses flexible door or side panels that resist dents. It is a front-engine, front-wheel drive car. *(1993 Saturn, Courtesy of Saturn Corporation.)* B: This sports car is made of high strength steel. It is a front-engine, rear-wheel drive vehicle. *(Courtesy of General Motors Corporation)* C: This is a future car or design study done to help manufacturers plan new models. *(Used with permission of Nissan Motor Corporation)* D: This is an ultra light experimental vehicle. It uses exotic plastics and composite materials to reduce weight and improve fuel economy and performance. Unique body repair methods would be needed with these materials when damaged. *(Courtesy of General Motor Corporation)*

HISTORY NOTE

Did you know that the first self-propelled vehicle was in an accident the very first time it was driven? The huge steam engine powered car, trying to avoid a horse drawn carriage, crashed into a brick wall. The vehicle, the brick wall, and its driver were all "hurt." As this first crash of the first motor vehicle, on its first drive points out, there will always be accidents and a need for well trained collision repair technicians.

COLLISION REPAIR TECHNICIAN

Collision repair technicians are skilled, knowledgeable people that know how to use specialized equip-

ment and highly technical methods to restore severely damaged vehicles. A collision repair technician must be a "jack-of-all-trades." He or she must possess the basic skills in the following areas:

1. *Metalworker*—A collision repair technician must be able to do all types of metalworking to properly form and shape sheet metal car bodies after an accident.

2. *Welder*—A collision repair technician must weld and cut steel and plastic efficiently during major body repairs.

3. *Auto repair technician*—A collision repair technician must remove and install mechanical systems, requiring some skill in automotive repair technology.

4. *Sculptor*—A collision repair technician must form plastic filler to match body shape, much like a sculptor shapes a piece of art.

5. *Plumber*—A collision repair technician must work with numerous lines, hoses, and fittings during power steering, brake system, and fuel system service.

6. *Electrician*—A collision repair technician must be good at testing and repairing wiring and electrical components after damage. Finding shorts, opens, and other wiring problems is essential to today's computer-controlled vehicles.

7. *Air Conditioning Technician*—A collision repair technician may be required to work on air conditioning systems.

8. *Computer Technician*—A collision repair technician should be able to scan and repair computer problems stemming from collision damage.

As this points out, today's collision repair technician must be a highly skilled professional. The day of the "Mud Builder" or "Parts Replacer" is over. Low skilled people can no longer survive and earn a living with modern, complex automotive technology.

OTHER PERSONNEL

The collision repair and paint technicians are the principals in any collision repair business. However, there are other jobs that must be done as well. The following describes other personnel that work in and with the collision repair shop.

The *shop owner* must be concerned with all phases of work performed. In smaller shops, the owner and shop manager are usually the same person. In large operations or dealerships, the owner might hire a shop manager. In all cases, the person in charge should understand all of the work done in the shop as well as its business operations.

The *shop supervisor* is in charge of the everyday operation of the shop. This job involves communication with all personnel that contribute to the body shop's success.

The *parts manager* is in charge of ordering all parts (both new and salvaged), receiving all parts, and seeing that they are delivered to the ordering technician. Since not every collision repair shop has an actual parts manager, the task of ordering parts can fall on each employee at one time or another.

The *bookkeeper* keeps the shop's books, prepares invoices, writes checks, pays bills, makes bank deposits, checks bank statements, and takes care of tax payments. Many shops hire an outside accountant to perform these tasks.

The *office manager's* duties include various aspects of the business such as handling letters, estimates, and receipts. In many small shops, the office manager also acts as the parts manager and bookkeeper.

A *receptionist* is sometimes employed to greet customers, answer the phone, route messages, and do other tasks.

A "helper" is an apprentice-type worker that learns new jobs while helping experienced personnel. He or she might help a technician mask a car before painting, run for parts, or help clean up the work area at the end of the day.

THE PROFESSIONAL

The term "professional" refers to the attitude, work quality, and image that a business and its workers project to customers. It is interesting to note that in Europe a shop cannot open without the presence of a "Meister" or "master" craftperson. A professional:

1. Is customer oriented.

2. Is up-to-date on vehicle developments.

3. Keeps up with advancements in the repair industry.

4. Pays attention to detail.

5. Ensures that his/her work is up-to-specs.

6. Participates in trade associations.

NOTE! OTHER AREAS OF EMPLOYMENT IN COLLISION REPAIR ARE SUMMARIZED THROUGHOUT THIS TEXTBOOK.

WHAT IS COLLISION REPAIR?

Collision repair involves fixing damage after a vehicle has been in a wreck or accident. Another term for collision repair is "auto body repair." Collision repair involves restoring the damaged vehicle back to its original condition, structurally and cosmetically. Refer to Figure 1–2.

With minor damage, this can be as simple as replacing a bumper or a grille, or fixing a small dent. With major damage, this can be a complicated process, requiring that you partially disassemble the vehicle, use frame straightening equipment, welding equipment, paint spraying equipment, and other specialized tools.

Many of the *mechanical systems*, including the steering, braking, and suspension components, can also be damaged in an accident. They too can require service by the collision repair technician.

Figure 1–2 During a collision, severe structural damage often occurs to the body, frame, mechanical, and electrical components in or near the impact area. (© American Honda Motor Co., Inc.)

Figure 1–3 Auto manufacturers are using more and more exotic materials in the design and construction of their vehicles. This increases the challenge to today's body technician. (Courtesy of General Motors Corporation)

Figure 1–4 When being manufactured, automated equipment normally assembles and welds the body structure to help form the frame. Because of this, collision damage repair can be very challenging. (Courtesy of General Motors Corporation)

WHAT IS A COLLISION?

A *collision,* commonly called a "crash" or "wreck," is accidental damage caused by an impact on the vehicle body and chassis. Since cars can weigh over a ton, metal parts can be crushed, bent, and torn. Plastic parts can be broken and deformed. The frame might even be forced out of alignment, all resulting from the tremendous force that can result from an accident.

The direction of impact, force of impact, type of body structure, and other factors are all important. For example, damage might have resulted when two vehicles hit each or when a vehicle hit a stationary object laying in or along the road. This kind of information can be useful to the estimator, body technician, insurance company, and police department.

A collision might be as minor as a "door ding" where someone accidentally opened their door and hit another car. Or, it might be severe enough of an accident to cause a "total loss," where repairs would be more expensive than the cost of buying another car. The insurance company would NOT pay for repairs but would give the driver enough money to purchase a similar year, make, and model vehicle.

VEHICLE CONSTRUCTION BASICS

Vehicle construction deals with how the factory made or manufactured the car or truck. There are many construction variations, as shown in Figure 1–3.

As a technician, you must understand construction differences. This information will greatly affect how you repair a vehicle. Various types of metal (steel, aluminum, stainless steel), plastics, and composite materials, in numerous combinations, are used in cars today. This makes the job of the body technician very challenging. Look at Figure 1–4.

NOTE! CHAPTER 3, VEHICLE CONSTRUCTION, WILL EXPLAIN HOW A CAR OR TRUCK IS MADE IN MORE DETAIL. REFER TO THIS CHAPTER FOR MORE INFORMATION ON THIS TOPIC IF NEEDED.

Frame and Body

The *frame* is usually a high strength metal structure used to support other parts of the vehicle. It holds the engine, transmission, suspension, and other parts in position. The frame can be separate from the body or the body can be welded together to form the frame. See Figure 1–5.

The vehicle *body* is a steel, aluminum, fiberglass, plastic, or composite skin forming the outside of the car. The body is normally painted to give the vehicle its attractive, shiny, colored appearance.

Figure 1–5 These are the two most common methods of frame construction. A: With unibody construction, the body structure is formed to provide a stiff, strong frame structure. This is the most common design used on passenger cars. *(© American Honda Motor Co., Inc.)* B: The separate frame was first used on the Model-T. Because of its strength, the full frame can still be found on many large luxury cars and trucks.

Frame Types. A *full frame* is a strong, thick steel structure that extends from the front to the rear of the vehicle. It is used on many full size cars and trucks. The frame serves as a foundation for the body and drive train.

Unibody describes a vehicle that has the body structure welded together to form an integral frame structure. Also called *space frame* or *unitized construction,* this is the most common type of body configuration. Unibody construction reduces weight, improves fuel economy, and has a high strength-to-weight ratio. Study Figure 1–6.

With unibody construction, other body parts (fenders, bumpers, etc.) bolt to the unibody frame structure. All parts, even the engine, work together to help give the frame and body its strength, Figure 1–7.

Parts and Components

The term "part" or "component" generally refers to the smallest units on a vehicle. An *assembly* is several parts that fit together to make up a more complex unit. For example, a car bumper assembly might be made up of several parts—bumper frame, bumper cover, bumper brackets, etc. Some of the basic parts of a car body are shown in Figure 1–8.

Figure 1–6 Three photos show different views of how car is made. *(Courtesy of Ford Motor Company)* A: Car body provides attractive exterior. It can be made of steel, Fiberglass, plastics, and composite materials. B: Body has been sectioned away to show engine and other mechanical–electrical assemblies under body. C: This view shows the power train for the same car. It is a front-engine, rear-wheel drive configuration.

Figure 1–7 Top view of unibody construction shows how structural members are added to support engine, suspension, and other mechanical systems. *(Courtesy of Ford Motor Company)*

Figure 1–8 Exploded view of car body shows various panels and pans. With this design, most of the panels are made of plastic. *(Used with permission of Nissan Motor Corporation)*

A *panel* is a general term that refers to a large removable body part. For example, a quarter panel is a large body section forming the rear side of the body over and behind the rear wheels. A rocker panel would be a body part along the bottom of a door opening.

Similarly, the term "pan" refers to a floor related component, front floor pan, rear floor pan. In auto body, the names of parts usually refers to the location and purpose of the part. This makes it relatively easy to remember automotive part names.

Chassis

The *chassis* includes everything under the body—suspension system, brake system, wheels and tires, steering system. It consists of the mechanical systems that support and power the car. Refer to Figure 1–9.

NOTE! THE CHASSIS IS EXPLAINED FURTHER IN CHAPTER 3, VEHICLE CONSTRUCTION AND CHAPTER 30, MECHANICAL REPAIRS.

SHOP OPERATIONS

Many types of personnel are involved in repairing a wrecked car. It is important for you to have a general idea of the duties of all personnel associated with a body shop. This will help you communicate and succeed on the job.

The next section of this chapter will explain the major tasks needed to fix a wrecked vehicle. Lets discuss what happens when a car is sent to be

Figure 1–9 Suspension and braking systems bolt directly to body with unitized construction. *(Courtesy of Ford Motor Company)*

repaired at a body shop after an accident, as shown in Figure 1–10.

Estimating

Estimating involves analyzing damage and calculating how much it will cost to repair the vehicle. It is critical that the quote on the repair is not too high nor too low. If too high, another shop with a lower bid will usually get the job. If too low, the shop's profits may not be enough to support the business. The shop could lose money!

In most shops, a well-trained *estimator* makes an appraisal of vehicle damage and determines the parts, materials, and labor needed to repair the vehicle to its original condition. This person must be well-versed in how cars and trucks are made. He or she must be good with numbers, computers, and communicating with people.

An *estimate*, also called *damage appraisal* or *physical damage report*, is a written or printed form that explains what must be done to repair the vehicle. The estimate must explain which parts can be repaired and which will require replacement, summarizing all aspects of the repair.

Manual estimating involves using an estimating sheet for writing out information about the vehicle, using crash estimating guides, and collision damage manuals to make the repair estimate. *Crash estimating books* and *collision damage manuals* contain vehicle identification information, the price of new parts, time needed to install the parts, refinishing or painting data, and other information. Refer to Figure 1–11A.

Computer estimating involves using electronic *hardware* (computer, printers, hard drives, CD-ROM drives) and *software* (floppy discs, computer programs, CDs) to speed up the estimating process. The estimator might use a hand-held unit to input which parts must be replaced or repaired. This saves time over writing the estimate out long hand. When this information is loaded into the office computer, the computer can streamline the estimating processes by automating many steps of writing the estimate, Figure 1–11B.

When making an estimate, the estimator must make sure no damage is overlooked. For example, with a major impact, he or she must check for damage to the chassis, engine, electrical system, and interior of the car. Many parts besides the body can be affected by a serious accident. Refer to Figure 1–12.

Most new cars now use an air bag. The *air bag system* uses impact sensors, the vehicle's on-board computer, an inflation module, and a nylon balloon in the steering column to protect the driver during a head-on collision. It can be expensive to service since the bag and all sensors often require replacement after inflation. The cost of the air bag system repair is another example of what must be considered when writing an estimate, Figure 1–13.

The estimate is usually given to the customer who turns the repair estimate into his or her insurance company. The insurance company will then select a

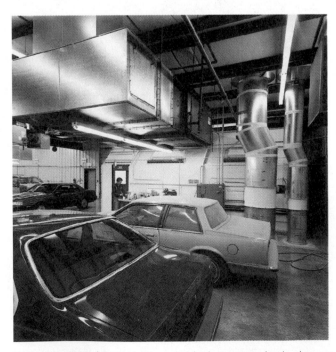

Figure 1–10 When a damaged vehicle enters a body shop, it goes through a series of preparation and repair steps to increase shop efficiency. *(Photo courtesy of Binks Manufacturing Company)*

A

B

Figure 1–11 Estimating is needed to find out how much the collision repair will cost the customer and insurance company. Most shops now use computer estimating to speed this process. *(Courtesy of Mitchell International, Inc.)* A: Various manuals are used by body shop personnel, stating part prices, labor time, body specs for frame straightening, and other data. B: Computerized estimating is a fast and efficient way of calculating repair costs. It is much more efficient than manual estimating.

A

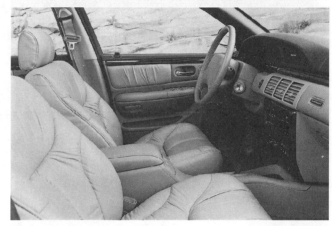

B

Figure 1–12 When making an estimate, estimator must also closely inspect for damage to all parts, not just body parts. A: Engine compartment can experience tremendous damage during frontal impact. The estimator must look for damage to the engine and its support systems. Wiring can also be damaged and must be accounted for in estimate. *(Courtesy of General Motors Corporation)* B: Interior can also be damaged in collision. Air bags can deploy. The steering wheel can be bent. A body can fly forward with enough force to damage the car's dashboard. Side impacts can also push a door into the passenger compartment, damaging seats and other parts. *(Courtesy of Chrysler Corporation)*

repair shop or give a check to the owner for completing the repair.

The *insurance adjuster* reviews the estimates and determines which one best reflects how the vehicle should be repaired. He or she may inspect the wrecked car to make sure the repairs will be done cost effectively.

Once the owner and/or the insurance company approves the repairs, the vehicle is turned over to the shop supervisor. The supervisor and sometimes a technician will then review the estimate to determine how to proceed with the repair.

Wash-up

When brought to the shop for repairs, the first step is wash-up. *Wash-up* involves a thorough cleaning of

the vehicle before beginning work. This is needed to remove mud, dirt, wax and water-soluble contaminants. These substances must be cleaned off before starting because they could contaminate your work area and the paint job. The car or truck must be completely dry before being moved to the metalworking area.

Bodywork

The *bodywork area* is where the vehicle body is repaired in the shop. The body damage can be either the result of a collision or deterioration. The repair tasks in this area of the shop are performed by colli-

A

B

C

Figure 1–13 Most new cars are equipped with air bags. A: Air bags deploy with frontal impact. Sensors detect impact and signal computer. Computer can then deploy air bag to help protect driver and passenger from injury. *(1993 Saturn, Courtesy of Saturn Corporation)* B: When deployed, driver and passenger side air bags prevent human body impact with dash and windshield. They deflate right after impact so driver can still see the road ahead if needed. *(Courtesy of General Motors Corporation)* C: Air bag module contains charge of pellets that produce gas pressure when electrically energized. *(Courtesy of General Motors Corporation)*

sion repair technicians and their helpers. Refer to Figure 1–14.

Depending upon the severity of the damage, you might have to remove and replace parts or simply use hand tools to work out small sheet metal dents.

Minor Repairs

Minor repairs are those that require minimum time and effort. Small dents, paint scratches, and damaged trim are typical examples. They require moderate skill and the use of hand tools, power tools, and body shop tools.

Hand tools generally include general tools used by both auto mechanics and auto body technicians. They would include wrenches, screwdrivers, pliers, and other common tools. They are commonly used to remove parts, fenders, doors, and similar assemblies.

Power tools use air pressure or electrical energy to aid repairs. This classification includes air wrenches, air and electric drills, sanders, and similar tools.

Body shop tools are most the specialized tools designed for working with body parts. A few are shown in Figure 1–15. They can be used to cut metal, hammer out small dents, and do similar tasks.

Panel straightening involves using various hand tools and equipment to bend or shape the panel back into its original contour. Dollies, body hammers, plastic filler, and sanders are a few of the tools and materials used to fix metal panel damage. Similar techniques are needed with plastic panels.

Panel replacement involves removing and installing a new panel or body part. You might have

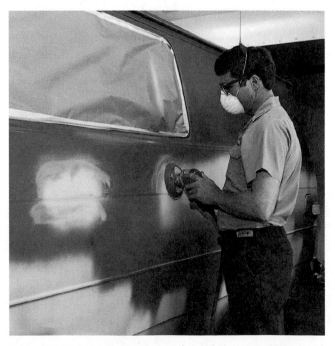

Figure 1–14 Minor body repair often involves using metalworking tools, plastic body filler and air sander to remove small dents. Here, technician has already masked windows and is using air sander to smooth surface on side of van. *(PPG Industries, Inc.)*

to unbolt and replace a fender, door, or spoiler, for example, Figure 1–16. With quarter panels and other welded body sections, you will have to cut off the damaged panel with power tools and then use a welder to install the new panel. This takes considerable skill.

Major Repairs

Major repairs is a general category that typically involves replacement of large body sections and frame straightening. To begin a major repair, you must normally remove severely damaged body

Figure 1–15 Many kinds of tools and equipment must be mastered in auto body repair. *(© The Eastwood Company—Used with permission)* A: Technician is using drill powered nibbler to cut off rusted section of body. B: This tool can be used to pop out minor dents. C: Special pliers are designed to fold metal over door frame during door skin replacement. D: Welding and cutting equipment is also needed to repair severe body damage.

Figure 1–16 Panel replacement sometimes is as simple as unbolting a part, like this fender. However, with welded-on panels the repair can be more time consuming. (Chief Automotive Systems, Inc.)

Figure 1–17 Major repairs typically involve replacement of large body sections and frame straightening. Before frame straightening, fenders, hood, and other parts must often be removed.

parts, like fenders, bumpers, etc. Then you can measure at specific body points to analyze the damage. See Figure 1–17.

Measurement systems allow you to check for frame or body misalignment resulting from a major collision. Various types of gauges and measuring devices can be used to compare known good body specs with the actual body measurements. The measurements will help you find out what must be done to straighten any frame or body misalignment. Study Figure 1–18.

Once you have measured to find the extent and direction of frame misalignment, you can use frame straightening equipment to pull the frame back into alignment.

Frame straightening equipment, also called a *frame rack,* uses a large steel framework, pulling chains, and hydraulic power to pull or force the frame back into its original position. The vehicle frame or body is clamped down onto the frame straightening equipment so it cannot move. Chains are then fastened to the damaged portion of the vehicle. Then, tremendous pulling hydraulic force is applied to the chains to pull the frame or body in the opposite direction of deformation. See Figure 1–19.

After pulling, more measurements are taken to determine if everything is returned to specs. If not, frame rails and other body sections may have to be cut off and replaced, as shown in Figure 1–20.

Figure 1–18 Measuring system is used to check location of specified points on frame or body structure. This will tell you if and how frame is bent so you can proceed with repairs. (Chief Automotive Systems, Inc.)

proofing is often a joint job of both the collision repair and paint technicians. Discussed later in this book, there are various methods of corrosion protection. Refer to Figure 1–21.

Corrosion Protection

Corrosion protection involves using various methods to protect steel body parts from rusting. When doing repairs, you must always use recommended methods of protecting repair areas from rust damage. Rust

Surface Preparation

Surface preparation or "surface prep" involves inspection and treatment of the old surface to prepare it for refinishing or painting. It is needed to make sure the repairs and new paint will hold up over time.

Figure 1–19 Frame rack or frame straightening equipment is very powerful. It will pull bent body or frame back to its original position. It takes considerable training and skill to use frame straightening equipment. *(Chief Automotive Systems, Inc.)*

Figure 1–20 When pulling with a rack, you may have to use heat to aid part straightening. If the part cannot be straightened, it must be cut off and a new piece sectioned or welded into place. *(Chief Automotive Systems, Inc.)*

Begin with *surface inspection* which involves looking closely at the old body surface to determine its condition. This will let you decide what must be done to the old surface to prepare it for a new layer of paint. Figure 1–22 shows a technician wiping down a car with cleaning agent while inspecting it for problems.

On one extreme, you might only have to sand the surface to ready it for painting. On the other extreme, if the old paint is cracked and peeling, you may need to strip off the old paint. *Stripping* is done by applying a chemical paint remover to soften and lift off the old paint. Stripping can also be done using air powered blasting equipment.

Discussed in later chapters, there are other methods of surface preparation before refinishing.

Sanding uses an abrasive coated paper or plastic backing to level and smooth a body surface being repaired. Sanding with coarse, rough paper might be

Figure 1–21 When doing body work, you must restore the manufacturer's rust or corrosion protection materials. Here, technician is spraying undercoating onto a freshly repaired door. *(3M Automotive Trades Division)*

done to level plastic filler. Sanding with fine, smooth paper might also be done to lightly scuff the old paint so the new paint will stick.

Paint Preparation

Paint preparation, or "paint prep" gets the vehicle ready for spraying or refinishing. During paint prep, you must:

1. Remove windshield wipers, emblems, nameplates, mirrors, and other trim pieces.
2. Clean the vehicle exterior by wiping down each area to be painted with an approved cleaning agent. This will remove grease, road tar, wax, and petroleum-based contaminants from the surface.
3. Machine and/or hand-sand chips and scratches.

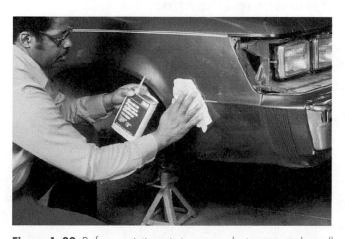

Figure 1–22 Before painting, it is extremely important that all surfaces to be sprayed are perfectly clean. Cleaning agents are available to remove wax, grease, oil, and other contaminants. *(3M Automotive Trades Division)*

4. Clean the interior carefully to remove all dust and dirt.

5. Double-check that all surfaces are properly cleaned before masking.

6. Closely inspect all surfaces to be painted for any remaining imperfections. Correct any surface problems you find!

NOTE! IF THE CAR OR TRUCK WENT THROUGH INITIAL CLEAN-UP, SOME OF THESE STEPS, SUCH AS INTERIOR CLEAN-UP, CAN BE IGNORED.

Masking

Masking protects surfaces and parts from paint overspray. Masking protects the parts of the vehicle such as windows, chrome, lights, and vinyl tops. Masking is done by placing special tape, paper, or plastic over areas NOT to be painted.

Masking can also be done by spraying a special water-soluble material over surfaces not to be painted. The masking material can then be washed off with soap and water after painting. Refer to Figure 1–23.

The *masking area* in the shop is usually equipped with masking paper and tape dispensers, tire covers, and other needed materials.

Paint overspray is an unwanted paint mist that spreads away from the surface being painted. It can stick to any uncovered or unmasked surface. Considerable time can then be wasted trying to clean off surfaces coated with a paint overspray. Masking is an important step before priming and painting.

Refinishing (Painting)

Refinishing or *painting* basically involves applying primer and paint over the properly prepared vehicle body. It is the most visible aspect of collision repair. Although it does not affect vehicle safety, it does affect your customer's evaluation of the repair because he or she can easily see paint defects. See Figure 1–24.

Not only do wrecked vehicles have to be painted, but older vehicles with weathered paint need refinishing to enhance their beauty. Sometimes the owner gets tired of looking at the same old color.

The *paint shop area* is where the vehicle is refinished. Here, a series of operations is performed on the vehicle to make sure the paint looks good and holds up over time.

Priming is primarily done to help smooth the body surface and help the top coats of paint adhere or stick

Figure 1–23 Masking involves covering any surface or part not to be painted. This technician is using high skill, custom masking techniques to paint pin stripes on vehicle. *(Badger Air Brush Co.)*

to the body. It is done before painting. Discussed in later chapters, various types of primer and other pre-painting steps may be required.

Paint selection involves finding out what type of paint materials must be used on the specific vehicle. It must be done properly to make sure the new paint matches the old (panel repair) and to assure long paint life. The technician must determine what kind of paint is on the car and then select the right paint for the job.

Paint mixing involves blending the paint and thinner or reducer to the correct thickness or *viscosity*.

Figure 1–24 When painting, technician must wear safety gear to keep chemicals off body and out of the lungs. Air powered spray gun is used to apply thin, even coats of primer and then paint. Note how lights and tire have been masked. *(PPG Industries, Inc.)*

Figure 1–25 Custom painting takes special talent and experience. Here, painter is using star-shaped mask and small air brush type spray gun to produce special paint effects. *(Badger Air Brush Co.)*

Figure 1–26 Wet sanding will smooth painted surface and is often used to remove small imperfections in freshly painted surfaces. Fine, waterproof sandpaper and water are used to smooth top of paint. *(Badger Air Brush Co.)*

Instructions on the paint will give information about the type of materials and ratio of paint-to-reducer or thinner required. Proper paint mixing is critical to how the paint flows out of the paint gun and onto the body. Incorrect mixing makes it impossible to do a good paint job.

Spraying is the physical application of paint using a paint spray gun. The technician methodically moves the spray gun next to the body while spraying accurate layers of paint onto the body. This requires a high degree of skill to prevent *paint runs* (excess paint thickness flows down or runs) and other painting problems.

When the vehicle moves into the spray booth, the painter takes over. Final cleaning is done at this point. Masking is removed after the paint has completely dried.

Custom painting involves forming various designs into the paint. Precut mask designs, air brush work, pin striping, and other techniques can be used with custom painting. See Figure 1–25.

Drying

Drying involves using different methods to cure the fresh paint. If only partially dry when returned to the customer, the new paint can be easily damaged.

Air drying is done by simply letting the paint dry in the atmosphere. This can take a long time with enamel if a hardening agent is not added to the paint.

Forced drying uses special heat lamps or other equipment to speed the paint curing process. Most shops use drying equipment to speed up drying. This

is especially useful in drying today's paints. Drying equipment designs vary.

Post-painting Operations

Post-painting operations include the tasks that must be done after painting and before returning the vehicle to the customer. This would include removal of masking tape, reinstalling parts, and cleaning of the vehicle.

Two simple examples are the common paint problems called *orange peel* and *paint runs.* If the painted surface has "orange peel" or a rough textured surface like the fruit peeling on an orange, you may have to wet sand the hardened paint, Figure 1–26. This will knock off the tiny bumps in the paint and smooth them out. A paint run results when too much paint is applied, too quickly. The thick wet coating of paint runs down or sags and then hardens into a large lump.

Wet sanding involves using a water resistant, ultra-fine sandpaper and water to level the paint. It can sometimes be done to fix small imperfections (orange peel, runs, etc.) in the paint. Wet sanding and buffing can also be done to a good paint job to make it even better looking.

Compounding or *buffing* is done to smooth newly painted surfaces, after wet sanding for example, or to remove a thin layer of old, dull paint. See Figure 1–27. It will make the paint smooth and shiny. An air or electric buffing machine equipped with a pad is used

Figure 1-27 After wet sanding on oxidized, dull paint, buffing with compound can restore the shine. *(Badger Air Brush Co.)*

to apply buffing compound to the paint. The abrasive action cuts off a thin layer of top coat to brighten the color and shine the paint.

Detailing is a final clean-up and touch-up on the vehicle. It involves washing any unpainted body sections, cleaning and vacuuming the interior, touching up any chips in sections not painted, and other tasks to improve vehicle cosmetics. Detailing can also involve other tasks such as polishing chrome, cleaning glass, installing trim, and cleaning the vinyl top and tires. This will ready the car or truck for return to the customer.

Mechanical-electrical Repairs

Mechanical repairs include tasks like replacing a damaged water pump, radiator, or engine bracket, for example. Mechanical components like these are often damaged in a major collision. Many mechanical parts are easy to replace and can be done by the auto body technician. However, other mechanical repairs may require special skills and tools. In this case, the vehicle would be sent to a professional mechanic. Refer to Figure 1-28.

Electrical repairs include tasks like repairing severed wiring, replacing engine sensors, and scanning for computer or wiring problems. During a collision, the impact on the vehicle body and the resulting metal deformation can easily crush wires and electrical components. For this reason, today's auto body technician must have basic skills needed to work with and repair electrical-electronic components.

NOTE! SEVERAL CHAPTERS IN THIS BOOK ARE DEVOTED TO HELPING YOU LEARN TO WORK ON MECHANICAL AND ELECTRICAL SYSTEMS.

Figure 1-28 Mechanical repairs are sometimes done in larger body shops. *(Hunter Engineering Company)* A: Alignment rack has all of the equipment needed to check and correct alignment of wheels. This is often needed after major repairs. B: Technician is under car making adjustments to steering and suspension systems to realign wheels.

BODY SHOP CLASSIFICATIONS

There are several ways to classify a body shop. A few of the most common will be discussed.

An *independent body shop* is one owned and operated by a private individual. The shop is NOT associated with other shops or companies.

A *franchise body shop* is tied to a main headquarters which regulates and aids the operation of the shop. The shop logo, materials used, costing, etc. are all set by the headquarters and the franchise must follow these guidelines.

A *dealership body shop* is owned and managed under the guidance of a new car dealership-Ford, GM, Chrysler, Toyota, etc. This type of shop often concentrates on repairs of the specific make of cars sold by the dealership.

Figure 1–29 Body shop personnel, if properly trained, can earn a good living. If you study and learn the contents of this book, you are on your way to a solid career in auto body repair. (Photo courtesy of Binks Manufacturing Company)

A *progression shop* often has an assembly line type of organization with specialists in each area of repair. One person might do nothing but frame work. Another technician might be good at "building the body" or installing parts and panels. The shop might have a wheel alignment technician, prep people, painter, and clean-up specialists. The vehicle will move from one area and specialist to the next until fully repaired.

A *specialty shop* concentrates on and only does specific types of repairs. For example, the body shop might send a radiator with a small hole in it to a specialty radiator shop for repair with their specialized equipment.

Complete collision services means the body shop might do wheel alignments, cooling system repairs, electrical system diagnosis and repair, suspension system work, and other repairs. Today, more and more collision repair shops are offering complete collision services. Refer to Figure 1–29.

Summary

- Collision repair involves fixing structural damage after a vehicle has been in a wreck or accident. Another term for collision repair is auto body repair.
- The collision repair and paint technicians are the principals in any collision repair business. Other personnel include the shop owner, shop supervisor,

parts manager, bookkeeper, office manager, receptionist, and helper.

- A collision is accidental damage caused by an impact on the vehicle body and chassis.
- There are several ways to classify a body shop. A few of the most common are: independent, franchise, dealership, progression, specialty, and complete collision services.

Technical Terms

collision repair technician	hand tools
shop owner	power tools
shop supervisor	body shop tools
parts manager	panel straightening
bookkeeper	panel replacement
office manager	major repairs
helper	measurement systems
progression shop	frame rack
professional	corrosion protection
collision repair	surface inspection
mechanical systems	stripping
electrical systems	sanding
collision	"paint prep"
total loss	masking
vehicle construction	paint overspray
frame	refinishing
body	priming
full frame	paint selection
unibody	paint mixing
component	spraying
assembly	paint runs
panel	custom painting
pan	drying
chassis	air-drying
estimating	forced drying
damage appraisal	post-painting operations
manual estimating	orange peel
computer estimating	wet sanding
air bag system	compounding
insurance adjuster	detailing
wash-up	mechanical repairs
minor repairs	electrical repairs
	specialty shop

Review Questions

1. What happened to the first self-propelled vehicle?

2. _____ _____ _____ are skilled, knowledgeable people that know how to use specialized equipment and highly technical methods to restore severely damaged vehicles.

3. List and explain the basic skills often required of a body technician.

4. The term "professional" refers to the _____, _____, and _____ that a business and its workers project to customers.

5. List six traits of a professional technician.

6. Define the term "collision repair."

7. What is a "total loss?"

8. Explain the difference between the frame and body of a car.

9. _____ describes a vehicle that has the body structure welded together to form an integral frame structure. It is also called _____ or _____ construction.

10. This refers to several parts that fit together to make up a more complex unit.
    a. Chassis
    b. Component
    c. Assembly
    d. None of the above

11. _____ involves analyzing damage and calculating how much it will cost to repair the vehicle.

12. What is the job of the insurance adjuster?

13. _____ _____ involves using various hand tools and equipment to bend or shape the panel back into its original contour.

14. Why would you use a measurement system?

15. _____ _____ _____, also called a _____ _____, uses a large steel framework, pulling chains, and hydraulic power to pull or force the frame back into its original position.

16. Explain two ways to strip off deteriorated paint quickly.

17. Give two reasons for sanding a body surface.

18. List five steps that must be done during "paint prep."

19. Basically, how and why do you mask a car?

20. _____ _____ _____ means the body shop might do wheel alignments, cooling system repairs, electrical system repair, suspension system work, and other repairs.

Activities

1. Ask a technician or shop owner to visit your classroom. Ask him or her to describe their duties and other questions.

2. Make a field trip to a body shop. Have the shop owner or supervisor give you a guided tour of the shop. Discuss the field trip in class the next day.

3. Ask a parent, relative, or friend if they were in an accident. Have them describe what happened during and after the accident when trying to get the car repaired.

4. Go to the library and look up information on different types of insurance—full coverage, liability, no-fault. Prepare a report on this subject.

CHAPTER 2

SAFETY, CERTIFICATION

Objectives

After studying this chapter, you should be able to:

■ List the types of dangers and accidents common to a body shop.

■ Explain how to avoid shop accidents.

■ Outline the control measures needed when working with hazardous substances.

■ Summarize hand and power tool safety.

■ Describe safety practices designed to avoid fire and explosions.

■ Explain the benefits of ASE certification.

■ Summarize the purpose of I-CAR.

■ Know the sources of professional training and certification available to collision repair shop personnel.

Introduction

This chapter will summarize the most important safety rules for a collision repair shop. It will explain the types of accidents that can happen and describe how to prevent them.

Safety involves using proper work habits to prevent personal injury and property damage. Always keep in mind that a body shop can be a very dangerous place to work if safety rules are not followed. Carelessness and the lack of good work habits can be deadly in today's industry!

WHAT CAUSES ACCIDENTS?

Remember! Accidents don't just happen; people cause accidents!

Accidents are unplanned events that hurt people, break tools, damage vehicles, or have other adverse effects on the business and its employees. Since a body shop has so many potential sources of danger, safety must be your number one concern.

TYPES OF ACCIDENTS

Care must be taken to prevent several kinds of accidents including asphyxiation, chemical burns, electrocution, fires, and explosions.

Asphyxiation refers to anything that prevents normal breathing. There are many mists, gases, and fumes in a body shop that can damage your lungs and affect your ability to breathe.

Chemical burns result when a corrosive chemical injures your skin or eyes. They can result from several chemicals in a body shop—paint removers, part chemicals, etc.

Electrocution results when electricity passes through your body. Severe injury or death can result.

A *fire* is rapid oxidation of a flammable material, producing high temperatures. A burn from a fire can cause permanent scar tissue and death. There are numerous *combustibles* (paints, thinners, reducers, gasoline, dirty rags) in a body shop. Any can quickly cause a fire.

Explosions are air pressure waves that result from extremely rapid burning. For example, if you were to weld near a gas tank, it could explode. The fumes in the tank could ignite and the tank could blow open.

A *physical injury* is a general category that includes cuts, broken bones, strained backs, and similar injuries. To prevent these painful injuries, constantly think and evaluate each step. Always think about what you are doing and try to do it safely.

TEXTBOOK SAFETY

Thousands of auto body technicians are injured or killed every year. Broken safety rules cause most of these accidents. Don't learn to respect safety rules the difficult way—by experiencing a painful injury. Learn to respect safety the easy way—by studying this book and following known safety practices.

Note that other chapters in this text give more specialized safety rules and cautions. However, these safety rules are generic and cannot cover every challenge you will encounter in the body shop. For this reason, you must always refer to manufacturer's instructions when in doubt.

Manufacturer's instructions are very detailed procedures for the specific product. They will be written to guide you in the use of the exact item, whether it be a piece of equipment or a certain type of paint.

Always refer to manufacturer's instructions. They can be in the owner's instruction manual for tools and equipment. With paint and chemicals, they are normally printed on the container's label.

OVERALL SHOP SAFETY

True professionalism and shop safety begins with how a technician performs his/her given work tasks. A professional understands the ever-present dangers in a body shop and strives to avoid making dangerous mistakes.

When working in a body shop, you will be using air and electric tools, welders, cutting torches, hydraulic frame straightening equipment, and hazardous materials. If you do not know or do not follow correct methods, you or someone else may be seriously injured or even killed.

Accidents have a far-reaching effect, not only on the victim, but also on the victim's family and friends. Therefore, it is the obligation of all employees and the employer to develop a safety program. A *safety program* is a written shop policy designed to protect the health and welfare of personnel and customers. It includes rules on everything from equipment use to disposal of hazardous chemicals.

In an effort to maintain strict safety measures, customers should never be allowed into the shop's work areas.

SHOP LAYOUT AND SAFETY

The *shop layout* is the general organization or arrangement of work areas. For various safety reasons, you should fully understand the layout of your shop. This will help you learn fire exit routes, fire extinguisher locations, storage areas, and other information to make you a better worker. Study the typical auto body shop layout in Figure 2–1.

A body shop is typically divided into these work areas:

1. Metalworking area.
2. Repair stall.
3. Frame rack.
4. Front end rack (alignment rack).
5. Tool & equipment storage room.

Shop Floor Plan

Figure 2–1 Body shop layouts vary but most have these areas. Learn the layout of your shop. Memorize fire extinguisher locations and fire exit routes.

6. Classroom area.
7. Paint prep area.
8. Finishing or paint booth area.
9. Office.
10. Locker room.

The *metalworking area* is where parts are removed, repaired, and installed. This is the largest area in the shop where many tasks are performed. Dangers in this area are many and varied—cutting metal, welding, grinding, etc.

A *repair stall* is a work area for one vehicle. Also termed a *bay,* it is usually marked off with painted lines on the floor. The stall has room in the front, rear, and sides for working on the vehicle. Stalls are often marked off in metalworking and prep areas.

The *frame rack* is a large piece of equipment designed to straighten badly damaged vehicle structures. It has powerful hydraulic rams and arms that require skill, training, and safety for utilization. It can exert tons of pulling force that can maim or kill. If a frame rack chain were to come loose or break, it could fly out with a tremendously destructive force.

A *front end rack* or *alignment rack* is used to measure and adjust the steering and suspension of a vehicle after repairs. It is needed to make sure the wheels

are aligned to factory specs. Dangers result from driving vehicles up and onto the rack and from using the small *pneumatic* (air) or *hydraulic* (oil-filled) equipment.

The *tool & equipment storage room* is an area for safely keeping specialized tools and equipment. It might have a pegboard wall or shelves for keeping tools when not in use. Dangers result only if tools are not stored and maintained properly.

A *classroom* may be provided for lectures, demonstrations, and meetings of shop personnel. If you get along with your instructor or supervisor, it is a fairly safe place.

The *paint prep area* is where the vehicle is readied for painting or refinishing. The vehicle is cleaned and masked in this area.

The *finishing* or *spray booth area* is where the body is painted. It normally has a large metal enclosure to keep out dirt and circulate clean, fresh air.

The *body shop office* contains business equipment. This area keeps the shop financially sound. Office workers keep track of paper work, making sure estimates are accurate, bills are paid, parts are ordered, and that payroll checks go out.

The locker room is for cleaning up after work, for changing work clothes, and using the restroom.

As you will learn, specific rules apply to each shop area.

IN CASE OF AN EMERGENCY

Have a list of *emergency telephone numbers* clearly posted next to the shop's telephone. These numbers should include a doctor, hospital, and fire and police departments.

A *first aid kit* includes many of the medical items needed to treat minor shop injuries. It will have sterile gauze, bandages, scissors, band aids, antiseptics and other items to help treat minor cuts and burns. A fully stocked first aid kit should always be kept in a handy location, usually near the office or restroom.

Safety signs give information that helps to improve shop safety. Signs are often provided to denote fire exit and fire extinguisher locations, dangerous or flammable chemicals, and other information. Safety signs should be located throughout the shop.

WORK AREA SAFETY

It is very important that the work area be kept safe. This involves a "team effort" with everyone working in the shop.

Keep all surfaces clean, dry, and orderly. Wipe up any oil, coolant, or grease on the floor. If someone were to slip and fall, it could result in serious injuries.

Keep workbenches clean and orderly. When things are stacked on benches and tables, they can easily fall. Generally, they cause a cluttered work area, which invites injury.

Hang tools up or put them away when not in use. Roll up idle hoses and air lines so they do not create traffic hazards.

Floor jacks, bumper jacks, jack stands, and creepers should be kept in their designated area, out of aisles and walkways.

FIRE SAFETY

Gasoline is a highly flammable petroleum or crude oil based liquid that vaporizes and burns rapidly. Always keep gasoline and diesel fuel in approved safety cans. Never use them to wash hands or tools.

Oily, greasy, or paint-soaked rags should be stored in an approved metal container with a lid. When soiled rags are left lying about improperly, they are prime candidates for *spontaneous combustion* (fire that start by itself). See Figure 2–2.

Use only approved explosion-proof equipment in hazardous locations. A *UL* (Underwriters Laborato-

Figure 2–2 After use, always keep dirty rags in an approved metal can with a metal lid. This will help prevent a fire due to spontaneous combustion. *(Photo Courtesy of Lab Safety Supply, Inc., Janesville, WI)*

ries) approved drum transfer pump along with a drum vent should be used when working with drums to transfer chemicals.

Keep all solvent containers closed, when not in use. Handle all solvents and other liquids with care to avoid spillage.

Store paints, thinners, solvents, pressurized containers, and other combustible materials in approved and designated storage cabinets or rooms. Storage rooms should have adequate ventilation, Figure 2–3.

Discard or clean all empty solvent containers. Solvent fumes in the bottom of a container are prime ignition sources.

Figure 2–3 Store all flammable materials (paints, solvents, etc.) in a metal fire cabinet. Never leave them lying around the shop. *(Photo Courtesy of Lab Safety Supply, Inc., Janesville, WI)*

Never light matches or smoke in the paint spraying area! The paint mist and fumes are like a bomb ready to go off.

Use extra caution when transferring flammable materials from bulk storage. Keep the drum grounded so that static electricity cannot cause an explosion. Refer to Figure 2–4.

Vehicle batteries often explode! Hydrogen gas floating around vehicle batteries can cause the battery to go off like a small bomb. Flying chunks of plastic and sulfuric acid can shoot out, blinding or killing someone. Only charge batteries in a well-ventilated area.

Do not use torches or welding equipment at the mixing bench or in the paint area.

NEVER use automotive type paints on household items such as toys or furniture. This could pose a dangerous health hazard to children who might ingest the paint.

Trash and rubbish should be removed from the shop area regularly. If not, serious fire and work area dangers can result.

Keep used paper towels and other paper products in a covered container separate from other trash. Empty it every day. Keep broken glass and jagged metal in separate containers. Recycle them if feasible.

Hold a rag around a fuel line fitting when disconnecting it.

You must release fuel pressure on many fuel injected vehicles before working because they can retain fuel pressure. Disconnect the battery before working on a fuel system.

Keep gas cylinders away from sources of heat like a furnace or room heater.

Never drop a gas cylinder. The head could break off and fly out as if shot from a cannon. Shut off the main gas valve on top of the tank after use. If a hose leak develops, this can prevent a major explosion.

Electrical Fires

Electrical fires result when excess current causes wiring to overheat, melt and burn. This often results when a wire or wires are short to ground while doing electrical work or after the collision cuts through wire insulation. To prevent electrical fires, always disconnect the battery when doing electrical work or when body damage may have cut through wires.

Fire Extinguishers

A *fire extinguisher* is designed to quickly smother a fire. There are several types available for putting out different kinds of fires.

Know where the fire extinguishers are and what types of fires they put out, Figure 2–5.

A multi-purpose dry chemical fire extinguisher will put out ordinary combustibles, flammable liquids, and electrical fires. During a fire, a few seconds time can be a "lifetime" for someone.

Never smoke while working on any vehicle or machine in the shop. There are too many flammables that could start a fire in a body shop.

In case of a gasoline fire, do not put water on it. The water will spread the fire. Use a fire extinguisher to smother the flames. Never open doors or windows unless it is absolutely necessary. The air draft will only make the fire worse.

A good rule is to call the fire department first and then attempt to extinguish the fire. Standing 6 to 10 feet (2 to 3 meters) from the fire, hold the extinguisher firmly in the recommended position. Aim the nozzle at the base and use a side-to-side motion, sweeping the entire width of the fire.

Figure 2–4 Study proper method for transferring flammable liquids from bulk storage. Note ground wires.

GUIDE TO FIRE EXTINGUISHER SELECTION

	Class of Fire	Typical Fuel Involved	Type of Extinguisher
Class **A** Fires (green)	**For Ordinary Combustibles** Put out a class A fire by lowering its temperature or by coating the burning combustibles.	Wood Paper Cloth Rubber Plastics Rubbish Upholstery	Water*[1] Foam* Multipurpose dry chemical[4]
Class **B** Fires (red)	**For Flammable Liquids** Put out a class B fire by smothering it. Use an extinguisher that gives a blanketing, flame-interrupting effect; cover whole flaming liquid surface.	Gasoline Oil Grease Paint Lighter fluid	Foam* Carbon dioxide[5] Halogenated agent[6] Standard dry chemical[2] Purple K dry chemical[3] Multipurpose dry chemical[4]
Class **C** Fires (blue)	**For Electrical Equipment** Put out a class C fire by shutting off power as quickly as possible and by always using a nonconducting extinguishing agent to prevent electric shock.	Motors Appliances Wiring Fuse boxes Switchboards	Carbon dioxide[5] Halogenated agent[6] Standard dry chemical[2] Purple K dry chemical[3] Multipurpose dry chemical[4]
Class **D** Fires (yellow)	**For Combustible Metals** Put out a class D fire of metal chips, turnings, or shavings by smothering or coating with a specially designed extinguishing agent.	Aluminum Magnesium Potassium Sodium Titanium Zirconium	Dry powder extinguishers and agents only

*Cartridge-operated water, foam, and soda-acid types of extinguishers are no longer manufactured. These extinguishers should be removed from service when they become due for their next hydrostatic pressure test.

Notes:

(1) Freezes in low temperatures unless treated with antifreeze solution, usually weighs over 20 pounds, and is heavier than any other extinguisher mentioned.

(2) Also called ordinary or regular dry chemical (sodium bicarbonate).

(3) Has the greatest initial fire-stopping power of the extinguishers mentioned for class B fires. Be sure to clean residue immediately after using the extinguisher so sprayed surfaces will not be damaged (potassium bicarbonate).

(4) The only extinguishers that fight A, B, and C classes of fires. However, they should not be used on fires in liquefied fat or oil of appreciable depth. Be sure to clean residue immediately after using the extinguisher so sprayed surfaces will not be damaged (ammonium phosphates).

(5) Use with caution in unventilated, confined spaces.

(6) May cause injury to the operator if the extinguishing agent (a gas) or the gases produced when the agent is applied to a fire is inhaled.

Figure 2-5 Chart shows four fire extinguisher classifications and types of fire they put out.

Stay low to avoid inhaling the smoke. If it gets too hot or too smoky, get out. Remember, never go back into a burning building for anything.

AVOIDING FALLS

Keep all shop floor drain covers snugly in place. Open drains have caused many toe, ankle, and leg injuries.

To clean up oil, use a commercial oil absorbent. Spread the absorbent on the spill. Rub it with your broom in a circular motion. Then use a dust pan and broom to pick up the absorbent.

Make sure that aisles and walkways are kept clean and wide enough for a safe clearance. Provide for adequate work space around any machines. Cluttered walking areas contain items waiting to cause accidents. Never leave tools or a creeper laying on the floor.

AVOIDING ELECTROCUTION

Keep all water off the floor. Remember that water is a conductor of electricity. A serious shock hazard will result if a live wire happens to fall into a puddle in which a person is standing. The floor must be dry when using electric power tools.

Electrocution results when a small amount of electric current passes through the human body. This can affect heart and brain functions, possibly causing death.

Disconnect electrical power before performing any service on the machine or tool.

Some late model vehicles have heated windshields. Over 100 AC volts are sent to the windshield to quickly warm the glass for melting ice and snow. This can be enough voltage and current to cause electrocution.

AVOIDING ASPHYXIATION

Make certain the work area is well lit and *ventilated.*

Car and truck engine exhaust produces deadly *carbon monoxide* (CO) gas which is odorless and invisible. Connect a shop vent hose to the tailpipe of any vehicle being operated in the shop.

Check and service furnaces and water heaters in the shop at least once every six months.

Asbestos dust used in the manufacture of older brake and clutch assemblies are cancer-causing agents. Never blow this dust into the shop. Use a vacuum system while wearing a filter mask to clean off asbestos dust safely. Refer to Figure 2–6.

Proper ventilation is also important in areas where caustics, degreasers, undercoats, and finishes are used. Ventilation can be by means of an air-changing system, extraction floors, or central dust extraction system.

When running an engine, set the parking brake when working on the vehicle. If it is an *automatic transmission* (shifts through gears automatically using hydraulic system), place it in park.

With a *manual transmission* (must be hand shifted through each forward gear), it should be in reverse (engine off) or neutral (engine on) unless instructed otherwise for a specific service operation.

AVOIDING EYE INJURIES

Remember that your eyes are irreplaceable. Your eyes are very delicate and can be permanently damaged in a split second. Human eyes are sensitive to dust, flying particles from grinding, and to mists or vapors from spraying. Such exposure could cause severe eye injury and possibly the loss of sight.

When risks to your eyes exist, wear appropriate eye or face protection. Refer to Figure 2–7.

A good pair of *safety glasses* are suitable with only minor danger, as when blowing off dust or sanding with an air sander.

Wear a *full-face shield* with more danger from flying particles, as when grinding.

Figure 2–6 Use a vacuum system to remove asbestos. dust or any other harmful substance from vehicle. Asbestos is a powerful cancer-causing agent. *(Hako)*

Wear chemical splash *goggles* when handling solvents, thinners, reducers, and other similar liquids. Because the eyes are very susceptible to irritation, approved safety goggles should also be worn when paint mists are present.

A welding helmet or welding goggles with the proper shade lens must be worn when welding. These will protect your eyes and face from flying molten metal and harmful light rays. Look at Figure 2–8.

AVOIDING CHEMICAL BURNS

There are many sources of chemical burns in a body shop. Cleaners, some paints, refrigerants, and solvents can cause skin and eye burns. A few rules to follow to prevent chemical burns include:

• Remove solvent-soaked clothing as the cloth will hold these chemicals against the skin, causing skin irritation or a chemical burn. Wear long sleeves for complete protection.

A

B

Figure 2–8 Welding helmet protects eyes and face from molten spatter and blinding light of welding. Tinted glass in helmet must be dark enough to protect eyes from bright light. *(Courtesy of Sellstrom Mfg.)*

C

Figure 2–7 Note three basic types of eye protection. A: Safety glasses are the most comfortable way to protect your eyes. They are sufficient for moderate dangers from flying objects. *(Photo Courtesy of Lab Safety Supply, Inc., Janesville, WI)* B: Full-face shield protects eyes as well as face. It provides a little more protection from danger of flying debris, as when grinding. *(Photo Courtesy of Lab Safety Supply, Inc., Janesville, WI)* C: Goggles help protect all around the eyes. They prevent debris or caustic liquids from entering eyes from the side. *(Courtesy of Sellstrom Mfg.)*

- Wear *rubber* or *plastic gloves* to protect yourself from the harmful effects of corrosive liquids, undercoats, and finishes. Use impervious gloves when working with solvents or two-component primers and topcoats. These gloves offer special protection from the chemicals found in two-component systems.

Danger! Chemical paint remover is very powerful. When using it, use extreme caution and protective gear, Figure 2–9.

When washing hands, use a proper *hand cleaner.* Never use thinner as a hand cleaner. Many chemicals can be absorbed into the skin, causing eventual, long-term illnesses.

PERSONAL SAFETY

Personal appearance and conduct can help prevent accidents. Follow these general guidelines for personal safety.

Loose clothing, unbuttoned shirt sleeves, dangling ties, loose jewelry, and shirts hanging out are very

Figure 2–9 Chemical paint remover will quickly soften and lift hardened paint. It can cause serious burns! (© *The Eastwood Company—Used with permission*)

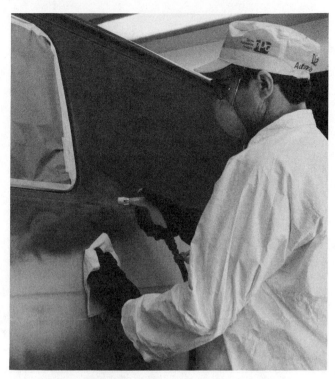

Figure 2–10 Technician is blowing off vehicle body in prep area to ready for new paint job. Note coveralls, cap, and respirator. *(PPG Industries, Inc.)*

dangerous. Instead, wear approved shop coveralls or jumpsuits. Pants should be long enough to cover the top of the shoes.

A clean *jumpsuit* or *lint-free coveralls* should be worn when in the paint spraying area. Dirty clothing can transfer dirt to freshly painted surfaces. Look at Figure 2–10.

Wear thick *leather shoes* that have nonslip soles to prevent falls and foot injuries. Good work shoes provide support and comfort for someone who is standing for a long time. Never wear tennis shoes or sandals in the shop. Toes can be broken or severed if a heavy object falls on them.

To keep hair safe and clean, wear a *cap* when sanding, grinding, and doing similar jobs, Figure 2–10. Wear a protective *painter's stretch hood* in the spray booth. *Bump caps* should be worn when working beneath the hood or under the vehicle. Keep clothing away from moving parts when an engine or a machine is running.

Tie long hair securely behind your head before beginning to work. If hair becomes tangled in moving parts or air tools, it can painfully rip out chunks of scalp.

Any loose or hanging clothing, such as shirttails, ties, cuffs, or scarves, creates a risk of getting wrapped up in moving parts of the vehicle or machinery, causing serious bodily injury. Remove all jewelry before working.

Use a portable shop light when working in dark areas, such as under a vehicle. This will increase work speed and quality.

When lifting and carrying objects, bend at your knees, not your back. Do not bend your waist when lifting. Remember, heavy objects should be lifted and moved with the proper equipment for the job or get someone to help you.

Never overreach! Maintain a balanced stance to avoid slipping and falling while working.

Proper conduct can also help prevent accidents. Horseplay is dangerous. Such things as air nozzle fights, creeper races, or practical jokes have no place in the shop. For example, technicians have been killed by air blow nozzles. If air enters your bloodstream, a blood clot can cause death.

Do not risk injury through the lack of knowledge. Use shop equipment or machinery only after receiving proper instruction.

Metalworking air hammers, the piercing noise of grinding, and the radio blaring full blast can all make it difficult to hear anything else. Some shop noise is enough to deafen or cause hearing loss.

When in metalworking areas, wear *earplugs* or *earmuffs* to protect your eardrums from damaging noise levels. Refer to Figure 2–11.

To prevent serious burns, avoid contact with hot metal parts such as the radiator, exhaust manifold, tailpipe, catalytic converter, and muffler.

During metalworking, it is very easy to be cut by sharp, jagged metal. Use caution, Figure 2–12.

When driving a vehicle in a shop, watch out for other vehicles and people. It is best to have someone act as a guide. Leave the window open and the radio off, so that the helper's directions can be heard.

If vehicle covers are available, by all means use them.

A

B

Figure 2–11 Many noises in the shop can cause hearing loss—grinders and air chisels for example. Wear earplugs or earmuffs when sound or decibel levels are high. A: Earplugs are easy to wear. *(Photo Courtesy of Lab Safety Supply, Inc., Janesville, WI)* B: Earmuffs provide slightly better protection but are somewhat clumsier. *(Courtesy of Sellstrom Mfg.)*

Sharp metal

Forming tool

Figure 2–12 Cuts are the most common injury in metalworking area. Sharp metal can easily lacerate skin. Technician is using special tool to form lip on sheet metal during rust repair. *(©The Eastwood Company—Used with permission)*

TOOL AND MACHINE SAFETY

Auto body tools and machines can inflict serious injuries if basic safety rules are NOT observed. Some general tool rules include the following:

Keep tools clean and in workable condition. Greasy or oily tools can easily slip out of your grasp, possibly causing injury.

Check all tools for cracks, chips, burns, broken teeth, or other dangerous conditions before using them. If tools are defective, replace them.

Be careful when using sharp or pointed tools that can cause injury. If a tool should be sharp, keep it sharp.

Do not use any hand tools for any job other than that for which they were specifically designed.

Never carry screwdrivers, punches, or other sharp hand tools in your pockets. You could be injured or damage the vehicle.

When using an electric power tool, make sure that it is properly grounded. The third round ground prong sends electricity flow to the ground if the tool shorts out, not through your body.

Check the wiring insulation for cracks and bare wires. When using electric tools, never stand on a wet or damp floor to avoid electrocution.

Do not operate a power tool or machine without its safety guard(s) in place.

When power grinding, cutting, sanding, or doing similar operation, always wear safety glasses.

When using power equipment on small parts, never hold the part in your hand. It could slip and injure your hand. Use vise grips or a bench vise instead.

Before plugging in any electric tool, make sure the switch is OFF to prevent serious injury. When you are through, turn the tool off to ready it for the next person.

Use *jack stands* to support a vehicle whenever you must work under it. Never trust *hydraulic jacks* alone; they are for raising the vehicle, not holding it. Numerous people have been crushed and killed when a vehicle fell on them. See Figure 2–13.

Never use a machine or tool beyond its stated capacity. If a grinding wheel spec is 2000 rpm (revolutions per minute), do not install it in a grinder with a higher operating speed. The wheel could explode if operated at a higher rpm.

Only use a tool or machine for its designed task. Never misuse or modify equipment.

Keep hands away from moving parts when the machine or tool is under power. Running vehicle engines often cause injuries. Never clear debris when the machine is under power and never use your hands.

Use caution with compressed air. Pneumatic tools must be operated at the pressure recommended by their manufacturer. The downstream pressure of com-

Raise With Floor Jack

A

Support on Stands Before Working

B

Figure 2–13 Take steps to keep a vehicle lifted and secured to avoid injury. A: Use floor jack to raise car. Transmission should be in neutral with wheels blocked while raising so wheel can turn. Never work under car on floor jack. B: Position and lower car on jack stands before working. After on stands, place transmission back into park or in gear and block wheels on ground. *(Courtesy of Ford Motor Company)*

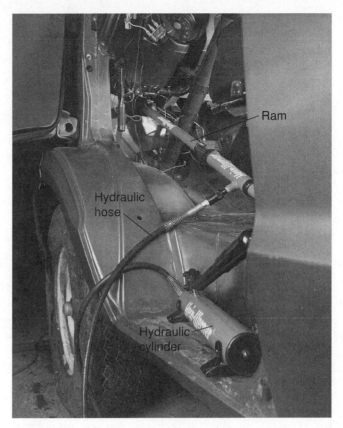

Ram

Hydraulic hose

Hydraulic cylinder

Figure 2–14 Hydraulic equipment, like this power ram, can exert tons of force. Make sure equipment is secure and stand to one side when applying pressure. *(Hein-Werner® Corporation)*

pressed air used for cleaning purposes must remain at a pressure level below 30 psi (2.1 K/cm^2).

Do not use compressed air to clean clothes. Even at low pressure, compressed air can cause dirt particles to become embedded in your skin, which can result in infection. Air entering an artery could cause death.

Store all parts and tools properly by putting them away neatly. This practice not only cuts down on injuries, it also reduces time wasted looking for a misplaced part or tool.

When working with a hydraulic press or power unit, apply hydraulic pressure in a safe manner. It is generally wise to stand to the side when operating hydraulic tools, Figure 2–14. Always wear safety glasses.

If the shop has a hydraulic lift, be sure to read the instruction manual. Check the pads to see that they are making proper contact with the frame. Then raise the vehicle about 6 inches (15 centimeters) and check to make sure it is well balanced on the lift.

If there are any rattling or scraping sounds, it means that the vehicle is not positioned properly. If this happens, lower the lift and realign the pads. Test it again. Look at Figure 2–15.

Figure 2–15 After raising car to desired height on lift, engage mechanical safety catch. This will prevent lift from accidentally lowering. *(Rotary Lift/A Dover Industries Co.)*

After lifting the vehicle to full height, engage the *lift safety catch* to ensure that the lift cannot lower while working underneath the vehicle.

Never permit anyone—technician or customer—to remain in the vehicle while it is being lifted.

Make sure you are properly trained before using a frame rack. Personal injury and major vehicle damage can result if you use improper methods.

When welding or cutting near vehicle interiors, remove seats and carpets to prevent a fire. Always have a pail of water and a fire extinguisher nearby.

PAINT SHOP SAFETY

Many paints and paint-related products present serious health hazards unless proper precautions are taken. The issue of paint shop safety has grown more important in recent years. More vehicles are now being refinished with urethane enamels, which contain harmful chemicals. The amount of exposure to chemicals has increased, and some are more toxic. These chemicals can cause nose, throat, and lung irritation. They can also cause acute respiratory problems. Symptoms can include shortness of breath, tightness in the chest, dizziness, nausea, abdominal pain, and vomiting.

RESPIRATORS

Respirators are needed in the paint shop to keep airborne materials from being inhaled. They must often be used even when adequate ventilation is provided. There are three primary types of respirators available to protect technicians: dust or particle respirator, cartridge filter respirator, and the hood or air-supplied respirator.

Respirator Types

A *dust* or *particle respirator* is a filter that fits over your nose and mouth to block small airborne particles. It is not designed to stop paint mist and fumes. A dust respirator is used when sanding or grinding to keep the dangerous materials out of your lungs.

Sanding operations create dust that can cause bronchial irritation and possible long-term lung damage. Protection from this health hazard is often overlooked. Just because the sanding dust does not cause immediate symptoms, does not mean that they will not cause problems when you get older. An approved dust respirator should be worn whenever sanding or grinding operations are performed.

Follow the instructions provided with the dust respirator to ensure proper fit. Bend or shape them so that air cannot leak around your face, nose, and mouth. Remember that inexpensive dust masks or respirators do not protect against vapors and spray mists.

Cartridge filter respirators protect against vapors and spray mists of nonactivated enamels (no hardener added), lacquers, and other nonisocyanate materials. If the refinishing materials contain no isocyanates, an air-purifying cartridge filter respirator with organic vapor cartridges and prefilters can be used.

The cartridge filter respirator consists of a rubber face piece designed to conform to the face and form an airtight seal. It includes replaceable prefilters and cartridges that remove solvent and other vapors from the air. The respirator also has intake and exhaust valves, which ensure that all incoming air flows through the filters.

Cartridge filter respirators are available in several sizes. Purchase one that fits your face.

Remember that cartridge filter respirators should be used only in well-ventilated areas. They must not be used in environments containing less than 19.5 percent oxygen.

To maintain the cartridge filter respirator, keep it clean and change the prefilters and cartridges as directed by the manufacturer.

An approved *air-supplied respirator* consists of a half-mask, full face piece, hood, or helmet, to which clean, breathable air is supplied through a hose from a separate air source. It provides protection from the dangers of inhaling isocyanate paint vapors and mists, as well as from hazardous solvent vapors. Note Figure 2–16.

The fresh air supply respirator is comfortable to wear and does not require fit testing. The fresh air supply respirator may include a self-contained oilless pump to supply air to either one hood or two half mask respirators.

The pump's air inlet must be located in a clean air area. Some shops mount the pumps on an outside wall, away from the dust and dirt generated by shop operations. If shop-compressed air is used, it must be filtered with a trap and carbon filter to remove oil, water, scale and odor. The air supply must have a valve to match air pressure to respirator equipment specs and an automatic control to sound an alarm or shut down the compressor in case of overheating and contamination. Overheating frequently causes carbon monoxide contamination of the air supply.

Respirator Testing and Maintenance

It is very important that an air-purifying cartridge filter respirator fits securely around your face. This will

Hood

Coveralls

Fresh
air hose

Figure 2–16 When applying some types of more harmful paints, wear a mask or hood supplied with outside or filtered fresh air. A pump circulates the air through the mask or hood to protect your lungs. *(PPG Industries, Inc.)*

prevent contaminated air from entering your lungs. To check for respirator air leaks, a *fit test* should be performed prior to using the respirator, making both negative and positive pressure checks.

To make a *negative pressure test*, place the palms of your hands over the cartridges and inhale. A good fit will be evident if the face piece collapses onto your face.

To perform a *positive pressure test*, cover up the exhalation valve and exhale. A proper fit is evident if the face piece billows out without air escaping from the mask.

Another form of fit testing consists of exposing amyl acetate (banana oil) near the seal around the face. If no odor is detected, a proper fit is evident.

Here are a few other maintenance tips for cartridge respirators:

Replace the prefilters when it becomes difficult to breathe through the respirator. Replace the cartridge(s) at proper intervals, and always at the first sign of solvent odor. Regularly check the mask to make sure it does not have any cracks or deformities. Store the respirator in an airtight container.

Note that facial hair might prevent an airtight seal, presenting a health hazard. Therefore, refinish-

ers with facial hair should use a fresh air supply respirator.

Follow the manufacturer's instructions to ensure proper maintenance and fit.

DUSTLESS SANDING SYSTEMS

A *dustless sanding system* uses a blower or air pump to draw airborne dust into a storage container, much like a vacuum cleaner. Depending on the system, vacuum pumps, vacuum pullers, brush motors, or turbine motors can be used to provide sufficient air volume. This action pulls airborne sanding dust through holes in a special sanding pad or through a shroud that surrounds the sanding pad.

Some dustless system manufacturers claim that their machines can trap over 99 percent of the toxic dust created by sanding lead- or chrome-based automotive paints and primers.

MANUFACTURER'S WARNINGS

Manufacturer's warnings give important procedures for safe use of their products. Study and follow instructions and warnings given by product and equipment manufacturers. Follow them to the letter.

Most of the products used in a collision repair shop carry warning and caution information that must be read and understood by users. Likewise, all federal (including Occupational Safety and Health Administration [OSHA], Mine Safety and Health Administration [MSHA], and National Institute for Occupational Safety and Health [NIOSH]), state, and local safety regulations should not only be fully understood, but also strictly observed.

Material safety data sheets (MSDS), available from all product manufacturers, detail chemical composition and precautionary information for all products that can present a health or safety hazard.

Employers must know the general uses, protective equipment, accident or spill procedures, and other information for safe handling of hazardous material. This training must be given to employees as part of their job orientation.

The best way to protect yourself when using paint and body products is to be familiar with the correct application procedures. Follow all safety and health precautions found on MSDS and on product labels.

RIGHT-TO-KNOW LAWS

In collision repair and refinishing shops, hazardous wastes are generated. As a result, every employee is protected by Right-to-Know Laws.

Right-to-Know laws give essential information and stipulations for safely working with hazardous materials. They began with OSHA's Hazard Communication Standard. This document was originally intended for chemical companies and manufacturers that require employees to handle potentially hazardous materials in the workshop. Since then, the majority of states have enacted their own Right-to-Know laws. The federal courts have decided that these regulations should apply to all companies, including the auto collision repair and refinishing professions.

EMPLOYER RESPONSIBILITIES

The general intent of the law is for employers to provide their employees with a safe working place as it relates to hazardous materials. Specifically, there are three areas of employer responsibility:

All employees must be trained about their rights under the legislation, the nature of the hazardous chemicals in their workplace, the labeling of chemicals, and the information about each chemical posted on material safety data sheets (MSDS).

The shop must maintain documentation on the hazardous chemicals in the workplace. It must show proof of training programs, records of accidents and/or spill incidents. The shop must show satisfaction of employee requests for specific chemical information.

Complete *EPA* (Environmental Protection Agency) lists of hazardous wastes can be found in the Code of Federal Regulations. Materials and wastes of most concern to the technician are organic solvents: wastes that contain heavy metals, especially lead, and ignitable, corrosive, and/or toxic materials.

It should be noted that no material is considered hazardous waste until the shop is finished using it and ready to dispose of it. For instance, a caustic cleaning solution with a heavy concentration of lead in the cleaning tank is not considered hazardous waste until it is ready to be replaced. Then it must be handled accordingly. The EPA says it is the owner's responsibility to determine whether the waste is hazardous, but the owner must have adequate test results to support the shop's claim.

WASTE DISPOSAL

Many shops use "full-service" haulers to test and remove hazardous waste from the property. Besides hauling the hazardous waste away, the hauler will also take care of all the paperwork, deal with the various government agencies, even advise the shop on how to recover disposal costs.

The collision repair shop is ultimately responsible for the safe disposal of hazardous wastes, even after they leave the shop. Be sure that any hauling contract is in writing.

In the event of an emergency hazardous waste spill, you or the shop owner must contact the National Response Center (1-800-424-8802) immediately. Failure to do so can result in a $10,000 fine, a year in jail, or both.

LIABILITY

You must also be aware of the liability question resulting from auto collision work. *Liability* means that you are financially responsible for damage or injuries resulting from improper repairs. There have been several lawsuits recently in which improper repairs were blamed for personal injury. Basically, if you do not do the job right, you and your shop can be held responsible or liable.

Collision repair facilities and insurance companies have the highest exposure to liability responsibility. The technician must set high standards personally and for the shop in terms of quality. Achieving these standards and employing the latest repair techniques will reduce the chance of being held liable.

TECHNICIAN LIABILITY

There are several principles of liability the collision repair technician should be familiar with:

Take "due care" to do the work thoroughly and correctly. The shop and technician(s) are liable for any faulty work. The shop is liable for failure to repair damage, which is acknowledged to exist, unless the customer specifically directs that it should not be repaired.

Warn the customer about anything that might be wrong with the vehicle after the repair. If the customer or insurance company does agree to allow you to fix the problem, put it in writing. Have the customer or insurance agent sign the work order. This will protect you and assure that the customer knows that the vehicle is not in perfect condition.

Ignorance is no defense! In the eyes of the law, the collision repair shop, technician, and insurance personnel are expected to be knowledgeable about the latest available techniques for safe, sound repair. Failure to learn and apply those techniques could result in liability.

ASE CERTIFICATION

ASE Certification is a testing program to help prove that you are a knowledgeable auto body technician. Just as doctors, accountants, electricians, and other professionals are licensed or certified to practice their profession, collision repair and refinishing technicians can also be certified.

Certification protects the general public and the professional. It assures the general public and the prospective employer that certain minimum standards of performance have been met.

ASE tests include multiple-choice questions pertaining to the service and repair of a vehicle. They do not include theoretical questions. To prepare for ASE auto body tests, study the material in this book carefully.

To help prepare for the Body Repair and/or Painting and Refinishing tests, some test questions at the end of service chapters in this text are similar to those used by ASE.

Collision repair and refinishing technicians can get certified in one or more technical areas by taking and passing written certification tests. The *National Institute for Automotive Service Excellence (ASE)* offers a voluntary certification program that is recommended by the major vehicle manufacturers in the United States. The Body Repair and Painting and Refinishing tests contain 40 questions in various areas.

Craftspeople who pass the written tests are awarded a certificate and a shoulder emblem for their work clothes. See Figure 2–17.

Many employers now expect their collision repair and refinishing technicians to be certified. The certified technician is recognized as a professional by the public, employers, and peers. For this reason, the certified technician usually receives higher pay than one who is not certified.

For further information on the ASE certification program write:

ASE
1305 Dulles Technology Drive
Herndon, VA 22071-3145

I-CAR

The *Inter-Industry Conference on Auto Collision Repair,* or *I-CAR,* is an advanced training organization dedicated to promoting high-quality practices in the collision repair industry. It is made up of vehicle manufacturers, collision repair shops, insurance companies, independent appraisers, recyclers, educators, and tool-equipment-material manufacturers.

Figure 2–17 After you pass ASE test, you will be given a shoulder patch for your work uniform.

I-CAR has emerged as the leading advanced collision repair training organization. I-CAR classes are offered in the U.S., Canada, and New Zealand.

Courses offered to auto body professionals by I-CAR include:

1. Collision Repair (eight parts)
2. Plastic Repair, Retexturing, and Refinishing
3. Finish Matching to Restore Pre-Accident Appearance
4. Advanced Vehicle Systems
5. Steering and Suspension

Upon completion of a course, a certificate of achievement is awarded for that area, as shown in Figure 2–18. This is also an excellent way to upgrade your skills after becoming employed and to prepare for ASE tests.

For information about the I-CAR courses and when they are given, write:

I-CAR
3701 Algonquin Road
Suite 400
Rolling Meadows, IL 60008-3118

or,

In the U.S., call: 1-800-ICAR-USA (1-800-422-7872) or for class schedules: 1-800-ICAR-456 (1-800-422-7456)

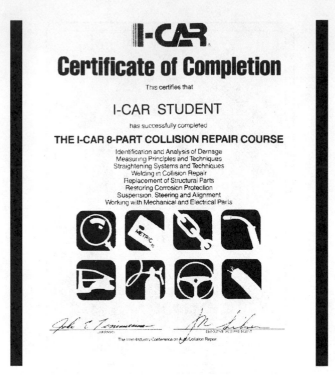

Figure 2–18 After graduation from school and when on the job, you should consider I-CAR training. It will help you keep up-to-date with technical advances. *(I-CAR)*

I-CAR Canada
1305 Pickering Parkway, Suite 202
Pickering, Ontario L1V 3P2

or,

In Canada, call: 1-800-565-ICAR (1-800-565-4227)
In Ontario, call: 1-800-461-ICAR (1-800-461-4227)

I-CAR New Zealand
P.O. Box 36-067
Northcote, Auckland

or call: (09)-419-0042

Many equipment and finish manufacturers have training programs designed to educate their customers in the use of their products. These training programs run throughout the course of the year. In most cases, they are scheduled in major cities across the United States and Canada, or at their training facilities. Training programs vary in duration and can be tailored to individual requirements. Shops should contact local sales representatives for more information.

DON'T BE FOOLISH!

Safety is your responsibility! Follow recommended safety practices at all times.

For example, if you think it is inconvenient or uncomfortable to wear a respirator mask, you are not thinking! After prolonged exposure, your lungs will be damaged. You will suffer health problems at an older age because of your laziness and lack of wisdom. Plan a long healthy life by protecting yourself now from work hazards!

Summary

- Care must be taken to prevent several types of accidents including asphyxiation, chemical burns, electrocution, fires, and explosions.

- A *safety program* is a written shop policy designed to protect the health and welfare of personnel and customers. It includes rules on everything from equipment use to disposal of hazardous chemicals.

- In case of an emergency, be sure the following are available and easily seen: emergency telephone numbers, a first aid kit, and safety signs denoting fire exits, fire extinguishers and dangerous chemical information.

- Certification protects the general public and the technician. *ASE* Certification assures the general public and the prospective employer that certain minimum standards of performance have been met.

- The *Inter-Industry Conference on Auto Collision Repair* or I-CAR is an advanced training organization dedicated to promoting high-quality practices in the collision repair industry. I-CAR classes are offered in the U.S., Canada, and New Zealand.

Technical Terms

safety	*frame rack*
accidents	*front end rack*
asphyxiation	*alignment rack*
chemical burns	*pneumatic (air)*
electrocution	*hydraulic (oil-filled)*
fire	*tool & equipment storage*
combustibles	*room*
explosions	*classroom*
physical injury	*paint prep area*
manufacturer's	*finishing area*
instructions	*paint booth area*
safety program	*body shop office*
shop layout	*emergency telephone*
metalworking area	*numbers*
repair stall	*first aid kit*
bay	*safety signs*

gasoline
spontaneous combustion
UL (Underwriters
    Laboratories)
electrical fires
fire extinguisher
ventilated
carbon monoxide (CO)
asbestos dust
automatic transmission
manual transmission
safety glasses
full-face shield
    goggles
rubber gloves
plastic gloves
hand cleaner
jumpsuit
lint-free coveralls
leather shoes
cap
painter's stretch hood
bump caps
earplugs
earmuffs
jack stands
hydraulic jacks

life safety catch
respirators
dust respirator
particle respirator
cartridge filter
    respirators
air-supplied respirator
fit test
negative pressure test
positive pressure test
dustless sanding system
manufacturer's warnings
materials safety data
    sheets (MSDS)
Right-to-Know laws
EPA (Environmental
    Protection Agency)
liability
ASE Certification
ASE tests
National Institute for
    Automotive Service
    Excellence (ASE)
Inter-Industry
    Conference on Auto
    Collision Repair
I-CAR

Review Questions

1. Safety involves using proper work habits to prevent _____ and _____.

2. List six kinds of accidents that are common in a body shop.

3. What are some combustible materials found in a body shop?

4. Name ten body shop work areas.

5. How is a frame rack dangerous?

6. When soiled rags are left lying about improperly, they can cause:
   a. Spontaneous combustion.
   b. Chemical burns.
   c. Explosion.
   d. None of the above.

7. Asbestos dust is inert and does not pose a health problem. True or False?

8. Wear _____ or _____ to protect yourself from the harmful effects of corrosive liquids, undercoats, and finishes.

9. What can happen if you wear tennis shoes and drop a heavy part on your foot?

10. When using an electric power tool, make sure that it is properly _____. The _____ ground _____ sends electricity flow to the ground, not through your body if the tool shorts out.

11. Numerous people have been crushed and killed when a vehicle fell on them. How could this have happened?

12. These are needed in the paint shop to keep paint mists and fumes from being inhaled.
    a. Face shield
    b. Mouth piece
    c. Respirator
    d. Shop rag

13. Technician A leaves his shirt sleeves unbuttoned in the shop. Technician B wears loose clothing instead of coveralls. Who is correct?
    a. Technician A
    b. Technician B
    c. Both A and B
    d. Neither A nor B

14. Which of the following is an important shop safety feature?
    a. Jack stands
    b. Attitude
    c. Approved metal containers
    d. All of the above

15. When running an engine in a vehicle with an automatic transmission, place it in _____.
    a. Neutral
    b. Reverse
    c. Park
    d. Drive

16. Which of the following statements is correct?
    a. Gasoline is an ideal cleaning solvent.
    b. Never keep more than ten day's worth of paint outside of approved storage areas.
    c. Oily rags should be stored in approved metal containers.
    d. All of the above.

17. Which type of fire involves electrical equipment?
    a. Class A
    b. Class B
    c. Class C
    d. Class D

18. With which type of respirator can facial hair prevent an airtight seal?
    a. Cartridge filter type
    b. Air-supplied type
    c. Full face type
    d. Hood type

19. Why should you become ASE certified?

20. What is I-CAR?

Activities

1. Inspect your shop. List anything that might be a safety hazard. Turn the report in to your instructor.

2. Select one hand tool and one power tool. Make a chart showing how you could be injured while improperly using each.

CHAPTER 3

VEHICLE CONSTRUCTION

Objectives

After studying this chapter, you should be able to:

- Define the most important parts of a vehicle body and frame.

- Explain body design and frame variations.

- Compare unibody and body-over-frame construction.

- Identify the major structural parts, sections, and assemblies of body-over-frame vehicles.

- Identify the major structural parts, sections, and assemblies of unibody vehicles.

- Summarize how to classify vehicles by body, engine, and drive train configurations.

Introduction

Vehicle construction refers to how a vehicle is made. As mentioned in Chapter 1, if you know how a vehicle is "put together" or constructed, you will be prepared to fix it properly when damaged. You must be able to identify the basic parts of a vehicle and compare design variations. This will give you the vocabulary to fully grasp information in later text chapters. So study carefully!

As you will learn, the modern motor vehicle is no longer a simple "buggy with an engine." The present-day motor vehicle is now a maze of interacting mechanical–electrical systems. In fact, over 15,000 parts are used in a typical vehicle. Damage to one part can affect the operation of another seemingly unrelated part. As a result, you must understand the whole vehicle and its systems to safely and effectively repair collision damaged vehicles.

CRASH TESTING

Automobile manufacturers are challenged by having to design vehicles that are light, *aerodynamic* (have low wind resistance), and are yet strong and safe.

Computer simulated crash testing is used before building a *prototype*, or first real vehicle, to determine how well the vehicle might survive a crash.

It is critical that the passenger compartment is strong enough to help prevent injury to the driver and his or her passengers.

Certified crash tests are done using a real vehicle and sensor-equipped dummies that show how much impact the people would suffer during a collision. Computer readings from the sensors in the dummies give feedback about each crash test for body structure evaluation, Figure 3–1.

Crush zones are built into the frame or body to collapse and absorb some of the energy of a collision. The front and rear of the vehicle collapses while the passenger compartment tends to retain its shape. This helps reduce the amount of force transmitted to the occupants, Figure 3–2.

An *insurance rating system* uses a number scale to rate the vehicle's accident survivability. It indicates

A

B

Figure 3–2 A: Arrows show how impact force is spread out. B: Front and rear of car are designed with crush zones to absorb energy of impact and protect passenger compartment. *(Saab Cars USA, Inc.)*

how well the vehicle will survive a crash and how much it will cost to repair it. A negative five is the worst rating (most damage) and positive five is the best (least damage). A zero rating would be average.

VEHICLE CLASSIFICATIONS

Vehicle classification relates to the construction, size, shape, number of doors, type of roof, and other criteria of a motor vehicle. To communicate properly in body repair, you must understand these basic terms.

FRAME CONSTRUCTION

The *frame* is the vehicle's foundation. The body and all major parts of a vehicle are attached to the frame. It must provide the support and strength needed for other mechanical parts attached to it.

There are three main types of vehicle frame construction: body-over-frame, unibody, and space frame. Each has its own unique repair challenges.

Conventional Frames

Body-over-frame vehicles have separate body and chassis parts bolted to the frame. The engine and other major assemblies are mounted on the frame. This type of frame consists of two side rails connected by a series of crossmembers. Refer to Figure 3–3.

Figure 3–1 Cars and trucks must pass motor vehicle safety crash certification tests to assure adequate passenger safety. *(BMW of North America)*

Figure 3-3 Conventional frame is a thick steel structure. Body and chassis parts bolt to frame. This type of frame is used in many full-size cars, vans and trucks. Note frame parts. *(Courtesy of Chrysler Corporation)*

Most conventional frames are wide at the rear and narrow at the front. The narrow front construction enables the front wheel to make a sharper turn. A wide frame at the rear provides better support of the body.

Other characteristics of a separate frame are:

1. Full frame vehicle is heavier.

2. High amounts of energy are absorbed by frame during a collision.

3. Suspension and drive train parts can be quickly assembled on the frame.

4. Heavy frame is made of thick sheet metal approximately ⅛ inch (3 mm) thick.

5. The vehicle profile is generally high off the ground.

The *frame rails* are the long steel members that extend along the sides of the vehicle. The *torque boxes* are the structural parts of the frame designed to allow some twisting to absorb road shock and collision impact. The *frame horn* is the very front of frame rails where the bumper attaches.

Crossmembers are thick metal stampings that extend sideways across the frame rails. They are often used to support the engine, suspension, and other chassis parts. *Spring hangers* are sometimes formed on the frame to hold the suspension system springs. *Rubber body insulators* are used between the frame and body to reduce noise and vibration.

Although unibody construction is the trend, body-over-frame construction is still being used. Full or partial frame construction is used on some full-size, luxury vehicles, most full-size pickup trucks, some small pickups, and most full-size vans.

The *conventional frame* is an independent, separate part, because it is not welded to any of the major

units of the body shell. The strong side rails are normally made of U-shaped channel or box-shaped sections. Various brackets, braces, and openings are provided for the parts of the chassis.

A *perimeter frame,* as its name implies, has the frame rail near the outside or perimeter of the vehicle. It is the most common type of full frame. It utilizes full length side rails with torque boxes in the four corners of the center section. A perimeter frame has good side impact strength. See Figure 3–4A.

An *X-frame* has two long members crossing over in the middle of the frame rails. Also called a *backbone frame,* it has a single thick beam in the middle section. Refer to Figure 3–4B. A *combination frame* has both perimeter and x-members. It is one of the strongest frame designs, Figure 3–4C.

A *ladder frame* has long frame rails with a series of straight crossmembers formed in several locations. It is a seldom used modification of the perimeter frame.

A *partial frame* is a cross between a solid frame and a unibody. *Sub-frame assemblies* are used at the front and rear while the unibody supports the middle area of the vehicle. The sub-frame is used to support the suspension and drivetrain.

Unibody Construction

Unibody construction uses body parts that are welded and bolted together to form an integral frame. No separate heavy gauge steel frame under the body is needed. In unibody designs, heavy-gauge, cold-rolled steels have been replaced with lighter, thinner, high-strength steel alloys or aluminum alloy. One example is shown in Figure 3–5.

The concept of unibody construction first proved successful in the aircraft industry. Lightweight, high-strength fuselages were needed. Adapted to the auto industry, unitized construction eliminated the need for a separate, rigid frame. The strength and rigidity of the vehicle was integrated into the body shell.

The body shell is formed by welding sheet metal into a box- or egg-like configuration. Strength is achieved through shape and design of the individual parts instead of their mass and weight. The entire inner structure works together for structural integrity.

The eggshell concept is an ideal model for understanding the principle of unibody design. Even when pressing hard on an eggshell, it is comparatively difficult to destroy its thin structure. All the force applied by your finger is not concentrated in one place but is dispersed over the shell surface. In engineering, this concept is called a *stressed hull structure.*

Similar to a unibody, a *space frame* has a metal body structure covered with an outer skin of plastic or composite panels. It is a relatively new type of vehicle

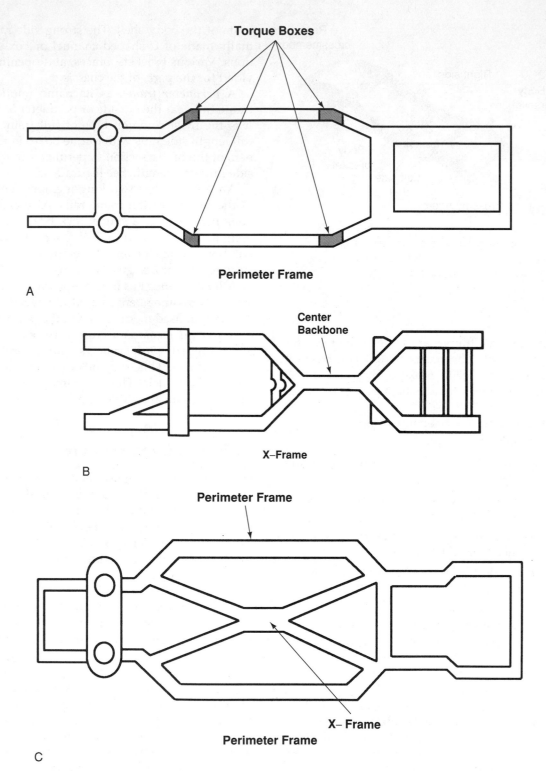

Figure 3–4 Conventional frame types.

construction. A space frame design is currently used on some vans and economy vehicles. Quite often, the roof and quarter panels are NOT welded to the structure as they are with traditional unibodies. Exterior body panels are attached with mechanical fasteners or adhesives. Look at Figure 3–6.

After a collision, a space frame is more likely to have hidden damage because of the ability of plastic panels to hide more severe damage. Corrosion protection is also important since the plastic body panels may look good but the hidden metal frame structure may become deteriorated.

Figure 3–5 Unibody construction has body panels forming frame. No separate, thick steel framework is needed. This body is made of corrosion resistant aluminum that will not rust. (© American Honda Motor Co., Inc.)

Basically, unibody frames are made up of numerous simple parts. Single layer stamped steel panels, channels, and boxed or closed steel sections form the unibody, Figure 3–7.

Support members are often bolted to the bottom of the unibody to hold the engine, transmission, and

suspension in alignment. They are needed in high stress areas to reduce body flex.

JOINING PARTS

Stationary parts, like the floor, roof, and quarter panels, are permanently welded or adhesive bonded into place. *Hinged parts,* like doors, hood, and decklids, will swing up and open.

Fastened parts are held together with various fasteners (bolts, nuts, clips, etc.). Many parts, like the fenders, hood, and grill bolt into place. These bolted on parts also add to the strength of the vehicle, Figure 3–8.

Welded parts are permanently joined by melting the material so that it flows together and bonds when cooled. Both metal and plastic parts can be welded.

Press-fit or *snap-fit parts* use clips or an interference fit to hold parts together. This assembly method is becoming more common to reduce manufacturing costs.

Adhesive bonded parts use a high strength epoxy or special glue to hold the parts together. Both metal and plastic parts can be adhesive joined.

Body Structure

Hood

Roof Panel

Trunk Lid

Rear Bumper

Door Skin

Grille

Left Quarter Panel

Front Bumper

Left Fender

Rocker Panel Skin

Space Frame

Figure 3–6 Note space frame construction. The structure is a steel space frame, built from steel stampings to which polymer exterior panels are attached. These plastic panels are flexible to resist door dings and small dents. (1992 Saturn, Courtesy Saturn Corporation)

Box or Closed Section

Open Hat Channel

Single Layer

Figure 3–7 Unibody parts can be single layer, hat channel, box, or other shapes. Curves in panels increases strength. *(I-CAR)*

Structural adhesive can also be used to bond parts together. Refer to Figure 3–9.

A *composite unibody* is made of specially formulated plastics and other materials, like carbon fiber, to form the vehicle. The frame is made totally of plastics, keeping metal parts to a minimum. This cuts weight while increasing strength, rigidity, performance, and fuel economy. Although not mass produced, several manufacturers are experimenting with composite unibody construction.

MAJOR BODY SECTIONS

For simplicity and to help communication in auto body repair, a vehicle is commonly divided into *three*

Figure 3–8 Many parts bolt to unibody structure, fenders for example. Engine and other assemblies bolted to body help increase structural integrity. *(Photograph provided courtesy of Mercedes-Benz North America, Inc.)*

body sections—front, center, and rear. You should understand how these sections are constructed so that you can properly repair them. Study Figure 3–10.

The *front section,* also called *nose section,* includes everything between the front bumper and the firewall. The bumper, grille, frame rails, front suspension parts, and usually the engine are a few of the items included in the front section of a vehicle.

The nickname "front clip" or "doghouse" is used to refer to the front body section. They are often purchased and cut off from a wreck in one piece from an *automotive recycler* or "salvage yard." The empty engine compartment forms the "doghouse."

The *center section* or *midsection* typically includes the body parts that form the passenger compartment. A few parts in this section include the floor pan, roof panel, cowl, doors, door pillars, glass, and related parts. A slang name for the center section is "greenhouse" because it is surrounded by glass.

The *rear section, tail section,* or *rear clip,* commonly consists of the rear quarter panels, trunk or rear floor pan, rear frame rails, trunk or deck lid, rear bumper, and related parts. Also called "cathouse," it is often sectioned or cut off of a salvaged vehicle to repair severe rear impact damage.

When discussing collision repair, body shop personnel often refer to these sections of the vehicle. It simplifies communication because everyone knows which parts are included in each section.

PANEL AND ASSEMBLY NOMENCLATURE

A *panel* is a stamped steel or molded plastic sheet that forms a body part. Various panels are used in a vehicle. Usually, the name of the panel is self explanatory.

Structural Adhesive

Quarter Panel

Structural Adhesive

Figure 3–9 Structural adhesive is now common. It helps hold parts securely together to make body quieter and stronger. *(Courtesy of Chrysler Corporation)*

Figure 3–10 Vehicle is commonly divided into three sections for better communication in auto body repair. Study external parts in each section. *(BMW of North America)*

When panels are joined into a large part, it is called an *assembly.*

The *vehicle left-side* is the steering wheel side, on vehicles and trucks built for American roads. The *vehicle right-side* is the passenger side or side opposite the steering wheel. Remember that vehicles built for other countries will often have their steering wheel on the right-side because they drive on the left side of the road.

Another way to determine the right- and left-sides of a vehicle is to stand behind the vehicle. Your right hand would be on the right-side and left hand would

Figure 3–11 Note part names at front and rear of body. *(BMW of North America)*

be on the left-side of the vehicle. Panels and parts are often called out as left- or right-side, as shown in Figure 3–11.

FRONT SECTION PARTS

The *frame rails* are the box frame members extending out near the bottom of the front section. They are usually the strongest part of a unibody.

The *cowl* is the body parts at the rear of the front section, right in front of the windshield. This includes the top cowl panel and side cowl panels.

The *front fender aprons* are inner panels that surround the wheels and tires to keep out road debris. They often bolt or weld to the frame rails and cowl.

The *shock towers* or *strut towers* are reinforced body areas for holding the upper parts of the suspension system. The coil springs, and strut or shock absorbers fit up into the shock towers. They are normally formed as part of the inner fender apron. Look at Figure 3–12.

The *radiator core support* is the framework around the front of the body structure for holding the cooling system radiator and related parts. It often fastens to the frame rails and inner fender aprons.

Figure 3–12 Frame rails are most important structural parts in front section of unibody vehicle. Other major parts fasten to rails. *(Used by permission of Tech-Cor, Inc.)*

The *hood* is a hinged panel for accessing the engine compartment (front-engine vehicle) or trunk area (rear-engine vehicle). *Hood hinges,* bolted to the hood and cowl panel, allow the hood to swing open. The hood is normally made of two or more panels welded or bonded together to prevent flexing and vibration.

The *dash panel*, sometimes termed *firewall* or *front bulkhead,* is the panel dividing the front section and the center, passenger compartment section. It normally welds in place.

The *front fenders* extend from the front doors to the front bumper. They cover the front suspension and inner aprons. They normally bolt into place around their perimeter.

The *bumper assembly* bolts to the front frame horns or rails to absorb minor impacts.

CENTER SECTION PARTS

The *floor pan* is the main structural section in the bottom of the passenger compartment. It is often stamped as one large piece of steel.

With front-wheel drive vehicles, the floor pan can be relatively flat. With rear-wheel drive vehicles, a *tunnel* is formed in the floor pan for the transmission and drive shaft. The drive shaft needs room to extend back to the rear axle assembly.

Pillars are vertical body members that hold the roof panel in place and protect in case of a rollover accident. Refer to Figure 3–13.

The *front pillars* extend up next to the edges of the windshield. They must be strong to protect the passengers. Also termed *A-pillars,* they are steel box members that extend down from the roof panel to the main body section.

Figure 3–13 Pillars hold roof in place and provide opening for doors. They must be extremely strong. *(© American Honda Motor Co., Inc.)*

Figure 3–14 Study basic construction of door assembly. Regulator allows window to go up and down. (*Courtesy of Chrysler Corporation*)

Center pillars or *B-pillars* are the roof supports between the front and rear doors on four-door vehicles. They help strengthen the roof and provide a mounting point for the rear door hinges.

Rear pillars extend up from the quarter panels to hold the rear of the roof and rear window glass. Also called *C-pillars*, their shape can vary with body style.

Rocker panels or *door sills* are strong beams that fit at the bottom of the door openings. They normally are welded to the floor pan and to the pillars, kick panels, or quarter panels. The *kick panels* are small panels between the front pillars and rocker panels.

The *rear shelf* or *package tray* is a thin panel behind the rear seat and in front of the back glass. It often has openings for the rear stereo speakers. The *rear bulkhead panel* separates the passenger compartment from the rear trunk area.

The *doors* are complex assemblies made up of an outer skin, inner door frame, door panel, window regulator, glass, and related parts. *Door hinges* bolt between the pillars and door frame. The *window regulator* is a gear mechanism that allows you to raise and lower the door glass. Look at Figure 3–14.

Side impact beams are metal bars or corrugated panels that bolt or weld inside the door assemblies to protect the passengers. Primarily, they prevent the door from opening upon impact. They also help keep anything from intruding into the passenger area, Figure 3–15.

The *roof panel* is a large multipiece panel that fits over the passenger compartment. It is normally welded to the pillars. Sometimes it includes a sunroof or removable top pieces, termed T-tops.

The *dash assembly*, sometimes termed *instrument panel*, is the assembly including the soft dash pad, instrument cluster, radio, heater and AC controls, vents, and similar parts.

Figure 3–15 Side impact beams are located inside of doors. (*Courtesy of Chrysler Corporation*)

REAR SECTION PARTS

The *trunk floor panel* is a stamped steel part that forms the bottom of the rear storage compartment. Quite often, the spare tire fits down into this stamped panel. It often welds to the rear rails, inner wheel houses, and lower rear panel.

The *deck lid* or *trunk lid* is a hinged panel over the rear storage compartment, Figure 3–16. A *rear hatch* is a larger panel and glass assembly hinged for more access to the rear of the vehicle.

The *quarter panels* are the large, side body sections that extend from the side doors back to the rear bumper. They are welded in place and form a vital part of the rear body structure.

The *lower rear panel* fits behind the rear bumper and between the quarter panels.

Rear shock towers hold the top of the rear suspen-

Figure 3–16 Deck lid is mounted on two hinges. Torsion bars, springs, or shocks keep lid in raised position when needed. Striker engages latch to hold lid closed. (© American Honda Motor Co., Inc.)

: Indicates undercoating coated portions.

Figure 3–17 Undercoating or anticorrosion material is often applied to underbody areas exposed to road salt, water, and other debris. This helps protect underbody from rust damage. *(Used with permission of Nissan Motor Corporation)*

sion. The *inner wheelhousings* surround the rear wheels.

GASKETS AND SEALS

Various *gaskets* and *rubber seals* are used to prevent air and water leakage between body parts. Seals or *weatherstripping* are often used around doors and the rear deck lid. The rubber seal is partially compressed when the door or lid is closed to form a leakproof connection. Another example, a rubber gasket often seals the stationary glass where it fits into the body.

ANTICORROSION MATERIALS

Anticorrosion materials are used to prevent rusting of metal parts. Various types of anticorrosion materials are available. For example, *undercoating* is often a thick tar or synthetic rubber-based material sprayed onto the underbody of the vehicle. After performing repairs, you must restore all corrosion protection. Refer to Figure 3–17.

SOUND DEADENING MATERIALS

Sound deadening materials are used to help quiet the passenger compartment. They are insulation materials that prevent engine and road noise from entering the passenger area.

ENGINE LOCATIONS, DRIVE LINES

There are four basic drive train designs: front-wheel drive *(FWD)*, rear-wheel drive *(RWD)*, rear-engine,

rear-wheel drive *(RRW)* and mid-engine, rear-wheel drive *(MRD)*. The vast majority of unibody vehicles on the road today are FWD with the engine in the front. These variations affect vehicle construction and repair methods.

A *longitudinal engine* mounts the crankshaft centerline front to rear when viewed from the top. Front-engine, rear-wheel drive vehicles use this type of engine mounting.

A *transverse engine* mounts sideways in the engine compartment. Its crankshaft centerline extends toward the right and left of the body. Both front-engine, and rear-engine vehicles use this configuration.

A *front-engine, front-wheel drive (FWD)* vehicle has both the engine and transaxle in the front. Constant velocity or CV-axles extend out from the transaxle to power the front drive wheels. This is one of the most common configurations, Figure 3–18.

A *front-engine, rear-wheel drive (RWD)* vehicle has the engine in the front and the drive axle in the rear.

Engine and transaxle

Figure 3–18 Study typical front-engine, front-wheel drive design. *(Courtesy of Chrysler Corporation)*

Figure 3–19 This is a high performance, rear-engine, rear-wheel drive car. Weight of engine is over drive wheels for good traction upon acceleration. *(Photograph used by permission from Porsche Cars North America, Inc.)*

The transmission is often right behind the engine and a drive shaft transfers power back to the rear axle. A few vehicles have the engine in the front and the transmission in the rear, however.

A *rear-engine, rear-wheel drive (RRD)* vehicle has the engine in the back and a transaxle transfers power to the rear drive wheels. Traction upon acceleration and cornering is good because the weight of the engine and transaxle are over the rear drive wheels, Figure 3–19.

A *mid-engine, rear-wheel drive (MRD)* vehicle has the engine located right behind the front seat or centrally located. This helps to place the center of gravity in the middle so that the front and rear wheels hold the same amount of weight. This improves cornering ability.

All-wheel drive uses two differentials to power all four drive wheels. This is a relatively new design used on several makes of passenger vehicles, Figure 3–20.

Four-wheel drive systems use a transfer case to send power to two differentials and all wheels. The transfer case can be engaged and disengaged to select two- or four-wheel drive as desired. It is common on off-road vehicles.

NOTE! FOR MORE INFORMATION ON VEHICLE CONSTRUCTION (AIR BAGS, DRIVE LINES, ETC.) AND RELATED SUBJECTS, REFER TO TEXTBOOK INDEX. FOR EXAMPLE, CHAPTER 30 EXPLAINS THE OPERATION AND REPAIR OF MECHANICAL SYSTEMS.

VEHICLE SIZES

A *compact car,* also termed *economy car,* is the smallest body classification. It normally uses a small,

Figure 3–20 All-wheel drive has drive train that powers all four wheels, all of the time. This one is for a mini van. *(Courtesy of Chrysler Corporation)*

4-cylinder engine, is very lightweight, and gets the highest gas mileage.

An *intermediate car* is medium in size. It can use a 4, 6, or 8 cylinder engine, has average weight, and physical dimensions. It usually has unibody construction, but a few older vehicles have body-over-frame construction.

A *full-size car* is the largest classification. It is large, heavy, and often uses a high performance V-8 engine. Full-size cars can have either unibody or body-over-frame construction.

ROOF DESIGNS

A *sedan* refers to a body design with a center pillar that supports the roof. Sedans come in both 2- and 4-door versions.

A *hardtop* does not have center pillar to support the roof. The roof must be reinforced to provide enough strength. A hardtop is also available in both 2- and 4-door versions.

A *hatchback* has a large third door at the back. This design is commonly found on small compact cars so that more rear storage space is available.

A *convertible* uses a retractable canvas roof with a steel tube framework. The top folds down into an area behind the seat. Some convertibles use a removable hardtop.

A *station wagon* extends the roof straight back to the rear of the body. A rear hatch or window and *tailgate* open to allow access to the large storage area.

VANS AND TRUCKS

A *van* has a large box-shaped body to increase interior volume or space. A full-size van normally is front-engine, rear-wheel drive with a full perimeter frame. A *mini van* is smaller and often uses front-engine, front-wheel drive with unibody construction.

A *pickup truck* normally has a separate cab and bed. A front-engine, rear-wheel drive is typical.

Summary

- *Vehicle classification* relates to the construction, size, shape, number of doors, type of roof, and other criteria of a motor vehicle.

- There are three main types of vehicle frame construction: body-over-frame, unibody, and space frame. Each has its own unique repair challenges.

- A vehicle is commonly divided into three body sections:
  1. *front*, or *nose* section
  2. *center section* or *midsection*
  3. *rear section*, *tail section*, or *rear clip*.

- There are four basic drive train designs:
  1. front-wheel drive (FWD)
  2. rear-wheel drive (RWD)
  3. rear-engine, rear-wheel drive (RRW)
  4. mid-engine, rear-wheel drive (MRD).

- The three vehicle sizes are compact (or economy), intermediate, and full size.

Technical Terms

certified crash tests	*conventional frame*
crush zones	*perimeter frame*
insurance rating system	*ladder frame*
vehicle classification	*x-frame*
frame	*partial frame*
body-over-frame	*unibody*
frame rails	*stressed hull structure*
torque boxes	*space frame*
frame horn	*support members*
crossmembers	*stationary parts*
spring hangers	*hinged parts*
rubber body insulators	*fastened parts*

snap-fit parts	*window regulator*
welded parts	*roof panel*
adhesive bonded parts	*instrument panel*
structural adhesive	*trunk floor panel*
three body sections	*quarter panel*
front section	*inner wheel housing*
center section	*undercoating*
rear clip	*sound deadening*
composite body	*material*
panel	*FWD*
vehicle left-side	*RWD*
frame rails	*MRD*
cowl	*longitudinal engine*
front fender aprons	*transverse engine*
shock tower	*all-wheel drive*
radiator support	*four-wheel drive*
hood	*compact car*
firewall	*intermediate car*
front fender	*full-size car*
floor pan	*sedan*
tunnel	*hardtop*
pillars	*hatchback*
rocker panel	*station wagon*
kick panels	*tailgate*
rear shelf	*mini van*
bulkhead panel	

Review Questions

1. How many parts are used in a typical vehicle?
   a. 1,000
   b. 10,000
   c. 15,000
   d. 50,000

2. _____ are built into the frame or body to collapse and absorb collision energy.

3. What are three main types of vehicle construction?

4. Describe some characteristics of a separate frame.

5. _____ are used between the frame and body to reduce noise and vibration.

6. What is a perimeter frame?

7. Explain how the concept of unibody construction was first developed.

8. What is a space frame?

9. A car has been hit hard in the front. All major front section parts must be replaced. The owner has no insurance and must pay for the repairs. Technician A says to call automotive recyclers or salvage yards to find a front clip. Technician B

says to order new parts to assure a good repair. Who is correct?

a. Technician A
b. Technician B
c. Both technicians
d. Neither technician

10. Describe the term "doghouse."

11. How do you tell the right- and left-side of a vehicle?

12. This is the area at the rear of the front section, right in front of the windshield.
    a. Kick panel
    b. Crossmember
    c. Side panel
    d. Cowl

13. What is the difference between FWD and RWD vehicles regarding the floor pan?

14. This part helps strengthen the roof and provide a mounting point for the rear door hinges.
    a. A-pillar
    b. B-pillar

c. C-pillar
d. D-pillar

15. The _____ are the large, side body sections that extend from the side doors back to the rear bumper. They are welded in place and form a vital part of the rear body structure.

Activities

1. Have a class discussion comparing the advantages and disadvantages of conventional frame versus unibody construction.

2. Examine a vehicle in the shop. See how many parts you can identify. Study how the vehicle is constructed.

3. Discuss front- and rear-wheel drive vehicles. What are the advantages and disavantages of each?

4. Name the makes and models of vehicles that use steel, aluminum, and plastic or fiberglass construction. Discuss each.

CHAPTER 4

HAND TOOLS

Objectives

After studying this chapter, you should be able to:

■ Identify general purpose hand tools.

■ Explain the use of general purpose hand tools.

■ Identify the most important body shop hand tools.

■ Explain the use of body shop hand tools.

■ Compare the advantages and disadvantages of different tools.

■ List typical safety rules for hand tools.

■ Properly select the right tool for the job.

■ Maintain and store tools properly.

Introduction

Professional auto body technicians invest thousands of dollars in their tools. A good set of tools will speed repairs and improve work quality. The importance of having the right tools for the job cannot be overstated.

Remember! Tools serve to increase the abilities of your hands, arms, legs, back, eyes, and ears. They allow you to do things that would be impossible otherwise. Neither you, nor the very best technician, can do quality work using inferior tools.

PURCHASE QUALITY TOOLS

Never buy cheap, low grade tools. Cheap tools slow down your work rate and efficiency because they are heavier, more clumsy and break more easily. You usually get what you pay for. Good tools will pay for themselves in a short period of time.

A *lifetime tool guarantee* means the tool will be replaced or repaired if it ever fails or breaks. Some guarantees are for the life of the tool; some are NOT. Even though guaranteed tools are more expensive, they will save money in the long run.

TOOL STORAGE

Always store tools properly when NOT in use. This will protect them from damage or loss. It will also speed your work because you will be able to find tools more quickly. Keep related tools together in one drawer. Keep heavy tools in one drawer and small or delicate tools in another. This will keep the delicate tools from being damaged.

After use, wipe oil and grease off of tools. This increases safety and professionalism. A dirty, messy looking set of tools implies a dirty, sloppy technician.

Tool holders are clip racks, pouches, or trays that help you organize small tools. Tool holders allow you to carry the tool set to the job easily. This saves you from having to walk back and forth to and from your tool box.

A *tool box* stores and protects your tools. Most tool boxes are made up of a large, bottom roll-around cabinet and an upper tool chest. The *upper chest* often holds commonly used tools at eye level. The *lower cabinet* often stores heavier tools. See Figure 4–1.

■ *Danger!* NEVER open more than one tool box drawer at the same time because the box can flip over. Death or injury could result! Close each drawer before opening the next one.

GENERAL DUTY HAMMERS

Hammers are used for striking and exerting an impact on a part. Always use the right hammer for the task and use it properly. Look at Figure 4–2.

A *ballpeen hammer* has a flat face for general striking and a round peen end for shaping sheet metal, rivet heads, or other objects.

The *brass* or *lead hammer* will make heavy blows without marring the metal surface. The soft metal head will dent and protect the part.

A *plastic hammer* is for making light blows where parts can be easily damaged. It is used on delicate parts.

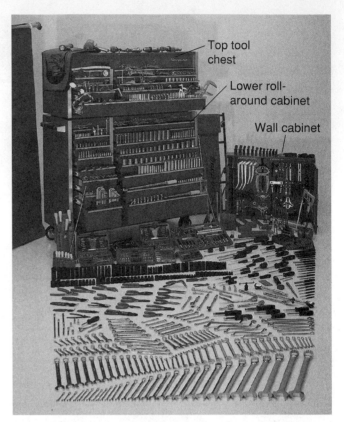

Figure 4–1 A quality tool box is the foundation for your set of tools. Lower rollaround cabinet often holds heavier, bulkier tools. Upper chest is for smaller, more commonly used tools. *(Courtesy of Snap-On Tools Corporation)*

A *dead blow hammer* has a metal face filled with lead shot (balls) to prevent rebounding. It will NOT bounce back up after striking. It is good for driving operations where part damage must be avoided.

A *rubber mallet* has a solid rubber head that is fairly heavy. It is often used to gently bump sheet metal without damaging the painted finish. They are also used to install wheel covers. Rubber mallets can be used in conjunction with a suction cup on soft

Figure 4–2 An assortment of hammers is essential. A: Brass hammer B: Rubber hammer C: Plastic hammer D: Dead blow hammer E: Ball peen hammer F: Ball peen hammer with rubber handle grip G: Claw hammer should not be used in body repair: it is for woodworking. *(Courtesy of Snap-On Tools Corporation)*

"cave-in" type dents. While pulling on the cup, the mallet is used to tap lightly all around the surrounding high spots. A "popping sound" occurs as the high spots drop and the low spot springs back to its original contour.

BODY HAMMERS

Body hammers are designed to work with sheet metal. They often have a point on one end and a flat head on the other or a head of an odd shape. They come in many different designs. Each style is designed for a special use. Refer to Figure 4–3.

Picking hammers have a sharply pointed head and will remove many small dents. The pointed end is used to raise small dents from the inside. The flat end is for hammer-and-dolly work to remove high spots and ripples. Picking hammers come in a variety of shapes and sizes. Some have long picks for reaching behind body panels. Some have sharp points; others are blunted.

Bumping hammers are used to bump out large dents. They can have a round or square face. The surfaces of the faces are nearly flat and large enough that the force of the blows are spread over a large area. These hammers are used for initial straightening on damaged panels. They are also used for working inner panels and reinforced sections that require more force but NOT a finished appearance.

Finishing hammers are used to achieve the final sheet metal contour. The face on a finishing hammer is smaller than that of the heavier bumping hammer. The surface of the face is crowned to concentrate the force on top of the ridge or high spot.

Shrinking hammers are finishing hammers with a serrated or cross-grooved face. They are used to shrink spots that have been stretched by excessive hammering.

Remember! When using hammers, make sure the head is tight on its handle. Injury could result if the head were to fly off. Try to hit the object squarely and hold the handle securely.

DOLLIES AND SPOONS

Dollies or *dolly blocks* are used like a small, portable anvil. They are generally held on the backside of a panel being struck with a hammer. Together the hammer and dolly work high spots down and low spots up to reshape the damaged body panel. Look at Figure 4–4.

Body spoons are used sometimes like a hammer and other times like a dolly. They are available in a variety of shapes and sizes to match various panel shapes. The flat surfaces of a spoon distribute the striking force over a wide area to prevent hammer dents. They are particularly useful on creases and ridges.

HOLDING TOOLS

A *vise* will secure or hold parts during hammering, cutting, drilling, and pressing operations. It normally bolts on a workbench.

Vise caps are soft lead, wood, or plastic jaw covers that will protect a part from marring. Vise jaws are often knurled and the small teeth will damage parts if NOT covered.

> *WARNING! Never hammer on a vise handle when tightening it. Only use your hands to tighten a vise handle.*

A *C-clamp* is a screw attached to a curved frame. It will hold objects on a work surface or drill press while working.

PUNCHES AND CHISELS

Punches and chisels are necessary in every body repair tool chest. There are several types.

Punches are used for driving and aligning operations. They come in a number of different shapes for different tasks.

A *center punch* is pointed to start a drilled hole or mark parts. The indentation will keep a drill bit from wandering out of place.

A *drift* or *starting punch* has a fully tapered shank. It will drive pins, shafts, and rods partially out of holes. A *pin punch* has a straight shank for use after a starting punch. It will push a shaft completely out of a hole.

An *aligning punch* is long and tapered and used to align body panels and other parts. It can be used to line up fender bolt holes and bumpers, for example.

Chisels are handy for some cutting operations. For example, a chisel can be used to shear off rivet heads or separate sheet metal parts, Figure 4–5.

Keep the ends of chisels and punches ground and shaped correctly. If the end becomes mushroomed or enlarged, grind it down. The sharp deformed end could cause hand injuries.

WRENCHES

Wrenches are used to rotate or turn nuts and bolts. Various types of hand wrenches are in Figure 4–6.

Figure 4-3 Body hammers come in various shapes. A: Flat head of body hammer is commonly used to beat down high areas in body panels. B: Pointed tip on body hammer will concentrate impacts in smaller area for working smaller size dents.

Dollies

Spoons

Figure 4–4 Dollies and spoons are essential in body repair. Dollies are often placed on back of panel so hammer blows work metal more effectively. Spoons are also used with hammers for less severe dents and creases. *(Courtesy of Snap-On Tools Corporation)*

Wrench size is the distance across the wrench jaws. Wrenches come in both conventional (inch) and metric (millimeter) sizes. The size will be stamped on the side of the wrench. The width of the jaw opening determines the size of a wrench.

For example, a ½-inch wrench has a jaw opening from face-to-face of approximately ½ inch. The actual size is slightly larger than its normal size so that the wrench can fit around a nut or bolt head of equal size.

Most standard or *SAE (Society Of Automotive Engineers)* wrench sets include sizes from ³⁄₁₆ to 1 inch. Metric sets usually include 6- to 19-millimeter wrenches. Smaller and larger wrenches can be purchased but are rarely used in collision repair.

It is important to remember that metric and SAE size wrenches are NOT interchangeable. For example, a ⁹⁄₁₆-inch wrench is ³⁄₁₀ millimeter larger than a 14-millimeter nut. If the ⁹⁄₁₆-inch wrench is used to turn or hold the 14-millimeter nut, the wrench will probably slip, rounding the points on the nut.

When using a wrench, PULL on the wrench—don't push. If the wrench comes off the bolt, there is less

chance that you will hurt your hand. Never extend the length of a wrench with a pipe for leverage. Excess force can bend or break the wrench.

Wrench Types

An *open end wrench* has three-sided jaws on both ends. This type of wrench is good if the bolt or nut is NOT very tight. The open jaws are weak. If a bolt is extremely tight, the open end wrench will bend or flex outward and strip the bolt head.

A *box end wrench* has closed ends that surround the bolt or nut head. It is a stronger design than an open end. It is available in 12-point and 6-point types. A 6-point will grip the head better and should be used on very tight, rusted, or partially stripped fastener heads.

A *combination wrench,* as implied, has both types of ends—box end and open end. It provides the features of two wrench types.

A *tubing, flare nut,* or *line wrench* has a small split in its jaw to fit over lines and tubing. It can be slipped over fuel, brake, and power steering lines. Avoid using an open end wrench on tubing nuts because they will round off and strip easily. Tubing nuts are very soft.

An *Allen wrench* is a hex, hexagon, or six-sided wrench. It will install or remove set screws. Set screws are often used on pulleys, gears, and knobs. See Figure 4–7.

A *crescent* or *adjustable wrench* has movable jaws to fit different head sizes. It can be used when a correct size wrench is NOT available. For example, if a bolt is badly rusted, an adjustable wrench may be set to fit the odd head dimension.

A *pipe wrench* is another type of adjustable wrench for holding and turning round objects. Its sharp jaw teeth dig into and grasp the part. A pipe wrench will mar and damage part surfaces and should only be used when necessary.

A *chain wrench* is also used to grasp and turn round objects. It is used to remove stuck or damaged engine oil filters or to adjust exhaust systems.

Specialized body wrenches come in a variety of designs to meet specific demands. For example, the frame wrench is designed to bend the lip of heavy gauge frame rail.

Socket Wrenches

Socket wrenches are cylinder-shaped, box end wrenches for rapid turning of bolts and nuts. They come in a variety of designs—deep sockets, swivel sockets, impact sockets, etc.

Figure 4–5 Study use of punches and chisels. A: Center punch will make small indentation in part. This will keep drill bit from moving around. B: Starting or drift punch is tapered and will start driving operation. C: Pin punch has straight sides and will completely drive out part. D: Chisels are named after their shape. Note chisel names. Cold chisel is most common in body repair. (© Stanley Tools, New Britain, Connecticut, 06050)

Figure 4–6 Study hand wrench names. A: Open end wrench B: Open end wrench with socket on other end C: Box end wrench D: Curved box end wrench E: Ratchet wrench F: Open end and flare nut wrench G: Angled head open end wrench H: Open end and flare nut wrench I: Curved box end wrench J: Combination wrenches K: Offset box end wrench L: Long open end wrench M: Long offset box end wrench (Courtesy of Snap-On Tools Corporation)

Figure 4–7 Allen wrenches are needed to turn hex head, set screws. An assortment of U.S. and metric sizes are needed. *(Courtesy of Snap-On Tools Corporation)*

Deep sockets are longer for reaching over stud bolts. *Swivel sockets* have a universal joint between the drive end and socket body. *Impact sockets* are thicker and case hardened for use with an air powered impact wrench. Impact sockets are often black in color. *Conventional sockets* or non-impact sockets are usually chrome plated.

Socket drive size is the size of the square opening for the drive handle. Common drive sizes are ¼, ⅜, ½, and ¾ inches. Small ¼-inch drive sockets are often used when working on an instrument panel with its many small screws. Large ½-inch drive sockets would be needed on larger suspension system parts.

Sockets are also made in 4-point, 6-point, 8-point, and 12-point configurations. Again, a 6-point is the strongest and will NOT strip the bolt or nut head easily.

A *ratchet* has a small lever that can be moved for either loosening or tightening bolts and nuts. It is a common type of socket drive handle. One type is in Figure 4–8.

A *breaker bar* provides the most powerful way of turning bolts and nuts. Also called a *flex handle*, it will break loose large or extremely tight fasteners.

A *speed handle* can be rotated to quickly remove or install loose bolts and nuts.

Extensions fit between the socket and its drive handle. They allow you to reach in and install the socket when surrounded by obstructions. See Figure 4–9.

A *universal joint* allows you to reach around objects with a socket wrench and extension. It will flex, allowing you to rotate the socket from an angle. Separate universal joints and swivel sockets are available.

A *torque wrench* is used to measure tightening force. *Torque* is a measurement of twisting force. It is given in both inch-pounds, foot-pounds, as well as metric measurements of Newton meters. Look at Figure 4–10.

If the fastener is tightened to a value less than its specification, the fastener can vibrate loose. If tightened too much, the threads can strip or the fastener can break. In either case, damage to other automobile parts can result. This can also endanger the driver and passengers of the vehicle.

Always torque all bolts and nuts to the *manufacturer's specifications* (factory values given in service manual). If there are no specifications listed, use the general torque specifications chart. One is given in the back of this book.

PRY BARS

Pry bars are used to gain leverage for shifting heavy parts. They are hardened steel bars with various end shapes. Pry bars are often used to adjust engine belt tension. They will also shift parts to align holes. This will aid in hand starting bolt threads. Refer to Figure 4–11.

SCREWDRIVERS

Screwdrivers allow you to rotate screws for installation or removal. Many threaded fasteners used in the automotive industry are driven by a screwdriver. Each fastener requires a specific kind of screwdriver.

Figure 4–8 Ratchet is most common socket drive handle. This one has a swivel head for reaching and turning sockets in tight quarters. *(© Stanley Tools New Britain, Connecticut 06050)*

Figure 4–9 A: Storage box. B: Socket set. C: Ratchet. D: Breaker or flex bar. E: T-handle. F: Extensions. *(K-D Tools)*

A well-equipped technician will have several sizes or types of each.

When selecting a screwdriver, select a tip wide and thick enough to almost fill the screw head opening. If NOT the right size, screwdriver and screw damage will result. Refer to Figure 4–12.

A *standard screwdriver* has a tip with a single flat blade for fitting into the slot in the screw. A *Phillips screwdriver* has two crossing blades for a star-shaped screw head. *Torx,* and *square head screwdrivers* have specially shaped tips, which are shown in Figure 4–13.

Stubby screwdrivers have a very short shank. They can fit into tight or restricted areas. For example, you might use them to install trim around a wheel opening. *Offset screwdrivers* have the shank at a 90-degree angle to the tip. They are also for restricted areas, like inside glove boxes.

An *impact driver* is hit with a hammer to rotate tight or stuck screws. The body of the driver can be rotated to change directions for installing or removing screws.

Figure 4–11 Pry bars are helpful when trying to align or shift parts into position. They are used when adjusting engine belts, for example. *(Courtesy of Snap-On Tools Corporation)*

Figure 4–10 Torque wrench should be used to properly tighten critical bolts on steering and suspension systems. It will measure twisting force accurately. *(I-Car)*

PLIERS

Pliers are used for working with wires, clips, and pins. They will grasp and hold parts, like your fingers. The collision repair technician must own several types.

NOTE! DO **NOT** USE PLIERS IN PLACE OF A WRENCH. THEY WILL SCAR AND DAMAGE PARTS. SEE FIGURE 4–14.

Slip-joint or *combination pliers* will adjust for two sizes. They are the most common design used by the auto body technician.

Figure 4–12 Study names of screwdrivers. A: Stubby screwdrivers B: Standard screwdrivers C: Phillips screwdriver D: Standard screwdriver with wood handle E: Phillips screwdriver with wood handle. *(Courtesy of Snap-On Tools Corporation)*

Figure 4–13 Note screwdriver and screw head names. *(Klein Tools, Inc.)*

A *sheet metal gauge* is used to measure body or repair panel thickness or gauge size. It has small openings with the gauge size stamped next to it. Gauge size is a number system that denotes the thickness of sheet metal. Look at Figure 4–16.

To use a thickness gauge, find the opening that fits the sheet metal. The number equals sheet metal thickness. Generally, a larger gauge number means thinner sheet metal. Ten gauge sheet metal would be thicker than 20 gauge.

Tin snips are the most common metal cutting tool. They can be used to cut straight or curved shapes in sheet metal. They are also used to trim panels to size.

Panel cutters will precisely cut sheet metal, leaving a clean, straight edge that can be easily welded. They are used to make straight or curved cutoffs in panels, often to repair rust damage.

FILES

Files are used to remove burrs, sharp edges, and to do other smoothing tasks. Various files shapes and coarseness of teeth are available, Figure 4–17.

In general, a *coarse file* works well on soft materials, such as brass, aluminum, and plastics. A *fine file* will give a smoother surface in harder materials. A fine file is normally used on steel to smooth its surface.

When using a file, always have a handle securely in place. The sharp tang, if NOT covered, can easily puncture your hand or wrist. Only apply filing pressure on the forward stroke. Lift the file on your backstroke.

Never press too hard or file too rapidly. This will quickly dull the file. Do NOT hammer on a file. Never pry with a file. It is very brittle and can shatter. When clogged, clean the file with a stiff wire brush or card brush.

Body files have very large, open teeth for cutting plastic body filler. They often have a separate blade that fits into a handle. They are commonly used when metal finishing damaged areas. See Figure 4–18.

SAWS

A *hacksaw* is sometimes needed to cut metal parts in auto body repair. Most hacksaws have an adjustable frame that accepts different blade lengths. When installing a hacksaw blade, the blade teeth should point AWAY from the handle.

A reciprocating saw has a handle with the blade extending out one end. No frame is used. After mak-

Rib joint or *channel lock pliers* have several jaw settings for grasping different size objects. They will open wider than combination pliers.

Needle nose pliers have long, thin jaws for reaching in and grasping small parts. Never twist on needle nose pliers or you will spring the jaws out of alignment. *Snap ring pliers* have tiny tips for fitting into circlips or snap rings. Both external and internal types are available.

Vise grip or *locking pliers* have jaws that lock into position on parts. The jaws can be adjusted to different widths. Then, when clamped down, they will hold the part and free your hand to do another task. Special locking pliers with extended jaws are available for welding or working with sheet metal. Refer to Figure 4–15.

Diagonal cutting pliers have cutting jaws that will clip off wires flush with a surface. Another name for these are *side cut pliers*.

SHEET METAL TOOLS

Various tools are used by the technician to work body sheet metal. The following are the most common.

Figure 4–14 Study names of common pliers. A: Slip joint pliers. B: Electrician's pliers. C: Needle nose pliers. D: Offset needle nose pliers. E: Stubby needle nose pliers. F: Channel lock pliers. G: Side cut pliers. H: Nose cutting pliers. I: Crimping plier *(Courtesy of Snap-On Tools Corporation)*

(A) Vise Grip Wrench

(B) Vise Grip Sheet Metal Clamp

(C) Vise Grip C–Clamp

Figure 4–15 Vise grip or locking pliers are handy because they will lock and stay on part. They will hold two parts together like a clamp.

Thickness of Sheet

Figure 4–16 Standard gage or sheet metal gauge can be fitted over metal to find its thickness. Number system denotes gauge thickness.

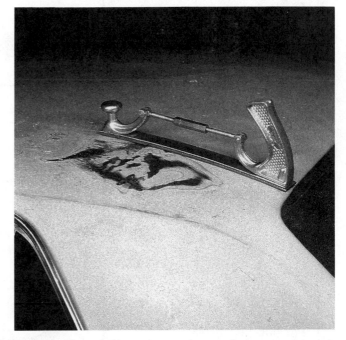

Figure 4–18 Body file is often used to rough shape and smooth body filler before complete hardening. This body file was used to shape filler on fender. *(Oatey Bond Tite)*

Figure 4–17 Note names of files and file accessories. A: Round file. B: Flat file. C: Diamond file. D: Half round file. E: Rat tail file. F: Body file. G: Small files. H: File cleaning card. I: Body file handles. J: File handles. *(Courtesy of Snap-On Tools Corporation)*

ing a starting hole, a jab saw can be used to cut into a blind panel, not accessible from the back.

Hacksaw blade coarseness is rated in teeth per inch or millimeter. It also comes in different teeth configurations. Select the correct blade for the material to be cut.

Generally, at least two teeth must contact the material at the same time. This will help prevent one tooth from catching and being broken off, Figure 4–19.

When using a hacksaw, place one hand on the handle and the other on the frame. Push down lightly when pushing forward and release down pressure on the backstroke.

As a general rule, count one thousand one, one thousand two, and so on to time each stroke. If cuts

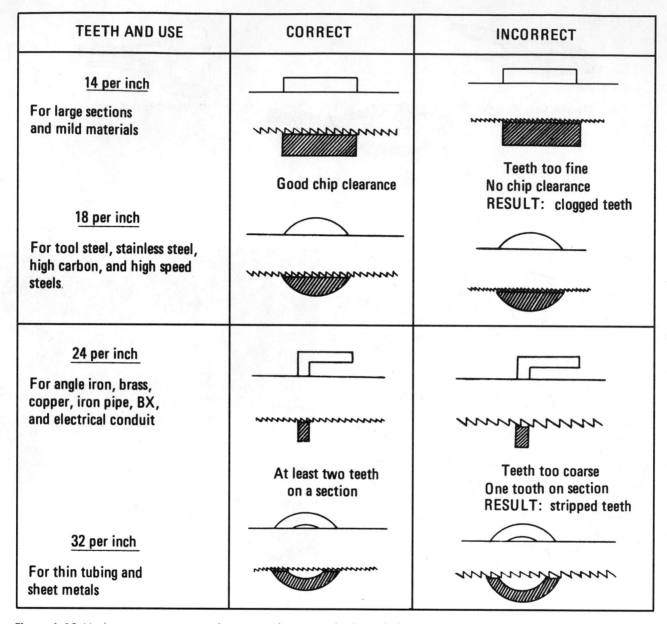

TEETH AND USE	CORRECT	INCORRECT
14 per inch For large sections and mild materials	Good chip clearance	Teeth too fine No chip clearance RESULT: clogged teeth
18 per inch For tool steel, stainless steel, high carbon, and high speed steels.		
24 per inch For angle iron, brass, copper, iron pipe, BX, and electrical conduit	At least two teeth on a section	Teeth too coarse One tooth on section RESULT: stripped teeth
32 per inch For thin tubing and sheet metals		

Figure 4–19 Hacksaw is sometimes used to cut metal parts. Study chart which explains hacksaw blade applications.

are too fast, the blade will quickly overheat and dull. This method of timing stroke speed works for saws and files.

CLEANING TOOLS

Auto body technicians sometimes have to clean parts when working. For example, if they must replace mechanical parts (suspension or steering system parts, for example), parts may be covered with oil or grease.

Hand scrapers will easily remove gaskets and softened paint (paint stripping chemicals used). They are used on flat surfaces. To prevent cuts, never scrape toward yourself. They can be made of steel for tough jobs or hard plastic to protect from gouging the surface.

Steel brushes are sometimes used to remove rust and dirt from parts. They are slow but are suitable in some situations. A wire brush should be used sparingly on bare metal because it can leave scratches in the metal. Wire brushes are ideal for cleaning weld joints.

Softer bristle brushes are often used with parts cleaning solvent to remove oil and grease.

CREEPERS, COVERS

A *creeper* allows you to lie and move around on the shop floor while working. It also allows you to slide around and under a car without getting dirty. A *stool creeper* is a small seat with caster wheels. You can lay your tools on the creeper to keep them handy.

Covers protect the vehicle from damage. A *fender cover* is often placed over the body to protect the paint from chips and scratches while working.

Seat covers protect the vehicle seats from being stained. Always use covers when needed. One stained seat or paint scratch will teach you the economy of protecting the vehicle.

HYDROMETERS

Hydrometers are used to measure the *specific gravity* or density of a liquid. They are used to check antifreeze, battery acid, and other liquids. Refer to Figure 4–20.

An *antifreeze tester* is a hydrometer for testing the strength of the cooling system solution. It detects the water-to-antifreeze concentration. An indicating arrow or the number of floating balls indicates the freeze-up protection of the antifreeze. If the cooling system does NOT have enough antifreeze, major engine and radiator damage can result during cold weather.

Figure 4–20 Hydrometers will measure concentration of antifreeze solution, battery acid or other liquids. *(Edelmann)*

FLUID HANDLING TOOLS

Funnels are needed to pour fluids into small openings. They might be needed when adding oil to an engine or brake fluid to a master cylinder.

Spouts are designed to install into can for handy pouring. They too are often used in oil cans.

A *grease gun* is used to lubricate high friction points on a vehicle's steering and suspension systems. Some body shop equipment also requires lubrication.

The grease gun tip is installed over grease fittings so that heavy grease can be injected into the part or fitting. Replaceable *grease cartridges* are often used with a grease gun.

An *oil can* is often used to lubricate parts and air tools. It has a long spout for applying oil to hard-to-reach areas. A *suction gun* can be used to remove or extract liquid. By pulling on the handle, a fluid can be pulled up into the gun.

TIRE TOOLS

A *tire pressure gauge* will accurately measure tire air pressure. Various designs are available. By pressing the gauge over the tire valve stem, the gauge will read pressure in psi or kilopascals. You should always check tire air pressures before releasing a vehicle to the customer. Low air pressure is common and can be dangerous. Recommended tire pressure is printed on the sidewall of the tire.

A *tread depth gauge* will quickly measure tire wear. The gauge is placed over the most worn area of the tire tread. A small pin on the gauge is pushed down into the tread. The gauge reading equals tire tread depth. The tire should be replaced or recommended for replacement if worn thinner than about 1/8 of an inch (3 mm).

PULLERS, PICKS

Wheel pullers are used to remove steering wheels, engine pulleys, and similar pressed-on parts. They are often bolted or mounted on the part, then a large screw is tightened to force the part off. Look at Figure 4–21.

A *slide hammer* is another type of puller that uses a hammering action to remove parts. Various ends can be installed on a slide hammer, as is shown in Figure 4–22.

A *dent puller* is a slide hammer with a threaded tip, a hook tip, or a suction cup. The threaded tip screws into a drilled or punched hole in the body panel. The slide hammer is then briskly slid along the steel shaft and struck against its handle. This produces a power-

Steering Wheel

Turn Wrench

Puller Screw

Wheel Puller

Bolts

Figure 4-21 Wheel pullers will remove pressed-on parts, like a steering wheel. Wear eye protection! *(OTC, a Division of SPX Corporation)*

ful pulling force to help remove dents in sheet metal panels.

Creases in sealed body panels or panel sections that cannot be reached from the back can be pulled out with a dent puller or pull rod. Use of either tool may require one or more holes drilled or punched in the crease. However, you can also weld a rod onto the panel for pulling. After pulling, the welded-on rod can be ground off flush, without having to drill a hole in the body.

Pull rods have a handle and curved end for light pulling of dents. A small dent or crease can be pulled up with a single pull rod, but three or four may be used simultaneously to pull up larger dents. A body hammer can also be used with a pull rod. The high crown of a dent can be bumped down, while the low spot is pulled up. Simultaneous bumping and pulling returns the panel to its origi-

A

B

C

D

E

Figure 4-22 Note uses of slide hammer puller. A: Slide hammer with hook attachment will grasp and pull exposed surfaces. B: Screw threaded into part is common for pulling small dents. C: Hole can be drilled in part or screw can be spot welded to panel so holes do not have to be drilled. D: Suction cup attachment will let you "pop out" or remove some minor dents. E: Cutter attachment can also be mounted on slide hammer.

Figure 4–23 Pull rods are often used in conjunction with body hammer. Pulling up on dent while hammering down will help reshaping.

nal shape with less danger of stretching the metal. Refer to Figure 4–23.

Picks are used to reach into confined spaces for removing tiny dents or dings. They are made of strong case hardened, spring steel. The pick is used to pry up low spots. Picks vary in length and shape, and most have a U-shaped handle. See Figure 4–24.

Figure 4–24 Pick tool is often used during dent removal. Pick will reach behind hidden or blind panel to carefully push out small dents and door dings.

Picks are commonly used to remove small dents in doors, quarter panels, and other sealed body sections. Picks are often preferred to slide hammers and pull rods because they do NOT require drilling holes in the sheet metal. They are used during *paintless dent removal* (removing small body dings or dents without painting panel).

NOTE! STRAIGHTENING TOOLS AND TECHNIQUES ARE DISCUSSED MORE IN OTHER TEXT CHAPTERS. REFER TO THE INDEX FOR ADDITIONAL INFORMATION.

MISCELLANEOUS BODY SHOP TOOLS

A variety of other miscellaneous hand tools will be useful from time to time. Many are inexpensive and have several uses. A few are very expensive but may be provided by the shop.

A common *utility knife* with a retractable blade is handy for cutting or trimming. Most come with extra blades stored in the handle. Remember that they will cause deep skin lacerations (cuts).

A *windshield knife* is designed to cut through the sealant used on some windshields. It has a sharp cutter blade and two handles. You hold one handle to guide the cutter and pull on the other handle to force the knife through the sealant. An electric heated windshield knife can be used to cut the adhesive. Air or pneumatic windshield cutters are also available.

Trim pad tools are designed to reach behind interior panels to pop out and remove clips. They often have a flat fork end that will surround the clip and push on the trim panel to prevent damage. They are often needed to remove inner door trim panels.

A door hinge *spring compressor* is used to remove and install the small spring used on some door hinges. To use this tool, the screw is tightened to compress the spring. The spring is then shortened so that it can be installed or removed.

A *door striker wrench* is a special socket designed to fit over or inside door striker posts. It will allow you to turn and loosen the post for adjustment or replacement.

A *door alignment tool* can be used to slightly bend and adjust sprung doors and hatches. It has steel knurled blocks that fit next to the door hinge. Depending upon the placement of the tool, when the door is partially closed, you can quickly realign a door. One is pictured in Figure 4–25.

A *locksmith tool,* also termed "slim jim," is used to open locked doors on cars and trucks. If you do NOT have a key or someone locked their keys in the vehi-

Figure 4–25 Door alignment tool is positioned next to door hinge. By trying to push door closed, you can raise or lower door as needed. *(Morgan Mfg. Inc.)*

cle, this type of tool will often trip and unlock the door for entry into the passenger compartment. Although designs vary, one type simply slips down between the door glass and door frame to move the lock mechanism.

Suction cup tools have a large synthetic rubber cup for sticking onto parts. They are often used to hold window glass when holding or moving the glass. They can also be used to pop out large surface area dents in panels. Refer to Figure 4–26.

Dispensers or *cartridge guns* are used to apply adhesive or sealer to body panels. They are often spring loaded. When you press the trigger, spring tension acts on the cartridge to force the material out of its tip.

A *smoke gun* can be used to find air leaks around doors and windows. With the vehicle's blower on, one technician blows smoke around all potential leakage points. Another technician stands outside to find smoke coming out of the passenger compartment, locating the leak.

A *body filler dispenser* is used to squeeze the desired amount of plastic filler and hardener onto your mixing board. By turning a handle, the material is forced out of the machine. This helps keep debris out of the filler. One type is in Figure 4–27.

Spreaders or *spatulas* are used to apply filler to low spots in body panels. They are usually made of plastic or sometimes rubber. They come in various widths for different size dents or low spots.

A *masking machine* is designed to feed out masking paper while applying masking tape to one edge of the paper. It speeds your work because the tape is already bonded onto the paper. You can quickly apply the masking paper to the body with a masking machine. See Figure 4–28.

Pin stripe brushes are used to apply paint in small, controlled areas. Some custom paint specialists use them to pin stripe cars, trucks, and vans. Small paint brushes can also be used to touch up chips along the lower body panel that were not painted. Pin stripe brushes come in different widths and lengths.

Figure 4–26 Suction cup tools are often used to hold windshield during installation. *(Saab Cars USA, Inc.)*

Figure 4–27 This is handy filler and hardener dispenser. By turning handles, you can feed out right amount of materials. Machine keeps filler perfectly clean and free of dust and debris. *(Oatey Bond Tite)*

A

B

C

D

Figure 4–28 Masking machines save time. A: Mobile masking machine has handle for carrying to job. B: This masking machine has step or seat for convenience. C: Arms on masking machine hold different sizes of paper and tape. D: This machine is for vinyl or plastic masking materials. *(Oatey Bond Tite)*

Summary

- Purchase quality tools with lifetime guarantees. Quality tools will pay for themselves in a short period of time.
- Proper tool storage will protect tools and speed your work when they are easy to locate.
- Some of the more widely used tools in collision repair work include: general duty hammers, body hammers, dollies and spoons, holding tools, punches and chisels, wrenches, pry bars, pliers, sheet metal tools, files, saws, cleaning tools, creepers, covers, hydrometers, fluid handling tools, tire tools, pullers, picks, and knives.

Technical Terms

tool holders	ratchet
tool chest	breaker bar
ball peen hammer	speed handle
plastic hammer	extension
dead blow hammer	universal joint
rubber mallet	torque wrench
tool guarantee	manufacturer's
tool holders	specifications
tool chest	standard screwdriver
picking hammer	Phillips
bumping hammer	stubby screwdriver
finishing hammer	impact driver
shrinking hammer	pliers
dolly	slip-joint pliers
body spoon	channel lock pliers
vise	needle nose pliers
vise caps	diagonal cutting pliers
c-clamp	vise grip pliers
center punch	snap ring pliers
starting punch	sheet metal gauge
pin punch	tin snips
aligning punch	panel cutters
chisel	files
wrench size	body file
SAE	hacksaw
open end wrench	hand scraper
box end wrench	creeper
combination wrench	fender cover
line wrench	hydrometer
Allen wrench	specific gravity
crescent wrench	antifreeze tester
pipe wrench	funnel
chain wrench	spout
socket wrench	grease gun
drive size	tire pressure gauge
tread depth gauge	door striker wrench
wheel puller	door alignment tool
dent puller	locksmith tool
pull rod	suction cup tool
pick	cartridge gun
paintless dent removal	smoke gun
utility knife	spreader
windshield knife	masking machine
trim pad tool	pin stripe brush
hinge spring compressor	

Review Questions

1. A good set of tools will speed _____, and improve _____.

2. What is a tool guarantee? Why would you want one?

3. Which tools would you put in the top chest of a tool box and in the lower roll-around cabinet?

4. This type of hammer is often used to install wheel covers.
   a. Lead hammer
   b. Plastic hammer
   c. Dead blow hammer
   d. Rubber mallet

5. _____ are used to achieve the final contour. The face on a _____ is smaller than that of the heavier bumping hammer.

6. How are dollies or dolly blocks used?

7. _____ are used sometimes like a hammer and sometimes like a dolly.

8. Never hammer on a vise handle when tightening it. True or false?

9. This type of punch is pointed to start a drilled hole or mark parts.
   a. Drift punch
   b. Starting punch
   c. Center punch
   d. Aligning punch

10. What is wrench size?

11. A car has damage to the front suspension and a brake line has to be removed. Technician A says to use vise grips first to make sure the fitting comes loose. Technician B says to use a combination wrench to protect the fitting nut from damage. Who is correct?
    a. Technician A
    b. Technician B
    c. Neither A nor B
    d. Both A and B

12. List the most common socket drive sizes.

13. This tool provides the most powerful way of turning bolts and nuts.
    a. Ratchet
    b. Flex handle
    c. Speed handle
    d. Impact driver

14. Never twist on _____ pliers or you will spring the jaws out of alignment.

15. Generally, a larger gauge number means a thinner sheet metal. Ten gauge sheet metal would be thicker than 20 gauge. True or false?

16. Explain when you would use a coarse file instead of a fine file.

17. What are body files?

18. A _____ is a small seat with caster wheels.

19. Explain the use of a slide hammer dent puller.

20. _____ have a handle and curved end for light pulling of dents.

Activities

1. Tour your shop. Note the location of all hand tools. Prepare a report on your findings.

2. Visit an outside body shop. Talk with other technicians about the tools they use. Discuss with the class anything you learned about new tools or techniques.

3. Order catalogs from tool manufacturers. Compare the quality, price, and warranty of each manufacturer.

CHAPTER 5

Body Shop

POWER TOOLS AND EQUIPMENT

Objectives

After studying this chapter, you should be able to:

- Identify power tools found in a body shop.

- Explain the purpose of each type of power tool.

- Summarize how to safely use power tools.

- Identify the typical types of equipment used in collision repair.

- Describe how to use body shop equipment.

- Explain safety precautions for using shop equipment.

- Select the right power tool or piece of equipment for the job.

- Explain low emissions spray equipment and regulations.

- Explain the operation of spray booths and drying rooms.

- Summarize atomization and how it relates to spray gun operation.

- Identify the various types of spray guns and explain how each type operates.

Introduction

Understanding when and how to use power tools and equipment is critical to your success as an auto body technician. Power tools and equipment speed repairs and allow you to do otherwise impossible repair operations.

Power tools and equipment utilize electrical energy, compressed air, or hydraulic power for operation. Drills, sanders, grinders, cut-off tools, and frame racks all use various forms of power to do their work. This chapter summarizes how to properly select and use power tools and equipment.

Danger! Power tools and equipment can be very dangerous if NOT used correctly. Always follow the instructions given in the owner's manual for the specific tool or piece of equipment. The information in this chapter is general and cannot cover all tool variations. If in doubt about any tool or piece of equipment, ask your instructor or shop foreman for a demonstration.

> *WARNING! The use of air-driven or electric power tools requires safety glasses or a face shield. For hazardous operations, wear both. Also, never wear loose clothing that could get caught in a tool.*

Refer to Chapter 2 for more information on power tool and equipment safety.

AIR SUPPLY SYSTEM

The shop's *air supply system* must provide clean, dry, air pressure for numerous tools and equipment. It has an air compressor, metal lines, rubber hoses, quick disconnect fittings, a pressure regulator, filters, and other parts.

AIR COMPRESSOR

An *air compressor* is made up of an electric motor, air pump, and large air storage tank. The motor spins the air pump which works like a small, reciprocating, piston engine. The air pump piston action pushes the air into a large, thick steel storage tank. The "heart" of any paint shop is its air compressor. Look at Figure 5–1.

A *compressor air filter* prevents airborne dust and dirt from entering and damaging the air pump's moving parts. The filter must be cleaned or changed at recommended intervals.

A *compressor circuit breaker* protects the electric motor from overheating damage. The circuit breaker will open to stop current flow to the motor if motor temperature and current become too high. When a circuit breaker trips, a button on the side of the motor must be pressed to reset the breaker.

A *compressor drain valve* on the bottom of the tank allows you to drain out water. The compression of the air tends to make moisture condense out of the air. This moisture must be drained out periodically to prevent it from entering the air lines.

Figure 5–1 Note major parts of air compressor, the "heart" of your air tools and equipment. *(Photo courtesy of Binks Manufacturing Company)*

A *compressor pressure sensor* is an electrical device that cuts current to the motor when normal system pressure is reached. It normally mounts in a small metal box at the air outlet line from the tank.

A *compressor pressure relief valve* prevents too much pressure from entering the tank. It is a spring-loaded valve that opens at a predetermined pressure, usually around 90 to 120 psi (8.4 K/cm^2). If the relief opens, the pressure sensor is faulty.

An *air tank shut-off valve* is a hand valve that isolates the tank pressure from shop line pressure. It should be closed at night or when the compressor is NOT going to be used. If NOT closed, the compressor would run all night if a hose leaked or ruptured.

Compressor oil plugs are provided for filling and changing air pump oil. The oil level in the compressor should be checked and changed periodically. Normally use single weight, non-detergent oil or the oil recommended by the manufacturer.

AIR LINES

Shop air lines are thick steel pipes that feed out from the tank and to several locations in the body shop.

Flexible synthetic rubber *air hoses* connect the metal pipes to the air tools and equipment.

Air hoses sizes are ¼ inch (6 mm), ⁵⁄₁₆ inch (8 mm) and ⅜ inch (10 mm) inside diameters (ID). There is less restriction using larger hose. The preferable size diameter is ⁵⁄₁₆ inch (8 mm) and it is used in many shops.

Air couplings allow you to quickly install and remove air hoses and air tools. Couplings should also have a large enough inside diameter to prevent air flow restrictions.

By sliding back on the outer fitting sleeve and pushing, you can connect or disconnect a tool to a hose. By sliding the fitting sleeve back and pulling, you can quickly disconnect tools.

AIR PRESSURE REGULATOR AND FILTER

An *air pressure regulator* is used to precisely control the amount of pressure fed to air tools and equipment. A regulator is commonly used to reduce air pressure sent to paint spray guns. However, pressure regulators may NOT be used between the compressor and many air tools, like impact guns. They require the power of full line pressure. See Figure 5–2.

The air pressure regulator has a thumb screw, spring-loaded valve, and pressure gauge. By turning the thumb screw while watching the gauge, you can set pressure to the desired level. The regulator pressure gauge often reads in pounds per square inch (psi). Some also read in metric values.

An *air line filter-drier* is used in the air line to remove moisture and debris from the air flowing through the air lines. It is designed to trap and hold water and oil that passes out of the compressor air pump. If any of these materials were to enter your paint spray gun, they would ruin the paint job.

An *air filter drain valve* allows you to remove trapped water and oil from the filter. It should be opened every evening to purge this unwanted material.

AIR TOOLS

Air tools include small hand held blow guns, spray guns, impact guns, and other tools used in the body shop. It is critical that you know how to identify and use them safely. There are various types of air tools. They run cool, are very dependable, and increase your profits.

Main pressure gauge

Regulated pressure gauge

Pressure regulator

Shut-off valves

Filter-drier

Filter drain valve

Figure 5–2 Pressure regulator can be set to match recommended pressure for specific tool, paint spray gun for example. Filter-drier is needed before paint gun to keep impurities out of gun and paint job. *(Photo courtesy of Binks Manfacturing Company)*

Air Blow Gun

An *air blow gun* is used to blow dust and dirt off the vehicle and its parts. It has a trigger that can be pressed to release a strong stream or blast of air. A blow gun is used to remove debris along trim pieces, bumpers, and other enclosed areas.

> *WARNING! Never direct a blow gun air blast at yourself or others. If air enters your bloodstream, death could result.*

Impact Wrenches

An *impact wrench* is a portable hand held, reversible air-powered tool for rapid turning of bolts and nuts.

When triggered, the output shaft spins freely over 2,000 rpm. The socket snaps over the square drive head and shaft. Study Figure 5–3.

When the impact wrench meets resistance, a small spring-loaded hammer strikes an anvil attached to the drive shaft. Thus, each impact moves the socket around a little until torque equilibrium is reached, the fastener breaks, or the trigger is released. This produces a powerful rotating force to loosen or tighten fasteners.

For all their torquing power, air impact wrenches have practically no recoil. Holding one is rather easy, but this can be misleading. The stream of air blowing through the wrench is very strong. Therefore, the wrench should be held tightly.

When using an air impact wrench, it is important that only *impact sockets* and *impact adapters* (usually black color) are used. Other types of sockets and adapters (chrome plated) might shatter and fly off, endangering everyone in the immediate area.

■ **Danger!** *Never use a conventional universal joint on an impact gun. The spinning joint can rip a hole in your hand or fly apart and explode. Only use special impact type swivel joints with an impact wrench.*

A ½ *inch impact* has a ½-inch size drive head and is shaped like a pistol with a hand grip hanging down. It can tighten fasteners to over 100 foot-pounds of torque. Remember that this is enough to snap off or stretch most bolts. It is commonly used on bolt and nut head sizes over about ⁹⁄₁₆ inch (14 mm). A ½ inch impact is frequently used to service wheel lug nuts.

A ⅜ *drive impact* has a drive head of a smaller size for working with fastener heads under ⁹⁄₁₆ inch (14 mm). It is lighter and more handy for working with small bolts and nuts on body panels.

The *air ratchet* wrench, like the hand ratchet, has a special ability to work in hard-to-reach places. Its ⅜-inch angle drive reaches in and loosens or tightens where other hand or power wrenches cannot fit. An air ratchet is handy for working behind panels, in tight quarters. The air ratchet wrench looks like an ordinary ratchet. It has a larger hand grip that contains the air vane motor and drive mechanism.

Remember that there is no reliable adjustment with an air ratchet or impact wrench. Where accurate torque is required, use a torque wrench! The air regulator on air-powered wrenches can be employed to adjust torque only to an approximate tightness. Adjust the impact to assure you do NOT overtighten. Then, use the hand torque wrench to final tighten the bolt or nut to specs.

Air Hammer

An *air hammer* uses back and forth hammer blows to drive a cutter or driver into the work piece. It works like a conventional hammer and chisel or punch but much quicker. Different shaped tools can be installed in the air hammer. For cutting, flat, forked, and curved cutters are useful.

An *air chisel* is similar but it is smaller and is often equipped with a cold chisel type of cutter. Refer back to Figure 5–3.

When using an air hammer or chisel, make sure the tool is held against the work before pulling the trigger. This will prevent the cutter from possibly flying out of the tool. Avoid running into hidden hardware, frame rails, and wiring with cutting tools. Keep the cutters sharp at all times.

Drills

Drills are used to make accurately sized holes in metal and plastic parts. Both air and electric drills are available.

Air drills use shop air pressure to spin a drill bit. They can be adjusted to any speed and are more commonly used than electric drills. They are usually available in ¼-, ⅜-, and ½-inch sizes. Air drills are smaller and lighter than electric drills. This compactness makes them a great deal easier to use for most tasks.

Drill bits of different sizes fit into the chuck on drills for making holes in parts. As in Figure 5–4, they come in various sizes. The size is usually stamped on the upper part of each bit.

Figure 5–3 Study names of air tools. A: One-half inch air impact wrench B: Air drill C: Air hammer D: Three-eighths-inch drive impact. (Courtesy of Snap-On Tools Corporation)

Figure 5–5 Hole saws will quickly and accurately make large diameter holes. *(Cooper Tools)*

Air Cutters

An *air nibbler* is used like tin snips to cut sheet metal. It has an air-powered snipping blade that moves up and down to cut straight or curved shapes in sheet metal panels. Several are in Figure 5–7.

An *air cutoff tool* uses a small abrasive wheel to rapidly cut or grind metal. It is handy for cutting when a confinement prevents the use of a nibbler. See Figure 5–7.

An *air saw* uses a reciprocating (back and forth) action to move a hacksaw type of blade for cutting parts. It works just like a hacksaw but will cut much more quickly.

Air Sanders

An *air sander* uses an abrasive action to smooth and shape body surfaces. Different coarseness sand papers can be attached to the pad on the sander. *Coarser sandpaper* removes material more quickly. *Fine sandpaper* produces a smoother surface finish. Air sanders are one of the most commonly used air tools in auto body repair.

A *circular sander* simply spins its pad and paper around and around in a circular motion. This type of sander is seldom used in auto body repair. Refer to Figure 5–8.

An *orbital* or *dual action sander* moves in two directions at the same time. This produces a much smoother surface finish. A dual action or *DA* sander is used to featheredge a repair area. It is the workhorse of body technicians. One is pictured in Figure 5–9.

The *sander pad* is a soft mounting surface for the sand paper. Disc adhesive or self-stick paper holds the sandpaper onto the pad. *Disc adhesive* is special non-hardening glue that comes in a tube. It can be placed on the pad to adhere the paper to the sander. Self-stick paper already has a non-hardening glue on it.

Figure 5–4 A good set of drill bits is a must. They should be sharp and ready to use. *(Courtesy of Snap-On Tools Corporation)*

A *key* is used to tighten the chuck. The *chuck* has movable jaws that close down and hold the bit. The key has a small gear that turns a gear on the chuck.

Never leave a key in a drill when NOT tightening. Also, unhook the air hose when installing a bit. Otherwise, injury could result. This also applies to a large drill press.

Hole saws are special cutters for making large holes in body panels. They fit into a drill like a drill bit. See Figure 5–5.

A *spot weld drill* is specially designed for removing spot welded body panels, Figure 5–6. It has a clamp type head and lever arm for accurately drilling through spot welds. The cutter will NOT deviate from the weld center during cutting.

Figure 5–6 Spot weld drills have a special fixture mounted over the drill. It helps hold drill over spot weld for accurate removal. *(NCG Company/Spotle Distributor)*

Figure 5–7 Note various types of metal cutting tools. A: Disc type cutoff tool B: Air nibbler C: Smaller air nibbler D: Air snips *(Courtesy of Snap-On Tools Corporation)*

Figure 5–9 Orbital or dual action is most common with auto body sanders. It will produce a smoother sanded surface.

Figure 5–8 Circular motion is not commonly used for sanding operations in auto body repair. The sanding disc would leave deep sanding marks. Circular motion is only used on grinders and polishers.

An *air file* is a long, thin air sander for working large flat surfaces on panels, Figure 5–10. It is handy when you must true or flatten a large repair area. It will plane down filler so that a large area is flat. An air file is often used for rough shaping operations.

GRINDERS

Grinders are used for fast removal of material. They are often used to smooth metal joints after welding and to remove paint and primer. They come in various sizes and shapes.

The most commonly used portable air grinder in collision repair and refinishing shops is the *disc-type grinder*. It is operated like the single-action disc sander. An air grinder should be used carefully. It can quickly thin down and cut through body panels, causing major problems.

Danger! If an air grinder will cut metal, it can certainly cut bone and flesh. Wear leather gloves and a full face shield when grinding.

A *bench grinder* is a stationary, electric grinder mounted on a work bench or pedestal stand. It is used to sharpen chisels, punches, and to shape other tool tips.

Trigger

Air motor

Orbital sander

Round sanding pad

A

Trigger

Dual action sander

Pad

B

Air File

Long, thin pad

C

Figure 5–10 Study common types of air sanders. *(Courtesy of Snap-On Tools Corporation)* A: Disc type orbital sander is most common design used. It is small and easy to handle. Its rounded sandpaper will let you work curved surfaces. B: This dual-action sander is good for featheredging repaired areas. C: Air file uses long, rectangular sheets of sandpaper. It is good for sanding large flat panels.

When using a bench grinder, keep the tool rest close to the stone or wire wheel. Otherwise, the tool or part can be pulled into the grinder. This can force your hand into the wheel or brush, causing a painful injury. Also, keep the shield in place over the top of the stone or brush and wear eye protection.

POLISHERS

An *air polisher* is used to smooth and shine painted surfaces by spinning a soft buffing pad. Polishing or buffing compound is rubbed over the paint with the polisher pad. This removes minor paint imperfections to increase *paint gloss* or shine.

A *polishing pad* is a cotton or synthetic cloth cover that fits over the polisher's backing plate. Sometimes the pad and backing plate are *integral* or one-piece.

A *pad cleaning tool* is a metal star wheel and handle that will clean dried polishing compound out of the pad. The wheel is held onto the spinning pad to clean out and soften the cloth material.

PNEUMATIC TOOL MAINTENANCE

Air tools need little upkeep. However, you will have problems if basic maintenance is NOT performed. For instance, moisture gathers in the air lines and is blown into tools during use. If a tool is stored with water in it, rust will form and the tool will wear out quickly.

Air tool lubrication should be done on all air tools. A few drops of special air tool oil, lightweight motor oil, or a mixture of oil and automatic transmission fluid should be used. Most air tool manufacturers recommend the use of special oil.

Squirt a couple of drops of oil into the air inlet or into special oil holes on the tool BEFORE AND AFTER use. This will prevent rapid wear and rusting of the vane motor and other parts of the tool. Run the tool after adding the oil. Wipe off excess oil on the tool to keep it off body parts.

An *in-line oiler* is an attachment that will automatically meter oil into air lines for air tools. It can be used on lines used for air tool but NOT for spray guns.

Remember, do NOT use in-line oilers in the paint area. Never over-oil sanders, grinders, and other air tools. You could contaminate the vehicle's surface with oil.

All air tools have recommended air pressures. If the tool is overworked, it will wear out sooner. If something is wrong with the tool, fix it. If the defect is NOT repaired, a chain reaction might occur and the other parts will become defective as well. The air compressor, in turn, will become overworked and could put out contaminated air.

Never forget! Your tools and equipment cannot function correctly without good care. To do good body and paint work, maintain your tools and equipment. More jobs are ruined because of the lack of care than by any other single cause.

BLASTERS

Blasters are air powered tools for forcing sand, plastic beads, or another material onto surfaces for paint removal. For example, they are handy when trying to remove surface rust from body panels. They will blast out all of the rust without further thinning of the panel.

With today's thin gauge, high strength steel, blasting is often recommended over grinding to clean out rust pockets. Grinding thins the metal and makes it weaker.

A *hand blaster* is a small, portable tool for blasting parts and panels on the vehicle. Silica sand or another abrasive is installed into the blaster cup or container. Air flow through the tool pulls a metered amount of abrasive out of the tool and forces it against the work piece. This will quickly remove paint, primer, rust, scale to take the surface down to bare metal.

A *cabinet blaster* is a stationary enclose equipped with a sand or bead blast tool. A window and rubber gloves in the cabinet allow you to blast parts without being exposed to the abrasive dust. It is often used on small parts removed from the car or truck.

SPRAY GUNS

Spray guns are used to apply sealer, primer, paint, and other liquid finishing materials to the vehicle. Spray guns must atomize the liquid, often paint, so that it flows onto the body surface smoothly and evenly.

A spray gun must *atomize* the liquid or it must break the liquid into fine mist of droplets. This requires sufficient pressure and volume at the gun.

If you plan on being a good painter, you must know your painting equipment inside and out.

Spray Gun Parts

To use, service, and troubleshoot a spray gun properly, you must understand the operation of its major parts. Refer to Figure 5–11 as each spray gun part is discussed.

The *gun body* holds the parts that meter air and liquid. The body holds the spray pattern adjustment valve, fluid control valve, air cap, fluid tip, trigger, and related parts.

The *spray gun cup* often fits onto bottom of the body to hold the material to be sprayed. The top of the cup fits against a rubber seal to prevent leakage. The seal is mounted in a lid on the lower part of the gun body.

The spray gun's *fluid control valve* can be turned to adjust the amount of paint or other material emitted. It consists of a thumb screw or knob, needle valve, and spring. Turning the knob affects how far the trigger pulls the needle valve open. The *fluid needle valve* seats in the fluid tip to prevent flow or can be pulled back to allow flow.

The spray gun's *air control valve* controls how much air flows out of the air cap side jets. It has an *air needle* that can be slid back and forth to open or close the air valve.

The *spray gun trigger* can be pulled to open both the fluid and air valves. It uses lever action to pull back on the needle valves.

The *spray gun air cap* works with the air valve to control the spray pattern of the paint. It screws over the front of the gun head.

The *spray pattern* is the shape of the atomized spray when it hits the body. With little air flow out of the side jets on the cap, you would have a very round, concentrated spray pattern. As you adjust air flow up, the cap jets narrow and better atomize the paint flowing out of the gun.

For more information on this and other related subjects, refer to the text index.

Siphon Spray Guns

Siphon spray guns use air flow through the gun head to form a suction that pulls paint into the air stream. This is the most common type of gun. One is shown in Figure 5–12.

An *air vent hole* and hose on the siphon spray gun allow atmospheric pressure to enter the cup. This vent can become clogged with dry primer or paint. If the vent is plugged, paint will NOT flow out of the gun.

An exploded view of a siphon type spray gun is in Figure 5–13, page 82. Study the relationship of the parts carefully.

Mix Nozzle Types

An *internal mix nozzle* combines the air and liquid inside or under the cap. An *external mix nozzle* combines the air and liquid outside of the gun. The external mix is more common in auto body repair. See Figure 5–14, page 83.

Pressure Feed Spray Guns

Pressurized pot or *pressure cup spray guns* use air pressure inside the paint cup or tank to force the

Figure 5–11 Study internal passages and parts of spray gun. (DeVilbiss Automotive Refinishing Products, Maumee, OH)

material out of the gun. The major external parts of this type of gun are in Figure 5–15.

Pressure pot guns provide possible advantages over siphon cup guns. They allow more paint speed through a smaller nozzle. Smaller paint streams atomize better.

A pressure pot, by having a remote cup, makes the gun lighter and easier to handle. It also permits spraying with the gun horizontal for painting under flared parts without danger of "spitting." Also, with the cup or tank away from the vehicle, paint dripping from the gun cup vent is eliminated as a problem.

Pressure tank spray guns use a much larger storage container for paint materials. They hold enough paint for a complete paint job. This saves time. You are sure the paint will match throughout the whole job. This

might help with spraying hard to match metallic or pearl paints, for example.

Remember that pressure cups have seals that must be kept clean and regularly inspected for damage. A loss of cup pressure affects the delivery of fluid to the spray gun.

> *WARNING! Always adjust line pressure to specs to prevent damage or rupture of the cup or tank. The specs will be given by the manufacturer.*

Pressure cups also hold pressure AFTER being disconnected from the air source. This can be embarrassingly messy if you open the lid and paint sprays all

Figure 5–12 The siphon paint gun is most common. Air flow through head generates vacuum which pulls paint up and out of cup. *(Photo courtesy of Binks Manufacturing Company)*

Labels: Siphon cup, Gun, Rubber seal, Paint pickup

over the shop. Make sure you release cup pressure before opening the lid.

Pressure cups also require some bleed-down time if the cup is initially over-pressurized. For example, if a cup is pressurized to 10 psi (.7 kpcm^2) and the painter desires only 6 (.42 kpcm^2) psi, the cup maintains that 10 psi (.7 kpcm^2) pressure momentarily when the trigger is first pulled back. This could force out too much paint and cause problems.

Bleeder and Non-bleeder Guns

Bleeder spray guns allow air to pass through the gun at all times, even when the trigger is NOT pulled back. They do NOT have an air control valve. The trigger only controls fluid needle movement. Bleeder guns are generally used with heated air sources.

Non-bleeder spray guns release air only when the trigger is pulled back. They have an air control valve. The trigger controls both fluid needle movement and the air control valve.

Touch-up Spray Guns

Touch-up spray guns are very small and are ideal for painting small repair areas. Often called an "air brush" or "door jamb gun," they have a tiny cup for holding a small amount of material. They operate like a conventional siphon gun.

VOC Emissions

Volatile organic compound (VOC), is a harmful substance produced by many painting materials. Some

geographic regions require the use of high transfer efficiency spray equipment to cut VOC emissions. These laws are designed to reduce the amount of air pollutants entering the earth's atmosphere.

High Efficiency Spray Guns

High efficiency spray guns are designed to reduce VOC emissions by only using 10 psi (.7 kpcm^2) air pressure at the gun head. Check local ordinances to find out if you must use these types of guns.

High efficiency spray guns are called *HVLP* for high volume, low pressure or *LVLP* for low volume, low pressure. They use 10 psi (.7 kpcm^2) or less for reducing overspray and emissions.

Transfer efficiency describes the percentage of paint a spray gun is capable of depositing on the surface. Transfer efficiency for spray guns must be at least 65% to meet regulations in some geographic locations. This means that at least 65% of the material sprayed must remain on the vehicle.

High transfer efficiency means more paint applied will remain on the surface. There is less paint wasted as overspray. High transfer efficiency cuts VOC emissions and protects our atmosphere from damage.

Transfer efficiency ratings are affected by the type of gun, gun adjustment, air pressure, spray pattern, and reduction of spray material. Generally, to improve transfer efficiency, use lower air pressure, smaller spray pattern, and thicker materials.

Actual spray transfer efficiency will vary depending on a painter's skill and technique. As you become more familiar with the techniques used with HVLP equipment, transfer efficiency and skill will increase.

Gravity feed spray guns mount the cup on top of the spray gun head so the material flows down without external air pressure. Although clumsy, it is the simplest type of high efficiency gun.

With *turbine spray systems,* the unit produces its own pressure and does NOT use shop air. This is an advantage if the shop air compressor is already near capacity. Another advantage is that turbine air is dry and free of oil.

Heated air produced by turbines can help reduce the paint's viscosity, which improves atomization. It may also improve drying times of paint materials in colder climates.

Some possible disadvantages are that the turbine's electric motor is NOT explosion proof and cannot be placed in the spray booth. The heated air also evaporates the solvents in atomized material faster than conventional air sources. This may cause a drier spray and poor appearance if proper reducer, techniques, and spraying conditions are NOT used.

Air conversion units act as in-line regulators to convert high pressure main line air pressure to low

Ref. No.	Description
1	Air Cap/Retaining Ring
2	Retaining Ring for Ref. No. 3
3	Air Cap Less Retaining Ring
4	Air Cap, Adapter/Retaining Ring
5	Retaining Ring for Ref. No. 7
6	Air Cap
7	Adapter for 31733-190 Air Cap
	Adapter for 31736-491 Air Cap
8	Fluid Tip
9	Gasket Kit (Kit of 10) (Polyethylene)
10	Baffle and Seal Kit
11	O-Ring
12	Lock Nut
13	Fluid Inlet Adapter
14	Fluid Inlet, Nut & O-Ring Kit
15	Gasket Kit (Kit of 10) (Teflon)
16	Spring
17	Air Valve
18	U Cup Seal
19	Washer
20	Snap Ring
21	Air Valve Assembly
22	Packing Kit (Kit of 10)
23	Packing Nut Kit (Kit of 10)
24	Screw
25	Stud & Screw Kit
	(Kit Includes 3 Studs & 5 Screws)
26	Trigger, Stud & Screw Kit
	(Kit Includes 1 each)
27	Plug
28	Nipple
29	Fan Adjustment Assembly
30	Retaining Ring
31	O Ring (Viton)
32	Adjusting Screw
33	Spring Kit (Kit of 10)
34	Bushing
35	Bushing, Spring & Knob Kit
36	Fluid Needle
37	Gun Body

Figure 5–13 Exploded view shows every part of a typical spray gun. Study part names and locations carefully. (DeVilbiss Automotive Refinishing Products, Maumee, OH)

Internal Mix

Air Jets

External Mix

Figure 5–14 Note difference between internal and external mix guns. External mix has air jets that mix with and disperse fluid as it leaves gun. *(I-CAR)*

Figure 5–15 Pressure pot or pressure cup gun is handy and easy to use. Study parts of pressure cup gun. Note how hoses feed from cup to gun. *(Photo courtesy of Binks Manufacturing Company)*

pressure, high volume air. They use existing shop air from the compressor.

Air conversion units allow adjustment of air pressures up to 10 psi (.7 kpcm^2). They can be wall mounted or worn by the painter. Air conversion units are available in both electrically heated and unheated models.

Step-down guns internally restrict the inlet pressure of 40–100 psi (2.8–7 kpcm^2) to 10 (.7 kpcm^2) psi at the air cap. Step-down spray guns do NOT require the use of a turbine or air conversion unit. They use existing shop air from the compressor. A special orifice, venturi, or regulator mounted on the gun cuts pressure.

Electrostatic spray guns electrically charge the paint particles at the gun to attract them to the vehicle body. They operate on the theory that opposites attract. The charged paint particles are attracted to

the grounded metal body of the car or truck. VOC regulations also list electrostatic spray equipment as complying to the minimum 65% transfer efficiency requirement. Its operation is shown in Figure 5–16.

Electrostatic spray guns are used for spraying finishes in automotive assembly plants and fleet use. They have higher transfer efficiency than other types of spray equipment when spraying complex shaped parts. For example, bicycle frames can be sprayed with higher transfer efficiency because the material is attracted to all sides of the part.

Electrostatic spray guns do NOT help attract the paint to non-metal plastic parts. To spray plastics, an electrically conductive *primer* must be applied. This primer cannot be applied using electrostatic spray equipment. Maintenance and repairs are somewhat expensive. Also, the orientation of metallic flakes may be difficult to manage.

Before purchasing spray equipment, test the equipment in the shop. This will help you select the right equipment to reduce air pollution and still produce good paint jobs in minimum time.

Specialized Spray Guns

Specialized spray guns are designed to apply various materials. They can be used to spray rubberized chip resistant materials, anticorrosion materials, and so on.

Figure 5–16 Electrostatic spray equipment uses static electrical charges to pull paint onto metal surfaces.

SPRAY BOOTHS

A *spray booth* is designed to provide a clean, safe, well-lit enclosure for painting. It isolates the painting operation from dirt and dust to keep this debris out of the paint job. It also confines the volatile fumes created by spraying and removes them from the shop area. See Figure 5–17.

Spray booths are designed to conform to federal, state, and local safety codes. In some areas, automatically operated fire extinguishers are required because of the highly explosive nature of refinishing materials.

A workbench is often in the paint mixing room for reducing the paint and for filling the spray gun. Paint storage should always be outside the spray booth.

An *air makeup* or *air replacement system* is important because air must be exhausted from spray booths continuously during the spraying process.

In winter, the spray area can become cold and uncomfortable. Finish problems can arise from spray-ing cold materials on cold vehicles in cold air. To prevent this problem, an air makeup system will often provide even temperatures and clean filtered air.

Some shops employ an independent air replacement system designed for the spray booth. This provides clean, dry, filtered air from the outside, and even heats the air in colder weather. Replacement air can be delivered to the general shop area or directly into the booth for a completely closed system.

The *downdraft spray booth* forces air from the ceiling down through exhaust vents in the floor. It is the most popular air movement system used today. The downward flow of air from the ceiling to the floor pit creates an envelope of air passing by the surface of the vehicle.

By taking clean, tempered air and directing it downward, the downdraft prevents contamination and overspray from settling on the freshly painted surface of the vehicle. This air movement also helps to remove toxic vapors from the breathing zone of the painter, providing a safer working environment.

A *side draft* or *crossflow spray booth* moves air sideways over the car or truck. An air inlet in one wall pushes fresh air into the booth. A vent on the opposite wall removes the booth air.

Spray booth lighting is very important. Colors appear different under different types of light. For instance, incandescent light tends to highlight reds. This makes it very important to utilize *color correcting lights* in the spray booth to make color show up properly. They will provide a perfectly neutral light that makes accurate color matching possible. If you are only going to paint a fender for example, you want the freshly painted fender to match the color of the rest of the vehicle.

Figure 5–17 Paint spray booth is large metal and glass enclosure with special air handling equipment. *(Photo courtesy of Binks Manufacturing Company)*

PAINT DRYING EQUIPMENT

A dust-free *paint drying room* will speed up drying, produce a cleaner job, and increase the volume of refinishing work. Some drying rooms have forced air or permanent infrared units for the force drying of paint, particularly enamels. These oven-like units can speed up the drying time as much as 75 percent. Force drying of putties, primers, and sealers will reduce waiting between operations. Drying rooms can also be used for fast drying spot and panel repairs.

Infrared drying equipment use special bulbs to generate infrared light for fast drying of materials. They can be designed into booth systems. They range from portable panels for partial or sectional drying to large heating units capable of moving automatically along a track next to the vehicle for overall drying. Look at Figure 5–18.

> *WARNING! When using a drying room, caution must be taken NOT to overheat and destroy the finish. A surface thermometer will measure panel temperatures to prevent overheating damage. It also lets you know when the surface is hot enough for complete paint drying. Two types are in Figure 5–19.*

MEASURING SYSTEMS

A *measuring system* is used to gauge and check the amount of frame and body damage. It is a special

Figure 5–19 Special thermometers should be used with drying equipment. *(I-CAR)*

machine for comparing known good measurements with those on the vehicle being repaired.

In some designs, the measuring system mounts over the vehicle. Brackets and rods are positioned so that pointers aim at specific reference points on the body. Other systems use laser light to denote properly located reference points. If any reference point does NOT line up with a measuring system, the frame or unibody must be straightened or parts must be replaced.

STRAIGHTENING SYSTEMS

Hydraulic equipment uses a confined fluid or oil to develop the pressure necessary for operation. The pressure is achieved manually (pumping on a handle or lever) or by a small motor (either air or electrically driven) which drives a pump.

A *straightening system* is a hydraulic machine for pulling a badly damaged frame or unibody structure back into proper alignment. Also termed a *frame rack,* the vehicle is anchored to the shop floor or rack using clamps and chains. Then, pulling chains are attached to the bent or damaged areas of the vehicle. One type of frame rack is given in Figure 5–20.

Pulling posts are vertical uprights on the frame machine so the chains can pull in the needed directions to straighten the damage. See Figure 5–21.

Figure 5–18 Two infrared lights. *(Photo courtesy of Binks Manufacturing Company)*

Holding chain

Drive on rack

Body anchor clamps

Pulling towers

Figure 5–20 Note major parts of frame rack. Anchors hold vehicle down onto rack while pulling. Towers allow you to position pulling chains and different heights and positions to remove frame or body damage. *(Chief Automotive Systems, Inc.)*

There are two basic types of frame/panel straighteners on the market: portable and stationary.

Frame rack accessories are the many chains, special tools, and other parts needed. They will vary with the equipment manufacturer. To perform the many different straightening operations involving pushing, pulling, or holding a vehicle, a large assortment of adapters is included in a typical kit. See Figure 5–22.

Body jacks, also known as porta-powers, can be used with frame/panel straighteners or by themselves. A body jack has a small hand-operated pump that operates a hydraulic cylinder. Pumping the handle extends the cylinder ram to produce a powerful pushing action.

A *vehicle cart* is a set of caster wheels that is clamped to the vehicle. It allows you to move the vehicle around the shop during repairs. Look at Figure 5–23.

LIFTS

The traditional stationary in-ground lift was usually found only in service stations, muffler shops, transmissions shops, and tire dealers. Today, collision repair shops use lifts because it is easier to evaluate underbody damage and make repairs.

As shown throughout this book, there are several ways to get a vehicle off the ground. Four-post and two-post hoists allow total movement under the vehicle. However, they take up more than a work stall in length and width. Side post hoists are great for estimating, but some access to the sides of the vehicle is impaired. Old center post hoists make some areas under the vehicle hard to reach but take up less space.

Raising a vehicle on a lift or a hoist requires special care. Adapters and hoist plates must be positioned correctly on lifts to prevent damage to the underbody of the vehicle. The exhaust system, tie-rods, and shock absorbers could be damaged if the adapters and hoist plates are incorrectly placed.

For more information on lifts, refer to the text index.

ELECTRIC TOOLS

Electric power tools plug into shop wall outlet power of 120 or 230 volts *AC* (alternating current). Drill presses, heat guns, welders, and vacuum cleaners are

Figure 5–21 Pulling tower can mount on rack or be separate unit. With either, they must be anchored properly for safe pulling. *(Wedge Clamp International, Inc.)*

Figure 5–22 Many accessories are provided with frame rack. You would need to refer to equipment manual to learn all about each of them. *(Chief Automotive Systems, Inc.)*

all vital electric-only tools. In addition, tools such as drills, polishers, and sanders perform the same tasks as their pneumatic counterparts.

Most power tools are built with an external grounding system for safety. A wire runs from the motor housing, through the power cord, to the third prong on the power plug. When connected to a grounded, three-hole electrical outlet, the grounding wire will carry any current that leaks past the electrical insulation of the tool. It will carry this current away from you and into the ground of the shop's wiring. Refer to Figure 5–24.

Some electric power tools are self-insulated and do NOT require grounding. These tools have only two prongs since they have a non-conducting housing.

Never use an adapter plug that eliminates and disconnects the third ground prong or you could be electrocuted.

BATTERY CHARGER

A **battery charger** converts 120 volts AC into 13 to 15 volts *DC* for recharging drained batteries. One is in Figure 5–25.

To use a battery charger, connect red to positive and black to negative. The red lead on the charger goes to the positive terminal of the battery. The black lead goes to ground or the negative battery terminal.

After connecting the charger, adjust its settings as needed (12 volt battery, fast or slow charge, etc.).

Danger! *A battery explosion could result if you connect a charger to a battery with the charger running.*

MULTIMETER

A **multimeter** is a voltmeter, ammeter, and ohmmeter combined into one electrical tester. Also called a VOM (volt-ohm-milliammeter), a multimeter is often used for many types of electrical tests. Look at Figure 5–26A.

An **analog meter** uses a needle that swings right and left for making measurements. This is an older design that is being replaced by digital meters. A **digital meter** uses a number display to show readings.

Wheels on frame
rack setup

Figure 5–23 This technician has car on dolly wheels for moving it around shop. Hold-down clamps from frame rack remain on unibody structure. *(Wedge Clamp International, Inc.)*

Grounded Outlet Box

Grounding prong is longest of the 3 prongs.

Figure 5–24 Never remove a ground prong from electrical cords. It prevents any short in tool from causing electric shock.

WARNING! Never use a low impedance (low resistance) meter to test modern electronic circuits. The low resistance and high current through the meter can damage and ruin delicate computer and electronic circuits. Use only high impedance (high internal resistance) meters.

An *inductive meter* clips around the outside insulation of wiring to take electrical readings. It is time saving when making current (amp) measurements, Figure 5–26B.

Figure 5–25 Battery charger is often needed with dead batteries. Connect charger to battery before turning it on. Set controls so as not to overcharge battery. *(Courtesy of Snap-On Tools Corporation)*

SCAN TOOLS

Scanners or *scan tools* are used to diagnose or troubleshoot vehicle computer system and wiring problems. A scanner connects to the vehicle's diagnostic connector or *ALDL* (assembly line diagnostic link). The scanner's electronic circuits can then communicate with the vehicle's on-board computer to help find problems.

Figure 5–26 Electrical test instruments are used by auto body technicians. Wiring is often damaged in collision and technician may have to find and fix minor wiring troubles. A: Multimeter will make voltage, current, and resistance measurements. This is a high impedance, digital meter acceptable for use on delicate computer circuits. (OTC, a Division of SPX Corporation) B: Inductive or clip-on meter will make rapid current measurements. You do not have to unhook wires to put meter in series with circuit. (TIF Instruments, Inc.)

A *scanner cartridge* is installed into the scanner for the specific make and model car or truck being tested. The cartridge holds the information needed for that vehicle.

When there is a computer system problem, the vehicle's computer will generate a trouble code. The *vehicle trouble code* is a number that denotes a certain area of the wiring or a component with an abnormal electrical value. You must refer to the service manual to find out what the number means.

Some scanners convert the trouble code number into detailed information for fixing the electrical problem. They will convert trouble code numbers into instructions for finding the computer system or wiring problem. They will tell you which part or leg of a circuit might be faulty. The scanner might tell you that a circuit or component has a high resistance, for example. You would then use a multimeter to verify the exact problem.

ENGINE ANALYZER

An *engine analyzer* is a large group of test instruments mounted in a rollaround cabinet. It can be used to find various kinds of troubles in the ignition, fuel injection, charging, and other electrical systems.

PERSONAL COMPUTER

The *personal computer* or *PC* is now an important tool for doing various body shop tasks. It is used to keep track of business transactions, complete damage reports, and even perform electrical tests on vehicles. A computer can find and manipulate huge amounts of data about all aspects of the shop operation. It is finding wider, more varied uses. See Figure 5–27.

Portable computers are small hand held units often used during estimating. They have small keyboards for inputting data. Some have a *bar code reader* which can convert printed bar codes (printed lines) into part numbers and other needed information. See Figure 5–28.

SOLDERING GUN

A *soldering gun* is used to heat and melt solder for making electrical repairs. It has a transformer that converts the AC into DC. The DC is sent through the gun tip which heats the tip enough to melt solder.

Solder is a mix of lead and tin for joining electrical wires and components. *Rosin core solder* is designed for doing electrical repairs. The *rosin* serves as a flux to make the melted solder adhere to the parts being joined.

Acid core solder is used for doing nonelectrical repairs, as on radiators. It should NOT be used for electrical repairs because the acid can corrode connections and affect their electrical resistance.

Figure 5–27 Personal computer is gaining importance as tool for body shops. It will help automate damage estimating and many other business related tasks. *(Courtesy of Mitchell International, Inc.)*

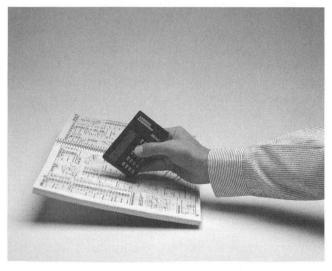

Figure 5–28 Hand held computer will read printed bar codes. This allows estimator to quickly input part numbers, prices and other data for making electronic estimate or for ordering parts. *(Courtesy of Mitchell International, Inc.)*

PLASTIC WELDER

A *plastic welder* is used to heat and melt plastic for repairing or joining plastic parts. It works like a sol-

dering gun but operates at a lower temperature. One is shown in Figure 5–29.

AIR CONDITIONING TOOLS

Because air conditioning parts are often damaged in frontal impacts, you should understand the use of basic air conditioning tools and equipment.

Air conditioning gauges are used to measure operating pressures in a vehicle's air conditioning system.

The A/C gauges are connected to *service ports* (small test fittings) in the system. The engine is then started and the A/C is set to maximum cooling. Gauge pressures are compared to known good readings. If pressures are too high or low, refer to troubleshooting charts to help find the problem.

A *leak detector* is a tool for finding refrigerant leaks in lines, hoses, and other parts of an air conditioning system. The tester is turned on and moved around possible leakage points. Since air conditioning refrigerant is heavier than air, the probe should be moved below possible leakage points. The tester will emit an audible tone or noise if a leak is present. This would help you find and fix refrigerant leaks more quickly. Note Figure 5–30.

Figure 5–29 Plastic welders are used to weld small tears in plastic parts. *(I-CAR)*

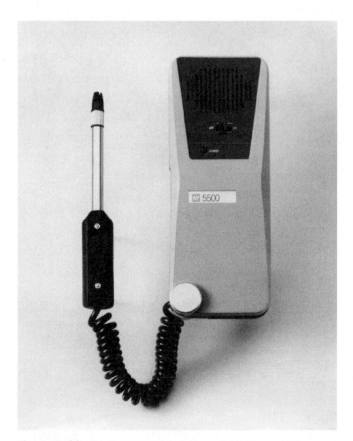

Figure 5–30 Electronic leak detector will make audible sound or change sound pitch if refrigerant leak is present. *(TIF Instruments, Inc.)*

A *charging station* is a machine for automatically recharging an air conditioning system with refrigerant. It has pressure gauges, a tank of refrigerant, and electronic controls for metering the right amount of refrigerant into the system. Refer to Figure 5–31.

A *recovery station* is used to capture the old, used refrigerant so that it does NOT enter and pollute the atmosphere. It consists of a large metal tank and vacuum pump. The recovery station pulls the refrigerant out of the vehicle and forces it into the storage tank. The station will then filter, clean, and dry the used refrigerant so that it can be recycled. See Figure 5–32.

OTHER EQUIPMENT

Many other types of equipment are used in body shops. You should have a basic understanding of their purpose.

A *tire changer* is a machine for quickly dismounting and mounting tires on and off wheels. It uses *pneumatic* (air) pressure to easily force the tire bead off or onto the wheel rim. One is pictured in Figure 5–33.

A *wheel balancer* is used to locate heavy areas on a wheel and tire assembly. It spins the wheel and tire and measures vibration. It will denote where *wheel weights* should be positioned on the wheel to equalize the weight and prevent vibration.

Figure 5–31 Charging station has gauges, refrigerant tank, timing, scale, and other parts for automatic refilling of air conditioning systems. *(Courtesy of Snap-On Tools Corporation)*

Figure 5–33 Tire changer will force tires on and off of wheels quickly and easily. *(FMC Automotive Equipment Division)*

Station Layout

Control Panel

Separator Drain Switch

Separator Drain Hose

Drain Oil Bottle

Filter Element

Refrigerant Tank

Figure 5–32 Recovery station is used to capture old refrigerant from vehicles. Refrigerant damages the atmosphere if released into the air. *(Courtesy of Snap-On Tools Corporation)*

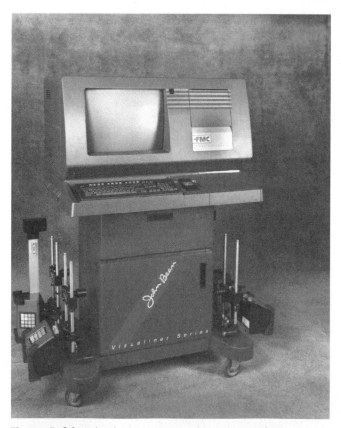

Figure 5–34 Wheel alignment machines vary. They measure the angle of each wheel so that you can adjust wheel alignment angles after major repairs. *(FMC Automotive Equipment Division)*

Figure 5–35 Headlight aiming equipment will let you quickly adjust the direction of car or truck headlights. Some use float type bubbles, others use electronic indicators. *(Hopkins Manufacturing Corporation)*

A *wheel alignment machine* is used to measure wheel alignment angles so they can be adjusted. After major collision repairs, the wheels of the vehicle often need realignment. The wheel alignment machine will show actual wheel angles so that they can be adjusted back to specifications, Figure 5–34.

Headlight aimers are used to adjust the direction of the vehicle headlights. Shown in Figure 5–35, they normally mount over the headlights. Leveling bulbs in the aimers will let you know if each bulb is aiming too high, too low, or correctly. By turning headlight aiming screws on the headlights, you can readjust the beams to aim correctly in front of the vehicle.

Summary

- Power tools and equipment utilize electrical energy, compressed air, or hydraulic power for operation.
- The use of air-driven or electric power tools requires safety glasses or a face shield. For hazardous operations, wear both.
- Some of the most common power tools used in collision repair are air compressors, air pressure regulators and filters, air blow guns, impact wrenches, air hammers, drills, air cutters, air sanders, grinders, polishers, blasters, and spray guns.

- Pneumatic tools should be lubricated BEFORE AND AFTER use to prevent wear and rusting of the vane motor and other parts of the tools.
- Volatile organic compound (VOC) is a harmful substance produced by many painting materials. Some geographic regions require the use of high transfer efficiency spray equipment to cut VOC emissions.
- The Personal Computer (PC) has become an important tool for accomplishing various body shop tasks. It is used to keep track of business transactions, complete damage reports, and even perform electrical tests on vehicles.

Technical Terms

air supply system	polishing pad
air compressor	integral
compressor drain valve	pad cleaning tool
pressure relief valve	swirl marks
compressor oil plugs	blaster
shop air lines	hand blaster
air hose sizes	cabinet blaster
air couplings	spray gun
air pressure regulator	atomize
air line filter-drier	gun body
air filter drain valve	spray gun cup
air blow gun	fluid control valve
air tool lubrication	fluid needle valve
in-line oiler	pattern control valve
impact wrench	spray gun air cap
½ inch impact	spray pattern
⅜ drive impact	primer
air ratchet	siphon spray gun
air hammer	air vent hole
drills	pressurized pot
air drills	pressure tank
key	bleeder spray gun
chuck	non-bleeder spray gun
spot weld drill	touch-up spray gun
air nibbler	volatile organic
air cutoff tool	compound
air saw	transfer efficiency
air sander	high efficiency spray gun
circular sander	HVLP
dual action sander	LVLP
sander pad	gravity feed spray gun
disc adhesive	turbine spray system
air file	air conversion unit
grinders	step-down gun
disc-type grinder	electrostatic spray gun
bench grinder	spray booth
air polisher	air replacement system

downdraft spray booth
side draft spray booth
color corrected lights
paint drying room
infrared drying
  equipment
surface thermometer
measuring system
hydraulic equipment
straightening system
pulling posts
frame rack accessories
body jack
battery charger
multimeter
analog meter
digital meter
low impedance
inductive meter

scanner
scanner cartridge
vehicle trouble code
engine analyzer
personal computer
soldering gun
rosin core solder
acid core solder
plastic welder
air conditioning gauges
service ports
leak detector
charging station
recovery station
tire changer
wheel balancer
wheel alignment machine
headlight aimers

Review Questions

1. List the major parts in a shop's air supply system.

2. What is a shop air compressor?

3. This valve must be opened every night to remove moisture from the compressor's storage tank.
   a. Pressure relief valve
   b. Drain valve
   c. Bypass valve
   d. Oil valve

4. How do you use air hose couplings?

5. What is the purpose of an air pressure regulator?

6. Why is air tool lubrication important and how do you do it?

7. An _____ is a portable hand held, reversible air-powered wrench for rapid turning of bolts and nuts.

8. It is OK to use conventional, chrome plated sockets on impact wrenches. True or False, and why?

9. Describe some common uses for a ½ inch impact.

10. A key is used to tighten the _____. The _____ has movable jaws that close down and hold the drill bit.

11. This type of sander moves in two directions as it moves, producing a much smoother surface finish.
    a. Circular
    b. Reciprocating
    c. File
    d. Orbital

12. A spray gun must _____ the liquid, that is, break the liquid into fine mist of droplets.

13. List and describe the major parts of a typical paint spray gun.

14. A siphon cup type spray gun is NOT working properly. Paint is NOT spraying out of the gun when the trigger is pressed. Technician A says that there may be too much thinner in the cup. Technician B says to check for a clogged vent hole. Who is correct?
    a. Technician A
    b. Technician B
    c. Neither technician
    d. Both technicians

15. What are some potential advantages of a remote pot or tank type spray gun?

Activities

1. Tour your shop and note the location of all power tools and equipment. Discuss with the class any questions you might have on power tool or equipment use.

2. Visit an outside shop. Watch technicians as they use power tools and equipment. Have a class discussion about how technicians used the tools.

3. Disassemble and reassemble a shop spray gun. Note the condition of all parts. Report on the condition of the gun.

4. Inspect your shop air compressor. Find the tank drain valve, shut off valve, and other parts.

CHAPTER 6

Body Shop

BASIC MEASUREMENT, SHOP MANUALS

Objectives

After studying this chapter, you should be able to:

■ Explain the many types of measurements needed in collision repair.

■ Make accurate linear, angle, pressure, volume, and other measurements.

■ Compare U.S. and metric measuring systems.

■ Identify and use basic measuring tools common to auto body repair.

■ Use conversion charts.

■ Properly mix paints and other materials.

■ Summarize how to measure with a paint mixing cup.

■ Make paint thickness measurements.

■ Use shop manuals efficiently.

Introduction

Measurements are number values that help control processes in collision repair. Measurements are needed to evaluate structural damage, correct that damage, mix paint, determine paint thickness, adjust a spray gun, and numerous other tasks. If you cannot make accurate measurements, you cannot be a good auto body technician. See Figure 6–1.

Remember that modern vehicles are precision manufactured using the latest technology. This includes the use of robotic assembly and laser measurement technology. This creates tighter tolerances than ever before. In fact, accurate measurement is one of the most important aspects of body repair.

Vehicle manufacturers give *specifications,* or measurements for numerous body dimensions and mechanical parts. In the course of your work you will have to refer to and understand these factory specifications. This chapter will help prepare you for these factory specifications.

CUSTOMARY	CONVERSION	METRIC	CUSTOMARY	CONVERSION	METRIC
Multiply	by	to get equivalent number of:	Multiply	by	to get equivalent number of:
LENGTH			**ACCELERATION**		
Inch	25.4	millimeters (mm)	Foot/sec2	0.304 8	meter/sec^2 (m/s^2)
Foot	0.304 8	meters (m)	Inch/sec2	0.025 4	meter/sec^2
Yard	0.914 4	meters	**TORQUE**		
Mile	1.609	kilometers (km)	Pound-inch	0.112 98	newton-meters (N·m)
AREA			Pound-foot	1.355 8	newton-meters
Inch^2	645.2	millimeters^2 (mm^2)	**POWER**		
	6.45	centimeters^2 (cm^2)	Horsepower	0.746	Kilowatts (kW)
Foot^2	0.092 9	meters^2 (m^2)	**PRESSURE OR STRESS**		
Yard^2	0.836 1	meters^2	Inches of water	0.249 1	kilopascals (kPa)
VOLUME			Pounds/sq. in.	6.895	Kilopascals
Inch^3	16 387.	mm^3	**ENERGY OR WORK**		
	16.387	cm^3	BTU	1055.	Joules (J)
	0.016 4	liters (l)	Foot-pound	1.355 8	joules
Quart	0.946 4	liters	Kilowatt-hour	3 600 000.	joules (J = one W's)
Gallon	3.785 4	liters		or 3.6 x 10^6	
Yard^3	0.764 6	meters^3 (m^3)	**LIGHT**		
MASS			Foot candle	1.076 4	lumens/meter^2 (lm/m^2)
Pound	0.453 6	kilograms (kg)	**FUEL PERFORMANCE**		
Ton	907.18	kilograms (kg)	Miles/gal	0.425 1	kilometers/liter (km/l)
Ton	0.907	tonne (t)	Gal/mile	2.352 7	liter/kilometer (l/km)
FORCE			**VELOCITY**		
Kilogram	9.807	newtons (N)	Miles/hour	1.609 3	Kilometers/hr. (km/h)
Ounce	0.278 0	newtons			
Pound	4.448	newtons			
TEMPERATURE					
Degree Fahrenheit	(†°F-32) ÷ 1.8	degree Celsius (C)			

°F
-40   0   32   40   80   98.6   120   160   200   °F 212

-40   -20   0   20   37 40   60   80   100
°C   °C

Figure 6–1 Chart gives conversion factors for U.S. and metric systems. Read through to compare values for each measurement. *(Courtesy of General Motors Corporation)*

ENGLISH AND METRIC SYSTEMS

The *English Measuring System* was first developed using human body parts as the basis for measurements. The length of the human arm was used to standardize the yard and the human foot devised the foot. It is primarily used in the United States, but NOT other countries. This makes it important for you to understand both systems. Specifications are usually given in both English and metric values.

The English System uses fractions and decimals for giving number values. *Fractions* are acceptable when precision is not critical. They divide the inch into thirty-seconds, sixteenths, and larger parts of an inch. *Decimals* are used when high precision is important. They can be used to divide an inch into tenths, hundredths, one-thousandths, ten-thousandths and more divisions.

The *metric measuring system*, also called *Scientific International (SI) System* uses a power of ten as its base. It is a more precise and simple system than our conventional system. This is because multiples of metric units are related to each other by the factor *ten*. Every metric unit can be multiplied or divided by a factor of ten to get larger units (multiples) or smaller units (submultiples). There is less chance for a math error when using the metric system.

The United States passed the *Metric Conversion Act* which committed to a voluntary and gradual transition from its customary system to the metric system. To date, only a few industries—including automotive—have made any movement toward adopting the metric system. Shop manuals give values in both English and metric numbers.

CONVERSION CHARTS

Conversion charts are handy for changing from one measuring system to another or from one value to another.

An *English-Metric conversion chart* allows you to change numbers to the other system. It gives multipliers that can be used to convert from English to metric or from metric to English values. For example, if a value is given in metric and you want to measure with a conventionally marked measuring tool, you would use a conversion chart.

A *decimal conversion chart* allows you to quickly change from fractions, to decimals, to millimeters. This is often used for various tasks, such as selecting drill bits. One is shown in Figure 6–2.

LINEAR MEASUREMENTS

Linear measurements are straight line measurements of distance. They are commonly used when evaluating major structural damage after a collision. There are many types of tools used for linear measurements.

FRACTION	DECIMAL	MILLIMETERS
1/64	.01563	.3969
1/32	.03125	.7938
	.03937	1.0000
3/64	.04688	1.1906
1/16	.06250	1.5875
5/64	.07813	1.9844
	.07874	2.0000
3/32	.09375	2.3813
7/64	.10938	2.7781
	.11811	3.0000
1/8	.12500	3.1750
9/64	.14063	3.5719
5/32	.15625	3.9688
	.15748	4.0000
11/64	.17188	4.3656
3/16	.18750	4.7625
	.19685	5.0000
13/64	.20313	5.1594
7/32	.21875	5.5563
15/64	.23438	5.9531
	.23622	6.0000
1/4	.25000	6.3500
17/64	.26563	6.7469
	.27559	7.0000
9/32	.28125	7.1438
19/64	.29688	7.5406
5/16	.31250	7.9375
	.31496	8.0000
21/64	.32813	8.3344
11/32	.34375	8.7313
	.35433	9.0000
23/64	.35938	9.1281
3/8	.37500	9.5250
25/64	.39063	9.9219
	.39370	10.0000
13/32	.40625	10.3188
27/64	.42188	10.7156
	.43307	11.0000
7/16	.43750	11.1125
29/64	.45313	11.5094
15/32	.46875	11.9063
	.47244	12.0000
31/64	.48438	12.3031
1/2	.50000	12.7000

FRACTION	DECIMAL	MILLIMETERS
	.51181	13.0000
33/64	.51563	13.0969
17/32	.53125	13.4938
35/64	.54688	13.8906
	.55118	14.0000
9/16	.56250	14.2875
37/64	.57813	14.6844
	.59055	15.0000
19/32	.59375	15.0813
39/64	.60938	15.4781
5/8	.62500	15.8750
	.62992	16.0000
41/64	.64063	16.2719
21/32	.65625	16.6688
	.66929	17.0000
43/64	.67188	17.0656
11/16	.68750	17.4625
45/64	.70313	17.8594
	.70866	18.0000
23/32	.71875	18.2563
47/64	.73438	18.6531
	.74803	19.0000
3/4	.75000	19.0500
49/64	.76563	19.4469
25/32	.78125	19.8438
	.78740	20.0000
51/64	.79688	20.2406
13/16	.81250	20.6375
	.82677	21.0000
53/64	.82813	21.0344
27/32	.84375	21.4313
55/64	.85938	21.8281
	.86614	22.0000
7/8	.87500	22.2250
57/64	.89063	22.6219
	.90551	23.0000
29/32	.90625	23.0188
59/64	.92188	23.4156
15/16	.93750	23.8125
	.94488	24.0000
61/64	.95313	24.2094
31/32	.96875	24.6063
	.98425	25.0000
63/64	.98438	25.0031
1	1.00000	25.4000

PERFECT CIRCLE®

Figure 6–2 Decimal conversion chart will let you quickly change fractions to decimals or to metric equivalents. *(Illustration Courtesy of Perfect Circle, Dana Corp.)*

Figure 6–3 Review the divisions of a ruler. Most read in sixteenths or sixty-fourths.

SCALES

A *scale* or *ruler* is the most basic tool for linear measurement. It has an accuracy of approximately ¹⁄₆₄ in. or 0.5 mm. You may wish to study how to read a conventional rule in Figure 6–3.

An *English rule* often has markings in fractions of an inch (½, ¼, ⅛, ⅟₁₆) or as decimal parts of an inch (.10, .20, .30, .40). A *metric rule* or *meter stick* is marked in millimeters and centimeters. The numbered lines usually equal ten millimeters (one centimeter). In Figure 6–4, see how to read one.

Figure 6–5 compares fractional, metric, and decimal inch scales.

Parallax error results when you read a rule or scale from an angle. Instead of looking straight down, viewing at an angle causes you to read the wrong line on the scale. Always look straight down when reading a rule.

A *pocket scale* or rule is very small (typically 6 in. or 152 mm long). It will clip into your shirt pocket and can be handy for numerous small measurements. A *yardstick* or *meter stick* may also be used for some larger linear measurements.

A *tape rule* or *tape measure* will extend out for making very long measurements. A tape measure is commonly used to make large distance measurements during body damage evaluation.

Figure 6–4 The small gradations on a metric rule equal millimeters. Numbered lines equal centimeters.

Figure 6–5 Compare values on fractional inch, metric, and decimal inch scales.

Since many body measurements are made at holes in the body, the tip of the tape rule must be small or ground to a point. This will prevent measurement errors.

A *tram gauge* is a special body dimension measuring tool, Figure 6–6. It is usually a lightweight frame with pointers. The pointers can be aligned with body dimension reference points to determine the direction and amount of body misalignment damage.

NOTE! TRAM GAUGES ARE DETAILED IN THE CHAPTER ON MEASURING SYSTEMS.

Figure 6–6 Tram gauge is specialized measuring tool used during major collision damage. It will quickly measure between body reference points to see if major frame or body straightening is required.

Types of Calipers

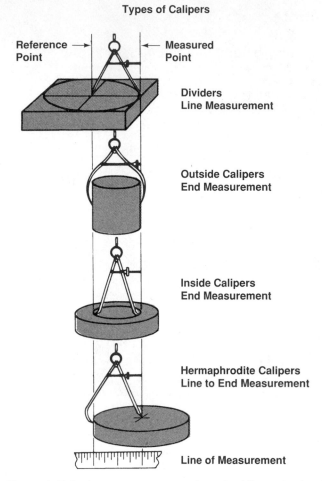

Figure 6–7 Study measurements made with different kinds of calipers.

DIVIDERS AND CALIPERS

Dividers have straight, sharp tips for taking measurements or marking parts for cutting. In auto body, dividers are sometimes used for layout or marking cut lines. They will scribe circles and lines on sheet metal and plastic. They will also transfer and make surface measurements. Dividers are sometimes used when fabricating repair pieces for rustout repair. Look at Figure 6–7.

Outside calipers will make rough external measurements when ¼₄ in. (0.40 mm) is accurate enough. The calipers are placed over the outside of parts. They are adjusted to just touch the parts. When placed next to a rule, part size can be determined. See Figure 6–7.

Inside calipers are designed for measuring inside of parts. They are used the same way. They are also accurate to about ¼₄ in. (0.40 mm). See Figure 6–7.

Hermaphrodite calipers have one straight tip and one curved tip. They will measure cylindrical shapes easily.

Figure 6–8 Digital sliding calipers are easy to use and read. They make outside, inside, and depth measurements. *(Compliments of the Fred V. Fowler Co., Inc.)*

Sliding calipers will measure inside, outside, and depth dimensions with high accuracy. Most sliding calipers measure to accuracy of .001 in. (0.025 mm). It is a very convenient tool, especially digital readout, electronic calipers, when high accuracy is necessary. See Figure 6–8.

MICROMETERS

Micrometers are sometimes used when measuring mechanical parts when high precision is important. Often called a "mike," it can easily measure one-thousandths of an inch (.001 in.) or one-hundredths of a millimeter (0.01 mm).

You might use one to measure the thickness of a brake system rotor. If worn too thin, this would tell you to replace the rotor. The basic parts of an outside micrometer are in Figure 6–9.

To learn to read a micrometer, refer to Figure 6–10. It details the steps for reading an English micrometer. The procedure for reading a metric micrometer is in Figure 6–11.

A digital readout micrometer gives readings as a decimal in a number window on the tool. It is much faster than having to use several steps to calculate the measurement. Look at Figure 6–12.

When using a micrometer, hold the frame in the palm of your hand. Rotate the thimble with your thumb and finger. Adjust the tool down until it drags lightly on the part. Do NOT tighten it. Then, read the micrometer.

Check the accuracy of a micrometer if dropped or after extended use. Measure a known size feeler gauge and check its reading or give it to your tool salesperson for an accuracy check.

Figure 6–9 Note parts of outside micrometer. *(Courtesy of the L.S. Starrett Company)*

DIAL INDICATORS

A *dial indicator* is often used to measure part movement and out-of-round in thousandths of an inch (hundredths of a mm). For example, the indicator might be used to check for wheel damage. It is mounted against the wheel or tire. When the tire is rotated, the dial indicator will show how much the wheel is bent. This would let you know that the wheel should be replaced. Look at Figure 6–13.

To use a dial indicator, mount the tool base so it will not move. A magnetic base will stick to metal parts or a metal plate placed on the floor. Position the tool arm and indicator stem against the part. Turn the outside of the dial to zero the needle. Move or rotate the part and take your reading.

FEELER GAUGES

Feeler gauges measure small clearances inside parts. Blade thickness is given on each blade in thousandths of an inch (.001, .010, .020) or in hundredths of a millimeter (0.01, 0.07, 0.10).

Flat feeler gauges are for measuring between parallel surfaces. *Wire feeler gauges* are round and are for measuring slightly larger distances between nonparallel or curved surfaces. Refer to Figure 6–14, page 104.

SPRING SCALE

A *spring scale* will measure pulling force. It is often used to check the force needed to turn a steering wheel. This will help determine if there is damage to the steering mechanism from the collision. One is shown in Figure 6–15, page 104.

To use a spring scale, hook the tool over the part (steering wheel, for example) and pull. Read the force or weight needed to move the part off the tool. Compare your measurement to specs.

Figure 6–10 Study steps for reading conventional micrometer. Basically, you must add whole divisions showing on barrel scale with thousands showing on thimble scale.

READING METRIC MICROMETERS

Whole Millimeters
(1.0, 2.0, 3.0, etc. mm)

Hundredths of
Millimeters
(0.00 to 0.50)
Thimble

Half Millimeters
(0.50 mm)
Lower Row on Barrel

Example:

Whole mm lines visible on barrel	3 = 3.00 mm
Additional half mm line (lower) visible on barrel	1 = .50 mm
Lines on thimble which have passed long line on barrel	36 = .36 mm
Reading of measurement Total	= 3.86 mm

Figure 6–11 Study steps for reading a metric micrometer.

PRESSURE AND FLOW MEASUREMENTS

You will have to make pressure and flow measurements when working. Pressures are important for air tools, spray guns, and other equipment. Adequate airflow is important when working in a paint spray booth, for example.

A *pressure gauge* reads in pounds per square inch (psi) or kilograms per square centimeter (K/cm^2). A few pressure gauges also show or measure vacuum. Note the two scales given on the pressure gauge in Figure 6–16.

Air pressure gauges are used on the shop's air compressor, on pressure regulators, or at the spray gun. Tire pressure gauges are also needed to check for proper tire inflation. Hydraulic pressure gauges can be found on hydraulic presses and other similar equipment.

Remember! Excessive pressure can be dangerous or damage parts. Low air pressure may keep the tool from working properly.

Figure 6–12 Digital readout mike is fast because you do not have to add barrel and thimble readings. *(Courtesy of DoAll Company, Des Plaines, Illinois)*

A *vacuum gauge* reads vacuum, negative pressure, or "suction." It reads in inches of mercury (in./hg.) or kilograms per square centimeter (K/cm^2).

A *flow meter* measures the movement of air, gas, or a liquid past a given point. A *manometer* or airflow meter is designed for use in a paint booth. Airflow meters can register in feet per minute or meters per minute. Liquid flow meters often register in gallons per hour or liters per hour.

ANGLE MEASUREMENTS

Angle measurements divides a circle into 360 or more parts, called *degrees.* You will learn to read angles in degrees when doing wheel alignment, for example. This will be explained in later chapters.

TEMPERATURE MEASUREMENTS

Temperature is usually measured in degrees Fahrenheit (F) or Celsius (C). In the body shop, temperatures are important in the drying of various materials such as primers, paints, adhesives.

Thermometers are used to measure temperature. For example, paint manufacturers often give different mixing values and recommend different thinners and reducers for different *ambient* (outside or room) temperatures.

A *mercury thermometer* encloses liquid mercury in a hollow glass rod to indicate temperature. Any change in temperature makes the mercury expand and contract. To read a thermometer, view the level of mercury next to the scale.

A *dial thermometer* is similar, but it has a needle that shows temperature. This type is often used when

Radial Runout

Lateral Runout

A

B

1. **Tire and Wheel Asm. Mounted on Car or Balance Machine**
2. **Dial Indicator**
3. **Stand**
4. **Roller Wheel**
5. **Run Tape Around Center Tread of Tire. Measure Radial Runout of Taped Surface.**
6. **Measure Lateral Runout at Point Where Tread Ends. Position Dial Indicator Perpendicular To Tire at That Point.**

Figure 6–13 Dial indicator is commonly used for measuring part runout or movement. A: Note parts of dial indicator. B: Mount indicator stand next to part. Position stem against part and zero needle. Slowly turn tire to measure out-of-round which might mean a bad tire or bent wheel.

Figure 6–14 Feeler gauges will measure clearance between parts. A: Set of flat feeler gauges. B: Wire feeler gauges. C: Spark plug gap feeler gauges. *(Courtesy of Snap-On Tools Corporation)*

checking the output of an air conditioning system. It is inserted into the center vent with the system and blower on high. If the reading is too warm (above specs), the system is not cooling properly.

Surface temperature thermometers are available in several different designs—magnetic thermometers, paper thermometers, digital thermometers.

Before applying any type of material during collision repairs, the vehicle, and material to be used, must be at room temperature. A vehicle's surface temperature must be brought to room temperature prior to applying fillers and paint materials. Failure to do so may result in formation of condensation on the surface.

Magnetic surface thermometers will stick to metal body panels for measuring temperatures during paint drying or curing. When using infrared heaters after painting, keep in mind that magnetic surface thermometers have more mass than the panel they are attached to. This may result in a lower temperature reading than the panel.

Disposable *paper thermometers* will show the highest temperature a surface reaches, but not necessarily the current temperature of the panel. They work well with infrared heaters.

A *digital thermometer* is an electronic instrument for measuring temperature. It has a digital readout that will show temperature in Fahrenheit or Celsius. Special surface types are often used in collision repair.

Most digital thermometers usually have several different probe tips. A round, hollow tip is for air temperature measurements. A flat, blunt tip is for surface temperature measurements. A tip with a strand of wire is for checking temperatures of fluids.

Figure 6–15 Spring tension gauge will measure pulling force, as when checking for steering problems.

PAINT-RELATED MEASUREMENTS

Mixing scales are often used by paint suppliers to weigh the toners in the paint itself. This will help them add the right amount of each toner. Called *paint formulations,* the supplier adds different pigments to make the paint with the desired color. Look at Figure 6–17.

When mixing and using paint and solvents or other additives, you must measure and mix their contents accurately. This is essential to doing good paint and body work. You must be able to properly mix reducers or thinners, hardeners, and other additives into the paint. If NOT, serious paint problems will result.

A *graduated pail* is often used to measure liquid materials when mixing. It has measurement lines on it like a kitchen measuring cup. Liquid is poured into the pail until it is next to the scale for the amount needed.

Mixing instructions are normally given on the material's label. This might be a percentage or parts of one ingredient compared to the other.

Figure 6–16 Pressure gauges are common measuring tools in auto body. Most have two scales to show both English and metric values. *(Photo courtesy of Binks Manufacturing Company)*

Figure 6–17 Electronic scales are used by manufacturers and suppliers to mix ingredients in paint and other materials. *(Sartorius)*

A *percentage reduction* means that each material must be added in certain proportions or parts. For instance, if a paint requires 50% reduction, this means that one part reducer or thinner (solvent) must be mixed with two parts of paint.

Mixing by parts means that for a specific volume of paint or other material, a specific amount of another material must be added. If you are mixing a gallon of paint in a spray gun pressure tank for example, and directions call for 25% reduction, you would add one quart of reducer. There are four quarts in a gallon and you want one part or 25% reducer for each four parts of paint.

Proportional numbers denote the amount of each material needed. The first number is usually the parts of paint needed. The second number is usually the solvent (thinner or reducer). A third number might be used to denote the amount of hardener or other additives required.

For example, the number 2:1:1 might mean add one part solvent and one part hardener to two parts of paint. For a half gallon of paint, you would add a quart of solvent and a quart or catalyst. This can vary so always refer to the exact directions on the materials.

A *mixing chart* converts a percentage into how many parts of each material must be mixed. One is given in Figure 6–18. Study the percentages and parts of each material that must be mixed.

PAINT MIXING STICKS

Graduated *paint mixing sticks* have conversion scales that allow you to easily convert ingredient percentages into part proportions. They are used by painters to help mix paints, solvents, catalysts, and other additives right before spraying. See Figure 6–19.

Paint mixing sticks should NOT be confused with *paint stirring sticks* (wooden sticks) for mixing the contents after being poured into the spray gun cup or a container.

VISCOSITY CUP MEASUREMENT

A *viscosity cup* is used to measure the thickness or fluidity of the mixed materials, usually paint. It is a small, stainless steel cup attached to a handle, Figure 6–20.

To use a viscosity cup, dip it into the mixed paint until submerged. Lift the cup out and hold it over the paint container. As soon as the cup is lifted out, start timing how long it takes for the cup to empty. The paint will leak out of a small specific size *orifice* (hole) in the bottom of the cup.

Use the second hand on your watch or a stop watch to time draining. When the paint stream breaks into drops, note how much time was needed. This equals the paint viscosity in seconds.

The paint manufacturer will give a recommended viscosity value in *viscosity cup seconds*. It will vary between 17 and 30 seconds depending upon the type of paint and type of cup used. Refer to the paint specifications for an exact value.

If the paint drains too quickly out of the viscosity cup, you have added too much solvent. More paint would be needed. If the cup drains too slowly, you have not added enough solvent. Remix until the paint passes the viscosity cup test.

If the paint is TOO THICK, your paint will develop orange peel or a rough film. If paint is TOO THIN, excess solvent can cause the paint to have poor hiding and other problems.

PAINT THICKNESS MEASUREMENT

Paint thickness is measured in *mils* or thousandths of an inch (hundredths of a millimeter). Original OEM paints are typically about 2 to 6 mils thick. With basecoat/clearcoats, the basecoat is approximately 1 to 2 mils thick. The clearcoat is about 2 to 4 mils thick. This is approximately the thickness of a piece of typing paper.

Reduction / Thinning Percentage		Reduction / Thinning Proportions	Paint		Solvent
10%	=	5 parts paint / 1 part solvent		10%	
25%	=	4 parts paint / 1 part solvent		25%	
33%	=	3 parts paint / 1 part solvent		33%	
50%	=	2 parts paint / 1 part solvent		50%	
75%	=	4 parts paint / 3 parts solvent		75%	
100%	=	1 part paint / 1 part solvent		100%	
125%	=	4 parts paint / 5 parts solvent		125%	
150%	=	2 parts paint / 3 parts solvent		150%	
200%	=	1 part paint / 2 parts solvent		200%	
250%	=	2 parts paint / 5 parts solvent		250%	

Figure 6–18 Chart shows possible mixing percentages with conversion to parts of each material. Study paint and solvent parts needed for each percentage.

Figure 6–19 Mixing sticks have scales on them for mixing different materials—paints, solvents, hardeners. They are handy reference tools for measuring out materials. *(BASF)*

Figure 6–20 Viscosity cup will measure consistency or fluidity of paint. A mixed paint specification is often given in seconds. If you mix the paint properly, the amount of time needed for sample to drain out of small cup should equal spec time. *(PPG Industries, Inc.)*

If a panel has been repainted, paint thickness will increase. If too much paint is already on the vehicle, it may have to be removed prior to refinishing. Paint buildup should be limited to no more than 12 mils. The OEM finish and one refinish usually equal just under 12 mils. Exceeding this paint thickness could cause cracking in the new finish. Chemical stripping or blasting would be needed to remove the old paint buildup.

A *mil gauge* can be used to measure the thickness

of the paint on the vehicle. This can be done before refinishing, after refinishing, and during other finishing operations. See Figure 6–21.

There are three types of mil gauges—pencil, gauge, and digital types. The *pencil gauge mil* paint measuring tools are spring-loaded and have markings for mil thickness. They have a magnet in them that is placed against the metal body or paint. It is pulled away from the body and a reading is taken. A scale on either tool will read in mils.

The *electronic mil gauge* is similar but has a digital readout showing paint thickness. When placed and held on the surface, the tool will automatically register paint thickness.

A

Mil Gauge

B

Figure 6–21 Paint thickness or mil gauges will tell you if paint already on vehicle is too thick for repainting without stripping or removal of old paint. A: Place mil gauge against panel. Magnet will be attracted to steel panel. Slowly pull tool away from panel while reading gauge which shows paint thickness. *(Talsol Corporation)* B: Electronic mil gauge will give almost instant readout of paint thickness. *(I-CAR)*

VIN NUMBERS

A good technician must have a complete understanding of commonly used terms that identify parts and assemblies of a vehicle. If the technician is NOT familiar with this language, it is difficult to order parts and read a repair order.

The *Vehicle Identification Number (VIN) plate* and *number* is used to accurately identify the body style, model year, engine, and other data about the vehicle. Since 1981, the VIN plate is riveted to the upper left corner of the instrument panel, visible through the windshield. Note Figure 6–22.

Prior to 1981 and on foreign vehicles, check the service manual for the location of the VIN, vehicle certification label, or body plate. Service manuals and crash estimating guides also contain all of the necessary VIN number decoding information.

Become familiar with each vehicle manufacturer's method of vehicle identification and the specific information it contains. Remember that you must obtain all of the information possible about the vehicle being worked on.

The *body ID number* or *service part number* gives information about how the vehicle is equipped. It will give paint codes or numbers for ordering the right type and color paint; lower and upperbody colors if a two-tone paint. The body ID number will also give trim information. This number will be on the body ID plate on the door, console lid, or elsewhere on the body.

BODY SHOP PUBLICATIONS

Various manuals or publications are used by a collision repair shop. It is important that you understand the purpose and use of each.

All automobile companies publish yearly *service manuals* that describe the construction and repair of their vehicle makes and models. These manuals give important details on repair procedures and parts. Also called shop manuals, they give instructions, specifications, and illustrations for their specific cars and trucks. Service manuals have information on mechanical as well as body repair.

The *contents page* of a service manual lists the broad categories in the manual and gives their page numbers. Each *service manual section* then concentrates on describing that area of repair.

Figure 6–22 Vehicle manufacturers place labels or ID plates to give information about how vehicle is equipped. Refer to service manual to locate and explain number codes. *(Courtesy of General Motors Corporation)*

Service manual abbreviations represent technical terms or words and save space. Each manufacturer uses slightly different abbreviations.

Aftermarket repair manuals are published by publishing companies (Mitchell Manuals, Motor Manuals, Chilton Manuals) rather than the manufacturer. They can give enough information needed for most repairs.

Repair charts give diagrams that guide you through logical steps for making repairs. They can vary in content and design. Most use arrows and icons (graphic symbols) that represent repair steps.

Diagnosis charts or *troubleshooting charts* give logical steps for finding the source of problems. Mechanical, body, electrical, and other types of troubleshooting charts are provided in service manuals.

They give the most common sources of problems for the experienced symptoms.

Paint reference charts in service manuals give comparable paints manufactured by different companies. This will help you match the color of the new paint with the paint already on the vehicle. See Figure 6–23.

COLLISION REPAIR PUBLICATIONS

Several types of books are published to help make estimates and also repair collision damaged vehicles. You should understand their purpose.

Collision estimating manuals or guides give information for calculating the cost of repairs. They have part numbers, prices, section illustrations, and other

AFTERMARKET PAINT REPAIR PRODUCTS

COLOR NAME	CHRY. CODE	PPG	BASF	DuPONT	S-W ACME M-S	AKZO/SIKKENS
Black Cherry P.C.	FM9	4043	18221	B8822	37297	CHA88:FM9
Radiant Red Met. C.C.	LRF	4447	22116	B9230	45860	CHA92:LRF
Lt. Driftwood S.G.	MFA	4569	22110	B9263	46579	CHA92:MFA
Char-Gold S.G.	MJ8	4677	23044	B9327	46947	CHA93:MJ8
Emerald Green P.C.	PGF	4639	23042	B9328	46976	CHA92:PGF
Teal P.C.	LP5	4445	21094	B9232	45858	CHA92:LP5
Med. Water Blue S.G.	KBF	4270	21075	B9135	44042	CHA91:KBF
Black C.C.	DX8	9700	15214	99	34858 90-5950	CHA85:DX8
Ascot Gray C.C.	PAB	35560	24070	B9457	48759	CHA94:PAB
Bright White C.C.	GW7	4037	18238	B8833	37298	CHA88:GW7

COLOR NAME	CHRY. CODE	PPG/UCV	BASF	DuPONT	S-W ACME M-S
Agate	AZ	9856/2-1461	22135	C9208	45994
Agate/Med. Quartz (LAZ/HD5)	AD	9856/2-1461 34618/1346	22135 19133	C9208 C8904	45994/ 40075
Agate/Med. Driftwood (LAZ/MF6)	AF	9856/2-1461 27468/2-1502	22135 23061	C9208 C9301	45994/ 47481
Dk. Slate/Slate Blue (MBR/KB7)	BB	35586/2-1501 17125/2-1426	23060 21095	C9302 C9116	47457/ 44568
Dk. Driftwood/Med. Driftwood (LF8/MF6)	FF	27243/2-1463 27468/2-1502	22137 23061	C9247 C9301	45999 47481

LOWER FASCIA	CHRY. CODE	PPG	BASF	DuPONT	S-W ACME M-S	AKZO/SIKKENS
Med. Quartz (HD2)*	HD2	4321	20214	B8948	41562	CHA89:HD2

*All lower fascias that are not body color are medium quartz (HD2).

Figure 6–23 Service manuals will sometimes give charts for purchasing recommended aftermarket paints. Simply use body ID number for paint color. Then find aftermarket paint number for that color in chart. *(Courtesy of Chrysler Corporation)*

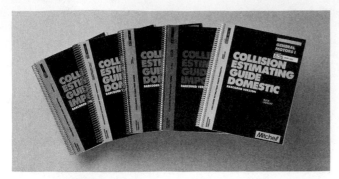

Figure 6–24 Collision estimating guides give information needed for quoting repair costs. *(Courtesy of Mitchell International, Inc.)*

Figure 6–25 Vehicle dimension manuals give structural measurements. If the measurements on the wrecked car or truck do not equal specs in manual, major body or frame straightening would be needed on frame rack. *(Courtesy of Mitchell International, Inc.)*

data to help the estimator, Figure 6–24. Discussed in later chapters, electronic or computer-based estimating guides are also available.

A *vehicle dimension manual* gives body and frame measurements from undamaged vehicles. Dimensions are given for every make and model car and truck. These known good dimensions can be compared to actual measurements taken off of a wrecked car or truck. This will let you know how badly the vehicle is damaged and what must be done to repair it. Refer to Figure 6–25.

It is important to follow the directions in a dimension manual. See Figure 6–26. Note how it gives measurements for a door opening. You would measure across the door opening on the vehicle. If any measurements are not correct, you could determine how the

Figure 6–26 Note how measurements are given across specific points of door opening. In collision, door opening can be bent or pushed out of alignment. Hydraulic equipment could then be used to realign door opening. *(Courtesy of Mitchell International, Inc.)*

Figure 6–28 Color matching manuals give information that will help you match the original paint. *(BASF)*

Figure 6–27 These are some of the symbols given in body repair manuals. Know them! *(Hein-Werner® Corporation)*

impact affected the door opening. Frame straightening and/or portable hydraulic equipment could then be used to push or pull the opening back into alignment.

As with service manuals, various symbols are used in body dimension manuals. The most typical are in Figure 6–27.

COLOR MATCHING MANUALS

Color matching manuals contain information needed for finishing panels so that the repair has the same appearance as the old finish. They have paint code information, color chips, blending and tinting data, tinting procedures, and other information. See Figure 6–28.

Summary

- Vehicle manufacturers give specifications, or measurements, for numerous body dimensions and mechanical parts. In the course of your work you will have to refer to and understand these factory specifications.

- The English Measuring System is primarily used in the United States, while the Metric System, also called Scientific International (SI) System, is used worldwide.

- Linear measurements are straight line measurements of distance. They are commonly used when evaluating major structural distance after a collision.

- Angle measurements are measured in degrees. Angle measurements are used in wheel alignment.

- Pressure measurements are measured in pounds per square inch (psi), or kilograms per square centimeter (K/cm^2).

- Temperature is usually measured in degrees Fahrenheit (°F) or Celsius (°C). In the body shop, temperatures are important in the drying of various materials such as primers, paints, and adhesives.

- The Vehicle Identification Number (VIN) is used to accurately identify the body style, model year, engine, and other data pertaining to the vehicle.

Technical Terms

measurements	mixing scales
U.S. Measuring System	graduated pail
fraction	percentage reduction
decimal	mixing by parts
metric measuring system	proportional numbers
conversion chart	mixing chart
U.S.–Metric conversion	paint mixing sticks
decimal conversion chart	paint stirring sticks
linear measurement	viscosity cup
scale	orifice
parallax error	viscosity cup seconds
pocket scale	paint thickness
tape rule	mil gauge
tram gauge	VIN number
dividers	body ID number
outside calipers	service manuals
inside calipers	service manuals
sliding calipers	abbreviations
micrometer	aftermarket repair
dial indicator	manuals
feeler gauges	diagnosis charts
spring scale	paint reference charts
pressure gauge	collision estimating
vacuum gauge	manuals
flow meter	vehicle dimension
angle measurement	manual
thermometer	color matching manuals
surface temperature	

Review Questions

1. _____ are number values that help control processes in collision repair.
2. Explain how you might use conversion charts.
3. How do you avoid parallax error when reading a scale?
4. In auto body, _____ will mark circles and lines on sheet metal and plastic.
5. Sliding calipers will measure _____, _____, and _____ dimensions to an accuracy of _____ in. _____.
6. Explain how you use an outside micrometer.

7. This tool is often used to measure part movement and out-of-round in thousandths of an inch (hundredths of a mm).
   a. Outside micrometer
   b. Inside micrometer
   c. Feeler gauge
   d. Dial indicator
8. Describe the three types of tips available for digital thermometers.
9. If a paint requires 50% reduction, how would you mix the paint and its solvent?
10. When mixing paint materials, what might the numbers 2:1:1 mean?
11. A _____ is used to measure the actual consistency or fluidity of the mixed materials, usually paint.
12. Paint buildup should be limited to no more than this amount.
    a. 12 mils   c. 50 mils
    b. 2 mils   d. 100 mils
13. What can happen if the paint on the vehicle is too thick?
14. The _____ is used to accurately identify the body style, model year, engine, and other data about the vehicle.
15. This type of manual gives information for calculating the cost of collision repairs.
    a. Service manual
    b. Dimensions manual
    c. Estimating manual
    d. Paint code manual

Activities

1. Find the VIN number on several vehicles. Write down the location of the VIN number for several cars. Look up the VIN number data in a service manual.

2. Use a paint thickness gauge to check for excess paint layers on several cars. Did different panels have more paint than others. How many vehicles had paint thicker than normal? Could you see any paint cracking or other surface problems when the paint was too thick?

3. Use a micrometer to measure the blades of a feeler gauge. Did your measurements equal the actual blade thicknesses?

CHAPTER 7

FASTENERS

Objectives

After studying this chapter, you should be able to:

■ Identify the various fasteners used in body construction.

■ Remove and install bolts and nuts properly.

■ Explain when specific fasteners are used in body construction.

■ Explain bolt and nut torque values.

■ Summarize the use of chemical fasteners.

■ Identify hose clamps.

Introduction

Fasteners make up the thousands of bolts, nuts, screws, clips and adhesives that literally hold a vehicle together.

As an auto body technician, you will constantly use fasteners when removing and installing body parts. This makes it important for you to be able to identify and use fasteners properly. This chapter will summarize the proper utilization and selection of bolts, nuts, screws, clips, adhesives, epoxies, and other fasteners found in a body shop.

Remember that each fastener is engineered for a specific application. Always replace fasteners with exactly the same type that was removed from the *original equipment manufacture (OEM)* assembly. Never try to "re-engineer" the vehicle. Keep in mind that using an incorrect fastener or a fastener of inferior quality can result in failure and possible injury to the vehicle occupants.

BOLTS

A *bolt* is a metal shaft with a head on one end and threads on the other. A *cap screw* is a term that describes a high strength bolt. Bolts and cap screws are usually named after the body part they hold, fender bolt, hood hinge bolt, etc. Their shape and head drive configuration also helps name them.

Bolt Terminology

To work with bolts properly, you must understand basic bolt terminology. See Figure 7–1.

The *bolt head* is used to torque or tighten the bolt. A socket or wrench fits over the head, which enables the bolt to be tightened. Some English and metric sockets are very close in size. It is important NOT to use metric sizes for English bolts, or English sizes for metric bolts; bolt heads may be rounded off and damaged.

H - Head
G - Grade Marking (Bolt Strength)
L - Length (Inches)
T - Thread Pitch (Thread/Inch)
D - Nominal Diameter (Inches)

H - Head
P - Property Class (Bolt Strength)
L - Length (Millimeters)
T - Thread Pitch (Millimeters)
D - Nominal Diameter (Millimeters)

Figure 7–1 Bolt measurements are needed when working. Know the dimensions of both English and metric bolts. *(Courtesy of Ford Motor Company)*

Bolt length is measured from the end of the threads to the bottom of the bolt head. It is NOT the total length including the bolt head.

Bolt diameter, sometimes termed *bolt size,* is measured around the outside of the threads. For example, a ½ inch bolt has a thread diameter of ½ inch while its head or wrench size would be ¾ inch.

Bolt head size is the distance measured across the flats of the bolt head. In *USC (United States Customary),* head size is given in fractions, just like wrench size. A few common sizes are ⁷⁄₁₆, ½, and ⁹⁄₁₆ inch. In the metric system, 3, 4, 5 millimeter head sizes are typical. Common USC and metric bolt head sizes are given in Figure 7–2.

Bolt thread pitch is a measurement of thread coarseness. Bolts and nuts can have coarse, fine, and metric threads. Bolt threads can be measured with a *thread pitch gauge.* One is in Figure 7–3.

A number of terms have been used over the years to identify the various types of threads. The terms

Common English (U.S. Customary) Head Sizes	Common Metric Head Sizes
Wrench Size (inches)*	Wrench Size (millimeters)*
3/8	9
7/16	10
1/2	11
9/16	12
5/8	13
11/16	14
3/4	15
13/16	16
7/8	17
15/16	18
1	19
1-1/16	20
1-1/8	21
1-3/16	22
1-1/4	23
1-5/16	24
1-3/8	26
7/16	27
1-1/2	29
	30
	32

* The wrench sizes given in this chart are not equivalents, but are standard head sizes found in both inches and millimeters.

Figure 7–2 These are common bolt head and wrench sizes. Never use a standard wrench on metric bolts and vice versa. This will round off bolt head.

Figure 7-3 Gauges can be used to measure thread, bolt, or nut sizes. A: Thread pitch gauge. Thread pitch gauge is fit against threads. Threads that match gauge equal pitch number printed on gauge. B: Bolt and nut size gauge. Bolts and nuts can be fitted into bolt and nut gauge to quickly tell sizes. *(Dorman Products)*

used in the automotive trade—the **United States Standard (USS)**, the **American National Standard (ANS)**, and the **Society of Automotive Engineers Standard (SAE)**—have all been replaced the Unified National Series.

The two common metric threads are coarse and fine and can be identified by the letters SI (System International or International System of Units) and ISO (International Standards Organization).

Bolts and nuts are also available in right-and left-hand threads. *Right-hand threads* must be turned clockwise to tighten. Less common *left-hand threads* must be rotated in a counterclockwise direction to tighten the fastener. Left-hand threads may be denoted by notches or the letter "L" stamped on them.

Bolt Strengths or Grades

Bolt strength indicates the amount of torque or tightening force that should be applied. Bolts are made from different materials having various degrees of hardness. Softer metal or harder metal can be used to make bolts. Bolts are made with different hardnesses and strengths for use in different situations.

Bolt grade markings are lines or numbers on the top of the head to identify bolt hardness and strength. The hardness or strength of metric bolts is indicated by using a property class indicator on the head of the bolt.

Bolt strength markings are given as lines, Figure 7–4. The number of lines on the head of the bolt is related to the strength. As the number of lines increases so does the strength.

Metric bolt strength markings are given as numbers. The higher the number is, the stronger the bolt. These markings apply to both bolts and nuts, Figure 7–5.

SAE GRADE MARKINGS	⬡	⬡	⬡	⬡	⬡
DEFINITION	No lines: unmarked indeterminate quality SAE Grades 0-1-2	3 Lines: common commercial quality Automotive & AN Bolts SAE Grade 5	4 Lines: medium commercial quality Automotive & AN Bolts SAE Grade 6	5 Lines: rarely used SAE Grade 7	6 Lines: best commercial quality NAS & Aircraft Screws SAE Grade 8
MATERIAL	Low Carbon Steel	Med. Carbon Steel Tempered	Med. Carbon Steel Quenched & Tempered	Med. Carbon Alloy Steel	Med. Carbon Alloy Steel Quenched & Tempered
TENSILE STRENGTH	65,000 psi	120,000 psi	140,000 psi	140,000 psi	150,000 psi

Figure 7-4 Bolt tensile strengths are denoted on head of bolts. Slash marks (U.S.) or numbers (metric) are used. Always replace bolts with equal or higher rating to prevent failure.

Grade	Identification	Class	Identification
Hex Nut Grade 5		Hex Nut Property Class 9	
	3 Dots		Arabic 9
Hex Nut Grade 8		Hex Nut Property Class 10	
	6 Dots		Arabic 10
Increasing dots represent increasing strength		Can also have blue finish or paint dab on hex flat. Increasing numbers represent increasing strength.	

Figure 7–5 Quality nut strengths are also denoted. More dots or a higher number means more strength.

Tensile strength is the amount of pressure per square inch the bolt can withstand just before breaking when being pulled apart. The harder or stronger the bolt, the greater the tensile strength.

Never replace a high grade bolt with a bolt having a lower grade marking—the weaker bolt could break! If in the steering or suspension, this could seriously endanger the passengers of the vehicle.

Bolt Torque

Bolt torque is a measurement of the turning force applied when installing a fastener. It is critical that bolts and nuts are torqued or tightened properly. Over-tightening will stretch and possibly break the bolt. Under-tightening could allow the bolt or nut to loosen and fall out.

Torque specifications are tightening values for the specific bolt or nut. They are given by the manufacturer. Discussed in the tool chapter, a torque wrench must be used to measure torque values.

If you cannot find the factory torque specification for a bolt, you can use a *general bolt torque chart.* It will give a general torque value for the size and grade of bolt. One is given in Figure 7–6. Normally, the bolt threads should be lubricated to get accurate results. Refer to the service manual to see if the threads should be lubricated or dry.

A *tightening sequence,* or *torque pattern,* assures that parts are clamped down evenly by several bolts or nuts. Generally, tighten fasteners in a crisscross pattern. This will pull the part down evenly, preventing warpage. It is commonly recommended on wheels, as shown in Figure 7–7.

Metric Standard						SAE Standard / Foot Pounds					
Grade of Bolt	5D	.8G	10K	12K		Grade of Bolt	SAE 1&2	SAE 5	SAE 6	SAE 8	
Min. Tensile Strength	71,160 P.S.I	113,800 P.S.I	142,200 P.S.I	170,679 P.S.I		Min. Ten Strength	64,000 P.S.I	105,000 P.S.I	133,000 P.S.I	150,000 P.S.I	
Grade Markings on Head	5D	8G	10K	12K	Size of Socket on Wrench Opening	Markings on Head	●	⊕	✚	✴	Size of Socket or Wrench Opening
Metric		Foot Pounds			Metric	U.S. Standard	Foot Pounds				U.S. Regular
Bolt Dia.	U.S. Dec Equiv.				Bolt Head	Bolt Dia.					Bolt Head / Nut
6 mm	.2362	5	G	8	10	10 mm	1/4	5	7	10	10.5	3/8	7/16
8 mm	.3150	10	16	22	27	14 mm	5/16	9	14	19	22	1/2	9/16
10 mm	.3937	19	31	40	49	17 mm	3/8	15	25	34	37	9/16	5/8
12 mm	.4720	34	54	70	86	19 mm	7/16	24	40	55	60	5/8	3/4
14 mm	.5512	55	89	117	137	22 mm	1/2	37	60	85	92	3/4	13/16
16 mm	.6299	83	132	175	208	24 mm	9/16	53	88	120	132	7/8	7/8
18 mm	.709	111	182	236	283	27 mm	5/8	74	120	167	180	15/16	1.
22 mm	.8661	182	284	394	464	32 mm	3/4	120	200	280	296	1-1/8	1-1/8

Figure 7–6 This is a general bolt torque chart. It gives different values for each bolt tensile strength rating.

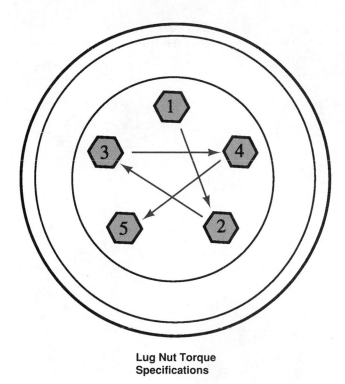

**Lug Nut Torque
Specifications**

Figure 7–7 When tightening several bolts that hold one part, a wheel for example, always use a crisscross pattern. This will prevent part warpage and problems.

Basically, tighten the fastener in steps. Begin at approximately half-torque, then continue to three-fourths torque, and then full torque at least twice.

Be careful when tightening bolts and nuts with air wrenches. It is easy to stretch or break a bolt in an instant. The air wrench can spin the bolt or nut so fast that it can hammer the fastener past its yield point. This can strip threads or snap off the bolt.

When torque is not critical, do NOT use the air impact to run the nut full speed onto the bolt. Instead, run it up slowly until it contacts the work. Then mark the socket and watch how far it turns. Smaller air-powered speed wrenches do NOT produce the severe force of impact wrenches and are much safer to use.

NUTS

A *nut* uses internal (inside) threads and an odd shaped head that often fits a wrench. When tightened onto a bolt, a strong clamping force holds the parts together. Many different nuts are used by the automotive industry. Several are in Figure 7–8.

Castellated or *slotted nuts* are grooved on top so that a safety wire or cotter pin can be installed into a hole in the bolt. This helps prevent the nut from working loose. For example, castellated nuts are used with the studs that hold wheel bearings in position.

Figure 7–8 Nuts also come in varied designs. Know their names. A: Hex nut B: High or deep nut C: Flange nut D: Castle or slotted nut E: Wing nut. *(Dorman Products)*

Slotted nuts are also used on steering and suspension parts for safety.

Self-locking nuts produce a friction or force fit when threaded onto a bolt or stud. The top of the nut can be crimped inward. Some have a plastic insert that produces a friction fit to keep the nut from loosening. Sometimes, locking nuts must be replaced after removal. Front-wheel drive spindles sometimes use self-locking nuts.

Jam nuts are thin nuts used to help hold larger, conventional nuts in place. The jam nut is tightened down against the other nut to prevent loosening.

Wing nuts have two extended arms for turning the nut by hand. They are used when a part must be removed frequently for service or maintenance. Air cleaners sometimes use wing nuts. See Figure 7–8.

Acorn nuts are closed on one end for appearance and to keep water and debris off the threads. They can be used when they are visible and looks are important.

Special types of nuts are used to hold parts onto the vehicle. Sometimes a washer is formed onto the nut. Termed *body nuts*, the flange on the nut helps distribute the clamping force of the thin body panel or trim piece to prevent warpage. Look at Figure 7–9.

Several applications for special nuts are shown in Figure 7–10.

THREAD REPAIRS

An auto body technician must frequently repair damaged threads. A *tap* is a tool for cutting inside threads in holes. A tap is used to repair damaged threaded holes. It is rotated down into the threaded hole to recut the threads. A *die* cuts threads on the outside of bolts or studs. It too is rotated over the threads to clean them up.

Figure 7–9 Body nuts are specially designed for specific holding applications. A: Counter boring nut B: Hex barrel nut C: Washer nut D: Washer nut with rubber gasket E: Pal or locknut F: Acorn nut G: Plate nut. *(A and B—Courtesy of American Engineered Components, C–G—Courtesy of Palnut)*

Lock Nut Keeps Ordinary Hex Nut Tight on Clamp Holding Cable.

Self-threading Nuts, Washer Type, Are Used on Tail Light Assembly.

Removable Pushnut® Fasteners are Slipped Over Integral Molded Studs to Secure Speaker.

Lock Nut Supports Expansion Shell That in Turn Prevents Loosening of Bolt.

Figure 7–10 Note some typical uses for jam nuts. *(Courtesy of Palnut)*

Special *t-handles* fit over the tap or die for turning. You must hold the tool perfectly square to cut good threads. Oil the threads. Then, rotate the tap or die about one-half of a turn and then back it out about one-fourth turn. This will clean metal shavings out and prevent tool breakage.

A *Helicoil®* or *thread insert* can be used to repair badly damaged internal threads. Basically, to use a thread insert, drill the hole oversize. Then tap the hole with new threads. Use the special tool to install rotate the insert into the freshly threaded hole. This will allow you to use the original size bolt. See Figure 7–11.

WASHERS

Washers are used under bolts, nuts, and other parts. They prevent damage to the surfaces of parts and provide better holding power. Several types are in Figure 7–12.

Flat washers are used to increase the clamping surface area. They prevent the smaller bolt head from pulling through the sheet metal or plastic.

A *wave washer* adds a spring action to keep parts from rattling and loosening.

Body or *fender washers* have a very large outside diameter for the size hole in them. They provide better holding power on thin metal and plastic parts.

Copper or *brass washers* are used to prevent fluid leakage, as on brake line fittings. *Spacer washers* come in specific thicknesses to allow for adjustment of parts. *Fiber washers* will prevent vibration or leakage but cannot be tightened to a great extent.

Finishing washers have a curved shape for a pleasing apprearance. They are used on interior pieces.

Split lock washers are used under nuts to prevent loosening by vibration. The ends of these spring-hardened washers dig into both the nut and the work to prevent rotation.

Figure 7–12 Know the washer types. A: Plain flat washer B: Wave or spring washer C: Spacer washer D: Fender washer E: Fiber washer F: Finishing washers G: Split lock washer H: External lock washer I: Internal lock washer. (Dorman Products)

Figure 7–11 Study basic thread repair procedure using thread repair insert. A: Drill hole out one size larger or as needed. B: Run correct size tap down through hole to cut new threads. C: Use special tool to screw insert down into threaded hole. D: Original size bolt can now be used in hole again. (Helicoil, Fastening Systems Division)

Shakeproof or *teeth lock washers* have teeth or bent lugs that grip both the work and the nut. Several designs, shapes, and sizes are available. An external type has teeth on the outside and an internal type has teeth around the inside.

A "rule of thumb" about lock washers. If the part did NOT come with one, do NOT add one. Lock washers are extremely hard and tend to break under severe pressure. If the bolt or nut has a lock washer, use one. The manufacturer would not use one if it did not have a purpose.

SCREWS

Screws are often used to hold nonstructural parts on the vehicle. Trim pieces, interior panels, etc. are often secured by screws. Refer to Figure 7–13.

Machine screws are threaded their full length and are relatively weak. They come in various configurations and will accept a nut.

Set screws frequently have an internal drive head for an Allen wrench. They are used to hold parts onto shafts.

Sheet metal screws have pointed or tapered tips. They thread into sheet metal for light holding tasks.

Self-tapping screws have a pointed tip that helps cut new threads in parts.

Trim screws have a washer attached to them. This improves appearance and helps keep the trim from shifting.

Headlight aiming screws have a special plastic adapter mounted on them. The adapter fits into the headlight assembly. Different design variations are needed for different makes and models of vehicles.

NON-THREADED FASTENERS

Non-threaded fasteners, as implied, do NOT use threads. They include keys, snap rings, pins, clips, adhesives, etc.

Figure 7–13 Know the common screw names. A: Pan head sheet metal screw B: Flat head sheet metal screw C: Oval head D: Round head E: Phillips head screw F: Threaded screw G: Oval head sheet metal screw H: Hex or nutdriver screw I: Hex screw with flange or integral washer J: Clutch head K: Torx head L: Trim screw M: Self-taping screw N: Body screw O: Headlight aiming screw. *(Dorman Products)*

Various *keys* and *pins* are used by equipment manufacturers to retain parts in alignment. It is important to be able to identify these keys and pins, order replacements, and replace them.

Square keys and *Woodruff keys* are used to prevent hand wheels, gears, cams, and pulleys from turning on their shaft. These keys are strong enough to carry heavy loads if they are fitted and seated properly. See Figure 7–14.

Round *taper pins* have a larger diameter on one end than the other. They are used to locate and position matching parts. They can also be used to secure small pulleys and gears to shafts. Refer to Figure 7–15.

Dowel pins have the same general diameter their full length. They are used to position and align the parts of an assembly. One end of a dowel pin is chamfered, and it is usually 0.001 to 0.002 inch (.025 to .05 mm) greater in diameter than the size of its hole. When replacing a dowel pin, be sure that it is the same size as the old one.

Cotter pins help prevent bolts and nuts from loosening or they fit through pins to hold parts together. They are also used as stops and holders on shafts and rods. All cotter pins are used for safety and should NEVER be reused.

The cotter pin should fit into the hole with very little side play. If too long, cut off the extra length of cotter pin. Bend it over in a smooth curve. Sharply angled bends invite breakage. Bend the ends with needle nose pliers. Final bending of the prongs can be done with a soft-faced mallet.

Snap rings are non-threaded fasteners that install into a groove machined into a part. They are used to hold parts on shafts. See Figure 7–15. Special snap ring pliers are designed to flex and install or remove snap rings. They have special tips that will hold the snap ring. Look at Figure 7–16.

Danger! Wear safety glasses when removing or installing snap rings. Being constructed of spring steel, they can shoot out with great force.

Body clips are specially shaped retainers for holding trim and other body pieces requiring little strength. The clip often fits into the back of the trim piece and through the body panel, Figure 7–17.

Figure 7–14 Keys and set screws are both used to align parts on shafts. A: Key and keyway B: Set screw application. *(Florida Dept. Of Voc. Ed.)*

Figure 7–15 Know the non-threaded fastener names. A: Internal snap or retaining ring B: External snap-ring C: E-clip or snap ring D: Cotter pin E: Clevis pin F: Hitch pin G: Split rollpin H: Tapered pin I: Straight dowel pin J: Linkage clip. *(Dorman Products)*

Push-in clips are usually made of plastic and they force fit into holes in body panels. Push-in clips are used to hold interior door trim panels, for example. They install easily, but can be difficult to remove, Figure 7–18.

Pop rivets can be used to hold two pieces of sheet metal together, Figure 7–19. They can be inserted into a blind hole through two pieces of metal and then drawn up with a riveting tool or gun. This will lock the pieces together. There is no need to have access to the back of the rivets.

Pop rivets should NOT be used in areas that are subject to excessive vibration or for structural panels. The rivets can work loose and weaken the repair.

REPLACING FASTENERS

When replacing fasteners, observe the following precautions:

1. Always use the same number of fasteners.

Figure 7–16 Note special retainer and E-clip used on this lock cylinder. (© American Honda Motor Co., Inc.)

Figure 7–17 Various types of retainers or clips are used to hold trim or molding on vehicle body. (Courtesy of Chrysler Corporation)

2. Use the same diameter, length, pitch, and type of fasteners.

3. Observe the OEM's recommendations given in the service manual for tightening sequence, tightening steps (increments), and torque values.

4. Always replace a used cotter pin.

5. Replace stretched fasteners or fasteners with any signs of damage.

6. Use the correct washers and pins as specified by the OEM.

7. Always replace "one-time" fasteners. They can be found in suspension and steering assemblies.

HOSE CLAMPS

Hose clamps are used to hold radiator hoses, heater hoses, and other hoses onto their fittings. See Figure 7–20.

A *spring hose clamp* is made of spring steel with barbs on each end. Squeezing the ends opens and expands the clamp. Special hose clamp pliers should be used to remove or install round wire type clamps. The pliers have a deep groove that will keep the clamp from slipping out of the jaws. Conventional pliers will work fine on spring strap clamps.

Worm hose clamps use a screw that engages a slotted band. Turning the screw reduces or enlarges clamp diameter. This is the most common replacement type of hose clamp.

ADHESIVES

Adhesives provide an alternate means of bonding parts together. The two types of adhesives most often used with automotive metals are acrylic resin and epoxy.

Acrylic resin adhesive is a two-part, somewhat flexible adhesive (liquid and powder) used on small surface areas. It is waterproof and NOT affected by gasoline or water.

Follow the manufacturer's directions for mixing materials. Drying and setting times are controlled by the amounts mixed. For example, three parts of powder to one part of liquid will set in about five minutes at 70°F (21°C). Changing these proportions will allow for faster or slower drying and setting times.

While acrylic resin provides a very strong bond, it sets too fast for large area work and is generally used for heavy-duty repairs on smaller objects. Acetone can be used as a cleaning solvent for acrylic resin adhesive.

Epoxy is a two-part bonding agent that dries harder than adhesive. It comes in two separate containers, usually tubes. One contains the epoxy resin and the other contains a hardener. Epoxy does NOT shrink when it hardens, is waterproof and heat-resistant at moderate temperatures.

Read the instructions for the proper quantity to use. If both resin and hardener are NOT in proper proportion, the bond might fail. Some epoxy tubes

Figure 7–18 Here are a few of the special plastic retainers available. These types are often used in interior. They quickly press into a hole. To remove them, you must carefully pry next to retainer with flat, forked trim tool. *(TRW Plastic Fasteners and Retainers Division, Westminster, MA and Roseville, MI)*

Figure 7-19 Pop rivets provide a quick way of holding sheet metal parts or panels. They are handy when backside of panel is not accessible.

Figure 7-20 Note hose clamp types. A: Wire spring hose clamp B: Wire strap hose clamp C: Worm hose clamp D: Screw-nut hose clamp E: Plastic hose clamp. *(Dorman Products)*

automatically dispense the correct amount of resin and hardener.

Once mixed, the epoxy remains in a workable condition for only a brief time. Therefore, try to mix only as much as is required and use it as quickly as possible. Clamp the work while the glue cures, which can take several hours. Do NOT apply epoxy in low temperatures (below 50°F or 10°C), because it will NOT harden. Once an epoxy is applied, it is difficult to remove it from a surface.

NOTE! ADHESIVES ARE DISCUSSED IN MORE DETAIL IN OTHER CHAPTERS. REFER TO THE TEXT INDEX IF NEEDED.

Summary

- Fasteners make up the thousands of bolts, nuts, screws, clips, and adhesives that literally hold a vehicle together.
- Always replace fasteners with exactly the same type that was removed from the original equipment manufacturer (OEM) assembly. An incorrect fastener, or one of inferior quality, can result in failure and possible injury to the vehicle occupants.
- Bolt strength indicates the amount of torque or tightening force that should be applied.
- Non-threaded fasteners, as implied, do not use threads. Examples of non-threaded fasteners are keys, snap rings, pins, clips, and adhesives.

Technical Terms

fasteners	*Helicoil*
bolt	*washer*
cap screw	*flat washer*
bolt head	*fender washer*
bolt length	*split lock washer*
bolt diameter	*shakeproof lock washer*
bolt head size	*machine screw*
USC	*set screw*
thread pitch	*sheet metal screw*
thread pitch gauge	*self-tapping screw*
right-hand threads	*trim screw*
left-hand threads	*headlight aiming screw*
bolt strength	*key*
bolt grade markings	*Woodruff key*
tensile strength	*taper pin*
bolt torque	*dowel pin*
torque specifications	*cotter pin*
torque pattern	*snap ring*
nut	*body clip*
slotted nut	*push-in clip*
self-locking nut	*pop rivet*
jam nut	*hose clamp*
wing nut	*spring hose clamp*
acorn nut	*worm hose clamp*
body nut	*adhesive*
tap	*acrylic resin adhesive*
die	*epoxy*

Review Questions

1. _____ include the thousands of bolts, nuts, screws, clips, and adhesives that literally hold a vehicle together.

2. Define the term cap screw.

3. What is bolt thread pitch and how is it measured?

4. If you turn right-hand threads clockwise, what will happen?

5. Which of these bolts is strongest?
   a. Three head markings
   b. Two head markings
   c. No head markings
   d. One head marking

6. When installing a wheel on an older car, no service manual can be found for getting a factory torque specification.
   Technician A says to use an impact on medium setting. Technician B says to use a general torque chart and a torque wrench. Who is correct?
   a. Technician A
   b. Technician B
   c. Both Technicians
   d. Neither Technician

7. What general sequence should be used when tightening a series of bolts or nuts?

8. How do you use a thread repair insert?

9. All cotter pins are used for safety and should NEVER be reused. True or false?

10. Body clips are specially shaped retainers for holding _____ and other body pieces requiring little strength.

Activities

1. Inspect a car or truck. Write down the various types of fasteners you can locate. Create a chart listing their names and applications.

2. Read the directions on a few types of body shop adhesives. Write a short report on their use.

3. Visit a body shop supply house or hardware store. Inspect the various types of fasteners available.

CHAPTER 8

AUTO BODY HARDWARE
AND MATERIALS

Objectives

After studying this chapter, you should be able to:

- Select the right materials for the job.

- Explain the basic purpose of common materials.

- Compare the use of similar shop materials.

- Summarize when to use different kinds of filler.

- Know how to select the right type of primer and paint.

- Understand the importance of using a complete paint system.

Introduction

Body shop materials include more than just refinishing or paint materials. It includes the various fillers, primers, sealers, adhesives, sandpapers, and other compounds common to body shops. It is critical that you understand their selection and use. This chapter will summarize the purpose of these basic types of materials. Later chapters will explain how to use these materials in more detail.

When a consumer or layperson looks at a car's paint job, they often only see a shiny, bright color. They seldom understand all of the technology involved in producing that long lasting, tough, durable, high gloss finish. There is much hidden technology under the surface of the paint.

A professional technician comprehends all of the "chemistry" and skill needed to do a good repair. This chapter will introduce you to the materials needed to do competent repairs.

NOTE! THIS CHAPTER ONLY GIVES YOU A WORKING KNOWLEDGE OF COMMON BODY SHOP MATERIALS. IT DOES NOT EXPLAIN HOW TO APPLY OR USE THEM. LATER CHAPTERS WILL GIVE YOU THIS INFORMATION.

REFINISHING MATERIALS

A vehicle body is protected by a complete finishing system. All parts of the system work together to protect the vehicle from ultra-violet (U.V.) radiation, weathering, pollutants, and corrosion.

Refinishing materials is a general term referring to the products used to repaint the vehicle. Refinishing material chemistry has changed drastically in the past few years. New paints last longer but require more skill and safety for proper application.

The *substrate* is the metal, fiberglass, or plastic material used in the vehicle's construction. It will affect the selection of refinishing materials.

The vehicle's paint or finish performs two basic functions—to beautify and to protect. Can you imagine what a car body would look like without paint? For a day or so, it would be the drab, steel gray of bare sheet metal. Then, as rusting ate into the metal, the body would turn an ugly, reddish brown. Finally, this degeneration would continue until the body was coated with solid rust.

The term *paint* generally refers to the visible topcoat. The most elementary painting system consists of a compatible primer and final topcoat over the substrate. This process can vary considerably and is usually more complex, as you will learn later.

UNDERCOATS AND TOPCOATS

A basic finish consists of several coats of two or more different materials. The most basic finish consists of:

1. Undercoat or primer coat.
2. Topcoat (color coat or basecoat/clearcoat).

The *primer* or *undercoat* has to improve adhesion of the topcoat. It is often the first coat applied. Paint alone will not stick or adhere as well as a primer. If you apply a topcoat to bare substrate, the paint will peel, flake off, or look rough. This is why you must "sandwich" a primer undercoat between the substrate and the topcoat. Undercoats also prevent any chemicals from bleeding through and showing in the topcoats of paint.

The terms *topcoat* or *colorcoat* refer to the paint applied over the undercoat. It is usually several light coats of one or more paints. The topcoat is the "glamour coat," because it features the eye-catching color, color effects, and gloss.

Basecoat/clearcoat paint systems use a colorcoat applied over the primer with a second layer of clearcoat over the colorcoat. This is the most common paint system used today. The clear paint brings out the richness of the underlying color and also protects the color. It makes the paint shine more than a single layer of color not using a clearcoat.

PAINT TYPES

There are three general types of paint:

1. Lacquer
2. Enamel/urethane
3. Waterbase paint

As you will learn, there are variations within these categories. It is important that you know what type of finishes manufacturers use because there are slightly different methods required for refinishing them. Refer to Figure 8–1.

Lacquer is an older paint that dries quickly because of solvent evaporation. Lacquers have been phased out for more durable enamel and urethane paints by both OEMs and body shops.

Lacquer topcoats usually must be compounded or rubbed with a compound or polish to bring out their gloss. The acrylic lacquer basecoat/clearcoat finish can allow a lacquer basecoat to be clearcoated with an enamel topcoat. This helps eliminate the need for compounding or polishing to bring out the gloss.

> **WARNING!** *Never spray lacquer over the top of enamel. The enamel can lift and cause problems. You can spray enamel over an old lacquer finish, however.*

Enamel finishes dry with a gloss and do not require rubbing or polishing. This is because it dries through a chemical change rather than by solvent evaporation. Enamel dries in two stages: first by evaporation of the solvent and then by oxidation of the binder, Figure 8–1.

Since enamels generally dry slower, there is more of a chance for dirt and dust to stick in the finish. While there is generally a slight amount of surface roughness in an enamel film, too much will cause a lower gloss.

Two-stage paints consist of two distinct layers of paint: basecoat and clearcoat. *Basecoat/clearcoat enamel* is now the most common system used to repaint cars and trucks. First, a layer of color is applied over the undercoat of primer. Next, while the basecoat is still wet, a second coat of clear is sprayed over the color basecoat.

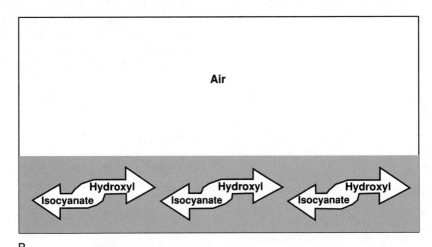

Figure 8–1 Know how paints dry or cure. *(PPG Industries, Inc.)* A: Enamels dry by evaporation of reducer or solvent first, then by oxidation. Resin reacts with oxygen in air for drying. Heat speeds this action. B: Urethane and polyurethane enamels dry by molecular cross linking.

Acrylic enamel and *acrylic urethane enamel* are two specific types of enamel paint. Both are commonly used in the industry. Acrylic urethanes are slightly harder than plain acrylics. Each is available in a variety of colors.

It can be difficult to tell the difference between lacquer and enamel, especially if the vehicle has been refinished. As you become more familiar with automotive refinishing, it will be easier to distinguish between them. This will be discussed later.

Waterbase paint, as implied, uses water to carry the pigment. They dry through evaporation of the water. Some manufacturers are starting to use waterbase paints on new vehicles. This is to help satisfy stricter emission regulations in some geographic areas. The basecoat of color is water-based. Then, an enamel topcoat is applied over the waterbase paint to protect it from the environment.

Waterbase primers have been used for years as a fix for lifting problems. Waterborne primers serve as an excellent barrier coat when there are paint incompatibility problems.

OEM FINISHES

Today's passenger car and light truck *OEM finishes* (factory paint jobs) are either "thermo-setting" acrylic enamel (paint is furnace hardened at factory), new high solids basecoat/clearcoat enamels, or waterbase, low emission paints. Common enamel finishes are baked in huge ovens to shorten the drying times and cure the paint. This is done before installing the interior and other non-metal parts.

Vehicle manufacturers use several different types of finish materials, coating processes, and application processes. Each type of finish requires different planning and repair steps.

The most common types of OEM coating processes include:

1. Single stage
2. Two-stage (basecoat/clearcoat)
3. Three-stage paint (Tri-coat)
4. Multi-stage

These will be explained fully in later chapters of this book.

CONTENTS OF PAINT

A paint's chemical content includes the following:

1. Pigments
2. Binders
3. Solvents
4. Additives

Each of these ingredients has a specific function within the paint formula.

Paint Pigments

The *pigments* are fine powders that impart color, opacity, durability, and other characteristics to the primer or paint. It is a non-volatile film forming ingredient. The main purpose of the pigment is to hide everything under the paint.

Pigment particles size and shape are also important. Pigment particle size affects hiding ability and appearance. In addition, pigment shape affects strength. Pigment particles may be nearly spherical, rod- or plate-like. Rod-shaped particles, for example, reinforce paint film as do "iron bars" in concrete.

Medium size reflective pigment particles, such as mica, are added to *pearl paints* to give the paint a luster or shine that tends to change color with viewing angle. As you will learn later, pearlescent paints are now common and are the most difficult to match when repainting.

Large reflective pigment flakes are added to *metallic paints.* The size, shape, color, and material in the flakes can vary. Often called "metal flakes," the flakes can be made of tiny but visible bits of metal or polyester. When light strikes the flakes, it reflects the light at different angles, looking like tiny "glittering stars" inside the paint.

If this is new to you, start looking at paint jobs more closely. See if you can see the difference between a solid color, a pearl, and a metallic.

Paint solids are the non-liquid contents of the paint or primer. *High-solids paints* are needed to reduce air pollution or emissions when painting. *Low-solids paints* are less desirable because they contain more solvents that pollute the air.

Paint Binders

The *paint binder* is the ingredient in a paint that holds the pigment particles together. It is the "backbone" or "film-former" of the paint. The binder helps the paint stick to the surface. Various materials are used in the binder. The binder determines the type of paint—lacquer or enamel.

The binder is generally made of a natural resin (such as rosin), drying oils (linseed or cottonseed), or a manufactured plastic. The binder dictates the type of paint because it contains the drying mechanism.

Binder is usually modified with plasticizers and catalysts. They improve such properties as durability, adhesion, corrosion resistance, mar-resistance, and flexibility.

Solvents

The *paint solvent* is the liquid solution that carries the pigment and binder so it can be sprayed. Thinners and reducers are composed of one or several solvents. They provide a transfer medium. Solvents are the volatile part of a paint. They are used to reduce a paint for spraying. Solvents give the paint its flow characteristics. They evaporate as the paint dries.

Most solvents are made from crude oil or petroleum. However, water-based paints are increasing in use to meet strict pollution regulations. The solvent reduces or thins the binder and transfers the pigment and binder through the spray gun to the surface being painted.

When used with lacquer, the solvent is called a *thinner.* When used with enamel, the solvent is called a *reducer.* This is an important distinction. The respective products are so labeled.

Remember! You "thin" lacquer and "reduce" enamel. Thinning and reducing are needed to make the mixture the right "thickness" or *viscosity* to flow out smoothly onto the surface.

Waterbased paints come *premixed* (ready to spray) and they are NOT normally reduced. In an emergency, distilled water can be added to make a thinner, more liquid solution.

When using waterborne materials, the water used for equipment cleaning:

1. Contains hazardous materials and should be disposed of as hazardous waste

2. Cannot be poured down the drain for disposal

3. Must not be combined with other waste solvents such as reducers or thinners. Keep a separate container for storing water wastes

Due to clean air regulations, some solvents are no longer being used. To meet clean air regulations, traditional solvents are being replaced by water or other solvents. Check local ordinances.

Paint Additives

Paint additives are ingredients added to modify the performance and characteristics of the paint. Additives are used to:

1. Speed up or slow down the drying process.
2. Lower the freezing point of a paint.
3. Prevent the paint from foaming when shaken.
4. Control settling of metallics and pigments.
5. Make the paint more flexible when dry.

DRYING AND CURING

Drying is the process of changing a coat of paint or other material from a liquid to a solid state. Drying is due to evaporation of solvent, chemical reaction of the binding medium, or combination of these causes. See Figure 8–2.

The term "drying" refers to a paint material that evaporates its solvent to harden. The term "curing" refers to a chemical action in the paint or other material itself that causes hardening.

Flash is the first stage of drying where some of the solvents evaporate, which dulls the surface from a high gloss to a normal gloss.

A *retarder* is a slow evaporating thinner or reducer used to retard or slow dry. It is a slow-drying solvent often used in very warm weather. If a paint dries too quickly, problems can result.

An *accelerator* is a fast evaporating thinner or reducer for speeding the drying time. It is needed in very cold weather to make the paint dry in a reasonable amount of time. The term "accelerator" also refers to a hardener or catalyst in some paint systems.

A general rule to follow in selecting the proper thinner or reducer is: the faster the shop drying conditions, the slower drying the thinner or reducer should be. In hot, dry weather, use a slower-drying thinner or reducer. In cold, wet weather, use a fast-dry thinner or reducer.

A *catalyst* is a substance that causes or speeds up a chemical reaction. When mixed with another substance, it speeds the reaction but does not change itself. Catalysts are used with many types of materials—paints, putties, fillers, fiberglass, plastics, Figure 8–3.

A *paint catalyst, drier,* or *hardener* is an additive used to make enamel paints cure quickly. Seldom is an enamel paint used alone. A hardener is almost

Curing

Drying

Figure 8–2 Drying is a process where solvents evaporate from paint. Curing is a chemical reaction that changes the molecular makeup of the paint. (I-CAR)

Figure 8–3 A catalyst or hardener is added to primer or paint to make it cure faster. (PPG Industries, Inc.)

always used by professional painters. The hardener speeds curing and makes the paint more durable.

The hardener is added to the paint right before it is sprayed. When an enamel catalyst is used, the paint can be wet sanded and compounded (polished) the next day, like a lacquer paint. If you make a mistake (paint run, dirt in paint, etc.), you can fix the problem after the short curing time. The hardener will make the enamel cure in just a few hours. Also, the car can be released to the customer sooner with less chance of paint damage.

> ***Danger! Isocyanate resin*** *is a principal ingredient in some urethane catalysts and hardeners. Because this ingredient has toxic effects, you must always wear an NIOSH approved respirator.*

PRIMERS AND SEALERS

Primers come in many variations—primer, primer-sealer, primer-surfacer, primer-filler, etc. It is important to understand the functions of subcoating or undercoat materials. You must follow manufacturer instructions. Deviation from these directions will result in unsatisfactory work.

A plain primer is a thin undercoat designed to provide good adhesion for the topcoat. Primers are generally used by automobile manufacturers rather than paint and body shops. However, primers can be used when the surface is very smooth and there is no potential problem with bleeding. If properly applied, primer does not require sanding. Refer to Figure 8–4.

Primers are usually enamel- or epoxy-based products because they provide better adhesion and corrosion resistance than lacquers.

A *self-etching primer* has acid in it to treat bare metal so that the primer will adhere properly. Some primer-sealers and primer-surfacers have an etching material in them.

SEALERS

Bleeding or *bleedthrough* is a problem where colors in the undercoat or old paint chemically seep into the new topcoats. This can discolor the new paint.

A *paint sealer* is an innercoat between the topcoat and the primer or old finish to prevent bleeding. Sealers differ from primer-sealers in that they cannot be used as a primer. Sealers are sprayed over a primer or primer-surfacer, or a sanded old finish. Sealers do not normally need sanding but some are sandable.

Sealers are sometimes used when a sharp color difference is visible after sanding. They are also used to prevent sand scratch swelling problems.

A *primer–sealer* is an undercoat that improves adhesion of the topcoat and also seals old painted surfaces that have been sanded. It will solve two potential problems (adhesion and bleed) with one application. Look at Figure 8–5.

Primer–sealers provide the same protection as primers—adhesion and corrosion resistance. But they also have the ability to seal over a sanded old finish to provide uniform color holdout.

Figure 8–4 Primers are needed to bond to substrate. There are many variations including primers, primer-surfacers, and primer sealers. *(Marson Corp.)*

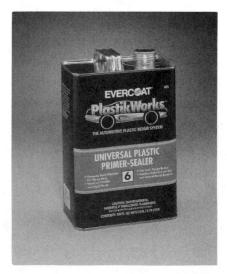

Figure 8–5 This primer-sealer is formulated for plastic parts. *(Evercoat Fibreglass Co., Inc.)*

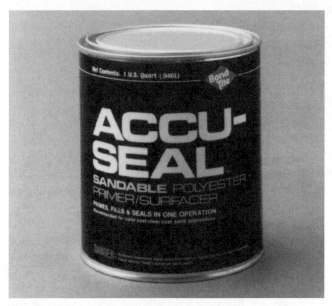

Figure 8–6 Sealer is needed to prevent undercoats from bleeding through into new paint. New formulas combine sealer into primer–surfacer to save steps. *(Oatey Bond Tite)*

PRIMER-SURFACERS

A *primer–surfacer* is a high-solids primer that fills small imperfections and usually must be sanded. It is often used after a filler to help smooth the surface. Primer–surfacers are used to build up and level feathered areas or rough surfaces and to provide a smooth base for topcoats. See Figures 8–6 and 8–7.

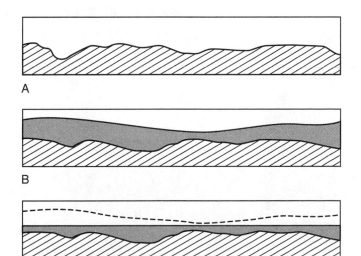

Figure 8–7 Primer–surfacer is the "workhorse" of auto body repair industry. *(PPG Industries, Inc.)* A: Magnified view of cross-section shows that surface is slightly rough. This might be due to sanding or texture of plastic filler. B: Primer–surfacer has been sprayed over surface. It has a high solids content that flows and fills indentations. C: Sanding primer–surfacer will quickly level and smooth surface. This readies surface for topcoats.

A good primer–surfacer should have the following characteristics:

1. Adhesion
2. Rust and corrosion resistance
3. Buildup
4. Sanding ease
5. Color holdout
6. Quick drying speed

Strong adhesion is the first prerequisite of a primer. All automotive topcoat colors require the use of a primer or primer–surfacer as a first coat over bare substrate. A good primer–surfacer should be ready to sand in as short a period as 30 minutes.

A *primer–filler* is a very thick form of primer–surfacer. It is sometimes used when a very pitted or rough surface must be filled and smoothed quickly. It might be used on a solid, but badly rusted and pitted body panel for example.

The industry trend is to use combination materials (primer–sealers or primer–surfacers) over singe purpose materials (sealer, primer, etc.). This will save time, money and help improve the quality of your work.

EPOXY PRIMERS

An *epoxy primer* is a two-part primer that cures fast and hard. Some material manufacturers recommend epoxy primer prior to the application of body fillers. Using an epoxy primer greatly increases body filler adhesion and corrosion resistance over bare metal. Epoxy primers most closely duplicate the OEM primers used for corrosion protection.

Body fillers, once mixed with the appropriate catalyst, starts a chemical reaction. This reaction in turn causes heat. The heat on bare metal will tend to cause condensation that may corrode the metal. Eventually, the plastic body filler will crack and loosen, leaving a corroded area. An epoxy primer protects against moisture entrapment caused by condensation. It can make your repair last longer.

USE A COMPLETE SYSTEM!

Remember! Always use a complete paint system. A *paint system* means all materials (primers, catalysts, paints) are compatible and manufactured by the same company. They are designed to work properly with each other. If you mix materials from different manufacturers, you can run into problems. The chemical contents of the different systems may not work well together. See Figure 8–8.

Figure 8-8 When painting, always use a complete paint system produced by one manufacturer. You are then sure that all chemicals used in the products will work together without problems. (PPG Industries, Inc.)

OTHER PAINT MATERIALS

A *prep solvent* or wax and grease remover is a fast drying solvent often used to clean a vehicle. It will remove wax, oil, grease, and other debris that could contaminate and ruin the paint job.

A *flattener* is an agent added to paint to lower gloss or shine. It can be added to any color gloss paint to make it a semi-gloss or flat (dull) color. For example, some factory and custom hoods are painted semi-gloss or flat black for a high performance look. A flattening agent would be used in this instance. They can also be used where reflection off a high gloss paint could affect driver visibility.

A *fisheye eliminator* is a paint additive that helps smooth the paint when small craters or holes in the paint film are a problem. Contaminants make the paint flow away from small debris in the paint film. Fisheye eliminator is an oil-based material that makes

the paint flow over the top of the contaminant. It should only be used when absolutely necessary. However, always have fisheye eliminator on hand for emergencies.

A *flex agent* is an additive that allows primers and paints to flex or bend without cracking. It is commonly added to paints being applied to plastic bumper covers, for example. Also called an *elastomer,* it is a manufactured compound with flexible and elastic properties that can be added to primers and paints.

Anti-chip coating, also called *gravel guard, chip guard,* or *vinyl coating,* is a rubberized material used along a vehicle's lower panels. It is designed to be flexible or rubbery to resist chips from rocks and other debris flying up off the tires. Anti-chip coatings are usually applied with a special spray gun, like the one in Figure 8–9.

Many manufacturers are using special chip resistant coatings in areas that are exposed to stones and gravel. These coatings are generally between the E-coat primer and the topcoats. Some chip resistant coatings are clear and can be applied over the topcoat. If a vehicle has chip resistant coatings, they must be replaced during the refinishing process.

Rubberized undercoat is a synthetic-based rubber material applied as a corrosion or rust preventive layer. It can be applied using a production gun or a spray can.

A *metal conditioner* is a phosphoric acid used to etch bare sheet metal before priming. A metal conditioner is a chemical cleaner that removes rust and

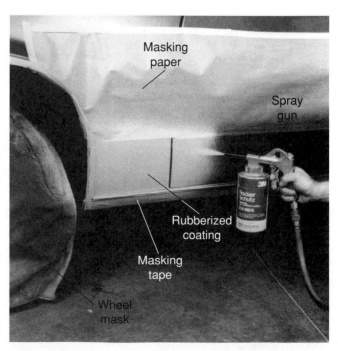

Figure 8-9 Antichip coating is rubberized material often sprayed along lower panels of vehicle to help resist chips. (3M Automotive Trades Division)

corrosion from bare metal and helps prevent further rusting.

Remember the following about metal conditioners:

1. Acid cleans the metal.

2. Dissolves light surface rust.

3. Etches metal, improving adhesion.

4. Needs to be completely neutralized with water after applying.

5. May have to be diluted, following product directions.

6. Is always followed by conversion coating.

7. Wear rubber gloves and eye protection.

A *conversion coating* is a special metal conditioner or primer used on galvanized steel, uncoated steel, and aluminum to prevent rust. It is applied after acid etching or metal conditioning.

Corrosion is a chemical reaction of air, moisture, or corrosive materials on a metal surface. Corrosion of steel is usually referred to as *rusting* or oxidation.

Paint stripper is a powerful chemical that dissolves paint for fast removal of an old finish. If the old paint is cracking or peeling, you may have to use a chemical stripper. It is applied over the old paint. After it soaks into and lifts the paint, a plastic scraper is used to remove the softened paint, Figure 8–10.

A *tack cloth* can be used to remove dust and lint from the surface right before painting. It is a cheesecloth treated with nondrying varnish to make it tacky. A tack cloth must be wiped gently over the surface to keep the varnish from contaminating the paint.

PLASTIC BODY FILLERS

A *filler* is any material used to fill (level) a damaged area. There are several types of filler. You should understand their differences.

Body filler or *plastic filler* is a heavy-bodied plastic material that cures very hard for filling small dents in metal. It is a compound of resin and plastic used to fill dents on car bodies. Note Figure 8–11.

Body fillers come canned and in plastic bags. When in a plastic bag, a dispenser is used to force the filler onto your mixing board. This keeps the filler perfectly clean. A *mixing board* is the surface (metal, glass, plastic) used for mixing the filler and its hardener.

Light body filler is formulated for easy sanding and fast repairs. It is used as a very thin, top coat of filler for final leveling. It can be spread thinly over large surfaces for block or air tool sanding the panel level.

Fiberglass body filler has fiberglass material added to the plastic filler. It is used for rust repair or where strength is important. It can be used on both metal and fiberglass substrates. Because fiberglass-reinforced filler is very difficult to sand, it is usually used

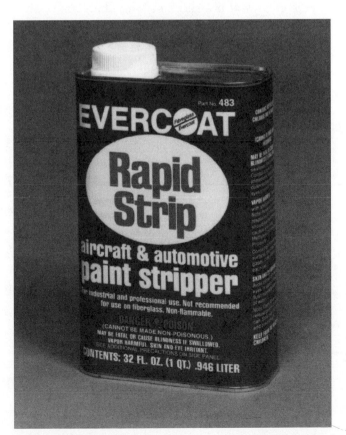

Figure 8–10 Paint stripper is a powerful chemical that will quickly dissolve old paint. It is needed only if old paint is peeling, cracking, and will not take new topcoat. Wear protective gear when using paint stripper as it will cause chemical burns. (Evercoat Fibreglass Co., Inc.)

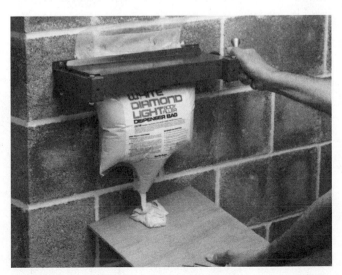

Figure 8–11 Plastic filler comes in cans, buckets, and plastic bags. Dispenser will save time and keep filler uncontaminated. (Oatey Bond Tite)

Figure 8–12 Fiberglass reinforced filler is used to improve repair strength. It is much stronger than plain plastic filler. Fiberglass impregnated filler looks and works like regular plastic filler. It is stronger than plastic filler and is usually waterproof, which makes rust repairs last longer. (U.S. Chemicals and Plastics, Inc., Canton, Ohio)

under a conventional, lightweight plastic filler. Look at Figure 8–12.

Short-hair fiberglass filler has tiny particles of fiberglass in it. It works and sands like a conventional filler, but is much stronger. *Long-hair fiberglass filler* has long strands of fiberglass for even more strength. It is commonly used when you must repair holes in metal or fiberglass bodies.

Cream hardeners are used to cure body fillers. They usually come in a tube. Once the hardening cream is mixed in, the plastic filler will heat up and harden. See Figure 8–13.

NOTE! THE MOST COMMON MISTAKE OF THE APPRENTICE IS TO USE <u>TOO MUCH CREAM HARDENER!</u> THE PLASTIC FILLER WILL SET UP OR HARDEN IN A COUPLE OF MINUTES, BEFORE YOU HAVE TIME TO SPREAD IT ON THE BODY. LITERALLY "TONS" OF PLASTIC FILLER HAVE BEEN WASTED BECAUSE OF HARDENER OVERUSE. USING TOO MUCH CREAM HARDENER CAN ALSO CAUSE PROBLEMS WITH ADHESION AND PINHOLING.

FIBERGLASS

Fiberglass resin is another form of plastic body repair material. It is a thick resin liquid that comes in a can. The fiberglass resin must be mixed with its own special type of hardener to cure. If you accidentally use

Figure 8–13 Cream hardeners are added to filler to make it cure. Note that hardeners can differ and can deteriorate with age. Always use the type recommended by the filler manufacturer. (Oatey Bond Tite)

cream hardener in fiberglass resin, it will not harden and you will have a mess to clean up. See Figure 8–14.

Fiberglass mat is a series of long fiberglass strands irregularly distributed to form a patch. It is used to strengthen and form a shape for the resin liquid.

Fiberglass cloth is made by weaving the fiberglass strands into a stitched pattern.

Fiberglass tape will stick to the repair surface to help form the body shape. This is a fast method of applying fiberglass for repairs. Resin can be applied over the tape.

GLAZING PUTTY

Glazing putty is a material made for filling small holes or sand scratches. It is similar to primer-surfacer but it has more solid content. Putty is applied over the undercoat of primer-sealer or primer-surfacer to correct small surface imperfections. The purpose of glazing putties is to fill excessively rough surfaces or imperfections that CANNOT be filled with a primer-surfacer.

Spot putty is the same as glazing putty except it has even more solids. Spot putty is recommended for scratches or nicks up to $\frac{1}{16}$ inch (1.5 mm) deep. It should NOT be used to fill large surface depressions. For larger depressions, use plastic filler or catalyzed putty.

One-part putty often comes in a tube. A rubber spreader is often used to work the putty into small holes in the primer. After fully drying, the putty is sanded smooth. Only the small pin holes or scratches remain filled with putty.

A

B

Figure 8–14 Fiberglass resin and mat or cloth is often used to repair fiberglass body panels and parts. It is sometimes used for rust repair. *(Oatey Bond Tite)* A: Clear resin cures to a hard, brittle solid. Special catalyst is needed. Do not use cream hardener. B: Fiberglass cloth, mat, or tape is used with resin. Cut pieces to size, coat them with resin, and apply them over repair area.

Two-part putty comes with its own hardener for rapid curing. This is the main advantage of two-part putty. It dries much more quickly. If you paint over partially dried putty, it can shrink and cause problems.

> *WARNING! A common mistake is to try to use putty like a filler. Putty is very weak and will not adhere to metal or filler. Only use putty over the top of primer to fill small pin holes or sand scratches. Don't be a "putty builder" or your work will be very weak.*

MASKING MATERIALS

Masking materials are used to cover and protect body parts from paint overspray. *Overspray* is unwanted paint spray mist floating around the spray gun. It can stick to glass and body parts and take considerable time to clean off.

Masking paper is special paper designed to be used to cover body parts not to be painted. It comes in a roll. When mounted on a masking machine, masking tape is automatically applied to one edge of the paper, speeding your work. See Figure 8–15.

Masking plastic is used just like paper to cover and protect parts from overspray. It also comes in rolls and can cover large body areas more easily than paper.

Plastic wheel masks are preshaped plastic covers for going over the vehicle's wheels and tires. Preshaped plastic antenna, headlamp, and mirror covers are also available.

Masking tape is used to hold masking paper or plastic into position. It is a high tack, easy to tear tape. It comes in rolls of varying widths, ¾ inch (19 mm) wide being the most common. Refer to Figure 8–16.

Figure 8–15 Masking is needed to keep overspray off of panels and parts not to be painted.

Masking Tape

Molding

Fine Line
Masking Tape

1. **Apply Masking Tape to Within 1/8" (3mm) of Edge.**

2. **Apply Masking Paper.**

3. **Mask to Edge of Part with 1/4" (6mm) Fine Line Tape.**

4. **Leave a Tail or Handle.**

5. **Remove Fine Line Tape While Paint is Still Wet.**

Figure 8–16 Know the applications of masking tape. Note example of how fine line tape is used along rubber molding to produce good paint edge. Paper masking tape is then used to hold paper in place next to fine line tape.

Fine line masking tape is a very thin, smooth surface plastic masking tape. Also termed *flush masking tape,* it can be used to produce a better *paint part edge* (edge where old paint and new paint meet). When the fine line tape is removed, the edge of the new paint will be straighter and smoother than if conventional masking tape were used.

Fine line tape can help a painter mask flush mounted parts. It may be better to mask these parts than to remove them. Door handles, side trim, mirror mounts, and moldings are a few examples. Fine line tape is also used where two different paint colors come together, as when painting stripes or two-tone finishes.

Duct tape is a thick tape with a plastic body. It is sometimes used to protect parts from damage when grinding, sanding, or blasting. Duct tape is thicker than masking tape and provides more protection for the surface under the tape.

Masking liquid, also called *masking coating,* is usually a water-based sprayable material for keeping overspray off of body parts. Some are solvent based. Masking liquid comes in a large, ready-to-spray container or drum. These materials are sprayed on and form a paint-proof coating over the vehicle.

Some masking coatings are tacky and used only during priming and painting. They form a film which can be applied when the vehicle enters the shop. Others dry to a hard, dull finish.

Masking coatings can be removed when the vehicle is ready to return to the owner. It washes off with soap and water. Local regulations may require that liquid masking residue be captured in a floor drain trap, and not put into the sewer system.

ABRASIVES

An *abrasive* is any material, such as sand, crushed steel grit, aluminum oxide, silicon carbide, or crushed slag, used for cleaning, sanding, smoothing, or material removal. Many types of abrasives are used by the auto body technician.

Grit refers to a measure of the size of particles on sandpaper or discs. A *coarse* sandpaper would have large grit. A *fine* sandpaper would have smaller grit.

Grit Ratings

A *grit numbering system* denotes how coarse or fine the abrasive is. For example, 16 grit would be one of the coarsest and 1500 grit would be one of the finest. The grit number is printed on the back of the paper or disc.

Very coarse grit of 16 to 60 is generally used for fast material removal. It will quickly remove paint and take it down to bare metal. This grit is commonly used on grinding discs and air files for rapid cutting.

A *coarse grit* of 36 to 60 is basically used for rough sanding and smoothing operations. This coarseness might be used to get the general shape of a large plastic filler area.

Medium grit of 80 to 120 is often used for sanding plastic filler high spots and for sanding of old paint.

Fine grit of 150 to 180 is normally used to sand bare metal and for smoothing existing painted surfaces.

Very fine grit ranges from 220 to about 2000 and is used for numerous final smoothing operations. Larger grits of 220 to 320 are for sanding primer-surfacers, and old paint. Finer grits of 400 to 2000 are for color-coat sanding, and sanding before polishing or buffing. Very fine grits are usually wet sandpaper to keep the paper from becoming clogged or filled with paint.

Generally, start your work with the coarsest grit that is practical. This will remove and smooth the work quickly. Then, gradually go to finer paper to achieve the desired surface smoothness. This procedure will be detailed in later chapters. See Figure 8–17.

Open and Closed Coat Grits

Sandpaper and discs come in either open coat or closed coat types of grit.

With an *open coat,* the resin that bonds the grit to the paper only touches the bottom of the grit. About 50–70% of its surface is covered by grit materials. Open coat grit will not clog as quickly.

With a *closed coat,* the resin completely covers the grit. This bonds the grit to the paper or disc more securely. About 90% of the surface is covered by grit materials. Closed coat will clog faster than open coat.

GRINDING DISCS

Grinding discs are round, very coarse abrasives used for initial removal of paint, plastic, and metal (weld

GRIT	ALUMINUM OXIDE	SILICON CARBIDE	AUTO BODY USE
Ultra Fine		1500 1200 800	Color-Coat Wet Sanding.
Very Fine		600	Color-Coat Wet Sanding Before Polishing.
	400 320 280 240	400 320 280 240	Sanding Primer-surfacer and Paint Before Painting. Wet or Dry Sanding Paper
	220	220	Dry Sanding Top Coat. Also Available for Wet Sanding.
Fine	180 150	180 150	Final Sanding of Bare Metal and Smoothing Old Paint. Dry Paper.
Medium	120 100 80	120 100 80	Smoothing Paint and Plastic Filler. Dry Paper.
Coarse	60 50 40 36	60 50 40 36	Rough-Sanding of Filler and Plastics. Dry Paper.
Very Coarse	24 16	24 16	Coarse Sanding or Grinding to Remove Paint. Dry Paper.

Figure 8–17 Note how sandpaper is made and classified by coarseness. *(I-CAR)* Study common grits of sandpaper and their common uses.

joints). Some are very thick and do not require a backing plate. Others are thinner and require a *disc backing plate* mounted on the grinder spindle. They are used for material removal operations.

Grinding disc size is measured across its outside diameter. The most common grinding disc sizes are 7 and 9 inch (175 and 225 mm). The hole in the center of the disc must also match the shaft on the grinder or sander.

SANDPAPERS

Sandpaper is a heavy paper coated with an abrasive grit. It is the most commonly used abrasive in auto body repair. There are several kinds, shapes, and grits of sandpaper. *Sanding discs* are round and are normally used on an air-powered orbital sander. They might have a self-stick coating or you may have to use disc adhesive to hold the sandpaper onto the tool pad, Figure 8–18.

Sanding sheets are square and can be cut to fit sanding blocks. Long sheets are also available for use on air files.

Dry sandpaper is designed to be used without water. Its resin is usually an animal glue. Its glue is not water resistant and will dissolve when wet, ruining the sandpaper.

Dry sandpaper is often used for coarse-to-medium grit sanding tasks, like shaping and smoothing plastic

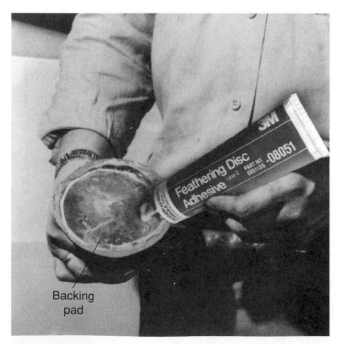

Figure 8–18 Disc adhesive is sometimes used to hold sandpaper onto air tool's pad. Only use a small amount. Spread it over pad surface with back of sandpaper. *(3M Automotive Trades Division)*

Backing pad

filler. One example, 80-grit dry sandpaper is often used on plastic filler. It will quickly cut the filler down but will not leave deep sand scratches in the paint surrounding the filler.

Wet sandpaper, as implied, can be used with water for flushing away sanding debris that would otherwise clog fine grits. Wet sandpaper comes in finer grits for final smoothing operations before and after painting. Wet sandpaper is available in grits from about 220 to 2000.

Wet sandpaper is commonly used to block sand paint before compounding or buffing. Wet sanding will knock down any imperfections in the paint film. Buffing or compounding is then needed to make the paint shiny again.

When using sandpapers:

1. Sand in one direction only, usually along the line of sight. If several grades of sandpaper are used on one area, cross sand to eliminate scratches.

2. Use the finest abrasive possible to do the job.

3. Start with as fine a grade as possible. If too fine, go to a coarser grade then work back to the finer grade.

4. Adjust one grade finer for hand versus machine sanding.

5. Support the abrasive with a block or pad to avoid finger marks and crowning.

6. Adjust two grades finer when wet sanding, due to faster cutting abrasives.

7. Choose one manufacturer's line so you can learn its cutting characteristics.

8. Follow the manufacturer's recommendation for use.

SCUFF PADS

Scuff pads are tuff synthetic pads used to clean and lightly scratch the surface of paints. Being like a sponge, they are handy for scuffing irregular surfaces, like on door jambs, around the inside of the hood and deck lids, and other obstructed areas. This will clean and lightly scuff these areas so the paint will stick.

COMPOUNDS

Compounding involves using an abrasive paste material to smooth and bring out the gloss of the applied topcoat. It can be applied by hand or with a polishing wheel on an air tool. A compound has a fine volcanic pumice or dust-like grit in a water-soluble paste. When rubbed on a painted surface, a thin layer of paint is removed. It will remove the very top layer of

Finer polishing
compound

Coarse rubbing
compound

Figure 8–19 Compounds are used to final smooth painted surfaces. Some are coarser than others. Some are designed for hand application and others for machine use. Always read label directions. *(U.S. Chemicals and Plastics, Inc., Canton, Ohio)*

old, weathered paint, leaving a new fresh surface of paint.

A *hand compound* is designed to be applied by hand on a rag or cloth. *Machine compound* is formulated to be applied with an electric or air polisher. It will not cut as fast and will not break down with the extra friction and heat of machine application.

Rubbing compound is the coarsest type of hand compound. It will rapidly remove paint but will leave visible scratch marks. Rubbing compound is designed for hand application, not machine application. It is often used on small areas to treat imperfections in the paint surface.

Polishing compound or *machine glaze* is a fine grit compound designed for machine application. A polisher is used to carefully run the compound over the cured or dried paint. Polishing compound is often used after a rubbing compound or after wet sanding. It will make the paint shiny and smooth.

Hand glazes are for final smoothing and shining of the paint. They are the last process used to produce a professional finish. They are applied by hand using a circular motion, like a wax.

Compounds come in other formulations as well. Read the label on the compound to learn about its use. Look at Figure 8–19.

Remember, a painter will generally use:

1. Rubbing compounds to remove surface imperfections in paint

2. Machine glazes to restore paint gloss after wet sanding

3. Hand glazes to remove swirl marks after machine buffing

ADHESIVES

Adhesives are special glues designed to bond parts to one another. Various types are available.

Weatherstrip adhesive is designed to hold rubber seals and similar parts in place. Weatherstrip adhesive dries to a hard rubber type consistency. This makes it ideal for holding door seals, trunk seals, and other seals onto the body. Look at Figure 8–20.

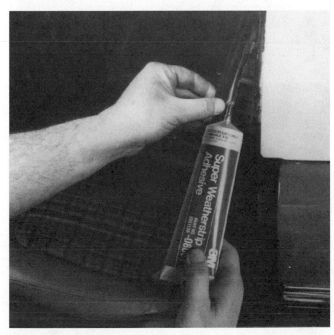

Figure 8–20 Weatherstrip adhesive is commonly used to install rubber seals around doors and trunks. Black color adhesive is best on black rubber seals. *(3M Automotive Trades Division)*

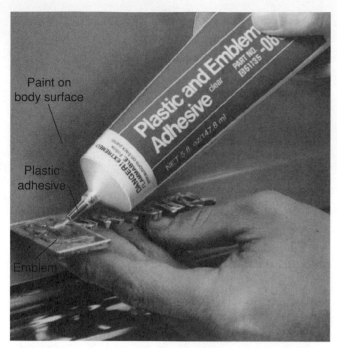

Figure 8–21 Plastic adhesive dries harder than weatherstrip adhesive. It is often used on trim pieces that bond directly to paint. (*3M Automotive Trades Division*)

Figure 8–23 Release agent will dissolve adhesive so that you can remove glued-on parts easily. (*3M Automotive Trades Division*)

Plastic adhesive or *emblem adhesive* is designed to hold hard plastic and metal parts. It is used to install various types of emblems and trim pieces onto painted surfaces. See Figure 8–21.

Vinyl adhesive is designed to bond a vinyl top to the vehicle body. This type of adhesive is often used when installing or repairing vinyl tops, interior roof liners, and similar parts. Refer to Figure 8–22.

An *adhesive release agent* is a chemical that dissolves most types of adhesives. It is used when you want to remove a part without damage. The agent is sprayed onto the adhesive. This softens the adhesive so the part can be lifted off easily. Refer to Figure 8–23.

EPOXIES

An *epoxy* is a two-part glue used to hold various parts together. The two ingredients are mixed together in equal parts. This makes the mixture cure through a chemical reaction. Always use the type of epoxy suggested by the auto manufacturer. Look at Figure 8–24.

SEALERS

Sealers are used to prevent water and air leaks between parts. They are flexible, which prevents cracking. Sealers come in several variations, Figure 8–25.

Seam sealers are designed to make a leakproof joint between body panels. It is often needed where two panels butt or overlap each other. Seam sealers come in different forms and each is applied differently. Read the directions.

Tube sealers are applied directly from the tube or by using a caulking gun. They squirt out like "toothpaste" and cure in a few hours.

Apply primer before applying seam sealer. Seam sealers are paintable but might need to be re-primed,

Figure 8–22 Vinyl adhesive is commonly used to bond vinyl roof to body. Spray can allows for smooth coating of adhesive so roof covering will lay flat and smooth. (*3M Automotive Trades Division*)

Figure 8–24 Numerous types of two-part epoxies are used to help bond parts. Make sure you use the type recommended by manufacturer. *(3M Automotive Trades Division)*

if product directions specify. Silicone sealers are NOT paintable and should NOT be used in auto body repair. Follow instructions on the product for finishing sealers.

Ribbon sealers come in strip form and are applied by hand. They are a thick sealer that must be worked onto the parts with your fingers.

NOTE! THE PROPER USE OR APPLICATION OF THESE MATERIALS WILL BE EXPLAINED LATER IN THIS BOOK. REFER TO THE INDEX IF YOU NEED MORE INFORMATION NOW.

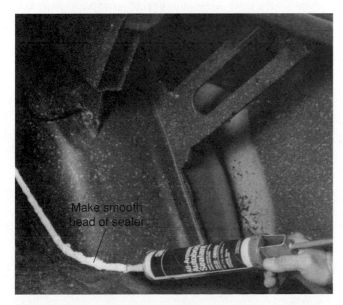

Make smooth bead of sealer

Figure 8–25 Various types of sealers are used to prevent leakage between body parts. Technician is using caulking gun to seal newly installed trunk floor panel. *(3M Automotive Trades Division)*

Summary

- Body shop materials include the various fillers, primers, sealers, adhesives, sandpapers, and other compounds common to body shops.
- The substrate is the metal, fiberglass, or plastic material used in the vehicle's construction. It will affect the selection of refinishing materials.
- There are three general types of paint: lacquer, enamel, and waterbase.
- A filler is any material used to fill (level) a damaged area.
- Masking materials, such as masking plastic, masking tape, and duct tape are used to cover and protect body parts from paint overspray.
- Sealers are used to prevent water and air leaks between parts. They are applied in the form of seam sealers, tube sealers, and ribbon sealers.

Technical Terms

refinishing materials	primer
substrate	self-etching primer
paint	bleeding
prime coat	paint sealer
undercoat	primer–sealer
topcoat	primer–surfacer
colorcoat	primer–filler
basecoat/clearcoat	epoxy primer
lacquer	paint system
enamel	prep solvent
two-stage paint	flattener
waterbase paint	fisheye eliminator
OEM finish	flex agent
pigment	anti-chip coating
pearl paints	rubberized undercoat
metallic paints	conversion coating
high-solids paints	corrosion
paint binder	paint stripper
paint solvent	tack cloth
thinner	body filler
reducer	mixing board
premixed paint	light body filler
additives	fiberglass filler
drying	long-hair fiberglass filler
curing	cream hardeners
flash	fiberglass resin
retarder	fiberglass mat
accelerator	fiberglass cloth
catalyst	glazing putty
hardener	spot putty
isocyanate	one-part putty
resin	two-part putty

masking paper
masking plastic
masking tape
fine line masking tape
duct tape
masking coating
abrasive
grit
grit numbering system
open coat
closed coat
grinding disc
sandpaper
sanding disc
sanding sheet
dry sandpaper

wet sandpaper
scuff pad
compounding
hand compound
machine compound
rubbing compound
polishing compound
hand glazes
adhesives
weatherstrip adhesive
emblem adhesive
vinyl adhesive
adhesive release agent
sealers
ribbon sealers

Review Questions

1. A _____ is the metal, fiberglass, or plastic material used in the vehicle's body construction.

2. What are two functions of a vehicle's paint or finish?

3. Define the terms "undercoat" and "topcoat."

4. List and explain the three basic types of automotive paints.

5. This refers to a factory paint job.
   a. Lacquer
   b. Enamel
   c. OEM paint
   d. ASE paint

6. Name the four ingredients in a paint.

7. What is the difference between thinner, reducer, and premix?

8. The term _____ refers to a paint material that evaporates its solvent to harden. The term _____ refers to a chemical action in the paint or other material itself that causes hardening.

9. What is a catalyst?

10. This is an undercoat that improves adhesion of the topcoat and seals old painted surfaces that have been sanded.
    a. Primer
    b. Primer–sealer
    c. Primer–filler
    d. Primer–surfacer

11. A _____ is a high-solids primer that fills small imperfections and usually must be sanded. It is often used after a filler to help smooth the surface.

12. What is corrosion or rust?

13. What is masking liquid or masking coating?

14. In detail, explain the sandpaper grit numbering system and how it is used.

Activities

1. Visit a paint supply house. Read the labels on several different kinds of products. Write a report on the hazards of using different body shop materials.

2. Check out different types of sandpaper. Inspect their grits and determine whether they are open or closed coat. Mount different sandpapers on a piece of cardboard and explain each.

3. Apply different types of adhesive and epoxy to a piece of cardboard. Study how long it takes each to dry or cure. Write a report on your findings.

CHAPTER 9

WELDING, HEATING, AND CUTTING

Objectives

After studying this chapter, you should be able to:

- Describe when to use and when NOT to use certain welding processes for collision repair.

- List safety precautions taken during welding.

- Name the parts of a MIG welder.

- Summarize how to set up a MIG welder.

- Describe differences between MIG electrode wires.

- Determine if a given 115-volt welder is powerful enough for the application.

- Explain the variables for making a quality MIG weld.

- Know the right techniques for MIG welding.

- Describe the various types of MIG welds and joints.

- Explain the resistance spot welding process.

- Know how to visually inspect and destructive test MIG welds and resistance spot welds.

- Explain the differences in welding aluminum as compared to steel.

- Describe plasma arc cutting.

Introduction

This chapter will introduce welding methods common to the collision repair industry. It will define technical terms and compare different types of welding found in a body shop.

With major collision repair work, many of the panels on a vehicle must be replaced and welded into place. As you will learn, this requires considerable skill and care. The structural integrity of the vehicle is dependent upon how well you weld and install panels.

NOTE! IF NOT ALREADY TRAINED, YOU MAY WANT TO CONSIDER TAKING A MIG WELDING COURSE IN SCHOOL. ASK YOUR INSTRUCTOR OR GUIDANCE COUNSELOR FOR MORE INFORMATION ON WELDING COURSES IN YOUR SCHOOL OR AREA. WELDING IS AN ESSENTIAL SKILL IF YOU PLAN ON BECOMING A "MASTER AUTO BODY TECHNICIAN."

WHAT IS WELDING?

As defined by the American Welding Society, a *weld* is formed when separate pieces of material are fused together through the application of heat. The heat must be high enough to cause the softening or melting of the pieces to be joined. Once the pieces are heated, pressure may or may NOT be used to force them together. See Figure 9–1.

The *base material* is the material to be welded, usually metal or plastic. Both can be welded in the collision repair industry.

In many instances, *filler material* from a wire or rod is added to the weld joint. The filler material makes the weld joint thicker and stronger. This chapter will explain the welding of metals. Plastic welding is covered in Chapter 11.

WELD TERMINOLOGY

The *weld root* is the part of the joint where the wire electrode is directed. The *weld face* is the exposed surface of the weld on the side where you welded.

Visible *weld penetration* is indicated by the height of the exposed surface of the weld on the back side. Full weld penetration is needed to assure maximum weld strength.

A *burn mark* on the back of a weld is an indication of good weld penetration. *Burn-through* results from penetrating too much into the lower base metal which burns a hole through the back side of the metal. Note Figure 9–2.

Fillet weld parts include the following. The *weld legs* are the width and height of the weld bead. The *weld throat* refers to the depth of the triangular cross section of the weld.

Joint fit-up refers to holding work pieces tightly together, in alignment, to prepare for welding. It is critical to the replacement of body parts!

Throat

Leg 1

Leg 2

Leg 1 = Leg 2 = Thickness of Base Metal (+1/8")

Figure 9–2 Weld legs should be equal in size and slightly larger than base metal. *(I-CAR)*

WELDING CATEGORIES

The three types of heat joining in collision repair are fusion welding, pressure welding, and adhesion bonding.

Fusion welding is joining different pieces of metal together by melting and fusing them into each other. The pieces of metal are heated to their melting point, joined together (usually with a filler rod), and allowed to cool. Molecules of the metals combine. MIG, TIG, stick arc, and oxyacetylene welding are all fusion processes. Refer to Figure 9–3.

There are two general types of gas metal arc welding methods: *metal inert gas (MIG)* and *tungsten inert gas (TIG)*.

MIG welding is a wire-feed fusion welding process commonly used in collision repair. MIG stands for "Metal Inert Gas," even though some shielding gases used may be active. It is the accepted industry name for *Gas Metal Arc Welding (GMAW)*. MIG is sometimes called "wire-feed" because wire is automatically fed into the weld. MIG welding is the only approved method of structural welding on unibody vehicles.

Today's steels demand a technique that leaves a narrow heat-affected zone. Oxyacetylene and stick arc welding create too large a heat-affected zone which will weaken the steel. Also, unibody vehicle

Figure 9–1 Welding is a vital aspect of auto body repair. Proper training is needed to make quality welds safely.

Figure 9–3 MIG stands for ***metal inert gas.*** Machine automatically feeds small wire electrode out of center of gun. MIG is recommended method for repairing collision damage.

Figure 9–5 TIG uses filler rod, NOT fed through gun. Gun provides arc and shielding gas to make welds on thicker metals. MIG welding is being used to repair this aluminum cylinder head.

designs require 100 percent fusion for most repairs. See Figure 9–4.

TIG is generally used in automotive engine rebuilding shops to repair cracks in aluminum cylinder heads and in reconstructing combustion chambers, but has very limited applications in collision repair. See Figure 9–5.

The once popular fusion welding methods of shielded arc welding or oxyacetylene welding have been replaced in unibody repair work by MIG welding. The reason is simply that the new steel alloys used in today's unibody vehicles cannot be welded properly with the two previous processes.

Shielded arc or ***stick arc welding*** uses a welding rod coated with a flux for fusion welding. The flux

coating acts as the shielding agent. Stick arc welding requires you to use a pointed hammer to chip off slag (hardened flux residue) after welding. It is primarily suitable for welding thicker parts, like engine brackets, frame brackets or when repairing full perimeter frames. Stick arc welding is NOT used on body panels. Refer to Figure 9–6.

Figure 9–6 Stick arc welding is no longer common in collision repair. It spreads too much heat for thin body panels and you must chip off slag after welding. Worker is stick arc welding plates for fabrication.

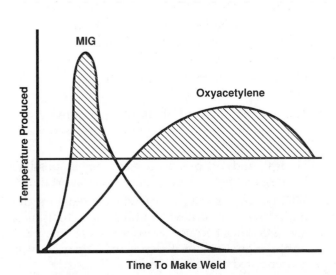

Figure 9–4 Graph compares time and temperature for oxyacetylene and MIG processes. Note how MIG is much hotter but takes less time, so heat spreads less over panel.

Even though there is full fusion, stick arc welding is NOT recommended for repairs on HSS. The high heat used with stick arc welding weakens **high strength steels (HSS).** Stick arc welding can be used on body-over-frame vehicles and low carbon steel frames, however.

Oxyacetylene welding is a form of fusion welding in which oxygen and acetylene are used in combination. The process is simple. The two are mixed in a chamber, ignited at the torch tip, and used to join a welding filler rod and base metal, Figure 9–7.

Adhesion bonding uses oxyacetylene to melt a filler metal onto the work piece for joining. *Brazing* is a form of adhesion bonding. It weakens HSS by applying too much heat, and is NOT recommended for collision repair.

Oxyacetylene and shielded arc (stick) welding are also NOT recommended for most collision repair. They create too much heat for use with high-strength steels (HSS). However, they can still be used to repair some thick metals.

Pressure welding uses high heat and clamping pressure to join metals. No filler material is added to the weld. Current flow through the metals produces enough heat to melt the base metals.

Figure 9–7 Oxyacetylene outfit can be used to weld, braze, or cut metals. It is no longer acceptable for structural welds on vehicles. Oxyacetylene torch can be used to braze fill joints when manufacturer recommends braze filling. Torch is often used to heat parts for cleaning before welding or cutting.

Squeeze-type resistance spot welding uses electric current through the base metal to form a small, round weld between the base metals. It is the only accepted form of pressure welding for collision repair. Resistance spot welding focuses the heat onto a small area. A series of pressure spot welds are often used to secure replacement panels onto the body structure of wrecked cars or trucks. This process is discussed shortly.

MIG WELDING

The advantages of MIG welding over the other fusion methods used in collision repair are numerous. Vehicle manufacturers now recommend that it be used NOT only for HSS, but for all structural collision repair.

The advantages of MIG welding are:

1. MIG welding is easy to learn. The typical welder can learn to use MIG equipment in just a few hours of instruction and practice.

2. MIG produces 100 percent fusion in the base metals. This means MIG welds can be ground down flush with the surface (for cosmetic reasons) without loss of strength.

3. Low current can be used to MIG weld thin metals. This prevents heat damage that can cause strength loss and warping.

4. The arc is smooth and the weld puddle small. This ensures maximum metal deposit with minimum spatter.

5. Gaps can be spot welded by making several spot welds on top of each other—immediately. There is no slag to remove, as with stick arc welding.

6. Almost all steels can be MIG welded with one common type of weld wire, even aluminum body panels.

7. Metals of different thicknesses can be MIG welded.

8. The welder can control the temperature on the weld and the time the weld takes. Increased welding speed reduces labor costs.

9. Vertical and/or overhead welding is possible because the metal is molten for a very short time.

10. MIG welding is safer to use when making repairs under the vehicle next to brake lines, fuel lines, and fuel tanks because the wire is NOT energized until the gun trigger is depressed. Again, heat is concentrated at the weld joint.

11. With MIG welding, there is minimum waste of welding consumables.

MIG Welding Process

MIG welding uses a small diameter welding wire electrode that is automatically fed into the weld joint. The welding machine feeds the roll or wire out to and through the welding gun. A short arc is generated between the base metal and the wire. The resulting heat from the arc melts the welding filler wire and joins the metals. Look at Figure 9–8.

During the welding process, either an inert or active *shielding gas* protects the weld from the atmosphere and prevents oxidation of the base metal. The type of inert or active gas used depends on the base metal to be welded.

Several types of shielding gases and shielding gas mixtures are used with the MIG process. Argon and helium are primarily used for welding *nonferrous* (non-iron) metals and can also be used in combination. Carbon dioxide and argon/carbon dioxide mixtures are other popular shielding gases.

MIG Welder Parts

Figure 9–9 shows a MIG welder. The major parts of a MIG welder are:

1. *Power supply*—converts wall outlet AC in DC.

2. *Welding gun*—feeds wire and gas into arc when trigger is pulled.

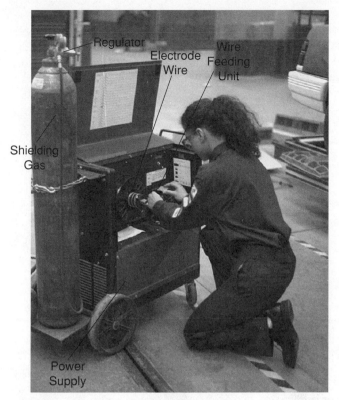

Figure 9–9 Know the parts of MIG welder. *(I-CAR)*

3. *Weld cable*—large wires that connect welding to vehicle.

4. *Electrode wire*—small welding wire feed down through center of gun.

5. *Wire feeder*—mechanism for pushing wire through gun and into weld arc.

6. *Shielding gas*—inert gas that surrounds and protects molten metal in weld.

7. *Regulator*—pressure control device for setting gas pressure.

8. *Weld clamp*—ground cable for connecting welder to vehicle.

A *welder amperage rating* gives the maximum current flow through the weld joint. The thickness of the metal being welded determines the amperage needed. Generally, one amp of welding current is needed for every .001 inch (.025 mm) of metal thickness.

A minimum of 90 amps is needed for collision repair, because working with two to three layers of .030 inch (.8 mm) metal is common. When welding on coated steel, the next higher heat (voltage) and wire speed (amperage) settings are used. The type of shielding gas used also affects the amperage required.

Figure 9–8 Note MIG welder components and their relationships. *(Lincoln Electric Co.)*

becomes enlarged with use, reducing current transfer efficiency.

The *MIG nozzle* protects the contact tip and directs the shielding gas flow. It must be kept clean. A dirty nozzle can cause holes (porosity) in the weld.

Anti-spatter compound spray may help spatter from sticking to the nozzle. Spatter build-up still has to be cleaned off occasionally. Spattering tends to stick to the nozzle, especially when welding steel, causing porosity. If spatter builds up, it can create a "bridge" between the contact tip and nozzle, and short out the welder.

MIG nozzle types include regular–tapered at the end and a straight type primarily for aluminum.

MIG Shielding Gas

MIG shielding gas protects the weld area from oxygen, nitrogen, and hydrogen which cause porosity in the weld. The gas also blows dirt and particles away. It is contained in a highly pressurized cylinder. See Figure 9–11.

The shielding gas cylinder has a flow meter/regulator which meters the gas out of the tank, Figure 9–9. It must be matched to the type of shielding gas used. The flow rate is measured in cubic feet per hour (cfh). The typical flow rate for shielding gases used in collision repair is from 25–30 cfh. This may be increased to 35 cfh if there is a breeze blowing through the work area. There are also preset flow meters that cannot be adjusted.

Figure 9–10 High quality welder is needed to do quality welds. *(Courtesy of Snap-On Tools Corporation)*

Duty cycle is how many minutes the welder can safely operate at a given amperage level continuously over 10 minutes. The duty cycle rating is a percentage. A machine with 40% duty cycle can run 4 out of 10 minutes continuously (at rated amperage). A machine with 60% duty cycle can run 6 out of 10 minutes continuously (at rated amperage).

MIG Welding Gun

The *MIG welding gun*, also called a *torch*, delivers wire, current, and shielding gas to the weld site. It consists of a neck and handle, an on/off trigger, contact tip (or tube), and nozzle, Figure 9–10.

The *MIG contact tip*, or *tube*, transfers current to the welding wire as the wire travels through. It is usually made of copper or copper alloy. Its inside diameter must match the diameter of the electrode wire used. This is usually stamped on the tip in millimeters. The tip needs to be changed when the inside hole

Figure 9–11 Shielding gas protects weld from airborne contaminants. Stick-out is distance wire electrode protrudes from tip. *(John W. Hogg)*

There are two types of shielding gas:

1. *Active gas* which combines with the weld to contribute to weld quality.
2. *Inert gas* which protects the weld but does NOT combine with the weld.

Shielding gas can be pure or mixed in various combinations. If the primary gas is active, the welding process is called *Metal Active Gas (MAG)*. When nearly equal active and inert combinations are used, the process is *MIG–MAG*. MIG is the accepted collision industry name for any of these processes.

Types of shielding gas include: Argon (inert), Helium (inert), Oxygen (active), and CO_2, or Carbon Dioxide (active). The right shielding gas depends on the metal being welded. A gas blend of 75% argon and 25% CO_2 for general quality welds on HSS and mild steel is often recommended. Pure CO_2 is NOT recommended for welding on HSS.

MIG Wire

MIG electrode wire comes in rolls that mount inside the MIG welder, Figure 9–12. Rollers grasp and force the wire out to the gun whenever the gun trigger is pulled.

The MIG wire is identified by an *American Welding Society (AWS)* code. This code reads AWS ER70S-6 and is explained in Figure 9–13. Choose the electrode wire made of the same type of metal being welded. Electrode wire comes in different diameters. Smaller diameters are best for thin gauge steel because less heat is required to melt them.

Common diameters for collision repair include .023 inch (.6 mm), .030 inch (.8 mm) and .035 inch (.9 mm).

Figure 9–12 MIG welding wire is on roll that is fed out to gun. Set up wire feed mechanism as directed in operating manual.

Different welding machines will have different recommendations. Generally, .023 inch (.6 mm) can be used on all thicknesses and is a general recommendation for most collision repair. Use .030 inch (.8 mm) wire only on 22 gauge and heavier thicknesses. Use .035 inch (.9 mm) only on 18 gauge and heavier thicknesses.

MIG flux core wire has its own flux contained in a tubular electrode and does NOT require a shielding gas. As with stick welding, the flux forms slag that must be chipped off. Flux core electrode wire is NOT recommended for most collision repair work.

Recently, MIG welders have been made available that run on low voltage. While low-voltage MIG welders do produce more weld spatter, they are used by smaller shops as a means of cutting down on expenses.

MIG Welding Variables

Most welders used for collision repair are 220 volt. There are also welders available that use a standard 110-volt outlet. The higher voltage welders are more expensive but usually provide better adjustments and resulting weld quality.

The operator has control over several variables when MIG welding. These include:

1. Heat (voltage)
2. Wire speed (amperage)
3. Travel speed and direction
4. Electrode stick-out
5. Gun angle
6. Polarity
7. Electrode diameter
8. Shielding gas type and flow rate.

The quality of the finished weld will depend on all of these variables, Figure 9–14. Weld quality will also depend upon weld position, surface condition, part alignment and how well the work pieces fit together (joint fit-up). The skill of the operator is the final controlling factor of weld quality.

The *heat setting,* or *voltage,* determines the length of the arc. The more voltage, the longer the arc. The longer the arc, the wider and flatter the weld, since the weld wire melts off in larger drops. Too long of an arc for the wire diameter used results in spattering. Too short of an arc for the wire diameter results in a pulsing sound.

Setting the wire speed when MIG welding also sets the amount of amperage applied to the weld. Changing wire speed and amperage mainly affects weld bead, penetration, height, and width.

Rod

Solid Wire

AWS ER70S-6

American Welding Society Standard

Electrode

70,000 PSI Tensile Strength

Chemical Makeup

Figure 9–13 Note what each part of AWS number code means. *(I-CAR)*

Welding Variables to Change	Desired Changes							
	Penetration		Deposition Rate		Bead Size		Bead Width	
	Increase	Decrease	Increase	Decrease	Increase	Decrease	Increase	Decrease
Current and Wire Feed Speed	Increase	Decrease	Increase	Decrease	Increase	Decrease	No effect	No effect
Voltage	Decrease	Increase	No effect	No effect	Increase	Decrease	Increase	Decrease
Travel Speed	Little effect	Little effect	No effect	No effect	Decrease	Increase	Increase	Decrease
Stickout	Decrease	Increase	Increase	Decrease	Increase	Decrease	Decrease	Increase
Wire Diameter	Decrease	Increase	Decrease	Increase	No effect	No effect	No effect	No effect
Shielding Gas Percent CO_2	Increase	Decrease	No effect	No effect	No effect	No effect	Increase	Decrease
Gun Angle	Backhand to 25°	Forehand	No effect	No effect	No effect	No effect	Backhand	Forehand

Figure 9–14 Study how to change variables to get better welding results.

To get a steady arc with a steady sound and correct penetration, both the heat (voltage) and wire speed (amperage) must be matched to each other. Set the heat, then the wire speed.

Travel speed is how fast you move the gun across the joint. The slower the travel speed, the deeper the weld penetration, the wider the weld, and the more bead height. Look at Figure 9–15.

If weld penetration or width is NOT right, changing travel speed is a second consideration. Changing voltage and wire speed are first considerations. If the height of the weld bead is not right, adjust travel speed first.

Travel direction refers to whether to push or pull the welding gun along the joint. *Push welding* means you aim or angle the gun ahead of the weld puddle.

CORRECT

A

TOO FAST

B

TOO SLOW

C

Figure 9–15 Welding speed or how fast you move gun affects weld bead. A: Correct weld has full penetration, proper width, and height. Weld would be very strong. B: Moving gun too quickly would cause poor penetration. A bead would only form near top of base metals. Weld would break easily. C: If you move gun too slowly, too much heat will melt bead down into joint too much.

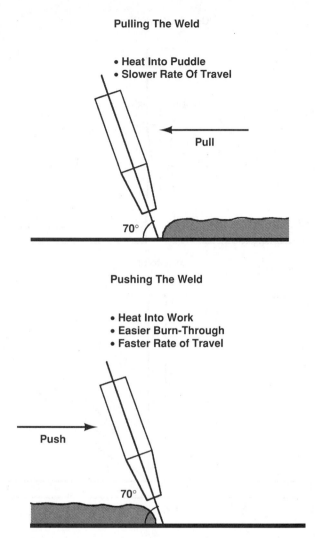

Pulling The Weld

• Heat Into Puddle
• Slower Rate Of Travel

Pull

70°

Pushing The Weld

• Heat Into Work
• Easier Burn-Through
• Faster Rate of Travel

Push

70°

Figure 9–16 When pulling gun, tilt gun in direction of weld. When push welding, tilt gun away from direction of weld. An approximately 70-degree angle should be formed with either method. *(I-CAR)*

Pull welding means you aim or angle the gun back toward the weld puddle. This is shown in Figure 9–16.

Electrode *wire stick-out* is the distance between the end of the gun's contact tip and the metal being welded. This is regardless of whether the tip is sticking out of the nozzle or recessed.

Electrode stick-out is also called *tip-to-work distance* or *contact tip height.* It should be kept between ¼–⅜ inch (6–9 mm) for .023 inch (.6 mm) wire. Wire stick-out should also be longer for larger diameter wires, because of the higher heat (voltage) setting used.

Support the welding gun with the free hand, whenever possible, to control stick-out. Too much electrode stick-out lowers weld penetration. The wire becomes preheated, and melts before penetrating deep enough into the weld.

Not enough electrode stick-out increases weld penetration, because the wire is too hot when contacting the work piece.

Gun angle consists of two different angles:

1. The angle of the gun to the work piece.

2. The angle of direction of travel.

The angle of the gun to the work piece varies, depending on the type of joint. For butt joints, hold the gun 90 degrees. For "T" joints, hold the gun at 45 degrees. For lap joints, hold the gun between 60 and 75 degrees. The thicker the work piece, the greater the angle. The angle of direction of travel is always about 70 degrees from the work piece, regardless of the type of joint. Look at Figure 9–17.

Even though the welder is plugged into an AC outlet the AC is changed to DC inside the welder. The polarity of the DC power source helps in determining how deep the penetration will be into the work piece.

Straight polarity, or "DC straight" is when the electrode is negative. It is also used when the work

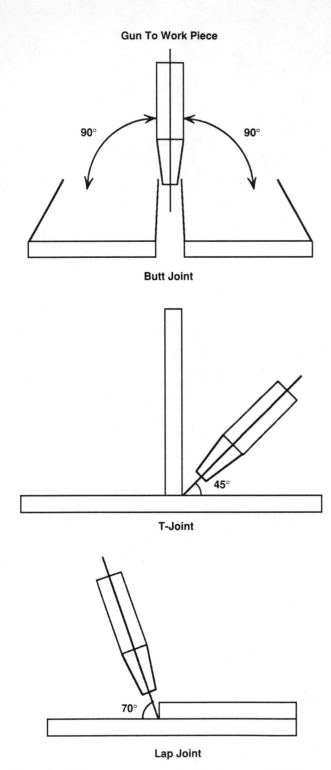

Gun To Work Piece

90°   90°

Butt Joint

45°

T-Joint

70°

Lap Joint

Figure 9–17 Typical gun angles for different joints. *(I-CAR)*

piece, through the work clamp, is positive. In DC straight, most of the heat is on the work piece.

Straight polarity can be used when welding very thin metal (24 gauge and lighter), to prevent burning through the metal. Straight polarity is also recommended for all positions when welding with flux cored wire.

Reverse polarity, or "DC reverse" is when the electrode is positive and the work piece is negative. In DC reverse, most of the heat is at the arc. Reverse polarity is commonly used for collision repair, because it provides the best fusion, leaving less weld on the surface to grind off. It also has a more stable arc.

You can change polarity with a toggle switch if welder has one. You can also reverse cable power supply hookups.

MIG Weld Types

The types of MIG welds include tack, continuous, butt, fillet, and plug welds. You should understand each, Figure 9–18.

A MIG *tack weld* is a short bead used for set up of a permanent weld. Tack welds help joint fit-up. They are usually placed about every 2 inches (51 mm) along a joint. Tack welds are ground flat if the permanent weld will be on the same side. This is done so there will be no break in the continuous weld.

It is possible to make spot welds with a MIG welder using a spot weld nozzle. A MIG *spot weld* fuses the top piece to the bottom piece without pre-drilling a hole. This type of weld is made by holding the nozzle at 90 degrees directly on the base metal and triggering the gun. It is hard to keep consistent quality and strength with MIG spot welds. Plug welds help assure even penetration and strength.

A *continuous weld* is a single weld bead along a joint. It could be a single pass weld. It could also be a series of short welds connected together to make one weld.

Skip welding produces a continuous weld by making short welds at different locations to prevent overheating, Figure 9–19A. All of the small welds are finally joined to produce the continuous weld. This prevents heat build-up in one location on the part.

Stitch welding is a continuous weld in one location, but with short pauses to prevent overheating. The operator can pause the machine manually to allow cooling. Some welders can also be programmed to pause automatically to prevent overheating, Figure 9–19B.

MIG *butt welds* are formed by fitting two edges of adjacent panels together and welding along the mating edges. They are often used to make two joints when sectioning frame rails, rocker panels, and door pillars. For butt welds, keep a gap between the two pieces the thickness of one piece. This helps weld penetration and prevents expansion and contraction problems. Also, hold the gun at 90 degrees to the joint.

Figure 9–18 Six MIG welding techniques.

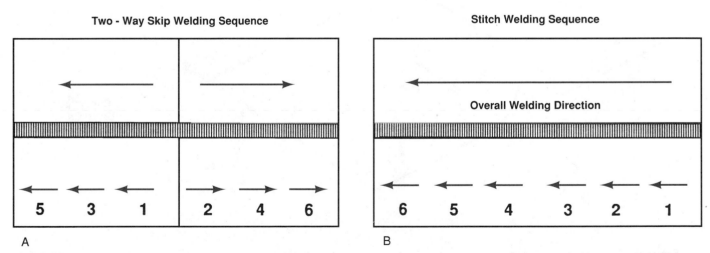

Figure 9–19 Compare stitch and skip welding methods. A: Two-way skip welding involves running short beads in sequence shown. Start in middle and work your way outward following numbers. B: Stitch welding is often programmed into MIG welder. Welder will automatically cycle on and off to allow cooling time between short beads. *(I-CAR)*

An *insert,* or *backing strip,* made of the same metal as the base metal can be placed behind the weld. The backing helps proper fit-up and supports the weld. See Figure 9–20.

A MIG *fillet weld* is a weld joining two surfaces with their edges or faces at about right angles to each other. The joint may be a lap joint or T-joint. Refer back to Figure 9–18.

MIG *lap joints* are welds made on overlapping surfaces. They are commonly used on front and rear rails and floor pans. When welding a lap joint the gun angle is kept between 60 and 75 degrees. If the lower

Face

Weld Bead Not Wider Than 3-4 Times Base Metal Thickness

Height Above Base Metal Not More Than Twice the Base Metal Thickness

Burn Mark About 2-3 Metal Thicknesses Visible Penetration Not More Than 1/8" (3 mm) Wide or 1/16" (1.5 mm) High

Figure 9–20 If possible, backing piece should be placed behind butt welds as shown. This will simplify welding and increase weld strength. *(I-CAR)*

Plug Welds On Top

Vehicle Front

Continuous Bead On Bottom

Back Piece Overlaps Front

Figure 9–21 Sometimes, it is best to use a combination of weld types. With this lap joint of a floor pan, plug welds have been used along top of panel. Continuous weld was placed along bottom. *(I-CAR)*

piece is thicker than the top piece, angle more at the lower piece. Look at Figure 9–21.

A MIG *plug weld* is made through a hole drilled in the top pieces, Figure 9–22. It is started by drilling or punching holes in the top piece or pieces. The hole is filled with a weld nugget. Drill or punch ³⁄₁₆- to ³⁄₈-inch (5–9 mm) holes in top piece or pieces.

Start around edge of hole, then fill in the hole. A ⁵⁄₁₆-inch (8 mm) hole works well for most collision repair. A ³⁄₁₆-inch (5 mm) hole is better with very thin

Figure 9–22 A: When plug welding, start on edge of hole and circle inward until hole is filled with weld puddle. B: If plug weld is very small, you can often hold gun stationary. C: Top layers of metal must be drilled. With three layers, drill top layer slightly larger than second. Do not drill bottom layer.

metals (24 gauge and lighter). A ⅜-inch (9 mm) hole is better with heavier metal (14 gauge and heavier), Figures 9–23 and 9–24.

When plug welds are used to join three or more panels together, holes are punched or drilled in every piece except the bottom piece. The holes are made progressively smaller from the top down. This is done to get better fusion of each layer to the adjacent ones.

Typical hole size combinations are as follows. With three layers of metal, use ⁵⁄₁₆-inch (8 mm) and ⅜-inch (9 mm) holes. With four layers, use ¼-inch (6 mm), ⁵⁄₁₆-inch (8 mm) and ⅜-inch (9 mm) diameter holes.

Where MIG plug welds are used to replace factory spot welds:

1. Follow manufacturer's recommendations for number, size, and location of plug welds.

2. If this information is NOT available, duplicate the number, size, and location of original factory welds.

Figure 9–23 Note typical specs for plug welds. Weld diameter should be slightly larger than hole in top piece. Also note bead height and penetration. *(I-CAR)*

Figure 9–24 Combination plug and lap welds are often recommended when sectioning structural members. *(I-CAR)*

WELDING POSITIONS

Weld position refers to the orientation of the work pieces.

In *flat welding* the pieces are parallel with the bench or shop floor. Flat welding is the easiest because gravity pulls the puddle down into the joint. Flat is used whenever possible. It provides best control. The weld bead does NOT flow away from the weld area.

In *horizontal welding* the pieces are turned sideways. Gravity tends to pull the puddle into the bottom piece. The gun can be pulled to the right or left. Pulling directs the heat at the puddle just laid, helping control penetration. When horizontal welding, drop the gun angle about 5 degrees and tip slightly in the direction of travel.

In *vertical welding* the pieces are turned upright. Gravity tends to pull the puddle down the joint. Welding in a vertical position works best when starting from the top and pulling the gun downward. The gun can be tipped downward slightly. A vertical up

directs heat into the weld puddle, increasing penetration. Too much heat in the weld puddle makes it fluid, allowing gravity to pull it downward.

In *overhead welding* the piece is turned upside down. This is the most difficult type of weld position. Gravity tries to pull the puddle off the pieces and into the welder tip. Welding in an overhead position can be done by pulling the gun in either direction. Overhead welding takes the most skill because it is usually NOT as easy to control stickout and gun angle. The size of the weld bead must be carefully controlled. Too large of a weld bead can cause the molten metal to fall and clog the nozzle.

In collision repair, the welding position is usually dictated by the location of the weld on the vehicle. Welding parameters can be affected by the welding position. MIG welding can be done in any position, depending on the location of the base metal.

Always make test welds on same type and thickness scrap metal in positions to be used before attempting to weld on the vehicle.

WELDING SAFETY

Use common sense while welding. The most important welding safety rules include:

1. Welding voltages and amperages can kill. Keep cables and connections in good shape.

2. Do NOT place the machine on a wet floor, or stand on a wet floor when welding. Keep the shop floor dry.

3. Arc rays are ultraviolet and can cause burns. Sparks or pieces of metal can also shoot out from the weld. Wear a welding helmet with face shield and filter plate.

   A *welding filter lens*, sometimes called *filter plate*, is a shaded glass welding helmet insert for protecting your eyes from ultraviolet burns. They are graded with numbers, from 4 to 12. The higher the number, the darker the filter. AWS recommends grade 9 or 10 for MIG welding.

   Note that there are *"self-darkening filter lenses"* available which instantly turn dark when the arc is struck. There is no need to move the face shield up and down. These filter plates work well, but have one disadvantage in that their viewing window is somewhat small.

4. Wear a heavy shirt with long sleeves. Fasten the top button. Wear pants without cuffs and welding gloves. A leather apron provides good protection.

5. Breathing welding fumes can cause respiratory problems, especially when welding zinc coated steel. Have adequate ventilation. Wear a respirator when welding.

6. Never have matches or butane lighter in pockets. They can ignite or explode from the ultraviolet rays of welding.

7. To protect the glass and other areas from sparks, use a welding blanket.

8. Protect computers and other electronic parts while welding. They can be easily damaged. Do NOT allow cables to pass near computers or sensors. Remove the computer from vehicle if welding within 12 inches (305 mm) of the computer.

9. Disconnect and isolate the negative battery cable, or both cables as an extra precaution (negative first).

10. Keep the current path short by placing the work clamp close to the weld location. Keep the power supply as far away from vehicle as possible.

WELDING SURFACE PREPARATION

To prepare the surface for welding, you must first remove paint, undercoating, rust, dirt, oil, and grease.

Use a plastic woven pad, grinder, sander, blaster, or wire brush. Avoid removing galvanized coatings. Apply weld-through primer to all bare metal mating surfaces.

The surfaces to be welded must be bare, clean metal. If NOT, contaminants will mix with the weld puddle and may result in a weak, defective weld. Be sure to use a weld-through primer on ungalvanized steel or where zinc has been removed.

HOLDING PARTS

Locking jaw pliers (vise grips), C-clamps, sheet metal screws, and special clamps are all necessary tools for welding. Clamping panels together correctly will require close attention to detail. See Figure 9–25.

Clamping both sides of a panel is NOT always possible. In these cases, a simple technique using self-tapping sheet metal screws or rivets can be employed.

When using the plug weld technique, the temporary panels are held in place by setting a screw in every other hole. The empty holes are then plug welded. After the original holes are plug welded, the screws are removed and the remaining holes are then plug welded.

Fixtures can also be used in some cases to hold panels in proper alignment. Fixtures alone, however, should NOT be depended upon to maintain tight clamping force at the welded joint. Some additional

Welding Gun

Vise Grip

Figure 9–25 Fit-up involves making sure all areas of panel fit together tightly and are in proper locations. Clamping pliers are used to hold parts in contact while welding. Try to position them close to the area to be welded.

clamping will be required to make sure that the panels are tight together and NOT just held in proper alignment.

WELD-THROUGH PRIMER

Weld-through primer is used to add corrosion protection to weld zones. This primer must be applied to clean surfaces. Most weld-through primers have poor adhesion qualities. Do NOT overuse them. Always follow directions closely, Figure 9–26.

Weld-through primer can be applied to galvanic mating surfaces where the coating was removed during repair. After welding, remove the excess primer, because it has poor adhesion qualities.

Be sure to select a weld-through primer and NOT just a galvanized spray coating which may interfere with welding.

After mechanical cleaning, the next step is to chemically clean the metal. Start as soon as possible after finish sanding, to avoid the formation of light surface rust.

USING MIG WELDER

Before operating the MIG welder, be sure to:

1. Read the owner's manual carefully. Remember that when in doubt, follow directions.
2. Use the proper power source, ideally on a separate circuit.
3. Use proper wire and shielding gas.
4. Set all drive rollers, cable liners, and tensions to manufacturer's specifications.

5. Set the machine to the proper voltage and write speed suggested for the thickness of the metal.
6. Adjust the shielding gas flow rate to the recommended settings.
7. Cover upholstery and glass to prevent spark damage. Sparks can be lessened by making sure the welding area is clean, reducing the voltage setting, and making sure the wire stick-out distance is correct.
8. Allow the weld to cool naturally. Do NOT use water or compressed air to cool the weld. Forced cooling can cause cracking. If the weld can be touched, it is cool enough.

Follow the recommendations for welder maintenance provided in the owner's manual.

MIG BURNBACK

Most MIG welders have a burnback setting to control the amount of time that the electrode is energized after releasing the trigger. *Burnback* occurs when the electrode wire melting rate is faster than the wire speed. The electrode wire melts back inside the contact tip and melts to the tip. When this happens, the wire cannot feed and the tip will need replacing.

Adjust the burnback setting while doing test welds. Always perform test welds on a piece of scrap similar to the piece being worked on. There also might be a mode setting for switching the welder to stitch, spot, or continuous mode.

Settings are different based on type of metal being welded. The recommended settings on the welder will usually be for uncoated steel. Coated steel, compared to uncoated steel, requires heat (voltage) and wire speed (amperage) settings for next higher gauge metal. Also use a slightly slower travel speed and more vertical gun angle.

WIRE SPEED

MIG *wire speed* is how fast the rollers feed the wire into the weld puddle. An even, high-pitched buzzing sound indicates the correct wire-to-heat ratio producing a temperature in the 9000°F (4982°C) range. A steady, reflected light is desirable; it will start to fade in intensity as the arc is shortened and wire speed is increased.

If the wire speed is too slow, a hissing and plopping sound will be heard as the wire melts away from the puddle and deposits the molten glob. There will be a much brighter reflected light.

Too much wire speed will choke the arc. More wire is being deposited than the head and puddle can

Before Operation

**Apply Weld - Through Primer
To The Whole Surface,
Including The End Face.**

Figure 9–26 Weld-through primer should be applied to bare metal before welding. It can be applied with spray can or brush. Use only a light coat. This will restore proper corrosion protection to bare metal.

absorb. The result is the wire melts into tiny balls of molten metal that fly away from the weld, creating a strobe light arc effect.

When welding overhead, the danger of having too large a puddle and balls is obvious. The balls are pulled down by gravity into the contact tip or into the gas nozzle. Therefore, overhead welding should always be done at a higher wire speed, with the arc and balls kept small and close together. Pressing the gas nozzle against the work will keep the wire in the puddle.

SHIELDING GAS FLOW RATE

MIG *gas flow rate* is a measurement of how fast gas flows over the weld puddle. Precise gas flow is essential for a good weld. If the flow of gas is too high, it will flow in eddies and reduce the shielding effect. If there is NOT enough gas, the shielding effect will also be reduced. Adjustment is made in accordance with the distance between the nozzle and the base metal, the welding current, travel speed, and welding environment (nearby air currents). The standard flow rate is 25 cubic feet per hour (.75 cubic meters per hour).

HEAT BUILD-UP PREVENTION

Mentioned briefly, too much heat when welding or heating distorts and weakens the metal. Always make sure you do not allow excess heat to transfer into any area of a panel. Use stitch or skip welding methods described earlier.

Stitch and skip welding will prevent costly and time consuming panel warpage. Another method of preventing heat build-up is heat sink compound.

Heat sink compound is a paste that can be applied to parts to absorb heat and prevent warpage. It comes in a can that can be applied and reused. The heat sink compound is sticky and can be placed on the panel next to the weld. Heat will flow into the compound and out of the metal to prevent heat damage.

CLEAN AFTER WELDING

Weld areas must also be cleaned after welding. Corrosion will form first in pitted weld areas. Proper surface preparation is a must. A few rules:

1. Thoroughly clean with sand or plastic media blaster or plastic abrasive.

2. Grind cosmetic areas flush with surface. Use caution NOT to thin the base metal or remove zinc needlessly.

3. Use compressed air to blow the area clean.

RESISTANCE SPOT WELDING

Squeeze-type resistance spot welding has two electrode arms that apply pressure and electric current to the metals being joined. No filler metal or shielding agent is needed. This type is often recommended by most European and Japanese vehicle manufacturers. It can be used to replace factory spot welds on some panels.

Squeeze-type resistance spot welding is primarily used for cosmetic panels when accessible from both sides. It is used for some structural parts like pillars and rocker panels only when recommended by the vehicle manufacturer. This process cannot be used on aluminum.

Resistance spot welding is NOT new, but there are some recent equipment developments. Modern spot welders for the shop are generally lighter, easier to use, and more effective for making strong welds. Refer to Figure 9–27.

Squeeze-type resistance spot welding is a type of pressure welding. It is the main process used in the factory. Over 90% of factory welds are resistance spot welds. Factory spot welds are usually done by robots. Extremely high current and pressures are used.

Squeeze-type resistance spot welders for collision repair are less powerful, but use the same process. Two or three sheets of metal are pressed between elec-

Figure 9–27 Technician is using resistance spot welder to install roof panel.

trode tips. Low voltage, high current passes through the material. Resistance of the metal to current flow heats and melts the metal, forming a weld as the molten metal cools. Spot weld strength depends on amount of pressure, current, and weld time, as well as the fit-up of the metal layers in the joint.

Resistance spot welding is fast, usually less than a second per weld. There is little heat effect so it will NOT warp metal. Zinc coating will only vaporize at point between electrode tips. Surrounding zinc flows into spot to keep corrosion protection.

A few drawbacks to resistance spot welding should be considered. It requires access to both sides of panel being welded. Aligning and sizing of tips is critical. A hand-held unit is heavier and more awkward than a MIG gun. It is NOT recommended for welding panels with a combined thickness of over ⅛ inch (3 mm).

Many manufacturers recommend both MIG plug welds and resistance spot welding for replacing factory spot welds. They recommend resistance spot welding for repairs on body panels and some structural areas, including radiator core supports, pillars, rocker panels, exposed pinch weld areas on window and door openings and roofs.

At least one vehicle manufacturer recommends removing the galvanized coating from outside the joint before resistance spot welding. Unless otherwise directed, do NOT remove the galvanized coating. This removes corrosion protection.

Resistance Spot Welder Settings

Basic *resistance spot welding parts* include:

1. *Transformer with controls*—converts AC into regulated DC.

2. *Arm sets*—hold welding tips and conduct current to tips.

3. *Electrode tips*—allow current flow through spot weld.

Three separate transformer controls are needed for quality welds, including a pressure multiplier, current adjuster, and a timer. These three settings depend on each other for good resistance spot welds. There are also computer controlled spot welders available that automatically adjust settings depending on the thickness of material dialed in.

On conventional type spot welders, consider each setting separately.

The *pressure multiplier* usually applies welder arm pressure in a range from 100 pounds (45 kg) for two thicknesses of 25 gauge metal, to about 265 pounds (120 kg) and higher for three thicknesses or thicker metals. This allows clamping pressure to be adjusted for metal thickness. The pressure multiplier can be spring or pneumatically assisted.

Gun Arm

Electrode Tip

Use The Minimum Possible Length of Arm.

A

Short Arms

B

Long Arms

C

Figure 9–28 Spot weld arm length affects clamping pressure. A: Use shortest arm lengths that will work. B: Short arms will reach many weld areas. *(Used with permission of Nissan Motor Corporation)* C: Longer arm length might be needed on very large panels. *(Used with permission of Nissan Motor Corporation)*

Spot welders for collision repair must be able to apply a maximum of at least 250 pounds (113 kg). If there is NOT enough active and follow-up pressure, metal will be thrown out of the weld. If the spot welder relies on operator grip for needed pressure, it cannot be used for collision repair.

Note that pressures at the tips will be less than the settings indicate when using longer arm sets. Generally, doubling the length of arms reduces pressure by ⅓ or more, Figure 9–28.

The pressure multiplier is NOT used to clamp the pieces to be welded together. Work pieces need to be fit-up tightly with clamps, screws, or other fasteners before welding. Remember that even the slightest gap results in poor welds or no weld.

The *current adjuster* is usually adjustable by percentage of peak current. Generally, the thicker the metal, the higher current required. Zinc coated steel needs current setting for the next thickest metal.

For collision repair, the welder needs a peak capacity of at least 7,500 amps measured at the electrodes (NOT at transformer). The manual should state that the current capacity is measured at the electrodes. Current set too high is another cause for metal throw out.

The *spot weld timer* adjusts the time that the current passes through the joint, usually in ⅓₀-, ½-, and 1-second intervals (2, 30, and 60 cycles). It may be automatically set if the welder is computer equipped. The weld timer determines weld size. Generally, the longer the time, the larger the weld diameter.

Excessive spot weld time may cause the electrode tips to mushroom, resulting in no focus of current and a weak weld. A *short spot weld time* will result in poor penetration and a weak weld. Choose the shortest that will do the job. Longer arm sets need more current and pressure. Straight 5 inch (126 mm) length is used most often.

Electrodes for most collision repair on two to three thicknesses of 22–24 gauge steel have ⅜-inch (9 mm) diameter tips. The electrode diameter at the tips increases with use. This spreads the heat and pressure too much, weakening the weld. Keep electrode tips maintained. Before each extended use, check the tips for wear and size.

Use a hand-held electrode shaper to maintain spot weld tips. A shaper that attaches to a drill is also available. A file can be used, but is NOT as accurate. The ridges left by filing need to be polished with emery cloth or the tips will NOT make full contact with the work piece. See Figure 9–29.

The spot welder tips must be aligned in a straight line as seen from the front and side. If the tips come together at an angle, the weld will be weak. If the tips do NOT come together at all, the weld area will be offset resulting in no weld. Always check tip alignment before welding and between groups of welds. Look at Figure 9–30.

The electrode tips also need to be tightly fastened to the arm sets. They tend to loosen during use, affecting current flow and tip alignment.

When servicing welder parts, follow the instructions in the operating manual. It will give directions for the specific make and model of welder.

Resistance Spot Welding Techniques

Check the vehicle's body repair manual to find the original factory welds and number of replacements recommended. You may also compare the num-

Figure 9–29 Keep spot welder tips in good condition. Use tip cutter and dresser to keep tip size correct. *(Illustration courtesy of Toyota Motor Sales, U.S.A., Inc.)*

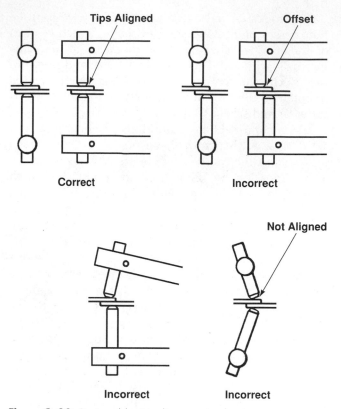

Figure 9–30 Spot welder tip alignment is also important.

ber of spot welds on the original panel. Refer to Figure 9–31.

The spot welds should be in the center of the flange without riding the edge. Make sure the original spot weld locations were NOT used. Check that the pitch of the welds is a little shorter than the factory welds. Make sure the spots are evenly spaced (ensuring strength).

Body repair manuals recommend certain spacing, or *pitch*, between resistance spot welds, Figure 9–32.

Panel Thickness mm (In.)	Pitch (P) mm (In.)	Edge Distance (E) mm (in.)
0.6 (0.024)	11 (0.43) or more	5 (0.20) or more
0.8 (0.031)	14 (0.55) or more	5 (0.20) or more
1.0 (0.039)	18 (0.71) or more	6 (0.24) or more
1.2 (0.047)	22 (0.87) or more	7 (0.28) or more
1.6 (0.063)	29 (1.14) or more	8 (0.31) or more

Figure 9–32 Weld pitch or spacing and distance from edge of panel are important. Note chart recommendations for different panel thicknesses. *(Illustration courtesy of Toyota Motor Sales, U.S.A., Inc.)*

Pitch, and the distance from the end of the panel, determine the strength of individual spot welds. The smaller the pitch, the tighter the bond. However, if welds are too close together, current will flow to a

Figure 9–31 When making spot welds, do not weld over old spot welds. Use new locations to assure tight fit and good weld. *(Illustration courtesy of Toyota Motor Sales, U.S.A., Inc.)*

spot already welded and may reduce weld strength. If welds are too close to the edge, current will flow to the edge of the joint, and may also weaken the weld.

Using 30 percent more welds than the original number of factory spot welds is recommended by some vehicle and some spot welder manufacturers. Repair spot welders do NOT have the high amperage of factory welders. Also, OEM spot welds are larger—¼″ (6 mm)—than repair spot welds which are ⁵⁄₃₂″ (4 mm). These two factors make for a stronger OEM weld in each individual nugget.

Spot weld current, time, and pressure settings are adjusted for:

1. Type of metal
2. Metal thickness
3. Length of arm sets
4. Distance electrode tips are from the metal edge.

When welding three thicknesses of metal, set weld current and weld time for the combined thicknesses. Do NOT weld the same spot twice. This can cause metal throw out and weaken the weld.

As a starting current setting, adjust weld current 30 percent to 50 percent. Adjust timer, if NOT computer controlled, to about 5 or 10 cycles (¹⁄₁₂–¹⁄₆ second). Position the electrode tips and squeeze the lever. As pressure is applied, a built-in switch automatically turns the current on and off for a set length of time. Keep pressure on the switch momentarily after the current shuts off to fuse the weld together.

Check that there are no dents exceeding half the thickness of the panel. A shallow dent is a sign of a strong weld. There should be no visible pin holes nor a lot of spatter. Refer to Figure 9–33.

NOTE! A GLOVE SHOULD **NOT** CATCH ON THE SURFACE WHEN RUBBED ACROSS IT. THIS WOULD INDICATE A LOT OF THROW OUT, OR TOO MUCH CURRENT USED WHEN WELDING.

There are two basic types of weld inspection: visual inspection and destructive testing.

Visual weld inspection is the most practical method on a repaired vehicle because the weld is NOT taken apart. Visual weld inspection involves looking at the weld for flaws, proper size and proper shape.

Destructive testing forces the weld apart to measure weld strength. Force is applied until the metal or weld breaks.

Basically, you have a good weld if metal tears off with weld. You have a bad weld if two pieces break cleanly at the weld with no metal tear-out.

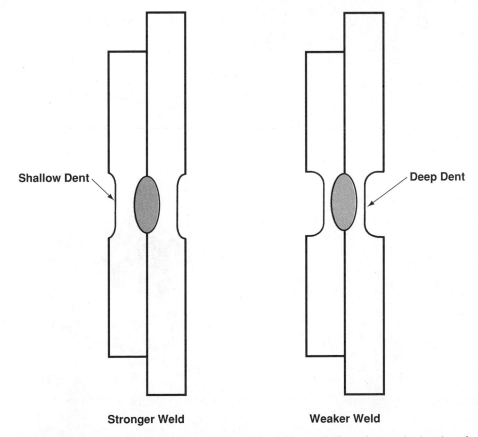

Stronger Weld   **Weaker Weld**

Figure 9–33 Visually inspect spot weld. There should be a shallow dent on both sides. If dent is too deep or not deep enough, weld will be weak. *(I-CAR)*

Before making a weld on the vehicle, make a practice weld that you can visually and destructively test. It is important to duplicate the actual weld conditions when testing using the same material, metal thickness, number of pieces, and primer application.

The test weld must be made under the same conditions as the weld that will be made on the vehicle. Part of metal from one piece should tear away. If two pieces break cleanly, make another test weld after increasing weld current slightly. If the weld fails again, increase current again and make another weld. If the weld still fails, increase weld time and test again.

Pull test welds apart until the weld is good, then use the same settings for the welds on the vehicle. See Figure 9–34.

Plug welds should have a $\frac{5}{16}$- inch (8 mm) hole. They should have a face diameter between $\frac{3}{8}$–$\frac{1}{2}$ inch (9.5–13 mm). Plug welds should be no more than $\frac{1}{8}$ inch (3 mm) above base metal on the face side. They

A

Weld

Chisel

Vise

B

C

Figure 9–34 Destructive testing of welds is best way to assure good strength. It can be done on test pieces of same thickness and material as welds to be made on vehicle. A: Make test weld on scrap pieces. Then use hammer and chisel to force weld apart. B: Wedge chisel down between pieces at weld point. *(I-CAR)* C: Bad weld will break at weld joint. Base metal will not tear because of weld weakness.

should have a burn mark on the back side ⅜–½ inch (9.5–13 mm) in diameter. Plug welds should have no more than ¹⁄₁₆ inch (1.5 mm) back side visible penetration and have no burn-through.

Butt joints with a backing strip should have a face width 3 to 4 times the thickness of the thinnest base metal. A burn mark width on the back side should be about 2 to 3 times the thickness of the thinnest base metal. There should be visible penetration on the back side no more than ¹⁄₁₆ inch (1.5 mm) below base metal or more than ⅛ inch (3 mm) wide. There should NOT be any burn through.

Fillet welds on lap joints should have equal leg sizes. Each should NOT be more than ⅛ inch (3 mm) thicker than the thickness of either base metal. There should be a face no more than 3 metal thicknesses wide. No visible penetration more than ¹⁄₁₆ inch (1.5 mm) below base metal should be visible. There should be no burn-through.

There should be no flaws in the weld measuring over ⅛ inch (3 mm) at their widest point. The ability to recognize weld flaws and possible causes is a good skill to develop.

WELD PROBLEMS

A welding problem causes a weak or cosmetically poor joint that reduces quality. The chart in Figure 9–35 lists weld problems and their possible causes.

1. *Weld Porosity*—holes in the weld
2. *Weld Cracks*—cracks on the top or inside the weld bead
3. *Weld Distortion*—uneven weld bead
4. *Weld Spatter*—drops of electrode on and around weld bead
5. *Weld Undercut*—groove melted along either side of weld and left unfilled
6. *Weld Overlap*—excess weld metal mounted on top and either side of weld bead)
7. *Too little penetration*—weld bead sitting on top of base metal
8. *Too much penetration*—burn through beneath lower base metal

WELDING ALUMINUM

Several vehicles now have body, frame, and chassis parts made of aluminum. Whole bodies made of aluminum are now available. As a result, the information needed for welding aluminum is growing.

Aluminum is light and relatively strong. It is naturally corrosion resistant. Aluminum forms its own corrosion barrier of aluminum oxide when exposed to air. A disadvantage of aluminum is its high cost.

There are some major differences to keep in mind when working with aluminum as opposed to steel, particularly when it comes to welding. Pure aluminum is lightweight and useful more for its ability to be formed than for its strength. When used on vehicles, it is alloyed with other elements and heat-treated for additional strength.

Concerning welding, pound for pound, aluminum is the best conductor of electricity. It conducts heat three times faster than steel. Aluminum becomes stronger, NOT brittle in extreme cold. It is also easily recyclable. Aluminum conducts heat faster than steel, and also spreads heat faster. Therefore, it requires special attention when welding.

Aluminum looks similar to magnesium which, if welded, could start a flash fire. To make sure the part is aluminum, brush the part with a stainless steel brush. Aluminum turns shiny. Magnesium turns dull gray.

Danger! *If the part is found to be magnesium, do NOT try to weld it. It can start to burn with tremendous heat.*

When welding aluminum, be sure to protect wire harnesses and electronics from potential damage spreading by heat. Aluminum takes more voltage and amperage for the same thickness of material.

Use the following guidelines when MIG welding aluminum:

1. Use aluminum wire and 100 percent argon shielding gas.
2. Set the wire speed faster than with steel.
3. Hold the gun closer to vertical when welding aluminum. Tilt it only about 5 to 10 degrees from the vertical in the direction of the weld.
4. Use only the forward welding method with aluminum. Always push—never pull. When making a vertical weld, start at the bottom and work up.
5. Set the tension of the wire drive roller lower to prevent twisting. But do NOT lower the tension too much or the wire speed will NOT be constant.
6. Use about 50 percent more shielding gas with aluminum.
7. Because there tends to be more spatter with aluminum, use an antispatter compound to control build-up at the end of the nozzle and contact tip.
8. Shop squeeze-type resistance spot welders do NOT have enough amperage for aluminum. Do NOT use resistance spot welders on aluminum.

Defect	Defect Condition	Remarks	Probable Causes
Pores/Pits (Porosity)		Holes form when gas is trapped in the weld metal.	Rust or dirt on the base metal. Rust or moisture adhering to the wire. Improper shielding action (the nozzle is blocked or the gas flow volume is low). Weld is cooling off too fast. Arc length is too long. Wrong wire used. Gas is sealed improperly. Weld joint surface is not clean. Electrode contamination.
Undercut		The overmelted base metal creates grooves or an indentation. The base metal's section is made smaller and, therefore, the weld zone's strength is severely lowered.	Arc length is too long. Improper gun angle. Welding speed is too fast. Current is too high. Torch feed is too fast. Torch angle is tilted.
Improper Fusion		An absence of fusion between weld metal and base metal or between deposited metals.	Improper torch feed operation. Voltage is too low. Weld area is not clean. Improper gun angle.
Overlap		Apt to occur in a fillet weld rather than a butt weld. Causes stress concentration and results in premature corrosion.	Welding speed is too slow. Arc length is too short. Torch feed is too slow. Current is too low.
Insufficient Penetration		Insufficient deposition made under the panel.	Welding current is too low. Arc length is too long. The end of the wire is not aligned with the butted portion of the panels. Groove face is too small. Gun speed is too fast. Improper electrode extension.
Excess Weld Spatter		Shows up as speckles and bumps along either side of the weld bead.	Arc length is too long. Rust on the base metal. Gun angle is too severe. Worn tube or drive rolls. Wire spool too tight. Voltage is too high. Wire speed too slow.
Spatter (short throat)		Prone to occur most often in fillet welds.	Current is too high. Wrong wire used.
Waviness of Bead		Uneven bead pattern usually caused by torch mishandling.	Wavering hands. Electrode extension too long.

Figure 9–35 Study weld problems and causes carefully.

Defect	Defect Condition	Remarks	Probable Causes
Cracks		Usually occur on the top surface only.	Stains on welded surface (paint, oil, rust, etc.). Voltage is too high. Wire speed is too fast. Gun speed is too slow.
The Bead Is Not Uniform.		The weld bead is misshapen and uneven rather than streamlined and even.	The contact tip hole is worn or deformed and the wire is oscillating as it comes out of the tip. The gun is not held steady during welding.
Burn Through		Holes in the weld bead.	The welding current is too high. The gap between the metal is too wide. Gun speed is too slow. The gun-to-base metal distance is too short. Reverse polarity to straight polarity (gun negative, work positive).

Figure 9–35 *(Continued)*

9. Always use skip and stitch welding techniques to prevent heat warping. Set wire speed slightly faster. Hold gun closer to vertical compared to steel.

10. Use only the push method when welding aluminum. Pushing helps take away any remaining aluminum oxide which must be cleaned off before welding. When vertical welding aluminum, always start at the bottom and work up.

11. When welding aluminum, there will be more spatter, but the spatter will NOT stick to the nozzle as with steel.

A MIG gun for welding aluminum can be either the standard equipment, or self-contained with a motor in the handle and aluminum wire spool mounted on top. The nozzle is straight, NOT tapered in at the end.

Aluminum electrode wire is classified by series according to the metal or metals the aluminum is alloyed with, and whether the aluminum is heat-treated or NOT. The series are set up by the Aluminum Association, NOT the AWS. The number does NOT indicate the strength of the electrode.

Special cleaning instructions are needed for aluminum. Remove all aluminum oxide with a stainless steel brush before welding. The metal might look clean, but aluminum oxide always needs to be brushed off. Clean the metal until shiny.

Never use a brush and sanding disc on aluminum after they have been used on steel. If already used on steel, iron powder will remain on the surface of the aluminum and contaminate the weld.

The typical procedure for MIG welding aluminum is as follows:

1. Clean the weld area completely, both front and back. Use wax and grease remover and a clean rag.

2. If the pieces to be welded are coated with a paint film, sand a strip about ¾ inch (19 mm) wide to the bare metal, using a disc sander and No. 80 disc. Do NOT press too hard, or the sander will heat up and peel off aluminum particles, clogging the paper.

3. Clean the metal until shiny with a stainless steel wire brush.

4. Load 0.030 (.8 mm) aluminum wire into the welder. Trigger it to extend about 1 inch (25 mm) beyond the nozzle.

5. Set the voltage and wire speed according to the instructions supplied with the welding machine. Remember that the wire speed must be faster than for steel. Make a practice weld on scrap pieces.

6. Position the two pieces together and lay a bead along the entire joint. The distance between the contact tip and the weld should be 5/16 to 9/16 inch (8 to 15 mm).

7. If the arc is too large, turn down the voltage and increase the wire speed. The bead should be uniform on top, with even penetration on the backside.

The high heat conduction of aluminum means that the technician must protect against warpage. There are two methods for doing this: stitch welding and center out welding, explained earlier.

Parts made of aluminum are usually 1½ to 2 times as thick as steel parts. When damaged, aluminum feels harder or stiffer to the touch because of work hardening.

With steel, the use of heat is avoided whenever possible to prevent reducing the strength of the metal. With aluminum, heat must be used to restore flexibility caused by work hardening. If NOT, it will crack when straightening force is applied.

Before straightening, heat is often applied to the damaged area of the aluminum. It is easy to apply too much heat since aluminum does NOT change color when heated. It also melts at a relatively low 1220°F (660°C). Careful heat control is very important.

Heat crayons or thermal *paint* can be used to determine the temperature of the aluminum or other metal being heated. They will melt at a specific temperature and warn you to prevent overheating.

As in Figure 9–36, the crayon or paint is applied next to the aluminum area to be heated. The mark will begin to melt when the crayon's or paint's melting point is almost reached. The melting will let you know that you are about to reach the melting point of the aluminum.

OXYACETYLENE WELDING

Even though oxyacetylene is no longer used for auto body welding, it can still be used for cleaning and heating on unibody vehicles. Therefore, oxyacetylene welding basics should be understood.

A typical *oxyacetylene welding outfit*, Figure 9–37, consists of the following:

1. *Cylinders*—steel tanks that hold the oxygen and acetylene.
2. *Regulators*—diaphragm valves that reduce pressure coming from the tanks to hoses.
3. *Hoses*—lines from regulators to torch.
4. *Torch*—mixes oxygen and acetylene in the proper proportions and produces a flame capable of melting steel.

Each regulator has a cylinder pressure gauge and a working pressure gauge. The gauges show the settings of the regulators. Working *oxygen pressure* ranges from 5 to 100 psi (.35 to 7 K/cm^2). Working *acetylene pressure* ranges from 1 to 12 psi (.07 to .84 K/cm^2).

There are two main types of torches: welding and cutting. A *welding torch* has two valves for adjusting gas flow. A *cutting torch* has a third oxygen valve and a lever or trigger for increased oxygen flow. The heat of the flame, combined with the blast of oxygen, will rapidly cut thick steel.

> **WARNING!** *The acetylene line pressure must never exceed 15 psi (1.05 K/cm^2). Free acetylene has a tendency to become unstable at pressure above 15 psi (1.05 K/cm^2) and could cause an explosion.*

Figure 9–36 Thermal paint or crayon can be used to prevent overheating. Aluminum does not change color when heated like steel. It is easy to overheat aluminum and blow holes in parts. Thermal paint or crayon will melt when melting point of aluminum is almost reached. (© American Honda Motor Co., Inc.)

Figure 9–37 Study parts of oxyacetylene outfit.

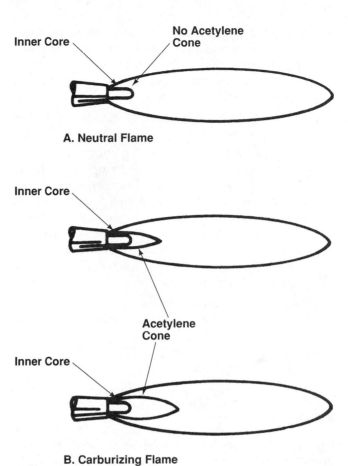

Figure 9–38 Note types of oxyacetylene flames.

All oxyacetylene welding should be done with a number 4, 5, or 6 tinted filter lens. A *spark lighter* is a necessity for producing a spark and igniting an oxyacetylene torch.

Flames and Adjustment

When acetylene and oxygen are mixed and burned, the condition of the flame varies depending on the ratio of oxygen and acetylene used.

Shown in Figure 9–38, there are three types of flames:

A *neutral flame* or standard flame is produced by mixing acetylene and oxygen in a 1 to 1 ratio. A neutral flame has a brilliant white core surrounded by a clear blue outer flame.

A *carburizing flame,* also called a reducing flame, is obtained by mixing slightly more acetylene than oxygen. Figure 9–38B shows that this flame has three parts. The core and the outer flame are the same as the neutral flame. However, between them is a light-colored acetylene cone enveloping the core. The length of the acetylene cone varies according to the amount of surplus acetylene in the gas mixture. For a carburizing flame, the oxygen-acetylene mixing ratio is about 1 to 1.4. A carburizing flame is used for heating and welding aluminum, nickel, and other alloys.

An *oxidizing flame* is obtained by mixing slightly more oxygen than acetylene. It resembles the neutral flame in appearance, but the inner core is shorter and its color is a little more violet. The outer flame is shorter and fuzzy at the end. Ordinarily, this flame oxidizes melted metal, so it is NOT used in the welding of mild steel.

Oxyacetylene Torch Flame Adjustment

When using an oxyacetylene welding torch, proceed as follows:

1. Attach the appropriate size tip to the end of the torch. Use the standard size tip for mild steel. Keep in mind that each torch manufacturer has a different system for measuring the size of the tip orifice.

2. Set the oxygen and acetylene regulators to the proper pressure.

3. Open the acetylene hand valve about half a turn and ignite the gas. Continue to open the hand valve until the black smoke disappears and a reddish yellow flame appears. Slowly open the oxygen hand valve until a blue flame with a yellowish white cone appears. Further open the oxygen hand valve until the center cone becomes sharp and well defined. This is a neutral flame and is used for welding mild steel.

4. If acetylene is added to the flame or oxygen is removed from the flame, a carburizing flame will result. If oxygen is added to the flame or acetylene is removed from the flame, an oxidizing flame will result.

Brazing

Brazing is like soldering at relatively low temperatures around 800°F (427°C). An adhesion bond is made by melting a filler metal and allowing it to spread into the pores of the work piece. The natural flow of the filler material into the joint is called *capillary attraction.* In brazing, the filler metal does NOT fuse with the work piece.

Brazing is still recommended by some vehicle manufacturers mainly as a sealer for weatherproofing lap joints. It is applied after the panel is already joined by fusion welding.

Braze welding is classified as either soft or hard brazing, depending on the temperature at which the brazing material melts. *Soft brazing* or *soldering* is done with brazing materials that melt at temperatures BELOW 900°F (468°C). *Hard brazing* is done with brazing materials that melt at temperatures ABOVE 900°F (468°C).

Brazing is applied only for sealing purposes. This is a method of welding whereby a filler rod, whose melting point is lower than that of the base metal, is melted without melting the base metal. Brass brazing is frequently applied to automotive bodies.

The basic characteristics of brazing are:

1. The pieces of metal are joined at a relatively low temperature where the base metal does NOT melt. Therefore, there is a lower risk of distortion and stress in the base metal.

2. Brazing filler metal has excellent flow characteristics. It penetrates well into narrow gaps and it is convenient for filling gaps in body seams.

3. Because the base metal does NOT melt, it is possible to join metals that would otherwise be incompatible.

4. Since there is no penetration, it has very low strength. Brazed joints cannot resist repeated loads or impacts.

Shutting Down Oxyacetylene Equipment

Always turn off the oxyacetylene torch when NOT in use. Never lay down a lit torch. Turn the torch off when NOT being held in your hand. Do this by first closing the acetylene hand valve, then the oxygen hand valve. Shutting off the acetylene valve first will immediately extinguish the flame. If the oxygen is shut off first, the acetylene will continue to burn, throwing off a great deal of smoke and soot.

Close the main valves on the tops of the cylinders when finished. Then, crack open the torch valves to bleed the hoses of pressure. Then, close the torch valves to ready it for the next use.

PLASMA ARC CUTTING

Plasma arc cutting creates an intensely hot air stream over a very small area which melts and removes metal. Extremely clean cuts are possible with plasma arc cutting. Because of the tight focus of the heat, there is no warpage, even when cutting thin sheet metal. See Figure 9–39.

Plasma arc cutting is replacing oxyacetylene as the best way to cut metals. It cuts damaged metal effectively and quickly but will NOT destroy the properties of the base metal. The old method of flame cutting just does NOT work that well anymore.

In plasma arc cutting, compressed air is often used for both shielding and cutting. As a shielding gas, air covers the outside area of the torch nozzle, cooling the area so the torch does NOT overheat.

Air also becomes the cutting gas. It swirls around the electrode as it heads toward the nozzle opening. The swirling action helps to constrict and narrow the gas. When the machine is turned on, a pilot arc is formed between the nozzle and the inner electrode. When the cutting gas reaches this pilot arc, it is super heated—up to 60,000°F (3298°C). Look at Figure 9–40.

The gas is now so hot it ionizes and becomes capable of carrying an electrical current (ionized gas is plasma). The small, narrow opening of the nozzle accelerates the expanding plasma toward the work piece. When the work piece is close enough, the arc crosses the gap, with the electrical current being carried by the plasma, forming the cutting arc.

A

Figure 9–40 Know the plasma arc cutting process.

Figure 9–39 Plasma arc welder is designed to rapidly cut metal. A: Note external parts of plasma arc cutter. *(HTP America, Inc.)* B: Technician is using plasma arc cutter.

The extreme heat and force of the cutting arc melt a narrow path through the metal. This serves to dissipate the metal into gas and tiny particles. The force of the plasma literally blows away the metal particles, leaving a clean cut.

A 10- to 15-amp plasma arc cutter is generally adequate for mild steel up to ³⁄₁₆ inch thick, a 30-amp unit can cut metal up to ¼ inch thick, and a 60-amp unit will slice through metal up to ½ inch thick.

Controls are usually quite simple. Plasma arc cutters made specifically for thinner metals might only have an on/off switch and a ready light. More elaborate equipment can include a built-in air compressor, variable output control, on-board coolant, and other features.

On some units, a switch is provided that allows the operator to alter the current mode depending on the surface being cut. When cutting painted or rusty metal, a continuous high-frequency arc is best.

Two critical parts of the torch are the cutting nozzle and the electrode. These are the only consumables (besides air) in plasma arc cutting. If either the nozzle or the electrode is worn or damaged, the quality of the cut will be affected. They wear somewhat with each cut. However, moisture in the air supply, cutting thick materials, or poor technique will make them fail more quickly. Keep a supply of electrodes and nozzles on hand and replace them when needed.

Today's plasma arc cutters do an excellent job using clean, dry compressed air. The air can be supplied through an external or built-in air compressor or by using a cylinder of compressed air. Look for equipment designed to run on less air pressure. Cylinders of air can be expensive, while shop air is almost free. To reduce contaminants, use a regulator with a filter.

Also, check the air pressure regularly. Using the wrong pressure can reduce the quality of the cuts, damage parts, and decrease the cutting capacity of the machine.

Operating a Plasma Arc Cutter

To operate a typical plasma arc cutter, proceed as follows:

1. Connect the unit to a clean, dry source of compressed air with a minimum line pressure of 60 psi at the air connection.

2. Connect the torch and ground clamp to the unit. After plugging the machine in, connect the ground clamp to a clean metal surface on the vehicle. The clamp should be as close as possible to the area to be cut.

3. Move the cutting nozzle into contact with an electrically conductive part of the work. This must be done to satisfy the work safety circuit.

4. Hold the plasma torch so that the cutting nozzle is perpendicular to the work surface. Push the plasma torch down. This will force the cutting nozzle down until it comes in contact with the electrode. Then the plasma arc will start. Release downward force on the torch to let the cutting nozzle return to its normal position. While keeping the cutting nozzle in light contact with the work, drag the gun lightly across the work surface.

5. Move the plasma torch in the direction the metal is to be cut. The speed of the cut will depend on the thickness of the metal. If the torch is moved too fast, it will NOT cut all the way through. If moved too slowly, it will put too much heat into the work piece and might also extinguish the plasma arc.

Other pointers that should be remembered when using a plasma arc cutter are:

1. When piercing materials ⅛ inch (3 mm) thick or more, angle the torch at 45 degrees until the plasma arc pierces the material. This will allow the stream of sparks to shoot off away from the gas diffuser.

   If the torch is held perpendicular to the work when piercing heavy-gauge material, the sparks will shoot back up at the gas diffuser. The molten metal will collect on the diffuser. This might plug the air holes and shorten the life of the diffuser.

   ■ *Danger! When angling the torch, be aware that the sparks can shoot off as far as 20 feet (6 m) away. Be sure that there are no combustibles or other workers in the area.*

2. Torch cooling is important to extend the life of the electrode and nozzle. At the end of a cut, the air continues to flow for several seconds. This prevents the nozzle and electrode from overheating. Some equipment suppliers also recommend "idling" the unit for a couple of minutes after the cut is made.

3. When making long straight cuts, use a metal straightedge as a guide. Simply clamp it to the work to be cut. For elaborate cuts, make a template out of thin sheet metal or wood and guide the tip along that edge.

4. When cutting ¼-inch materials, start the cut at the edge of the material.

5. When making rust repairs on cosmetic panels, it is possible to piece the new metal over the rusted area and then cut the patch panel at the same time that rust is cut out. This process also works when splicing in a quarter panel.

6. Be aware of the fact that the sparks from the arc can damage painted surfaces and can also pit glass. Use a welding blanket to protect these surfaces.

7. Make sure there is nothing behind the panel that can be damaged. Check for wiring, fuel lines, sound deadening materials, and other objects that could cause a fire.

Summary

- A weld is formed when separate pieces of material are fused together through the application of heat. The heat must be high enough to cause the softening or melting of the pieces to be joined.

- The three types of heat joining in collision repair are fusion welding, pressure welding, and adhesion bonding.

- MIG (metal inert gas) welding is a wire-feed fusion welding process commonly used in collision repair. TIG (tungsten inert gas) is generally used in automotive engine rebuilding shops to repair cracks in aluminum cylinder heads and in reconstructing combustion chambers, but has very limited applications in collision repair.

- The major parts of a MIG welder are: power supply, welding gun, weld cable, electrode wire, wire feeder, shielding gas, regulator, and wire clamp.

- The types of MIG welds are tack, continuous, butt, fillet, and plug welds.

- Plasma arc cutting creates an intensely hot air stream over a very small area, which melts and removes metal. It is replacing oxyacetylene as the best way to cut metals.

Technical Terms

weld	*weldface*
base material	*weld penetration*
filler material	*burn mark*
weldroot	*burn-through*

weld legs
weld throat
joint fit-up
fusion welding
MIG
TIG
stick arc welding
oxyacetylene welding
adhesion bonding
high-strength steels
resistance spot welding
shielding gas
nonferrous
welder amperage rating
duty cycle
MIG welding gun
contact tip
nozzle
active gas
inert gas
MAG
MIG–MAG
AWS
heat setting
travel speed
push welding
pull welding
wire stick-out
gun angle
straight polarity
reverse polarity
tack weld
spot weld
continuous weld
skip welding
stitch welding
butt weld
backing strip
fillet weld
lap joint

plug weld
flat welding
horizontal welding
vertical welding
overhead welding
welding filter lens
self-darkening filter lens
weld-through primer
burnback
wire speed
gas flow rate
heat sink compound
resistance spot welding
arm sets
electrode tips
pressure multiplier
current adjuster
spot weld timer
pitch
visual weld inspection
destructive testing
weld porosity
weld cracks
weld distortion
weld spatter
weld undercut
weld overlap
heat crayons
oxygen pressure
acetylene pressure
cutting torch
spark lighter
neutral flame
carburizing flame
oxidizing flame
capillary attraction
soft brazing
hard brazing
plasma arc cutting

Review Questions

1. Explain the difference between a welding base material and a filler material.

2. Define the term "weld penetration." How can you tell if it is correct?

3. List ten advantages of MIG welding.

4. This term refers to metals NOT containing iron.
   a. Nonalloy
   b. Alloy
   c. Nonferrous
   d. Ferrous

5. List and explain eight parts of a MIG welder.

6. The _____ protects the contact tip and directs the shielding gas flow.

7. This type of welding gas combines with the weld to contribute to weld quality.
   a. Inert gas
   b. Active gas
   c. Biodegradable gas
   d. Butane gas

8. Explain the effects of the voltage setting on a MIG welder.

9. _____ is how fast you move the gun across the joint.

10. How does moving more slowly or quickly affect the answer in question nine?

11. Explain the difference between push and pull welding.

12. What is the difference between skip and stitch welding?

13. This is the most difficult welding position.
    a. Horizontal
    b. Vertical
    c. Flat
    d. Overhead

14. A _____ primer is used to add zinc anti-corrosion protection to weld zones.

15. Body repair manuals recommend certain spacing, or _____, between resistance spot welds. Pitch, and the _____ from the _____ of the panel, determine the _____ of individual spot welds.

16. List and explain eight welding problems.

Activities

1. Visit your guidance counselor. Ask about welding courses offered in your area. Give a report to the class about your findings.

2. Practice destructive tests of welds. Make MIG and spot welds on scrap metal. Tear them apart with a hammer and chisel. Visually inspect the welds and write a report on your findings.

3. Visit a body shop. While wearing all protective gear and a helmet with an approved lens, observe experienced auto body welders working. Write a report on what you have learned.

MINOR REPAIRS

CHAPTER 10

METAL STRAIGHTENING FUNDAMENTALS

Objectives

After reading this chapter, you should be able to:

- Describe different types of metals used in vehicle construction.

- Explain the strength ratings of metals.

- Summarize the deformation effects of impacts on steel.

- Use a hammer and dolly to straighten metal.

- Explain how to bump dents with spoons.

- List the steps for shrinking metal.

- Prepare a surface for filler.

- Properly mix filler and cream hardener.

- Correctly apply filler.

- Use recommended methods for shaping filler.

- List common mistakes made when using filler and spot putty.

Introduction

This chapter will introduce you to basic metal-working methods. It will explain how to analyze minor damage to sheet metal before showing you how to repair the damage. Good metal-working skills are critical to your success as an auto body technician.

An untrained person can spend more time shaping and sculpting plastic filler than properly reworking the damaged metal. Not only does this waste valuable shop time, but the quality of the repair also suffers. An improperly straightened panel will have tension that can cause the plastic filler to crack, lose adhesion, or fall off. This, of course, does nothing to build customer satisfaction.

To do quality sheet metal repairs, you must first know how to return the sheet metal to its original shape. Then, you can use a thin layer of filler to smooth the surface above the panel. This chapter will help you develop these essential skills.

SHEET METAL

There are two types of sheet metal used in automobile construction—hot-rolled and cold-rolled.

Hot-rolled sheet metal is made by rolling at temperatures exceeding 1,472°F (792°C). It has a standard manufacturing thickness range of $\frac{1}{16}$ to $\frac{5}{16}$ in. (1.6 to 7.9 mm). It is used for comparatively thick parts such as frames and crossmembers.

Cold-rolled sheet metal is hot-rolled sheet metal that has been acid rinsed, cold rolled thin, then annealed. It has a dependable thickness accuracy, surface quality, and better workability than hot-rolled steel. Most unibodies are made from cold-rolled steel.

Low-carbon or *mild steel* has a low level of carbon and is relatively soft and easy to work. Much of the sheet metal used in collision repair today is low-carbon or mild steel. It can be safely welded, heat shrunk, and cold worked without seriously affecting its strength. Mild steel has a yield strength of up to 30,000 psi (2,100 K/cm²).

Because MS is easily deformed and relatively heavy, vehicle manufacturers have begun using high-strength steels in load carrying parts of the vehicle.

High-strength steel (HSS) is stronger than low-carbon or mild steel because of heat treatment. Most new vehicles contain HSS in their structural components. It has a yield strength of up to 60,000 psi (4,200 K/cm²). HSS experiences an increase in stress, exceeding this yield strength, when deformed during a collision.

The same properties that give strength offer some unique challenges. When high-strength steel is deformed on impact, it is more difficult to restore than mild steel.

STEEL STRENGTH

When flat sheet steel is formed into a shape for a part, it takes on certain properties that harden it.

For example, a roof panel is relatively flat. If hit lightly in the center, the panel will usually bend and then pop back to its original shape. However, if you hit a panel with a curved shape, the panel will hardly move. Although both are the same steel, the one that has been changed the most will be stronger and more resistant to bending.

The same is true for panels whose shape has been changed during a collision. The structure of the metal in the affected areas has changed, causing the metal to become harder and more resistant to corrective forces. See Figure 10–1.

To repair collision damage, a technician should understand what property changes have taken place in the metal.

Deformation refers to the new, undesired bent shape the metal takes after an impact or collision.

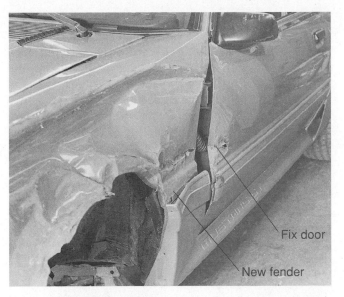

Figure 10–1 Before starting work on straightening a panel, evaluate damage. Would it be cheaper to purchase a new or used panel? If labor time is low enough, panel straightening would be cost effective.

There are various ways to measure the strength of a metal. All relate to the metal's ability to resist deformation.

1. *Tensile strength* is the property of a material that resists forces applied to pull it apart. *Tension* includes both yield stress and ultimate strength. *Yield stress* is the amount of strain needed to permanently deform a test specimen. *Ultimate strength* is a measure of the load that breaks a specimen. The tensile strength of a metal can be determined by a tensile testing machine.

2. *Compressive strength* is the property of a material to resist being crushed.

3. *Shear strength* is a measure of how well a material can withstand forces acting to cut or slice it apart.

4. *Torsional strength* is the property of a material that withstands a twisting force.

Strength is expressed in pounds per square inch (psi) or kilograms per centimeter squared (K/cm²).

Even though most types of steel look alike, there are differences in their chemical makeup and crystalline structure. These invisible differences can affect strength and sensitivity to heat. There is a variety of high-strength steels. All have unique properties that dictate the way in which they can be repaired.

PHYSICAL STRUCTURE OF STEEL

Steel, just like all matter, is composed of atoms. These very small particles of matter are arranged to form grains that can only be seen with a microscope. Grains are formed into patterns called the grain structure.

The *grain structure* in a piece of steel determines how much it can be bent or shaped. To change the shape of flat sheet steel, you must change the shape and position of all the individual grains that are located in the area of the creases, folds, or curves.

In mild steels, the individual grains can withstand a considerable amount of change and movement before splitting or breaking. To demonstrate this, bend a welding rod back and forth several times. Notice that in the bend, the metal will become very hot. The heat is generated by the internal friction created as the individual grains move against each other.

EFFECT OF IMPACT FORCES

The grain pattern of a metal will determine how it reacts to force. Sheet metal's resistance to change has three properties: elastic deformation, plastic deformation, and work hardening. All of these properties are related to the yield point.

Yield point is the amount of force that a piece of metal can resist without tearing or breaking.

Elastic deformation is the ability of metal to stretch and return to its original shape. For example, take a piece of sheet metal and gently bend it to form a slight arc. When released, it will spring back to its original shape.

Spring-back is the tendency for metal to return to its original shape after deformation. It will occur in any area that is still relatively smooth. Many such areas will spring back to shape if they are released by relieving the distortion in the buckled areas.

Plastic deformation is the ability of metal to be bent or formed into different shapes. When metal is bent beyond its elastic limit, it will have a tendency to spring back. However, it will NOT spring back all the way to its original shape. This is because the grain structure has been changed.

Plasticity is important to the collision repair technician because both stretching and permanent deformation take place in various areas of most damaged panels.

WORK HARDENING

Work hardening is the limit of plastic deformation that causes the metal to become hard where it has been bent. For example, if a welding rod is bent back and forth several times, a fold or buckle will appear at the point of the bend. The plastic deformation has been so great that the metal will be very hard and stiff at the bend.

The importance of understanding how metal stiffens, making it stronger in areas that are bent or worked, cannot be overemphasized. It is the basis of practically all collision repair.

KINDS OF DAMAGE

A part is *kinked* when:

1. It has a sharp bend of a small radius, usually more than 90 degrees over a short distance, Figure 10–2.
2. After straightening, there is a visible crack or tear in the metal or there is permanent deformation that cannot be straightened to its pre-accident shape without the use of excessive heat.

A part is *bent* when:

1. The change in the shape of the part between the damaged and undamaged areas is smooth and continuous.
2. Straightening the part by pulling restores its shape to pre-accident condition without any areas of permanent deformation.

USING BODY HAMMERS

The body hammer is often used to remove small dents in sheet metal parts. The body hammer is designed to strike the sheet metal and rebound off the surface. A driving action would create additional damage in the sheet metal. Refer to Figure 10–3.

A *high spot* or *bump* is an area that sticks up higher than the surrounding surface. A *low spot* or *dent* is just the opposite, it is recessed below the surrounding

Figure 10–2 Radius of bend determines whether or not you have a kink or a bend. Kink generally results when metal is folded over 90 degrees.

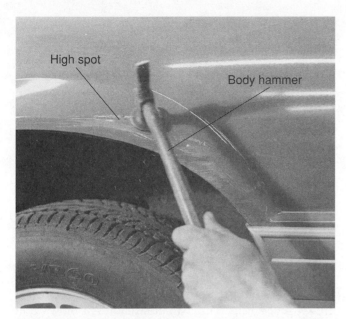

Figure 10–3 Body hammer is used to lower high spots. When using hammer, swing from your wrist so that hammer hits flat. If you swing with your arm and you do not hit squarely, edge of hammer head will form a dent.

surface. Minor low and high spots in sheet metal can often be fixed with a body hammer.

The term *raising* means to work a dent outward or away from the body. The term *lowering* means to work a high spot or bump down or into the body.

The secret of metal straightening is to hit the right spot at the right time, with the right amount of force. When using a body hammer, swing in a circular motion at your wrist. Do not swing the hammer with your whole arm and shoulder. Hit the part squarely and let the hammer rebound off the metal. Space each blow ⅜ to ½ inch (9.5 to 12.7 mm) apart until the damaged metal is level.

The face of the hammer must fit the contour of the panel. Use a flat face on flat or low-crown panels. Use a convex-shaped or high-crown face when bumping inside curves.

Heavy body hammers should be used for roughing out the damage. *Finishing*, or *dinging hammers* should be used for final shaping. The secret to finish hammering is light, rapid taps. It is also important to hit squarely. Hitting with the edge of the hammer will put additional nicks in the metal.

BUMPING DENTS WITH SPOONS

Spoons can be used to pry out damage, struck with a hammer to drive out damage, and as a dolly in hard-to-reach areas. Some are even designed to be used in place of a body hammer.

Spring hammering is a method of bumping damage with a hammer and a dinging spoon. The dinging spoon is lightweight and has a low crown. When used, hold the spoon firmly against a ridge or crease. Hit the spoon with a ball peen or bumping hammer to work the high spot down, Figure 10–4. Always keep firm pressure on the spoon when spring hammering. It must never be allowed to bounce.

The force of the blow on the spoon is distributed over a large area of the ridge. Begin at the ends of the ridge and work toward the high point, alternating from side to side.

Spoons can be used to back up the hammer or in combination with a slapper spoon. With a long body spoon, you can often reach into restricted places. Pressure can be applied to tension areas with the spoon, while high areas are bumped down. See Figure 10–5.

Spoons can also be used to pry up metal or to drive out deep dents. In Figure 10–6, note how a double-end spoon is being used to pry out a dent in a door panel. The door is supported on blocks of wood to provide clearance for the panel. Use care not to stretch the metal by prying it out too much. Once the dent is

Figure 10–4 Large dinging spoon can be used to lower ridge formed in damaged panel. Start at outer ends of ridge and work your way to the center.

Figure 10–5 Use curved spoon to reach in behind damaged panel to serve as a dolly. Tap on outside of panel with hammer while pressing spoon in from backside.

Figure 10–6 You can also use curved spoon to pry out dents in panels, a door panel in this example. Pieces of wood should be used to raise door or panel off work surface.

roughed out, a body hammer can be used to finish the area.

BUMPING DENTS WITH DOLLIES

In the rough-out phase, a dolly block is used as an impact tool. The backside of the metal can be hit with the dolly to raise low areas and to unroll buckles. The dolly is also used as a backing block for the hammer.

The contour of the dolly must fit the contour of the backside of the damaged area. As you hit the panel, the dolly tends to rebound slightly. This creates a secondary lifting action on the metal. You control rebound by the pressure exerted against the dolly and by the size of the dolly. A greater lifting action is also obtained when the hammer blows are close to the dolly. The further away the blows are from the dolly, the less the metal is moved.

HAMMER-ON-DOLLY

Hammer-on-dolly is a method used to stretch metal. Hammer-on-dolly repairs are used to smooth small, shallow dents and bulges. Look at Figure 10–7.

To lower a bulge, place the dolly against the backside of the panel directly behind the bulge and use a hammer from the front side. There will be a slight rebound as your hammer hits the dolly. The dolly will then hit the backside of the panel. As the force of the dolly pressing against the panel is increased, the flattening action will also increase.

Any shrunken metal on a crown can be stretched to its normal level easily with the hammer-on-dolly method. Hammer-on-dolly is used only if there is access to the backside of the panel. If not, dent pullers and filling are used. Refer to Figure 10–8.

Note that improper hammer blows placed on a crown will shrink rather than stretch. All blows that are designed to stretch should be hard and accurate. An inaccurate hard blow can damage the panel.

Keep in mind that light hammer blows are for straightening, not stretching. In other words, when using the hammer-on-dolly technique, hit hard and do not miss!

HAMMER-OFF-DOLLY

Hammer-off-dolly is used to straighten metal just before the final stage of straightening. In this procedure, hold the dolly under the lowest area, and hit the high area with your hammer. Look at Figure 10–9.

Generally, use the hammer and dolly to roll out the damage in reverse order than it was formed. The damage must be rolled out working toward the center. The dolly is held tightly under the channel at the outer end where the least degree of bend is present.

Figure 10–7 With hammer-on-dolly method, place dolly right behind damage and hit metal right over dolly to straighten metal.

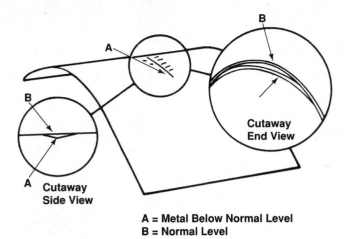

A = Metal Below Normal Level
B = Normal Level

Figure 10–8 The panel was damaged and has been roughed out. However, it is still low in the area of the buckle. Because the damage shows no evidence of a pressure area, the panel is low at point A. The only way point A can be raised to the original level (point B) is by stretching. The stretching has to be along the line of the rolled buckle. Picking up the low area will not correct the condition. The hammer-on-dolly method should be used at point A. For a small, long dent, final spread in the same direction as the long area of the dent. If you wipe sideways across the dent, the spreader will sink into the dent. For larger dents wider than the spreader, spread in the same direction. Do not wipe in different directions.

Figure 10–9 With hammer-off-dolly method, place dolly next to area to be hit. Then, strike high spots next to dolly.

Use a flat-faced dinging hammer to direct light to medium blows at the outer ends of the ridge closest to the dolly. The blows from the hammer gradually force down the ends of the ridge. The dolly pressure forces the end of the channel upward. The same procedure is repeated on the other end of the channel and the adjacent ridges.

Use the hammer-off-dolly method to gradually work toward the center. Work on the greatest degree of bend in the ridges and channels first. As the pressure is released, the metal tends to move back to its original position. The dolly can also be used as a driving tool to help work the channel.

If the dolly does NOT move when the channel is hit upward, there is still too much pressure on the ridges and/or channel. More dollying must be done to relieve the tension.

In Figure 10–10, study the procedure for reshaping a damaged body panel. Note sequence of areas to be worked.

Once the area has been brought back to its basic shape, use the hammer-on-dolly method to smooth and level the area. You are then ready for metal finishing or filling procedures.

USING PICKING HAMMERS

Picking hammers, picks, a dolly edge, and a scratch awl can be used to pick up metal. When picking up a small dent, it is better to use several light blows. After an area has been raised, use a file or grinder to level the damaged area.

Picks can be used to pry up meal in areas that cannot be reached with a dolly or spoon. A vehicle door is a good example, Figure 10–11. A pick can sometimes be inserted through a drainage hole. This eliminates the need to remove the inside door trim or to drill holes in the outer panel for pulling the dent.

When picks are used to remove small dents without having to repaint the panel, it is termed *paintless dent removal.* This method only works with very small dents that do not damage the finish.

When prying with a pick, be careful not to stretch the metal by exerting too much pressure. Start with the point of impact or the lowest point. Slowly pry up the damaged area. On the larger areas, use a flat blade pick rather than a pointed one. Tap down pressure areas, while prying up low tension areas.

PULLING DAMAGED AREAS

Dents can be pulled out with a number of tools: suction cups, pull rods, and dent pullers. Pulling is often needed because access to the inside of many panels is blocked by reinforcements and other parts. With a puller, you can repair a simple dent in a minimal amount of time.

First, study the damage to determine the point and angle of the impact. Then, you can find where pulling force is needed to remove the damage.

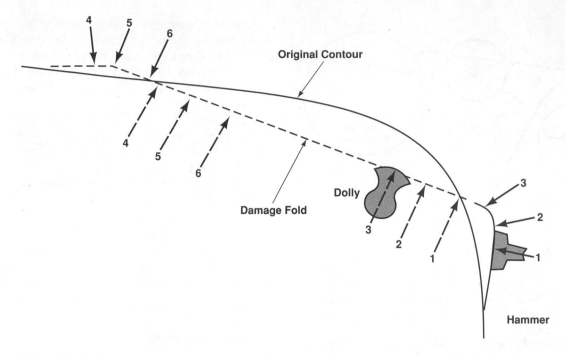

Figure 10–10 Note steps for removing damage from curved shape using hammer and dolly. First, start at one end of damage, on right. Then, work damage on other side. Roll out damage toward middle. Filler would then be needed to obtain final contour.

Figure 10–11 Picks are often used to remove small dents from doors and other hard-to-reach areas. Pry on dents with pick while applying light taps from hammer on other side. Picks will fit through small openings in side of door or other part.

Pulling Dents with Suction Cup

A *suction cup* can be used to pull out large, shallow dents. Wet the area and install the cup. If hand held, pull straight out on the cup's handle. If mounted on a slide hammer, use a quick blow to pop the dent out.

A *vacuum suction cup* uses a remote power source (separate vacuum pump or air compressor airflow) to produce negative pressure (vacuum) in the cup. This increases the pulling power because the cup will be forced against the panel tightly. Larger, deeper dents can be pulled with a vacuum suction cup.

Pulling Dents with Screws

A *screw-on slide hammer* will remove deeper dents and creases. Drill or punch holes one inch (25 mm) apart along the crease. Punching is better than drilling because punching leaves more metal for the screw tip to grab.

Beginning at the point of impact, thread the screw tip on the dent puller into the first hole. Hold the handle of the dent puller in one hand and forcefully slide the weight straight back against the handle. This will pull the dent or crease outward.

Caution! Be careful not to pinch your fingers between the weight and the handle of a slide hammer.

To gradually work the damage out, pull the first hole slightly. Then, go on to the next hole. Work from the lowest spot of damage in both directions.

After pulling out each hole slightly, repeat the process. Work the surface as close to the finished contour as possible without pulling the metal beyond the original surface. Tap high spots down with a body hammer to relieve pressure in ridge areas. Holes must be welded closed and low spots can be filled with body filler.

Shallow, small dents in enclosed panels can be pulled out with one or more pull rods. Again, a body hammer should be used to tap high spots down while pulling.

Keep in mind that it is senseless to pierce a large number of holes in the surface of a panel that could have been straightened by other means. The result is often an unsatisfactory job. Worse, it may be the case that more time was required to do it wrong than would have been required to do it correctly.

Pulling with Studs

A *stud spot welder* joins pull rods on the surface of a panel so that you do not have to drill holes. It is the best way to pull dents. Pulling with spot-welded studs avoids drilling or punching through the metal and undercoating, which can lead to corrosion. Refer to Figure 10–12.

To use a stud welding gun, grind the area down to bare metal. Install a stud into the gun. Press the gun against the dented area. Pull the trigger to weld the pin onto the surface of the panel. Weld enough pins onto the area to remove the damage. Look at Figure 10–13.

Next, attach a slide hammer to each of the pins and pull out the damage in steps, Figure 10–14. You could also use a pulling chain on a frame rack if needed, Figure 10–15. After bringing the surface of the dent almost out to the desired level, grind off the studs, Figure 10–16. This will allow you to remove the dent without drilling holes in the panel.

Figure 10–12 Stud pulling kit has special spot welder that welds studs onto panel. No holes must be drilled or punched for screws.

Figure 10–13 Use stud gun to weld small metal studs onto area to be pulled.

Figure 10–14 Attach slide hammer to each stud. Use slide hammer blows and body hammer to work metal outward.

Figure 10–15 Hydraulic frame straightening chain can also be used to pull on studs to remove dent.

Figure 10–16 Cut off studs when done. Then grind them flush with surface. Use plastic filler to final shape repair area.

SHRINKING METAL

Shrinking metal removes strain or tension on a damaged, stretched sheet metal area. During impact, the metal can be stretched. When pulled or hammered straight, the area can still have tension or strain on it. This is because the stretched metal no longer fits in the same area. The metal will tend to pop in and out when you try to finally straighten it. You would have to use heat to shrink the metal back to its original dimensions.

If a strained area is filled with plastic filler, road vibrations can cause the panel to make a popping or flapping noise. After prolonged movement of the strained area, the filler can crack or fall off. Eventually, you will be required to spend extra time correcting the work that should have been done properly in the first place.

Principles of Shrinking

A steel bar will expand (lengthen) when heated and contract (shorten) when cooled. If heated while butted against a solid object at both ends, it cannot lengthen and will bulge out in the middle or hottest area. Then when cooled, the length of the bar will decrease. This is the principle of shrinking metal.

Shrinking a steel bar also applies to the shrinking of a warped area in a piece of sheet metal. A small spot in the center of the warped area is heated to a dull red. When the temperature rises, the heated area swells and attempts to expand outward toward the edges of the heated circle. Since the surrounding area is cool and hard, the panel cannot expand. As a result, a strong compression load is generated.

If heating continues, the stretching of the metal is centered in the dull red hot portion, pressing it out. This causes it to thicken, thus relieving the compression load. If the red hot area is suddenly cooled, the steel will contract and the surface area will shrink.

A variety of welding equipment can be used to heat metal for shrinking. Attachments are available for spot and MIG welding equipment to transform them into shrinking tools; the most commonly used tool is the oxyacetylene torch with a No. 1 or No. 2 tip.

Torch Shrinking

Torch shrinking uses the heat of an oxyacetylene torch to release tension in the panel. To shrink an area with a torch, heat a small spot in the bulge to a cherry red.

Shrink in the highest spot of the stretched area, then in the next highest spot, until the area has been shrunk back to its proper position.

The size of the area to be heated, or "hot spot," is determined by the amount of excess metal. The larger the area, the harder the heat is to control. An average-sized area to heat is usually about the size of a quarter. Smaller areas should be used on flat panels because they tend to warp easily. The area should never be larger than the size of the hammer face being used.

Use a neutral flame and a No. 1 or No. 2 tip to heat the panel. Bring the point of the cone straight down to within ⅛ inch (3 mm) of the metal. Hold the torch steady until the metal starts to turn red. Then move the torch slowly outward in a circular motion until the area is cherry red.

> *WARNING!* *Do not heat the metal past a cherry red. It will start to melt, and a hole may be burned through the metal. Also, remember that aluminum will not change color or turn red when heated.*

The metal usually will bulge up instead of down because the top of it is heated first. When it starts to bulge, the rest of the metal in the area follows. When the area has been heated, tap around it to drive the molecules of metal closer together. You may have to support the panel with a dolly to prevent the metal from collapsing. Push the dolly *lightly* under the metal. When the redness disappears, use a hammer and dolly to level the area around the shrink.

> *WARNING!* *Never use hard, hammer-on-dolly blows to level the area when shrinking. This will restretch the metal.*

Once the redness has disappeared and the area has been smoothed, cool the area with a wet rag or sponge. This will cause metal contraction. A slight amount of distortion could result. Straighten any warpage before heating the next spot.

Remember! It is easy to overshrink. When this occurs, the metal in the area last heated is usually collapsed or pulled flat. Sometimes the metal surrounding the heated area can even be pulled out of the proper contour. To fix overshrinking use hard, hammer-on-dolly blows to stretch the affected area.

Shrinking a Gouge

A *gouge* is caused by a focused impact that forces a sharp dent or crease into a panel. A gouge causes the metal to be stretched. Gouges must be shrunk to their original size to properly repair the damage. Simply picking up the low area would distort the panel. Filling the gouge with filler without restoring the panel's original contour will leave tension in the panel that could cause the filler to crack or pop off.

To shrink a gouge, heat the lowest point of the gouge with an oxyacetylene torch until the metal is cherry red. Use a dolly to hammer up the shrink. This will increase the tension on the soft area, forcing it to swell and return to its original position.

While the metal is still hot, hold the dolly directly under the groove and tap down the ridges on either side of the groove. This will not only drive down the ridges, but will also bump up the gouged metal.

If the gouge is long, repeat this process several times to raise the whole length of the gouge. Only heat as much of the gouge that can be worked before the metal cools.

IDENTIFYING STRETCHED METAL

Stretched metal has been forced thinner in thickness and larger in surface area by impact. When metal is severely damaged in a collision, it is often stretched in the badly buckled areas. These same areas are also sometimes stretched slightly during the straightening process. Most of the stretched metal will be found along ridges, channels, and buckles in the direct damage area. When there are stretched areas of metal, it is impossible to correctly straighten the area back to its original contour. The stretched areas can be compared to a bulge on a tire. There is no place for the area to fit within the correct panel contour.

When an area is stretched, the grains of metal are moved farther away from each other. The metal is thinned and work hardened. Shrinking is needed to bring the molecules back to their original position and to restore the metal to its proper contour and thickness.

Before shrinking, dolly the damaged area back as close to its original shape as possible. Then you can accurately determine whether or not there is stretched metal in the damaged area. It will usually pop in and out if stretched. If stretched, you must shrink the metal.

Kinking Stretched Metal

Kinking involves using a hammer and dolly to create pleats, or kinks, in the stretched area to shrink the area's surface area. Instead of using heat to shrink the metal, kinking is another way to deal with stretched metal.

To kink metal, hit the stretched area with a picking hammer slightly off-dolly. This will lower the area slightly below the rest of the panel. Fill the low area with body filler. Then file and sand the area level with the rest of the panel.

FILING THE REPAIR AREA

When the area has been bumped and pulled as level and smooth as possible, use a body file to locate any remaining high and low spots. File across the damaged area to the undamaged metal on the opposite side. This will keep the filing action on the correct plane with the good part of the panel. Look at Figure 10–17.

Push the file forward by its handle for the cutting stroke. Control file downward pressure and direction by holding the front of the file. Use as long a stroke as possible.

When filing relatively flat areas, hold the file at a 30-degree angle and push straight. You can also hold the file straight and push it at a 30-degree angle, Figure 10–18. On a crowned panel, hold the file straight with the length of the flattest crown. Push to one side at a 30-degree angle or less, Figure 10–19.

The scratch pattern created by the file on the metal identifies any high and low spots. You can then further work the metal into shape before using plastic filler.

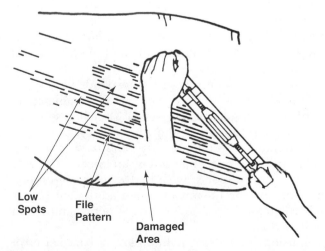

Low
Spots

File
Pattern

Damaged
Area

Figure 10–17 Filing will help you locate high and low spots that need further work. Low spots will NOT have file marks.

Figure 10–18 Shown are two methods for filing. Top: Push file sideways while holding it at 30-degree angle. Bottom: Hold file straight and push it sideways at 30-degree angle. Always put equal pressure on both ends of file.

Figure 10–19 Note two methods for filing crowned or curved surface. Top: Push file straight along crown to true top of crown. Bottom: Angle and push file off to side to shape and true curves on sides of crown. Twist file with your wrists to match curved shape.

WORKING ALUMINUM

Aluminum is used for a variety of automotive panels, such as hoods and deck lids. The repair of aluminum requires much more care than working steel panels. Aluminum is much softer than steel, yet it is more difficult to shape once it becomes work hardened. It also melts at a lower temperature and distorts readily when heated.

Because aluminum is soft, it responds very readily to the hammer-on-dolly method. If hammered too hard or too much, the panel will stretch. Use several light strokes rather than a few heavy blows.

Aluminum does not readily bend back to its original shape after being buckled by an impact. Therefore, it does not respond well to the hammer-off-dolly method. Be careful not to create additional damage when attempting to lower ridges with hammer and dolly blows.

Raising small dents with a picking hammer or pry bar is an excellent way to repair aluminum panels. However, do not raise the panel too far and stretch the soft aluminum.

Spring hammering with a hammer and spoon is an excellent way to unlock stress in high-pressure areas of aluminum. The spoon distributes the force of the blow over a wider area.

Because aluminum is soft, reduce hand pressure on the body file. Use a file with rounded edges to avoid scratching and gouging the metal.

Grind carefully on aluminum. A coarse grit grinding disc will quickly burn through aluminum. The heat from grinding can also warp the panel. A No. 36 grit open coat disc can be used, but grind carefully to remove only paint and primer, not the metal. Make two or three passes, then quench the area with a wet rag to cool the metal in the panel.

Featheredging of aluminum should be done with a dual-action sander. Use No. 80 or No. 100 grit paper and a soft, flexible backing pad.

Heat shrink stretched aluminum slowly to avoid distorting the panel. Do not heat the spot over 1,200°F (584°C). Use a thermal crayon or paint to monitor heating. Mark the part with the crayon when it is still cold. When the stated temperature has been reached, the crayon or paint mark will liquefy.

Unlike steel, aluminum does not turn red as it is heated. Instead, it turns ash gray just before it melts. Thus, a lack of caution will result in a melted panel. Also, quench or cool the heated area very slowly to avoid distortion.

USING BODY FILLER

After the damaged metal has been bumped, pulled, pried, and dinged, apply body or plastic filler next.

Body fillers, also called *plastic fillers,* are designed to cover up minor surface irregularities that remain after metal straightening. Keep in mind that the quality of the repair and finish is adversely affected by the wrong choice of filler. The chart in Figure 10–20 shows various types of filler and their uses.

NOTE! FOR MORE INFORMATION ON BODY FILLERS AND RELATED MATERIALS, REFER BACK TO CHAPTER 8.

Preparing Surface for Filler

One of the most important steps in applying plastic body fillers is surface preparation. Begin by washing the repair area with soap and water to remove dirt and grime. Then clean the area with wax and grease remover to eliminate wax, road tar, and grease. Use a cleaner that will remove the *silicones* often present in automotive waxes.

Wash brazed or soldered joints to neutralize the acids in the flux. Do not grind these areas before neutralizing the acids. Grinding simply drives the acids deeper into the metal.

Mask any trim, parts, or adjacent panels that could be damaged by grinding, sanding, and filling. Use masking tape or duct tape to protect them.

Grind the area to remove the old paint 3 to 4 in. (75 to 100 mm) around the area to be filled. Remember! Never apply body filler over paint! Only apply filler to bare metal. Filler will NOT bond properly to paint, causing problems.

Use a No. 24 or No. 36 grit grinding disc to remove the paint. Grinding also etches the metal to provide better adhesion, Figure 10–21. Only grind enough to remove the finish. Do not grind too much or you will thin and weaken the metal.

If applying filler over a metal patch, do not hammer down the excess weld bead. Grind it level with the surface. Hammering a weld down distorts the metal, creates stress, and increases the area to be filled.

After grinding away the finish from the repair area, blow away the sanding dust with compressed air and wipe the surface with a tack rag to remove any remaining dust particles.

PREPARING SURFACE FOR FILLER
Surface Preparation Problems

Surface preparation involves the many steps needed to clean, straighten, and smooth the surface before refinishing. Many problems are linked to improper surface preparation. Below is a list of rules to follow to prepare for applying filler.

1. Before applying filler, sand or grind surface to the bare metal, making sure all rust, spots of paints, weld scale, etc., are removed.

2. After sanding or grinding, blow off area with high pressure air gun. Wipe with a clean cloth to remove any fine dust or moisture that may be left on the surface.

WARNING! Anything that remains between the bare metal and filler will probably result in adhesion failure.

3. Make sure no solvents are used to clean sanded area before applying filler. Trapped vapors will result, causing pinholing and poor adhesion.

4. If body filler is to be applied to brazed seams or panel joints, thoroughly wash the area to neutralize the acids in the flux.

5. Avoid applying filler over seams or joints that were pop riveted. Too much movement takes place, which will cause the filler to crack.

6. For best results, the filler, shop, and parts should be above 65°F (18°C).

7. With high humidity conditions, use a heat lamp to warm and dry the area to be prepared. This will eliminate moisture accumulation between the bare metal and filler which will cause poor adhesion.

Mixing Filler

Mix the can of filler to a uniform and smooth consistency. It must be free of lumps and not wet on top. Heavyweight fillers should be shaken on a paint shaker for several minutes.

COMPARING BODY FILLERS

Filler	Composition	Characteristics	Application
Conventional Fillers			
Heavyweight fillers	Polyester resins and talc particles	Smooth sanding; fine feather-edging; nonsagging; less pinholing than lightweight fillers	Dents, dings, and gouges in metal panels
Lightweight fillers	Microsphere glass bubbles; fine grain talc; polyester resins	Spreads easily; nonshrinking; homogeneous; no settling	Dings, dents, and gouges in metal panels
Premium fillers	Microspheres; talc; polyester resins; special chemical additives	Sands fast and easy; spreads creamy and moist; spreads smooth without pinholes; dries tack-free; will not sag	Dings, dents, and gouges in metal panels
Fiberglass-Reinforced Fillers			
Short strand	Small fiberglass strands; polyester resins	Waterproof; stronger than regular fillers	Fills small rustouts and holes. Used with fiberglass cloth to bridge larger rustouts.
Long strand	Long fiberglass strands; polyester resins	Waterproof; stronger than short strand fiberglass fillers; bridges small holes without matte or cloth	Cracked or shattered fiberglass. Repairing rustouts, holes, and tears.
Specialty Fillers			
Aluminum filler	Aluminum flakes and powders; polyester resins	Waterproof; spreads smoothly; high level of quality and durability	Restoring classic and exotic vehicles
Finishing filler/ polyester putty	High-resin content; fine talc particles; microsphere glass bubbles	Ultra-smooth and creamy; tack-free; nonshrinking; eliminates need for air dry type glazing putty	Fills pinholes and sand scratches in metal, filler, fiberglass, and old finishes.
Sprayable filler/ polyester primer-surfacer	High-viscosity polyester resins; talc particles; liquid hardener	Virtually nonshrinking; prevents bleed-through; eliminates primer/glazing/ primer procedure	Fills file marks, sand scratches, mildly cracked or crazed paint films, and pinholes. Seals fillers and old finishes against bleed-through.

Figure 10–20 Chart shows general composition, characteristics, and applications for various types of filler.

Proper *filler mixing* is needed to prevent these problems:

1. The filler in the upper portion of the can will be too thin. This results in runs and sags when applying filler.

2. The filler can cure slowly or not at all.

3. The filler can have a gummy, soft condition when sanded. It can have a very tacky surface after curing that will clog your sandpaper.

4. The filler can cause poor featheredging. It will tear off the metal and form a small lip at its outer edge.

5. The filler can blister and lift when coated with primers and refinishing materials.

6. The filler in the bottom of the can will be too thick. When you use the bottom, the filler will be very coarse and grainy.

7. The filler will have pinholing or small air holes will form in the filler.

Figure 10–21 Before applying filler, grind area to remove all paint and rust. Coarse grind marks will help filler bond to metal. Mask trim or adjacent panels so you do not accidentally damage surfaces not being repaired. Use compressed air to blow off dust from repair area.

8. The filler will cause poor color holdout when the area is coated with primers and refinishing materials.

Kneading the Hardener

Kneading hardener is done by squeezing the tube back and forth with your fingers to mix the material. Loosen the tube cap to release the air. Knead the tube thoroughly to assure a smooth, pastelike consistency. The hardener should be like toothpaste when squeezed out.

If you do NOT knead the hardener, the result can be the same problems listed for poor filler mixing.

If the hardener is kneaded thoroughly and remains thin and watery, you have *spoiled hardener.* It should not be used because it has been chemically broken down. Hardener can spoil if frozen or if stored too long.

Mixing Filler and Hardener

Numerous problems can occur from improper *catalyzing* (mixing) of *cream hardener* (filler catalyst) and filler. Before catalyzing, make sure the materials (filler and hardener) to be used are compatible. They should be manufactured by the same company and be recommended for each other.

The following tips will help eliminate problems relating to mixing filler and its catalyst. Open the can of filler without bending its lid. Remove the desired amount of filler. Use a clean putty knife or spreader.

Place the filler on a smooth, clean filler mixing board. A *filler mixing board* is a clean, nonporous sur-

face for mixing filler and hardener. You can use a sheet metal, glass, or hard plastic, Figure 10–22.

> WARNING! *Cardboard should NOT be used as a mixing board filler. It is porous and contains waxes for waterproofing. These waxes will be dissolved in the mixed filler and cause poor bonding. Cardboard also absorbs some of the chemicals in the filler and hardener, changing the filler's curing quality slightly. Cardboard fibers can also stick in the filler and ruin the finish. Mixing boards with a handle are also available.*

Add hardener according to the proportion indicated on the can, usually 10 percent hardener (one part hardener for each ten parts filler). Too little hardener will result in a soft, gummy filler that will not adhere properly to the metal. It will also not sand or featheredge cleanly. See Figure 10–23. Too much hardener will produce excessive gases, resulting in pinholing. Look at Figure 10–24.

A general rule, for each "golf ball size glob" of filler, use a one inch (25 mm) bead of hardener. If the filler is as big as a "baseball," use about a six-inch (150 mm) bead of hardener. However, always refer to the manufacturer instructions for exact mixing instructions, Figure 10–25.

Filler over-catalyzation results when you use too much hardener for the amount of filler. It must be avoided when adding hardener to the filler. In addi-

Figure 10–22 Place amount of filler needed on mixing board. Add recommended amount of cream hardener to filler. Then mix together.

Figure 10–23 If you do not use enough hardener, filler will not bond to panel properly and will not featheredge or sand properly.

Figure 10–24 A common mistake is to use too much hardener. This will cause excess gas and pinholes in hardened filler. Filler may also harden on your mixing board before you have time to apply it to vehicle.

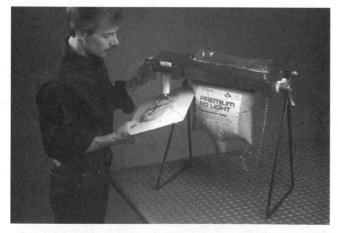

Figure 10–25 Technician is using filler and hardener in dispenser. This helps keep filler fresh and clean. *(Oatey Bond Tite)*

tion to paint color bleed-through and pinholing, a reverse curing action may occur, causing poor adhesion and poor sanding properties.

Filler under-catalyzation is caused by NOT using enough hardener in the filler. It will result in the filler not curing properly, resulting in tack surfaces and poor adhesion properties.

With a clean putty knife or spreader, use a scraping motion (back and forth) to mix the filler and hardener together thoroughly and achieve a uniform color. Scrape filler off both sides of the spreader and mix it in. Every few back and forth strokes, scrape the filler into the center of your mixing board by circling inward.

NOTE! DO NOT STIR THE FILLER. STIRRING WHIPS AIR INTO THE FILLER, AND CAUSES AIR POCKETS AND PINHOLES WHEN APPLIED.

If the filler and hardener are NOT thoroughly mixed to a uniform color, soft spots will form in the cured filler. The result is an uneven cure, poor adhesion, lifting, and blistering.

Reinstall the cover on the can of filler right away. This will keep out dust and dirt. It will also help prevent liquids in the filler from evaporating.

Always use clean tools when removing the filler from the can and mixing the filler and hardener together. Do NOT redip the knife, spreader, or mixed filler into the can. This will cause the whole can of filler to harden with time. Hard lumps of filler might form in the can and/or applied filler. This will cause problems the next time you try to use the filler.

Use different spreaders to mix and apply the filler. A small amount of unmixed filler will always remain on the mixing spreader. If any is applied, you will have soft spots in the cured filler. The paint finish may peel.

Applying the Filler

Apply the mixed filler as soon as you are done mixing. First, apply a thin coat of filler to the repair area. Press firmly to force filler into the sand scratches and holes. This will strengthen the bond.

Work the filler patch in two directions (left to right, then top to bottom). This will greatly reduce pinholing. Build-up layers should NOT be more than 1/8 in. (3 mm) thick.

Spread the filler approximately 3 in. (75 mm) beyond the repaired area. This will assure better adhesion, and allows you to featheredge the patch.

When this layer cures, apply more coats to build up the repair area to a proper contour. Allow each application to set up before applying the next coat of filler.

Build up the final layer of filler slightly above the panel surface. Make the filler slightly thicker than needed. This will allow you to sand off the waxy film that forms on the surface of the filler. You will also be able to sand the filler down smooth on an equal plane with the existing panel. Look at Figure 10–26.

Figure 10–26 When applying filler, work quickly because filler cures quickly. Build filler up slightly higher or thicker than needed. Also, spread filler out over slightly larger area than repair area, but not over paint. This will let you work filler down to correct contour and featheredge around repair.

Always use a clean plastic *spreader* or *spatula* to apply filler. Chunks of old filler could fall into the new soft filler. This can cause large pockets to be gouged as you spread the filler. Also, for your final coating of filler, make sure the spreader has a smooth edge. If worn and nicked, used spreaders will not make a smooth layer of filler.

If needed, you can use your fingers to bend the spreader to match the shape of the contour. Use a smaller spreader on small repair areas. A larger spreader will fill large areas more easily.

Avoid using filler in cold temperatures. When the filler, shop, or panel are cold, the filler will NOT cure properly. It will have a tacky surface and poor sanding properties. Large pinholes could also form. Filler should be stored at room temperature (65° to 70°F or 18° to 21°C). Use a heat lamp to warm cold surfaces if needed.

In winter, moisture can form on metal surfaces when a cold vehicle is brought inside. In summer, condensation might form on the metal. Again, use a heat lamp to dry damp surfaces before applying filler. If the repair area is not first warmed to remove moisture, poor adhesion, featheredging, pinholing, and lifting could result.

Make sure all holes, gaps, joints, cracks, etc., are welded. Holes left under filler allow moisture to accumulate between the metal and filler, eventually resulting in bond failure.

Filing the Filler

Allow the filler to cure to a semi-hard consistency. This usually takes 15 to 20 minutes. Scratch the filler with your fingernail. If the scratch leaves a white mark, the filler is ready to be filed. See Figure 10–27.

Filler filing involves using a coarse "cheese grater" or body file to rough shape the semi-hard filler. You will knock off the high spots and rough edges. Since the filler is only partially hard, the body file will quickly remove excess filler. It will force the semi-soft filler through the large holes in the file face.

If you do NOT rough shape the filler with a grater, you will waste time and sandpaper. Sandpaper will become loaded quickly. They will also create unwanted dust.

To use the cheese grater file, hold it at a 30- to 40-degree angle. Pull it lightly across the semi-hard filler, Figure 10–28. Work the file in several directions. Stop filing when the filler is slightly above the desired level. This will be sufficient for sanding out the file marks and for feathering the edges. If the filler is undercut, additional filler must be applied.

Applying Filler to Body Lines

Many vehicles have sharp body lines in doors, quarter panels, hoods, etc. Maintaining the sharpness of these lines when doing filler work is difficult, especially in recessed areas. The best way to get straight, clean lines is to file each plane, angle, or corner separately.

Apply masking tape along one edge. Then apply filler to the adjacent surface. Before the filler sets up, pull the tape off. This will remove the excess filler from the body line.

After the first application is dry and sanded, tape the opposite edge. Apply masking tape along the

Figure 10–27 Curing time for filler will vary with shop temperature and other factors. You need to be ready to file when filler partially hardens.

A

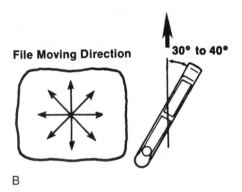

File Moving Direction

30° to 40°

B

Figure 10–28 Use a body file or "cheese grater" to rough shape filler when partially cured. A: Body file will quickly remove high spots from filler. It is faster than sanding and does not produce dust. B: Hold body file flat and move in all directions to true flat surface. Hold file at 30- to 40- degree angle.

OEM Mastic Joint Seal

A

Spot Weld

Body Filler With a Groove Sanded Into It Looks Like a Factory Joint.

B

Joint Area is Damaged And Low, Requiring Filler.

Filler With Simulated "Joint" Sanded In

Crack in Filler

C

Rust Forming Under Filler

Figure 10–29 A: Joints between two panels may be filled with sealer. B: Never try to fill this type of joint with filler and then sand in a groove. C: Flexible joint will crack and rust if improper method is used.

body line and over the filler. Then, coat the adjacent surface with filler. When the tape is removed and the filler sanded, the result is a straight, even line or corner.

Applying Filler to Panel Joints

Many panels have joints that are factory finished with a *seam sealer* to allow the panel to flex and move. Often, both halves of the joint suffer damage and require filling. Never make the mistake of covering the seam sealer with body filler. The filler will crack over the body flex joint.

Figure 10–29 shows what happens when the inflexible filler is subjected to the twisting action of the panels under normal road conditions. A crack can develop that allows moisture to seep under the filler, which causes rust to form on the metal surface. This eventually results in the failure of the filler-to-metal bond and a weakened sheet metal joint.

The original flexibility of the joint can be preserved by taping its alternate sides. As shown in Figure 10–30, apply tape to one panel. Then apply

filler to the other panel. Pull the tape up to remove excess filler. Then fill the other panel the same way. After you shape the filler on both panels, force a seam sealer into the joint.

Sanding the Filler

After filing, sand out all file marks, Figure 10–31. Use a No. 36 or No. 40 grit disc on a sanding board or block first. An air file can also be used on large flat areas. Then, follow with No. 80 grit sandpaper until all scratches are removed.

Danger! *Do not breathe the dust created when sanding filler. Wear a respirator mask to keep the plastic dust out of your lungs.*

Finally, smooth the filler with No. 180 grit sandpaper. A sanding block or air file can again be used, as well as a long sanding board. A DA will work fine on smaller areas.

Figure 10-30 These are proper steps for filling damaged panel flex joint with filler.

Be careful not to oversand. *Filler oversanding* results in the filled area being below the desired level, which makes it necessary to apply more filler.

Filler undersanding leaves the filled area high or thicker than the surrounding panel. A hump would be formed at the filled area.

After final sanding, blow with an air gun and wipe with a tack cloth. This removes any fine sanding dust that might be hiding surface pinholes. It also exposes holes lying just below the surface. These holes and remaining sand scratched must be filled.

Run your hand or straightedge over the surface to check for evenness. Do not trust "eye balling" for accuracy. Paint does NOT hide imperfections; it highlights them. Do not be satisfied until the repaired surface is perfectly smooth.

Remember! If you can feel the slightest bump, paint will make it show up much more. The dull sur-

face of filler and sanded paint does not visibly show surface imperfections.

Featheredging

Featheredging involves sanding the repair area until the filler and old paint blend smoothly into each other. You must use fine sandpaper, 180 grit or finer. Sand until you remove any small lip where different materials on the surface meet. Look at Figure 10-32.

Featheredging is commonly done with a DA sander. When sanding, hold the sander float on the surface. Avoid tilting the sander to remove material more quickly. This will sand a small hole into the filler. By holding the sander flat, you will plane off the filler smoothly. Refer to Figure 10-33.

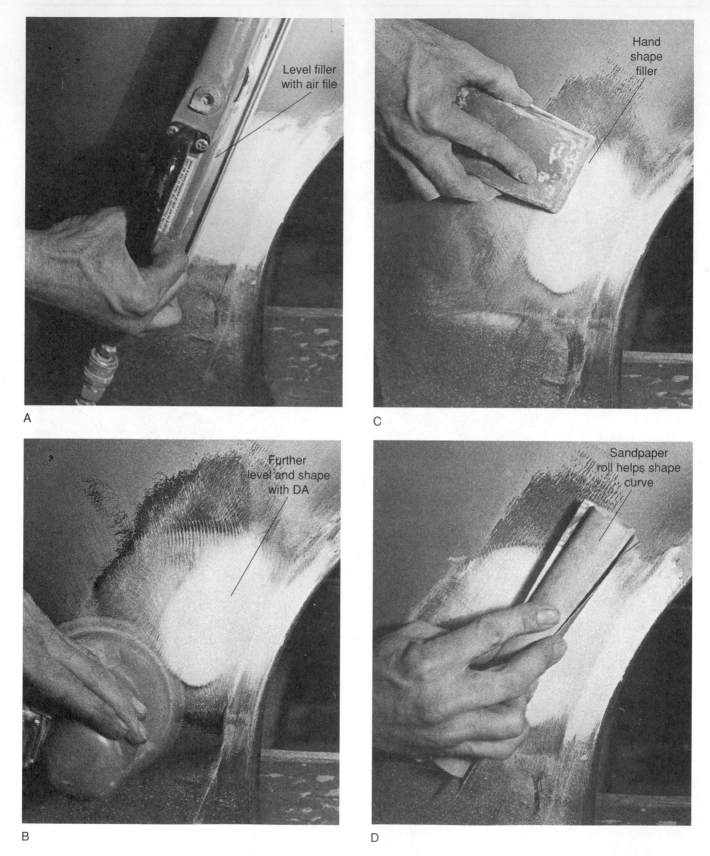

Figure 10–31 When sanding filler, make sure you select correct method of sanding. This will save time and improve repair quality. A: If large enough area, first sand with air file. Its large surface area will help true large flat areas. Roll air file to help round contour if needed. B: After air file, use disc sander to further shape filler. Move sander in directions needed to featheredge and shape filler to match panel contour. C: Hand block sand area to carefully lower filler to same plane as metal. You want a smooth featheredge. You should not be able to feel any lip where filler and metal meet. D: On curves, round cardboard sandpaper area to help match filler and metal shapes.

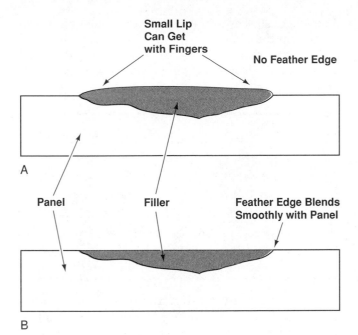

Figure 10-32 Poor and good filler featheredge. A: Filler has not been featheredged properly. You would be able to feel a small lip at edge of filler. B: Filler has good featheredge and blends smoothly into panel.

Figure 10-34 On large areas, you should not sand through to metal in center area of filler. This would mean you have a metal high spot. It would show up easily as large hump when painted.

On large areas with filler, use an air file with 180 grit or finer sandpaper. The large sandpaper surface area will help you quickly straighten doors panels, fenders, and other large, relatively flat panels. See Figure 10-34.

Priming

Priming is done directly after filling to cover any bare metal as well as the filler. After using filler, primer-surfacer is often sprayed on the repair area. Since primer-surfacer is very thick, it will help fill small sand scratches in the filler and paint. Refer to Figure 10-35.

For best and quickest results when applying primer-surfacer, spray two or three coats with a five to fifteen minute flash time between coats. You will actually save time by following flash recommendations versus spraying coats wet on wet.

It is difficult to tell when a thick coat of primer-surfacer is truly dry. The surface will appear dry while

Figure 10-33 When featheredging filler, hold sander flat so that edge of sandpaper does NOT dig into filler. Also, pay close attention so that you do not oversand filler. *(Courtesy Dynabrade™)*

Figure 10-35 After filler is sanded properly, apply a coat of primer or primer-surfacer. Primer-surfacer will help fill small imperfections and let you further sand repair area true.

there is still a lot of solvent trapped below the surface. The lower layer of primer-surfacer is still trying to dry and shrink.

On the other extreme, thin dry coats of primer-surfacer can cause loss of adhesion, not only to the substrate, but also to the topcoat color. Always spray wet coats of primer-surfacer. Wait an hour or more before sanding the primer-surfacer.

If the primer-surfacer is sanded before all of the solvent has evaporated, the material in the scratches will continue to shrink down in the scratches. They will show up in the final finishing color topcoats as sanding scratches.

After the primer dries, you can dry or wet sand the filler to check your work. Some technicians like to apply a thin coat of a different color primer over the full coat of primer-surfacer. Then, by sanding the area, you can easily find high and low spots. If the second color primer does not sand off, you found a low spot. If it sands off too quickly, you have found a high spot.

Ideally, the second color primer should sand off at the same time. This shows that the surface is flat and ready for sealer, a topcoat and other operations.

Applying Glazing Putty

Once the primer is dry, small pinholes and scratches can be filled with *spot putty* or *glazing putty* as shown in Figure 10–36. If one-part putty, apply it directly to your spreader. If using a polyester putty, mix the putty and hardener according to the manufacturer's instructions.

Place a small amount of putty onto a clean rubber squeegee. Apply a thin coat over the primer.

Figure 10–36 After priming, you might find small surface imperfections. These can be filled with spot putty. Use spot putty sparingly. *(Marson Corp.)*

Use single strokes and a fast scraping motion. Use a minimum number of strokes when applying lacquer-based putties. They dry very fast. Repeated passes of the spreader might pull the putty away from the primer.

> *WARNING! A common mistake is to use spot putty as a filler. Spot putty is NOT as strong as filler. Only use spot putty to fill small imperfections in the primer. Do NOT apply it to bare metal or painted surfaces. Most are designed to be applied over primer.*

Allow the putty to dry completely before sanding smooth with No. 240 grit sandpaper. Sanding the putty too quickly results in sand scratches in the finish.

NOTE! EXCESSIVE USE OF GLAZING PUTTIES IS USUALLY AN INDICATION OF A LACK OF SKILL AND TRAINING. THEY SHOULD BE USED ON SMALL PINHOLES AND OTHER SMALL SURFACE PROBLEMS IN THE PRIMER.

MORE INFORMATION

NOTE! THE REPAIR IS NOW READY FOR FINAL PRIMING, SEALING, AND PAINTING. THIS WILL BE DETAILED IN LATER CHAPTERS. REFER TO THE INDEX FOR MORE INFORMATION ON THESE SUBJECTS IF NEEDED NOW.

SUMMARY

- The two types of sheet metal used in auto body work are hot-rolled and cold-rolled. Hot-rolled sheet metal is used for comparatively thick parts such as frames and crossmembers. Cold-rolled sheet metal is used for most unibodies.

- The various tools used to straighten metals include body hammers, spoons, dollies, picking hammers, suction cups, screw-on slide hammers, and spot-welded studs.

- Shrinking metal removes strain or tension on a damaged, stretched sheet metal area.

- Aluminum is used for a variety of automotive panels such as hoods and deck lids. It is much softer than steel, yet it is more difficult to shape once it becomes work hardened. It also melts at a lower temperature and distorts readily when heated.

- Body fillers, also called plastic fillers, are designed to level minor surface irregularities that remain after metal straightening.
- Featheredging involves sanding the repair area until the filler and old paint blend smoothly into each other.
- Priming is done after sanding body fillers to prepare the surface for refinishing.

Technical Terms

mild steel
high-strength steel
deformation
tensile strength
yield
stress
compressive strength
shear strength
torsional strength
grain structure
yield point
elastic deformation
spring-back
plastic deformation
work hardening
kinked
bent
high spot
low spot
dinging hammer
spoons
spring hammering
hammer-on-dolly
hammer-off-dolly
paintless dent removal

vacuum suction cup
screw-on slide hammer
stud spot welder
shrinking metal
stretched metal
torch shrinking
gouge
kinking
body fillers
silicones
kneading hardener
spoiled hardener
cream hardener
mixing board
filler over-catalyzation
filler under-catalyzation
spreader
filler filing
seam sealer
filler undersanding
filler oversanding
featheredging
priming
spot putty

Review Questions

1. What is the difference between mild steel and high-strength steel?

2. This term refers to a measure of how well a material resists a twisting force.
   a. Tensile strength
   b. Torsional strength
   c. Yield stress
   d. Compression strength

3. _____ _____ is the ability of metal to stretch and return to its original shape.

4. _____ _____ is the limit of plastic deformation that causes the metal to become hard where it has been bent.

5. When is a part kinked?

6. When is a part bent?

7. Explain the difference between a high spot and a low spot on a panel.

8. The term _____ means to work a dent outward or away from the body. The term _____ means to work a high spot or bump down or into the body.

9. Describe the difference between hammer-on- and hammer-off-dollying.

10. A vacuum suction cup uses a remote power source (separate vacuum pump or air compressor airflow) to produce negative pressure (vacuum) in the cup. True or false?

11. What is the main advantage of using a stud spot welder over a screw-in puller?

12. When should you shrink metal?

13. How do you torch shrink metal?

14. Aluminum turns "cherry red" when heated near its melting point. True or false?

15. _____ _____, also called _____ _____, are designed to cover up minor surface irregularities that remain after metal straightening.

16. List seven rules to prepare for applying plastic filler.

17. This is done to mix a tube of cream hardener.
   a. Knurling
   b. Shaking
   c. Spreading
   d. Kneading

18. Why should cardboard not be used as a mixing board for filler?

19. Explain how you should file filler.

20. _____ _____ results in the filled area being below the desired level, which makes it necessary to apply more filler.

Activities

1. Obtain a damaged panel (fender, hood, door, or lid) from a salvage yard. Use a hammer to place a small dent in a flat area of the panel. Use the information in this chapter to grind, fill, and smooth the dent using filler.

2. Featheredge, prime, and spot putty the area filled in activity number one.

3. Read the mixing instructions on several brands of filler. Make a report on your findings. What differences in mixing hardener and filler did you find?

CHAPTER 11

PLASTIC AND
FIBERGLASS REPAIR

Objectives

After studying this chapter, you should be able to:

- List typical plastic applications in body construction.

- Identify automotive plastics through the use of international symbols (ISO codes) and by making a trial-and-error weld.

- Describe the basic differences between welding metal and welding plastic.

- Outline the basics of hot-air and airless welding.

- Repair interior and unreinforced hard plastics.

- Perform two-part adhesive repairs.

- Repair RRIM and other reinforced plastics.

Introduction

The term *plastics* refers to a wide range of materials synthetically compounded from crude oil, coal, natural gas, and other natural substances. Unlike metals, plastics do NOT occur in nature and must be manufactured. Because plastic is much lighter in weight than sheet metal, it has become an important part of today's vehicles. Today, more and more plastic is being used in automobile manufacturing. Look at Figure 11–1.

Plastic parts include bumpers, fender extensions, fascias, fender aprons, grille openings, stone shields, instrument panels, trim panels, fuel lines, and engine parts, Figure 11–2. Fuel saving and weight reduction programs by auto makers have made plastic parts more common. See Figure 11–3.

Many of the new reinforced plastics are almost as strong and rigid as steel. Some are even more dimensionally stable. Plastic parts are also extremely corrosion resistant. Tests are being made on plastic engine blocks and plastic frame parts. Plastic suppliers are projecting increased use of plastic in floor pans, windows, steering shafts, springs, wheels, bearings, and other mechanical components.

This increasing use of plastic has resulted in new approaches to collision repair. Many plastic parts can be repaired more economically than they can be replaced, especially if the part does NOT have to be removed. Cuts, cracks, gouges, tears, and punctures are all repairable. When necessary, some plastics can also be re-formed back to their original shape after distortion. Repair is also quicker than replacement. Since parts are NOT always available, this means less downtime for the vehicle.

Figure 11–1 Plastics are now very common in modern vehicles. This car uses a plastic skin over many parts. This increases impact resistance, improves corrosion resistance, and reduces vehicle weight for increased fuel economy. *(1993 Saturn, Courtesy of Saturn Corporation)*

TYPES OF AUTO PLASTICS

Two general types of plastics are used in automotive construction: thermoplastics and thermosetting plastics.

Thermoplastics can be repeatedly softened and reshaped by heating, with no change in their chemical makeup. They soften or melt when heated and harden when cooled. Thermoplastics are weldable with a plastic welder.

Thermosetting plastics undergo a chemical change by the action of heating, a catalyst, or ultraviolet light. They are hardened into a permanent shape that CANNOT be altered by reapplying heat or catalysts. Thermosets are NOT weldable, but can be repaired with flexible parts repair materials.

The table in Figure 11–4 shows some of the more common plastics with their full chemical name, common name, and their locations on a vehicle.

Composite plastics, or "hybrids," are blends of different plastics and other ingredients designed to achieve specific performance characteristics.

NOTE: A Standard Symbol is Stamped on the Side Under Each Resin Part to Show the Type of Material Used.

No.	Part Name	Material
①	Headlight Lid	PA6/PPE-M (Polyamide/Polyphenylene ether)
②	Front and Rear Bumpers	PBT-P (Polybutylene terephthalate)
③	Front and Rear Skirts	PP (Polypropylene)
④	Door Mirror Housing	ABS (Acrylonitrile butadiene styrene)
⑤	Side Sill Panel	PA6/PPE-M (Polyamide/Polyphenylene ether)
⑥	Trunk Lid Spoiler	UP-G (Polyster unsaturated thermoset)
⑦	Fuel Lid	PA6/PPE-M (Polyamide/Polyphenylene ether)

Figure 11–2 Note the types of plastic parts used on this rustproof aluminum body car. *(© American Honda Motor Co., Inc.)*

Figure 11-3 Study locations of different kinds of plastics on typical vehicle. *(Used with permission of Nissan Motor Corporation)*

SYMBOL, CHEMICAL NAME, TRADE NAME, AND DESIGN
APPLICATIONS OF COMMONLY USED AUTOMOTIVE PLASTICS

Symbol	Chemical Name	Trade Name	Design Applications	Thermosetting or Thermoplastic
AAS	Acrylonitrile-styrene	Acrylic Rubber	—	Thermoplastic
ABS	Acrylonitrile-butadiene-styrene	ABS, Cycolac, Abson, Kralastic, Lustran, Absafil, Dylel	Body and dash panels, grilles, headlamp doors	Thermoplastic
ABS/MAT	Hard ABS reinforced with fiberglass	—	Body panels	Thermosetting
ABS/PVC	ABS/Polyvinyl chloride	ABS Vinyl	—	Thermoplastic
EP	Epoxy	Epon, EPO, Epotuf, Araldite	Fiberglass body panels	Thermosetting
EPDM	Ethylene-propylene-diene-monomer	EPDM, Nordel	Bumper impact strips, body panels	Thermosetting
PA	Polyamide	Nylon, Capron, Zytel, Rilsan, Minlon, Vydyne	Exterior trim panels	Thermosetting
PC	Polycarbonate	Lexan, Merlon	Grilles, instrument panels, lenses	Thermoplastic
PPO	Polyphenylene oxide	Noryl, Olefo	Chromed plastic parts, grilles, headlamp doors, bezels, ornaments	Thermosetting
PE	Polyethylene	Dylan, Fortiflex, Marlex, Alathon, Hi-fax, Hosalen, Paxon	Inner fender panels, interior trim panels, valances, spoilers	Thermoplastic
PP	Polypropylene	Profax, Olefo, Marlex, Olemer, Aydel, Dypro	Interior moldings and panels, inner fenders, radiator shrouds, bumper covers	Thermoplastic
PS	Polystyrene	Lustrex, Dylene, Styron, Fostacryl, Duraton	—	Thermoplastic
PUR	Polyurethane	Castethane, Bayflex	Bumper covers, front and rear body panels, filler panels	Thermosetting
TPUR	Polyurethane	Pellethane, Estane, Roylar, Texin	Bumper covers, gravel deflectors, filler panels, soft bezels	Thermoplastic
PVC	Polyvinyl chloride	Geon, Vinylete, Pliovic	Interior trim, soft filler panels	Thermoplastic
RIM	"Reaction injection molded" polyurethane	—	Bumper covers	Thermosetting
RRIM	Reinforced RIM-polyurethane	—	Exterior body panels	Thermosetting
SAN	Styrene-acrylonitrite	Lustran, Tyril, Fostacryl	Interior trim panels	Thermosetting
TPR	Thermoplastic rubber	—	Valance panels	Thermosetting
UP	Polyester	SMC, Premi-glas, BMC, Selection Vibrin-mat	Fiberglass body panels	Thermosetting

Figure 11–4 Chart lists plastic symbols, chemical names, trade names, applications, and plastic types.

A good example of the change in unibody vehicles centers around the use of fiber-reinforced composite plastic panels, commonly known as *sheet molded compounds (SMC).* The reason for using SMC is simple. It is light, corrosion proof, dent resistant, and relatively easy to repair compared to the more traditional materials.

The use of SMC and other *fiber-reinforced plastics (FRP)* is NOT new. They have been used in various applications on automobiles for years. The use of large external body panels of reinforced plastic is NOT unusual either. What is new is that, unlike the external panels on earlier vehicles, these panels now are bonded to a metal space frame using structural adhesives, adding overall structural rigidity to the vehicle.

PLASTICS SAFETY

Working with plastics and fiberglass requires you to think about safety at all times. The resin and related ingredients can irritate your skin and stomach lining. The curing agent or hardener can produce harmful vapors.

Read and understand the following safety points before using any of these types of products:

1. Read all label instructions and warnings carefully.

2. When cutting, sanding, or grinding plastics, dust control is important.

3. Wear rubber gloves when working with fiberglass resin or hardener. Long sleeves, buttoned collar, and cuffs are helpful in preventing sanding dust from getting on your skin. Disposable paint suits will keep dust away from clothes.

4. A protective skin cream should be used on any exposed areas of the body.

5. If the resin or hardener comes in contact with the skin, wash with borax soap and water or alcohol.

6. Safety glasses are always a necessity.

7. Always work in a well-ventilated area.

8. Wear a respirator to avoid inhaling sanding dust and resin vapors.

PLASTIC IDENTIFICATION

There are several ways to identify an unknown plastic. One way to identify a plastic is by *international symbols,* or *ISO codes,* which are molded into plastic parts. Many manufacturers are using these symbols. The symbol or abbreviation is formed in an oval on the backside of the part. One problem is that you usually have to remove the part to read the symbol.

If the part is NOT identified by a symbol, the *body repair manual* will give information about plastic types used on the vehicle. Body manuals often name the types of plastic used in a particular application.

The *burn test* involves using a flame and the resulting smoke to determine the type of plastic. It is no longer recommended for identifying plastics. First, an open flame in a collision repair shop creates a potential fire hazard. Second, it is environmentally unsound. Finally, the burn test is NOT always reliable. Many parts are now being manufactured from composite plastics that use more than one ingredient. A burn test is of no help in such cases.

A reliable means of identifying an unknown plastic is to make a trial-and-error weld on a hidden or damaged area of the part. Try several different filler rods until one sticks. Most suppliers offer only a few types of plastic filler rods; the range of possibilities is NOT that great. The rods are color coded. Once you find a rod that works, the base material is identified.

PRINCIPLES OF PLASTIC WELDING

Plastic welding uses heat and sometimes a plastic filler rod to join or repair plastic parts. The welding of plastics is NOT unlike the welding of metals. Both methods use a heat source, welding rod, and similar techniques (butt joints, lap joints, etc.). Joints are prepared in much the same manner, and evaluated for strength. There are differences, however, between welding metal and welding plastics.

Plastics have a wide melting range between the temperature when they soften and the temperature when they char or burn. Also, unlike metals, plastics are poor conductors of heat. This makes them difficult to heat uniformly. Plastic filler rod and plastic surface will burn before the material below the surface becomes fully softened. A plastic welder must work within a much smaller temperature range than a metal welder.

Because a plastic rod does NOT become completely molten, a plastic weld might appear incomplete. The outer surface of the rod becomes molten while the inner core remains semi-solid. The plastic rod will not look completely melted, except for molten flow on either side of the bead. Even though a strong and permanent bond has been formed, you may think you have a weak, cold-joint weld.

When plastic welding, force the rod into the joint to create a good bond. When heat is taken away, the rod reverts to its original form. A combination of heat and pressure is used when plastic welding. Normally, apply pressure on the welding rod with one hand, while applying heat with the tool. Use a constant fanning motion with hot air from the welding torch.

NOTE! TOO MUCH PRESSURE ON THE ROD TENDS TO STRETCH THE BEAD. TOO MUCH HEAT WILL CHAR, MELT, OR DISTORT THE PLASTIC. COMPETENT PLASTIC WELDING TAKES PRACTICE.

HOT-AIR PLASTIC WELDING

Hot-air plastic welding uses a tool with an electric heating element to produce hot air (450° to 650°F or 230° to 340°C) which blows through a nozzle and onto the plastic. The air supply comes from either the shop's air compressor or a self-contained portable compressor that comes with the welding unit.

Most hot-air welders use a tip working pressure of around 3 psi (.21 K/cm²). Air pressure regulators reduces the air pressure first to around 50 psi, and then to the working pressure of about 3 psi (.21 K/cm²). A typical hot-air welder is illustrated in Figure 11–5.

The torch is used in conjunction with the welding rod, which is normally 3/16 inch (5 mm) in diameter. The plastic welding rod must be made of the same material as the plastic being repaired. This will ensure proper strength, hardness, and flexibility of the repair. See Figure 11–6.

One of the problems with hot-air welding is that the plastic welding rod is often thicker than the panel to be welded. This can cause the panel to overheat before the rod has melted. Using a smaller diameter rod with the hot-air welder can often correct such warpage problems.

Three types of welding tips are available for use with most hot-air plastic welding torches. They are:

Tacking tips—shaped to tack weld broken sections of plastic together before welding. If necessary, tack welds can be easily pulled apart for realigning.

Round tips—used to make short welds, to weld small holes, to weld in hard-to-reach places, and to weld sharp corners, Figure 11–5.

Figure 11–5 A: Know the parts of plastic welder. B: Note welder tip types. *(Seelye, Inc.)*

Figure 11–6 When plastic welding, you must use proper combination of heat and pressure. Hand pressure is needed to force plastic rod down into weld joint. Fan welder over joint to heat rod and base material properly.

Figure 11–7 Note construction of high speed plastic welding tip.

Speed tips—hold, feed and automatically preheat the plastic welding rod. This design feeds the rod into the base material, thus allowing for faster welding speeds. They are used for long, fairly straight welds, Figure 11–7.

Some hot-air welder manufacturers have developed specialized welding tips and rods to meet specific needs. Check the product catalog for more information.

Using Hot-air Plastic Welders

No two hot-air plastic welders are exactly alike. For specific instructions, always refer to the owner's manual and other material provided by the welder manufacturer.

Some manufacturers advise against using their welder on plastic thinner than ⅛ inch (3.2 mm) because of distortion. It is sometimes acceptable to weld thin plastics if they are supported from underneath while welding.

To set up a typical hot-air welder, proceed as follows:

1. Close the pressure regulator valve by turning it counterclockwise until loose. This will prevent possible damage to the gauge from a sudden surge of air pressure.

2. Connect the air pressure regulator to a supply of either compressed air or inert gas. If inert gas is used, a pressure-reducing valve is needed.

3. Turn on the air supply. Starting pressure depends upon the wattage of the heating element. Check the operating manual for specifications.

4. Connect the welder to a common 120-volt AC outlet. Use a three-prong grounded plug.

5. Allow the welder to warm up at the recommended air pressure. Air or inert gas must flow through the welder at all times, from warm-up to cool-down. This will prevent burnout of the heating element and damage to the gun.

6. Select the proper tip. While wearing work gloves insert the tip into the torch with pliers to avoid touching the barrel while hot.

7. After the tip has been installed, the temperature will increase slightly due to back pressure. Allow 2 to 3 minutes for the tip to reach operating temperature.

8. Check the temperature by holding a thermometer ¼ inch (6 mm) from the hot air end of the torch. For most thermoplastics, the temperature should be in the 450° to 650°F (230° to 340°C) range. Information supplied with the welder usually includes a chart of welding temperatures.

9. If the temperature is too high to weld the material, increase the air pressure slightly until the temperature goes down. If the temperature is too low, decrease the air pressure slightly until the temperature rises. When increasing and decreasing the air pressure, allow at least 1 to 3 minutes for the temperature to stabilize.

10. Remember, the element can become overheated by too little air pressure. When decreasing air pressure, never allow the round nut that holds the barrel to the handle of the welder to become too hot to the touch. This indicates overheating.

11. A partially clogged dirt screen in the regulator can also cause overheating. Watch for these symptoms.

12. When you are done welding, disconnect the electrical cord. However, allow the air to flow through the welder for a few minutes or until the barrel is cool to the touch. Then disconnect the air supply.

AIRLESS PLASTIC WELDING

Airless plastic welding uses an electric heating element to melt a smaller ⅛ inch (3 mm) diameter rod with no external air supply. It has become very popular. Airless welding with a smaller rod helps eliminate two troublesome problems: panel warpage and excess rod build-up.

When setting up an airless welder, set the temperature dial at the appropriate setting. This will depend upon the specific plastic being worked on. It will normally take about 3 minutes for the welder to fully warm up.

Make sure the rod is the same material as the damaged plastic or the weld will be unsuccessful. Many airless welder manufacturers provide rod application charts. When the correct rod has been chosen, it is good practice to run a small piece through the welder to clean out the tip before beginning.

ULTRASONIC PLASTIC WELDING

Ultrasonic plastic welding relies on high-frequency vibratory energy to produce plastic bonding without melting the base material. Hand-held systems, Figure 11–8, are available in 20 and 40 kHz frequencies. They are equally adept at welding large parts and tight, hard-to-reach areas. Welding time is controlled by the power supply.

Most commonly used injection-molded plastics can be ultrasonically welded without the use of solvents, heat, or adhesives. Ultrasonic weldability depends on the plastic's melting temperature, elasticity, impact resistance, coefficient of friction, and thermal conductivity. Generally, the more rigid the plastic, the easier it is to weld ultrasonically. Thermoplastics such as polyethylene and polypropylene are ideal for ultrasonic welding, provided the welder can be positioned close to the joint area.

In the typical ultrasonic system, the vibration is generated in the transducer and then transmitted through the *sonotrode,* which is the equivalent of an electrode. The sonotrode tip directly contacts the work piece. An anvil supports the assembly. The best

Figure 11–8 Ultrasonic welder uses high frequency vibration to join plastic parts.

results are achieved when the sonotrode tip and anvil are contoured to accommodate the specific shape of the parts being joined.

When sonotrode tips begin to show wear, they may be reconditioned by cleaning and burnishing. Light sanding with 400 grit paper is usually sufficient. If the wear is excessive, the tips should be replaced.

Occasionally, the tip might tend to stick to the weld surface, particularly if improper machine settings are used. The sticking can be avoided by increasing the clamping force or decreasing the welding time. You can also apply a lubricant, such as a diluted soap solution, to the surfaces being joined. You can also prevent tip sticking by using a welding tip with an insert of tungsten carbide.

PLASTIC WELDING METHODS

The basic methods for hot-air and airless welding are very similar. To make a good plastic weld with either procedure, keep the following factors in mind:

1. Plastic welding rods are frequently *color coded* to indicate their material. Unfortunately, the coding is NOT uniform among manufacturers. It is important to use the reference information provided. If the rod is NOT compatible with the base material, the weld will NOT hold.

2. Too much heat will char, melt, or distort the plastic. Too little heat will NOT provide weld penetration between the base material and the rod.

3. Too much pressure stretches and distorts the weld.

4. The angle between rod and base material must be correct. If too shallow, a proper weld will NOT be achieved.

5. Use the correct welding speed. If the torch movement is too fast, it will NOT permit a good weld. If the tool is moved too slowly, it can char the plastic.

The basic repair sequence is generally the same for both processes. That is,

1. Prepare the damaged area.
2. Align the damaged area.
3. Make the weld.
4. Allow it to cool.
5. Sand. If the repair area has pinholes or voids, bevel the edges of the defective area. Add another weld bead. Then, resand.
6. Apply a flexible filler and topcoat.

HOT-AIR PLASTIC WELDING PROCEDURE

The typical hot-air plastic welding procedure is as follows:

1. Set the welder to the proper temperature (if a temperature adjustment is provided).
2. Wash and clean the part with soap and water. Allow it to dry. Then clean the part with a plastic cleaner. Do NOT use conventional prep solvents or wax and grease removers. To remove silicone materials, use a conventional cleaner first, making sure to completely remove all residue.
3. V-groove the damaged area.
4. Bevel the part ¼ inch (6 mm) on each side of the damaged area. See Figure 11–9.
5. Tack weld or tape the brake line with aluminum body tape.
6. Select the welding rod and welding tip best suited to the type of plastic and the damage.

7. Make the weld. The plastic weld should penetrate 75 percent through the base material, Figure 11–10. Allow it to cool and cure for about 30 minutes.
8. Grind or sand the weld to the proper contour and shape.

When welding plastic, single- or double-V butt welds produce the strongest joints. When using a round or V-shaped welding rod, prepare the area by slowly grinding, sanding, or shaving the adjoining surfaces to produce a single- or double-V. Wipe any dust or shavings from the joint with a clean, dry rag. Do not use cleaning solvents because they can soften the plastic edges and cause poor welds.

PLASTIC TACK WELDING

On long tears where backup is difficult, small *tack welds* can be made to hold the two sides in place before doing the permanent weld. For larger areas, a patch can be made from a piece of plastic and tacked in place.

To tack weld, proceed as follows:

1. Hold the damaged area in alignment with clamps or aluminum body tape.
2. Using a tacking welding tip, fuse the two sides to form a thin hinge weld along the root of the crack. This is especially useful for long cracks because it allows for easy adjustment and alignment of the edges.
3. Start tacking by drawing the point of the welding tip along the joint. Press the tip in firmly, making sure to contact both sides of the crack. Draw the

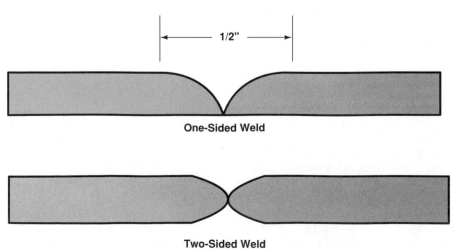

One-Sided Weld

Two-Sided Weld

Figure 11–9 Parts must be beveled on each side of repair. This will provide larger surface area and pocket below surface for welding rod. *(I-CAR)*

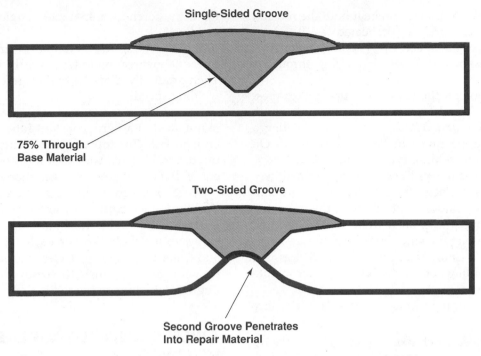

Single-Sided Groove

75% Through Base Material

Two-Sided Groove

Second Groove Penetrates Into Repair Material

Figure 11–10 With single-sided weld, weld must penetrate about 75 percent of base material. With two-sided weld, second weld should fuse with weld on other side. *(I-CAR)*

tip smoothly and evenly along the line of the crack. No welding rod is used when tacking.

4. The point of the tip will fuse both sides in a thin line at the root of the crack. The fused parts will hold the sides in alignment. Then, you can fuse the entire length of the crack.

WELDING A PLASTIC V-GROOVE

Prepare the rod for welding by cutting the end at an approximately 60-degree angle. When starting a weld, hold the nozzle about ¼ to ½ in. (6 to 12 mm) above and parallel to the base material. Hold the rod at a right angle to the work. Position the cut end of the rod at the beginning of the weld.

Direct the hot air from the tip alternately at the rod and the base material. Concentrate the heat more on the rod when starting to weld. Keep the rod lined up and press it into the seam. Light pressure is sufficient.

Once the rod begins to stick to the plastic, start to move the torch and use the heat to control the flow. After you start your weld, direct more of the heat into the base material. Be careful NOT to melt or char the plastic. As the welding continues, a small bead should form along the entire weld joint.

As you plastic weld and use up the rod, you must regrip the rod. Unless done carefully, you will lift the rod away from the weld. This will allow air to be trapped under the weld, weakening it. To prevent this, you must develop the skill of continuously applying pressure on the rod while repositioning

your fingers. This can be done by applying pressure with your third and fourth fingers while moving the thumb and first finger up the rod.

At the end of a weld, maintain pressure on the rod as the heat is removed. Hold the rod still for a few seconds to make sure it has cooled and does NOT pull loose. Then carefully cut the rod with a sharp knife or clippers.

Do NOT attempt to pull the rod from the joint after making the weld. About 15 minutes cooling time is needed for rigid plastic and 30 minutes for thermoplastics.

Smooth the weld area by grinding with No. 36 grit sandpaper. Excess plastic can be removed with a sharp knife before grinding. When grinding, do NOT overheat the weld area because it will soften. Use water to cool the plastic while grinding, if needed.

After rough grinding, check the weld visually for defects. Any voids or cracks are unacceptable. Bending should NOT produce any cracks. A good plastic weld is as strong as the part itself!

The weld area can be finish sanded using 220 grit sandpaper followed by a 320 grit. Either a belt or orbital sander may be used, plus hand sanding as required. If refinishing is to be done, follow the procedure designed specifically for plastics.

PLASTIC SPEED WELDING

As mentioned, *plastic speed welding* uses a specially designed tip to produce a more uniform weld and at a high rate of speed. You must preheat both the rod and base material. The rod is preheated as it passes through a tube in the speed tip. The base material is preheated by a stream of hot air passing through a vent in the tip.

A pointed shoe on the end of the tip applies pressure on the rod. You do not have to apply pressure to the rod. The shoe smoothes out the rod, creating a more uniform appearance in the finished weld. On panel work, speed welding is commonly used.

With speed plastic welding, the conventional two-hand method is replaced by a faster and more uniform one-hand operation. Once started, the rod is fed automatically into the preheat tube as the welding torch is pulled along the joint. Speed tips are designed to provide the constant balance of heat and pressure. The average welding speed is about 40 in. per minute (1,000 mm per minute).

Following are some techniques essential for quality speed welding.

1. Hold the speed torch like a dagger. Bring the tip over the starting point a full 3 inches (75 mm) from the base material. You do not want the hot air to affect the part.

2. Cut the welding rod at a 60-degree angle. Insert it into the preheat tube. Immediately place the pointed shoe end of the tip on the base material at the starting point.

3. Hold the torch perpendicular to the base material. Push the rod through until it stops against the base material at the starting point. If necessary, lift the torch slightly to allow the rod to pass under the shoe.

4. Keep a slight pressure on the rod and only the weight of the torch on the shoe. Then pull the torch slowly toward you to start the speed weld.

    Caution! Once the speed weld is started, do NOT stop. If you must pause for any reason, pull the speed tip off the rod immediately. If this is NOT done, the rod will melt into the preheat tube.

5. In the first inch or two (25–50 mm) of travel, push it into the preheat tube with slight pressure.

6. Once started, swing the torch to a 45-degree angle. The rod will now feed without a need for pressure. As the torch moves along, inspect the quality of the weld.

Controlling Speed Welding Rate

The angle between the torch and base material determines the *speed welding rate.* For this reason, hold the torch at a 90-degree angle when starting the weld.

Hold the torch at a 45-degree angle after you begin welding.

If the welding rate is too fast, bring the torch back to the 90-degree angle temporarily to slow it down. Then gradually move to the desired angle for proper welding speed.

Remember, once started, speed welding must be maintained at a fairly constant rate. The torch cannot be held still. To stop welding before the rod is used up, bring the torch back past the 90-degree angle and cut off the rod at the end of the shoe.

A good speed weld in a V-groove will have a slightly higher crown and more uniformity than the normal hand weld. It should appear smooth and shiny, with a slight bead on each side. For best results and faster welding speed, clean the shoe on the speed tip with a wire brush to remove any residue that might create drag on the rod.

AIRLESS MELT-FLOW PLASTIC WELDING

Melt-flow plastic welding is the most commonly used airless welding method. It can be utilized for both single-sided and two-sided repairs. Refer back to Figure 11–9 and Figure 11–10.

A typical melt-flow procedure is as follows:

1. With the welding rod in the preheat tube, place the flat shoe part of the tip in the V-groove.

2. Hold it in place until the rod begins to melt and flow out around the shoe.

3. A small amount of force is needed to feed the rod through the preheat tube. The rod will NOT feed itself. Care should be used NOT to feed it too fast.

4. Move the shoe slowly. Crisscross the groove until it is filled with melted plastic.

5. Work the melted plastic well into the base material, especially toward the top of the V-groove.

6. Complete a weld length of about 1 in. (25 mm) at a time. This will allow smoothing of the weld before the plastic cools.

PLASTIC STITCH-TAMP WELDING

Plastic stitch-tamp welding is used primarily on hard plastics, like ABS and nylon, to insure a good base/rod mix. It is also ideal to use these types of plastics.

After completing the weld using the melt-flow procedure, remove the rod. Turn the shoe over and slowly move the pointed end of the tip into the weld area to bond the rod and base material together. Stitch-tamp the entire length of the weld. After stitch-tamping, use the flat shoe part of the tip to smooth out the weld area.

SINGLE-SIDED PLASTIC WELDS

Single-sided plastic welds are used when the part cannot be removed from the vehicle. To make a single-sided weld, proceed as follows:

1. Set the temperature dial on the welder for the plastic being welded. Allow it to warm up to the proper temperature.

2. Clean the part by washing with soap and water, followed by a good plastic cleaner.

3. Align the break using aluminum body tape.

4. V-groove the damaged area 75 percent of the way through the base material. Angle or bevel back the torn edges of the damage at least ¼ in. (6 mm) on each side of the damaged area. Use a die grinder or similar tool.

5. Clean the preheat tube, and insert the rod. Begin the weld by placing the shoe over the V-groove and feeding the rod through. Move the tip slowly for good melt-in and heat penetration.

6. When the entire V-groove has been filled, turn the shoe over and use the tip to stitch-tamp the rod and base material together into a good mix along the length of the weld.

7. Resmooth the weld area using the flat shoe part of the tip, again working slowly. Then cool with a damp sponge or cloth.

8. Shape the excess weld build-up to a smooth contour, using a razor blade and/or abrasive paper.

TWO-SIDED PLASTIC WELDS

A *two-sided plastic weld* is the strongest type of weld because you weld both sides of the part. When making a two-sided weld, be sure to do the following:

1. Allow the welder to heat up. Then clean the preheat tube.

2. Clean the part with soap and water and plastic cleaner.

3. Align the front of the break with aluminum body tape, smoothing it out with a stiff squeegee or spreader.

4. V-groove 50 percent of the way through the backside of the panel.

5. Weld the backside of the panel using the melt-flow method. Move slowly enough to achieve good melt-in.

6. When finished, smooth the weld with the shoe.

7. Quick-cool the weld with a damp sponge or cloth.

8. Remove the tape from the front of the piece. V-groove deep enough that the first weld is penetrated by the second V-groove.

9. Weld the seam, filling the groove completely.

10. Use a razor blade or slow speed grinder to reshape the contour.

REPAIRING VINYL DENTS

Vinyl is a soft, flexible, thin plastic material often applied over a foam filler. Vinyl of foam construction is commonly used on interior parts safety. Common vinyl parts are the dash pads, armrests, inner door trim, seat covers, exterior roof covering. Dash pads or padded instrument panels are expensive and time consuming to replace. Therefore, they are perfect candidates for repair, Figure 11–11.

Most *dash pads* are made of vinyl-clad urethane foam to protect people during a collision. Surface dents in foam dash pads, armrests, and other padded interior parts are common in collision repair. These dents can often be repaired by applying heat as follows:

1. Soak the dent with a damp sponge or cloth for about half a minute. Leave the dented area moist.

2. Using a heat gun, heat the area around the dent. Hold the gun 10 to 12 in. (250 to 300 mm) from the surface. Keep it moving in a circular motion at all times, working from the outside in.

3. Heat the area to around 130°F (54°C). Do NOT overheat the vinyl or it will blister. Keep heating until the area is too uncomfortable to touch. If available, use a digital thermometer to meter the surface temperature.

4. Using gloves, massage the pad. Force the material toward the center of the dent. The area might have to be reheated and massaged more than once. In some cases, heat alone might repair the damage.

Figure 11–11 Study construction of typical dash pad.

5. When the dent has been removed, cool the area quickly with a damp sponge or cloth.

6. Apply vinyl treatment or preservative to the part.

WELDING VINYL-FOAM CUTS

To plastic weld a cut in vinyl-foam parts, a dash pad for example, proceed in the following manner:

1. Set up the welder for the proper temperature for welding urethane.

2. Wash the pad with soap and water, dry, and clean with plastic cleaner.

3. If the damaged area is brittle, warm it with a heat gun. If there are curled or jagged edges, cut them away.

4. V-groove at least ¼ in. (6 mm) into the foam padding. Bevel the edges as much as possible. Rough up the area for about ¼ in. (6 mm) around the V-groove.

5. Turn the welder so the shoe is facing up. Feed the rod slowly through the welder. Start the weld at the bottom of the groove. Completely fill it with melted plastic until it is flush with the surface.

6. Smooth out the excess rod build-up. Feather it out over the beveled edges for at least ¼ in. (6 mm) on each side of the groove.

7. Cool the weld and grind away any remaining excess rod build-up. Rough up the vinyl for about 2 in. (50 mm) beyond the weld on each side for good filler adhesion.

8. Use a flexible filler material designed for use on vinyl to get the desired contour. Allow the filler to cure.

9. Contour sand to remove the tacky glaze. If any filler is accidentally sanded through, apply a skim coat and re-sand.

10. Spray on a vinyl re-texture material to match the grain of the existing vinyl. Blend it out to a break or contour line on the cover. This will help hide the repair.

11. Mask and paint the entire part the correct color vinyl paint. For more information on vinyl painting, refer to the text index.

HEAT RESHAPING PLASTIC PARTS

Many bent, stretched, or deformed plastic parts, such as flexible bumper covers and vinyl clad foam interior parts, can often be straightened with heat. This is because of "plastic memory," which means the piece wants to keep or return to its original molded shape.

If it is bent or deformed slightly, it will return to its original shape if heat is applied.

To reshape a distorted bumper cover, use the following procedure:

1. Thoroughly wash the cover with soap and water.

2. Clean with plastic cleaner. Make sure to remove all road tar, oil, grease, and undercoating.

3. Dampen the repair area with a water soaked rag or sponge.

4. Apply heat directly to the distorted area. Use a concentrated heat source, such as a heat lamp or high-temperature heat gun. When the opposite side of the cover becomes uncomfortable to the touch, it has been heated enough.

> **WARNING!** *Do not overheat textured vinyl or you will damage the vinyl surface.*

5. Use a paint paddle, squeegee, or wood block to help reshape the piece if necessary.

6. Quick-cool the area by applying cold water with a sponge or rag.

PLASTIC BUMPER TAB REPLACEMENT

When a bumper cover has been torn away from its mounting screws, the mounting tabs will often be broken or torn away. Mounting tabs must be repaired with a two-sided weld to provide enough weld strength.

If the material is a thermoplastic, either the hot-air or airless method may be used. If the piece is a thermosetting plastic, airless welding must be used. If welded properly, the repaired piece will be as strong as the original, undamaged part.

The following is the procedure for rebuilding a mounting tab that has been torn off:

1. Begin by cleaning the piece as described before.

2. Bevel back the torn edges of the mounting tab at least ¼ inch (6 mm) on both sides.

3. Rough up the plastic and wipe dust free.

4. Use aluminum body tape to build a form in the shape of the missing tab. Turn the tape edges up to form the thickness of the new tab.

5. Set the temperature dial on the welder for the type of plastic being repaired. Allow the unit to warm up.

6. Begin the weld. Push the rod slowly through the preheat tube. Slightly overfill the form, working the melted plastic into the base material.

7. Smooth and shape the weld. Quick-cool the weld area.

8. Remove the tape. V-groove along the tear line on the other side about halfway through the piece.

9. Weld the groove and quick-cool. Finish the weld to the desired contour using a slow-speed grinder with a No. 60 or 80 grit disc.

ULTRASONIC STUD WELDING

Ultrasonic stud welding uses high frequency movement and friction to generate heat which bond plastic parts together. It can be used to join plastic parts at a single point or at numerous locations. In many applications, a continuous weld is NOT required. The welding cycle is short, almost always less than half a second.

Ultrasonic stud welding is made along the circumference of the stud. Its strength is a function of the stud diameter and the depth of the weld. Maximum tensile strength is achieved when the depth of the weld equals half the diameter of the stud.

ADHESIVE REPAIR SYSTEMS

Adhesive repair systems are of two types: cyanoacrylate (CA) and two-part. Two-part is the most commonly used.

Cyanoacrylates, or *CAs* are one-part, fast curing adhesives used to help repair rigid and flexible plastics. They are used as a filler or to tack parts together before applying the final repair material. CAs are sometimes known as "super glues." They can be a valuable tool for the repair of plastic parts. CAs set up very quickly.

Although one-part, an activating agent can be used to accelerate the bonding process of a CA. Care must be used NOT to apply too much activating agent. If too much is used, the product foams causing a weaker bond.

CAs do NOT work equally well on all plastics. There is no hard and fast rule. When CAs are used, be sure to use products from reliable suppliers and follow the manufacturer's guidelines for using them.

Two-part adhesive systems consist of a base resin and a hardener (catalyst). The resin comes in one container and the hardener in another. When mixed, the adhesive cures into a plastic material similar to the base material in the part. Two-part adhesive systems are an acceptable alternative to welding for many plastic repairs.

Not all plastics can be welded, while adhesives can be used in all but a few instances. If adhesive repair is chosen, you must first identify the type of plastic. A good way to do this is through a plastic flexibility test.

To do a plastic flexibility test, use your hands to flex and bend the part and compare it to samples of plastic. Compare the flexibilities. Use the repair material that most closely matches the characteristics of the part's base material.

USE THE CORRECT ADHESIVE!

WARNING! When working with an adhesive system, use the manufacturer's categories to decide on a repair product and procedure. There are many plastic and repair material variations. The car or truck manufacturer's manual is the most accurate source of information. The service manual will recommend products and procedures for the exact type of plastic in the part.

It is important to keep in mind that there are differences between manufacturers' repair materials. When using plastic repair adhesives, remember that:

1. Mixing product lines is NOT acceptable. Choose a product line and use it for the entire repair.

2. Most product lines have two or more adhesives designed for different types of plastic.

3. The product line usually includes an adhesion promoter, a filler product, and a flexible coating agent. Use each as directed.

4. Some product lines are formulated for a specific base material. For instance, one manufacturer offers individual products for use with each type of plastic (TPO, urethanes, or Xenoy for example), regardless of plastic flexibility.

A product line might use a single flexible filler for all plastics, or there might be two or more flexible fillers designed for different types of plastic.

TWO-PART PLASTIC ADHESIVE REPAIRS

Regardless of which manufacturer's products are used, two-part adhesive repairs share the common preparation steps:

1. Clean the part. First, use soap and water and then a plastic cleaner. See Figure 11–12.

Figure 11–12 A: Wipe part clean with plastic cleaner. B: Spray adhesion promoter will assure that repairs bond to part properly.

2. Make sure both the part and the repair material are at room temperature for proper curing and adhesion.

3. Mix the two parts of the adhesive thoroughly and in the proper proportions.

4. Apply the material within the time guidelines given in the product literature. Use heat if indicated by the manufacturer.

5. Follow the cure time guidelines given in the product literature. Regulated heat can speed curing.

6. Support the part adequately during the cure time to ensure that the damaged area does NOT move before the adhesive cures. This would weaken the repair.

7. Follow the product literature for guidelines on when to reinforce a repair.

An *adhesion promoter* is a chemical that treats the surface of the plastic so the repair material will bond properly. Some plastics (TPO, PP, and E/P, for example) require an adhesion promoter. There is a simple test to perform that indicates whether or NOT the plastic will require an adhesion promoter. Lightly sand a hidden spot on the piece, using a high-speed grinder and No. 36 grit paper.

If the material gives off dust, it can be repaired with a standard structural adhesive system. If the material melts and smears or has a greasy or waxy look, then you must use an adhesion promoter. Many plastic fillers and adhesives contain an adhesion promoter. Check their labels.

In Figure 11–13, read the step-by-step procedure for repairing a flexible plastic part with two-part adhesive.

Here is a typical way to use a two-part epoxy adhesive to repair a flexible bumper cover:

1. Clean the entire cover with soap and water. Wipe or blow-dry. Then clean the surface with a good plastic cleaner.

2. V-groove the damaged area. Then grind about a 1½-in. (38 mm) taper around the damage for good adhesion and repair strength.

3. Use a sander with No. 180 grit paper to featheredge the paint around the damaged area. Then blow off the dust. Depending on the extent of the damage, the backside might need reinforcement. To do this, use steps 4 through 6.

4. To reinforce the repair area, sand and clean the backside of the cover with plastic cleaner. Then, if needed, apply a coat of adhesion promoter.

5. Dispense equal amounts of both parts of the flexible epoxy adhesive. Mix them to a uniform color. Apply the material to a piece of fiberglass cloth using a plastic squeegee.

6. Attach the plastic saturated cloth to the backside of the bumper cover. Fill in the weave with additional adhesive material.

7. With the backside reinforcement in place, Figure 11–14, apply a coat of adhesion promoter to the sanded repair area on the front side. Let the adhesion promoter dry completely.

8. Fill in the area with adhesive material. Shape the adhesive with your spreader to match the shape of the part. Allow it to cure properly.

9. Rough grind the repair area with No. 80 grit paper, then sand with 180 grit, followed by smoother 240 grit.

10. If additional adhesive material is needed to fill in a low spot or pinholes, be sure to apply a coat of adhesion promoter again.

A

Chamfel edges

B

Taper Edges

C

Part B

Mix thoroughly

D

Clamp parts in alignment if applicable

E

Rough Shape Adhesive

F

G

Figure 11–13 Study basic steps for repairing flexible plastic part with two-part adhesive. A: Lower flexible plastic cover has been torn. Clean part first. B: Die grinder will quickly cut groove in tear. C: Use grinder to bevel edges of tear. D: Mix adhesive in correct, usually equal, proportions. E: Use locking pliers or other means to hold repair in position. F: Rough sand repair to match contour of part. G: Apply another layer of repair material and fine sand until smooth.

**Adhesive Bond Backup
Patch on Large Holes**

Flexible
Plastic Part

Two-Part
Adhesive

Figure 11–14 On larger holes, a backup patch is needed to support repair material. Patch or backup is bonded to back of part. Then, repair material is applied to front to finish repair.

TWO-PART ADHESIVE DASH REPAIR

Some two-part adhesive products are made for dash pad repair. A typical repair procedure is as follows:

1. Thoroughly clean the part.
2. Sand or grind away the broken or loose vinyl covering to get to the foam beneath. A V-groove need NOT be used.
3. Apply the adhesive material according to the manufacturer's directions. Make sure the recommended cure times are followed.
4. After curing, sand or grind to contour. Apply a skim coat of adhesive if necessary. Allow the adhesive to cure. Then block sand with medium grit paper, followed by fine paper.
5. Apply a sealer. Then spray re-texture to as much area as needed to hide the repair.
6. Refinish the whole part as per paint system recommendations.

> *WARNING!* Some dash pad damage might be the result of age and exposure to sunlight. In these cases, repairs will NOT work. To check for this condition, press on the pad to flex the vinyl covering near the damage. If more cracks appear, it is beyond repair and should be replaced.

PLASTIC FLAME TREATING

Plastic flame treating uses a torch flame to oxidize and chemically prepare the plastic for adhesion. The purpose is not to heat or melt the surface. Flame treating is used to replace the action of adhesion promoters. Immediately following flame treatment, complete the repair using methods described earlier for a two-part adhesive. Do not touch and contaminate the plastic while using the adhesive.

REINFORCED PLASTIC REPAIRS

Reinforced plastic—including *sheet molded compound (SMC), fiber-reinforced plastic (FRP),* and *reinforced reaction injection molded polyurethane (RRIM)*—parts are being used in many unibody vehicles. They provide a durable plastic skin over a steel unibody. The table in Figure 11–15 provides an overview of reinforced plastic repair materials.

The damage that generally occurs in reinforced plastic panels includes:

1. One-sided damage, such as a scratch or gouge.
2. Punctures and fractures.
3. Panel separation, where the panel pulls away from the metal space frame.
4. Severe damage, which requires full or partial panel replacement.
5. Minor bends and distortions of the space frame, which can be repaired by pulling and straightening.
6. Severe kinks and bends to the space frame, which require replacement of that piece along factory seams or by sectioning.

Remember! Combinations of these types of damage often occur on a single vehicle. Depending on the location and amount of damage, there are four different types of repairs. These are:

REINFORCED PLASTIC REPAIR MATERIAL SELECTION CHART					
Type of Repair	Applicable Repair Product				
	Panel Adhesive	Patching Adhesive	Structural Filler	Cosmetic Filler	Glass Fiber Reinforcement
Panel Replacement	X				
Panel Sectioning	X		X$_1$	X$_1$	X
One-Sided Repairs				X$_1$	
Two-Sided Repairs	X$_2$	X$_2$	X	X	X

Notes: 1. Some panel adhesives can also be used as structural and cosmetic fillers, depending on sanding characteristics.
2. Panel adhesives can also be used as patching adhesives, but not vice versa.

Figure 11–15 Study reinforced plastic repair chart. It gives recommended repairs and materials.

1. Single-sided repair.
2. Two-sided repair.
3. Panel sectioning.
4. Full panel replacement.

To select a repair method, thorough examination of the vehicle is required. Examine all affected reinforced plastic panels. First, check the entire panel for signs of damage. Also check all panel seams for adhesive bond failure. Examine the back of the panel to determine the extent of the damage.

REINFORCED PLASTIC ADHESIVES

Many of the materials that are used for reinforced plastic repair are two-part adhesive products. Two-part adhesive means a base material and a hardener must be mixed to cure the adhesive. Each must be mixed together in the proper ratio. Both parts must be thoroughly mixed together before use.

Work life or *open time* is the time when it is still possible to disturb the adhesive and still have the adhesive set up for a good bond. This work life time will be provided by the manufacturer. The cure time of some adhesives used in reinforced plastic repair can be shortened with the application of heat. Temperature and humidity can affect work life and cure time.

After mixing, remember that each product has a work life or open time. If you move or disturb the adhesive as it starts to harden, you will adversely affect its durability.

REINFORCED PLASTIC, FILLERS AND GLASS CLOTH

Two filler products are specifically formulated for use on reinforced plastic. They are cosmetic filler and structural filler.

Cosmetic filler is typically a two-part epoxy or polyester filler used to cover up minor imperfections. Do NOT use fillers designed for sheet metal on reinforced plastic.

Structural filler is used to fill the larger gaps in the panel structure while maintaining strength. Structural fillers add to the structural rigidity of the part.

All two-part products will shrink to some degree. The use of heat will help to speed the drying time and will eliminate some of the shrinkage.

Check with the product manufacturer for temperatures and dry times. If the product is NOT properly heated to a full cure, shrinkage will occur as the product cures with time. The "rule of thumb" is to heat the material to a surface temperature higher than any temperatures that the vehicle will be subject to when it is on the road. If it is a black vehicle sitting in the sun in mid-summer in Florida, this could be about 170°F (77°C) or more.

Check with the product manufacturer for recommendations for heat curing. Generally, 200° to 250°F (93° to 121°C) for 20 to 40 minutes should do it. Remember that at lower temperatures, the product will have to be heated longer. Also, if there is high humidity, the cure process will take longer.

There are several different types of glass cloth available. Rovings and mattings are NOT appropriate for reinforced plastic repair. Choose unidirectional cloth, woven glass cloth, or nylon screening. The cloth weave must be loose enough to allow the adhesive to fully saturate the cloth, leaving no air space around the weave. See Figure 11–16.

REINFORCED PLASTIC, SINGLE-SIDED REPAIRS

Single-sided damage is surface damage that does NOT penetrate or fracture the rear of the panel. Damage might pass all the way through a panel, but no pieces of the panel have broken away. If the break is clean and all of the reinforcing fibers have stayed in place, then a single-sided repair would be adequate.

For a single-sided repair, you must bevel deep to penetrate the fibers in the panel. The broken fibers must come into contact with the adhesive.

The following is a typical single-sided repair procedure for reinforced plastic:

1. Clean the repair area with soap and water.
2. Clean again using mild wax and grease remover.
3. Remove any paint from the surrounding area by sanding with No. 80 grit sandpaper.
4. Scuff sand the area surrounding the damage.
5. Bevel the damage to provide an adequate area for bonding.
6. Mix two-part filler according to the manufacturer's instructions.
7. Apply the filler and cure as recommended.

Once the filler has been sanded, apply additional coats as required and resand. The product manufacturer will provide grit recommendations.

Fiberglass mat   Fiberglass cloth

Figure 11–16 Fiberglass mat or roving has random layer of strands. Fiberglass cloth is woven and is recommended for repairs of reinforced plastics.

TWO-SIDED REPAIRS OF REINFORCED PLASTIC

A two-sided repair is normally needed on damage that passes all of the way through the panel. This would include damage to the reinforcing fibers.

A *backing strip* or *backing patch* is bonded to the rear of the repair area to restore the reinforced plastic's strength. The patch also forms a foundation for forming the exterior surface to match the original contour of the panel.

To make a two-sided repair in a reinforced plastic panel, proceed as follows:

1. Clean the surface surrounding the damage with a good wax and grease remover. Use a No. 36 grinding disc to remove all paint and primer at least 3 in. (75 mm) beyond the repair area.
2. Grind, file, or use a hacksaw to remove all cracked or splintered material away from the hole on both the inside and outside of the repair area.
3. Remove any dirt, sound deadener, and the like from the inner surface of the repair area. Clean with reducer, lacquer thinner, or a similar solvent.
4. Scuff around the hole with No. 80 grit paper to provide a good bonding surface.
5. Bevel the inside and outside edge of the repair area about 30 degrees to permit better patch adhesion.
6. Clean the repair area thoroughly.
7. Cut several pieces of fiberglass cloth large enough to cover the hole and the scuffed area. The exact number of pieces will depend on the thickness of the original panel.
8. Prepare a mixture of resin and hardener. Follow the label recommendations.
9. Using a small paintbrush, saturate at least two layers of the fiberglass cloth with the activated resin mix, Figure 11–17.
10. Apply the material to the inside or back surface of the repair area. Make sure the cloth fully contacts the scuffed area surrounding the hole.
11. Saturate three more layers of cloth with the mix. Apply it to the outside surface. These layers must also contact the inner layers and the scuffed outside repair area.
12. With all of the layers of cloth in place, form a saucer-like depression in them. This is needed to increase the depth of the repair material. Use a squeegee to work out any air bubbles.
13. Clean all tools with a lacquer thinner immediately after use.

Figure 11–17 To make a filler patch, use layers of structural adhesive with fiberglass cloth as shown. Waxed paper will allow you to pick up and apply patch to part. It can then be pulled off. *(I-CAR)*

14. Let the saturated cloth patch become tacky. An infrared heat lamp can be used to speed up the process. If one is used, keep it 12 to 15 in. (300 to 375 mm) away from the surface. Do NOT overheat the repair area because too much heat will cause distortion.

15. With No. 50 grit paper, disc sand the patch slightly below the contour of the panel.

16. Prepare more resin and hardener mix. Use a plastic spreader to fill the depression in the repair area. You need a sufficient layer of material for grinding down smooth and flush.

17. Allow the patch to harden. Again, a heat lamp can be used to speed the curing process.

18. When the patch is fully hardened, sand the excess material down to the basic contour. Use No. 80 grit paper and a sanding block. Finish sand with No. 120 or finer grit paper.

There are several ways to hold the patch in place from the front side of the panel. One method is to use a pull rod. Drill a hole in the middle of the patch. Insert the end of the rod. Position the patch, and pull it snug with the pull rod. Apply heat using a heat gun on the front, or have someone else apply the heat to the back of the patch.

This same two-sided repair can be made by attaching sheet metal to the backside of the panel with sheet metal screws. Sand the sheet metal and both sides of the part to provide good adhesion. Before fastening the sheet metal, apply resin and hardener mix to both sides of the rim of the hole. Follow the procedures described earlier for the remainder of the repair.

When the inner side of the hole is NOT accessible, apply a fiberglass patch to the outer side only. After the usual cleaning and sanding operations, apply several additional layers of fiberglass cloth to the outer side of the hole. Before it dries, make a saucer-like depression in the cloth to provide greater depth for the repair material.

REINFORCED PLASTIC PANEL REMOVAL AND REPLACEMENT (R&R), SECTIONING

Proper sectioning requires that you understand which areas are most appropriate for sectioning. You must also know how to avoid problems with horizontal bracing, rivets, and concealed parts.

The replacement panel used will depend on the amount and location of the damage. Using the left rear quarter panel as an example, there are three possibilities. The entire panel can be ordered, or simply a front, or rear half.

Remember that reinforced plastic is a very forgiving and workable material. Just because quarter panels come split at the wheel well, the sectioning point does NOT have to be located there. With proper backing strips to reinforce the joints, sectioning can be done almost anywhere.

The *mill and drill pads* are used to help the factory hold panels in place while the adhesive cures. These mill and drill pads will also help you to hold, align, and level replacement panels. If a panel is to be sectioned, it should be done between mill and drill pad locations.

REMOVING PLASTIC REINFORCED PANELS

First, remove the interior trim to locate the horizontal bracing and mill and drill pads. Examine the back of the panel to gauge the extent of panel damage. Also determine the location of the horizontal bracing, mill and drill pads, and electrical and mechanical components.

Once the interior trim is removed, a "window" can be cut. Controlling the depth of the cut is very important. Space frame components, as well as electrical lines and heating/cooling elements, may be located behind the panels. When cutting the window, know what is behind the panel being cut into, or limit the depth of the cut to ¼ inch (6 mm) to avoid doing damage.

Now that the window has been cut, the rest of the panel can be removed from the space frame. This can be done using heat and a putty knife, or by carefully using an air chisel. Choose a flat chisel, beveled on one side only. Be careful NOT to damage the space frame.

If the door surround panels are to be left attached to the vehicle, the air chisel method may NOT be the best choice for separating the seam between two panels. Use the heat and putty knife method to separate the seams to avoid doing damage to the door surround pieces.

The adhesive bond must be broken to remove the remaining quarter panel. Using approximately 400°F (202°C), heat the outboard section of the panel. Concentrate the heat in the area of the bond. Heat a span of about 5 to 7 in. (125 to 175 mm). After a short time, the adhesive will soften. Then the panel can be removed using a panel cutter, chisel, or pry bar. More than one person may be needed to assist in the heating and prying operations. Apply the heat and pry at the same time.

As shown in Figure 11–18, there is sometimes a horizontal panel reinforcement. It can be made of reinforced plastic and is bonded to the back of the panel. This reinforcement contains the mill and drill pad bolts and acts as a spacer to hold the panel in its correct place. When replacing a panel, use this reinforcement as a sectioning point and anchoring point for the new panel. Leave several inches of the reinforcement bonded to the space frame. Determine the sectioning location. Make the cut, using extra care to avoid cutting through the reinforcement. Cut through the outer panel only at the sectioning location.

Decide how much of the reinforcement will be kept. Make a cut on the scrap side of the panel. Cut through both the panel and reinforcement. Remove the scrap panel in the usual way. Then remove the strip of panel left attached to the reinforcement.

On the replacement panel, mark off the corresponding piece of panel reinforcement that must be removed to fit the panel. Be cautious when estimating how much reinforcement must be removed from the replacement panel. Leave enough reinforcement to enable the part to be trimmed to fit.

FITTING PLASTIC REINFORCED PANELS

After removing the scrap panel, prepare the space frame for the new panel. First, remove the old adhesive from the space frame. In some cases, the adhesive can just be peeled away from the frame. You may also have to use heat and a putty knife or a sander. Remove all of the adhesive since the heat will beak down the adhesive.

Bevel the outside edges of the existing panel to a 20-degree taper. Sand and clean the backsides of the panel where the backing strips will be attached. Backing strips are made using scrap material which duplicates the original panel contour as closely as possible. They should extend about 2 in. (50 mm) beyond either side of the sectioning location. Clean the backing strips. Remove the paint from those places where adhesive will be applied.

Measure the replacement panel for fit. Trim the panel to size. Check the fit again. Leave a ½ in. (12

Figure 11–18 Reinforced plastic panels are normally bonded over steel unibody structure. Reinforcements are also located behind the plastic pads.

mm) gap between the existing panel and the replacement panel. When proper fit has been established, the new panel can be prepared for the adhesive. Sand or grind bevels into the panel where they mate to the existing panel.

Bevel the mating edges of the new panel to a shallow taper, just like on the existing panel. Make sure to bevel all of the way through the panel. Do NOT leave a shoulder.

Apply the adhesive material in a continuous bead all of the way around the panel. Make sure the bead is ⅜ to ½ in. (9 to 12 mm) in diameter. Check for horizontal bracing, and apply a bead of adhesive to correspond with it. Then fit the panel onto the vehicle and clamp it into place. Install the mill and drill pad nuts and tighten securely.

The work life will be recommended by the adhesive manufacturer. This time should be followed to ensure that the proper fit has been achieved.

USING MOLDED CORES

A *molded core* is a curved body repair part made by applying plastic repair material over a part and then removing the cured material. Naturally, holes are much more difficult to repair in a curved portion of a reinforced plastic panel than those on a flat surface. Basically, the only solution (short of purchasing a new panel section) is to use the molded core method of replacement. This is often the quickest and cheapest way to repair a curved surface.

1. Locate an undamaged panel on another vehicle that matches the damaged one. It will be used as a model or pattern. A new or used vehicle can be used since it will NOT be harmed.

2. On the model vehicle, mask off an area slightly larger than the damaged area. Apply additional masking paper and tape to the surrounding area, especially on the low side of the panel. This will prevent any resin from getting on the finish.

3. Coat the area with paste floor wax. Leave a wet coat of wax all over the surface. A piece of waxed paper can be substituted for the coat of wax. Make sure the waxed paper is taped firmly in place.

4. Cut several pieces of thin fiberglass mat in sizes large than the area to be repaired.

5. Mix the fiberglass resin and hardener following the label instructions.

6. Starting from one corner of the mold area, place pieces of fiberglass mat on the waxed area so each edge overlaps the next one; use just one layer of matting.

7. Apply the resin/hardener to the matting with a paintbrush. Force the mixture into the curved surfaces and around corners with the tips of the bristles.

8. Use the smaller pieces of matting along the edges and on difficult curves. Additional resin/hardener can be applied if needed, brushing in one direction only to force the material into the indentations. In all cases, use only one layer of matting.

9. After matting has been applied to the entire waxed area, allow the molded core to cure a minimum of one hour.

10. Once the molded core has hardened, gently work the piece loose from the model vehicle. The core should be an exact reproduction of this section of the panel.

11. Remove the wax or waxed paper from the model vehicle. Then polish this section of the panel.

12. Since the molded core is generally a little larger than the original panel, place it under the damaged panel and align. If necessary, trim down the edges of the core and the damaged panel slightly where needed for better alignment. The edges of the damaged panel and core must also be cleaned.

13. Using fiberglass adhesive, cement the molded core in place on the inside of the panel. Allow the core and panel to cure.

14. Grind back the original damaged edges to a taper or bevel, maintaining the desired contour.

15. Lay a fiberglass mat, soaked in resin/hardener, on the taper or bevel and over the entire core. Once the mat has hardened, level it with a coat of fiberglass filler. Then prepare it for painting.

In some instances it might NOT be possible to place the core on the inside of the damaged panel. In this case, the damaged portion must be cut out to the exact size of the core. After the panel has been trimmed and its edges beveled, tabs must be installed to support the core from the inside. These tabs can be made from pieces of the panel or from fiberglass strips saturated in resin/hardener.

After cleaning and sanding the inside sections, attach the tabs to the inside edge of the panel and bond with fiberglass adhesive. Clamping pliers can be used to hold the tabs in place. Taper the edge of the opening and place the core on the tabs. Fasten the core to the tabs with fiberglass adhesive. Grind down any high spots so that layers of fiberglass mat can be added.

Place the saturated mats over the core, extending about 1½ to 2 in. (38 to 50 mm) beyond the damaged area in all directions. Work each layer with a spatula or squeegee to remove all air pockets. Additional resin/hardener can be added with a paintbrush to secure the layers. Allow sufficient curing time. Then sand the surface level. For a smooth surface, use fiberglass filler to finish the job.

REPAIRING RRIM

Reinforced reaction injection molded (RRIM) is a two-part polyurethane composite plastic. Part A is the isocyanate. Part B contains the reinforced fibers, resins, and a catalyst. The two parts are first mixed in a special mixing chamber, then injected into a mold. RRIM parts are becoming more common in fenders and bumper covers.

Since RRIM is a thermosetting plastic, heat (100° to 140°F or 37° to 59°C) is applied to the mold to cure the material. The molded product is made to be stiff yet flexible. It can absorb minor impacts without damage. This makes RRIM an ideal material for exposed areas.

Gouges and punctures can be repaired using a structural adhesive. If the damage is a puncture that extends through the panel, a backing patch is required. To make a typical backing patch repair, proceed as follows:

1. Clean the damaged area thoroughly using the plastic cleaner recommended by the manufacturer and a clean cloth. Wipe dry.

2. Remove any paint film in and around the damage with an orbital sander and No. 180 grit disc.

3. Using a No. 50 grit disc, enlarge the damaged area, tapering out the damage for about 1 in. (25 mm). Wipe or blow away any loose particles.

4. Clean the backside of the damaged area with the plastic cleaner.

5. Use a No. 50 grit disc to scuff sand the area. Extend the area to about 1½ inches (38 mm) beyond the damage. Align the front of the panel with body tape, if necessary.

6. Cut a piece of fiberglass cloth to cover the damaged area and the part of the panel that has been scuff sanded.

7. Mix the adhesive according to the manufacturer's recommendations. Apply a layer of adhesive to the backside of the panel about ⅛ inch (3 mm) thick.

8. Place the fiberglass patch into position on the adhesive. Cover it with a sheet of waxed paper. Use a roller to force the adhesive into the fibers of the patch.

9. Remove the waxed paper and add another layer of adhesive. Work out the adhesive to just beyond the edges of the patch. Allow the adhesive to cure following the manufacturer's recommendation.

10. Now move to the front side of the panel. Apply a layer of adhesive, completely covering the damaged area. Build it up to slightly higher than the surrounding contour. Allow it to cure.

11. Apply heat to help speed the cure of the patch.

12. Contour the adhesive to the adjoining surface by block sanding using No. 220 grit paper.

13. Finish by feathering with an orbital sander and a No. 320 disc.

14. Follow the recommendations given in Chapter 16 for priming and painting.

SPRAYING VINYL PAINTS

Vinyl repair paints are usually ready for spraying as packaged. Since application properties cannot be controlled with thinners or other additives, air pressure is an important factor.

When applying vinyl paints by siphon feed guns, the normal air pressure range is between 40 and 50 psi (2.8 and 3.5 K/cm²) at the gun. With pressure systems, the air pressure is reduced to 30 to 40 psi (2.1 to 2.8 K/cm²). Overspray can be controlled by decreasing the air pressure.

There is no retardant for vinyl paints. If blushing occurs, allow the initial coat to set up and reapply the color in a much lighter coat.

Vinyl and soft ABS plastics should be thoroughly cleansed with vinyl cleaner and allowed to dry. Then treat the surface with vinyl prep. *Vinyl prep* is a chemical solution that opens the pores of the vinyl material. Wipe off the vinyl prep right after it is applied. The surfaces are then ready for color and/or clearcoating.

Summary

- Plastics refers to a wide range of materials synthetically compounded from crude oil, coal, natural gas, and other substances. Bumpers, fender extensions, fascias, fender aprons, grille openings, stone shields, instrument panels, trim panels, fuel lines, and engine parts can be constructed of plastic.

- Two general types of plastics are used in automotive construction: thermoplastics and thermosetting plastics. Thermoplastics can be repeatedly softened and reshaped by heating with no change in their chemical makeup; thermosetting plastics undergo a chemical change and are hardened into a permanent shape that CANNOT be altered by reapplying heat or catalysts.

- One way to identify a plastic is by international symbols, or ISO codes, which are molded into plastic parts. If there is no ISO code, refer to the body repair manual for information. Finally, the burn test is an option, though it is no longer recommended for identifying plastics.

- Plastic welding uses heat and sometimes a plastic filler rod to join or repair plastic parts. The types of plastic welding include hot-air, airless, and ultrasonic.

Technical Terms

plastics	melt-flow plastic welding
thermoplastics	
thermosetting plastics	plastic stitch-tamp welding
composite plastics	
sheet molded compounds	single-sided plastic weld
fiber-reinforced plastics	two-sided plastic weld
ISO codes	vinyl
body repair manual	plastic memory
burn test	cyanoacrylates
plastic welding	two-part adhesive
hot-air plastic welding	adhesion promoter
airless plastic welding	plastic flame treating
ultrasonic plastic welding	work life
sonotrode	cosmetic filler
rod color code	structural filler
tack weld	backing strip
plastic speed welding	molded core
speed welding rate	RRIM
	vinyl prep

Review Questions

1. Define the term "plastics."

2. Technician A says the burn test is a reliable means of identifying plastics. Technician B says it is NOT. Who is correct?
   a. Technician A
   b. Technician B
   c. Both A and B
   d. Neither A nor B

3. In speed welding, the torch is held at a _____-degree angle to the base material to start the weld.

   a. 45
   b. 90
   c. 30
   d. 120

4. Explain the difference between a thermoplastic and a thermosetting plastic.

5. When Technician A grinds the base material, it melts and smears, so he or she uses an adhesion promoter to make the repair. Under the same circumstances, Technician B says that an adhesion promoter is NOT needed. Who is correct?
   a. Technician A
   b. Technician B
   c. Both A and B
   d. Neither A nor B

6. Why is plastic flame treating sometimes used?

7. A _____ _____ is a curved body repair part made by applying plastic repair material over a part and then removing the cured material.

8. The _____ and _____ _____ are used to help the factory hold panels in place while the adhesive cures.

9. What is a backing strip or patch?

10. Which of the following is the correct repair method for RRIM?
    a. Adhesive
    b. Welding
    c. Both a and b
    d. Neither a nor b

Activities

1. Inspect plastic body parts. Try to find an identification code on the back of each part. Make a report on the type of plastic used for different parts.

2. Make a one-side repair on a plastic part. Summarize the repair in a report. Describe the type of plastic, damage, and steps for repairing the part.

3. Visit a body shop. Talk to technicians about new methods of repairing plastics. Report your findings to the class.

CHAPTER 12

REPLACING HOODS, BUMPERS, FENDERS, GRILLES, AND LIDS

Objectives

After studying this chapter, you should be able to:

- Remove and install fenders.

- List the various methods for adjusting mechanically fastened panels.

- Perform hood-to-hinge, hood height, and hood latch adjustments.

- Remove, install, and adjust deck lids.

- Remove, install, and adjust bumpers.

- Replace grilles and other bolt-on body parts.

Introduction

A collision-damaged vehicle can require a variety of repair operations. Repair steps will depend on the nature and location of the damage. Panels with minor damage can often be straightened and filled with plastic. Minor bulges, dents, and creases can be fixed using the techniques discussed in earlier chapters. However, quite often the damage is too great and part replacement is the only logical answer.

This chapter covers replacement procedures for hoods, fenders, bumpers, deck lids, and similar bolt-on parts. As Figure 12–1 shows, many major parts bolt on to the vehicle.

Figure 12–1 Even with unibody designs, vehicles still have many bolt-on parts and panels. It is important that you know how to properly remove and replace them. *(Photograph provided courtesy of Mercedes-Benz North America, Inc.)*

HOW ARE PARTS FASTENED?

The methods of fastening parts to cars and trucks has changed in the past few years. Many parts that were held with bolts and screws in the past now snap into place. Plastic retainers now hold these parts onto the vehicle. This is done to save time during vehicle manufacturing. The part is simply pressed or "popped" into position on the assembly line.

Fastener variations can make repair more challenging, Figure 12–2. Parts can be held by screws, bolts, nuts, metal or plastic clips, adhesives, and other methods. To efficiently replace parts, you must carefully study part construction. Inspect parts closely to find out how they are held on the vehicle. This will let you make logical decisions on which parts to remove first, second, and so on, and the methods needed.

Keep in mind! On-the-job experience is the only way to become competent and fast at body part *R&R* (removal and replacement). Sometimes you must remove one part at a time. In other instances, it is bet-

Bumper cover

Mirror

Rear spoiler

Fog lights

Headlights

Fender

Door

Figure 12–2 Note some of the parts that bolt onto this unibody car. *(Courtesy of Mitsubishi Motor Sales of America, Inc.)*

ter to remove several parts as an assembly. This chapter will give you the background information to make this learning process easier.

REFER TO ESTIMATE

When starting work, refer to the estimate to get guidance on where to begin. The estimator will have determined which parts need repair and which should be replaced. Use this information and shop manuals to remove and replace parts efficiently.

The estimate is an important reference tool for doing repairs. It must be followed. The insurance company and estimator have both determined which parts must be repaired. If you fail to follow the estimate, the insurance company might not pay for your work.

The estimate is also used to order new parts. You may want to make sure all ordered parts have arrived. Compare new parts on hand with the parts list. If anything is missing, have the parts person order them. This will save time and prevent your stall from being tied up waiting for parts.

WHERE TO START?

Generally, start removing large, external parts first. For example, if the front end has damage, you must remove the hood first. This will give you more room to access rear fender bolts. This will also allow more light into the front for finding and removing hidden bolts in the frontal area. Use this kind of logic to remove parts efficiently.

If in doubt about how to remove a part, refer to the vehicle's service manual. Factory service manuals normally have a body repair section. The *body repair section* of the manual explains and illustrates how parts are serviced. The manual will give step-by-step instructions for the specific make and model vehicle. It will give bolt locations, torque values, removal sequences, and other important information.

As one example of a repair variation, look at Figure 12–3. The rear quarter panels on this car bolt in place. Most cars have welded quarter panels. This car also has aluminum body panels that must be repaired differently than steel.

HOOD REMOVAL AND REPLACEMENT

The *hood* provides an external cover over the front of the vehicle. It is one of the largest, heaviest panels on a car or truck. In a front-engine vehicle, it provides

Figure 12–3 Hood, deck lid, fenders, and doors commonly bolt onto unibody. A unique design, rear quarter panels also bolt on with this rear-engine, high performance, aluminum bodied car. (© American Honda Motor Co., Inc.)

access to the engine compartment. With a rear-engine car, it serves as a trunk lid.

Before removing the hood, analyze part conditions. Open and close the hood. Check for binding and bent hinges. If applicable, inspect hood alignment with the fenders and cowl. This will help you determine what must be done during repairs.

To remove a hood, first disconnect any wires and hoses. Wires often connect to an underhood light. Hoses might run to the hood for the windshield washer system. Refer to Figure 12–4.

Next, remove the hood hinge bolts. If the hood is not badly damaged and will be reused, mark hood hinge alignment. To mark the hood, make alignment marks around the sides of the hood hinge where it contacts the hood. You may also want to mark the hinge where it mounts on the body. You can then use these marks to rough adjust the hinges and hood during reinstallation. See Figure 12–5.

To prevent part damage, have someone help you hold the hood. Place your shoulder under the hood while holding the bottom edge of the hood with one hand. This will keep the hood from sliding down and hitting the cowl or fenders. Use your shoulder to support the weight of the hood. With your free hand, remove the hood bolts. Your helper should do the same. Do not let the weight of the hood rest on the bolts as you loosen them.

Figure 12–4 Study the parts of typical hood assembly and cable hood release mechanism. (© American Honda Motor Co., Inc.)

WARNING! *Do not make the mistake of removing the hood bolts without you and someone else holding it securely. It is easy for the hood to slip and scratch the fenders or cowl. If these parts were not originally damaged, you will have to fix them on your own time.*

Note the location of any *hood hinge spacers* that help adjust the hood. If there is no major damage, you may need to reinstall the spacers in the same loca-

tions. Place the hood out of the way, where it will not fall over. Spacers are shown in Figure 12–4.

Hood Hinge Removal and Replacement

Hood hinges allow the hood to open and close while staying in alignment. They must hold considerable weight while keeping the hood open. They are often damaged in a frontal impact.

If badly bent, you will have to replace the hood hinges. If equipped with large coil springs, you may also have to install the old springs on the new hinges.

Figure 12–5 If hood is not heavily damaged and shifted out of alignment, mark the hood next to the hinges. This will save time when initially installing hood after other repairs. *(Courtesy of General Motors Corporation)*

A *hood hinge spring tool* should be used to stretch the spring off and on. It is a hooked tool that will easily pry the end of the spring off and on of its mount.

Danger! Hood hinges are very strong. Wear eye protection. Also keep your fingers away from the spring as it is stretched. Your fingers could be severely pinched and cut by this spring.

If needed, unbolt the hinges from the inner fender panels. Again, mark their alignment if the panels are not damaged. Install the new hinges. Snug the bolts down; do not tighten them. You will have to adjust the hood and hinges later.

Hood Adjustment

Install the hood in reverse order of removal. Again, have someone help you hold the hood while installing its bolts. Snug down but do not tighten the hood bolts. You will need to adjust the hood before tightening the bolts fully. A misaligned hood is shown in Figure 12–6.

WARNING! After installing the hood, close the hood slowly. If not centered, it could hit and dent the fenders. It may be a good idea to place tape over the fender edges to protect them.

Hood adjustments are made at the hinges, at the adjustable stops, and at the hood latch. You can adjust the hood up or down and forward or rearward. This allows you to align the hood with the fenders and cowl vertically and horizontally. The holes in the hinges are slotted. This allow the hinges to be raised or lowered at the cowl or fender and to allow the hood to be moved forward or rearward at the hinges.

Hood hinge adjustments control the general position of the hood in the fenders and the rear hood height. By loosening the hood-to-hinge bolts, you can move the front end of the hood right or left. You can also slide the hood to the front or back. Tighten them down when the hood is centered in the opening. You want an equal gap around the hood's perimeter. There should be enough of a gap at the back edge to clear the cowl panel. Refer to Figure 12–7A.

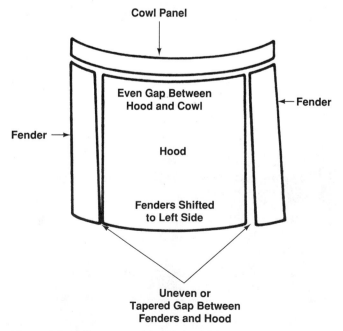

Figure 12–6 Gap around hood should be the same. Problems may be due to fenders out of alignment.

Figure 12-7 Study basic methods of adjusting a hood. *(Courtesy of Chrysler Corporation)* A: With hood-to-hinge bolts loose, shift hood as needed to position it on body. Align hood straight on body and obtain correct clearance at back of hood. B: Turn bumpers up or down to make front of hood level with fenders and other parts. C: Close hood slowly. Hood should not shift sideways when striker engages latch. Center latch in striker and adjust latch up or down to pull hood lightly down against bumpers.

By partially loosening the hinge-to-body bolts, you can raise or lower the rear height of the hood. Do not loosen the bolts too much or the weight of the hood will push the hinge all the way down. Tap on the hinges with a mallet to shift them as needed. The back of the hood should be level with the fenders and cowl when fully closed.

Generally, adjust the hood hinges so that the hood is centered in the fenders. Adjust it to have the proper gap around its perimeter. A *part gap* or *clearance* is the distance measured between two adjacent parts, hood-to-fender gap for example. Then, adjust the hinges to raise or lower the back of the hood.

The *hood stop adjustment* controls the height of the front of the hood. It is usually made up of rubber bumpers mounted on threaded studs. By loosening the locknut, you can rotate to raise or lower the stops and hood. Adjust the hood stops so that the hood is even with the front of the fenders and fascia. Tighten the locknuts after adjustment. See Figure 12-7B.

Hood Latch Removal, Replacement, and Adjustment

The *hood latch mechanism* keeps the hood closed and releases the hood when activated. Some hood latches are opened by moving a lever behind the grille. Most have a cable release that runs into the passenger compartment. All have slots for adjustment, Figure 12-7C.

A *cable hood release,* as shown in Figure 12-8, consists of:

1. The *hood release handle* can be pulled to slide a cable running out to the hood latch. It is normally mounted on the lower left side of the passenger compartment.

2. The *hood release cable* is a steel cable that slides inside a plastic housing. One end fastens to the release handle and the other to the hood latch.

3. The *hood latch* has metal arms that grasp and hold the hood striker. The spring-loaded arms lock over the hood striker when the hood is closed. When the cable release is pulled, the arms release the striker so the hood can open.

4. The *hood striker* bolts to the hood and engages the hood latch when closed.

To remove a hood latch, scribe mark its location if needed. Remove its bolts and disconnect any cable. Slots in the latch mount provide up and down and side to side adjustment.

Hood latch adjustment controls how well the hood striker engages the latch mechanism. Basically, with the hood centered and set at the right height, adjust the latch for proper closing.

Slowly lower the hood while watching to see if the striker centers itself in the latch. The hood should not pivot right or left when it engages the latch. If the hood moves to one side when closed, shift the latch right or left as needed.

The latch should also produce a slight downward compression of the rubber stops. This keeps the hood from bouncing up and down. If you must slam the hood down to engage the latch, raise the latch. If the hood will move up and down when latched, lower the latch.

After adjustment, tighten the latch bolts. Make sure it releases the hood properly. Always check the vehi-

Figure 12–8 Study parts and adjustment of hood release mechanism. (© American Honda Motor Co., Inc.)

cle's service manual for specific hood adjustment procedures.

BUMPER REMOVAL, REPLACEMENT, AND ADJUSTMENT

New vehicle *bumpers* are designed to withstand minor impact without damage. Bumpers used to be made of heavy chrome plated steel. They protect other parts from light impact with shear mass and bulk.

Now, bumper designs are light, yet strong. Many use an outer covering of flexible plastic with a heavy steel or aluminum inner bumper. Some have a plastic honeycomb or foam structure behind their flexible cover. The trend is also to a large one-piece cover over the lower front half of the vehicle nose. This is shown in Figure 12–9.

To remove a bumper, first disconnect the wiring going to any lights. Procedures vary so you may need to refer to a service manual. Some bolts can be hidden behind parking lights, inner fender panels, etc.

Bumpers can be heavy and clumsy. Before removing the last mounting bolts, support the bumper. Get a helper or use a floor jack. If they are to be repaired or reused, place a block of wood or piece of thick foam rubber on the jack saddle. Raise the jack to support the weight of the bumper. Remove the bolts. Then, you can work the bumper and jack away from the vehicle. These general procedures also apply to the rear bumper, Figure 12–10.

A

B

Figure 12–9 Note construction of modern bumper assemblies. A: Cutaway of rear bumper shows plastic honeycomb that backs up outer skin. *(1992 Saturn, Courtesy of Saturn Corporation)* B: A metal, often aluminum, inner bumper holds and supports out skin of bumper.

Bumper shock absorbers are used to absorb some of the impact of a collision and reduce damage. They will compress inward to help prevent bumper and other part damage during a low speed impact. One design is shown in Figure 12–11. When bumper shock absorbers are used, bolts or nuts on the shocks often hold the bumper in place.

With major front end damage, sometimes it is best to remove the large assemblies, like the front clip or bumper-spoiler assembly. This will let you gain access

Figure 12–10 Replacement of rear bumper is similar to that of front bumper. Always remember to disconnect all wires so they are not damaged when you lift bumper off. *(© American Honda Motor Co., Inc.)*

Figure 12–11 Some bumpers mount on shock isolator or energy absorber. It helps absorb impact energy to protect other parts from damage. *(Courtesy of Chrysler Corporation)*

to hard-to-reach parts on the assembly more easily. This may allow you to service damaged bumper, lights, brackets, and other front end parts in less time, Figure 12–12.

FENDER REMOVAL, REPLACEMENT, AND ADJUSTMENT

To remove a fender, find and remove all of the bolts securing it to the vehicle. Also remove any wires going to fender-mounted lights. Fenders are usually bolted to the radiator core support, inner fender panels, and cowl. Bolts are often hidden behind the doors, inner fender panels, and under the vehicle. Refer to Figure 12–13.

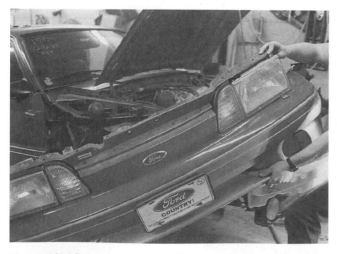

Figure 12–12 Sometimes it is efficient to remove bumper and related parts as an assembly. This makes it easier to transfer parts and access parts under assembly. *(Courtesy of Ford Motor Company)*.

With all of the bolts removed, carefully lift the fender off, Figure 12–14. Transfer any needed parts (trim, body clips, etc.) from the old fender over to the new fender.

Install the replacement fender in reverse order of removal. If the doors or cowl are undamaged, place masking or duct tape over their edges. This will protect their finish from scratches when installing the fender.

When installing the fenders, hand start the fender bolts. Do not tighten them. Leave the bolts loose enough that you can adjust the fender. Shift the fender on its bolts so that it aligns with other body parts properly. Shift the fender forward or backward until the fender, door, and cowl have the correct spacing or gap. Also adjust the fender in and out so that it is flush with the door and parallel with the hood. Tighten the fender bolts after you have the fender in alignment.

Fender shimming is an adjustment method that uses spacers under the bolts that attach the fender to the cowl or inner fender panel. By changing shim thicknesses, you can move the position of the fender for proper alignment.

Often the fender and hood adjustments must be made simultaneously to achieve a satisfactory result. The gap between fender and hood should be to factory specifications. The front of the fender and the hood should be aligned as well. The result will be even spacing all around the fender.

GRILLE REMOVAL AND REPLACEMENT

Grilles are often held in place with small screws and clips. You might have to remove a cover to access grill fasteners, Figure 12–15. An air ratchet is handy for reaching down and unscrewing grille bolts. When installing a grille, make sure all clips are undamaged and installed. Since most grilles are plastic, be careful to not overtighten any bolts or screws. You could crack the grille.

Most grilles can be adjusted. They have slotted or oversized holes in them, Figure 12–16. By leaving the bolts loose, you can shift and align the grille with other parts. Once aligned, tighten the grille fasteners slowly.

DECK LID REMOVAL, REPLACEMENT, AND ADJUSTMENT

The deck lid is very similar to the hood in construction. Two hinges connect the deck lid to the rear body panel. The trailing edge is secured by a locking latch.

Weatherstrip

Clip

Front Fender

Inner Fender

Figure 12–13 Fender bolts are located around outside of fender. Some are hidden behind inner fender panel or at rear behind front of door around cowl. (© American Honda Motor Co., Inc.)

A

J5-048

B

J5-411

Figure 12–14 Note basic methods for R&R of fender. (Courtesy of Chrysler Corporation) A: Bolts are often located at rear bottom of fender. B: Bumper had to be removed first before you could remove these fender bolts.

Figure 12-15 When servicing grille and other front end parts, you often have to remove a cover panel over front of vehicle. Small screws normally hold this cover. *(Courtesy of Chrysler Corporation)*

Figure 12-16 Most new grilles are made of plastic. Small clips and screws hold the grille in place. *(Courtesy of Chrysler Corporation)*

Deck lid or hatch door removal and replacement is similar to a hood. See Figure 12-17. The deck lid must be evenly spaced between the adjacent panels. Slotted holes in the hinges and/or caged plates in the deck lid allow it to be moved. To adjust the deck lid forward or rearward, slightly loosen the bolts on both hinges. Close and adjust the deck lid as required. Then raise the lid and tighten the bolts.

Weatherstripping is a rubber seal that prevents leakage at the joint between the movable part (lid,

hatch, door) and the body. To prevent air and water leaks, the deck lid must contact the weatherstripping evenly when closed. The latch must be adjusted so that it holds the lid or hatch closed against the weatherstripping.

Deck lids and hatches usually do not have exterior or interior door handle mechanisms. They operate with a key (or instrument panel switch on powered units) and lock mechanism.

Lock cylinders contain a tumbler mechanism that engages the key so that you can turn the key and disengage the latch. When you insert your key into a door or lid, it engages the lock cylinder. The lock cylinder then transfers motion to the latch.

The lock cylinder on door and deck lids is usually held on the panel with a retainer. A sealing gasket may also seal out water and dust. To remove a lock cylinder, pry the retainer sideways. This will free the lock cylinder. Sometimes, lock cylinders are held by small screws. If needed, lubricate a lock cylinder with dry powdered graphite.

Lid shock absorbers are usually spring-loaded, gas filled units that hold the lid open and cause it to close more slowly. The shocks often engage small ball sockets mounted on the body. The ends of the shocks snap-fit over the ball sockets. *Bad lid shock absorbers* will no longer support the weight of the lid. They should be replaced.

Lid torsion rods are spring steel rods used to help lift the weight of the lid. They extend horizontally across the body and engage a stationary bracket. Some torsion rod brackets have adjustment slots. You can change tension on the torsion rods by moving them in these slots. Refer to Figure 12-18.

PANEL ALIGNMENT

After installing all new body parts, you must check overall panel alignment. Make sure that clearance between parts is equal. As shown in Figure 12-19, the gap around all parts must be within specifications. Also check that all panel surfaces are even with each other. Take the time to double-check all panels to assure good alignment. This is a sign of a professional technician.

TRUCK BED REMOVAL AND REPLACEMENT

Truck beds are usually bolted to the frame. To remove the bed, simply remove the bolts that extend up through brackets on the frame. Keep track of bolt lengths and rubber mounting cushion locations. They

Tailgate Edge Cushion
Turn as Necessary, to
Make the Tailgate Fit
Flush with the Body at
Rear and Side.

Striker

Striker Adjustment
Adjust Tailgate Fit
to Gate Opening
by Moving Striker

Clip

Support Strut Mounting Bolt

Clip

Frame
Garnish

Frame
Garnish

High Mount
Brake Light

Bracket

Tailgate Lining

Tailgate

Clip

Grommet

Direction of
Harness Removal

Tailgate Support
Strut

Rear Shele

Mounting Bolt

Cover

Tailgate Mounting Bolts

Hinge

Hinge Mounting Nuts

Headliner

Figure 12–17 Study parts of rear hatch lid. (© American Honda Motor Co., Inc.)

must be reinstalled in their original locations. See Figure 12–20.

Truck tailgates mount on two hinges. A steel cable often limits how far down the tailgate will open, Figure 12–21. Latches in the sides of the tailgate engage strikers on the body. The handle on the outside of the tailgate moves small linkage rods that run out to the latches.

The tailgate hinges must be adjusted as described earlier for other parts. Generally, leave the hinge bolts loose while shifting the tailgate as needed. Then, tighten the hinge bolts and recheck adjustment.

> **WARNING!** *Truck tailgates are surprisingly heavy. Ask someone to help you when removing or installing one.*

INSTALLING SOUND-DEADENING PADS

Sound-deadening pads are often bonded to the inside surface of trunk cavities and doors to reducing noise,

Figure 12–18 Deck lids can also be held open by torsion rods. Some can be adjusted by moving location of rod in mount. (Courtesy of Ford Motor Company)

vibration, and harshness. Sound-deadening material is made of a plastic or asphalt-based material. It prevents the thin sheet metal panels from acting like large metal sounding drums to quiet the passenger compartment. The original factory material is bonded and, sometimes, heat formed to the surface.

■ **Danger!** Sound-deadening material is a combustible and must be removed from any area to be welded or flame cut.

During collision repair, sound-deadening pads must be replaced to match pre-accident performance. After repair, the area must be properly refinished to provide corrosion protection before the sound-deadening material is applied.

Some pads are available as factory service parts. Be sure to check the factory body repair manual for details. If a factory pad is not available, the sound-deadening qualities must be restored with a suitable replacement product. These should be available from several sources.

One sound-deadening product is available with an adhesive on the back. Cut it to size and shape. Peel off the backing, and apply. The sheets can be heated with a heat gun to make them flexible to conform to the contour of the sheet metal.

CUSTOM BODY PANELS

Custom body panels are aftermarket parts that alter the appearance of the vehicle. Customizing is a growing trend. Many vehicle owners, when faced with the need to replace damaged panels, spend the extra money to give their vehicles a performance facelift. They have a body shop install custom ground effects and spoilers.

Sometimes, the aftermarket custom parts cost no more than the original parts. A number of companies sell spoiler and air dam kits that enhance vehicle appearance.

NOTE! WARN CUSTOMERS THAT THEY MAY BE AFFECTING THEIR FACTORY WARRANTY BY INSTALLING AFTERMARKET PARTS.

Air dams improve aerodynamics by restricting air passing under the vehicle body, thus reducing turbulence and resistance to airflow. If designed properly, this can increase fuel economy.

A *rear spoiler* mounts on the deck lid to alter the airstream at the rear of the body to increase body down force. This helps rear wheel traction at highway speeds.

Spoilers, side skirts, air dams, and other aftermarket parts are commonly made from molded polyurethane plastic. Before installing them, clean the parts with a wax and grease remover. Then, scuff sand the parts with No. 240 grit sandpaper followed by No. 320 grit paper to improve adhesion.

Figure 12–19 After installing panels, double-check their fit. You want even gaps or clearances between all parts. (Illustration courtesy of Toyota Motor Sales, U.S.A., Inc.)

Figure 12-20 Truck bed normally bolts to full frame. After removing all bolts, wires, and other parts, bed can be lifted off frame. *(Courtesy of Chrysler Corporation)*

Figure 12-21 Truck tailgate is serviced like other hinged parts. It must align properly when closed and engage strikers properly. *(Courtesy of Chrysler Corporation)*

Most custom body panels utilize original fasteners. They simply bolt in place in the same way as the original panel. Double-sided adhesive tape is sometimes used to fit custom panels tightly against the original panels. To use double-sided tape, clean the area with wax and grease remover. Scuff sand the area to ensure a positive bond between the vehicle and the new panel.

When installing add-on panels, read and follow the kit instructions carefully.

Summary

- When starting work, refer to the estimate to get guidance on where to begin. The estimator will have determined which parts need repair and which should be replaced. Use this information to begin removal and replacement (R and R).

- Hood hinges allow the hood to open and close while staying in alignment. They must hold considerable weight while keeping the hood open. They are often damaged in a frontal impact.

- A cable hood release consists of the hood release handle, hood release cable, hood latch, and the hood striker.

- Bumpers today are designed to be light, yet strong. Many use an outer covering of flexible plastic with a heavy steel or aluminum inner bumper. Some have a plastic honeycomb structure behind their flexible cover. The trend is also to a large one-piece cover over the lower front half of the vehicle nose.

- Fender shimming is an adjustment method that uses spacers under the bolts that attach the fender to the cowl or inner fender panel. By changing shim thicknesses, you can move the position of the fender for proper alignment.

- After installing all new body parts, you must check overall panel alignment. Make sure that clearance between parts is equal and that the gap around all parts is within specifications.

- Custom body panels are aftermarket parts that alter the appearance of the vehicle.

Technical Terms

removal and repair	*hood release handle*
(R&R)	*hood release cable*
hood	*hood latch*
panel spacers	*hood striker*
hood hinges	*hood latch adjustment*
hinge spring tool	*bumpers*
hood adjustments	*bumper shock absorber*
part gap	*fender shimming*
hood stop adjustment	*weatherstripping*
hood latch mechanism	*lock cylinders*
cable hood release	*lid shock absorbers*

lid torsion rods
sound-deadening pads
custom body panels

air dam
rear spoiler

Review Questions

1. Many parts that were held with bolts and screws in the past now snap fit into place. True or false?

2. List five ways parts can be held together.

3. A vehicle has a badly damaged fender. The estimate says to "R and R" the fender. This means you should:
   a. remove and repair the fender.
   b. remove and replace the fender.
   c. replace and realign fender.
   d. None of the above

4. When starting work on a damaged vehicle, what would you do first?

5. Factory service manuals normally have a _____ _____ section that explains and illustrates how body parts are serviced.

6. How and why might you want to mark a hood before removal?

7. Where are hood adjustments made?

8. This adjustment controls the height of the front of the hood.

   a. Hinge-to-body adjustment
   b. Hinge-to-hood adjustment
   c. Hood stop adjustment
   d. None of the above

9. Describe the parts of a cable hood release.

10. Fender _____ is an adjustment method that uses spacers under the bolts that attach the fender to the cowl or inner fender panel.

11. What is the purpose of weatherstripping?

12. Bad lid _____ _____ will no longer support the weight of the lid. They should be replaced.

Activities

1. Inspect several cars. Determine if their bolt-on panels are adjusted properly. Is the gap between parts equal all the way around all panels? Make a report of your findings.

2. Using a service manual, summarize the procedures for removing a hood and fender from three different makes of cars. Write a report on how these procedures vary.

3. After getting instructor permission, loosen the bolts on a hood latch and hood. Move the hood and latch out of alignment. Adjust the hood and latch.

CHAPTER 13

SERVICING DOORS, GLASS, LEAKS

Objectives

After studying this chapter, you should be able to:

- R and R, and adjust a door.

- Replace both welded and adhesive-bonded door skins.

- Replace an SMC door skin.

- R and R, and adjust a door regulator.

- R and R a windshield.

- R and R other stationary glass.

- Find and fix air and water leaks.

- Describe gasket, full cutout, and partial cutout glass replacement procedures.

- Describe the basics of vent window and tailgate door glass service.

Introduction

Doors are the most used—and abused—parts of a vehicle. They are opened and closed thousands and thousands of times over the life of a car or truck. They must do this while still being strong enough to stay closed and protect the driver and passengers from injury during a collision. Doors must also seal out water and wind noise to keep the interior dry and quiet. Look at Figure 13–1.

Glass also plays an important role in the safety and appearance of a vehicle. Glass adds to structural integrity and visibility. Windshields, door glass, stationary glass, and related parts must all be serviced properly to keep the vehicle safe to drive.

This chapter will give you the most important information for working on these vital parts. It will give you the background needed to use service manual instructions and specifications effectively.

Figure 13–1 Phantom view of car shows intrusion beams in doors and large glass areas. Modern vehicles are much stronger and lighter than in the past to protect passengers from injury during a collision. *(Saab Cars USA, Inc.)*

DOORS

Door Construction

There are two basic door designs: framed doors and hardtop doors. *Framed doors* surround the sides and top of the door glass with a metal frame, helping keep the window glass aligned. The door frame seals against the door opening. *Hardtop doors* have the glass extending up out of the door without a frame around it. The glass itself must seal against the weatherstripping in the door opening.

Illustrated in Figure 13–2, the basic parts of a door include the:

1. *Door frame*—the main steel frame of the door. Other parts (hinges, glass, handle, etc.) mount on the door frame.

2. *Door skin*—the outer panel over the door frame. It can be made of steel, aluminum, fiberglass, or plastic.

3. *Door glass*—must allow good visibility out of the door.

4. *Door glass channel*—serves as a guide for the glass to move up and down. It is a U-shaped channel lined with a low friction material, felt for example.

5. *Door regulator*—a gear and arm mechanism for moving the glass. When you turn the window handle or press the window button, the regulator moves the glass up or down.

6. *Door latch*—engages the *door striker* on the vehicle body to hold the door closed.

7. *Inner and outer door handles*—use linkage rods to transfer motion to the door latch, allowing you to activate the latch to open the door.

8. *Door trim panel*—an attractive cover over the inner door frame. Various parts (inner handle, window buttons, speakers) can mount in the inner trim panel.

9. A plastic or paper *door dust cover* fits between the inner trim panel and door frame to keep out wind noise.

10. *Door weatherstripping* fits around the door or door opening to seal the door to body joint. When the door is closed, the weatherstripping is partially compressed to prevent air and water leaks.

11. *Rear view mirror* can often mount on the outside of the door frame. A remote mirror knob may provide mirror adjustment on the inner trim panel.

Door Adjustments

Doors must be accurately adjusted so that they close easily, do not rattle, and do not leak. The door hinges must be adjusted to hold the door in the center of its opening when closed. The door striker must be adjusted to engage the latch smoothly. This section will describe various door adjustments.

Adjusting Door Hinges. Doors must fit their openings and align with the adjacent body panels.

When the doors on a four-door sedan need adjusting, start at the rear door. Since the quarter panel cannot be moved, the rear door must be adjusted to it. Once the rear door is adjusted, the front door can then be adjusted to fit the rear door. Then, the front fender can be adjusted to fit the front door.

On hardtop models, the windows can be adjusted to fit the weatherstripping. Hardtop windows are usually adjusted starting with the front edge of the glass and working toward the back. The vent assembly or glass is adjusted to fit the front door pillar. The front window is then adjusted to it. The rear door window is adjusted to the front window rear edge and the opening for the rear door assembly.

Doors are attached to the body with hinges. The bolted hinge can be adjusted forward, rearward, up, and down easily. The use of shims behind the hinge also allows the hinge to be moved as desired.

To adjust a door in its opening, follow these steps:

1. Determine which hinge bolts must be loosened to move the door in the desired direction.

Figure 13–2 Know the parts of typical door assembly. (© American Honda Motor Co., Inc.)

2. Use a jack and wooden block to support the weight of the door. The wooden block will prevent the jack saddle from chipping the paint on the door.

3. Loosen the hinge-to-body bolts just enough to permit movement of the door.

4. Move the door as needed to align it. Tighten the hinge bolts and check the fit to be sure there is no binding or interference with the adjacent panel.

WARNING! Do not slam the door after adjusting it. You could damage the latch or striker if they are no longer in alignment.

5. Repeat the operation until the desired fit is obtained. Then check the striker pin alignment for proper door closing.

6. Loosen the door striker and move it up or down as needed. If the door tends to move up, move the striker down. If the door tends to drop when engaging the striker, shift the striker upward. See Figure 13–3.

Figure 13–4 This technician is using a door stand to adjust door.

7. The door and glass must also be checked to assure proper alignment to the roof rail and vertical weatherstripping.

When door adjustments are necessary, it may be helpful to remove the striker plate. Doing so allows the door to be centered in the opening more easily.

On some vehicles, a special wrench must be used to loosen and tighten the hinge bolts. If the hinges are to be removed, a line should be scribed around each one to mark their position. This makes reinstallation easier. Be careful not to cut the paint or corrosion will result. Refer to Figure 13–4.

You might have to loosen the fender at the rear bottom edge to reach the bolts. If the hinge pins are worn out, replace the hinges. Some hinges use bushings around the pins. When these bushings are worn, replace them. This will remove clearance in the hinges and also readjust the door.

In-and-out adjustments are also very important. The door must be aligned in and out to fit the body panels. To adjust the door in or out, loosen the hinge-to-door bolts. Shift the door as needed and then tighten the hinge bolts.

If the top of the door is moved out, it will also move the opposite bottom corner in. If the bottom of the door is moved in on the hinge, it will move the opposite corner out.

The key is to move the door in or out equally on both hinges. Then it will only affect the front of the door because the amount of adjustment decreases toward the back. The center door post, striker pin, and lock will determine the position of the rear of the door. The front edge of the door should always be slightly in from the fender. This will help prevent wind noise from entering the gap between the door and fender.

Figure 13–3 Door striker should be loosened and adjusted to hold door tight against weatherstripping. If door tends to move up or down when engaging striker, raise or lower it. (© American Honda Motor Co., Inc.)

Some hinges are welded to both the door and body. Obviously, no adjustments can be made to the welded door hinge. If only slightly out of alignment, you can spring or bend the hinge mounts to adjust welded hinges. Look at Figure 13–5.

Door Inner Trim Panel R and R

To work on parts inside the door, you must remove the inner door trim panel and related parts. Remove any screws that hold on the armrest and other trim pieces. You may have to pop out small decorative plugs over some of the screws. Refer to the service manual if in doubt.

Remove the window crank handle. It can be held on by a screw or by a clip from behind, Figure 13–6.

With all screws out of the door inner trim panel, you will usually have to pop out a series of plastic clips. They install around the perimeter of the panel. Use a *forked trim tool* designed to remove clips in trim parts. Slide it between the door and panel. Then pry out the plastic clips without damaging the panel.

As you lift off the door inner trim panel, disconnect any wires going to the panel. Feed the wires through the panel.

With the door panel off, peel back the paper or plastic water shield over the door. Pull slowly so you

do not damage it. You now have access to the bolts and nuts securing the window regulator.

When replacing a door inner trim panel, check that all plastic clips are fully in the panel. They can slide out of position and not align with the holes in the door. Bond the paper or plastic water shield back into place, Figure 13–7. Then, feed any wires through the panel.

Fit the panel over the top lip on the door and down into position. Starting at one end, use your hand to pop each clip into the door. Lean down and check that each clip is started in its hole. Then use your hand to pop each clip into place. Install the other parts in reverse order of removal.

Window Glass and Regulator R and R, Adjustment

Small nuts and bolts secure the window regulator and glass guides or tracks in position. Usually, the glass bolts to the upper arms of the regulator. On a few older vehicles, the glass may be held on with special adhesive or epoxy.

To remove the glass, unbolt it from the regulator. You must then remove any parts that prevent you from sliding the glass out of the door. This can vary so refer to the manual if needed. Look at Figure 13–8.

If the glass was broken, use a vacuum cleaner to remove all broken glass from inside the door. Install the new glass and bolt it to the regulator. Make sure you use all rubber, plastic, and metal washers.

> *WARNING! Do not slam the door before adjusting the glass. With a hardtop, the glass can hit and break on the top door opening.*

To adjust the glass and regulator, roll the window all the way up. Make sure it is centered in the frame or door opening. If needed, loosen the regulator mounting fasteners. Shift the regulator and glass as needed. Turning the window crank one way or the other may help shift the regulator. When the glass is properly positioned, tighten the regulator fasteners.

Stops may also be provided to limit upward travel of the glass. Adjust the stops so they limit upward glass travel. Double-check the door glass adjustment with the door closed. Inspect where the glass contact the inner door channel or weatherstripping. It must fully seal the door opening.

If needed, lubricate high friction points on the regulator. Lubricate the large gear and the arms where

Figure 13–5 Pry bar fixture like this one can be used to do minor adjustment of door with welded hinges.

Figure 13–6 Note two common methods of holding window crank handles in place. A: Small screw under plastic bezel holds window crank. *(Courtesy of Ford Motor Company)* B: Spring clip holds this window crank. Hook, fork tool, or shop rag can be used to pop clip out of its groove. *(© American Honda Motor Co., Inc.)*

they rub together. The window glass should slide up and down easily without binding.

Door Lock and Latch R and R

Door lock assemblies usually consist of the outside door handle, linkage rods, the door lock mechanism, and the door latch. Various types of exterior door handles are available. With a push-button type handle,

the button contacts the lock lever on the latch to open the door. However, most exterior door handles operate through one or more rods.

Door handles can be replaced by raising the window and removing the interior trim, panel, and water shield to gain access to the inside of the door. Exterior door handles are often held on with screws or bolts. A short screwdriver or small, ¼ inch drive socket is often needed to remove an outside door handle.

Pad Back Paper or Plastic Cover

Adhesive

Figure 13–7 *Slowly pull back paper or plastic water shield behind door panel. It must be reused. (Courtesy of Chrysler Corporation)*

Some causes of exterior door handle problems are:

1. Worn bushings
2. Bent or incorrectly adjusted lock cylinder rods
3. No lubrication on handle, linkage, or latch
4. Worn or damaged latches

Inside door lock mechanisms are generally the pull handle type. The mechanisms are connected to the lock by one or more lock cylinder rods. Clips or bushings are used to secure the rods in place.

The door lock mechanism usually mounts through a hole in the door. A spring clip often fits over the inside of the lock to hold it in place. An arm on the lock transfers motion through a rod to the door latch.

To remove the lock, place a drop light inside the door. While looking through one of the large openings in the inside of the door, pop off the small clip holding the lock rod. Then, pry the clip off the lock. You can use a screwdriver or pliers depending upon the amount of space around the lock. Slide the lock and washer off the outside of the door.

Electric door locks often use electric solenoids to move the linkage to the door locks. When you turn the key or press a door lock button, current flows to the solenoids in the doors. The solenoids convert the electrical energy into motion. The solenoid motion moves the lock linkages and latches. This locks or unlocks the doors.

In Figure 13–9, note the solenoid-operated door lock mechanism. For more information on electrical systems, refer to the Chapter 26.

Station Wagon Rear Door Adjustments

Most unibody station wagons have a *three-way tailgate.* Compact wagons are the exception. They often have a hatchback style rear gate. The three-way tailgate has a unique hinge and locking arrangement. The three-way tailgate can be operated as a tailgate with the glass fully down or as a door with the glass up or down.

Before doing rear door adjustments, closely examine the door to find misalignment. You might have to remove the right upper striker pin and adjust the tailgate as a regular door. If the right lower striker pin forces the door up or down and out of alignment, readjust the pin to provide a smooth action.

Adjust the left hinges to position the tailgate in the opening and to align it flush with adjacent panels. Closely examine the hinges to determine what adjustments are available.

On some vehicles, the lower left hinge provides up-and-down as well as in-and-out adjustment for the tailgate. Some vehicles provide for adjustments on the body side of the hinge. Others allow adjustment to the door side of the hinge. After adjusting the left hinges, reinstall and adjust the strikers. If all adjustments are correct, the tailgate should operate smoothly and fit properly.

Door Skin Replacement

Like other damaged panels, a door skin can be bumped back into shape, pulled into shape, or replaced. The decision is based on the amount of door frame damage. Another option is replacement of just the door skin.

The door skin wraps around—and is flanged around—the door frame. The door skin is secured to the frame either by welding or with adhesives. Typical replacement procedures are needed for both types of skins.

Replacing Welded Door Skins

A *welded door skin* has spot welds that hold the skin onto its frame. To replace a welded door skin, follow manufacturer recommended procedures and these basic steps:

1. Before removing the door, check to see if the hinges are sprung. Check the alignment of the door with respect to its opening. If the door frame is bent, do not try to replace the door skin. Straighten the door frame or obtain a replacement door.

2. Inspect how the skin is fastened to the door. Determine how much interior hardware must be removed.

Figure 13–8 Study internal parts of door. Note adjustment points for window glass. *(© American Honda Motor Co., Inc.)*

3. Remove the trim panel and disconnect the negative side of the battery to isolate all power door accessories. Remove all hardware from the door.

4. To prevent loss, place all removed parts and hardware inside the vehicle or in a parts tray.

5. If it only has minor damage, straighten and/or align the inner door frame.

6. Remove the door glass to prevent breakage or pitting while repairing the door. Place it inside the vehicle for protection.

Figure 13–9 Most power door locks use solenoid to move lock mechanisms and latches. Switch on lock electrically energizes solenoid. Solenoid then converts electrical energy into motion. *(Courtesy of Chrysler Corporation)*

7. Remove the door and move it to a suitable work area.

8. Apply tape to the door frame and measure the distance between the lower line of the tape and the edge of the skin. Also measure the distance between the edge of the skin and the door frame.

9. Remove the paint from the spot welds in the *skin hem* (folded door edge). Using a drill and spot weld cutter or hole saw, remove the spot welds.

10. Use a plasma arc cutter or grinder to remove the brazed portion of the skin from the door frame.

11. Grind off the edge of the door skin hem flange, Figure 13–10A. Grind off just enough metal so that the skin can be separated from the flange. Do not grind into the frame. Also, do not use a cutting torch or power chisel to separate the panels. The frame can be distorted or be accidentally cut.

12. Separate the reinforcing strip on the top of the skin, if applicable.

13. Using a hammer and chisel, start to separate the skin from the frame. Use a pair of tin snips to cut around any spot welds that could not be cut or ground out.

14. When the skin moves freely, remove it. Use clamping pliers to remove what remains of the hem flange. Any remaining spot welds, braze, and rust should be ground or blasted off.

15. With the skin removed, examine the frame for damage. Repair any remaining inner door damage at this time. If necessary, remove damage to the inner flange with a hammer and dolly.

16. Apply weld-through primer to bare metal mating surfaces. Cover other bare metal with an anti-corrosion primer or other corrosion protection material.

17. Prepare the new skin for installation. Using a drill or hole punch, make holes for plug welds. Remove the paint from the weld and braze locations with a sander. Apply weld-through primer to the bare metal mating surfaces.

18. Some door skins have a silencer pad that must be attached to the skin. To do this, clean the skin with alcohol, then heat it and the silencer pad with a heat lamp. Finally, glue the pad to the skin.

19. Apply body sealer to the backside of the new skin. Apply the sealer evenly, ⅜ in. (9 mm) from the flange, in a ⅛-in. (3 mm) thick bead.

20. Using clamping pliers, attach the new skin to the door and align it properly. Braze where required.

21. Use a hammer and dolly to flange the hem. See Figure 13–10B. Cover the dolly face with masking tape to avoid marring the skin. Bend the hem flange gradually in three steps. Be careful not to bend or throw the skin out of alignment.

22. After working the flange within 30 degrees of the frame, use a flanging tool to finish the hem flange, Figure 13–10C. Check alignment of door in opening.

23. Weld the plug or spot weld locations of the glass opening. Then tack weld the hem flange.

24. Drill holes into the new door skin to accommodate moldings, trim, and so forth. Make sure all edges are cut-in prior to installing any parts.

Figure 13–10 Follow major steps for replacing a welded door skin. A: Grind off door skin hem flange as shown. B: Use hammer and dolly to straighten and fit hem flange. C: Use flanging pliers to force new skin down over door frame.

25. Install all door parts. Prepare the door surfaces for refinishing.
26. Place the door on the vehicle. Align the door with the adjacent panels. Check for proper operation.

Sealing Door Seams

Remember that all joints and seams must be protected from corrosion. Use an appropriate seam sealer to keep water and contaminants out of the door and provide long-term protection.

Allow seam sealer to dry properly before painting. Drying time depends on the type of sealer, its thickness, and the temperature and humidity in the area.

Normally, the lower the temperature, the longer the necessary dry time. Also, the higher the humidity, the longer the dry time.

NOTE! NEVER ATTEMPT TO USE A SEAM SEALER WITHOUT FIRST READING THE INSTRUCTIONS PROVIDED BY THE MANUFACTURER.

Replacing Adhesive-bonded Door Skins

An *adhesive-bonded door skin* is bonded, not welded, to the door frame. It requires different replacement methods.

1. After removing all hardware, trim material, and the glass, remove the door from the vehicle.

2. Use a grinder to grind the edge of the door. This will make it possible to safely separate and remove the damaged skin.

3. Peel off the remaining hem flange using a chisel.

4. Use sandpaper or a blaster to remove any rust from areas that are too tight for a grinder. Then sand or grind all areas where the door skin meets the door frame.

5. If necessary, straighten the door frame.

6. Thoroughly clean the edge of the door frame, inside and out, with a good adhesive cleaner.

7. Check the fit of the replacement door skin.

8. Prime both sides of the door frame with adhesive primer.

9. Cut the tip of the adhesive nozzle to provide a ⅛ in. (3 mm) bead of adhesive.

10. Apply the adhesive in a continuous bead. The adhesive can be applied to the inside of the door skin creases or to the door skin side of the door frame.

11. Carefully position the door skin on the frame.

12. Flange the door skin in the usual manner. Be sure to wipe away any excess adhesive along the flange. Check door alignment in opening before adhesive cures.

13. Seal the crimped seam with seam sealer.

14. To protect against rust and corrosion, apply an anti-corrosion compound to the inside of the door.

15. Bond or tack weld the tabs at the top edge of the door skin. Use the method that best suits the design of the door. This step may not be needed on certain vehicle makes.

16. Paint and reassemble the door.

Replacing SMC Door Skins

Sheet molded compound or *SMC* door skin panels are becoming popular. SMC is similar to fiberglass. Many doors are made completely of SMC, except for steel door intrusion beams, and steel lock and hinge reinforcements.

To replace an SMC door skin, proceed as follows:

1. Cut away the center of the skin. Air shears work well because cut depth is easily controlled. If you use a saw, be careful not to hit or cut internal door parts.

2. To remove the remaining door skin, heat the bonding areas with a heat gun. Then apply pressure with a pry bar or chisel to remove the rest of the material. Be careful not to damage the door flange.

3. Sand the door frame flange to remove all remaining adhesive. Clean the bonding areas of the replacement skin with soap and water. Allow it to dry. Sand the bonding areas to expose the SMC fibers. Wipe dry with a clean cloth.

4. Apply a bead of two-part adhesive to the door frame flange, as shown in Figure 13–11.

5. Set the skin on the door frame and lightly clamp it. Do not squeeze too tight. You want to leave adhesive between the skin and frame. Check door alignment in opening before adhesive cures.

To complete the job, allow the adhesive to cure, paint the door, and then reassemble and mount it on the vehicle.

Further information on the repairs of SMC panels can be found in Chapter 11.

Door Reinforcements

All the doors of unibody vehicles have inner metal reinforcements at various locations. There are some other door frame reinforcements, such as at the hinge locations and the door lock plate. Door intrusion beams are normally used inside side doors.

A *door intrusion beam* is welded or bolted to the metal support brackets on the door frame to increase door strength. Methods of strengthening doors are given in Figure 13–12.

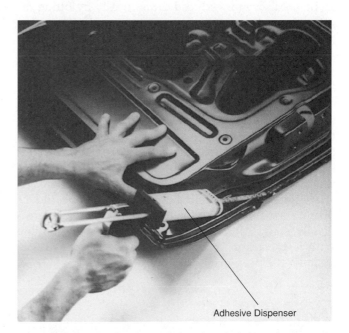

Adhesive Dispenser

Figure 13–11 Installing an adhesive-bonded door skin is similar to installing a welded-on skin. However, you must use a special two-part adhesive to bond skin onto frame.

Figure 13–12 *Study inner components relating to intrusion beams.*

GLASS

Windshields

Today's vehicles are built with a lot of glass that affords greater visibility for driving. Frequently, this glass is broken during a collision, flying gravel, or vandalism. Glass must also be removed from areas of major damage before the damage can be straightened.

Glass also plays an important role in aerodynamic styling. Air drag is reduced dramatically by fitting the glass accurately to the short metal, and eliminating trim. This approach reduces wind noise and provides a more sleek, uncluttered appearance.

Stationary glass panels in modern unibody vehicles also play an important role in the strength of the body structure. The stationary glass is an integral part of the upper body structure. It provides lateral bracing to help prevent roof collapse during a rollover. For this reason, when stationary glass is replaced, it must be installed in the same manner as it was by the manufacturer.

If the glass is installed incorrectly, you could be putting a vehicle back on the road that is not structurally sound. It is important for you to be familiar with the various techniques used to remove and install glass properly.

Types of Glass

For years, the glass used in most vehicles was either laminated or tempered. Both are considered safety glass because of their construction. Today, other types of glass are also found in modern unibody vehicles.

Figure 13–13 *Note how lamination holds glass together when windshield is broken.*

Laminated plate glass consists of two thin sheets of glass with a layer of clear plastic between them. It is used for windshields, Figure 13–13. When this type of glass is broken, the plastic material will tend to hold the shattered pieces in place and prevent them from causing injury.

Tempered glass is a single piece of heat-treated glass that shatters into small pieces when broken. However, it has more impact resistance than regular glass. It is used for side and rear window glass but never for windshields. When tempered glass is broken, it shatters into small pieces.

Both laminated and tempered glass can be tinted. *Tinted glass* contains a shaded vinyl material to filter out most of the sun's glare. This type is helpful in reducing eye strain and prevents fading of the interior. Some windshields are shaded to reduce the sun's glare by means of a dark tinted band or section across

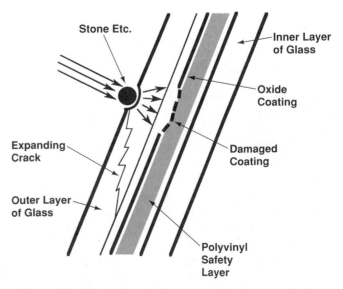

Figure 13–14 *Study what happens when laminated glass is broken. (I-CAR)*

the top. Tinted glass is usually recommended if the vehicle is to be equipped with air conditioning.

Glass can also be tinted by adding small quantities of metal powder to the other normal ingredients of glass to give it a particular color.

Glass can also be fitted with a defrosting circuit or antenna. *Self-defrosting glass* has a conducting grid or invisible layer that carries electric current to heat the glass. A grid type is common in rear windows. Windshields use a transparent conducting medium, Figure 13–14.

A *window antenna wire* for radio reception is placed either between the layers of laminated glass (windshield) or printed on the surface of the glass (rear window). Some glass has antenna wires and heating wires side by side.

Anti-lacerative glass has one or more additional layers of plastic affixed to the inside of the glass. This glass gives added protection against shattering and cuts during impact.

Modular or *encapsulated glass* has a plastic trim molding attached to its edge. It also fits the contours of a vehicle more closely than glass used in the past. Modular glass is the newest glass used in unibody applications.

Windshield Service

Replacement of the windshield involves two different methods: gasket installations or adhesive installations. The adhesive installation if further divided into two methods: the full cutout and the partial cutout method.

> **WARNING!** *When replacing glass, be aware of the following:*
>
> 1. *If you fail to restore the original structural integrity of a vehicle during repair, it could be violating federal law.*
> 2. *Butyl tape alone CANNOT be used to completely replace urethane because it has no structural bonding properties. It only holds the windshield in place and prevents leaks. NEVER use butyl tape ALONE to install a windshield.*

A *windshield gasket* is a rubber molding shaped to fit the windshield, body, and trim. The gasket installation method is common in older vehicles but still

Figure 13–15 Some windshields are held in place with a gasket or rubber seal. Note cross section of windshield gasket.

finds use in present day vehicles. The gasket is grooved to accept the glass, a sheet metal flange, and sometimes the exterior reveal molding, Figure 13–15. The gasket locking strip must be removed before the glass can be removed from the opening.

The *adhesive installation,* as the name implies, uses an adhesive material to secure the glass in place, Figure 13–16. The use of adhesives permits the windshield to be mounted flush with the roof panel, decreasing wind drag and noise. Rubber stops and spacers separate the glass from the metal.

Reveal moldings, covering the adhesive, are held in place by adhesive grooves in the body or by clips.

The *partial cutout method* of windshield replacement uses some of the original adhesive. The old adhesive must be in good condition and of sufficient thickness. It serves as a base for the new adhesive.

When the original adhesive is defective or requires complete removal, the *full cutout method* of windshield replacement is used. Both methods are shown in Figure 13–17.

Broken Glass

It is important to clean up pieces of broken glass from the seats, carpet, and air ducts before returning the vehicle to the customer. Vacuum the interior and blow out around the glass mounting area and vent ducts. Vacuum up as much glass as possible. Then, blow out glass from the heater and behind the dashboard with low pressure compressed air.

Figure 13–16 Study installation of adhesive-bonded windshield. Note cross section of adhesive-bonded windshield.

Figure 13–17 There are two ways to replace adhesive-bonded windshield. *(I-CAR)* A: With partial cutout method, you can use some of the old adhesive. B: With full cutout method, you must remove all of the old factory adhesive. Square ribbon sealer and adhesive are used to affix new windshield to body.

Danger! *If you fail to clean up broken glass properly, someone could be cut and injured. Also, if you fail to clean out dash ducts, glass can blow into people's eyes when the heater or A/C blower is turned on. Wear gloves and a full face shield!*

Windshield Gasket Method

Before removing the windshield, remove the interior and exterior moldings. Any garnish moldings on the interior face of the windshield are secured in place by screws or retaining clips. All of the garnish moldings should be removed first. If needed, the rearview mirror should be removed as well.

> *WARNING! The instructions in this text are for general purposes. Always refer to the service manual for the exact make and model vehicle. It will give the detailed instructions and specifications needed.*

On the exterior of the vehicle, remove the reveal moldings. The reveal molding is usually secured by

retaining clips attached to the body opening. A projection on the clip engages the flange on the reveal molding.

To replace a windshield using a gasket, proceed as follows:

1. Place protective covers over adjacent panels. Put on safety glass and gloves.

2. Be sure all moldings, trim, and hardware are removed. Remove the windshield wiper arms.

3. If the glass has a built-in antenna wire, disconnect the antenna leads. The wires are usually at the lower center of the windshield. Tape the leads to the glass.

4. Locate the locking strip on the outside of the gasket. Pry up the tab and remove the locking strip

to open the gasket all the way around the wind-shield.

5. Use a putty knife to pry the gasket away from the pinchweld inside and outside of the vehicle.

6. With an assistant in the passenger compartment, push the windshield and gasket out of the body opening. If the glass was not cracked and is to be reused, exert even pressure on the glass so it will not break.

7. Clean the windshield opening with solvent to remove any dirt or residual sealer.

8. Place the glass on a cloth-covered bench or table to protect the glass. If the glass was removed for body repairs, leave the gasket intact.

9. If the glass was replaced because it was broken, remove the gasket from the glass. Install the gas-ket on the replacement glass.

10. Cracks that develop in the outer edge of the glass are sometimes caused by low or high spots or poor spot welds in the pinchweld flange. Examine the body pinchweld and correct any problems.

11. Install setting blocks and spacers.

12. Carefully install the glass on the blocks to verify fit. Center the windshield. Check the gap between the glass and the pinchweld. The gap should be uniform around the entire pinchweld.

13. After the windshield is lined up, apply several strips of masking tape. Apply the tape from the glass to the vehicle body.

14. Slit each piece of tape at the end of the glass. Then lift the new windshield out and set it aside. To permanently install the windshield, you will line up the tape on the body with the tape on the glass.

15. Insert a cloth cord in the pinchweld groove of the gasket. Start at the top of the glass so the cord ends meet in the lower center of the glass. Tape the ends of the cord to the inside of the glass, Figure 13–18.

16. Squirt a soapy solution in the pinchweld groove for easier installation.

17. Apply waterproof sealer to the base of the gasket.

18. With an assistant, install the glass and gasket assembly in the body opening. Use your masking tape to align the gals. Slip the bottom groove over the pinchweld.

19. Slowly pull the cord ends so that the gasket slips over the pinchweld flange. Work the bottom sec-tion of the glass in first, then the sides, and finally the top. The glass might crack if the cord is only pulled from one end.

Figure 13–18 When installing windshield with large rubber gasket, install a piece of cloth cord inside gasket. Then, when you pull cord, it will force edge of rubber gasket over lip on body.

20. Dispense a small bead of waterproof sealer around the body side of the gasket.

21. Remove excess sealer with solvent.

22. Install the reveal and garnish moldings.

23. Check the windshield for water leaks using a low pressure stream of water.

24. Place a soapy solution in the locking strip groove. Replace the locking strip by spreading the groove. Feed the strip into the opening. The soapy solu-tion lubricates the groove and makes it easier to slide the strip through.

Windshield Full Cutout Method

When using the full cutout method, first remove the windshield according to the following procedure:

1. Protect both the interior and the exterior of the vehicle from damage. Cover the front seat and instrument panel. Also cover the painted surfaces next to the windshield area.

2. Remove the rearview mirror. Take off the wipers, antenna, moldings, and any other parts that might get in the way. Remove the cowl vent panel if it makes it easier to reach around the edge of the windshield.

3. Using a hook tool, lift the molding at the bot-tom of the windshield. Once it can be securely grasped, pull it out from around the windshield. Do this carefully so the molding is not dam-aged.

4. With a utility knife, score the exposed urethane all the way around the outside of the windshield. Cut as close to the glass as you can. This makes it easier to insert the vibrating power knife.

5. Using a power knife, cut through the adhesive next to the glass. Cut as close to the glass as possible.

Pneumatic windshield cutters use shop air pressure and a vibrating action to help cut the adhesive around glass. They have a variety of blade designs available for use on different windshields. Many have blades with depth stops to prevent pinchweld damage. With some designs, you may have to use two or more blades to remove some windshields.

Electric adhesive cutters either use 12 or 120 volt power supplies to produce a vibrating action to assist in cutting the adhesive around glass. They operate similar to pneumatic windshield cutters. Some power cutters are used on the outside of the vehicle. Others are designed to be used from inside the passenger compartment.

Piano wire (fine steel wire) can also be used to cut the adhesive, Figure 13–19. Use a 3- to 4-foot length of the lightest gauge wire that can be purchased. The cutting procedure with piano wire is a two-person job. After pushing the wire through to the interior, you and your helper must pull the wire around the windshield to cut the windshield free.

If removing a piece of modular or encapsulated glass, especially if it is undamaged, most auto-

makers recommend using the vibrating power knife to remove the glass instead of piano wire.

6. Carefully lift out the glass.

To prepare for the installation of the windshield, proceed in the following manner:

1. Cut out the remaining urethane adhesive from the pinchweld with a razor blade knife. Be careful not to cut or damage the headliner. Make sure no loose pieces of old adhesive are left. If the windshield had been replaced before with butyl tape or other unknown materials, it is especially important to remove this material thoroughly.

2. Check for rust in the pinchweld area. If there is rust, remove it with a wire brush, then sand if needed. Use a grit recommended by the adhesive manufacturer.

3. Dry set the new windshield. Check for at least ¼ in. (6 mm) of clearance around the windshield. Adjust setting blocks as needed to get proper alignment. After the windshield is lined up, apply several strips of masking tape. Bridge from the windshield to the body. See Figure 13–20.

4. Slit the pieces of tape at the edge of the glass. Lift the windshield out and set it aside. When you set the new windshield on the adhesive, line up the tape on the vehicle with the tape on the windshield to get it positioned.

5. Use a urethane adhesive cleaner on a lint-free dry cloth to wipe the pinchweld area. This removes any loose urethane. Let the cleaner dry.

6. Use a urethane primer in the pinchweld area. Do not use a liquid butyl primer or a ribbon sealer primer. Apply the primer to all bare metal in the pinchweld area.

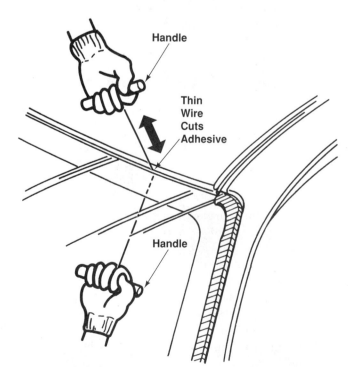

Figure 13–19 Piano wire can also be used to cut through adhesive holding windshield. Hold wire as close to glass as possible. Be careful not to cut yourself. (© American Honda Motor Co., Inc.)

Figure 13–20 Ask someone to help when lowering windshield straight down onto adhesive bead. Suction cups will help hold glass. (© American Honda Motor Co., Inc.)

7. Clean the windshield edge with a recommended solvent. Wipe dry with a clean, lint-free cloth.

8. Place a ½-in. (12 mm) coat of urethane primer on the inside contact surface of the windshield. Apply it all the way around. Let it dry for the required time.

9. Install square ribbon sealer to the inside edge of the pinchweld. For shallow pinchwelds, use $5/16 \times 5/16$ inch (8×8 mm). For deeper pinchwelds, use $3/8 \times 3/8$ inch (9×9 mm). *Square ribbon sealer* provides better support than round sealer. It also does not squeeze into the space needed for the urethane.

> *WARNING! Using an adhesive other than urethane can result in the shop and you being held liable. If the vehicle is involved in another collision and the glass reacts differently than the original installation, you and the shop could be sued.*

10. Apply a fast-curing, high-strength urethane adhesive following the manufacturer's instructions. Apply it directly behind the pinchweld, as shown in Figure 13–21. Hold the dispenser at a 45-degree angle. If too much adhesive is applied, excessive squeeze-out occurs.

> *WARNING! The adhesive must be strong enough to deflect a top-mounted air bag without allowing the windshield to be blown out.*

The final step is to install the windshield. This is done as follows:

1. Set the windshield into place. Line up the pieces of masking tape on the glass and body. Press firmly so the glass makes contact with the ribbon sealer and the urethane adhesive.

2. Look for squeeze-out along the edge of the windshield. Use a paddle to spread it evenly. Smooth the surface and remove any excess adhesive. Fill all spaces between the glass and the metal.

   Remember! At least ¼ inch (6 mm) of the windshield surface must be bonded to the vehicle body.

3. Install the moldings. Clean up the area with a liquid adhesive cleaner.

A

B

Figure 13–21 Apply adhesive slowly in recommended size, uniform bead. A: Technician is using dispenser to apply continuous bead of adhesive to flange for windshield. B: Use plastic spreader or putty knife to level off and remove excess adhesive.

4. Attach the cowl vent panel, wiper, antenna, and other parts.

The ribbon sealer will hold the windshield in place while the urethane adhesive cures. The urethane adhesive will reach its maximum strength in four or five days. Follow the manufacturer's recommendations for curing times. Curing times are affected by temperature and humidity.

Partial Cutout Method

The partial cutout method is recommended only under ideal curing conditions. Most of the steps are the same as in the full cutout method. One difference is that it is not necessary to remove all the old adhesive. The old adhesive left on the pinchweld serves as the base for the new adhesive.

If the old adhesive is not bonded securely to the vehicle body, do not use the partial cutout method. Remove all of the old adhesive and use the full cutout method. The same is true if butyl ribbon sealer or some other unknown material is discovered in the pinchweld.

Because there is no butyl ribbon sealer to hold the glass in position, allow enough time for the urethane to cure before driving the vehicle.

Inform the customer that the urethane will not achieve full strength until it is fully cured. Cure time will vary depending on temperature and humidity, but most are fully cured in 24 to 72 hours. If possible, keep the vehicle until the windshield adhesive is fully cured.

Other Glass R and R

The removal and replacement of rear and many stationary side windows follow the above methods closely. Procedures vary slightly for different vehicle makes. However, many of the operations are similar.

When working on small side windows, use duct or masking tape to secure the window while working. When inside the passenger compartment working, it is easy for the glass to fall out and break on the shop floor.

AIR AND WATER LEAKS

Air leaks will result in a complaint of wind noise in the passenger compartment. They often result from improperly adjusted doors, window glass, or damaged weatherstripping.

Water leaks will result in a complaint of water leaking into the passenger compartment or trunk. The most common causes of water leaks are poor seal around the windshield, window glass, sun roof, doors, or lids.

Improper door adjustment is the most common cause for both air and water leaks. The doors must provide a good seal between the weatherstripping and the body openings. The weatherstripping should be compressed sufficiently in the opening to prevent water, dust, and drafts from entering the vehicle. Door hinges wear and allow the doors to drop down, out of alignment.

To find body leaks, you can use several methods:

To conduct a *water hose test,* have someone squirt water onto the possible leakage areas while you watch for leaks inside the vehicle. Direct the water to flow over gaps in parts that might be leaking. Dripping water will result around any gap or leak in parts.

To conduct an *air hose leak test,* place a soapy water solution on possible leakage points and use low pressure air on the inside of the vehicle. When you find a leak, bubble will form in the soapy water.

An *air leak tape test* involves covering potential leaks with masking tape and driving the vehicle. If covering an area stops wind noise, you have found the air leak.

An *electronic leak detector* uses a signal generator tool and signal detector tool to find leaks. One person sits in the vehicle with the detector. Another person moves the generator tool around possible leakage points. The detector will make an audible "beep" if the signal passes through a body opening. This shows you the location of leakage points.

After finding the leak, you must adjust the door or lid, replace the weatherstripping, or seal the glass to fix the leak. You must use common sense and the procedures given in this and other chapters to stop the air or water leakage.

REAR VIEW MIRROR SERVICE

Both exterior and interior rear view mirrors require repair or replacement after collision damage, Figure 13–22.

External rear view mirrors normally bolt to the outside of the driver and passenger doors. Screws on the outside or inside of the door secure the mirrors. A gasket normally fits between the mirror and door surface.

If only the mirror is broken on external mirrors, you can sometimes replace the mirror glass. Heat the mirror with a heat gun to soften the adhesive. Then, pry off the broken pieces of mirror. Bond the new mirror into its housing with an approved adhesive.

Some interior rear view mirrors attach to the windshield with a special adhesive. You must clean the glass with a recommended cleaner. Spray on a clear primer agent. Then, apply a small bead of

Figure 13–22 Pry off old mirror.

adhesive. Hold the mirror mounting pad stationary on the windshield for a few minutes until the adhesive cures.

MORE INFORMATION

For more information on the subjects in this chapter, refer to the index. For example, heated windshields, power windows, and other related subjects are discussed in Chapter 26, Electrical Repairs.

Summary

- There are two basic door designs: framed and hardtop. Framed doors surround the sides and top of the door glass with a metal frame, helping keep the window glass aligned. The door frame seals against the door opening. Hardtop doors have the glass extending up out of the door without a frame around it. The glass itself must seal against the weatherstripping in the door opening.

- The basic parts of a door include the: door frame, door skin, door glass, door glass channel, regulator, door latch, handles, door trim panel, dust cover, weatherstripping, and rear view mirror.

- Laminated plate and tempered glass are among the two most common window glasses. Laminated plate glass consists of two thin sheets of glass with a layer of clear plastic between them. It is used for windshields. Tempered glass is a single piece of heat-treated glass that shatters into small pieces when broken. It is used for side and rear windows.

- Air leaks will result from improperly adjusted doors, window glass, or damaged weatherstripping. The most common causes of water leaks are poor seal around the windshield, window glass, sun roof, doors, or lids.

Technical Terms

framed doors	*self-defrosting glass*
hardtop doors	*window antenna wire*
door frame	*anti-lacerative*
door skin	*glass*
door glass channel	*modular or encapsulated*
door regulator	*glass*
door latch	*windshield gasket*
door striker	*reveal moldings*
door trim panel	*partial cutout method*
weatherstripping	*full cutout method*
door lock	*pneumatic windshield*
three-way tailgate	*cutter*
welded door skin	*electric adhesive cutter*
skin hem	*piano wire*
adhesive-bonded door	*water hose test*
skin	*air hose leak test*
door intrusion beam	*air leak tape test*
laminated plate glass	*electronic leak*
tempered glass	*detector*
tinted glass	

Review Questions

1. _____ are the most used—and abused—parts of a vehicle.

2. Explain the difference between a frame door and a hardtop door.

3. List and describe the 11 major parts of a door.

4. An older car needs its doors adjusted. The driver's door is sagging badly and will not close easily. Technician A says to check for worn hinges. Technician B says to loosen and adjust the hinges if not worn too much.
   Who is correct?
   a. Technician A
   b. Technician B
   c. Both Technicians
   d. Neither Technician

5. This tool should be used when removing interior door trim panels.
   a. Pneumatic knife
   b. Electric knife
   c. Forked tool
   d. Slide hammer

6. What can happen if you slam a hardtop door after adjusting a door?

7. This can cause exterior door handle problems:
   a. Worn bushings
   b. Bent or incorrectly adjusted lock cylinder rods
   c. No lubrication on handle, linkage, or latch
   d. All of the above
   e. None of the above

8. Summarize the five major steps in replacing an SMC door skin.

9. This type of glass shatters into tiny pieces when broken.
   a. Laminated glass
   b. Tempered glass
   c. Modular glass
   d. Encapsulated glass

10. What is the difference between the partial and full cutout methods of windshield replacement?

PRE-PAINTING PREPARATION

CHAPTER 14

VEHICLE PREPARATION

Objectives

After studying this chapter, you should be able to:

- Prepare a vehicle for painting.

- Properly clean a vehicle using soap, water, air pressure, and a wax-grease remover.

- Evaluate the condition of the old painted surface.

- Describe methods for removing the old paint if needed.

- Properly prepare and treat bare metal surfaces.

- Correctly sand and featheredge surfaces.

- Apply an undercoat.

- Mask a vehicle properly.

Introduction

Vehicle preparation involves all of the final steps prior to painting, including cleaning, sanding, stripping, masking, priming, and other related tasks.

Keep in mind that it is foolish to apply any kind of finish to a surface NOT properly prepared. The paint work will look bad or NOT hold up. Also, shop costs increase because the job usually has to be done again. Thorough vehicle preparation pays off in material savings, job quality, and customer satisfaction.

As you will learn, even if the original finish is in good condition, it should be lightly sanded or scuffed after washing to remove "dead film" and to block or smooth out small imperfections. If the old paint surface is in poor condition, the paint should be removed down to the bare metal. This way, a good foundation for your "new paint job" is achieved.

Before refinishing can begin, the vehicle must be properly prepared. You must:

1. Correct any surface defects.
2. Wash the vehicle with soap and water. The underside of the vehicle should also be washed.
3. Clean the area to be refinished with wax and grease remover.
4. Mask the vehicle.
5. Tack off the vehicle using a tack rag.
6. Check that all surface preparation has been completed.

VEHICLE CLEANING

The vehicle cleaning processes should include:

1. Power washing the underbody and wheel housings.
2. Cleaning the door and trunk or hatch jambs.
3. Cleaning under the hood.
4. Using a strong wax and grease remover to remove road tars.
5. Blowing off the entire vehicle with high pressure air before and after masking.
6. Blowing off wheel covers outside of the spray booth before placing them in the spray booth.
7. Washing the repair area with a mild cleaner.
8. Tacking off entire vehicle, including masking paper.

Initial washing involves a complete cleaning of the car or truck to remove mud, dirt, and other foreign matter. Washing should be done before bringing the vehicle into the shop. This will prevent road debris from entering the shop area. Look at Figure 14–1.

Wet the whole vehicle with a water hose. Concentrate water flow onto trim pieces, around windows, and other areas that can trap and hold debris. Dirt also collects in door jambs, around the trunk and hood openings, and in wheel wells.

> *WARNING! Failure to remove foreign matter from the vehicle can allow it to blow or fall into the wet paint when spraying. This avoidable problem is very frustrating and a waste of time and money!*

Scrub all surfaces thoroughly with a detergent and water. A sponge works well. Wash the top first, then the front, rear, and sides. Rinse the vehicle thoroughly and let it dry completely. Remember that all adjacent panels must be as clean as the area to be refinished.

> *Danger! Never use gasoline as a cleaning solvent. A tremendous fire could result. Gasoline is also a poor wax-removing solvent and can itself deposit contaminating substances on the surface.*

> *WARNING! Do NOT use synthetic reducers for cleaning. They absorb reducer into the paint film. Blistering or lifting of the new paint can result.*

Figure 14–1 Thoroughly wash vehicle using soap and water before bringing into shop. All dirt and debris must be removed.

Using Wax and Grease Remover

Paint will NOT adhere to a waxy surface. For this reason, thoroughly clean all surfaces to be painted with a wax and grease solvent. Concentrate on areas where heavy wax build-up can be a problem. This would include around trim, moldings, door handles, radio antennae, and behind the bumpers.

To apply wax and grease remover, fold a clean, dry cloth. Soak it with the solvent. Then, wipe the painted surface. While the surface is still wet, fold a second clean cloth and wipe off the wet solvent. Work small areas and wet the surface liberally. Never attempt to clean too large of an area. The solvent will dry before the surface can be wiped.

For best results, remember to wipe off the wax and grease remover while it is still wet.

> **NOTE!** ALWAYS USE NEW WIPING CLOTHS WHEN USING WAX AND GREASE REMOVER. LAUNDERING OR WASHING THE USED RAGS MIGHT NOT REMOVE ALL OIL, WAX, OR SILICONE RESIDUE.

To remove any last trace of moisture and dirt from seals and moldings, use compressed air at low pressure. Use a blow gun to blow out behind any area that could hold moisture.

Special attention should be paid to tar, gasoline, battery acid, coolant, and brake fluid stains. These can penetrate well beneath the surface of the paint film. These contaminants must be removed before sanding.

SURFACE EVALUATION

There are several characteristics of the finish that may affect the refinishing procedures. These finish characteristics include:

1. Type of existing finish
2. General appearance of old finish
3. Condition of existing finish

You should make a visual inspection of the condition and appearance of the finish. During the inspection, answer these questions:

1. Has the finish been damaged because of age?
2. Has the finish been damaged because of weathering?
3. Does the finish have environmental damage?
4. Has the finish faded?
5. Will the gloss of the finish cause problems with matching?
6. How much texture or orange peel does the finish have?
7. Which conditions must be repaired prior to refinishing?

Both the customer and appraiser should be informed of any additional work that will be required prior to refinishing.

There are several factors that may affect the aging and durability of an automotive finish. The life span of a finish can be affected by its exposure to acid rain, industrial fallout, ultraviolet (UV) radiation and hard water.

If a vehicle has been exposed to these elements, the damage may have to be repaired before refinishing. The finish may have to be removed before refinishing.

A *visual inspection* of the finish should include looking for:

1. Fading, dulling, whitening, or similar changes in gloss.
2. Cracking or checking (tiny spots are in paint film).
3. Blistering (paint film is lifting or bubbling).
4. Spotting (paint is discolored).
5. Cratering (deep cavities are formed in paint film).
6. Other paint problems.

Surface evaluation is a close inspection of the old paint to determine its conditions. Once the vehicle has been cleaned, inspect the paint surface carefully.

Look for any signs of *paint film breakdown,* including checking, cracking, or blistering. Pay particular attention to the gloss level; low gloss often indicates surface irregularities.

To do a *paint adhesion check,* sand through a small area of the old finish and featheredge it. If the featheredge does NOT break or crumble, the old paint may be adhered properly. If you cannot featheredge the old paint, it must be removed before repainting.

Most forms of paint failure are progressive (ongoing) and cannot be stopped. In fact, trying to paint over a failing paint will usually accelerate the deterioration. If the old finish is badly weathered or scarred, it is NOT suitable for refinishing.

Pre-existing Damage

Pre-existing damage includes paint cracking, scratches in paint, acid rain damage, and industrial fallout damage. If there is pre-existing damage, the vehicle's owner should be contacted, and the situation explained. It is then the decision of the vehicle owner whether to authorize additional repairs. Some types of pre-existing damage may have to be repaired before the new finish can be applied or match the existing finish.

Acid rain is caused by the release of various chemicals into the atmosphere. It results when these chemicals are absorbed by rain water and form acids. When it rains or snows these acids settle on the paint surface. They can become stronger as the water evaporates.

Acid rain damage may cause:

1. Craters to be etched into the paint film
2. Changes in pigment colors
3. Fading or dulling
4. Corrosion of metallic colors
5. Whitish spotting of clearcoats

Acid rain damage can be identified by:

1. Using a magnifying glass.
2. Feeling the surface for depressions.
3. Visual inspection. Craters can be as small as a pinhead or as large as a quarter.

Industrial fallout is when metallic particles are released into the atmosphere from steel mills, foundries, and railroad operations. This is another source of paint damage. The metallic particles fall onto the paint surface. They then rust when exposed to moisture. The resulting damage will appear as black or brown spots or rust colored rings on the paint surface. The particles can etch into the paint surface causing a coarse or sandy surface.

Industrial fallout damage can be identified by feel or wiping a terry cloth towel over the surface. The metallic particles will catch a small amount of the cloth and can be easily seen.

Hard water spotting damage forms when rain or tap water dries on the paint surface. The water evaporates leaving hard minerals on the paint surface. Hard water spotting:

1. Leaves a round white ring on the paint surface.

2. It is generally repairable because the mineral deposits are on top of the paint film.

UV radiation damage results from excessive exposure of the paint film to the sun's radiation. For example, exposure to UV radiation can cause:

1. Discoloration of the paint film

2. Cracking of the paint film

3. Fading or similar loss of gloss

4. Yellowing of the paint

When the old paint is badly aged or damaged, the old finish should be completely removed. There are three common ways of stripping paint from metal surfaces:

1. Chemical stripping

2. Blasting

3. Sanding or grinding

NOTE! FOR MORE INFORMATION ON SURFACE EVALUATION, REFER TO THE INDEX. THIS SUBJECT IS EXPLAINED IN SEVERAL OTHER LOCATIONS, THE CHAPTER ON PAINT PROBLEMS FOR EXAMPLE.

CHEMICAL STRIPPING OLD PAINT

Chemical stripping uses a chemical action to dissolve and remove old paint down to bare metal. A chemical paint remover is often used for stripping large areas of paint. Chemical stripping is effective in those places that a power sander cannot reach.

Before applying paint remover, mask off the area to ensure that the remover does NOT dissolve any paint NOT meant to be stripped. Use two or three thicknesses of masking paper to give adequate protection. Cover any crevices to prevent the paint remover from seeping to the bottom of a panel.

Danger! *Paint remover should be applied following the manufacturer's instructions. Pay attention to warnings regarding ventilation, smoking. Also wear protective clothing such as rubber gloves, long sleeve shirts, and goggles. If paint remover comes in contact with your skin or eyes, it can cause serious chemical burns.*

WARNING! *Some paint removers can harm any plastic beneath the paint. Also, the chemical residue can be difficult to remove completely. If the chemical residue is NOT cleaned off, it can cause paint adhesion problems.*

Before applying the paint remover, slightly score the surface of the paint to be stripped. Use a scratch awl or similar pointed tool to place deep scratches in the paint. This will help the chemical stripper penetrate and dissolve the paint more quickly.

To apply paint remover, brush on a heavy coat in one direction only to the entire area being treated. Use a soft bristle brush. Do NOT brush the material out. Allow the paint remover to stand and soak until the finish is softened.

Although paint remover is quickly effective on most topcoats, some surfaces can prove stubborn. For example, acrylic lacquer becomes sticky, making it more difficult to remove. More than one application of remover might be needed.

Caution should be taken when removing the loosened paint coatings. Some paint removers are designed to be neutralized by water. Others are more easily removed with a squeegee or scraper. See Figure 14–2.

Be sure to rinse off any residue that remains by using a cleaning solvent and steel wool. Follow immediately by wiping with a clean rag. This rinsing operation is essential. Many paint removers contain wax. If left on the surface, the residue will prevent the paint from adhering, drying, and hardening properly.

After chemical stripping, you will sometimes have to remove small patches of remaining semi-softened paint. For fast removal, use a scuffing disc mounted on a grinder, Figure 14–3. Scuffing wheels will work well in restricted areas, Figure 14–4.

BLASTING OFF OLD PAINT

Abrasive blasting involves using air pressure, a blasting gun, and an abrasive (sand or plastic beads) to remove old paint. Blasting leaves a clean, dry surface that is ideal for refinishing. Specialty shops have large blasters that can remove all of the paint from a vehicle in a few hours. Body shops often have smaller blasters for removing paint from smaller areas. Look at Figure 14–5.

A

B

Figure 14–3 Here technician is using grinder equipped with large scuff pad. It will quickly remove softened paint without scarring metal. (© The Eastwood Company—Used with permission)

C

Figure 14–2 If your evaluation finds serious problems with old paint, you may have to strip it off. (Sikkens, Inc.) A: Old paint is peeling and would not provide solid base for new paint. (MAACO Auto Painting & Bodyworks) B: Apply thick coating of chemical paint stripper. Wear protective gear to prevent chemical burns. C: After paint softens, scrape it off. Then clean residue off of metal.

Blasting will quickly reveal hidden rust that can result in scaling and other problems after the paint job has been finished. In addition, blasting makes hard-to-reach areas accessible. Also this method saves time when compared with sanding/grinding and chemical stripping.

Typically, blasting operations concentrate the pressure and flow of air and sand or plastic beads in a small area. On some models, the blaster can be adjusted to vary the blast volume and pattern.

NOTE! SANDBLASTING CAN WARP THIN SHEET METAL, ALUMINUM, PLASTIC, AND OTHER SUBSTRATES. SAND OR HARD MEDIA BLASTING IS NOT RECOMMENDED ON LARGE FLAT PANELS THAT COULD WARP EASILY.

Soft plastic stripping media, however, will remove paint from almost any surface without damage. Methods of using a soft plastic stripping media are similar to the conventional sandblasting methods, with the addition of these guidelines:

1. Use low (20 to 25 psi or 1.4 to 1.8 K/cm^2) air pressure at the nozzle.

2. Hold the nozzle at a shallow (20 to 30 degrees) angle to the panel.

3. Hold the gun 18 to 24 in. (450 to 600 mm) from the panel.

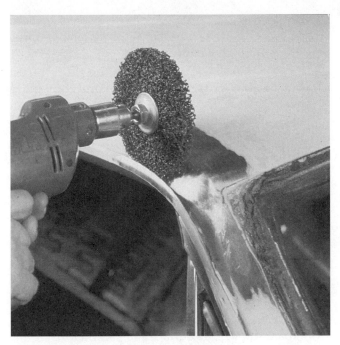

Figure 14–4 To get at hard-to-reach areas, a scuffing disc like this one will work well. (© The Eastwood Company. Used with permission)

4. Use a broad, sweeping back-and-forth motion.
5. Stop when the primer is reached.

Mentioned earlier in the text, some of the newer models provide dust-free or "captive" sandblasting. They contain a built-in vacuum and filtration system that vacuums up and recycles the abrasive.

GRINDING OFF OLD PAINT

Machine grinding is suitable for removing the old finish from small flat areas and gently curved areas.

Figure 14–5 Sandblasting is good on small rust areas. It will remove rust from pits without thinning metal. Soft media or plastic bead blasting is better on larger surface areas.

Start with a No. 24 grit open-coat disc. Hold the face of the disc at a slight angle to the surface. Work back and forth evenly over the area to remove the bulk of the old finish down to the metal. Follow this with a No. 36 and then a No. 80 close coat disc. Go over the entire repair area and surrounding surface to eliminate the troughs or steps caused by the coarse disc.

> **WARNING!** When using the grinder, care must be taken to prevent gouging, scarring, or heat warping the metal.

After all of the paint is removed, be sure to finish sand the area with an orbital sander. Use No. 80 grit paper to remove the metal scratches. Then finish sand using No. 180 grit paper to remove the grinding marks.

BARE METAL TREATMENT

Proper *bare metal treatment* prepares the metal for primer. It is often ignored or carried out in a haphazard manner. This can only result in poor adhesion, corrosion, and customer dissatisfaction.

Several metal treatment systems are available that ensure a good bond. One of the best is metal prep/conversion coating. To apply, proceed as follows:

1. Clean the metal to remove contaminants. Use a wax and grease remover. Work small areas, 2 to 3 square feet (18 to 27 sq. cm) at a time, wetting the surface liberally. While the surface is still wet, fold a second clean cloth and wipe dry.

2. Clean with metal conditioner. Mix the appropriate cleaner with water in a plastic bucket according to the label instructions. Apply with a cloth, sponge, or spray bottle. If rust is present, work the surface with a stiff brush or abrasive pad. Then, while the surface is still wet, wipe it dry with a clean cloth.

3. Apply conversion coating. Using the proper conversion coating for the metal (check manufacturer's recommendation), pour the conversion coating into a plastic bucket. Using an abrasive pad, brush, or spray bottle, apply the coating to the surface. Leave the conditioner on the surface 2 to 5 minutes to create a zinc phosphate coating on the steel. If the surface dries before the rinsing, reapply. Flush the coating from the surface with cold water. Wipe dry with a clean cloth. Allow to air dry completely. Primer or primer-surfacer can then be applied.

A *wash primer* is another type of sprayable surface treatment that eliminates the need for a conversion coating. The vinyl resin in the wash primer provides corrosion resistance. The reducer in the wash primer contains phosphoric acid for strong bonding. A wash primer with phosphoric acid reducer cleans and etches the metal to aid adhesion.

Before applying a wash primer carefully read and follow the manufacturer's directions and special instructions.

Typically, metal treatment and priming are considered separate surface preparation steps. However, some new products actually combine these steps.

Self-etching primers etch the bare metal to improve paint adhesion and corrosion resistance, while providing the priming and filling properties of primer-surfacer. Self-etching primers work best on lightly sanded surfaces where a slight-to-moderate amount of filling is required. They must be applied as directed by the manufacturer.

PREPARING METAL REPLACEMENT PARTS

Many manufacturers and parts suppliers prime replacement panels. The function of this *new part primer coat* is to protect the metal against corrosion. It does NOT necessarily provide a firm basis for a paint system. Although most primers do have this dual function, the supplier should always be consulted.

Remember that the primer on new body parts may not be intended to serve as the primer. A primer must be applied to these replacement parts or the color coat will NOT adhere properly.

Clean the new part with wax and grease remover. Then examine the part for scratches and other imperfections. Sand any imperfections until smooth but do NOT remove the coating completely. Scuff sand the entire panel. Then apply primer before painting. If in doubt about the coating, check with the manufacturer of the part for the recommended finishing procedure.

Clean any bare metal replacement panels protected with grease with a wax and grease solvent. Wash them with liberal amounts of solvent, changing rags frequently. Then treat the panels with a metal conditioner. Flush them down with water, and dry them off.

SANDING

One of the most important parts of surface preparation is *sanding.* Sanding prepares the surface for painting in several ways:

1. Chipped paint can be sanded to taper the sharp edges. Otherwise, the chip would show up as ridges under the new finish.
2. Cracking, peeling paint and minor surface rust can be removed by sanding before applying a fresh topcoat. If NOT, these conditions will continue to deteriorate and will eventually ruin the new finish.
3. Primed areas must be sanded smooth and level.
4. The entire surface to be refinished must be scuff sanded to improve adhesion of the new finish. Scuff sanding also removes any trace of contaminants on the existing finish.

Selecting Sandpaper

Because *coated abrasives* (sandpapers) are often used to prepare the vehicle surface for painting, using the correct abrasive is critical. You must select the proper sandpaper for optimum productivity, cost efficiency, and best finish.

Open coat sandpaper is good for sanding softer materials, such as old paint, body filler, plastic, and aluminum. Open coat can prevent premature loading or clogging of the sandpaper. *Closed coat sandpaper* generally provides a finer finish and is commonly used when wet sanding.

Mentioned in earlier chapters, *grit sizes* vary from coarse to micro fine grades. Sandpaper grits are ordered by number—the lower the number, the coarser the grit. Refer to Figure 14–6.

Here are some general uses for different sandpaper grits:

1. Very coarse papers, No. 24 to 80 grit are used to remove old paint and filler.
2. Medium grit papers, No. 320, No. 360, or No. 400 grit are used to level and sand the gloss off an old finish to be refinished.
3. Very fine and ultra fine grits are used primarily for color sanding.
4. Compounding papers, the No. 1250, No. 1500, and No. 2000 grits, are used to solve problems on newly painted surfaces.

Generally, select the finest grit paper that will do the job. Fine paper may remove material more slowly but it will leave a smoother surface.

A common mistake is to use too coarse of a sandpaper. Coarser paper will sand more quickly but will leave deep sanding marks that can show up in the new paint job. Finer paper would have to be used to sand the surface down to remove these scratches.

	SANDPAPER GRIT SIZES			
Grit	Aluminum Oxide	Silicon Carbide	Zirconia Alumina	Primary Use for Collision Repair
Micro fine	—	2000 1500 1250	—	Used for base coat/clear coat paint system
Ultra fine	—	800	—	Used for color sanding.
Very fine	—	600	600	Used for color sanding. Also for sanding the paint before polishing.
	400 320 280 240	400 320 280 240	400 — 280 240	Used for sanding primer-surfacer and old paint prior to painting.
	220	220	—	Used for sanding of topcoat.
Fine	180 150	180 150	180 150	Used for final sanding of bare metal and smoothing old paint.
Medium	120 100 80	120 100 80	— 100 80	Used for smoothing old paint and plastic filler.
Coarse	60 50 40 36	60 50 40 36	60 — 40 —	Used for rough sanding plastic filler.
Very coarse	24 16	24 16	24 —	Used on sander or grinder to remove paint.

Figure 14–6 Study uses of different sandpaper grits. You must know which coarseness of sandpaper to use for each task.

Disc Adhesive, Self-stick Paper

To apply nonstick sandpaper to the backing pad of a sander, squeeze a few drops of *disc adhesive* on the backing pad. Spread the adhesive evenly on the pad, Figure 14–7A. Then center the disc on the pad and press it into place, Figure 14–7B. To help make the adhesive more sticky, pull the paper on and off the backing pad a couple of times.

A

Center on Pad

B

Figure 14–7 Note how disc adhesive is used. A: Apply disc adhesive around backing pad. B: Place sandpaper disc over pad. Lift it on and off pad several times until adhesive holds paper securely.

Self-stick sandpaper has adhesive applied to it during manufacturing. This type of paper is slightly more expensive but saves time. When using a self-adhesive sanding disc, be sure to center the paper on the pad before pressing it into place.

After you are done sanding, remove the used sandpaper disc from the backing pad. If NOT removed right away, the adhesive will harden and cause the sandpaper to stick to the backing pad. Should this occur, use solvent on a rag to dissolve the adhesive and remove the sandpaper.

Abrasive grinding discs are used for rough jobs, such as grinding off rust and paint. They are available in grit sizes of No. 16 to No. 50, and in diameters of 3 to 9 in. (75 to 225 mm). The grinding disc is first assembled to the backing plate and then the disc/plate assembly is attached to the grinder.

Sanding Methods

Sanding can be done with a sanding block or by using power equipment. Most heavy sanding—such as removal of the old finish—is done by power sanders. Delicate final sanding operations are usually done by hand with a sanding block. Hand and power sanding can also be done wet (with water) or dry (without water). Sandpapers are available in dry or wet-or-dry types.

Block Sanding. *Block sanding* is a simple back and forth scrubbing action with the sandpaper mounted on a rubber blocking tool. It is often used on flat surfaces. Block sanding helps level the surface or make it flat.

Use the following general steps when block sanding:

1. Use sandpaper that fits the sanding block. If needed, cut the sheet of sandpaper to fit the block. Fit the sandpaper under the ends of the block.

2. Hold the block flat against the surface. Apply even, moderate pressure along the length of the block. Sand back and forth with long, straight strokes, Figure 14–8.

3. Do NOT sand in a circular motion. This will create sand scratches that might be visible under the finish. To achieve the best results, always sand in the same direction as the body lines on the vehicle.

4. Be sure to thoroughly sand areas where a heavy wax build-up can be a problem, such as around trim, moldings, door handles, radio antennas, and behind the bumpers.

5. To sand convex or concave panels, use a flexible sponge rubber backing pad, Figure 14–9. You can also use the side of your hand to hand sand *concave* (curved inward) surfaces. You can use the palm of your hand to hand sand *convex* (curved outward) surfaces. You must hold your hand to match the shape of the surface.

> *WARNING!* Never try to sand a flat surface while holding the sandpaper in your hand. An unleveled or irregular surface will result.

6. Carefully find and sand scratches using a finer grit paper.

7. When block sanding primer or putty, make certain to sand the area until it feels smooth and level. Rub your hand or a clean cloth over the surface to check for rough spots.

Remember! If you can feel the slightest bump or dip in the surface, it will show up after painting. A surface will look smooth when sanded dull or when in primer. However, when coated with a shiny, reflective paint, it will exaggerate or magnify any surface roughness.

Dry and Wet Sanding. Block sanding can be done wet or dry. *Dry sanding* is done with coarser non-waterproof sandpaper, without using water. It is commonly done to remove material quickly. The majority of acrylic primer-surfacers should be sanded dry.

Figure 14–8 Dry block sanding works well when using coarser papers. Dry sanding will quickly clog finer papers. Never sand flat surfaces by hand without using block.

Figure 14–9 Soft, flexible block should be used on curved panels.

Figure 14–10 Wet sanding is fast and efficient. Water will help flush away material so sandpaper does not clog up.

Wet sanding is done with finer waterproof sandpaper, using water to flush away sanded particles. Normally, use coarse dry sanding first to remove major surface imperfections, followed by wet sanding for final smoothing. Wet sanding also reduces the problem of paper clogging. See Figure 14–10.

Wax and silicone can penetrate beneath the surface. Because this contamination is NOT easily detected, you might want to add wax and grease remover or soap to the water when wet sanding. Look at Figure 14–11.

Scuff Pad

Scuff padding is done with a nylon pad on hard-to-reach areas to clean and scuff the surface. Scuff

Figure 14–11 When wet sanding, dip sponge in bucket of water. Squeeze water out and over area being sanded. (Carborundum Abrasives Co.)

padding is often done inside door jambs, around hood and trunk openings, and other restricted areas. Since the scuff pad is flexible, it will scuff irregular surfaces easily.

Paint scuffing is needed to make sure the new paint bonds properly. If you paint over a smooth, hard surface, the new paint will not have anything to bond to and it will peel off. Paint scuffing can be done with fine sandpaper or a scuff pad.

When scuff pad sanding, you can place the pad over a sanding block on flat surfaces. You can also use your hand to hold and shape the pad on curved or restricted areas.

NOTE! SCUFF PAD COARSENESS RATINGS CAN VARY. REFER TO MANUFACTURER DATA TO OBTAIN THE COARSENESS RATING NEEDED.

Power Grinding and Sanding

Power grinding is done to quickly remove large amounts of old paint and other materials. An air grinder is one of the fastest methods to remove material.

Danger! When grinding, position the grinding disc against the surface so that sparks fly away from your body. Wear leather gloves and a full face shield.

Power sanding normally uses an air sander to begin smoothing operations. Often, a disc orbital sander is used to level surface imperfections.

Danger! Always wear a dust mask when sanding or grinding. The dust can be harmful if inhaled.

When power sanding, replace the sandpaper when paint begins to cake or "ball up" on the paper. This paint build-up can scratch or gouge the surface and reduce the sanding action of the disc. Slowing down sander speed will also help prevent paint build-up and prolong sandpaper life.

Types of Sanding

There are several types of sanding that a painter must master. Most are done during the surface preparation stage, but are performed after priming.

Remember, the smoother the surface, the easier the refinishing work.

Bare metal sanding is done to smooth rough metal surfaces. If the metal work has been done properly, little sanding of bare metal should be required. But once in a while the metal is very rough from grinding or welding. In such cases, power sand it with No. 50 grit to level out burrs, nibs, and deep scratches.

Paint sanding is needed when the old finish is rough or in poor shape and to level and smooth primed areas. Since the primer-surfacer is primarily intended to fill low spots and scratches, thorough sanding must be done to leave material in the low spots and cut away the high spots. Block sanding is highly recommended for this purpose.

USING A GUIDE COAT

A *guide coat* is a very thin coat of primer or paint that assists in pointing out minor high and low spots. A guide coat is applied by spraying a very light coat of a different color primer or paint over the repair area. Sanding reveals the high spots and the low spots by contrasting the colors of the guide coat and the material under it.

A *surface high spot* shows up when sanding quickly cuts through the guide coat. A *surface low spot* shows up when sanding will NOT remove the guide coat.

When the surface is flat and ready for painting, the guide coat will sand off evenly or at the same time. Minor surface irregularities can be corrected by applying coats of primer-surfacer and resanding. Spot putty can be applied to fill deeper low spots and pits.

For the average wet sanding job, use No. 360 or No. 400 grit on acrylic lacquer or enamel topcoat. Use No. 320 grit when the topcoat is an alkyd enamel. Dry sanding runs 100 grit coarser because sanding dust partially fills in the grit.

Light sanding or *scuffing* should be done on all areas where the old finish is in good condition. The purpose is to partially reduce the paint gloss to improve adhesion. Use an orbital or dual action sander, or use a sanding block. Never use a rotary disc grinder or sander.

If the new topcoat will be lacquer or enamel, use a No. 360 or No. 400 grit sandpaper. If it will be alkyd enamel, use a No. 320 grit sandpaper. For the base coat/clear coat finishes, proper surface preparation is especially critical. It is important to sand all surfaces to be refinished with No. 400 grit or finer paper, followed by 600 grit. Sanding can be done wet or dry. Wet sanding is much faster and requires less sandpaper with finer grits.

Remember! Every square inch or square centimeter to be painted must be sanded. If you fail to scuff any glossy surface thoroughly, the paint can peel off.

It is a good idea to carefully inspect the vehicle surfaces after sanding and scuffing. If you can see any shiny area on the old paint, sand or scuff that area. This will assure that the new finish adheres properly.

FEATHEREDGING

If a new coat of paint is accidentally applied over a broken area of the old finish, the broken film will be very noticeable through the topcoat. The broken areas must be featheredged. *Featheredged* means that the sharp edge of the broken paint film must be gradually tapered down by sanding. Then the bare metal areas are filled with a primer-surfacer and the entire area is sanded smooth and level.

Hand featheredging with a sanding block is usually a two-step procedure:

1. Cut down the edges of the broken areas with a coarse No. 80 grit paper and follow with No. 240 grit.
2. Complete the taper of the featheredge with either a No. 360 or No. 400 grit paper and water. This will produce a finely tapered edge and eliminate coarse paper scratches.

When *power featheredging* with an air sander, use an orbital or dual action sander with a flexible backing pad. Use a No. 80 grit for the rough cut, followed by a No. 180 or 240 grit for the fine work.

Start by positioning the sanding disc flat against the work surface. Using the outer edge, or approximately 1 inch (25 mm) of the sanding disc, cut away the rough paint edges. Do NOT hold the sander at an angle greater than 10 degrees from the surface or it will cut a deep gouge in the paint.

After initially leveling the rough paint edges, lay the sander flat on the panel. Finish tapering the paint layers by moving the sander back and forth in a cross-cutting pattern. Start over the chipped area and work in an outward direction. Stop frequently and run your hand over the sanded area to feel for rough edges. When the surface feels smooth where the old paint and primer meet, featheredging is complete.

> *WARNING! A common mistake when using a DA is to tilt the sander to remove small surface imperfections. This will cause an indentation in the surface that will show up after painting. Normally, hold the sander flat on the surface to avoid this problem.*

Remember! The dust from sanding and grinding operations can often cause a major health problem. As

A

B

C

Figure 14–12 To protect your lungs from airborne dust from sanding, always work in well-ventilated area or use dust collection system on sanding equipment. *(Dynabrade)* A: This is a complete portable sander-dust collection system. B: During use, sanding dust is pulled through hose by vacuum source and captured in disposable bag.

shown in Figure 14–12, there are several dust control systems available.

UNDERCOAT SYSTEMS

Proper *undercoats* of primer is the foundation for an attractive, durable topcoat of paint. If the undercoat—or combination of undercoats—is NOT correct, the topcoat appearance will suffer, possibly cracking or peeling.

Undercoats can be compared to a sandwich filler that holds two slices of bread together. The bottom slice of bread is called the substrate (or surface of the vehicle). That surface can be bare metal or plastic, or a painted or preprimed surface. The undercoat is the sandwich filler applied to the substrate. It makes the substrate smooth and provides a bond for the topcoat. The upper slice is the topcoat, the final color coat that the customer sees.

There are four basic types of undercoats:

1. Primer
2. Primer-surfacer
3. Primer-sealer
4. Sealer

Most surfaces must be undercoated before refinishing for several reasons:

1. To fill scratches
2. To provide a good base for the topcoat
3. To promote adhesion of the topcoat to the substrate
4. To ensure corrosion resistance

A *primer* alone, however, will NOT fill sand scratches or other surface flaws. *Primer-surfacers* are used to provide both priming and filling in one step. *Primer-sealers* are applied to prevent solvents in the topcoat from being absorbed into the porous primer-surfacer. These three undercoats—primer, primer-surfacer, and primer-sealer—can be used together, singularly, or in various combinations. This will depend on the surface condition and size of the job.

Sealers are used to improve adhesion between the old and new finishes. To provide good adhesion, use a sealer over an old lacquer finish when the new finish is to be enamel. Under other conditions, a sealer is desirable but NOT absolutely necessary.

Before applying any undercoat, be sure to treat all bare metal with metal conditioner. Reduce the undercoat according to the manufacturer's instructions. Be careful to select the proper solvent for the weather conditions and mix the materials thoroughly.

Apply the first coat of undercoat and allow it to flash dry. Follow the recommendations on the label for flash time. Then apply two or three more medium wet coats for additional film build-up. Again, allow flash time between each coat. When making a spot repair, extend the additional coats several inches out from the first coat.

Allow the undercoat to dry thoroughly. After the undercoat is dry, block sand the area until it is smooth. For best results, use No. 320 grit sandpaper. If very fine scratches still appear, another coat of undercoat might be all that is required to fill them.

USING SPOT PUTTY

Discussed earlier in the text, some sand scratches might require additional filling with glazing putty. *Glazing* or *spot putty* is used to fill small scratches and pinholes after priming.

To apply the spot putty, squeeze a small amount of the tube onto the edge of a squeegee. Quickly press the putty onto the repair area. Level it off with a flat scraping motion. Use moderate pressure to assure that the putty fills the depression completely. Make additional passes quickly, if necessary.

> *WARNING! Use spot or glazing putty sparingly. Do NOT use it as a plastic filler or you will have major problems, like shrinkage.*

Allow the putty to air dry until it is hard. Test with a fingernail for hardness before sanding. If it is sanded too soon, the putty will continue to shrink, leaving part of the scratch unfilled. Once it hardens, dry sand the putty with No. 80 to 180 grit paper. You can also wet sand the putty with No. 320 grit paper. Wet sanding requires special paper and plenty of water.

After sanding the puttied area, clean the surface and then reprime. If the putty has been wet sanded, make sure to dry the surface thoroughly before applying primer-surfacer.

Lacquer-based glazing putties are being replaced by *two-part putties*. Two-part putties include *polyester putties* (finishing fillers) and *polyester primer/fillers*. Both products must be mixed with hardener and can be applied to filler, bare metal, or old paint finishes. The use of these high-viscosity, finely textured "two-part putties" eliminates the traditional primer/putty/primer process. Because they chemically harden, they cure quickly and can be primed and refinished without the worry of sand scratch swelling commonly associated with lacquer-based glazing putties.

For more information on these topics, refer to Chapters 8 and 10.

MASKING

Masking keeps paint mist from contacting areas other than those to be refinished or painted. It is a very important step in the vehicle preparation process. Masking has become even more important because of two-component type paints. Once these paints dry, the overspray CANNOT be removed with a thinner or other solvent. It must be removed with a rubbing compound or by other time-consuming means.

There are several ways of masking the parts of a vehicle:

1. Masking paper and masking tape
2. Plastic sheeting and masking tape
3. Special shaped cloth or plastic covers (for wheels, antenna, rear view mirrors)
4. Liquid masking material

> *WARNING! Traditional masking products may not work with waterborne paints because of their high water content. If using waterborne products, check with your supplier for masking papers and tapes made for use with them.*

Using Masking Paper and Tape

Masking paper is a roll of paper designed to cover parts of a vehicle. Automotive masking paper comes in various widths—from 3 to 36 inches (75–915 mm). It is heat resistant so that it can be used safely in baking ovens. It also has good wet strength, freedom from loose fibers, and resistance to solvent penetration.

> *WARNING! Never use newspaper for masking a vehicle since it does NOT meet any of these requirements. Newspaper also contains printing inks that are soluble in some paint solvents. These inks can be transferred to the underlying finish or bleed into the new paint, causing staining.*

Masking tape is very sticky paper tape designed to cover small parts and to also hold the masking paper in place. Automotive masking tape comes in various widths—from ¼ to 2 in. (6.4 to 50 mm). Larger width tapes are used only occasionally because they are difficult to handle.

Automotive masking tape should NOT be confused with tape bought in hardware or paint stores for home use. This kind of tape will NOT hold up to the demanding requirements of automotive refinishing.

A *masking paper dispenser* automatically applies tape to one edge of the paper as the paper is pulled out, Figure 14–13. This saves time when masking a car or truck. The average size vehicle can take two rolls of tape to be completely masked. The use of masking paper and tape dispensing equipment makes it easy to tear off the exact amount needed. Some dispensers permit tape to adhere to both edges of the paper as it is rolled out.

Fine line masking tape is a very thin, smooth surface plastic masking tape. Also termed *flush masking tape,* it can be used to produce a better *paint part edge* (edge where old paint and new paint meet). When the fine line tape is removed, the edge of the new paint will be straighter and smoother than if conventional masking tape were used.

Masking Covers

Masking covers are specially shaped cloth or plastic covers for masking specific parts. There are several types of masking covers available. They can save time when masking.

One is the *tire cover* that eliminates the need for masking off the tire. Others include a body cover and a frame cover. Covers are also available in a variety of sizes and shapes to mask headlights, taillights, antennas, mirrors, etc.

Masking Procedures

Before any types of masking materials are applied, the vehicle must be completely cleaned and all dust blown away. Masking tape will NOT stick to surfaces that are NOT clean and dry. It is important that the tape is pressed down firmly and adheres to the surface. Otherwise, paint will creep under it.

In the case of a two-color job where the color break is NOT hidden by a stripe or molding, use fine line masking tape and press its edge down firmly.

There are no clear ground rules on when to mask and when to remove parts. This would include parts like trim, moldings, door handles, etc. The decision to remove or mask depends upon the design of the vehi-

Figure 14–13 Masking tape–paper dispenser is a time saver. This unit has different widths of paper on it.

cle, and the expectations of the customer. If a part can be removed easily, this is better than trying to mask around the part. Also, if you cannot sand and clean right up to the part, the part should be removed. If it will be difficult to mask the piece, you might save time removing the part from the vehicle. Each part will require an individual decision.

Removal of trim is more often necessary when using a base coat/clear coat system than with a single stage finish. The film build-up can be greater with base coat/clear coats. This additional thickness makes the paint edge more likely to crack or chip.

It is wise to completely clean and detail the vehicle before masking and again after the refinishing job is completed. This is because masking over a dirty vehicle can cause a "dirty paint job!"

If the painting environment is cold and damp, the masking tape may NOT stick to the glass or chrome parts. Condensation on them can prevent the tape from sticking properly. Wipe the parts off before masking them. When masking door jambs, be sure to cover both the door lock assembly and the striker bolt. They can become filled and clogged with paint if NOT masked.

Although masking tape is elastic, do not stretch the tape when making a straight line, Figure 14–14. Only stretch masking tape to cover curved surfaces. This is especially true when masking newly applied finishes that are still soft underneath. It is also wise to avoid stretching the tape because this can increase the degree of tape marking on the finish.

Figure 14-14 When using masking tape, pull lightly on tape with one hand without stretching tape. Moving up or down in hand will control direction of tape application. Other hand is used to press tape down securely on surface.

Figure 14-15 Small parts can be covered completely with masking tape. Make sure edge of tape does not cover surface to be painted.

When applying masking tape, hold and peel the tape with one hand. Use your other hand to guide and secure the tape to the vehicle, Figure 14–15. This provides tight edges for good adherence. This also allows you to change directions and go around corners.

To cut the tape easily, quickly tear upward against your thumbnail, as shown in Figure 14–16. This permits a clean cut of the tape without stretching.

WARNING! Be careful that the masking tape does NOT overlap any area to be painted. After painting, you can remove paint from parts but you cannot add missing paint to the body. Loop or overlap the inner tape edge to follow curves. The tape will stretch to conform to the curves. Difficult areas such as wheels can be masked using this process, but more often covers are used to save time.

When masking large areas, such as bumpers, tape the paper to the middle of the bumper first. Then each side can be secured without the paper dragging on the floor and getting in the way.

Before masking glass areas, remove accessories such as wiper blades. The wiper shafts can be protected in the same manner as radio antennas and door handles. Use tape or special covers.

To mask glass, first apply tape along the very top and along the edges of the moldings. Then, use

two pieces of masking paper to cover the glass, Figure 14–17. Overlap the tape on the paper with the tape already on the molding. The top piece of paper should overlap the bottom piece of paper. If necessary, fold and tape any pleats in the paper to prevent dust and paint seepage.

An *overspray leak* results when you do not seal the masking paper or plastic and overspray gets on unwanted surfaces. You would have to then take the time to use solvent or compound to remove the overspray problem.

Fine line tape can be used to protect existing stripes from overspray. Also use fine line tape for precise color separation in two-color painting and for creating vivid, clean stripes. Its added flexibility makes painting of curved lines easier, with less reworking.

Double masking uses TWO LAYERS of masking paper to prevent bleed-through or finish-dulling from

Figure 14-16 Paper can be cut or torn using fingernail to hold tape down while pulling sideways with other hand.

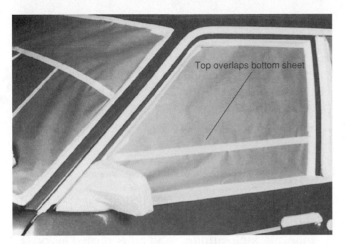

Figure 14–17 Two pieces of masking paper are often used to cover glass. Apply lower sheet first, then upper sheet. Tape over where paper edges meet to prevent overspray leakage.

solvents. It is needed when spraying horizontal surfaces (hood, trunk, etc.) next to other horizontal surfaces. Overspray will tend to soak through the adjacent masked area and onto the old paint.

A *reverse masking* method requires you to fold the masking paper back and over the masking tape, Figure 14–18. It is often used during spot repairs to help blend the painted area and make it less noticeable. This also helps prevent bleed-through. The paper is taped on the inside and allowed to bellow slightly, which keeps it lifted a bit from the surface.

A door edge or body line next to a refinished panel can sometimes show a slight difference in an otherwise acceptable color match, particularly with metallics. This situation can be avoided by crossing the line and sanding the adjacent panel when preparing for refinishing. Then reverse mask the adjacent panel and refinish as desired.

Figure 14–18 Reverse masking will help blend a repair area. Overspray will hit paper and blend more smoothly into old paint.

If there is a slight difference after removing the masking paper, just paint across the line and blend in smoothly as with any spot repair. Reverse mask very carefully. Any overmasked or undermasked areas will lead to extra work after the vehicle is painted.

Overmasked areas mean that the painter must touch up the part of the vehicle that should have been painted. On the other hand, *undermasked* areas must be cleaned with solvent or polishing compound to remove overspray. Each would detract from the appearance of an otherwise good job.

Liquid Masking Material

Liquid masking material seals off the entire vehicle to protect undamaged panels and parts from paint overspray. It is the newest masking system available to painters. Liquid masking is used on areas where masking is necessary but difficult to apply, including wheel wells, headlights, grille, underbody chassis, and even the engine compartment.

Masking liquid, also called masking coating, is usually a water-based sprayable material for keeping overspray off body parts. Some are solvent based. Masking liquid comes in a large, ready-to-spray container or drum. These materials are sprayed on and form a paint-proof coating over the vehicle.

Some masking coatings are tacky and used only during priming and painting. They form a film that can be applied when the vehicle enters the shop. Others dry to a hard, dull finish.

Masking coatings can be removed when the vehicle is ready to return to the owner. It washes off with soap and water. Local regulations may require that liquid masking residue be captured in a floor drain trap, and not put into the sewer system.

To mask a vehicle using the liquid masking system, proceed as follows:

1. Partially mask the area to be painted by going around it with masking paper. Fold the paper over onto the area to be painted, Figure 14–19. Secure the paper with masking tape.

2. Apply the liquid masking material. Use a heavy, single overlapping coat. Apply the material to all surfaces not to be painted. This would include bumpers, grilles, doors, windshields, body panels, wheels, wheel wells, door jambs, and even the entire compartment, Figure 14–20.

   An airless spray system is generally recommended for applying the masking material.

3. Fold the masking paper back over the liquid masking material, Figure 14–21. Wipe away any material from the area to be painted with a damp sponge. Allow the surface to dry.

Figure 14–19 Partially mask around area to be painted. Fold paper over area to be painted.

Figure 14–20 Spray liquid mask onto areas NOT to be painted.

Figure 14–21 Fold masking paper back over and away from area to be painted. Tape down so it cannot fall into paint.

Figure 14–22 After paint has hardened sufficiently, wash off liquid masking material.

4. Prepare the surface. Then apply primer and paint according to the manufacturer's instructions.

5. Allow the paint to dry, then unmask the vehicle. Liquid masking may be used in both air dry or bake conditions.

6. After the paint is cured, wash off the dried liquid masking material with a garden hose or pressure washer, Figure 14–22.

Summary

- Vehicle preparation involves all of the final steps prior to painting, including cleaning, sanding, stripping, masking, priming, and other related tasks.

- Open coat sandpaper is good for sanding softer materials, such as old paint, body filler, plastic and aluminum. Closed coat sandpaper generally provides a finer finish and is commonly used in wet sanding.

- Proper undercoats of primer is the foundation for an attractive, durable topcoat of paint. If the undercoat—or combination of undercoats—is NOT correct, the topcoat appearance will suffer, possibly cracking or peeling.

- Masking keeps paint mist from contacting areas other than those to be refinished or painted. Some masking materials include masking paper and tape, plastic sheeting, cloth, plastic covers, and liquid masking material.

Technical Terms

vehicle preparation	*surface low spot*
surface evaluation	*featheredged*
paint film breakdown	*undercoats*
paint adhesion check	*primer*
chemical stripping	*primer-surfacer*
abrasive blasting	*primer-sealer*
machine grinding	*sealer*
bare metal treatment	*polyester putties*
wash primer	*masking*
self-etching primers	*masking paper*
new part primer coat	*masking tape*
sanding grit sizes	*masking paper dispenser*
disc adhesive	*fine line masking tape*
self-stick sandpaper	*masking covers*
block sanding	*overspray leak*
dry sanding	*double masking*
wet sanding	*reverse masking*
scuff pad	*overmasked*
paint scuffing	*undermasked*
guide coat	*liquid masking material*
surface high spot	

Review Questions

1. What sandpaper grit size is used to remove an old paint film?
   a. No. 24
   b. No. 400
   c. No. 1250
   d. No. 2000

2. Technician A uses a circular motion when block sanding. Technician B block sands in a back-and-forth direction. Who is correct?
   a. Technician A
   b. Technician B
   c. Both A and B
   d. Neither A nor B

3. Paint film breakdown will show up as _____, _____, or _____.

4. How do you do a paint adhesion check?

5. _____ are used to provide both priming and filling in one step.

6. Which of the following statements concerning masking is INCORRECT?
   a. Newspaper works well and saves money as paint masking paper.
   b. Removal of trim, as opposed to masking, is preferred in some instances.
   c. Masking tape will NOT stick to surfaces that are NOT clean and dry.
   d. Using plastic covers on tires eliminates the need for masking them.

7. List four ways of masking the parts of a vehicle.

8. Name three common ways of stripping paint from metal surfaces.

9. Define the term "abrasive blasting."

10. Why is plastic bead blasting often preferred over sandblasting?

11. _____ _____ etch the bare metal to improve paint adhesion and corrosion resistance, while providing the priming and filling properties of primer-surfacer.

12. Explain four ways that sanding prepares the surface for painting.

13. Describe four general uses for different sandpaper grits.

14. How do you use a guide coat?

15. Lacquer-based glazing putties are being replaced by two-part putties. True or false?

Activities

1. Visit a body shop. Ask the owner to let you watch worker prepare a vehicle for painting.

2. Make a chart showing the steps for preparing a vehicle for painting.

CHAPTER 15

SHOP AND EQUIPMENT PREPARATION

Objectives

After reading this chapter, you should be able to:

■ Describe the recommended maintenance program for a spray booth.

■ Explain the importance of proper paint atomization, paint viscosity, and paint temperature.

■ Measure the viscosity of paint using a Ford cup and a Zahn cup.

■ Describe the advantages of a captive spray gun system.

■ Operate and maintain a spray gun.

■ Complete a spray pattern test.

■ Adjust a spray gun to prepare for painting a vehicle.

Introduction

To complete a professional paint job, your shop and equipment must be in perfect condition! A dirty paint booth, a poorly maintained paint spray gun, contaminated air supply, and other avoidable situations will all ruin your work. Sloppy shop conditions will usually result in a "sloppy paint job."

This chapter summarizes the steps needed for preparing the finishing equipment and paint area for spraying the topcoat. There are a number of shop and equipment variables that affect the refinishing operation. These variables include the painting environment, as well as the painting equipment and their adjustments. ALL are important. You must pay close attention to these variables because they can affect the quality of your work. See Figure 15–1.

Remember! A professional painter will spend more time maintaining the shop and his or her equipment than on any other single task. Spraying the car only takes a very short amount of time by comparison.

NOTE! YOU SHOULD HAVE STUDIED CHAPTERS 3, 5, 6, AND 8 BEFORE COMPLETING THIS CHAPTER. THESE CHAPTERS GIVE VITAL INFORMATION FOR COMPREHENDING THIS MATERIAL.

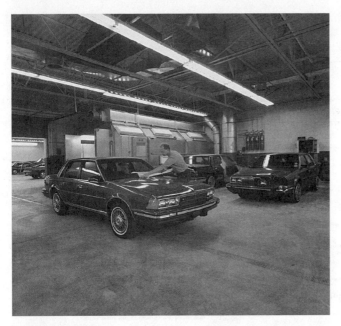

Figure 15–1 The cleanliness of your prep area, spray booth, and shop in general affects the quality of your work. Always keep all areas clean and organized. *(Photo courtesy of Binks Manufacturing Company)*

PAINTING ENVIRONMENT

A painter must have a suitable work environment. Automotive paint must be kept free of dust and dirt during spraying and while drying. In fact, today's clearcoat finishes will magnify any dust, dirt, or other flaws in the finish.

Figure 15–2 shows the basic work flow of a vehicle while going through a typical body shop. Note location of spray booth for painting and drying equipment.

The proper *painting environment* must address these variables:

1. Cleanliness—to keep dirt out of paint

2. Temperature/humidity—to provide proper paint curing or drying conditions

3. Light—to properly light vehicle and paint as it is applied

4. Compressed air/pressure—to send clean air, at the right pressure to gun

There are many ways of keeping dirt from becoming a problem in a finish. During body repairs, dirt can be controlled by:

1. Using a dustless, or vacuum, sanding system

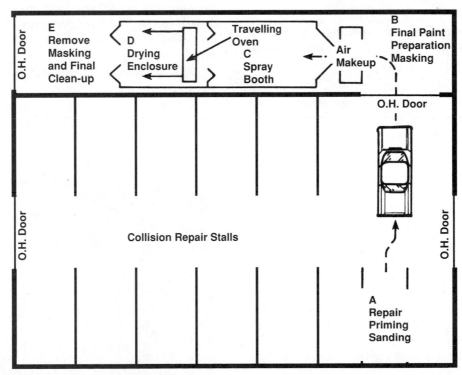

Figure 15–2 A: After making repairs, vehicle is moved into final prep area. B: It is a clean area for prepping surface and masking. C: It is then moved into paint booth for tacking and painting. D: After painting, another area is often provided for drying. E: After drying, vehicle is pulled into final clean-up area.

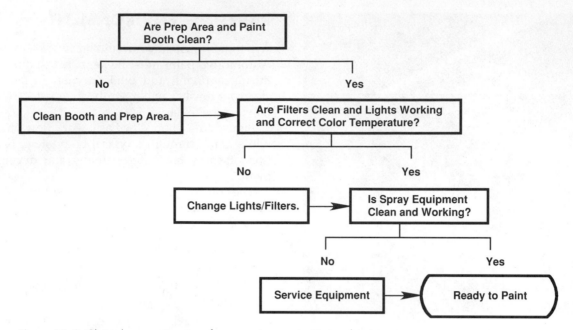

Figure 15–3 Chart shows major steps for preparing equipment and paint area.

2. Cleaning the vehicle before bringing it into the shop

3. Having the paint prep area separate from the body repair area

4. Using down draft prep stations

5. Maintaining the compressed air system's filters and water traps

Before beginning a refinish operation, you must *prep* (prepare) the equipment and paint area. As diagrammed in Figure 15–3, you should:

1. Clean the spray booth.

2. Check the spray booth filters for clogging and replace them if needed.

3. Replace any burned out bulbs.

4. Drain any moisture from the compressed air system. Check filters and dryers.

PREPARING PAINT BOOTH

Improper booth cleanliness may result in foreign matter entering the fresh paint. This can require you to sand out the debris and repaint the area. You will waste time and materials if you try to paint a car or truck in a dirty environment.

The *spray booth* must provide the painter with:

1. Clean environment, Figure 15–4.

2. Constant temperature. The paint, vehicle, and air flow should be at room temperature while spraying.

3. Daylight corrected lighting.

4. Proper air movement for removing hazardous fumes and overspray, and correct drying and curing of the paint film.

Before pulling the vehicle into the booth, make sure the area is perfectly clean and organized. Routine maintenance is necessary for proper spray booth performance. A regular program of cleaning, filter replacement, examining seals and lighting is important for the spray booth to operate properly.

Daily spray booth cleaning includes:

1. Remove all masking paper, empty cans, and other nonessential items. Clean up scrap, masking paper, rags, and so forth. Maintain and clean ALL equipment used in the booth.

Figure 15–4 Spray booth provides controlled, clean conditions for painting. *(Photo courtesy of Binks Manufacturing Company)*

Figure 15–5 Before pulling vehicle into spray booth, make sure booth is perfectly clean. Remove all unneeded objects, wipe down surfaces, and sweep out. *(Photo courtesy of Binks Manufacturing Company)*

2. Sweep the floor, Figure 15–5. The collected material should be stored in a fireproof container. Keep the booth free of dirt and overspray at ALL times. Floors and walls should be wiped down after every job.

3. To help keep any stray dust down, wet the spray booth floor before spraying.

4. Drain oil and water filters and traps.

5. Clean the air hoses by wiping with a damp rag or tack cloth. Clean ALL air hoses several times a day. Accumulations of dirt and dust on their outer surfaces might drop off onto the freshly painted surfaces.

6. Inspect filters and replace if necessary.

The continuous flow of air through the booth will eventually load the filters with dirt and over-spray, Figure 15–6. These filters should be inspected and replaced at the recommended intervals. When they are replaced, the filters recommended by the booth manufacturer should be used, Figure 15–7. Several types of filtration systems are available. See Figure 15–8.

Monitor the manometer readings daily and know what a normal reading should be. The *manometer* indicates when the intake filters are overloaded. Some booths have a pressure switch that shuts off the air supply and exhaust fan when the intake filter is clogged. Refer to Figure 15–9.

Danger! Clogged booth filters are a fire hazard because they could ignite under certain conditions.

Weekly spray booth cleaning includes the following:

1. Vacuum the top of the spray booth and blow off exterior glass and walls.

2. Secure access doors and blow off interior walls and ceiling with the fan running.

3. Clean the light fixtures. Periodically check the lighting inside the booth and replace weak or burned out bulbs. Improper lighting can lead to poor finishes.

To do a *monthly spray booth cleaning:*

1. Inspect the spray booth for air leaks and caulking and resealing when necessary.

2. Inspect and clean sprinkler heads. Replace plastic bags over sprinkler heads.

Annual spray booth cleaning includes these tasks:

1. Clean the plenum chamber and fan blade. Pay special attention to corners at the base of the

Figure 15–6 Airflow through booth and filters helps keep any dirt from entering wet paint.

Wet or Wash Type

A **Water Wash with Pump**   **No Pump**

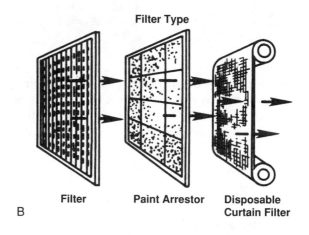

Filter Type

B **Filter**   **Paint Arrestor**   **Disposable Curtain Filter**

Figure 15–7 Filters should be checked and changed periodically. A: These are ceiling filters in paint booth. B: These are floor gratings over filters.

chamber. Paint dust accumulation in this area creates a flammable situation.

2. Oil the plenum and fan blade.

3. Inspect the exhaust stack for paint build-up in damper area. Excessive build-up here will prevent dampers (butterflies) from opening and closing properly.

Prep with Vehicle in Booth

After driving the vehicle into the spray booth, close the booth doors tightly, Figure 15–10. Turn on the air filtration system and allow it to run a few minutes. Then *tack-rag* the entire vehicle to remove any loose dust and other debris on surfaces. This is needed before proceeding with the painting operation.

C

Figure 15–8 Different methods of spray booth filtration: A: wet filtration, B: dry filtration, and C: a combination of water spray and centrifugal separation.

Figure 15–9 Manometer is mounted at paint booth. It will tell you when filters are becoming clogged, requiring replacement. (Photo courtesy of Binks Manufacturing Company)

The booth doors must be kept tightly closed during painting. If it becomes necessary to open a door, be sure the exhaust fan and air supply are turned off. In fact, many spray booths are equipped with door switches that automatically shut off the exhaust fan.

Personal cleanliness cannot be overemphasized. Never enter the booth wearing dirty clothes or shoes. The dirt can be easily transferred to the vehicle and into the finish. All clothing and gloves should be clean and lint-free.

PAINT MIXING AND STORAGE AREA PREP

The *paint mixing room* should provide a safe, clean, well-lit area for a painter to store, mix, and reduce paint materials. The mixing room. It should be located near the spray booth. It should also contain the mixing equipment if an inter-mix system is used. The

Figure 15–10 After cleaning paint booth thoroughly, you can pull vehicle into booth.

paint mixing room may also include a painter prep area. This area must be constructed to meet applicable building, fire, and electrical codes. The paint mixing area must be kept clean to reduce the amount of dust and dirt that can be introduced to the paint and painter.

A *painter prep area* is a shop area for:

1. A clean area for a painter to dress
2. Clean storage for painting suits
3. A place to clean and store personal safety equipment
4. A good location to have emergency eye wash and first aid equipment

Dirt can enter the paint as it is being mixed, so a clean, well-lit mixing area is required. Federal and local laws will dictate the type of mixing area the shop must have. In many cases, this means an enclosed space with its own ventilation system and explosion-proof lighting, as well as the following:

The mixing area must have adequate ventilation and fire protection (per local and state codes). It must also have proper mixing and measuring equipment such as paint shakers, paddle agitators, churning knives, paint mixing sticks, mixing cans, and other equipment.

Many refinishing materials are expendable. That is, they are used up in day-to-day shop activities. For this reason, it is very important to keep plenty of such items on hand. It is foolish to run out of a material while in the middle of a job. Have plenty of these expendable materials on hand:

1. Abrasive paper and sanding blocks
2. Clean wiping cloths or paper towels
3. Tack-rags
4. Paint paddles
5. Strainers
6. Mixing buckets
7. Masking paper and tape
8. Squeegees
9. Thinner/reducer
10. Cleaning solvent

NOTE! FOR MORE INFORMATION ON MATERIALS, REFER TO CHAPTER 8.

PREPARING SPRAY PAINT EQUIPMENT

If a spray paint equipment is NOT adjusted, handled, and cleaned properly, it will apply a defective coating to the surface. The most common problems and sug-

First Stage   **Second Stage**   **Third Stage**

Figure 15–11 Note three stages of atomization shown by cutaway view of spray gun.

gested remedies are given in the equipment service manuals. These variables can affect the appearance of the color and the outcome of the refinishing operation.

When preparing the spray equipment, you must:

1. Clean the spray equipment.
2. Set up the spray equipment with the proper fluid needle, fluid nozzle, and air cap for the material to be sprayed.
3. Adjust the temperature in the spray booth if necessary.
4. Adjust the air pressure.
5. Make a test spray pattern.

Compressed Air System Preparation

The compressed air system can be a source of problems for the painter. *Air supply system problems* can introduce dirt, moisture, and oil into the air supply. From there, this contamination can get into the paint. To avoid air supply problems:

1. Check and replace oil and water filters and traps on a regular basis.
2. Drain moisture from the system daily. Draining the system in the morning allows more moisture to be removed because it is cool and has condensed.
3. Replace air hoses as necessary. Deteriorated air hoses can also introduce dirt into the system.

Air lines should slope away from the compressor. This allows moisture to collect away from the compressor. Air hose fitting should be at the top of the metal air line. This will reduce the amount of moisture getting into the air filters and hoses.

Atomization Is Important!

A thorough understanding of atomization is the key to using a spray gun correctly. *Atomization* breaks paint into a spray of tiny, uniform droplets. When properly applied to the vehicle's surface, these

droplets flow together to create an even film thickness with a mirrorlike gloss. Proper atomization is essential when working with today's basecoat/clearcoat finishes.

Illustrated in Figure 15–11, atomization takes place in three basic stages.

In the first stage, the paint siphoned from the fluid tip is surrounded by air streaming from the annular ring. This turbulence begins the breakup of the paint.

The second stage of atomization occurs when the paint stream is hit with jets of air from the containment holes. These air jets keep the paint stream from getting out of control and aid in the breakup of the paint.

Gravity Feed Type   **Pressure Feed Type**

Syphon Feed Type

Compressed Air   **Pressure Tank**

Figure 15–12 Compare four basic types of paint spray guns.

Figure 15–13 Know the parts of typical spray gun. *(Illustration courtesy of Binks Manufacturing Company)*

In the third phase of atomization, the paint is struck by jets of air from the air cap horns. These jets hit the paint from opposite sides, causing it to form into a fan-shaped spray.

Basecoat/clearcoat finishes require very fine atomization. This is because the basecoat is so thin. Basecoat/clearcoat finishes will also NOT obtain proper hiding and coverage if NOT atomized properly.

In Figure 15–12, note the common types of spray guns. These were covered in detail in Chapter 5.

Spray Gun Parts Review

The principal components of a typical spray gun are illustrated in Figure 15–13.

The *air cap* directs the compressed air into the paint to atomize it and form the spray pattern. Each of the orifices has a different function, Figure 15–14. The *center orifice* located at the fluid nozzle creates a vacuum for the discharge of the paint. The *side orifices* determine the spray pattern by means of air pressure. The *auxiliary orifices* promote atomization of the paint.

Air flow through the two side orifices forms the shape of the spray pattern. When the pattern control knob is closed, the spray pattern is ROUND. As the knob is opened, the spray becomes more OBLONG in shape.

The fluid needle and the fluid nozzle both meter and direct the flow of paint from the gun into the air stream.

The *fluid nozzle* forms an internal seat for the fluid needle, allowing the *fluid needle* to open or shut off

the flow of paint. The amount of paint that leaves the gun depends on fluid nozzle size and how far the needle is pulled back (adjusted). Fluid nozzles are available in a variety of sizes to properly handle paints of various types and viscosities.

The fluid control knob changes the distance the fluid needle moves away from its seat in the nozzle when the trigger is pulled. This controls paint flow.

Like the fluid valve, the air valve is opened by the trigger. The distance the air valve opens is regulated by a screw adjustment. When the trigger is pulled

Figure 15–14 Center orifice located at fluid nozzle creates a vacuum for discharge of paint. Side orifices determine spray pattern by means of air pressure. Auxiliary orifices help atomize paint. *(PPG Industries, Inc.)*

partway, the air valve opens. When it is pulled a little farther, the fluid nozzle opens.

Note how the pressure feed spraying system is hooked up:

1. Connect the regulated air hose from the air control device on the tank to the air inlet on the gun.
2. Connect the mainline air hose from the regulator to the air regulator inlet on the tank.
3. Connect the fluid hose from the fluid outlet on the tank to the fluid inlet on the gun.

Paint pressure tanks are available in sizes from two quarts to 10 gallons (2–38 liters). They are available in single, dual, and non-regulated models.

MIXING PAINT AND SOLVENT

When preparing for spraying, you must thin or reduce the paint to the proper viscosity. Directions on the paint can will explain thinning or reducing procedures.

When mixing and using paint and solvents or other additives, you must measure and mix their contents accurately. This is essential to doing good paint and body work. You must be able to properly mix reducers or thinners, hardeners, and other additives into the paint. If NOT, serious paint problems will result.

Paint mixing instructions are normally given on the paint can label. This may be a percentage or parts of one ingredient compared to the other.

A *percentage reduction* means that each material must be added in certain proportions or parts. For instance, if a paint requires 50% reduction, this means that one part reducer or thinner (solvent) must be mixed with two parts of paint.

Mixing by parts means that for a specific volume of paint or other material, a specific amount of another material must be added. If you are mixing a gallon of paint in a spray gun pressure tank for example, and directions call for 25% reduction, you would add one quart of reducer. There are four quarts in a gallon and you want one part or 25% reducer for each four parts of paint.

Proportional numbers denote the amount of each material needed. The first number is usually the parts of paint needed. The second number is usually the solvent (thinner or reducer). A third number might be used to denote the amount of hardener or other additives required.

For example, the number 4:1:1 might mean to add four parts of color, one part hardener, and one part solvent. For a gallon of color, you would add one quart of hardener, and one quart of solvent. This can vary so always refer to the exact directions on the paint can.

A *mixing chart* converts a percentage into how many parts of each material must be mixed. Study the percentages and parts of each material that must be mixed.

Using Paint Mixing Sticks

Graduated *paint mixing sticks* have scale markings that allow you to easily mix paint, solvent, and additives in the correct proportions. They are provided by the paint system manufacturer. Several are needed to provide mixing guides for each type of paint. Look at Figure 15–15.

Each mixing stick will have a ratio or percentage printed at the top. Paint measurement marks and numbers are placed along the tool for pouring out the correct quantity of each material quickly. Select the mixing stick with the correct ratio and type of paint to be used, Figure 15–16.

Obtain a can, pail, or container with straight sides. Tapered sides on the container would upset your measurements. It should be big enough to hold ALL paint, hardener, and solvent needed for the job. A gallon or larger container saves mixing time for an overall or complete paint job. If you are only painting a small area and one cup will do, mix the materials in the spray gun cup. If you are using a pressure tank spray gun, measure and mix the materials in the tank.

For this example, let us say that the paint mixing stick is for a mixing ratio of 4:1:1 for color, hardener, and solvent.

1. Place the correct paint mixing stick for the type of paint into the container, Figure 15–17.

Figure 15–15 Mixing sticks are provided by paint manufacturers for adding correct amounts of paint, hardener, and solvent. They are designed to be used specifically with their paint systems.

A

B

Figure 15–16 Top of mixing stick will give mixing ratios. Ratio should be same as instructions given on paint can label.

Figure 15–17 Place correct mixing stick into clean container for mixing materials. Side of container must not be tapered.

4. Pour in the final ingredient (usually solvent) until it aligns with the same number in last column on the mixing stick. This is demonstrated in Figure 15–18.

After adding the correct amounts of each material, thoroughly mix them with your metal mixing stick. You can then fill your spray paint gun with properly mixed paint.

When filling your spray gun, always use a paint strainer over the cup. The *paint strainer* is a paper funnel-mesh strainer that keeps debris out of the spray gun. It should be used when anything is poured into your spray gun cup! Contaminants can accidentally get into new materials. Dirt and dust can also fall off the top of containers when you're pouring!

PAINT VISCOSITY PREPARATION

Paint viscosity refers to the paint's thickness or ability to resist flow. Using an incorrect viscosity paint will result in various finish defects. The paint must be thoroughly mixed and properly thinned or reduced.

Paint viscosity can be measured by means of a *viscosity cup.* This is another very accurate method of assuring proper paint thickness. The flow characteristics of liquids relate directly to the degree of internal friction. Therefore, anything that influences the internal friction (such as solvents, thinners, or temperature change) will influence flow. Similarly, paint flow affects how well the paint will atomize and "flow out" on the vehicle surface.

The two types of paint viscosity measuring cups are the *Ford cup* and the *Zahn cup.* Although the Ford cup is very accurate, its high cost limits its use. The Zahn type cup is inexpensive and more common.

2. Pour the amount of paint or primer you might use into the bucket. Stop pouring when the paint is even with any of the numbers on the left of the stick. Pour until the first material is even with any number on the left column. This might be 1 through 7 for example, depending on the quantity of paint needed.

For more paint, you might fill to lines 6 or 7. For a spot repair, you might only need to make material even with lines 2 or 3, for example. Make sure the paint is perfectly even with any of the numbers on the mixing stick. If color is listed on the left, the paint should be even with any number column in that column.

3. Pour in hardener until even with the same number (from step 2) in the next column on the stick. If the material already in the container aligned with 3, pour in hardener until it aligns with 3 but in the second column.

Pour to First Row Number

Pour to Second Row Number

Pour to Third Row Number

Color, Clear or Undercoat   Hardener   Reducer/Thinner

Figure 15–18 *Study basic steps for using mixing stick. (BASF) A: Depending upon information on top of mixing stick, paint or primer is usually poured in first. Pour in the amount of material needed for job. Stop when you reach the correct numbers on the mixing stick. B: If used, pour hardener or catalyst in next. Pour material in can until even with same number on mixing stick but in next column. If the paint was even with number 5, pour in hardener to number 5 on next or center column on stick. C: Pour in solvent until liquid is even with 5 on stick in right column. Pour all materials slowly so that you do not add too much. Stir materials with metal stick.*

The paint manufacturer will give a recommended viscosity value in *viscosity cup seconds.* It will vary between 17 and 30 seconds depending upon the type of paint and type of cup used. Refer to the paint specifications on the can for an exact value.

If the paint DRAINS TOO QUICKLY out of the viscosity cup, you have added too much solvent. More paint would be needed. If the cup DRAINS TOO SLOWLY, you have NOT added enough solvent. Remix until the paint passes the viscosity cup test.

If the paint is TOO THICK, your paint will develop orange peel or a rough film. If paint is TOO THIN, excess solvent can cause the paint to have poor hiding and other problems.

Make sure you use a thinner or reducer designed for the shop temperature and conditions. The amount of reduction should be the same regardless of temperature.

Various automotive finishes are manufactured to spray at specific viscosities. It is very important to follow the label directions for each type of material being mixed.

Using Ford Viscosity Cup

The Ford cup comes in two sizes: No. 3 and No. 4. The bottom of the cup is conical shaped with an orifice in the center. The No. 3 and No. 4 cups are distinguished by the diameter of this orifice. Look at Figure 15–19.

To measure the viscosity of paint with a Ford cup, proceed as follows:

1. Keep the temperature of the paint and cup at about 68°F (20°C).

2. Secure the cup to the frame. Place the glass plate on top.

3. Place the level on top of the glass plate. Adjust the frame with the level adjusting bolts. Then, place a container below the cup.

4. While supporting the bottom of the cup with one hand, place a piece of thick rubber over the orifice. Pour in the paint, being careful that no air bubbles enter.

5. Slide the glass plate horizontally over the top of the cup to remove any excess paint, then set it aside.

6. Release the piece of rubber supporting the orifice. Time how long the paint drains continuously with a stopwatch. Measure until the continuous

Figure 15–19 Ford cup is very accurate way of checking paint viscosity. Time how long it takes material to pour out of cup. This time (in seconds) should equal specs given by paint manufacturer. (BASF)

paint flow stops. This time is used as an indicator of the paint viscosity. For example, if it takes 15.4 seconds, the viscosity of the paint is 15.4 seconds at 68°F (20°C).

Using Zahn Viscosity Cup

The Zahn cup is also cylindrical in shape and has an orifice at the bottom. To determine viscosity with a Zahn cup, proceed as follows:

1. Prepare the paint to be tested. Mix, strain, and reduce as directed by the manufacturer.
2. Fill the cup by submerging it in the paint, Figure 15–20.
3. After removing the cup, release the flow of the paint and trigger the stopwatch. Keep your eyes on the flow, NOT on the watch.

4. When the solid stream of paint "breaks" (indicating air passing through orifice), stop the watch. A stopwatch is ideal for measuring paint viscosity with either viscosity cup. Most painters prefer a digital stopwatch because it is easily read.

As with the Ford cup, the result is expressed in seconds. Manufacturers recommend specific viscosities for their various types of paint.

PAINT TEMPERATURE

The temperature at which paint is sprayed and dried has a great influence on the smoothness of the finish. This involves NOT only the temperature of the shop, but the temperature of the work surface as well.

You should pull the vehicle into the shop and booth early enough before spraying so that its surfaces can warm up. Never spray warm paint on a cold surface or cool paint on a hot surface. This will upset the flow characteristics of the paint.

Appropriate thinners or reducers should also be used for warm and cold weather applications. For example, a *hot weather solvent* (reducer or thinner) is designed to slow solvent evaporation to prevent problems. A *cold weather solvent* is designed to speed solvent evaporation so the paint flows and dries in a reasonable amount of time.

CAPTIVE SPRAY GUN SYSTEM

Because different materials require different set-ups, many shops use a captive spray gun system. In a *captive spray gun system,* individual guns are set up and used for applying each type of material. Each would be clean, adjusted and ready for use. You would have separate spray guns for each type of material to be sprayed:

1. For applying primer-surfacers
2. For applying primer-sealers

A   B   C

Figure 15–20 Using a Zahn cup: A: Dip the cup into the paint until it is full. B: Remove the cup, and as it clears the surface of the paint, begin timing the flow of paint from the small hole in the bottom of the cup. C: Stop the timer when the stream of paint breaks.

3. For applying basecoats

4. For applying clearcoats

By having a gun adjusted for applying each material, you will save time. Also, your work will be better because you will know how each gun setting will apply its own material.

Adjusting the Spray

Proper spray gun operation is critical to refinishing. Spray guns are precision engineered tools. They must be treated as such.

A *good spray pattern* will deposit an even, oval-shaped, mist of paint on the surface being painted. The paint should go on smoothly in a medium to wet coat, without sagging or running.

A good pattern depends on the proper mixture of air and paint droplets. Adjusting the spray gun is much like fine-tuning an engine fuel system for the proper mixture of air and fuel.

There are three basic adjustments that will give the proper spray pattern, degree of wetness, and air pressure: air pressure, pattern control, and fluid control.

To adjust a typical paint spray gun:

1. Adjust the air pressure. If set at the dryer-regulator (or transformer), you must account for pressure loss through the hose and fittings. Due to friction, as air passes from the dryer-regulator to the gun, pressure will be lost. The air pressure at the dryer-regulator and at the gun varies depending on the length and diameter of the hose.

   A *gun mounted pressure gauge* or gun mounted gauge-regulator is the best method to measure and adjust spray gun air pressure. Install the gauge or regulator between the hose coupler and the gun. This will let you set actual pressure at the gun. Refer to Figure 15–21.

Figure 15–22 Fluid control knob on spray gun controls volume of paint leaving gun.

The optimum spraying pressure is the lowest needed to obtain proper atomization, flow rate, and pattern width. *High spray gun pressure* results in excessive paint loss through overspray and poor flow due to high solvent evaporation before the paint reaches the surface. *Low spray gun pressure* produces poor drying characteristics due to high solvent retention, and makes the paint film prone to bubbling and sagging.

Proper spray gun air pressure varies with the kind of material sprayed and type of gun. Many low volatile organic compound (VOC) regulations require 10 psi (.7 K/cm^2) or less at the air cap. Always follow the spray gun manufacturer's air pressure recommendations for the type of material to be sprayed.

2. Set the size of the spray pattern using the *pattern control knob.* Turn the pattern control knob all the way in to create a small, round pattern. Back the knob out to produce a wide pattern.

Figure 15–21 It is good idea to place pressure gauge or gauge-regulator at gun. This will set actual reading at gun without pressure loss through air line and fittings.

Figure 15–23 A long slender paint spray pattern should be formed on the masking paper during your test.

3. Use the *fluid control knob* to adjust the amount of fluid leaving the spray gun. Shown in Figure 15–22, regulate the volume of paint according to the selected pattern size. Back the fluid knob out to increase the paint flow. Screw the knob inward to decrease the flow.

Spray Pattern Test

A *spray pattern test* checks the operation of the spray gun on a piece of paper. Before attempting to paint the vehicle, it is very important to test the spray pattern.

Hold the gun 6 to 8 in. (150 to 200 mm) away from the paper if spraying lacquer. Hold the gun 8 to 10 in. (200 to 250 mm) away when spraying enamel. Pull the trigger all the way back and release it immediately. This burst of paint should leave a long, slender pattern on the test paper, Figure 15–23.

Balanced Pattern

Split Pattern

Heavy Center Pattern

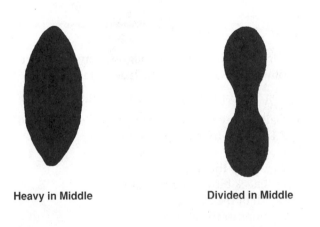

Heavy in Middle

Divided in Middle

Figure 15–25 With cap turned sideways on gun, test spray further. Spray a heavy coat of paint onto test paper to flood the pattern. Inspect the lengths of the runs. If all adjustments are correct, the runs will be almost equal in length.

Too Much Paint at Top or Bottom

Leaning to One Side

Figure 15–24 If your test shows incorrect spray patterns like these, there is something wrong with the gun. You would need to disassemble and clean gun or replace damaged parts. (I-CAR)

Figure 15–24 shows some incorrect spray patterns. These problems are usually caused by a clogged passage in the gun.

A spray pattern test that is:

1. Heavy in the middle could mean too little air flow.

2. Divided in the middle indicates too much air flow.

3. Too much paint at top or bottom might be caused by a restriction at the fluid needle or air cap horn.

4. Leaning to one side could mean that there is a restriction at the fluid needle or air cap horn.

5. If the pattern is heavy on one side or the top or bottom, try turning the air cap 180 degrees. If the pattern remains the same, replace the fluid needle and fluid nozzle. If the pattern rotates 180 degrees, then the problem is in the air cap horns.

Spraying primer-surfacer usually requires a smaller spray pattern. Turn in the pattern control knob until the spray pattern is 6 to 8 in. (150 to 200 mm) wide. For spot repair, the pattern should be about 5 to 6 in. (125 to 150 mm) from top to bottom.

If the paint droplets are coarse and large, close the fluid control knob about one half turn or increase the air pressure 5 psi (.35 K/cm^2). If the spray is too fine or too dry, either open the fluid control knob about one half turn or decrease the air pressure 5 psi (.35 K/cm^2).

Next, test the spray pattern for uniformity of paint distribution. Loosen the air cap retaining ring and rotate the air cap so that the horns are straight up and down. In this position, you will get a horizontal spray pattern instead of a vertical one.

Spray again on your test paper. However, hold down the trigger until the paint begins to run. This is known as flooding the pattern. Inspect the lengths of the runs. If ALL adjustments are correct, the runs will be almost equal in length. See Figure 15–25A.

The uneven runs in the split pattern shown in Figure 15–25B are a result of setting the spray pattern too wide or the air pressure too low. Turn the pattern control knob in one half turn or raise the air pressure 5 pounds (.35 K/cm^2). Alternate between these two adjustments until the runs are even in length.

If paint runs are longer in the middle than on the edges, too much paint is being discharged. Turn in the fluid control knob until the runs are even in length, Figure 15–25C.

> ■ **Danger!** *Always wear a suitable air respirator when doing any spraying.*

Summary

- A painter must have a suitable painting environment. The following variables must be addressed: cleanliness, temperature/humidity, light, and compressed air/pressure.

- Atomization breaks paint into a spray of tiny, uniform droplets. When properly applied, these droplets flow together to create an even film thickness with a mirrorlike gloss. Proper atomization is essential when working with today's basecoat/clearcoat finishes.

- Paint viscosity refers to the paint's thickness or ability to resist flow. It can be measured by means of a Ford cup or a Zahn cup. The Zahn cup is the more common, and less expensive, cup used.

- In a captive spray gun system, individual guns are set up and used for applying each type of material.

This system saves time, and improves work quality because each gun will already be at the correct setting when needed.

Technical Terms

painting environment	*pattern knob*
spray booth	*paint mixing instructions*
manometer	*percentage reduction*
tack-rag	*mixing chart*
paint mixing room	*paint mixing sticks*
painter prep area	*paint viscosity*
atomization	*viscosity cup*
gun air cap	*viscosity cup seconds*
cap center orifice	*hot weather solvent*
cap side orifices	*cold weather solvent*
fluid nozzle	*captive spray gun system*
fluid needle	*spray pattern test*
fluid control knob	

Review Questions

1. Clearcoat finishes will magnify any dust, dirt, or other flaws in the finish. True or false?

2. List four functions of a paint booth.

3. Daily spray booth cleaning requires you to do ALL of the following EXCEPT:
   a. remove ALL nonessential items.
   b. sweep the floor.
   c. check blower belt tension.
   d. all of the above.
   e. none of the above.

4. After pulling the vehicle into the spray booth, _____ the entire vehicle to remove any loose dust and other debris.

5. Name some expendable materials that should always be kept on hand.

6. To avoid air supply problems, do ALL of the following EXCEPT:
   a. check and replace oil and water filters on a regular basis.
   b. drain moisture from the system daily.
   c. replace deteriorated air hoses because they can introduce dirt into the system.
   d. ALL of the above.
   e. none of the above.

7. _____ breaks the paint into a spray mist of tiny, uniform droplets.

8. A spray paint gun has too much paint being applied on one side during a pattern test. Techni-

cian A says to check for a clogged side orifice in the cap. Technician B says to check for proper fluid needle adjustment.

Who is correct?

a. Technician A
b. Technician B
c. Both Technicians
d. Neither Technician

9. If the label on a can of material says to reduce 100 percent, what would you do?

10. Paint mixing sticks have scale markings that allow you to easily mix _____, _____, and _____ in the correct proportions.

11. In your own words, how do you use paint mixing sticks?

12. If the paint drains too quickly out of the viscosity cup, you have added too much paint. True or false?

13. What is captive spray gun system?

14. Summarize the three steps for adjusting a spray paint gun.

Activities

1. Inspect the condition of your spray booth. Is it ready for use? Make a report on its condition.

2. Make a wall chart showing how to use one type of paint mixing stick. Place callouts and steps on the chart for display in the classroom.

3. Make a spray pattern test of a spray gun. Try adjusting the gun knobs to make good and poor spray patterns.

CHAPTER 16

PAINTING FUNDAMENTALS

Objectives

After studying this chapter, you should be able to:

- Explain the difference between spot refinishing, panel refinishing, and overall refinishing.

- Properly use a spray gun.

- Describe how to spray different types of materials.

- Summarize the different kinds of spray coats.

- Outline general topcoat application procedures.

- Explain the key points to keep in mind when applying multi-stage finishes.

- Finish and/or retexture various types of automotive plastics.

- List general rules for painting a vehicle.

Introduction

From the customer's standpoint, the topcoat or color coat is the most important aspect of a paint job. The topcoat is what the customer sees and evaluates. Most customer complaints stem from problems with the topcoat. As a painter, you must therefore take special pride in producing a beautiful finish. To do this, you must understand the topcoat materials and how they are applied.

> **NOTE!** PREVIOUS TEXT CHAPTERS PROVIDED INFORMATION RELEVANT TO THIS CHAPTER. FOR MORE SPECIFIC INFORMATION ON PAINT TYPES, PAINT MIXING, SHOP PREP, AND VEHICLE PREP, REFER TO THE INDEX.

PREPARATION REVIEW

As detailed in Chapters 14 and 15, the vehicle should be ready for painting in a clean paint spray booth. Check all masking tape and paper one last time. Make sure none of the tape has pulled up or paper has been torn. Inspect all edges and paper closely for openings that could allow overspray leaks.

Make sure the air circulation system on the spray booth is turned on and working properly. While wearing protective gear, blow off any remaining dust with an air gun. As you blow off surfaces, wipe the vehicle down with a *tack cloth* (rag with coating that holds dust and debris). After wiping with a tack cloth, be careful NOT to touch the surface being refinished. Also, do NOT open the spray booth doors.

Make sure the paint has been thinned or reduced with the proper solvent to the desired viscosity. If needed, add the right amount of catalyst or hardener. Again, refer to the directions on the materials. Use a viscosity cup to check for proper paint viscosity.

Make sure the paint is mixed thoroughly. At least a one inch (25 mm) wide, flat bottom, stirring paddle or steel spatula works well. You can also use a mixing machine if available. Insufficient mixing is a common reason for paint problems.

Paint settling occurs when the paint sits idle and pigments, metallic flakes, or mica particles settle to the bottom. This can cause problems because the color sprayed out first will contain a high percentage of these heavier ingredients. When the spray gun cup is almost empty, the paint will be lighter and have less metallic or mica in it.

Remember! If a color with heavy pigments is allowed to stand in your spray gun for 10 to 15 minutes without being stirred, the pigment will settle. This can cause color variations when sprayed. Use a strainer when pouring the paint into the spray gun cup or tank. This will remove any large u.. could cause paint problems.

Check that spray gun air pressure is correct. Perform a spray test pattern on a sheet of paper. Make sure the spray gun is working properly before applying paint to the vehicle.

Check the temperature of the vehicle, the spray booth, and paint materials, Figure 16–1. They should all be equalized and within specs. Use a thermometer to check the surface temperature of the vehicle. If vehicle surface temperature is too cold or hot, painting problems will result.

REVIEW OF TOPCOATS

The most common types of topcoats that you will work with are:

1. Alkyd enamels

2. Acrylic lacquers

3. Acrylic enamels (including both hardener and two-part types)

4. Polyurethane enamels

5. Acrylic urethane enamels

Today, two-part enamels are the most common. The type of refinish system ultimately determines the attractiveness of the color, gloss, and overall finish. The type of paint also affects other variables.

The table in Figure 16–2 is a summary of the properties of topcoats used for refinishing. The table in Figure 16–3 compares the durability of various topcoat finishes.

Before applying the topcoat, carefully read the paint manufacturer's directions that appear on the paint can. Each has specific formulations for its products. For this reason, the best source of data on how to apply a specific brand of paint is the label. Another source of good information can be found in the manufacturer's literature.

Some of the more important label and literature data that should be checked include:

1. Viscosity recommendations

2. Air pressure recommendations

3. Use of additives, reducers, thinners, and activators

4. Application techniques

5. Number of coats required

6. Blending and mist coat procedures

7. Polishing and compounding recommendations

8. Clean-up procedures

Figure 16–1 Remember to check the surface temperature of the vehicle before refinishing.

SUMMARY OF TOPCOAT FEATURES

Nomenclature		One-Part Type			Two-Part Type	
		Alkyd Enamel	Acrylic Lacquer	Acrylic Enamel	Polyurethane	Acrylic Urethane Enamel
Spray characteristics		Excellent	Excellent	Good	Good	Good
Possible thickness per application		Fair	Fair	Good	Excellent	Excellent
Gloss	without polishing	Fair	Good	Good	Excellent	Excellent
	after polishing	Good	Good	Good	—	Good
Hardness		Good	Good	Good	Excellent	Excellent
Weather resistance (frosting, yellowing)		Fair	Fair	Good	Excellent	Excellent
Gasoline resistance		Fair	Fair	Fair	Excellent	Good
Adhesion		Good	Good	Fair	Excellent	Excellent
Pollutant resistance		Fair	Fair	Fair	Excellent	Excellent
Drying time	to touch	68°F 5-10 minutes	68°F 10 minutes	68°F 10 minutes	68°F 2-30 minutes	68°F 10-20 minutes
	for surface repair	68°F 6 hours 140°F 40 minutes	68°F 8 hours 158°F 30 minutes	68°F 8 hours 158°F 30 minutes	—	68°F 4 hours 158°F 15 minutes
	to let stand outside	68°F 24 hours 140°F 40 minutes	68°F 24 hours 158°F 40 minutes	68°F 24 hours 158°F 40 minutes	68°F 48 hours 158°F 1 hour	68°F 16 hours 158°F 30 minutes

Figure 16–2 Study characteristics of different types of topcoats.

Make sure you are using the correct type of refinishing materials for the job. Refer to the paint code information on the body plate to find the correct paint color and type needed. The *body ID number* or *service part number* gives information about how the vehicle is equipped. It will give paint codes or numbers for ordering the right type and color paint. Lower and upperbody colors will be given if a two-tone paint. The body ID number will also give trim information. This number will be on the body ID plate on the door, console lid, or elsewhere on the body.

Typical locations for paint codes are shown in Figure 16–4. An example of an actual body ID plate is given in Figure 16–5.

DETERMINING TYPE OF OLD FINISH

Before planning any refinishing job, you must find out what type of paint is on the vehicle. The vehicle might have its original paint or it could have been repainted with a different type paint. Methods for finding out the type of paint on a vehicle include the following.

1. With a *solvent application method,* rub the paint with a white cloth soaked in lacquer thinner to see how easily the paint will dissolve. If the paint film dissolves and leaves a mark on the rag, it is a type of air dried paint. If it does not dissolve, it is either an oven-dried or a two-part reaction type paint. Acrylic

COMPARING DURABILITY OF TOPCOATS

Figure 16–3 Note how two-part acrylic enamel and acrylic urethane enamel are more durable than other finishes.

urethane paint film will not dissolve as easily as an air-dried paint, but sometimes the thinner will penetrate sufficiently to blur the paint gloss.

2. With a *heat application method,* wet sand an area with No. 1000 grit sandpaper to dull the paint film. Then heat the area with an infrared lamp. If a gloss returns to the dulled appearance, the paint is acrylic lacquer.

3. With the *hardness method,* you must check the general hardness of the paint. Paints do not dry to the same hardness. Generally, two-part reaction and oven-dried paints dry to a harder film than air-dried paint.

4. With an *inspection method,* inspect closely for signs of repainting. Look for masking tape created paint lines, overspray, and other signs of repairing. If the vehicle has not been repainted, you can use the body color code identification plate to determine the type of paint on the vehicle.

Is the Above Correct? Are There Other Methods?

> *WARNING! Do NOT spray lacquer paint over the top of enamel. However, it is acceptable to spray enamel over lacquer. If you apply lacquer over enamel, problems can develop.*

SPRAY GUN APPLICATION STROKE

The *application stroke* is a side-to-side movement of the spray gun to distribute the paint mist properly on the vehicle. The proper stroke is critical to the paint job. Practice on masking paper. Any problems with the spray pattern must be corrected before painting the vehicle. Look at Figure 16–6.

To use a spray gun, hold the gun at the proper distance from the surface, Figure 16–7. *Spray gun distance* is measured from the gun tip to the surface being painted. Typically, hold the gun 6 to 8 inches (152 to 203 mm) away for lacquer and 8 to 10 inches (203 to 254 mm) away from the surface for enamel.

A *short spray distance* causes the high velocity mist to ripple the wet film. A *long spray distance* causes a greater percentage of the thinner to evaporate, resulting in orange peel or dry spray.

A slower drying thinner will permit more variation in the distance of the gun from the surface. However, it will produce runs if the gun gets too close. Excessive spraying distance also causes more overspray.

Spray gun angle refers to whether the gun is tilted up or down or sideways. Normally, hold the gun parallel and perpendicular to the surface. Keep the gun at a right angle to the vehicle. This should be done even when spraying curves in the body. Refer to Figure 16–8.

If you tilt the gun when spraying the sides of the vehicle, an uneven paint film will result, Figure 16–9. On flat surfaces such as the hood or roof, the gun should be pointed almost straight down. See Figure 16–10.

> *WARNING! When painting a hood, roof, or deck lid, the spray gun cup must NOT leak. If the seal around the cup is faulty, paint will drip out of the gun and onto the vehicle. If the drip will NOT flow out, you might have to sand and repaint the panel.*

Avoid fanning the gun with your wrist. Fanning the gun will deposit an uneven paint film. The paint film will be thicker right in front of your gun and thinner on the sides. The only time it is permissible to fan the gun is when blending a small repair spot. With a spot repair, you want the paint film thinner at the edges to blend out the spray.

Spray gun triggering involves stopping the paint spray before you stop moving the gun sideways.

Model	Position	Model	Position
Acura	9	Honda	8,10
Alfa Romeo	4,13	Hyundai	6,7
AMC	9,10	Isuzu	2,10
Audi	12,13	Lexus	7,8
Austin Rover	17	Mazda	1,2,3,4,6,8
BMW	4,5	Mercedes	2,7,9
Chrysler	3,5,16	Mitsubishi	7
Chrysler Corp	3,5	Montero / Pickup	3
Caravan / Voyager / Ram Van	6	Cordia / Tredia	4
Chrysler Imports	1,2,4	Others	1,2,3
Colt Vista	16	Nissan	1,3,4,6,8,15,*
Conquest	7	Peugeot	2,3,4,5,8
Diahatsu	1,6,7	Porsche	9
Datsun	2	Renault	1,3,4,5,8
Dodge D50	3	Rover	1,3,4,5
Ford	10	Saab	5,6,8
Ford Motor Co	10	Subaru	2
General Motors		Suzuki	7,11
A, J and L Bodies	14	Toyota Passenger	7,8,14
E and K Bodies	12	Truck	4
B,C,H and N Bodies	13	Volkswagen	2,11
GM Imports	2,12,13,14	Volvo	6,7,8
		Yugo	12

* Under Right Front Passenger Seat

Figure 16–4 Chart shows typical locations for paint codes for major makes of vehicles. (Courtesy of Mitchell International, Inc.)

When you pull halfway back on the trigger, only air blows out of the nozzle. When you pull all the way back, paint is atomized and sprayed out.

During the application stroke, release halfway on the trigger right before you stop moving the gun sideways. This will prevent too much paint being deposited when the gun changes direction. It will also keep air moving through the nozzle to help prevent sudden burst of paint. Release the trigger halfway at the end of each pass, then pull it back when beginning the pass in the opposite direction. Again look at Figure 16–7.

Spray gun speed refers to how fast the gun is moved sideways while painting. Move the gun with a steady, deliberate pass, about one foot (0.3 m) per second. The speed must be consistent or it will result in an uneven paint film. If you move the gun too quickly, NOT enough paint will be deposited on the surface. If you move too slowly, too much paint will deposit on the surface. Never stop the gun while spraying, or a paint sag and run will result.

A *banding coat* is done to deposit enough paint on edges or corners of surfaces. Spray these difficult areas first, Figure 16–11. Aim directly at the corner or edge so that half of the spray covers each side of the corner or edge. Hold the gun an inch (25–50 mm) or two closer than usual while moving the gun up or down along the edge. After all of the edges and

Figure 16–5 Body ID plate or service parts identification plate gives VIN and other data about vehicle. Note paint and trim code numbers. *(Courtesy of General Motors Corporation)*

corners have been sprayed, spray the face or front of the panel.

Generally, start spraying at the top of any upright surface, such as a door panel. The gun nozzle should be level with the top of the panel. The upper half of the spray pattern should hit and cover the masking paper. Move the gun all the way across the top of the panel. Make sure you hold the gun square with the panel and keep it the same distance from the panel.

Overlap strokes involves making each spray gun coat cover about half of the previous coat of paint. Make each pass in the opposite direction. Keep the nozzle level with the lower edge of the previous pass. Thus, one half of the spray pattern overlaps the previous coat. The other half of the paint pattern is applied to the unpainted area.

Always blend into the "wet edge" of the previous section sprayed. Proper triggering where the sections meet will avoid a double coat and the possibility of sags or paint runs. See Figure 16–12.

Continue the back-and-forth passes. Trigger the gun at the end of each pass and lower each successive pass one half the top-to-bottom width of the spray pattern. Make your last pass with the lower half of the spray pattern hitting below the surface being painted. This will assure enough paint film thickness at the bottom of the panel.

For a double coat, repeat the previous procedure. Allow flash time of several minutes between coats.

Two or three single coats are required for enamel top coats. Allow the first coat to set up or become tacky before applying additional coats. Refer to the paint label for details.

Figure 16–6 Before spraying vehicle, make sure spray gun is working properly. This will prevent time-consuming rework if gun is not working correctly. *(PPG Industries, Inc.)*

Figure 16–7 Note right and wrong ways of using spray gun. *(Illustration courtesy of Binks Manufacturing Company)* Wrong—If you fan gun, paint film will be thicker in middle and thinner, drier on sides. Right—Like a machine, hold gun perfectly straight and equal distance from surface as it is moved sideways. Release trigger at end of each stroke.

For painting very narrow surfaces, switch to a gun with a smaller spray pattern. This can also be accomplished by reducing the air pressure and spray pattern on a full-size gun.

PAINT THICKNESS MEASUREMENT

Paint thickness is measured in *mils* or thousandths of an inch (hundredths of a millimeter). Original OEM

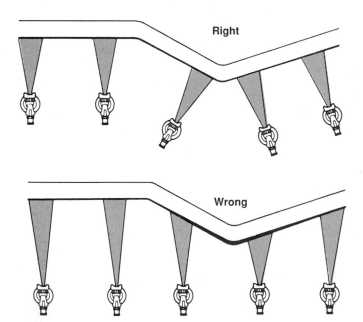

Figure 16–8 During normal painting, gun should always aim directly at surface and be kept an equal distance from surface. If surface curves, redirect gun to paint right at surface. Right—Gun is rotated so that it stays aimed directly at surface. Note correct distance from surface is also maintained. Wrong—Since gun is not kept aimed at surface and distance decreases at curved surface, paint would be too thick at curve. Running or sagging might result.

paints are typically about 2 to 6 mils thick. With basecoat/clearcoats, the basecoat is approximately 1–2 mils thick. The clearcoat is about 2–4 mils thick. This is approximately the thickness of a piece of typing paper.

When you repaint a vehicle, paint thickness will increase. If too much paint is already on the vehicle, it may have to be removed prior to refinishing. Paint build-up should be limited to no more than 12 mils. The OEM finish and one refinish usually equal just under 12 mils. Exceeding this paint thickness could cause cracking in the new finish. Chemical stripping or blasting would be needed to remove the old paint build-up.

A *mil gauge* can be used to measure the thickness of the paint on the vehicle. This should be done before refinishing.

For more information on mil gauges, refer to the Chapter 6.

GUN HANDLING PROBLEMS

The inexperienced painter is prone to making spraying errors. These include the following:

Gun heeling occurs when the gun is allowed to tilt. Because the gun is no longer perpendicular to the surface, the spray produces uneven film thickness, excessive overspray, dry spray, and orange peel.

Gun arching occurs when the gun is NOT moved parallel with the surface. At the outer edges of the stroke, the gun is farther away from the surface than at the middle of the stroke. The result is uneven film thickness, paint runs, excessive overspray, dry spray, and orange peel.

Incorrect gun stroke speed means you are moving the gun too slowly or quickly. If the stroke is made too quickly, the paint will NOT cover the surface evenly.

Figure 16–9 Do not let gun tilt up or down. This would also result in uneven paint film. *(Illustration courtesy of Binks Manufacturing Company)*

If the stroke is made too slowly, sags and runs will develop. Proper stroke speed is something that comes with experience. Generally, you must watch the paint go onto the surface to carefully watch for a proper coat.

Improper spray overlap means you are NOT covering half of the previous pass with the next pass. Improper overlapping results in uneven film thickness, contrasting color hues, and sags and runs. If you overlap coats too much, the paint can run. If

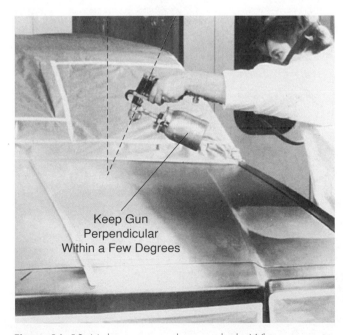

Figure 16–10 Make sure cup does not leak. When you paint horizontal surfaces, such as hood, you must aim gun almost straight down. Any leakage can drip on vehicle.

Figure 16–11 Banding coat assures that edges of panel receive enough paint. After making banding coats on edges, follow arrows to paint rest of door or panel.

18 To 36 Inches
(457–915 mm)

18 To 36 Inches
(457–915 mm)

4 Inch (100 mm) Overlap

Figure 16–12 When going from one section of vehicle to next, blend wet edge. Overlap next section a few inches or millimeters into already painted section. This will help paint flow out properly at edge of sections.

you do NOT overlap enough, poor coverage can result.

Improper coverage means the paint film thickness is NOT uniform or too thin. It is caused by NOT triggering exactly over the edge of the panel or from improper spray overlap.

NOTE! EXAMPLES OF THESE AND OTHER PAINT PROBLEMS ARE GIVEN IN CHAPTER 18.

TYPES OF SPRAY COATS

There are varying degrees of thickness for a spray coat: light, medium, or heavy. The easiest way to control thickness is by changing how fast you move the gun sideways. If you move the gun slower, a heavier, thicker coat will be applied. If you move more slowly, film thickness is decreased.

A *tack coat* or mist coat is a very light, mist coat applied to the surface first. It allows the application of heavier wet coats without sagging or runs. The tack coat dries quickly to bond and form a lightly textured paint film to hold the next coats in place. The tack coat will flash quickly, usually in a few minutes.

A *dust coat* is a light, dry coating that is similar to a mist coat. It is accomplished by holding the gun a short distance from the surface while moving the gun more quickly. It can be used to help even out coverage.

A *full wet coat* is a heavy, glossy coat applied over the tack coat. Spraying this coat requires skill and practice to prevent runs. The wet coat makes the paint lay down smooth and shiny. It prevents a dull dry paint surface or rough, textured "orange peel" type film. The last coat is usually wet coat.

Shading coats or *blend coats* are progressive applications of paint on the boundary of spot repair areas

so that a color difference is NOT noticeable. They are applied in two or more coats. The second and third coats are thinner and sprayed over a wider area than the first. See Figure 16–13.

PAINT BLENDING

Paint blending involves tapering the new paint gradually into the old paint. This makes any difference in the new paint less noticeable. It helps hide any slight differences in color or texture. Blending is the key to a successful spot repair. Look at Figure 16–14.

To blend paint, apply the topcoat with a fanning motion, working from the center outward. This allows each coat to blend out a bit further than the previous one.

An alternative method is to apply the finish in short strokes from the center outward. Again, extend each coat so that it blends out further than the previous one.

With either method, the spray pattern should be narrowed and the fluid delivery reduced. To minimize overspray, the air pressure may also have to be reduced, depending on the material being sprayed.

REFINISHING METHODS

Refinishing methods are selected according to several variables:

Blending Single Stage
Or Basecoat Colors

Blend Area

← **1st Coat** →

← **2nd Coat** →

← **3rd Coat** →

Figure 16–13 Blending is needed for spot repair of small area on panel or when using basecoat/clearcoat. When blending, you intentionally fan gun out away from repair. (I-CAR)

Figure 16–14 View shows how fanning gun at wrist will blend paint thinner near outer edges of repair area. Work the gun from the center outward. Where paint is thinner, it will gradually blend into existing paint to hide repair.

1. Condition of the original finish
2. Size of the area to be finished
3. Location of the repair on the vehicle

From these variables, you must determine how much of the vehicle must be painted. The three categories of paint repair are spot repair (area of panel painted); panel repair (complete panel painted); and overall refinishing (whole vehicle painted).

SPOT REPAIRS

Spot repair involves painting an area smaller than the panel. The paint must be blended out to match the existing finish.

Spot repair generally involves:

1. Minor body repair
2. Metal conditioning
3. Application of undercoat system
4. Application of topcoat to blend into the old finish surrounding the repair

Spot repairs are recommended where a complete panel repair is either uneconomical or impractical. This might be due to the tiny size of the damage, its hidden location, or another factor. It is also commonly used when two large panels have no break line. For example, when painting a quarter panel, the paint is blended into the sail panel where the roof joins the quarter panel.

Solid Color Spot Repairs

You must use experience and common sense as to the range of blending needed for spot repairs with solid colors. Blending with a solid color of paint is used for situations such as light damage to the fender edge.

In this case, there are two methods of blending: at the hood-to-fender gap and at the body line. When blending at a body line, you do NOT have to paint the upper portion of the fender where paint shading shows more. This can help avoid problems with color and texture differences.

As shown in Figure 16–15, when spot repairs are made with a solid color, the blend area should be treated with rubbing compound or sanded with 1000 grit sandpaper before refinishing.

Figure 16–15 Note basic steps for blending paint with solid color.

Metallic Color Spot Repairs

Matching metallic colors is complicated because you have to match the color and the density of the metallic flakes in the paint. If spot repairs are done with a metallic color, skill is required in matching the color and the metallic flakes through proper distribution of the paint. The blend area will be less noticeable if it is angled away from the body line. Refer to Figures 16–16 and 16–17.

PANEL REPAIRS

Panel repairs involves painting a complete body part separated by a definite boundary, such as a door or fender. Usually, you do NOT have to blend the paint with panel repairs. Blending is only needed when it is difficult to match the paint, as with a metallic color. However, blending is routinely done for such areas as between the quarter panel and roof panel.

Solid Color Panel Repairs

Panel repair with a solid color covers an entire panel (door, hood, etc.). The paint match is made at the panel joints. Panel repair is more common than spot repair. It usually results in a better looking repair and can be just as fast as spot repair on most panels.

Figure 16–17 Blend area will be less noticeable if it is angled away from body line.

For a complete panel repair, mask off the area NOT to be painted, Figure 16–18. If a panel has damage at two different locations, the whole panel should be repaired. Blending can be done to the molding or extended below the molding.

When blending new paint into old paint, you must use common sense to determine where to blend the paint. Try to find a body section that gives a natural break line or small area for blending.

Metallic Color Panel Repairs

New and old paint differences tend to be very noticeable with bright metallic colors. It is almost impossible to match the new metallic finish exactly with the previous one. You must extend the blending over a wide area to help hide the differences. This will make the repair less visible, Figure 16–19.

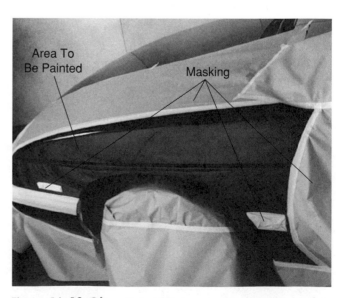

Figure 16–18 Often, it is just as easy to paint a complete panel.

Figure 16–16 Study basic steps for blending metallic color.

Figure 16–19 Note panel repair with metallic basecoat/clearcoat. Basecoat is blended only over repair area. Then, top section of fender or whole fender must be cleared.

If a panel has damage at both ends or if the whole panel is to be refinished, the blending might have to extend onto adjacent panels.

OVERALL REFINISHING

Overall refinishing involves painting the whole vehicle. This is usually done when the old paint has weathered and deteriorated. Surface prep is time consuming since the entire surface must be cleaned and sanded or scuffed. Any damage must be straightened. Also, all parts NOT to be painted (trim, glass, mirrors, etc.) must be masked or removed. There are several things you must remember when painting the whole vehicle.

For overall refinishing, keep a wet edge while maintaining minimal overspray on the horizontal surfaces. This prevents spray from settling onto dry surfaces, which would cause a gritty surface.

Avoid paint runs or sags by changing the point of overlap on each coat. *Paint overlap* refers to the area where one vertical painted area overlaps the new area being painted.

There is no universal sequence for overall refinishing of a vehicle. However, most experienced painters agree that the following method is an excellent technique for non-downdraft spray booths.

Start by painting the roof, then the rear, then the driver's side, front, and finally the passenger side. It will produce minimum overspray on horizontal surfaces. This will also help keep a wet edge when starting a new section.

The term *wet edge* means that the area just painted will still be wet when starting to paint a new adjoining area.

When using a downdraft spray booth, overall paint sequence is different. This is because of the direction of the airflow (top to bottom). Following this procedure allows the three main horizontal surfaces to remain wet while maintaining minimum overspray.

APPLYING BASECOAT/CLEARCOAT

Basecoat/clearcoat systems pose a major challenge to painters. Since more and more vehicles have basecoat/clearcoat finishes, it is very important to become familiar with them.

You must first spray the color basecoat over the repair area, Figure 16–20. The basecoat does NOT have to be sprayed where the old paint color is acceptable. Blend the basecoat of color out around the repair. Then, spray the whole panel with clear. This will normally make the old color and new basecoat blend and match.

When estimating a basecoat/clearcoat repair, carefully examine the finish on the area adjacent to the damage. If it is chalked, dulled, or otherwise impaired, color matching might prove impossible. Ideally, such repairs should be performed as overall refinishing jobs. This approach will eliminate many problems in repairing basecoat/clearcoat finishes that are severely weathered.

Figure 16–20 Basecoats/clearcoats are now one of most common finishes. When spraying basecoat, blend color out over repair area. Only spray color where needed. Then, spray half of panel with clear. After flashing, spray whole fender with clear. (I-CAR)

When spraying, two medium coats of basecoat should be applied. The basecoat does NOT have to be glossy, and only enough should be used to achieve hiding. Two or three medium wet coats of clear should be applied next. Allow at least 15 minutes flash time between coats.

Avoid sanding the basecoat. If sanding must be done because of dirt or imperfections, allow the paint time to dry. Wet sanding with 800 to 1200 grit sandpaper will minimize sand scratches. The sanded area must then be given another coat of basecoat to prevent streaking and mottling.

Several tips to remember when using basecoat/clearcoat finishes include:

1. On panel repairs, only spray the basecoat where needed. You do NOT have to basecoat the whole panel if the existing color is acceptable. Use as much of the existing color as possible to help avoid a color mismatch.

2. Do NOT load clearcoats on heavily. Because they are clear, it is easy to use too much trying to increase the desired glamour effect. As a result, the thick clear will "bury" the basecoat and hide the color.

3. Do NOT use thick viscosity clearcoats. Contrary to some opinions, clears do NOT perform better when they are under-reduced. Thin or reduce clearcoats according to the label instructions. Many clearcoats come *pre-thinned* (no additional thinning is needed) from the manufacturer.

4. Do NOT use economy thinners or reducers with clearcoats. These only weaken the performance of clears by trapping solvents. They also affect flow and leveling characteristics of the clearcoat. Use a quality thinner/reducer. Allow each coat to flash thoroughly before applying the next one.

APPLYING TRI-COAT FINISHES

Tri-coat finishes, like pearl paints, require somewhat different spraying techniques because they are difficult to match. However, they have much in common with basecoat/clearcoat finishes.

Follow the recommendations furnished by the tri-coat paint manufacturer. Pay close attention when the instructions call for the use of adhesion promoters, anti-static materials, and so on.

Before painting with a tri-coat, you should make a *let-down panel*. A let-down panel helps you find the correct amount of coats needed to achieve a color match with tri-coat finishes. Gun pressure, reduction, and spray technique can all affect the finished job. Therefore, the time spent spraying one or more let-down panels will be repaid by a job that satisfies the customer. A mismatch in the basecoat, mica, or clearcoats can affect the overall finish match.

NOTE! INSTRUCTIONS FOR MAKING LET-DOWN PANELS AND OTHER METHODS OF COLOR MATCHING ARE DETAILED IN CHAPTER 17.

REFINISHING RULES

There are several rules you should remember when refinishing a vehicle. Ask yourself these questions and answer them before painting:

1. Are the vehicle surfaces straight and ready for painting? A common mistake is to overlook a surface problem before painting. Since the surface is usually sanded dull, imperfections are easy to overlook. Double check metal straightening work, plastic filler, and primer before proceeding. Even overlooking a small paint chip can ruin the job.

2. Are all surfaces perfectly clean and scuffed? Paint will NOT adhere to a dirty or glossy smooth surface. If the paint peels, you will have hours of rework. Blow off and tack-rag the vehicle before painting.

3. Are you painting in an ideal environment? Are the spray booth and vehicle the right temperature? Are the booth filters and blower working properly? Do NOT try to paint a vehicle in an open shop. Dirt will almost always settle in the paint. Only paint in a spray booth!

4. Is the paint type and mixing correct? Use the right kind of paint and mix it following label directions. Are all additives mixed into the paint? If you forget to add hardener, you will NOT be able to wet sand or buff the paint for weeks.

5. Is the paint spray gun working properly? Test and adjust the gun spray pattern on a sheet of paper or old part. If the gun is spitting or NOT working properly, you do NOT want to try to paint the vehicle. This would result in hours of rework.

6. Does the spray gun cup leak? A leaking cup can drip and ruin the paint job. You must tilt the gun down when spraying the roof, hood, and trunk lid. If the cup is leaking, paint might drip out and onto these surfaces.

7. Are you allowing enough flash time between coats? Flash time is the time needed for a fresh coat of paint to partially dry. Flash time is needed to prevent the paint from sagging or running.

8. Are you applying the paint properly? Hold the gun the right distance from the surface, typically 8 to 10 inches (203 to 254 mm). Aim the gun directly at the surface while moving it at the correct speed. Do NOT fan the gun unless you are blending the paint.

9. Is the paint going on the surface properly? Closely watch the paint as it deposits on the surface being painted. Check for application problems—dry

coat, excessive wet coat, improper spray overlap, and so on. Constant inspection of the wet paint as it hits the surface is critical to doing good paint work. Is the lighting good enough to see the paint go onto all surfaces?

10. Are you applying the correct film thickness? A common mistake is to apply too much paint. Remember that "thin is in." You only want to apply enough paint to provide good color coverage and gloss. Film thicknesses are much less than in the past. Use the number of coats recommended by the paint manufacturer.

11. Could you accidentally touch the paint? Keep air hoses and yourself a safe distance from the wet paint. It is easy to brush up against the wet paint and damage it.

NOTE! INFORMATION RELATING TO PAINTING A VEHICLE IS GIVEN IN SEVERAL CHAPTERS OF THIS TEXT. REFER TO THE INDEX FOR ADDED INFORMATION IF NEEDED.

REMOVAL OF MASKING MATERIALS

If the finish has been force dried, remove the masking tape while the finish is still warm. If the finish is allowed to cool, the tape will be difficult to remove. It can also leave adhesive behind.

Pull the tape slowly so that it comes off evenly, Figure 16–21. Take care NOT to touch any painted areas because the paint might NOT be completely dry. Fingerprints or tape marks could result.

If you used liquid masking material, wash it off with soap and water. Do NOT wash the freshly painted surfaces until they are fully dry.

Never allow lacquer paint to dry thoroughly before removing the tape. This could cause the paint to peel

Figure 16–21 Remove masking tape slowly to avoid peeling off paint.

off along with the tape. With fast drying lacquer, it is best to remove the tape right after refinishing.

> *WARNING! Never mask a vehicle and let it sit for a prolonged period. Also, do NOT let the masking paper and tape get wet. Either will cause problems. The tape edge can roll up and allow paint to spray onto parts NOT meant to be painted. Also, the tape can stick and be difficult to remove. You might have to carefully wash off the adhesive.*

FINISHING AUTOMOTIVE PLASTICS

Follow the manufacturer's recommendations when refinishing automotive plastics. The manufacturer will explain if a special plastic primer, flex agent, or adhesion promoter is required. Figure 16–22 lists the more popular automotive plastics along with their suggested finishing systems.

Most rigid (hard) plastics generally require no primers. The paint will adhere properly to the plastic. Semi-rigid (flexible) plastics might require the addition of a flex agent to the finishing system. Semi-rigid plastics expand, contract, and bend more easily than other substrates. The *flex agent* keeps the paint film flexible so it can flex with the plastic without cracking.

Some manufacturers require that different flex additives be used in the various finishing systems. Others offer a universal flex additive that can be used in many systems.

Remember! It is best NOT to mix manufacturers' products. The flex additive, the topcoat, the undercoat, and solvent should all be provided by the same manufacturer whenever possible. Mixing brand names on the same job can yield poor results.

FINISHING RIGID EXTERIOR PLASTIC PARTS

While most rigid exterior plastics do NOT require a primer, some paint manufacturers nevertheless recommend a primer application before the topcoat. Conversion coatings, metal conditioners, self-etching primers, and flex agents should NOT be used.

The finishing procedure for rigid plastic is as follows:

1. Wash the part thoroughly with the recommended solvent.

FINISHING SYSTEMS FOR AUTOMOTIVE PLASTICS

KEY I Interior E Exterior P Primer NP No primer SP Special primer/adhesion promoter NA None approved * Flexible primer and/or additive recommended		Standard Lacquer System	Flexible Lacquer/ Enamel System	Polypropylene System	Vinyl System	Urethane System
ABS	Acrylonitrile-Butadiene-Styrene	I/NP E/NP				
ABS/PVC	ABS/Vinyl (Soft)		I/NP E/NP		I/NP	
EP I, EP II, or TPO	Ethylene Propylene			E/SP*		
PA	Nylon	E/P				
PC	Lexan	I/NP				
PE	Polyethylene	NA	NA	NA	NA	NA
PP	Polypropylene			I/SP		
PPO	Noryl	I/NP				
PS	Polystyrene	NA	NA	NA	NA	NA
PUR, RIM, or RRIM	Thermoset Polyurethane		E*			E
PVC	Polyvinyl Chloride (Vinyl)		E/NP I/NP		E/NP	E I/NP
SAN	Styrene Acrylonitrile	I/NP				
SMC	Sheet Molded Compound (Polyester)	E/P				
UP	Polyester (Fiberglass)	E/P				
TPUR	Thermoplastic Polyurethane		E*			E
TPR	Thermoplastic Rubber		E*			E

Figure 16–22 Chart shows refinishing systems for automotive plastics.

2. Sand the area to receive the basecoat with 400 grit sandpaper. The blend area to be cleared should be sanded with 600 grit or finer sandpaper.

3. Color coat using the appropriate acrylic lacquer, acrylic enamel, urethane, or basecoat/clearcoat system.

4. Only apply enough film thickness to achieve full hiding. This is usually two or three medium wet coats. The basecoat should be allowed to flash completely before the clearcoat is applied.

Flexible replacement panels are factory primed with an elastomeric enamel-based primer. Clean the surface with solvent. Sand with 400 grit sandpaper, and clean again.

If the OEM primer is scratched and has left the plastic substrate exposed, spray the exposed area with a flexible primer-surfacer prior to finishing. If the exposed surface is NOT primed, the area will be highlighted after the topcoats are applied. Use a fast evaporating solvent to reduce the primer-surfacer and prevent swelling of the base material. Swelling can be caused by absorption of the solvent into the plastic.

FINISHING POLYPROPYLENE PARTS

Finishing polypropylene (PP) parts involves the use of a special primer. Since polypropylene is hard, it can be color coated after priming with conventional interior acrylic lacquer. A special primer must be used for the undercoat and a flex agent added to the topcoat. If NOT, peeling will result.

If a PP bumper has major structural damage, it must be replaced. Replacement bumpers of this type are usually primed and ready to be painted. If they are NOT primed, apply the special PP primer over the entire bumper.

When applying an acrylic enamel topcoat, proceed as follows:

1. Apply properly reduced and mixed PP primer and flex additive as directed by the manufacturer. Allow 1 to 2 hours drying time before applying any color coats.

2. Apply reduced and mixed acrylic enamel and hardener additive. Flex additive should NOT be used in the topcoat.

3. Allow 8 hours (overnight if possible) drying time.

If an acrylic lacquer basecoat/clearcoat is being used, proceed as follows:

1. Apply properly reduced and mixed PP primer. Allow ½ to 1 hour drying time before the application of acrylic lacquer. Flex additives should NOT be used with color basecoat.

2. Apply properly thinned acrylic enamel clearcoat. Allow 8 hours (overnight if possible) drying time.

WARNING! Because polypropylene bumpers are made of thermoplastic resin, force drying at more than 212 degrees F (100 degrees C) could result in part deformation.

FINISHING URETHANE BUMPERS

Following is the procedure for finishing a colored urethane bumper:

1. Mask off the area to be finished. Clean it with a wax and grease remover. Insufficient cleaning will result in peeling or blistering.

2. Prepare the surface by wet sanding with 600 grit sandpaper. Apply a coat of primer-surfacer over the entire bumper. Because it is extremely difficult to match the topcoat for spot refinishing, the entire bumper should be done.

3. Clean the surface again.

4. Apply the color coat over a section of or the entire bumper if needed, Figure 16–23. Use a two-part acrylic urethane with a flex agent added. For metallics, allow proper flash time after applica-

Figure 16–23 If plastic part is flexible, you will need to add flex agent to paint so that it will not crack later.

tion. Then apply the clearcoat over the entire bumper.

5. Follow the dry time recommended by the manufacturer.

CLEANING THE SPRAY GUN

Like any precision piece of equipment, the refinisher's spray gun should be cleaned after use. Your livelihood depends upon the proper care of your equipment, and your spray gun is a vital tool.

After you use a spray gun, always clean it and other equipment (mixing sticks, containers, viscosity cup, etc.) right away. Neglect and lack of care is responsible for most spray gun problems. Besides cleaning, you must also lubricate all bearing surfaces and packings at recommended intervals.

WARNING! If the gun is NOT cleaned right after use, passages will usually clog. When used the next time, the gun may spit (eject pieces of dried paint) or form a poor spray pattern. This is of particular importance when dealing with enamel paints with additives.

Paints with hardeners or a catalyst can cure in the gun if NOT removed after use. The paint can set up in the cup and other parts of the gun. This can be a very costly mistake. Clean the gun completely after every use!

Danger! *When manually cleaning guns, wear rubber gloves, eye protection, and a respirator. Some paints pose a health risk when absorbed into the skin or inhaled.*

To manually clean a siphon feed gun, follow these steps:

1. Pour the unused paint out of the cup. Pour it into a container for proper disposal. Proper disposal is needed to protect our environment and to abide by environmental laws.

2. Place the cup back onto the gun but leave it loose. Loosen the air cap two or three turns.

3. Adjust line pressure at the gun to about five psi (34 kPa). Hold a folded cloth over the air cap and pull the trigger, Figure 16–24. This will force the paint in the gun back into the cup.

4. Clean the cup and cup cover with solvent and a thin bristle brush, Figure 16–25. Wipe off any residue with a clean rag soaked with solvent.

5. Pour a small amount of clean solvent into the cup. Spray the solvent through the gun to clean out the fluid passages.

6. Remove the air cap and soak it in thinner or solvent. Clean out clogged orifices with a round toothpick or broom straw, Figure 16–26. Also clean out the vent hole and tube in the cup lid because they can fill with paint.

> **WARNING!** *Never use wire or nails to clean the precision openings in a spray gun. This could enlarge or damage the openings and affect spray gun operation.*

7. Next, clean the fluid nozzle with a brush and solvent, Figure 16–27.

8. With a clean rag soaked with thinner, wipe the outside of the spray gun to remove all traces of paint, Figure 16–28.

9. Periodically, fully disassemble the spray gun. Remove the fluid and air needles, springs, and related parts. This will allow you to clean and lubricate parts more thoroughly. The manual for the spray gun will give details on how to clean and lubricate each part.

To clean a pressure feed spray gun, release the pressure in the cup first. Loosen the air cap. Then force the paint into the cup by triggering the spray gun. Empty the contents into a suitable container. Refill the cup with a clean, compatible solvent. The air cap can be left off. Spray the solvent out of the spray gun to wash out internal passages. If a tank is used, clean as directed by the manufacturer and reassemble.

Figure 16–24 After lowering air pressure, hold rag over nozzle and trigger spray gun. This will blow paint out of spray gun and into cup. *(BBV, Inc.)*

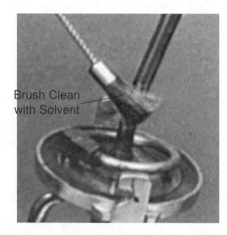

Brush Clean with Solvent

Figure 16–25 Wash all surfaces inside gun with solvent used to thin or reduce paint. *(BBV, Inc.)*

Figure 16–26 Use tooth·pick or similar soft tool to clean out passages in air cap and lid. Do not use metal wire or nail because they could damage opening and affect gun operation. *(BBV, Inc.)*

Using a Spray Gun Washer

Areas in the United States with air pollution problems, such as southern California, require the use of enclosed spray gun cleaning equipment. Spraying equipment (guns, cups, mixing sticks, and strainers) is placed in the tub of the *spray gun washer*. The spray gun washer will automatically clean them.

Figure 16–27 Make sure you clean off fluid tip under air cap. Periodically, remove needle valves for cleaning. *(BBV, Inc.)*

Figure 16–28 Wipe outside of spray gun with solvent-soaked rag. *(Aja)*

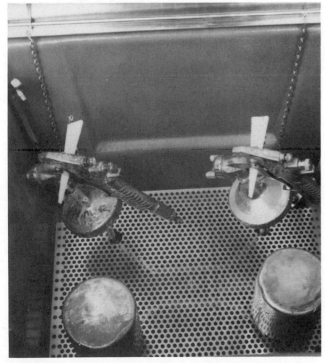

Figure 16–29 Gun washer will quickly clean gun and ready it for next job.

After the washer lid is closed, a pump circulates the solvent to clean the inside and outside of the equipment. In less than 60 seconds, the equipment is clean and ready for use. See Figure 16–29.

The spray gun washer saves time and increases safety. Compared with manual cleaning, the spray gun washer saves about ten minutes on each color change.

Check the owner's manual for complete operational details and the proper solvents to use. Always lubricate a spray gun after cleaning in a spray gun washer.

Spray Gun Lubrication

Spray gun lubrication involves placing a small amount of oil on packing and high friction points. Most manufacturers recommend daily lubrication of the parts shown in Figure 16–30.

WARNING! Do NOT overlubricate a spray gun. The excess oil could overflow into the fluid passages and mix with the paint. This could result in a defective paint job and "fish-eyes" (small dimples in paint film).

Always examine the needle and nozzle periodically for excessive wear. Packings, springs, needles, and nozzles will have to be periodically replaced due to normal wear. This should be done only in accordance with the manufacturer's instructions.

VOC TRACKING

VOC tracking systems help monitor and record materials used to abide by environmental regulations. Most computerized VOC tracking systems require a painter to enter general information about the job. This general information includes:

1. Date
2. Painter's name or initials
3. Repair order number
4. Customer and vehicle information
5. Gross vehicle weight or vehicle type
6. Size of mixing container or amount mixed

After entering all the general information, a painter enters information for the material to be sprayed. This includes: paint formulation number, reducers, cata-

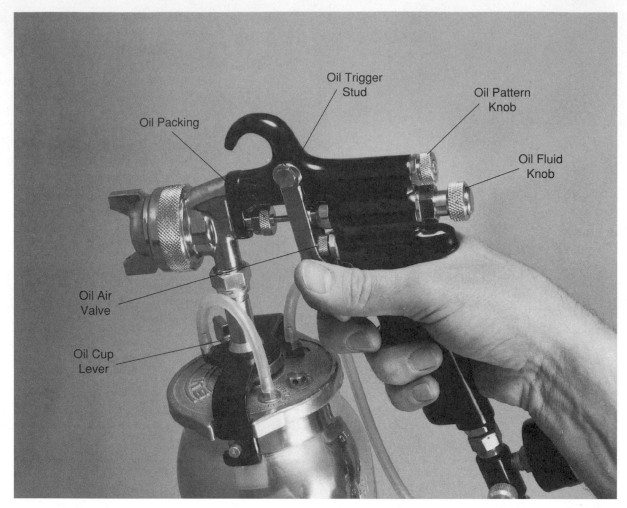

Figure 16–30 Note parts that should be lubricated on gun after cleaning. *(Photo courtesy of Binks Manfacturing Company)*

lysts or hardeners, and all other additives used in the mixture. As the product information is entered, the computer enters the VOC content of each material.

After applying the material, the painter enters the amount of material left in the spray gun. This allows the computer to calculate the exact amount of VOCs sprayed, NOT just the VOC total of the amount mixed. These steps are performed for each material used during the refinishing operation. The computer continues to enter the general information for each step.

By keeping records of this detail, a painter can use the computer to print the records needed to document total amount of VOCs sprayed.

Summary

- The most common types of topcoats are: alkyd enamels, acrylic lacquers, acrylic enamels, polyurethane enamels, and acrylic urethane enamels.

- Spray gun distance is measured from the gun tip to the surface being painted. Typically, hold the gun 6 to 8 inches (152–203 mm) away for lacquer and 8 to 10 inches (203–254 mm) away from the surface for enamel.

- When applying basecoat, two medium coats are sufficient. Use enough to achieve hiding, no more.

- VOC tracking systems help monitor and record materials used to abide by environmental regulations. As the product information is entered, the computer enters the VOC content of each material.

Technical Terms

tack cloth	*short spray distance*
paint settling	*long spray distance*
body ID number	*spray gun angle*
application stroke	*spray gun triggering*
spray gun distance	*spray gun speed*

banding coat
overlap strokes
paint thickness
mil gauge
spray gun heeling
spray gun arching
incorrect spray gun
  stroke speed
improper spray overlap
improper coverage
tack coat
dust coat

full wet coat
shading coats
paint blending
spot repair
panel repairs
overall refinishing
paint overlap
wet edge
let-down panel
spray gun washer
spray gun lubrication
VOC tracking systems

Review Questions

1. From the customer's standpoint, the topcoat or color coat is the most important aspect of a paint job. True or false?

2. How do you use a tack cloth?

3. What are some of the more important paint label information that should be checked before spraying?

4. A short spray distance causes the high velocity mist to _____ the wet paint _____. A long spray distance causes a greater percentage of the thinner to _____, resulting in _____ _____ or _____ spray.

5. How do you properly trigger a paint spray gun?

6. Spray gun speed refers to how fast the spray gun is moved _____ while painting.

7. What are overlap strokes of a spray gun?

8. What is the maximum paint film build-up allowable?
   a. 2 mils
   b. 5 mils
   c. 12 mils
   d. 50 mils

9. What can happen if the paint film is too thick after you paint a car or truck?

10. This refers to whether a paint film is uniform.
    a. Heeling
    b. Arching
    c. Spattering
    d. Coverage

11. Technician A says that the first coat of paint on an overall finish should be a very wet coat. Technician B says that the first coat should be a tack coat.

Who is correct?
a. Technician A
b. Technician B
c. Both Technicians
d. Neither Technician

12. Inspection finds uneven coverage when painting a vehicle. Technician A says to use a dust coat to help even out the coverage. Technician B says to use a full wet coat.
Who is correct?
a. Technician A
b. Technician B
c. Both Technicians
d. Neither Technician

13. _____ _____ or _____ coats are progressive applications of paint on the boundary of spot repair areas so that a color difference is NOT noticeable.

14. Explain the difference between a spot repair and a panel repair.

15. How do you avoid runs and sags in paint during application?

16. When repairing a small area with basecoat/clearcoat, you only need to spray the basecoat over the repair area but the whole panel should be cleared. True or false?

17. List ten rules or questions you should remember when refinishing a vehicle.

18. When manually cleaning spray paint guns, it is wise to wear _____, _____, and a _____.

Activities

1. Practice spraying on old body part. Prepare its surface properly using information in previous chapters and this chapter. You might be able to obtain mismatched paint for free from a body shop or supplier. Write a report on what you learned and any problems that you encountered. List the materials used for the job.

2. Completely disassemble and reassemble a spray gun. Follow manufacturer's instructions. Note if any parts are worn or dirty.

3. Practice spraying a metallic paint onto an old part or a sheet of sandpaper. Intentionally apply too much paint so that it runs or sags in one location. In another location, spray a dry mist of metallic by holding the spray gun too far away from the surface. After drying, inspect the difference in the metallic. Make a report of your findings.

REFINISHING

CHAPTER 17

COLOR MATCHING

Objectives

After studying this chapter, you should be able to:

- Describe color theory and how it relates to refinishing.

- Define the terms relating to color.

- Describe the use of a computerized color matching system.

- Make let-down and spray-out test panels.

- Explain how to tint solid and metallic colors.

- Summarize the repair procedures for multi-stage finishes.

Introduction

Color matching involves the steps needed to make the new finish match the existing finish on the vehicle. Even if you use the body color code numbers and correct paint formula, the new paint may NOT be the exact same color. With today's multi-stage finishes and factory robotic painting, it can be very difficult to match colors when making spot and panel repairs.

Multi-stage paints like metallic pearl paints, for example, are very difficult to match. Even if you have a new vehicle with a fresh OEM finish, it can be a challenge to make your repair look like the paint already on the vehicle. Today, there are many variables that affect the color and appearance of your paint work.

This chapter will help you develop the skills needed to match any type of paint. It will summarize color theory, color evaluation, color matching, computer analysis of paint, tinting, and other factors. See Figure 17–1.

Figure 17-1 Finish on today's car is much more difficult to match than in the past. Multi-stage metallic and pearl paints can be a challenge to match. *(Courtesy of Ford Motor Company)*

COLOR THEORY

Color is caused by how objects reflect light at different frequencies or wavelengths into our eyes. The color seen depends on the kind and amount of light waves the surface reflects. When these light waves strike the retina in your eye, they are converted into electrical impulses that the brain sees as color.

When the eye sees a colored object, that object is absorbing all of the light except for the color that it appears to be. A red ball appears red because the ball absorbs all of the colors in the light shining on it except for the reds. In contrast, a black object absorbs almost all light, while chrome absorbs none.

White light is actually a mixture of various colors of light. By passing light through a prism, light is broken down into its separate colors, called the *color spectrum.* This is the same principle of how rain breaks up light to form a rainbow. Refer to Figure 17-2.

The colors in the spectrum are easily remembered with the name "Roy G. Biv." which stands for the colors:

Red

Orange

Yellow

Green

Blue

Indigo

Violet

LIGHTING

Sunlight contains the entire visible spectrum of light. It is the standard by which other light sources are measured. Since the vehicle will be seen in sunlight, you should always use sunlight, or daylight corrected lighting, when making color evaluations.

Each light source has a different mixture of colored light. When light sources are plotted on a graph, a dif-

Composition of Light

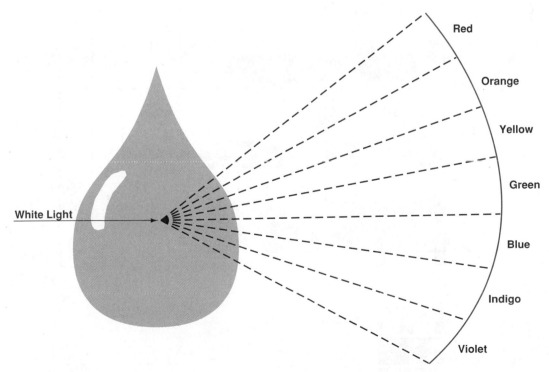

Figure 17-2 White contains all of the colors of the spectrum. When it is sent through a prism, these colors separate and can be seen. *(I-CAR)*

ference can be seen in the amount of colored light each light source contains. The same color of paint will look very different under different kinds of light. This is why it is so important to check the color match in daylight or under a balanced artificial light, Figure 17–3.

Compared to daylight, *incandescent light* has more yellows, oranges, and reds. *Fluorescent light* has more violets and reds. They should NOT be used when analyzing a color. See Figure 17–4.

The index for measuring how close a lamp in

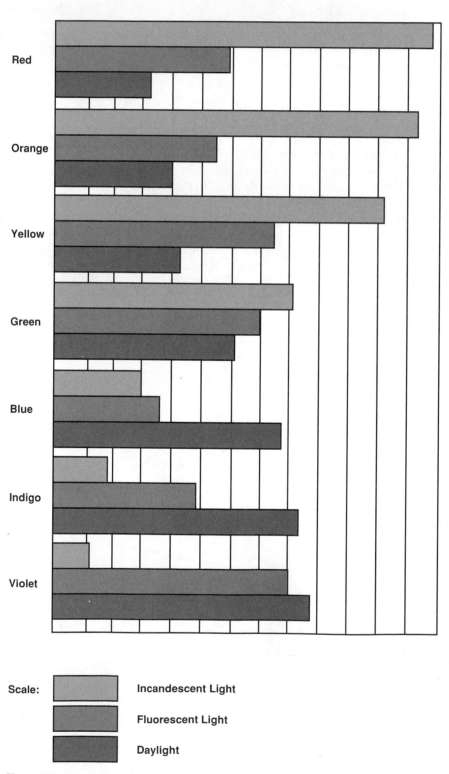

Comparison of Light

Red
Orange
Yellow
Green
Blue
Indigo
Violet

Scale:

Incandescent Light

Fluorescent Light

Daylight

Figure 17–3 Note how the type of lighting affects how we see light. *(I-CAR)*

Sunlight = Blue	Fluorescent = Blue	Incandescent = Yellow
Green	Light Yellow	Light Red
Yellow	Red	
Red		

Figure 17–4 When evaluating paint color, use sunlight or color corrected lighting. Colors will look different under fluorescent or incandescent lighting.

indoor lighting is to actual daylight is the *Color Rendering Index*, abbreviated *CRI.* A CRI of 100 duplicates daylight. A range of 85 to 100 is preferred for spray booth lighting.

Lamps may also have a *lumen rating* for brightness. Lamps are normally between 1,000–2,000 lumens, with a higher lumen rating producing a brighter light.

Lamps may also be rated for *light temperature* in "Kelvin." Daylight is 6,200 Kelvin. For painting, a lamp rating of 6,000–7,000 Kelvin is recommended.

What the eye sees as color is really light reflected from an object. The eye might see different shades of a color depending on the type of light source used. Look at Figure 17–5.

Always evaluate and match paint colors in daylight or while using daylight corrected lighting. The characteristics of the light in the shop will affect how you perceive the color of paint on a vehicle. The color of the paint on the panel does NOT change. What changes is the amount of colored light reflected from the panel.

For this reason, choose lamps that are closest to simulating actual sunlight. The spray booth manufacturer or representative may have recommendations.

COLOR BLINDNESS

Color blindness makes it difficult for a person's eye to see colors accurately. If problems arise in matching certain colors, it might be wise to have your eyes checked for color vision. Nearly 10 percent of all men have trouble seeing one or more colors. Blue-greens are most often the problem. However, almost no women have this difficulty. This is one of the reasons women do the touch-up work in auto plants. If you have a color vision problem, ask someone in the shop to help you match colors.

To do finish matching, the painter must be able to recognize colors as they actually are. It is important NOT only to see the color that is to be worked on, but also the overtones within that color, including the shades of darkness or lightness and the richness or fullness of the color.

DIMENSIONS OF COLOR

Many people describe color in terms of what they see. For example, you might have heard these descriptions: sky blue, ruby red, grass green, or midnight blue. These terms cause confusion when describing colors.

To minimize the confusion when painting, color should be based upon three *dimensions of color*, which are:

1. Value—lightness or darkness
2. Hue—color, cast, or tint
3. Chroma—saturation, richness, intensity, muddiness

These three dimensions are used to organize colors into a logical sequence on a color tree. The *color tree* is used to locate colors three-dimensionally when matching colors. Colors move around the color tree in a specific sequence—from blue to red to yellow to green, Figure 17–6. This sequence is easier to remember if you think of "BRYG." These are the first letters of blue, red, yellow, and green.

Value refers to the degree of lightness or darkness of the color. It is one dimension of color, Figure 17–7. When using the color tree, the value scale runs vertically through the tree. It is white at the top and black at the bottom. It is neutral gray at the center.

Hue, also called color, cast, or tint, describes what we normally think of as color. Hue is the color that is seen, moving around the outer edge of the color tree. It moves from blue to red to yellow to green. See Figure 17–7. When using the color tree, the hue scale shows color position around the color tree. It uses four main colors: blue, red, yellow, and green.

Chroma refers to the color's level of intensity, or the amount of gray (black and white) in a color. It is also called saturation, richness, intensity, or muddiness. It moves along the spokes that radiate outward from the central gray axis of the color tree. Weak, washed-out colors with the least chroma are at the core of the color tree. Highly chromatic colors that are rich, vibrant, and intense are at the outer edge. When using the color tree, chroma increases as it moves out-

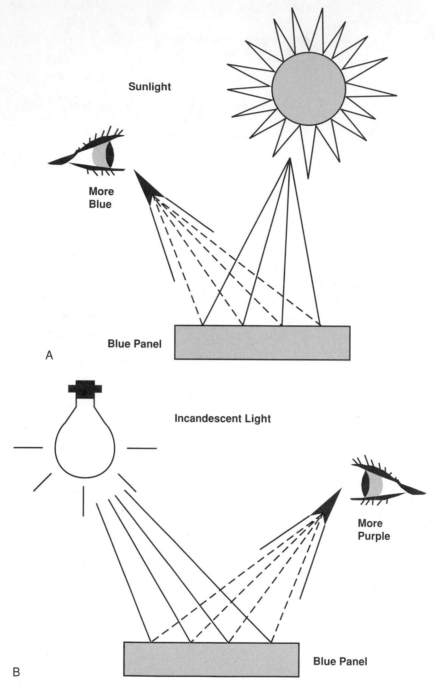

Figure 17–5 Sunlight is best lighting to use when evaluating color. (I-CAR) A: Sunlight will show blue panel correctly. B: Incandescent light will make blue panel look more purple.

ward from the neutral gray center. It decreases as it moves closer to the neutral gray center, Figure 17–7.

METAMERISM

Metamerism happens when different light sources affect paint pigments differently. A paint may have some blue in it which is NOT noticeable in daylight,

but which becomes very evident under street lights. The problem is that the refinish and OEM paint formulas are NOT made of the same pigments. This causes the pigments to look different under different light sources.

Paint manufacturers formulate refinish paints to minimize the effect of metamerism. Metamerism is most often a problem when a painter leaves the paint formula during tinting operations. That is why it is

Figure 17–6 Note graphic representation of three dimensions of color. *(Munsell Color Group)*

important to use only the tints called for in the formula.

PLOTTING COLOR

Plotting color is the process of identifying paint color in a graphic way based on value, hue, and chroma. This knowledge will help you become familiar with the refinishing evaluation process.

Plotting is NOT an exact science. It only has meaning when it is compared to the color on the vehicle. Plotting will help you recognize the differences between changes in value, hue, and chroma and adjust color as needed.

Evaluate colors in this order:

1. Value
2. Hue
3. Chroma

Solid Colors

Value:
• Adjusted First.
• Adding White Increases Value.
• Adding Black/Colored Pigments Decreases Value.
• Changes in Value Affect Chroma.
• Hue Adjustments Affect Value.

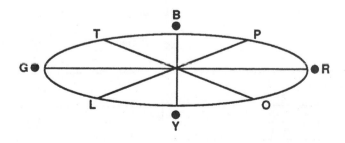

Hue:
• Adjusted Second.
• Adding Colored Pigments Moves Colors Around Color Wheel.
• Adding Colored Pigments Affects Chroma.

Chroma:
• Rarely Adjusted.
• Colored Pigments Affect Chroma.
• Increasing Chroma Decreases Value.
• Use Gray to Decrease Without Changing Value.

Figure 17–7 Note major steps for evaluating color using value, hue, and chroma. *(I-CAR)*

Using the plotting chart, develop a tinting plan which makes sense for all three dimensions of the color. In most cases only one dimension of a color will require adjustment.

For example, a plot for white paint is in Figure 17–8. Note how the vehicle color (V) is different from the paint (P). You would need to adjust the color. The value is too high. The hue is too red and the chroma is too low.

When working with colors that are between the four main colors on the color wheel, a painter should remember that:

1. Orange, bronze, and gold colors can move toward red or yellow.

2. Maroon and purple can move toward blue or red.

3. Lime can move toward green or yellow.

4. Aqua and turquoise can move toward green or blue.

When adjusting hue, a paint can be moved to either side of the dominant color, or toward one of two dominant colors if the paint is between major colors. Always use bluer, redder, yellower, or greener to describe how hue is to be moved.

Plotting White

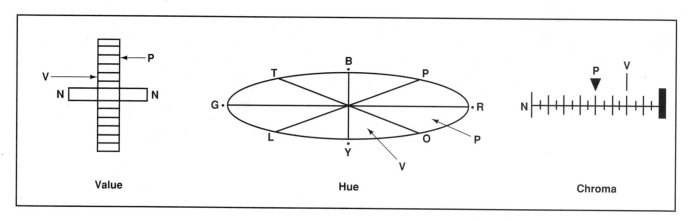

Value		Hue		Chroma

Metallics Only

Sidetone Value - Vehicle is :   ☐ Lighter   ☐ Darker

Sidetone Hue - Vehicle is More :   ☐ Blue   ☐ Red
☐ Green   ☐ Yellow

Color : White

Code	Tint	Amount	Weight
053	Ferrite Yellow	2.0	2.0
035	Red	3.5	5.5
006	Black	53.5	59.0
001	White	886.5	945.5

Figure 17–8 When plotting color, letter "V" stands for vehicle and "P" stands for paint. First, you would tint paint to adjust value. You would then adjust the hue by adding color to move hue around wheel. Chroma is rarely adjusted. *(I-CAR)*

PAINT COLOR MATCHING

Because a variety of factors can cause paint mismatch problems, it is very important to follow a step-by-step process on every job. There are acceptable variances in color that occur at both the refinishing and OEM levels.

In other words, paint can fall to either side of the color standard and still be acceptable. Thus, there can be a difference in the two finishes even though they are officially the same color. This can pose problems when painting.

Remember! Whatever the reason for color variance, you must match the only color standard that really matters—the vehicle itself. For better or worse, the vehicle is the standard!

Color Directory

A *color directory* is a publication containing color chips and other paint related information for most makes and models of vehicles. Most collision repair and refinishing shops have an aftermarket refinishing color directory. See Figure 17–9.

To use a color directory, locate the vehicle manufacturer's paint code. Then you can identify the color chip next to it. It is wise to compare the color chip with the vehicle color. There is always the chance that the vehicle has been repainted with a different color.

Figure 17–10 shows an actual page from a color matching manual. Note how it gives recommendations for changing a specific color.

The OEM has a group of sample panels, called *color standards,* for each vehicle color. These color standard panels are also provided to the aftermarket paint manufacturers for formulation of refinish colors. The OEM uses these color standard panels to identify

Figure 17–9 Color manuals give instructions, color chip samples, and charts for matching colors. Color matching manuals are provided by paint manufacturer. *(BASF)*

acceptable color variances. For example, a blue color can vary slightly to either the green or the red side of the standard and still be acceptable.

Remember! The vehicle must be the standard because it may already have been repaired before.

PAINT FORMULA

The *paint formula* gives the percentage of each ingredient that is needed to match an OEM color. The formula will be available from the mixing system or from the local paint jobber.

A *basecoat patch* is a small area on the vehicle's surface without clear to enable the painter to check for color match with tri-coat colors. The manufacturer masks the patch before clearcoating to help you match the color more easily. The basecoat patch is sometimes located on the driver's rocker panel. Other common locations for the exposed basecoat are somewhere under the deck lid or hood. If the color match is correct, order the topcoat by color stock number.

Refinish suppliers supply topcoat colors in two ways—factory colors and custom colors. If it is a recent model or a popular color, chances are they will have the paint ready-mixed. These ready-mixed paints are called *factory packaged colors.*

If it is an older color, they might have to mix it. *Custom-mixed colors* are those colors that are mixed to order at the paint supply distributor. Custom-mixed colors can always be identified easily. The contents of the can must be written or typed on the label by the person who mixed the paint.

An *intermix system* is a full set of paint pigments and solvents that can be mixed at the body shop. Most automobile paint manufacturers have made a color mixing system available to painters. With such an "intermix" system, it is possible to mix thousands of colors at a savings over the cost of factory-packaged colors or jobber mixing of colors.

An in-shop intermix system also allows you to remix the paint to better match the color of the vehicle more easily. You do NOT have to go back to the paint supplier for a remix.

SPECTROPHOTOMETER

A *spectrophotometer* is an electronic device for analyzing the color of the paint on a vehicle. It electronically reads the color frequencies in the finish to quickly and accurately find the correct paint formula for a color match. See Figure 17–11.

The spectrophotometer wand or box is placed on the surface (either vehicle or test panel) to be checked. Most systems require that a test panel be sprayed for

If you have a RED METALLIC color and you want to:

	ALPHA-CRYL		MIRATHANE & MIRACRYL		SUPER-MAX		DIAMONT	
Make it more BLUE	AT-120	AT-155	MB-214	MB-633	TE-20		BC-300	BC-833
	AT-151		MB-255	MB-643			BC-402	BC-838
	AT-153		MB-557				BC-405	BC-840
	AT-154		MB-630				BC-470	BC-880
Make it more RED	AT-150	AT-162	MB-550	MB-630	TE-50	TE-79	BC-810	BC-840
	AT-151	AT-163	MB-551	MB-633	TE-51		BC-820	BC-880
	AT-152	AT-165	MB-552	MB-643	TE-65		BC-825	
	AT-153	AT-170	MB-554	MB-731	TE-66		BC-830	
	AT-154	AT-179	MB-557		TE-67		BC-833	
	AT-155	AT-1613	MB-559		TE-78		BC-838	
Make it more YELLOW	AT-174		MB-560	MB-731	TE-72	TE-86	BC-600	BC-805
	AT-176		MB-566	MB-733	TE-74	TE-87	BC-605	BC-810
	AT-180		MB-568	MB-763	TE-78		BC-610	BC-850
	AT-184		MB-711	MB-764	TE-80		BC-620	
	AT-186		MB-716	MB-765	TE-84		BC-710	
	AT-187		MB-722		TE-85		BC-800	
Make it LIGHTER	AT-111	AT-118	MB-073	MB-084	TE-13		BC-110	BC-170
	AT-112	AT-1101	MB-074	MB-085	TE-14		BC-113	BC-180
	AT-113	AT-1102	MB-075	MB-086	TE-17		BC-115	
	AT-114	AT-1173	MB-081				BC-120	
	AT-115	AT-1174	MB-082				BC-140	
	AT-116	AT-1175	MB-083				BC-145	
Make it DARKER	AT-141		MB-431		TE-41		BC-200	
	AT-142		MB-451		TE-42		BC-209	
	AT-143		MB-455		TE-43		BC-250	
Make it BRIGHTER & More SPARKLE	AT-112		MB-084		TE-14		BC-170	
	AT-115		MB-085		TE-17		BC-180	
Make it GRAYER	AT-141		MB-431		TE-31	TE-42	BC-200	
	AT-142		MB-451		TE-32	TE-43	BC-209	
	AT-143		MB-455		TE-41		BC-250	
Make the PITCH LIGHTER (Basecoat only)	AT-104		MB-040				BC-101	
	# 850		# 850					

Automotive Refinishing Products

Section 3 – page 7

Figure 17–10 Study typical page from a color manual. It gives formulas for making paint match vehicle more closely. *(BASF)*

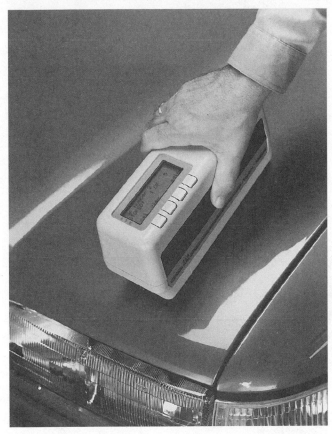

Figure 17-11 Spectrophotometer or electronic color analyzer uses electronic technology to read actual color of vehicle. It can then communicate with computer system and paint formula software to mix correct paint color. *(PPG Industries, Inc.)*

a comparison. The multi-angle spectrophotometers get a reading at 45, 25 and 75 degrees. Each angle is read for several variables.

Depending upon the type of system, they will read:

1. *LAB* or lightness, red to green hue, and yellow to blue hue.

2. *LCH* or lightness, chroma, and hue.

Most systems compare the vehicle and test panel to one another. The painter will get a reading on the relative lightness/darkness, hue, and chroma of the vehicle to the panel checked. It is still up to the painter to decide how to move the paint closer to the vehicle. Decisions on which tint and how much will be added must still be made using human judgment.

COMPUTERIZED PAINT MATCHING SYSTEMS

Computerized paint matching systems use data from the spectrophotometer to help in how to match the paint color. Many spectrophotometer systems can input their color data into a computer. The computer can then use its stored data to help determine how to mix or tint the paint.

Depending upon the sophistication of the system, computerized paint matching system may be able to:

1. Compare the actual color of the vehicle to a computer stored set of color formulations.

2. Make a recommendation on which tint in the formula will move the sample panel closer to the vehicle.

3. Automatically keep a record of the mixing or tinting procedure. This will let you quickly match the paint if the vehicle returns for another repair.

COLOR VARIANCE PROGRAMS

Color variance programs compare the color of refinish paints to OEM color standards and actual painted parts obtained from shops. If a particular OEM finish variation is noted often enough, a paint company may develop a *color variation formula* to match the OEM finish.

Variance chips are several samples of color used to help match paint color variations. One paint code may have a series of variance chips on each side of a typical color. They can be used to adjust the paint formulation more precisely than by just using one chip. The chips are organized into books by the paint manufacturer. Many paint manufacturers have color variance programs.

To use variance chips, lay the chips on the vehicle under proper lighting. Find the variance chip that best matches the color on the vehicle. Using the number for this chip, the computer will then give instructions for mixing the paint to match the variance chip and vehicle. Computerized formulas will give variance to change the color as needed.

SPRAY METHODS AFFECT COLOR

Although a painter cannot control the variables that can affect colors at the manufacturing plant, there are variables in the shop that can be controlled. For example, a painter can control the:

1. Agitation of the paint

2. Application techniques

3. Amount of material applied

4. Spray gun set-up

5. Atomizing air pressure

6. Type and amount of solvent used for reduction

7. Identification of the correct paint code and mixing formula

All of these will help you make the new paint match the existing finish. Refer to Figure 17–12.

Varying the spraying technique can affect color. That is, the application technique could cause the color to vary. Painters who spray wet end up with a darker color than those who spray drier, especially with metallics.

MATCHING SOLID COLORS

For many years all vehicles were solid colors, such as black, white, tan, blue, green, maroon, and so on. Solid colors reflect light in only one direction. Solid colors are still used on vehicles, but to a lesser degree when compared with a few years ago.

Matching solid colors is easier than matching metallic or mica paints. You only need to match the color pigment and NOT the metal or mica flakes suspended in the paint.

Oddly enough, a mismatch in a panel repair will usually show up more than a mismatch in a spot repair—even though the spot repair is smaller. That is because a panel, such as a vehicle door, has a distinct edge. And the repair, obviously, cuts off at that edge. Mismatched panels, as in the case of front and rear doors, will be right next to each other and will show a sharp contrast.

A spot repair, on the other hand, is performed by blending the repair into the surrounding area. In spot repairs, the first coat is applied to the immediate area being repaired. Subsequent coats extend beyond this

Effects Of Gun Setup

Changing Of Color Tone Spraying Condition	Color Becoming Lighter	Color Becoming Deeper	Degree Of Effect
Evaporation Speed Of Solvent	Fast	Slow	Medium
Paint Viscosity	Low	High	Large
Paint Discharge Quantity	Small	Large	Large
Spray Pattern Width	Wide	Narrow	Medium
Gun Speed	Fast	Slow	Medium
Gun Distance	Apart	Close	Medium
Air Pressure	High	Low	Large
Paint Film Thickness	Thin	Thick	Large

Note : Color Tone Will Become Vivid By Clearcoating.

Figure 17–12 Chart shows effects of gun setup. Study them carefully. *(I-CAR)*

area gradually. Finally, a blend coat extends beyond the color coats. Thus, if there is a slight mismatch, the blend coat and the last color coat will allow enough show-through of the old finish to make the color difference a gradual one.

MATCHING METALLIC FINISHES

Metallic paints contain small flakes of aluminum suspended in liquid, Figure 17–13. The position of the flakes and the thickness of the paint affect the overall color. The flakes reflect light while the color absorbs a higher amount of the light. The thicker the layer of paint, the greater the light absorption.

A *dry metallic paint spray* makes the paint appear lighter and more silver. The aluminum flakes are trapped at various angles near the surface of the paint film. Light reflection is NOT uniform. The light has less paint film to travel through, little of it is absorbed. The result is non-uniform light reflection and minimum light absorption.

A *wet metallic paint spray* makes the color appear darker and less silver. The flakes have sufficient time to settle in the wet paint. The flakes lie parallel to and deeper within the paint film. Light reflection is uniform and, because the light has to go farther into the paint film, light absorption is greater. The result is a painted surface that appears deeper and darker in color.

NOTE! METALLIC COLORS MUST BE STIRRED AND MIXED THOROUGHLY BEFORE USE. THE PIGMENT QUICKLY SETTLES BELOW THE BINDER.

ALSO, THE ALUMINUM FLAKES SETTLE BELOW THE PIGMENT. IF FLAKES STAY AT THE BOTTOM OF THE CAN, THE PAINT WILL NOT MATCH THE SAME COLOR ON THE VEHICLE BEING REFINISHED.

An *agitator paint cup* will help keep the metallic flakes mixed and evenly distributed in the cup. As shown in Figure 17–14, a small air motor in the gun moves a mixing paddle up and down. This helps keep the paint stirred.

In summary, the shades of metallic colors are controlled by:

1. Choice of solvents
2. Color reduction
3. Air pressure
4. Wetness of application
5. Spraying techniques

A good painter must know how to handle metallic colors. They are very sensitive to the solvents with which they are reduced and the air pressure with which they are applied. Metallic colors are also affected by a number of variables. This would include spraying conditions such as temperature, humidity, and ventilation. It also involves the spraying process such as amount of reduction, evaporation, speed of solvents, air pressure, and type of equipment.

To darken a metallic color:

1. Use a larger fluid needle and fluid nozzle.
2. Increase fluid flow.
3. Decrease fan width.

Metallic Topcoat

Figure 17–13 Metallic flakes in paint will reflect almost all light back out. Location and orientation of flakes is critical to matching metallic finishes.

Figure 17–14 *Agitator spray gun will help keep paint mixed to prevent problems with metallic and multi-stage paints. (Photo courtesy of Binks Manufacturing Company)*

4. Decrease air pressure.

5. Decrease travel speed.

6. Use a slower evaporating solvent.

To lighten a metallic color, do just the opposite.

MATCHING MULTI-STAGE FINISHES

Another type of glamour finish is the multi-stage finish. Shown in Figure 17–15, *multi-stage finishes* generally consist of:

1. Metal treatment (phosphate)

2. E-coat

3. Primer coats

4. Colored basecoat

5. Mica intermediate coat

6. Two coats of clearcoat

A multi-stage system may use a fluorine clear over a urethane clearcoat. The *fluorine clearcoat* is used for the following reasons:

1. It improves resistance to UV radiation.

2. It aids protection from weathering, chalking, oxidation, and industrial fallout.

3. It improves luster of the finish.

4. It reduces required maintenance, such as waxing and polishing.

Mica and carbon graphic pigments have special requirements when it comes to color evaluation. In automotive finishes, mica may be coated with titanium dioxide. The thickness of the titanium dioxide coating determines the colors that are reflected and allowed to pass through.

ZONE CONCEPT

The *zone concept* divides the horizontal surfaces of the vehicle into zones defined by character lines and moldings. It requires refinishing of an entire zone or zones with basecoat, mica intermediate coats, and clearcoats.

COLOR FLOP

Flop, also termed *flip-flop,* refers to a change in color hue when viewing from head-on and then from the side. The lightness or darkness of a color varies from head-on to side-tone views. Flop occurs most often in paints containing metallic pigments, but a type of flop can also occur in mica paints. Solid colors do NOT exhibit flop. See Figure 17–16.

To understand flop, think of the flakes in metallic and pearl paints as tiny mirrors. When light shines onto a mirror's surface, it is reflected back in exactly the opposite direction. Similarly, when light shines onto the aluminum flakes in a vehicle's metallic finish, it is reflected back in a straight line in the opposite direction. The brightness caused by this reflection is greatest when you are standing in the angle from which the light is reflecting. The brightness could drop off rapidly as you walk to one side or away from this angle. The direction and intensity of the light being reflected back by the flakes in the paint film is what causes the flop phenomenon.

Head-on view compares the test panel to the vehicle straight on, or perpendicular. *Side-tone view* compares the test panel to the vehicle on a 45–60 degree angle. Compare the test panel to the vehicle on both angles with metallic finishes. The position of the metallics in the paint film can cause the color of the paint to change from head-on to side-tone.

The first approach to correcting the problem is to adjust the spraying technique to compensate for this effect. Spraying the fender a little wetter will slightly darken the appearance when looking directly into the panel. When viewed from an angle, the resulting appearance is lighter.

Spraying the panel slightly dryer reverses the effect, giving a lighter appearance when looking directly at the panel. This is because the aluminum flakes are close to the surface. The result is a darker appearance viewed at an angle, as light becomes trapped.

If spray techniques cannot correct the condition, the addition of a small amount of white will eliminate the sharp contrast from light to dark when the surface is viewed at various angles. The white acts to dull the transparency, giving a more uniform, subdued reflection through the paint film. Care should be taken

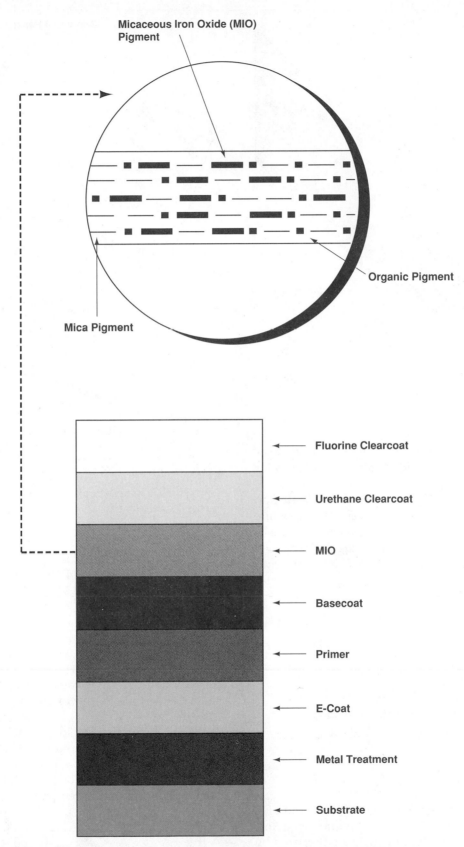

Figure 17–15 Cutaway shows basic makeup of multi-stage paint. *(I-CAR)*

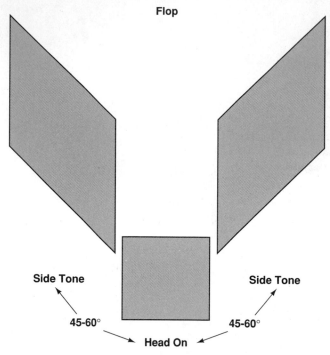

Figure 17–16 Flop occurs when a metallic or multi-stage paint looks different when viewed at different angles. *(I-CAR)*

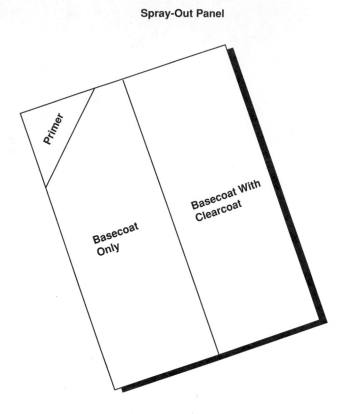

- **Use Correct Techniques**
- **Apply Basecoat To Full Hiding**
- **Allow Proper Flash**
- **Allow To Cure/Dry**

Figure 17–17 Spray-out panel tests paint match before applying paint to vehicle. *(I-CAR)*

when adding white since the change occurs quickly. Once too much white is added, recovering the color match becomes impossible.

When confronted with an extremely difficult flop condition, the best method involves adding white plus blending the color into the adjacent panels. When blending, extend the color in stages. Spraying a little wetter will darken the paint head-on, and lighten side-tone. Spraying drier will lighten the paint head-on, and darken side-tone.

CHECKING COLOR MATCH

There are three ways to check color match:

1. Spray-out panels—used with conventional paints
2. Let-down panels—used with multi-stage paints
3. Draw-down bar—used to check show-through

Spray-out Panel

The *spray-out panel* checks the paint color and also shows the effects of painter's technique on a test piece, Figure 17–17. Spray-out panels are prepared by applying the paint as near to actual spraying conditions as possible. When done properly, a spray-out panel shows the paint exactly as it will look when sprayed on a vehicle.

Before making a spray-out panel, double-check the paint code. Reduce the paint correctly. Set up the spray gun to the material that will be sprayed. Adjust the air pressure at the spray gun for the material to be applied.

When making a spray-out panel, apply a primer that matches the primer on the vehicle. Apply basecoat to full hiding. Allow proper flash time between coats. Apply clearcoat to half the panel. The panel should be fully dry or cured prior to evaluating color match.

When evaluating color match on basecoat/clearcoat systems, clear only half of the panel. The uncleared section can be used to check the color match of the basecoat prior to applying the clear. You can refer to any non-cleared patch on the vehicle.

NOTE! ON BASECOAT/CLEARCOAT FINISHES, THE BASECOAT CAN ALSO BE APPLIED TO A PIECE OF CLEAR PLASTIC. AFTER THE BASECOAT DRIES, THE SHEET IS TURNED OVER TO GIVE AN IDEA OF WHAT THE BASECOAT WILL LOOK LIKE WITH CLEAR APPLIED.

Let-down Panel

A *let-down panel* is used to evaluate color match on tri-coat and multi-stage paint systems, Figure 17–18. Directions for making a let-down panel are available from the manufacturer of the paint system used. Each coat of the mica intermediate coat will darken the appearance of the finish.

Here is how to make a letdown panel for a tri-coat finish.

1. Prepare the let-down panel with the same primers being used on the vehicle. If a primer-sealer is going to be used, apply the primer-sealer to the let-down panel also. Generally, a light color primer-surfacer (or primer-sealer) is preferred for tri-coat finishes.

2. Apply the basecoat color to hide the test sheet, using the same air pressure and spray pattern that will be used on the vehicle. Duplicating the actual spray techniques when preparing the let-down panel is an important point. Make sure NOT to vary your procedures.

3. After the panel has dried, divide it into four equal sections, Figure 17–18. Next, mask off the lower three quarters of the panel, exposing the top quarter.

Let-Down Panel

	Uncleared	Cleared

White Basecoat and
5 Coats of Pearl Luster

White Basecoat and
4 Coats of Pearl Luster

White Basecoat and
3 Coats of Pearl Luster

White Basecoat and
2 Coats of Pearl Luster

White Basecoat and
1 Coat of Pearl Luster

2"(50 mm) of Uncoated
Basecoat

Figure 17–18 Let-down panel tests multi-stage paint for match before spraying vehicle. You must mask each layer to apply different amounts of basecoat and clearcoat. You can then use the panel as a large paint chip for comparison to vehicle's finish. (I-CAR)

4. Apply one coat of mica midcoat color over the top quarter of the panel.

5. After the mica coat has flashed, remove the masking paper and move it down to the middle of the panel, exposing the top half.

6. Apply another coat of mica midcoat color over the exposed top half of the panel.

7. After this second coat has flashed, remove the masking paper and move it down to expose three quarters of the panel.

8. Apply another coat of mica midcoat color over the exposed three quarters of the panel.

9. After flashing, remove the masking paper entirely.

10. Apply a fourth coat of mica midcoat color. As always, spray the coating in the same way as would be done on the vehicle.

11. After the entire let-down panel has dried, mask off the panel lengthwise this time.

12. Apply the manufacturer's recommended number of clear coats to the exposed half. Refer to Figure 16–24 again.

13. Compare the different shades on the let-down panel with the paint on the vehicle. Use the same number of coats used on the matching section of the let-down panel to achieve the correct paint match.

Once made, the let-down panel can be kept and used on vehicles with the same color code. On the back of the panel note the color code, gun settings, and painter's name. One must be made for each different tri-coat color and each painter.

Draw-down Bar

The *draw-down bar* is a machined bar that evenly distributes 1 mil of unreduced paint to a card or sheet of plastic. It is used to check approximate color match. More than one coat may be required to achieve full hiding. See Figure 17–19.

The draw-down bar cannot show the effects of reduction and application technique. Do NOT depend on the draw-down bar to make a final color evaluation. A painter must always make a spray-out panel for final color evaluation. Draw downs cannot be used for tri-coat or multi-stage finishes.

BLENDING CLEARCOATS

Clearcoats may be blended by using additives provided by the manufacturer, or by painting technique. When working with basecoat/clearcoat finishes, remember:

1. Clearcoats are NOT perfectly clear. They will change the appearance of a color.

- **1 Mil Thickness**
- **Unreduced Paint**
- **Full Hiding**
- **Use Clear Film on BC/CC**

Figure 17–19 Draw-down bar can be used to spread thin layer of paint to check approximate color match. *(I-CAR)*

2. Blend the basecoat and clear the entire panel.

3. You may have to step-out the clearcoat if it must be blended.

4. You should clear the entire surface of horizontal panels.

5. Blend into the smallest area possible to help hide the repair.

FLUORINE CLEARCOAT REPAIRS

The basic steps for spot repair with a fluorine clearcoat system include:

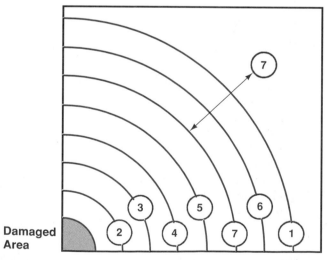

Figure 17–20 Compare numbers on illustration to the following: 1: Compound or sand with 1200–1500 grit sandpaper; 2: Apply first coat of basecoat; 3: Apply second coat of basecoat; 4: Apply third coat of basecoat or until hiding is obtained; 5: Apply color blender if necessary. Dry at 140°F (60°C) for 20 minutes; 6: Apply 3–4 coats of fluorine clearcoat. Dry properly between coats; 7: Polish with fine compound. *(Used with permission of Nissan Motor Corporation)*

1. Compound or sand with 1200-1500 grit sandpaper for better adhesion, Figure 17–20.

2. Apply first coat of basecoat.

3. Apply second coat of basecoat.

4. Apply third coat of basecoat or until hiding is obtained.

5. Apply color blender if necessary. Dry at 140°F (60° C) for 20 minutes.

6. Apply 3–4 coats of fluorine clearcoat. The area between 5 and 6 is faded out or blended if required. Dry at 60–70°F (16–21°C) for 10 minutes between coats. After applying final coat, force dry at 170° F (75°C) for 45 minutes.

7. Polish with fine compounds.

When working with tri-coat and multi-stage finishes, a painter must match the basecoat prior to applying the intermediate and clearcoats. Some vehicle manufacturers leave an area of basecoat that is NOT coated with mica or clear for comparing the basecoat spray-out to the vehicle.

TRI-COAT SPOT REPAIR

A *halo effect* is an unwanted shiny ring or halo that appears around a pearl or mica paint repair. It is caused by the paint being wetter in the middle and drier near the outer edges of the repair.

Avoid a halo effect by applying the first coat of mica to the basecoat only. The more intermediate mica coats that are applied, the darker the finish will appear. Allow a larger area in which to blend the mica intermediate mica coats. They require more room to blend than a standard basecoat. Keep the tri-coat repair area as small as possible.

This is one manufacturer's method for a spot or partial repair on a tri-coat system.

1. Apply adhesion promoter to all unsealed panels. Adhesion promoter should extend beyond the repair area.

2. Apply primer to area over the body filler.

3. Apply two or more coats of basecoat to areas to full hiding. Extend each coat slightly beyond the previous one, allowing to dry between coats. Look at Figure 17–21.

4. Check let-down panel for total number of coats of mica intermediate coats needed to match the OEM finish. Apply the intermediate coat to repair area, extending each coat beyond the last. Allow adequate flash time between coats.

5. Apply two coats of clear over entire panel. The clear may have to be blended into the sail panel.

Figure 17–21 Note spot repairing a multi-stage finish. You must blend pearl coat over area larger than repair. Then, clear the whole panel. *(Used with permission of Nissan Motor Corporation)*

TRI-COAT PANEL REPAIR

These are typical steps for a panel repair with a multi-stage finish:

1. Apply adhesion promoter to both doors.
2. Apply primer to area over the body filler.
3. Apply two or more coats of basecoat to areas to full hiding. Extend each coat slightly beyond the previous one, allowing to dry between coats. See Figure 17–22.

Figure 17–22 Note panel repair of multi-stage finish. You will usually have to blend pearl into adjacent panels. Then, clear the whole side of the vehicle. *(Used with permission of Nissan Motor Corporation)*

4. Check the let-down panel for total number of mica intermediate coats needed to match the OEM finish to areas. Extend each coat beyond the previous one, with only the last coat extending into adjacent panel. Allow adequate flash time between coats.
5. Apply two coats of clear to both doors.

BLENDING MICA COATS

This is a typical mica intermediate coat blending procedure:

1. Apply mica intermediate coat to the area covered by the basecoat.
2. Apply second mica intermediate coat well beyond the edge of the first coat.
3. Apply third mica intermediate coat so it extends just beyond the edge of the first coat but within the second coat.
4. Apply fourth mica intermediate coat to just beyond the edge of the second coat.

Spot repair recommendations for tri-coats are now available. However, the zone repair is still a workable repair option, and may be required on certain vehicles.

MATCHING MICA PAINTS

Many basecoat/clearcoat finishes contain mica pigments. Some of these finishes have proven to be especially challenging to match.

Because the finish may NOT provide full hiding, the color of the primer may show through enough to change the look of the paint. If the painter applies the refinish paint to full hiding, there may be a color mismatch because the primer color is no longer visible through the topcoat.

A color effect test panel is required for basecoat/clearcoat finishes which contain mica. To make this test panel:

1. Apply a primer that matches the primer color on the vehicle. Allow to dry.
2. Mask the panel into thirds.
3. Apply one coat of basecoat to the exposed section. Allow to dry.
4. Unmask the next section, and apply another coat of basecoat.
5. Unmask the last section of panel, and apply an additional two coats of basecoat to the entire panel. Allow to dry.

6. Apply two coats of clear to the panel. Allow to dry.

7. Compare the test panel against the vehicle to determine the number of basecoat coats that provide the best match.

Applying an extra coat of refinish basecoat to the vehicle may change the color to the point of NOT matching. Reds or other colors that traditionally provide poor hiding work best for making this panel.

When working with multi-stage finishes, do NOT tint the mica intermediate coat. Adjust the number of intermediate coats that are applied. Micas used in basecoat/clearcoat finishes are treated the same as metallic colors. They require special attention to side-tone angles. Mica will make the paint appear lighter and less chromatic on the head-on angle.

Mica will also reduce the metallic effect. For example, if the vehicle seems darker and more chromatic on the side-tone, add mica. If the test panel is darker and more chromatic on the side-tone, there is too much mica pigment.

Mica cannot be removed from the paint; however, this condition can be corrected by adding small amounts of both black and white. You can also add small amounts of the coarsest metallic in the formula.

Keeping good records during and after the tinting operation is important. Use the plotting chart or a separate record sheet.

WHY A COLOR MISMATCH?

Tinting should only be used as a last resort. If the color of the refinish job varies from the original, check the following possible reasons for the mismatch:

1. Has the original finish faded? Check the paint or unexposed areas such as door jambs or under the deck lid or hood to determine if the finish has faded. You can restore the paint's luster by compounding the original finish beyond the repair area. This will remove chalking and oxidation before making a color comparison.

2. Was the wrong color used? Check the vehicle manufacturer's paint code and the paint manufacturer's stock number of the color used to make sure that it is the right color.

3. Were the pigment and/or metallic flakes mixed thoroughly? Leaving pigment, metallic flake, or pearl in the bottom of the can could cause a mismatch. Be sure to agitate the paint thoroughly before and while painting.

4. Has the amount of thinner or reducer been measured carefully? Over-reducing will lighten or desaturate a color. Remember that it is easy to add more thinner or reducer, but it cannot be taken out.

5. When using a test panel, was enough time allowed for the paint to dry? Be sure to allow proper flash and dry times for each coat. The paint usually gets darker as it dries. Dry time can be shortened by using heat lamps, heat guns, or other drying methods.

6. If using a clear coat, remember that compounding the clear will make the paint appear darker. If testing a basecoat/clearcoat finish, color judgment cannot be made until the clear is applied to the basecoat.

TINTING

When the paint does NOT match the vehicle, you must determine if:

1. Paint code was properly identified.

2. Proper paint code was used, Figure 17–23.

3. Spray-out test panel was made properly.

Was the spray-out test panel checked:

1. Against a clean vehicle?

2. In the proper light?

3. On both face and side-tone views?

Finally, check the paint company variance chips for a formula that may obtain a better match. If there is NOT a variance formula, determine if the color is close enough to blend. If NOT, the paint must be tinted to have a blendable match.

A paint mismatch does NOT automatically mean tinting. There are a number of things to be checked first. Tinting should only be done to move the paint close enough for blending. Do NOT try to tint to a perfect match. Blending the paint out over a larger area takes care of any final color variations.

It must be remembered that the color might NOT be exactly right because all automotive finishes gradually change color over time. Some colors fade lighter, others go darker. Yellow, for instance, fades fairly rapidly. If the yellow fades to a cream, the color will usually go lighter and whiter.

Tinting involves altering the paint color slightly to better match the new finish with the old finish. Tinting may be one of the least understood tools of finish matching. There are three basic reasons for tinting:

1. To adjust color variations in shades to match the color from the manufacturer.

2. To adjust color on an aged or weathered finish.

3. To make a color for which there is no formula or for which there are no paint codes available.

Some computerized paint systems provide color variance information. Before making the decision to tint, determine if a color variance chip or formula is available. These may provide a blendable match, and reduce or eliminate the need to tint. Computerized paint systems also provide tinting information.

Before Tinting

| Paint Code | Ordered/Mixed Paint | Spray-out/Draw-down Panel |

Compare Paint to Vehicle in Daylight or Daylight Corrected Light.

Check Variance Chips

Figure 17–23 Note things to check before tinting. *(I-CAR)*

Computer tinting information may include:

1. A list of tints by number and name
2. Notes on tint strength, or hiding characteristics
3. Description on how each tint affects value, hue, and chroma
4. Cautionary notes, if needed, for using each tint

This computer matching information can be printed out with a copy of the paint formula when the paint is mixed.

The printout can be referenced during the tinting operation.

Review of Tinting

As a brief review of tinting, remember:

1. Tint only to blend.
2. Use only one tinting base at a time and check the color after every "hit."
3. Always tint within the formula.
4. Evaluate color match in daylight or under daylight corrected lighting.
5. Do NOT use a black tinting base unless absolutely necessary.
6. Do NOT use a white tinting base for metallic colors, unless absolutely necessary.
7. Evaluate color match against a clean vehicle.
8. Do NOT use the "dab" method of color match.

9. Adding small amounts of coarse metallic tinting base can darken side-tone.
10. Adding small amounts of metallic tinting base can lighten a metallic color.

Evaluating and tinting metallic colors is more difficult than evaluating and tinting solid colors. Evaluation of both metallic and solid colors should be done in this order:

1. Verify formula.
2. Plot the color on the plotting chart.
3. Compare the test panel to the vehicle.
4. Check and adjust value.
5. Check and adjust hue.
6. Check and adjust chroma.

Using kill charts and adding tints NOT in the formula will also move the color, but NOT around the outside of the color wheel. Adding tints suggested by a *kill chart* will move the paint more directly toward the gray center of the color wheel, affecting both hue and chroma.

There may be situations where this may be desirable, but as a rule of thumb, do NOT use kill charts to change hue. The proper tint for changing hue is already in the formula. Adding tints which are NOT in the formula may also cause problems with metamerism.

Adding paint instead of tints will add the dominant tint and all the other tints in that paint formula. Again, use only tint bases and do NOT add paint.

Figure 17–24 Follow major steps for tinting. *(I-CAR)*

Some paint companies produce metallic tinting bases designed to correct a specific problem, usually having to do with changes in side-tone. Use these products according to the manufacturer's recommendations. Using the paint formula and tinting guide, select the tinting base which will move the paint in the right direction.

When tinting, a painter should:

1. Use only half the can of paint.
2. Use only tint bases. Never add paint.
3. Use only tints that are in the paint formula.
4. Add tint bases in small amounts, and check the paint following each addition.

5. Keep records of each tint base and the amount added. This will be useful if more paint needs to be mixed.

A chart summarizing the tinting process is given in Figure 17–24. Read through it carefully.

Summary

- The colors in the spectrum are easily remembered by the name "ROY G. BIV" which stands for the colors red, orange, yellow, green, blue, indigo, and violet.
- The same shade of paint will look very different under incandescent and fluorescent lights. Therefore, it is very important to view a color in daylight or under a balanced artificial light.
- Color should be based upon value, hue, and chroma.
- Computerized paint matching systems use data from the spectrophotometer to help in how to match the paint color.
- The three ways to check color match are:
  1. Spray-out panels—used with conventional paints.
  2. Let-down panels—used with multi-stage paints.
  3. Draw-down panels—used to check show-through.

Technical Terms

color matching	custom-mixed colors
color	intermix system
white light	spectrophotometer
color spectrum	computerized paint
sunlight	matching systems
incandescent light	variance chips
fluorescent light	show-through
CRI	dry metallic paint spray
lumen rating	wet metallic paint spray
light temperature	agitator paint cup
color blindness	multi-stage finishes
color tree	fluorine clearcoat
value	zone concept
hue	flop
chroma	head-on view
metamerism	side-tone view
plotting color	spray-out panels
color directory	let-down panels
paint formula	draw-down bar
basecoat patch	halo effect
factory packaged colors	tinting

Review Questions

1. By passing light through a prism, light is broken down into its separate _____, called the _____.

2. When evaluating the color of a finish, it should be viewed under:
   a. sunlight.
   b. incandescent light.
   c. fluorescent light.
   d. drop light.

3. How do we see the color of a finish or any object?

4. _____ refers to the degree of lightness or darkness of the color.

5. _____, also called _____, or _____, describes what we normally think of as color.

6. _____ refers to the color's level of intensity, or the amount of gray (black and white) in a color.

7. What is a color directory?

8. A basecoat patch is a small area on the vehicle's surface without clear to enable the painter to check for color match. True or false?

9. This is a full set of paint pigments and solvents that can be mixed at the body shop.
   a. Factory packaged colors
   b. Custom-mixed colors
   c. Intermix system
   d. Manufacturer system

10. What is a spectrophotometer?

11. List three tasks that a computerized paint matching system may be able to do.

12. Explain variance chips in detail.

13. A dry metallic paint spray makes the paint appear darker and less silver. True or false?

14. List six ways to darken a metallic color.

15. Define the term "flop."

Activities

1. Obtain a color matching manual. Read its directions and use it to find a color match for a vehicle. Write a report on your findings.

2. Locate a shop with a computerized color matching system. Write a summary on how to use the equipment.

3. Make either a let-down or a spray-down panel. Make it into a display for the classroom.

CHAPTER 18

PAINT PROBLEMS,
FINAL DETAILING

Objectives

After studying this chapter, you should be able to:

- List and explain the most common paint problems.

- Repair common paint problems.

- Use a dirt-nib file.

- Wet sand to remove minor paint problems.

- Hand and machine compound a finish.

- Properly final detail a vehicle.

Introduction

After doing the body work and painting the vehicle, you must check your work quality, Figure 18–1. Ideally, the vehicle can be released to the customer after a minor clean-up. Sometimes, however, you will find small imperfections in the paint film that must be corrected. In rare occasions, you may have to solve major paint problems on existing or freshly painted surfaces.

This chapter will provide you with the information needed to analyze and correct paint problems. It will also outline how to final detail a vehicle.

Figure 18–1 When refinishing only a part of a body, it is critical that new paint's color matches existing paint on other parts. This can be a challenge with today's multi-stage paints.

SURFACE IMPERFECTIONS

The steps for correcting surface imperfections include:

1. Examining the finish for imperfections
2. Correcting the imperfection
3. Finesse finishing
4. Final detailing

There are a number of defects in the repair area that must be corrected before the vehicle is delivered to the customer. A few of these paint problems include runs, sags, orange peel, dirt or dust, and overspray.

SURFACE FINISH MEASUREMENTS

A good panel repair will have several desirable characteristics. It should not be rough, wavy, nor have surface flaws.

Surface roughness is a measurement of paint film or other surface smoothness in a limited area. If you look at any paint surface with a magnifying glass, it will have some surface roughness. Ideally, you want the paint to be as smooth as possible. Paint film roughness is normally due to improper mixing or application (spraying).

Surface waviness is a measurement of an area's general levelness or trueness. If a panel is supposed to be perfectly flat, there should be no waviness when viewed from an angle. Improper sanding or blocking of plastic filler or primer-surfacer is the main reason for waviness.

The first requisite for a good paint job is a smooth body surface. The body person will make it extra work for the painter if the body work is poor.

PAINT PROBLEMS

Paint problems include a wide range of troubles that can be found before or after painting. You must be able to inspect and analyze paint problems efficiently. If you fail to find a problem before painting, you will have extra work in fixing your mistake. You must also be able to find and solve paint problems that are found after you paint a vehicle.

The following is a detailed explanation of the most common paint problems.

Acid and Alkali Spotting

Acid and *alkali spotting* cause an obvious discoloration of the surface, as in Figure 18–2. Various paint pigments react differently when in contact with acids or alkalies. The cause of acid and alkali spotting is a chemical change of pigments. This chemical change results from atmospheric contamination, in the presence of moisture. This problem is found on older finishes that have been exposed to industrial pollution.

To remedy acid spotting, wash with detergent and water. Follow this with a vinegar bath. You might try wet sanding and compounding if there is only minor spotting. If the spots have absorbed deep into the finish, you will have to sand and refinish. If contamination has reached the metal or subcoating, the spot must be sanded down to the metal before refinishing.

To prevent acid spotting, warn the customer to keep the finish away from the contaminated atmosphere. Immediately following contamination, the surface should be vigorously flushed with cool water and detergent.

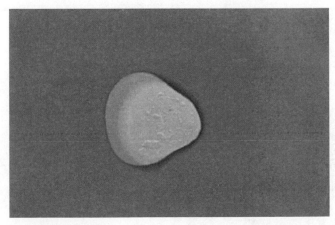

Figure 18–2 This is close-up of acid or alkali spotting of paint. (PPG Industries, Inc.)

Figure 18–3 This paint has suffered from bleeding. *(PPG Industries, Inc.)*

Bleeding

Bleeding is a discoloration of the surface of refinish color after painting. It is caused by solvent penetration from fresh color materials (old paints, fillers, putties, etc.) that absorb through the new paint. Usually, reds and maroons release a dye that comes to the surface of the fresh paint. A sample of bleeding is in Figure 18–3.

To remedy bleeding, remove all color coats and refinish. You can also allow the surface to cure. Then apply bleeder sealer and recoat.

To prevent bleeding, apply bleeder sealer over suspected bleeder colors before spraying new color.

Blistering

Blistering shows up as small, swelled areas on the finish, like a "water blister" on human skin. There will be a lack of gloss if blisters are small. You will find broken edged craters if the blisters have burst. See Figure 18–4.

Blistering is usually caused by rust under the surface. It is also caused by painting over oil or grease, by moisture in spray lines, and trapped solvents. Blistering can also be due to prolonged or repeated exposure of paint film to high humidity.

To remedy blistering, sand and refinish the blistered areas. It can be prevented by thoroughly cleaning and treating metal.

Frequently drain your air lines of water. Avoid overly fast drying thinners when temperature is high. Also allow proper dry time between coats.

Blushing

Blushing is a problem that makes the finish turn "milky looking." This is shown in Figure 18–5. It is caused by fast thinners in high humidity or condensation on the vehicle surface while painting.

To remedy blushing, add retarder to the thinner and respray. You may also have to sand and refinish.

To prevent blushing, keep paint and surface to be painted at room temperature. Select a good quality thinner. Use a retarder or reflow solvent when spraying in high humidity and warm temperatures.

Chalking

Chalking is a problem that causes a lack of gloss on the paint surface. Extreme cases will show up as a powdery surface. It is a natural weathering of the paint film. On a new finish, it can be due to a lack of thorough agitation of paint. Poorly balanced thinners can also create earlier chalking type failures. Look at Figure 18–6.

Figure 18–4 Here is a blistering paint problem. *(PPG Industries, Inc.)*

Figure 18–5 Blushing makes the paint look "milky." *(PPG Industries, Inc.)*

To repair chalking, sand to remove damaged surface material. Then clean and refinish. Minor chalking can be corrected by wet sanding and buffing.

To prevent chalking, agitate the paint thoroughly. Use recommended thinner for good balance.

Checking, Crazing, Cracking

Checking, crazing, and cracking are problems where the paint forms tiny cracks or lines in the paint film.

Checking usually shows up as a crowfoot separation in the paint film, Figure 18–7.

Crazing often is seen as a shattered glass type appearance in the paint film, Figure 18–8.

Cracking produces an irregular separation of the paint film, Figure 18–9.

Checking, crazing, and cracking are usually caused by insufficient drying of the paint film prior to recoating. These problems can also be due to repeated extreme temperature changes. Excessive heavy coats of paint or an excessive paint film thickness is another cause.

If your paint ingredients are not thoroughly mixed, it can also cause checking/crazing/cracking. If you add materials not designed for the paint system (incompatibility), checking, crazing, and cracking can result. If you fail to find this problem and you paint a previously checked finish, the problem will reoccur.

To fix checking, crazing, and cracking, you must remove the finish down through the checked paint film and refinish. With severe cases, you should strip the surface chemically or by blasting.

To prevent checking, crazing, and cracking, follow proper drying times between coats. Avoid extreme temperature changes. Spray uniform coats, avoiding excess, particularly with lacquers. Mix all ingredients thoroughly. Use only recommended balanced materials, thinners, etc. Remove a previously checked finish before recoating.

Figure 18–6 A chalking problem reduces gloss and gives the paint a powdery surface. *(PPG Industries, Inc.)*

Figure 18–8 Crazing causes an appearance of shattered glass. *(PPG Industries, Inc.)*

Figure 18–7 Note this line checking problem. *(PPG Industries, Inc.)*

Figure 18–9 Crowfoot checks look something like "bird tracks." *(PPG Industries, Inc.)*

Dirt in Finish

Dirt in finish is caused by foreign particles dried in the paint film. This is due to improper cleaning, not properly blowing off the vehicle, dirt on the painter, or failure to tack rag the surface before painting. This can also be due to a bad air regulator filter. A dirty work area or dirty spray gun can also deposit dirt in the finish. Refer to Figure 18–10 .

To correct light dirt in the finish, rub out finish with polishing compound. If dirt is deep in finish, sand and compound to restore gloss. Metallic finishes may show mottling with this treatment and will then require additional color coats.

To prevent dirt in the finish, blow out all cracks and body joints. Solvent clean and tack rag the surface thoroughly. Be sure all of your equipment and work area is clean. Replace inlet air filters if dirty or defective. Strain out foreign matter from the paint. Keep all containers closed when not in use to prevent contamination.

Dulled Finish

A *dulled finish* occurs where the spray pattern overlaps an already sprayed but dry area when painting, Figure 18–11. If a slow-dry thinner is used, the overspray will generally melt into the previously sprayed area. If it does not, the finish will be dull.

A dull paint finish can be caused by:

1. Compounding the new paint before thinner evaporates
2. Using a poorly balanced thinner or reducer
3. Poorly cleaned surface
4. Topcoats put on wet subcoats
5. Washing with caustic cleaners
6. Using inferior polishes

Figure 18–10 Dirt in finish can come from various sources. (PPG Industries, Inc.)

Figure 18–11 A dulled finish will lack normal gloss or shine. (PPG Industries, Inc.)

7. Inadequate flash time between coats
8. Insufficient film build-up

To remedy a dulled finish, allow finish to dry hard and rub with a mild rubbing compound. Then polish the finish to a high gloss.

To prevent a dulled finish, clean all surfaces thoroughly. Use recommended materials. Allow all coatings sufficient drying time.

Fisheyes

Fisheyes is a problem with separation of the wet paint film. Small indentations will form in the wet paint film. Sometimes, the previous finish under the new paint can be seen in these spots. An example is in Figure 18–12.

Fisheyes are usually caused by improper cleaning of the old surface. They can also be due to spraying over finishes that contain silicone.

To correct a fisheye problem, wash off the paint while still wet and respray. You can also add a fisheye preventer additive to the paint and respray over the problem. This will usually make the fisheyes flow out smooth. To prevent fisheyes, clean surface with wax and grease remover.

Lifting

Lifting shows up when the paint raises or swells when wet, Figure 18–13. It is often due to improper drying of previous coating. Lifting can also be caused by sandwiching enamel between two lacquers or acrylics. Spraying over a dusty surface can also cause lifting. Recoating improperly cured enamel is another reason for lifting.

To fix a lifting problem, remove lifted surfaces and refinish. To prevent this trouble, clean old surfaces properly. Allow all subcoats proper drying time. Seal old finishes.

Figure 18–12 Fisheyes are small indentations in surface film that look something like the eyes of a fish looking at you. *(PPG Industries, Inc.)*

Figure 18–14 Mottling is a streaking problem common to metallic paints. *(PPG Industries, Inc.)*

Figure 18–13 With lifting, the paint tends to raise up and swell. *(PPG Industries, Inc.)*

Figure 18–15 Orange peel is a rough, bumpy paint film. *(PPG Industries, Inc.)*

Mottling

Mottling is a streaking of the color, usually with metallic finishes. It is caused by excessive wetting or a heavier film thickness in some areas. Look at Figure 18–14.

To remedy mottling of a freshly applied paint, back the spray gun away when painting. Also increase air pressure for final coat. Avoid overreduction. On a dried finish, scuff down and apply additional color to correct mottling.

To prevent mottling, avoid excessive wetting or heavy film build-up in local areas. Be careful not to overreduce the color.

Orange Peel

Orange peel is a paint roughness problem that looks like tiny dents in the paint surface. It resembles the skin of an orange. An example is in Figure 18–15.

The droplets formed in the spray pattern hit the surface and dry before they have time to flow out. This causes a roughness in the surface.

When this occurs with primer–surfacers, excessive sanding is required to make the surface smooth enough to apply the topcoats. With lacquer topcoats, excessive compounding and polishing is required to produce a smooth, high-luster film. While there is always a slight amount of orange peel in an enamel film, too much will cause roughness, low gloss or both.

Orange peel is commonly caused by under reduction or an improper thinning solvent. The paint will lack proper flow. It can also be due to the surface drying too fast and improper air pressure at the spray gun.

To fix orange peel while still painting, you can often thin or reduce the final coat to its maximum limit and apply the last coat wet. This may make the orange peel flow out. If not, with enamel, rub surface with a mild polishing compound. With lacquer, sand or use rubbing compound. With severe cases, you may have to sand and refinish.

To prevent orange peel, properly adjust air pressure to the spray gun. Also make sure you have properly thinned or reduced the paint.

Peeling

Peeling shows up as a separation of a paint film from the subsurface. It is caused by improper surface preparation or incompatibility of one coat to another. See Figure 18–16.

To repair a peeling problem, you must remove peeling paint completely. Prepare the metal properly and refinish with compatible materials.

To prevent peeling, thoroughly clean and treat the old surface. Use recommended primers for special metals. Follow acceptable refinish practices using compatible materials.

Pin Holes or Blistering over Plastic Filler

Pin holes or blistering over plastic filler are noticed as air bubbles raising the paint film. These bubbles can then pop and cause craters when they erupt.

Some causes for pin holes over plastic filler are excessive amounts of hardener. Vigorous stirring or beating of the hardener will form bubbles in filler.

To fix this problem, sand thoroughly and recoat with a glaze coat of body filler or putty.

To prevent pin holes and blistering, mix in recommended quantities of hardener. Stir plastic filler mildly. Work out possible air trapped bubbles when applying filler.

Figure 18–17 Pitting or cratering looks similar to dry spray. (PPG Industries, Inc.)

Pitting or Cratering

Pitting or *cratering* is a problem where small holes form in the paint film. It can look like dry spray or overspray. It is caused by the same things as blistering (except blisters have broken). Corrections are also the same as for blistering. Refer to Figure 18–17.

Plastic Bleed Thru

Plastic bleed thru is a discoloration, often yellowing, of the paint due to chemical from the plastic filler. It is often caused by too much hardener or by applying the topcoat before the plastic filler is fully cured. See Figure 18–18.

To remedy plastic bleed thru, allow topcoat to cure and refinish. To prevent this problem, use right amount of hardener in plastic fillers. Allow adequate cure time before refinishing.

Figure 18–16 With peeling, a noticeable area of paint lifts. (PPG Industries, Inc.)

Figure 18–18 With a bleed-thru problem, colors under the paint are visible. (PPG Industries, Inc.)

Figure 18–19 Rust under a finish is due to improper surface preparation. *(PPG Industries, Inc.)*

Figure 18–20 Runs and sags are due to too much wet paint in one place. *(PPG Industries, Inc.)*

Rust under Finish

Rust under finish will cause the finish to peel or blister. You can also have raised spots on paint film. This problem is caused by improper metal preparation. Broken paint film has allowed moisture to creep under surrounding finish. Rust can also be caused if you have water in air lines. Look at Figure 18–19.

To remedy rust under the finish, seal off entrance of moisture from inner part of panels. Sand down to bare metal, prepare metal and treat with phosphate before refinishing. You can also prevent a rust problem by applying epoxy primer directly to metal. Locate any source of moisture and stop it.

When replacing ornaments or molding, be careful not to break paint film and allow dissimilar metals to come in contact. This contact can produce electrolysis that may cause a tearing away or loss of good bond with the film.

Runs

Runs occur when gravity produces a mass slippage of an overwet, thick paint film. The weight of the film will cause it to slide or roll down the surface. A large area of paint will flow down and form large globules of paint. See Figure 18–20.

Runs are caused by:

1. Overreduction with low air pressure
2. Extra slow thinners
3. Painting on cold surface
4. Improperly cleaned surface
5. Spray gun too close or moved too slowly
6. Too many coats of paint

To fix a run in a metallic paint, wash off the paint with solvent while still wet. Then, refinish the panel.

With solid colors, you can also allow the paint to dry. Then, wet sand the run or sag before buffing. This will not work with metallics.

To prevent runs, use recommended thinner at specified reduction and air pressure. Do not paint over cold surface. Clean surface thoroughly. Allow sufficient flash time between coats. Use proper gun spray pattern, speed, and distance from surface.

Sag

A *sag* is a partial slipping down of the paint created by a film that is too heavy to support itself. It appears something like a "curtain." A large area of paint is pulled down by gravity.

Sags are caused by:

1. Underreduction
2. Applying successive coats without allowing dry time
3. Low air pressure (lack of atomization)
4. Spray gun too close to surface
5. Spray gun out of adjustment
6. Moving spray gun too slowly

To fix a sag, sand or wash off and refinish. To prevent sags, use proper thinner at recommended reduction. Adjust air pressure and gun for correct atomization and move it at right speed. Keep gun at right distance from work.

Undercoat Show-thru

Undercoat show-thru is a problem where the color of the undercoat is seen through the paint. It is caused by insufficient color coats or repeated compounding. Undercoat show-thru can also be caused by not hav-

Figure 18–21 This is an undercoat show-thru problem. (PPG Industries, Inc.)

Figure 18–22 Water spotting dulls paint gloss. (PPG Industries, Inc.)

ing uniform color under the topcoat. To fix undercoat show-thru, sand and refinish. Refer to Figure 18–21.

To prevent undercoat show-thru, apply good coverage of color. Avoid excessive compounding.

Water Spotting

Water spotting is a dulling of gloss in spots. It can occur as a mass of spots that appear as a large distortion of the film. It is due to spots of water drying on finish that is not thoroughly dry. It can be caused by washing finish in bright sunlight. Refer to Figure 18–22.

To repair water spots, you can try wet sanding and polishing. However, you might have to sand and refinish.

To prevent water spotting, keep the fresh paint job out of rain. Do not allow water to dry on the new finish.

Wet Spots

Wet spots are a paint problem seen as off colored and/or slow drying spots of various sizes. It is usually due to improper cleaning. Heavy undercoats not properly dried is another reason. So is contamination with gasoline or other incompatible solvent.

To remedy wet spots, sand or wash off thoroughly and refinish. To prevent this trouble, clean surface with wax and grease remover. Allow undercoats to dry thoroughly. Use only water as a sanding lubricant.

Wrinkling

Wrinkling is a severe puckering of the paint film that appears like the skin of prune (fruit), more common

with enamel paints. There is a loss of gloss as paint dries. Minute wrinkling may not be visible to the naked eye. See Figure 18–23.

Wrinkling is caused by:

1. Underreduction
2. Air pressure too low causing excessive film thickness
3. Excessive coats of paint
4. Fast reducers creating overloading
5. Surface drying trapping solvents
6. Fresh film subjected to heat too soon

To fix wrinkling, break open top surface by sanding and allow to dry thoroughly. Then, remove paint and refinish.

To prevent wrinkling, reduce and apply enamels according to directions. Do not force dry until solvents have flashed off.

Metal Dust Damage

Metal dust damage, also known as "rail dust," occurs when metallic particles from industrial fallout settle

Figure 18–23 Wrinkling gives the paint a "prune look." (PPG Industries, Inc.)

onto the paint. The particles soon begin to rust, eating into the paint finish. Study Figure 18–24.

Metal dust damage can be identified on light colored paints by the visible small brown or black specks. On darker colored paints, you must feel the surface for prickly protrusion in the paint film. You can also rub a cotton towel across the paint. The iron particles will snag bits of cotton in the rag.

Metal dust damage is repaired by:

1. Blowing off the vehicle with compressed air

2. Washing and degreasing the vehicle

3. Treating with mild oxalic acid solution to dissolve the rust

4. Washing again to remove loose metallic particles

5. Color sanding, compounding, and glazing

Oxalic acid is also known as industrial fallout remover. It works by dissolving the rust holding the particles to the paint. To use the oxalic solution:

1. Soak rags in the solution.

2. Lay the cloths over the affected area. Work in small areas.

3. Remove the cloths and rinse thoroughly with clean water. Remove excess water with clean towels.

4. Check the paint surface for remaining signs of iron particles.

5. If more particles are present, repeat the above steps.

6. If the solution does NOT dislodge all of the particles, wet sand the affected area. Then try machine compounding and polishing the area. If you do not cut through the finish or clear, this will repair the damage. The area must be refinished if it has gone through the topcoat.

Danger! *Wear rubber gloves, respirator, and face shield when using oxalic acid. Protect yourself properly from the fumes and an accidental splash of acid.*

Acid Rain Damage

Acid rain damage varies because it is chemical damage from industrial fallout. The contents of the fallout varies with geographic locations. Various types of minerals sit on top of the paint film and damage it. Refer to Figure 18–25.

Minor acid rain damage produces shallow craters, dulling, fading, and chalking that do not eat fully through the topcoat. Minor acid rain damage can be removed by:

1. Washing the vehicle.

2. Neutralizing the acid by using a baking soda solution. The solution is a mixture of one tablespoon of baking soda per quart of water. The solution is applied with a spray bottle or by laying a saturated cloth on the area.

Figure 18–24 Metal dust fallout can etch into paint. A: Metal dust etched into clearcoat can be felt with hand or rag. B: After treatment, this damage can be repaired by wet sanding clearcoat and compounding.

Figure 18–25 Acid rain damage can also "eat" into paint. A: With minor acid rain damage, clearcoat is not penetrated. Wet sanding and buffing will usually fix damage. B: With major acid rain damage, damage is too deep and area must be refinished.

3. Rinsing with clean water.

4. Wet sanding with 1500 grit or finer sandpaper.

5. Compounding and glazing.

Test this in a small area on the worst acid rain damage first. If this does not restore the finish, there is major acid rain damage.

Major acid rain damage is severe chemical etching that has eaten completely through the topcoat. It may have eaten into the primer or all the way down to the body part. It requires that you strip all paint from the damaged areas. Otherwise, the acid residue will continue to eat through the paint from beneath.

NOTE! ONLY HORIZONTAL SURFACES (HOODS, DECK LIDS, ROOFS) USUALLY SUFFER MAJOR ACID RAIN DAMAGE AND REQUIRE STRIPPING. THE SIDES OF THE VEHICLE ARE USUALLY UNAFFECTED AND DO NOT HAVE TO BE STRIPPED.

Sand Scratches

Sand scratches result from two sources:

1. Final sanding with too coarse of a sandpaper.

2. Not allowing materials (usually primer-surfacer or spot putty) to dry fully before painting.

If a solid color, you might be able to wet sand and machine compound the area. If in a colorcoat of a basecoat/clearcoat system, you will usually have to resand and refinish the area. See Figure 18–26.

FINAL DETAILING

The objective in *final detailing* is to locate and correct any defect that may cause customer complaints. Corrective steps for final detailing are:

1. Sanding and Filing

2. Compounding

3. Machine Glazing

4. Hand Glazing

Each of these steps has its own requirements. As a general rule, finer and finer grades of products will be used for all of these steps. Progressively use finer wet sandpaper and compounds. Also, a single product line should be used throughout the repair. Manufacturer's recommendations should be followed.

Paint Surface Chips

Paint surface chips result from mechanical impact damage to the paint film: door dings, damage from

Primer-surfacer applied over sanded metal simulates the contours of the metal, with shrinkage more over deeper fills.

A

If sanded level before all solvents have evaporated, further evaporation of solvents will cause shrinkage leaving furrows over the sanding marks in the metal.

B

If the colorcoat is polished before all the thinner evaporates from the primer-surfacer and color, it will shrink back showing sand scratches. This condition may also be caused by using coarse rubbing compounds or too high of air pressure or too fast of solvent, when applying primer-surfacer.

C

Figure 18–26 If not due to too coarse a sandpaper, sand scratches can be due to not allowing materials under paint to dry before refinishing. A: Primer–surfacer has been applied to rough sanded surface. B: If sanded level before all solvents have evaporated, primer-surfacer will shrink more over sand scratches. C: If topcoat is then applied, sand scratches will appear in paint. *(PPG Industries, Inc.)*

road debris, etc. If the whole vehicle is not refinished, you should take the time to touch up chips in the old paint. Use the paint mixed for the repair. It will usually have hardener in it.

Degrease the area with wax and grease remover. If you use a small paint brush, slowly move the touch-up paint straight into each chip. If you are using a solid color, use a thicker viscosity touchup paint to fill the chip in one application. If you have metallic paint, use thinner touchup paint and several coats to help match the color.

Allow the paint to cure sufficiently before wet sanding and polishing the chip repairs level.

Paint Surface Protrusions

A *paint surface protrusion* is a particle of paint or other debris sticking out of the paint film after refinishing. This problems results from a lack of cleanliness. The spray gun, paint materials, or booth was contaminated.

If the protrusion is larger, repair it with a knife or single-edge razor blade as follows.

1. Cut off the protrusion, being careful not to take off more finish than is necessary. The tip of the knife or razor blade should be pointed slightly upward.

2. Smooth the area with a finesse sanding block or 3500 grit sandpaper.

3. Blow off any particles. Finish with an extra-fine rubbing compound.

Dirt-nib Filing

Dirt-nib files can be used to remove any defect which is on or above the surface of the paint. This includes runs, sags, and dirt. A dirt-nib file will remove the protrusion with minimum damage to the surrounding paint film. Dirt-nib files are available commercially, or you can make your own, as shown in Figure 18–27.

To make a dirt-nib file, cut off a short piece of a vixen body file. After dressing down the sharp corners on a grinder, place a piece of 400 grit sandpaper

Dress Sharp Corners

Sandpaper on Flat Surface

Properly Prepared Cutting Edges

Figure 18–27 Note how to make a dirt-nib file.

on a flat surface and draw the piece of file back and forth over the sandpaper until the teeth become smooth. A light machine oil will speed up the operation.

Danger! Do not try to break off a piece of the vixen body file. It can shatter!

To use a dirt-nib file, place the file lightly on the paint film. Use short, straight strokes in one direction only. Making two or three light passes will remove most defects. After filing, the area must be sanded to remove the file marks.

Finesse Sanding

After dirt-nib filing, *finesse sanding* can be used to level the protrusion with the surrounding paint film. Use a finesse sanding block as follows:

1. Dress the surface of the block with wet 220 grit sandpaper to make it smooth and flat.

2. Thoroughly soak the block in clear water.

3. Place the block over the protrusion and move it back-and-forth. If necessary, use a little water to help make the movement smoother. Refer to Figure 18–28.

4. When the protrusion has all but disappeared, blow off the loose particles and finish the job with rubbing, then polishing compound.

> *WARNING! If you fail to catalyze enamel paints with a hardener, you may not be able to file, wet sand and repair minor paint problems right away. If slight defects in finished surface should occur, they should not be compounded until the paint has had a chance to cure. This could involve a period of several days if not catalyzed.*

Wet Sanding

Wet sanding can be done to smooth the paint surface on larger areas, as when removing orange peel.

Wet sanding should normally be done with a *backing pad* or rubber sanding *block* to avoid crowning of the paint surface. A pad or block will help keep large, relatively flat surfaces level and uncrowned. On restricted and curved surfaces, you can use only your hand to wet sand. See Figure 18–29.

Figure 18–28 Finesse sanding block is soaked in water and then carefully rubbed over small paint imperfections to remove them. *(I-CAR)*

Figure 18–30 When wet sanding, keep area wet to help flush away paint particles. *(3M Automotive Trades Division)*

Sanding blocks and sandpapers are available in a variety of grit sizes. For surface repairs, use coarser wet sandpapers, 400 to 600. For finesse finishing, 1,000, 1,200, and finer grits of wet sandpaper are typically used.

Wet sand in a small circular motion. Use plenty of water to flush away paint debris. Dip the block in a bucket of water or use a hose to flow water over the area. A sponge can also be used to help keep the sandpaper wet. Refer to Figure 18–30.

Check the defect often when using a sanding block. You do not want to cut too deep into the finish. If you cut through the clearcoat or color, repainting will be necessary. Wash surfaces thoroughly with clean water and a sponge after wet sanding.

Rubbing compounds are available in various cutting strengths for both hand and machine compounding. *Hand compounds* are oil based to provide lubrication. Small areas or blended areas are best done by hand compounding. On large surfaces, machine compounding is recommended.

Rubbing compounds are used:

1. To eliminate fine sand scratches around a repair area

2. To correct a gritty surface

3. To smooth and bring out some of the gloss of lacquer topcoats

4. Sometimes as a final smoothing step to remove light scratches and small dirt particles before painting

Rubbing Compound

Rubbing compounds generally contain coarser grit abrasives than polishes. They are used to more rapidly cut the surface film by hand. Rubbing compounds produce a low surface gloss.

Figure 18–29 Under normal conditions, use a sanding block when wet sanding large, relatively flat surfaces. If not, crowning of paint can result. *(I-CAR)*

Hand Compounding

Fold a soft, lint-free flannel cloth into a thick pad or roll it into a ball and apply a small amount of hand compound to it. Use straight, back-and-forth strokes and medium-to-hard pressure until the desired smoothness is achieved.

Hand compounding takes a lot of elbow grease and is time consuming. To keep the compounding of lacquer topcoats to a minimum, it is important to apply the finish as wet as possible (without sags or runs) by using the proper thinner for the shop temperature.

When using hand polishes or glazes, apply the glaze to the surface using a clean dry cloth. Rub the glaze thoroughly into the surface. Then wipe dry. Glazes can fill and cover up some scratches which should be buffed out. These kinds of scratches will reappear after the vehicle has been washed a few times.

Figure 18–31 Buffing will return shine after wet sanding.

Machine Compounding

Machine compounds are water based to disperse the abrasive while using a power buffer. A buffing pad is rotated by an electric or air polisher to force the compound over the paint surface. If done properly, this will quickly bring it to a high gloss, Figure 18–31.

Edge Masking involves taping over panel edges and body lines prior to machine buffing or polishing to protect the paint from burn-through. Masking tape is applied to these surfaces to protect them.

Burn-through occurs when the pad removes too much paint on an edge or lip of a body surface. Since machine buffing will cut more quickly on these areas, always protect them with masking paper.

After the compounding is completed, remove the tape and compound the edge by hand—just enough to produce a smooth finish. Keep in mind that body lines usually retain less paint than flat surfaces and thus should get only minimum compounding.

Many finesse finishing systems recommend the use of specific buffing and polishing pads. They have replaced wool pads with finer, more uniform synthetic pads. Refer to Figure 18–32.

Apply machine compound over a small area using a medium-to-coarse bristled paintbrush or a squeeze bottle. Then compound using a slow-speed power buffer. It is important to use a slow-speed machine to avoid static build-up and high surface temperatures. Do not push down on the buffer. Let the weight of the machine do the work.

Because the compound has a tendency to dry out, do not try to do too large an area at one time. Always keep the machine moving to prevent cutting through or burning the topcoat. As the compound starts to dry out, lift up a little on the machine so pad speed increases. This will make the surface start to shine.

Polishing

Polishing involves using very fine compound to bring the paint surface up to full gloss. It is usually done after compounding. You can hand polish small or hard to reach areas. Machine polish larger areas to save time.

Instead of a circular action buffer, you should use an orbital action machine for final polishing. An *orbital action polisher* will move the polishing compound in a random manner to prevent swirl marks left from machine compounding. Swirl marks are tiny lines in the paint film from the abrasive action of the coarser compound.

Slight defects in the topcoat can be repaired by polishing. The choice of rubbing compound depends on the extent of the damage. Final polishing should

No More Than 5°

Figure 18–32 When buffing, do not press down on buffer. Let weight of machine do work. Also, do not tilt machine more than approximately five degrees. *(I-CAR)*

always be done with an extra-fine polishing compound.

Using Buffers and Polishers. When using buffing and polishing pads:

1. Inspect, clean, or replace pads often to avoid residue build-up.

2. Use separate pads for different grades and types of products.

3. When applying the compound, apply an "X" of the product to the surface. Work it around the face of the pad before hitting the machine's trigger. This will help prevent compound from flying all over.

The buffer has an effect on the cutting action. For example, the higher the rpm, the higher the cutting rate and the lower the rpm, the lower the cutting rate. The faster the orbital buffer is moved across the panel, the slower the cutting rate. The slower the buffer is moved, the higher the cutting rate.

Excessive buffing heat can cause swirl marks, warping, discoloring, hazing and the material can dry out too quickly. If the area is hot to the touch, there is too much heat. Cool it with water.

When using a buffer, a painter should:

1. Keep the pad flat or at about a 5 degree angle to the surface.

2. Let the weight of the machine do the work.

3. Use care around panel edges and character lines to avoid burn-through.

4. Check the repair area often and apply more product as needed.

5. Compound until the product begins to dry. Do not keep polishing on a dry surface.

Static electricity created during machine compounding causes the product to cling to the surface being repaired. Avoid static by grounding the vehicle. You might also want to add 25% rubbing alcohol to the water used to cool the surface.

When using rubbing compounds and machine glazes:

1. Use a single manufacturer's product line.

2. Follow the manufacturer's recommendations for use.

3. Use the materials sparingly.

4. Use the buffing wheel to evenly distribute the material evenly over the area to be repaired.

5. Keep the pad flat and directly over the surface being repaired.

6. Use a slow, circular motion.

7. Use the finest product possible. Using a finer product may take a little longer initially, but will generally require less time to complete the repair.

8. Reduce swirl marks by avoiding coarse products and worn buffing pads.

GET READY

Get ready is last, thorough clean-up before returning the vehicle to the customer. You must do all the "little things" that make a big difference to customer satisfaction. The interior and exterior of the vehicle should be cleaner than when the customer brought it in.

Vacuum the interior of the vehicle carefully. Clean the seats, door panels, seat belts, and carpets. If dusty, clean and treat the vinyl surface with a conditioner. Be sure to remove all excess reconditioner from the seat crevices and folds. Stubborn stains should be cleaned with a recommended carpet cleaning solution.

> *WARNING! Avoid using strong cleaning agents on the plastic parts in the dash panel. Some will dissolve and damage plastic, a costly mistake. You should also avoid having anything containing silicone in it.*

Carefully remove any overspray that may have been left on windows or chrome. If done without dripping on the new finish, use paint solvent (thinner or reducer). Clean and polish chrome, moldings, and bumpers. Thoroughly clean all the glass, including windows, mirrors, and lights.

> *WARNING! Steel wool should not be used to polish chrome because pieces of the wool can easily become embedded in the new finish. Instead, use a commercial chrome polisher polish.*

Use a brush with soap and water to clean the tires and wheels. Do not let dirty wheels spoil the appearance of an otherwise quality job. Coat them with a conditioner.

Use chassis black to blacken wheel openings and any other exposed undercarriage parts, since overspray often gets on these areas. The customer generally will not notice this, but it certainly will be noticed if not done.

Figure 18–33 Before releasing vehicle, make sure everything is perfectly clean. Clean windows, interior, and lights to satisfy customer. *(3M Automotive Trades Division)*

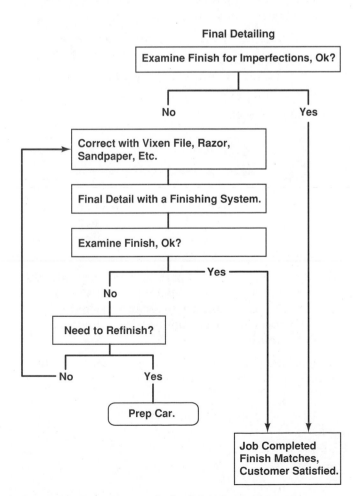

Figure 18–34 Study steps for final detailing. *(I-CAR)*

Replace wipers, moldings, and emblems that were removed before finishing. Take the time to clean off these items and be certain that everything is replaced.

If the vehicle has a vinyl top, do not forget to wipe it with a damp cloth or a commercial vinyl cleaner.

As a finishing touch, clean the engine compartment. The easiest way to do this is to spray it with a heavy-duty engine cleaner. Then flush the engine compartment out with high-pressure water. A clean engine compartment usually makes a big impression on the customer.

Finally, inspect the vehicle with a careful eye for details. If a window is smeared, clean it again, Figure 18–33. If a piece of masking tape remains, remove it. If an emblem is missing, replace it before the customer asks where it is.

If the vehicle gets dirty while waiting to be picked up, wipe it down with a clean cloth. The number one objective should always be a satisfied customer. Look at Figure 18–34.

CARING FOR NEW FINISH

A newly refinished vehicle must receive special care, as the paint can take several months to cure. Each paint manufacturer will have specific recommendations for caring for a new finish. Explain all precautions to the vehicle owner.

To care for a new finish, you and the customer should:

1. Avoid commercial car washes and harsh cleaners for 1–3 months.
2. Hand wash using only water and a soft sponge for the first month. Dry with cotton towels only. Do not use a chamois.
3. Avoid waxing and polishing for up to three months. After that time, use a wax designed for basecoat/clearcoat finishes, as they are the least aggressive.
4. Avoid scraping ice and snow near newly refinished surfaces.
5. Flush gas, oil, or fluid spills with water as soon as possible for the first month. Do not wipe off.

Summary

- Some of the most common paint problems include alkali and acid spotting, bleeding, blistering, mottling, running, and peeling.
- The steps for correcting surface imperfections include: examining the finish for imperfections; correcting the imperfection; finesse finishing; and final detailing.

- The objective in final detailing is to locate and correct any defect that may cause customer complaints. The four steps are: sanding and filing; compounding; machine glazing; and hand glazing.

- A newly refinished vehicle must receive special care, as the paint may take several months to cure. Know the specific manufacturer's recommendations and explain all precautions to the vehicle owner.

Technical Terms

surface roughness
surface waviness
acid and alkali spotting
bleeding
blistering
blushing
chalking
checking
crazing
cracking
dulled finish
fisheyes
lifting
mottling
orange peel
peeling
pitting
plastic bleed thru
run
sag

water spotting
wet spots
wrinkling
metal dust damage
oxalic acid
acid rain damage
sand scratches
final detailing
paint surface chips
paint surface protrusion
dirt-nib file
finesse sanding
sanding block
rubbing compound
hand compounds
machine compounds
edge masking
burn-through
polishing
get ready

Review Questions

1. List four steps for correcting surface imperfections.

2. _____ shows up as small, swelled areas on the finish, like a _____ _____ on human skin.

3. What is paint blushing?

4. Describe paint chalking problem.

5. How can you correct a small amount of dirt on a painted surface?

6. List eight reasons for a dull paint finish.

7. What causes fisheyes and how can you prevent and fix them?

8. This is a paint roughness problem that look like tiny dents in the paint surface.
   a. Paint protrusions
   b. Mottling
   c. Orange peel
   d. Peeling

9. List six reasons for paint runs.

10. Is fixing a run in a solid color and metallic the same? Explain your answer.

11. Technician A says to wet sand with a sanding block to keep from crowning the surface. Technician B says it is OK to use your hand to wet sand on curved surfaces.
    Who is correct?
    a. Technician A
    b. Technician B
    c. Both Technicians
    d. Neither Technician

12. What is the difference between a rubbing compound and a polishing compound?

13. _____ _____ are water based to disperse the abrasive while using a power buffer.

14. Why should you mask edges and body lines before buffing?

15. What is burn-through?

Activities

1. Inspect several older vehicles. How many paint problems can you find? Make a report of your findings. Is there any industrial fallout problem in your area?

2. Obtain an old painted part. Intentionally paint the part to produce various paint problems. Allow the paint to dry and try to repair some of the problems without repainting. Write a report on this activity.

3. Final detail a vehicle. Clean all interior and exterior surfaces with recommended products.

CHAPTER 19

DECALS, CUSTOM PAINTING, TRIM

Objectives

After studying this chapter, you should be able to:

■ Properly remove vinyl decals and striping.

■ Prepare the surface before applying adhesive overlay material or before custom painting.

■ Install adhesive tape and decals.

■ Explain various techniques for doing custom paint work.

■ Remove, align, and install molding and emblems.

Introduction

People of all ages often want their cars and trucks customized or personalized. Also, factory installed pin stripes and decorative tape is now common. If you can do this kind of work, you will find it to be in high demand and very profitable.

This chapter will introduce you to basic methods for doing custom paint work, for painting stripes, and applying custom decals or pin striping tape. The chapter will also summarize methods for working with moldings and emblems. See Figure 19–1.

Figure 19-1 There is a high demand for technicians who can do custom work. If you can do custom paint or install vinyl overlays, your value will increase.

Figure 19-2 To remove vinyl stripes and decals, mask around the material. Then spray on two coats of remover. After soaking, you can more easily peel off vinyl materials. *(Courtesy of Ford Motor Company)*

OVERLAYS AND TAPE STRIPES

An *overlay* is a larger, self-adhesive vinyl material applied to the finish. It provides an easy way to customize the looks of a vehicle. Overlays might be multicolor stripes, artwork, or artificial wood grain. Overlays can also be body color, mounting along the lower areas of the body to help protect the finish from stone chips.

Vinyl tape is a tough, durable decorative striping material adhered to the vehicle's finish. It has a pressure sensitive backing that bonds securely to the finish.

Vinyl decals are generally more complex and decorative pressure sensitive material than tape stripes. Both tape and decals can be original equipment or aftermarket installed.

When repairing collision damage, you may have to replace vinyl tape and decals. If you use established methods, this can be a rewarding task.

Overlay and Tape Stripe Removal

There are several ways to remove vinyl tape stripes and decals. These include:

1. Spray remover and scraper
2. Heat gun and scraper
3. Scuff pad (if repainting panel)

Vinyl overlay remover is a chemical that dissolves plastic vinyl to aid its removal. To use spray vinyl remover, mask the area around the stripe or decal with plastic, Figure 19-2. Scuff sand the decal with 220 grit sandpaper to help speed the action of the

chemical. Do not cut through the vinyl or sand the paint or you may have to repaint the panel.

If original equipment or if material on the other side of the vehicle is not going to be removed, measure the location of the existing stripe or decal before removal. Write down your measurements for later reference.

Spray the entire stripe or decal with remover spray. Use smooth steady strokes so that the material is evenly coated with the chemical, Figure 19-2. After a few minutes, spray the chemical on the vinyl again. Allow the remover to soak for about 15 minutes.

Danger! Follow all safety precautions when using vinyl remover. It is a powerful chemical. Only use it in a well-ventilated area and wear eye protection.

After soaking, peel the stripe or decal away from the panel. Start in one corner and try to peel in one piece. If needed, use a sharp plastic squeegee to help peel off the old material.

After removal of the stripe or decal, use the squeegee to remove any remaining adhesive from the panel. Then, use a rag and *adhesive remover* to clean off the remaining vinyl glue.

On smaller pressure sensitive overlays, a heat gun can sometimes be used to warm, soften, and remove the vinyl material. Without overheating, move the heat gun to gradually soften the stripe. As the vinyl and adhesive soften, slowly peel off the material. Then, clean the area with adhesive remover.

A scuff pad mounted on a air tool can also be used to remove narrow vinyl material, like pin stripes. It will abrade the soft plastic material without clogging. Sandpaper will quickly clog if ran over vinyl stripes or decals.

Overlay and Tape Stripe Application

Use a water soluble marker and tape measure to mark where you want to install the new striping or decal. Place tiny reference marks on the finish where needed. See Figure 19–3A.

Then place masking tape on the vehicle to serve as a guide. Align the tape with the marker reference marks.

Measure and mark locations for tape

A

Wash area thoroughly

B

Figure 19–3 Preparation before installing vinyl materials is important. A: Always measure location of existing overlays before removal. Then, you can mark their locations on body for properly locating new stripes or decals. B: Wipe down area with wax and grease remover. Then, wash with soap and water. Note masking tape to be used as straightedge when installing vinyl striping. *(Mustang Monthly Magazine)*

Before tape or decal application, make sure the surface of the panel is ready. It should be wet sanded and buffed if needed. Also, wipe the panel down with wax and grease remover. This will clean off any wax and other foreign matter. Look at Figure 19–3B.

Check that the temperature of the panel is about room temperature. It should be no cooler than about 60°F (16°C) or no hotter than 90°F (32°C). If brought in from outside, allow the temperature of the vehicle's surface to reach room temperature.

Refer to the instructions provided with the stripe or decal material. Methods can vary.

Installing Overlays

The *overlay wet method* of installation involves using soapy water to help simplify the application of larger decals and striping. Soapy water will allow you to shift and position the material without the adhesive instantly sticking to the panel. The water will also aid removal of the backing material from the overlay.

Fill a bucket of clean water. Then add some dish washing liquid to the water and mix. Place the decal into the soapy water. Peel off the backing material carefully so that you do not tear the vinyl, Figure 19–4A.

Position the overlay on the vehicle. Position it up against your alignment masking tape, Figure 19–4B. The soapy water will let you shift the overlay without it sticking tightly to the finish. Carefully straighten and align the material, removing any wrinkles. Working from the middle outward, use a rubber squeegee to flatten out the overlay. Make sure you have removed all air bubbles and wrinkles, Figure 19–4C. Then, use a rag to rub and adhere the overlay to the panel. As you rub toward the edges of the overlay, you will work any water out from under the vinyl. This will make the overlay stick to the finish.

Once the water is removed and almost dry, carefully peel off the carrier paper. Grasp at one edge of the carrier paper. Then, slowly peel it off the vinyl. Go slowly so that you do not lift and tear the vinyl. Refer to Figures 19–5A and B.

Next, if needed, cut off the ends of the overlay or stripe at the panel ends. Use a sharp razor blade knife to cut the material to the desired length. You may want the material to wrap around the panel edge or you may prefer it to stop right at the edge. See Figure 19–6.

To remove any remaining air bubbles, pierce the bubble with a needle. Then, rub the overlay with a rag to work the air out from under the vinyl.

Rubbing away from the overlay, double-check that all edges are adhered tightly to the finish. Rub over

Figure 19–4 Note basic steps for installing vinyl overlay wet. A: Wet vinyl overlay in soapy water and remove backing sheet over adhesive. B: Position overlay onto vehicle. Align it with your marks or masking tape. Move quickly before the water dries. C: Use rubber squeegee to remove wrinkles and air bubbles. Wipe outward or away from center of overlay. (Mustang Monthly Magazine)

Figure 19–5 Note how carrier paper is removed from vinyl striping. A: After overlay is smooth and dry, peel off carrier paper. Use your fingers to hold ends of material down if needed. B: Slowly remove carrier paper by pulling it straight back. You must not tear thin vinyl material. (Mustang Monthly Magazine)

all edges a couple of times. The result will be a long lasting attractive addition to the vehicle's appearance.

Installing Vinyl Pin Stripes

The *overlay dry method* of installation does not require soapy water to aid application. All surfaces are clean and dry. Narrow pin stripe tape can be installed dry without wrinkling or bubble problems. Generally, if an overlay is narrower than about 2 inches (50 mm), you can use the dry method of installation.

Pin stripe tape may or may not have a carrier paper. Both types are installed in about the same way. With carrier paper, you will just have to peel off the paper after adhering the tape to the vehicle's surface.

Figure 19–6 With carrier paper off, cut ends of striping to length. Cut them so they just start to wrap around panel edge. *(Mustang Monthly Magazine)*

A few rules for installing pin stripe tape include:

1. Make sure the surface is perfectly clean. Use soap and water. Then, wash the area with wax and grease remover. If not the tape will come off and your customer will return unhappy.

2. Use a grease pen or water soluble marker to locate where you want the striping. If needed, you can also lay down masking tape as a guide. With the dry method, the tape will stick to the surface and can be difficult to reposition.

3. Position and adhere one end of the tape stripe. You might want to place masking tape over the end to keep it from pulling off.

4. Use one hand to lightly stretch the tape and the other to lightly push and tack the tape into position. You want to lightly stick the tape in position first. Then, if not straight, you can pull the tape up and reposition it.

5. Never stretch the tape striping too tight. If you do, the tape will distort or come off after exposure to heat of the sun.

6. Do not overstretch the tape when rounding corners. Again, this will thin the material and cause it to lift later.

7. After using your finger to lightly tack the tape into position. Stand back and check its alignment and straightness. If not straight, pull the tape back off and realign it.

8. Once you are sure the tape is positioned properly, use a rubber squeegee to bond the tape securely to the finish. Start at the center of the stripe and wipe toward the ends. Do not use too much pressure near the ends or you can tear the tape.

9. If the pin stripe tape has a carrier paper, slowly pull if off. Then, check for kinks and air bubble. Work

them out. Again, rub a squeegee over the stripe to adhere it tightly to the finish.

10. Do not use your hand to try to bond pin stripe tape. It will tend to distort and wrinkle the tape. After using the squeegee, rub a soft rag over the tape to final bond it in place.

PAINTED PIN STRIPES

There are two common methods to paint on pin stripes. One uses vinyl masking tape to mask on each side of the paint stripe. The other uses a special striping tool to apply a thin line of paint over the finish. Painted on pin stripes are sometimes requested for a custom paint job or during a restoration job. A painted stripe will generally last longer and look better than vinyl tape.

Using Pin Stripe Masking Tape

Pin stripe masking tape uses two pieces of vinyl tape held with a paper carrier. Position and apply the tape as you would pin stripe tape. Then, remove the carrier paper.

Next, use a small pin striping brush to apply the paint in the area between the tape. Most painters use lacquer or catalyzed enamel so the strip will dry quickly. Use long smooth brush strokes parallel with the stripe. Using a brush saves time and material over a spray gun or air brush because you do not have to mask large areas around the stripe.

When the paint stripe has flashed, carefully remove the masking tape. Slowly pull it straight back and off the vehicle. Do not pull sideways or you could peel off some of the freshly painted stripe. Wet sand and polish the painted stripes if needed.

Using Pin Striping Tool

A *pin striping tool* uses a serrated roller to deposit a painted pin stripe. The tool holds the paint in a cylinder shaped cup. The roller, when moved over the surface, deposits the paint onto the finish. Various widths of roller can be installed in the tool to change paint stripe widths.

A *magnetic guide strip* can be used to help guide the tool for making straight or slightly curved pin stripes. It is a flexible plastic material filled with magnets. When placed on a steel body part, the guide strip will stay in place without damage to the finish. A guide rod on the pin striping tool contacts this guide when striping.

When the tool is held square and moved over the surface, it will make a uniform width pin stripe. If tilted, the width of the pin stripe will narrow. With practice, this will let you make pointed or curly ends on the painted pin stripes.

Using Pin Striping Brushes

Pin striping brushes have very long soft horse hairs on them. Special talent is needed to use them. Using a very steady hand, a freehand technique is sometimes used to pull the brush along the finish to apply painted pin stripes. Body lines or trim are often used as a guide when freehand striping.

NOTE! VERY FEW PEOPLE HAVE A STEADY ENOUGH HAND TO FREEHAND PIN STRIPE. MOST PAINTERS USE PIN STRIPING BRUSHES IN COMBINATION WITH MASKING TAPE TO STRIPE VEHICLES.

Painting Wider Stripes

Wider painted stripes are done by spraying a different color or tint over the existing finish after masking. Before painting, wet sand the area to be painted with very fine (1000 or finer grit) wet sandpaper. This will prepare the surface for good adhesion of the new paint.

Apply fine line masking tape where the stripes are wanted. Fine line tape is needed so the stripes have a smooth edge when the tape is removed. After carefully applying the fine line tape, mask the area on each side with paper or plastic and conventional masking tape.

Spray the color for the stripes onto the unmasked area. After drying, remove the masking material. Wet sand the area and buff to a high gloss. If the stripe is wide, use a full size spray gun. If the stripes are smaller, use an air brush or touchup gun to save materials and speed cleanup.

CUSTOM PAINTING

Custom painting involves using multiple colors, metal flake paints, multi-layer masking, and special spraying techniques to produce a personalized look. Multi-color stripes, flames, murals, landscapes, names, and other artwork can be added to the finish. Complex images require you to have special artistic talent. If you cannot paint an attractive image on paper, you will not be able to do it on a vehicle.

Custom painting requires considerable talent, skill and knowledge. You need to plan the custom job carefully. This will let you determine how to mask and spray or apply each color. Custom painters are good at using air brushes, striping tools, and masking materials.

Before custom painting, make sure the base finish is in good condition. You do not want to waste your time trying to paint over a weathered or problem finish. Wet sand and clean the area to be custom painted. Use surface preparation methods detailed in other chapters.

To produce a feathered custom stripe on a van, the area to be striped is masked and painted with the main color for the stripe. Then, an air brush and a different color paint is misted around the outside edge of the stripe. This color is misted over the edge of the masking paper. Then, when the masking is removed, the two colors blend into each other for a custom stripe effect.

Custom masks can be made by drawing a design on thin posterboard and then cutting them out. The posterboard design is then taped onto the vehicle and spray painted. Using an airbrush and translucent paint, various attractive effects can be produced.

Card masking involves using a simple masking pattern to produce a custom paint effect. Usually, an air brush is used to mist the paint over the edge of the masking card. The card can be moved to repeat the pattern to produce a wide range of paint effects.

Lace painting involves spraying through lace fabric to produce a custom pattern in the paint. Various lace designs can be purchased at fabric stores. The cloth pattern will allow the paint to pass through the holes in the lace but mask it in other areas.

A *marble effect* can be made by forcing crumpled plastic against a freshly painted stripe or area. When the plastic is lifted off, it will remove paint in random areas with a marble type effect.

Spider webbing is done by forcing paint through the air brush in a very thin, fibrous type spray. Air pressure from the gun can also be used to spread and smear the wet paint to produce a varying effect.

Painted flames are a custom painting technique often used on "hot rods" or older street rods. First, fine line masking tape is used to form the outline of the flames. Then, the area around this shape is covered with masking paper or plastic.

First, the base color for the flames is applied. Then, a second translucent color is blended. A third color may be used to darken the outer edges and center area of the flames. The flames are finally wet sanded and polished when dry.

Painted lettering involves masking off letters over the finishing and spraying or brushing them on with a

Figure 19–7 When installing self-stick emblems, make sure surface is clean and dry. Apply emblem adhesive if needed on used emblem to make sure emblem does not come off. (3M Automotive Trades Division)

different color. This can be time consuming but is sometimes requested by customers.

When doing custom paint work, do not "bite off more than you can chew." Start out simple with minor complexity. As you learn to successfully do custom work, you can progress to more complex paint work. Experience is the best teacher with custom paint work.

A good idea is to practice techniques on old parts using left over paint. Then, you can learn from your mistakes and successes without working on a customer vehicle.

MOLDINGS AND TRIM

Moldings and trim can either be held on with adhesive or mechanical fasteners. If adhesive held, the molding or emblem can usually be removed by warming with a heat gun. Then, force a *molding tool* under the part to separate it from the body. Pull outward on the molding or emblem as you work the tool behind the part.

When installing adhesive backed molding or emblem, make sure the body surface is perfectly clean. If not, the molding can come off in service.

If needed, use masking tape as a guide for molding installation. Carefully apply the masking tape down the side of the vehicle in a perfectly straight line.

Then, position the molding next to the masking tape before pressing it into place.

If you are reusing adhesive backed molding or emblems, use aftermarket emblem adhesive. Spread a thin coating of emblem adhesive on the back of the molding or emblem. Then, move the part straight into position without smearing the adhesive, Figure 19–7. Use masking tape to hold the part in place until the adhesive dries.

When molding is held by fasteners, you will have to gain access to them. This might involve removing door panels or inner fender aprons.

Summary

- An overlay is a self-adhesive vinyl material applied to the finish. It may be multicolor stripes, artwork, or artificial wood grain.

- There are several ways to remove vinyl tape stripes and decals, including: spray remover and scraper; heat gun and scraper; and scuff pad (if repainting panel).

- The overlay wet method of installation involves using soapy water to help simplify the application of larger decals and striping. The overlay dry method does not require water. Generally, if an overlay is narrower than 2" (50 mm), you can use the dry method.

- Custom painting involves using multiple colors, metal flake paints, multi-layer masking, and special spraying techniques to produce a personalized look. Stripes, flames, murals or names may also be added.

Technical Terms

overlay	*pin striping brushes*
vinyl tape	*custom painting*
vinyl decals	*custom masks*
vinyl overlay remover	*card masking*
adhesive remover	*lace painting*
overlay wet method	*marble effect*
overlay dry method	*spider webbing*
pin striping tool	*painted flames*
magnetic guide strip	*molding tool*

Review Questions

1. What is a vinyl overlay?

2. Why do you sand vinyl overlays before using overlay remover.

3. A large overlay must be installed on a car's hood. Technician A says to use the wet method is best. Technician B says the dry method of installation is faster.

   Who is correct?

   a. Technician A
   b. Technician B
   c. Both Technicians
   d. Neither Technician

4. List ten rules for installing pin stripe tape.

5. A _____ _____ uses a serrated roller to deposit painted pin stripes.

6. Explain card masking.

7. How do you do custom lace painting?

8. How do you produce a spider webbing effect when custom painting?

9. What is a molding tool?

10. Custom paint work is easy if basic methods are followed. True or false?

Activities

1. Obtain an old body part from a salvage yard with an overlay on it. Use proper methods to remove the vinyl overlay without damaging the finish.

2. Using old paint and a scrap part, practice doing custom paint work. Try doing lacing, flames, and other effects.

3. Attend a custom car show. Using a camera, document the types of custom paint effects found. Ask the car owners about their custom paint effects. Write a report on how some of the custom paint jobs were done.

MAJOR REPAIRS

CHAPTER 20

MEASURING VEHICLE DAMAGE

Objectives

After studying this chapter, you should be able to:

- Distinguish between body-over-frame and unibody vehicles.
- Explain how Impact Forces are transmitted through both frame and unibody construction vehicles.
- Describe how to visually determine the extent of impact damage.
- List the various types and variations of body measuring tools.
- Analyze damage by measuring body dimensions.
- Analyze impact damage to mechanical parts of the vehicle.
- Explain the importance of the datum plane and centerline concepts as related to unibody repair.
- Interpret body dimension information and locate key reference points on a vehicle, using body dimension manuals.
- Discuss the use of tram bars, self-centering gauges, and strut tower gauges.
- Diagnose various types of body damage, including twist, mash, sag, and side sway.
- Given a damaged vehicle and a body specification manual, locate and measure key points using a tape measure, tram bar, and self-centering gauges.
- Describe the two types of universal measuring systems.
- Explain the operation of the dedicated fixture system, including the use of bolt-on, pin-type, and MacPherson fixtures and bench extensions.

Introduction

When a car or truck is in a high speed crash, powerful impact forces can bend the frame or unibody structure of the vehicle. The frame or body is designed to absorb some of the energy of the collision and protect its occupants. When a heavily damaged vehicle enters the shop, the extent of the damage must be carefully evaluated. Sometimes, measurements are needed to help the estimator calculate the costs of the repairs. See Figure 20–1.

Vehicle measurement involves using specialized tools and equipment to measure the location of reference points on the vehicle, Figure 20–2. These measurements are then compared to published dimensions from an undamaged vehicle. By comparing known good and actual measurements, you can determine the extent of damage. The difference in the two measurements indicates the direction and amount of frame or body misalignment.

After studying damage measurements, frame straightening equipment is used to pull the frame or body back into alignment. Straightening procedures are explained in the next chapter.

Figure 20–1 An estimator and technician are carefully evaluating vehicle damage before starting repairs. If it appears unibody or frame is out of alignment, measurements must be taken. *(Rotary Lift)*

A

B

Figure 20–2 A vehicle measuring system is designed to check location of specific points on damaged vehicle. If any points are not where they should be, the frame or unibody must be straightened. A: This measuring system has telescoping rods and pointers that can be swung at various angles for quick measurements of body and chassis parts. *(Wedge Clamp International, Inc.)* B: This measuring system uses rods and pointers that mount at right angles to each other. When adjusted to proper lengths, you can quickly tell if parts have been forced out of alignment by collision. *(Car-O-Liner)*

WHY IS MEASUREMENT IMPORTANT?

There is good reason for close body structure tolerances. Steering and suspension systems, for instance, are mounted to the frame or unibody structure. Severe body or frame damage can change steering or suspension geometry or misalign mechanical parts. This can result in poor handling, vibration, and noise problems. Thus, the tolerances of critical manufacturing dimensions must be held to within a maximum value of less than ⅛ inch (3 mm).

The challenge faced by the collision repair industry is to find out which panels are out of place and in which direction and how far they have moved. Only then can a proper plan be devised to bring the vehicle back to pre-accident specifications. This process involves accurate measuring and monitoring of the entire vehicle.

To correctly analyze damage on a unibody vehicle, the entire structure must be considered. To do this, it is necessary to be able to take proper measurements to locate damage. It will also help to plan where to pull.

Measurement gauges are special tools used to check specific frame and body points. They allow you to quickly measure the direction and extent of vehicle damage.

Control or *reference points* are specific locations on the frame or body for making measurements. They may be holes, specific bolts, nuts, panel edges, or other locations on the vehicle. To repair a badly damaged vehicle, you must restore the reference points to their factory dimensions. This must be done while reference points in the undamaged area remain in their correct locations.

Therefore, the collision repair technician must work with the whole vehicle. This is done by measuring and recording dimensional changes. The most widely accepted method of checking body dimensions is to use the charts supplied in the body dimension manuals.

DAMAGE DIAGNOSIS

To repair a vehicle properly, you or the estimator must first accurately diagnose the collision damage. Someone must assess the severity and extent of damage and find all parts that have been affected. Once this has been determined, a plan can be made for repair.

Damage found from an inaccurately diagnosed vehicle will be uncovered during repair. When this happens, the repair method or procedure must be changed.

Generally, physical damage is rarely missed during an inspection by a competent estimator and body technician. However, the effects of the damage on unrelated systems and damage next to the impacted part are frequently overlooked. A visual inspection alone is generally inadequate with modern vehicles. Accident damage should be assessed by measurements with the proper tools and equipment.

The following is a basic diagnosis procedure:

1. Know the type of vehicle construction (full frame, partial frame, unibody).

2. Visually locate the point of impact.

3. Determine the direction and force of the impact. Once this is determined, check for possible damage.

4. Determine if the damage is confined to the body, or if it involves mechanical parts (wheels, suspension, engine).

5. Systematically inspect damage to the parts along the path of the impact and find the point where there is no longer any evidence of damage. For example, pillar damage can be determined by checking the door opening alignment.

6. Measure the major parts and check body height by comparing the actual measurements with the values in the body dimensions chart. Use a centering gauge to compare measurements of the height of the left and right sides of the body.

7. Check for suspension and overall body damage with the proper fixtures.

SAFETY

Before starting a vehicle damage evaluation, keep the following safety pointers in mind:

1. Once the vehicle is in the shop, check for broken glass edges and jagged metal. Edges of broken glass should be masked with tape and labeled "DANGER." Sharp jagged metal edges can be taped, but it is better to grind them down with a portable power grinder or a file.

2. If fluids, such as lubricants or transmission fluid, are leaking from the vehicle, wipe them up. This may prevent someone from slipping and falling.

3. Remove the gas tank before welding or cutting is begun on the vehicle. Never just drain the tank because the fumes are explosive.

4. Disconnect the battery. This will avoid the possibility of a charge igniting flammable vapors. It also protects the electrical system.

5. Make the damage diagnosis in a well-lit shop. If the damage involves functional or mechanical parts, a detailed inspection of the underbody, using a lift or a bench is required.

NOTE! FOR MORE SAFETY RULES, REFER TO THE INDEX IN THE BACK OF THIS BOOK.

IMPACT EFFECTS

A modern vehicle is designed to withstand the shocks of normal driving and to provide protection for the occupants during a collision. Special consideration is given to designing the body so that it will collapse and absorb the maximum amount of energy in a severe collision.

The front body and rear body are to some extent made to deform easily, forming a structure that absorbs impact energy. The center passenger compartment area is designed to stay unaffected. For example, during a head-on collision with a barrier at 30 mph (48 km/h), the engine compartment compacts by about 30 to 40 percent of its length, but the passenger compartment is compacted by only one to two percent of its length.

Described in earlier chapters, there are two basic types of automotive construction:

1. Body-over-frame (BOF) vehicles

2. Unibody (or monocoque) vehicles

In the body-over-frame construction, the passenger (pay-load) area is enclosed with cosmetic panels of steel attached to a structural frame. The frame also supports most of the drivetrain and mechanical accessories. In the unibody construction, the metal body panels are welded together making a structural unit.

With BOF vehicles, the collision damage can be cosmetic and/or structural. However, when a unibody vehicle is hit, the collision usually results in both cosmetic and structural damage.

Under the force of collision impacts, the frame type vehicle and the unibody type vehicle react quite differently. Also, damage assessment and repair techniques are different, even though the basic repair skills are similar.

When the collision damage has been identified using the proper identification and analysis procedures, anyone skilled in the mechanics of collision damage repair is capable of repairing the damage successfully.

ANALYZING COLLISION FORCES

The impact force of the collision and the extent of damage differ depending on how the accident occurred. The damage can be partly determined by understanding how the collision happened. To understand the circumstances of the collision, contact persons directly involved or eyewitnesses. It is quite possible for the person responsible for making the estimate to get a direct response from the customer. This method of damage assessment is sometimes necessary to estimate the cost of the repair. Therefore, the body technician should speak to the estimator or the person who prepares the estimate.

The body technician should know the following items:

1. The size, shape, position, and speed of the vehicles involved in the collision
2. Speed of the vehicle at the time of the collision
3. Angle and direction of the vehicle at the time of the impact
4. The number of passengers and their positions at the time of the impact

A good body/frame technician can usually determine what actually happened to cause the damage. Certain types of collision damage often occur in a predictable pattern and sequence.

If a driver's first reaction is to turn away from the danger, the vehicle will be forced to take the hit on the side, Figure 20–3. If the driver's reaction is to slam on the brakes, the direction of impact would be frontal,

Figure 20–4 Driver normally hits brakes before a collision, causing nose of car to dive downward. Impact can then cause frame or unibody sag. Front area will be forced up and area around cowl sags down.

Figure 20–4. A frontal collision where the point of impact is high on the vehicle could cause the cowl and roof to move rearward and the rear of the vehicle to move downward. If the point of impact is low at the front, the inertia of the body mass could cause the rear of the vehicle to distort upward, forcing the roof forward. This would leave an excessively large opening between the front upper part of the door and the roof line, Figure 20–5.

Given vehicles with similar weights traveling at the same speed, vehicle damage will vary depending on what is struck—another vehicle, a telephone pole, or a wall.

If the impact is spread over a larger area (as in hitting a wall), damage will be minimal, Figure 20–6A. Conversely, the smaller the area of impact, the greater the severity of the damage, Figure 20–6B. In this example, the bumper, hood, radiator, and so forth have been severely deformed. The engine has been pushed back and the effect of the collision has extended as far as the rear suspension.

Another consideration is when one vehicle hits another while moving. If vehicle Number One in Figure 20–7 drives into the side of vehicle Number Two while Number Two is moving, the motion of the first vehicle will drive the front end of the vehicle back. However, the motion of vehicle Number

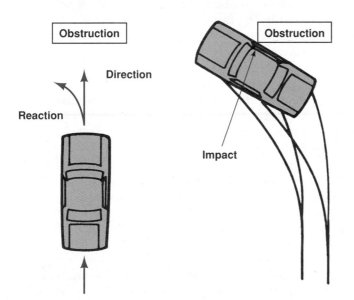

Figure 20–3 Direction of impact affects type of vehicle damage. If driver reacts and turns away from object, hit is on side, often causing sideways damage.

Figure 20–5 Hard frontal impact causes major or primary damage to front end. Minor, secondary damage occurs elsewhere from shock wave flowing through body.

Figure 20–6 Note impact damage differences. A: Vehicle hits wall straight on. Large area absorbs energy and damage is limited to front body parts. B: Vehicle hits power or light pole. Small area must absorb energy so damage travels much deeper into engine compartment.

Figure 20–7 Broadside collision often causes heavy frame or unibody damage. Vehicle One would suffer side sway, front end damage. Vehicle Two would suffer major side sway damage in center section.

Two will also "drag" that same front end to the side. There is only one collision but the damage is in two directions.

On the other hand, there might be two collisions in only one direction. This is a fairly common occurrence in freeway pile-ups. For example, a vehicle might collide with another vehicle. Then, it might leave the road and hit a pole or guardrail. This results in two completely separate types of damage.

There are many other variables and possible combinations of damage types. It is important to determine what actually happened before an accurate diagnosis can be made. Get as many facts as possible and combine them with physical measurements and centerline gauge readings to determine exactly the collision repair procedure that should be taken. A little extra time spent here can save many hours in the overall repair procedure. "Think time" saves hard work.

NOTE! FOR MORE INFORMATION ON ESTIMATING, REFER TO CHAPTER 28.

TYPES OF FRAME DAMAGE

Vehicle damage can be broken down into five categories:

1. *Side sway damage* results from collision impacts that occur from the side. It often causes side bending of the frame or unibody, Figure 20–8. Side sway usually occurs in the front or rear of the vehicle. Generally, it is possible to spot side sway damage by noting if there are buckles on the inside of one rail and buckles on the outside of the opposite side rail.

Side sway can be recognized by abnormalities such as a gap at the door on the long side and wrinkles on the short side. Look for impact damage obviously from the side. For example, hood and deck lid will NOT fit into proper opening.

2. *Sag damage* is a condition where a section of the frame or unibody is lower than normal, Figure 20–9. The structure has a swayback appearance. Sag damage generally is caused by a direct impact from the front or rear. It can occur on one side of the vehicle or on both sides, Figure 20–10.

Sag can usually be detected visually by an irregular gap between the fender and the door. The gap will be narrow at the top and wide at the bottom. Also look for a door hanging too low at the striker.

Enough sag can be present in the frame to prevent body panel alignment even though wrinkles or kinks are NOT visible in the frame itself.

Figure 20–8 Note various types of damage. A: Front side sway damage is present when frame or unibody is forced to one side. B: Rear side sway is similar but are back of vehicle from rear impact. C: Double side sway was caused by severe side impact.

Figure 20–9 Sag causes frame or unibody to drop lower from severe impact. A: Front sag is often in cowl area from buckling of frame rails. B: Rear sag is similar but at rear rails.

Figure 20–10 A: Side rail sag is due to front end collision. B: Side rail sag is due to rear collision.

Figure 20–11 A: Note mash damage on left front rail. B: Note mash damage on left rear rail.

Figure 20–12 A: Note heavy mash and buckling damage from front end collision. B: Same damage but from rear.

3. *Mash damage* is present when any section or member of the vehicle is shorter than factory specifications. Mash is usually limited to forward of the cowl or rearward of the rear window. Doors might fit well and appear to be undisturbed. See Figure 20–11.

Mash is indicated by wrinkles and severe distortion in fenders, hood, and possibly frame horns or rails. The frame or unibody will rise upward at the top of the wheel arch, causing the spring housing to collapse, Figure 20–12.

With mash damage, there is very little vertical displacement of the bumper. The damage results from direct front or rear collisions.

4. *Diamond damage* is a condition where one side of the vehicle has been moved to the rear or front. This type of damage causes the frame or unibody to be out of square. It will form a parallelogram and is caused by a hard impact on a corner or off-center from the front or rear. Diamond damage on a unibody vehicle usually results in a total loss. Refer to Figure 20–13.

Diamond damage affects the entire frame or unibody, NOT just the side rails. Visual indications are hood and trunk lid misalignment. Buckles might appear in the quarter panel near the rear wheel housing or at the roof to quarter panel joint. Wrinkles and buckles probably will appear in the passenger compartment and/or trunk floor. There usually will be some mash and sag combined with the diamond, Figure 20–14.

5. *Twist damage* is a condition where one corner of the vehicle is higher than normal; the opposite corner might be lower than normal. It is another type of total frame or unibody damage. Twist can happen when a vehicle hits a curb or median strip at high speed. It is also common in rear corner impacts. Look at Figure 20–15.

A careful inspection might reveal no apparent damage to the sheet metal; however, the real damage is hidden underneath. One corner of the vehicle has been driven upward by the impact. The adjacent corner may also be twisted downward. If one corner of the vehicle is sagging close to the ground as though a spring were weak, the vehicle should be checked for twist.

Figure 20–13 Diamond damage forces only one side of frame or unibody rearward. Hard impact affects one side only.

Figure 20–14 Study diamond condition. This often results in total loss because straightening would be too time consuming.

Figure 20–15 Twist damage forces one side of frame or body up and other down.

Unfortunately, most accidents result in a mix of one or more of these damage problems. Side sway and sag frequency occur almost simultaneously. Also, some of these collision solutions affect crossmembers, especially the front member. In a rollover accident, for example, the front crossmember on which the motor mounts are attached will be pulled or pushed out of shape because of the engine's weight. This will result in a sag of this crossmember.

UNIBODY VEHICLE DAMAGE

The damage that occurs to a unibody vehicle as the result of an impact can best be described by using the *cone concept.* The unibody vehicle is designed to absorb a collision impact. When hit, the body folds and collapses as it absorbs the impact. As the force penetrates the structure, it is absorbed by an ever increasing area of the unibody. This characteristic spreads the force until it is completely dissipated. Visualize the point of impact as the tip of the cone.

The centerline of the cone will point in the direction of impact. The depth and spread of the cone indicate the direction and area that the collision force traveled through the unibody. The tip of the cone and point of impact is the *primary damage* area, Figure 20–16.

Figure 20–16 Unibody vehicles use cone or egg shell principle to help absorb impact energy. *(Babcox Publications)*

Since unibodies are pieces of thin sheet metal joined together, the shock of a collision is absorbed by a large portion of the body shell. The effects of the impact shock wave as it travels through the body structure is called *secondary damage.* Generally, this damage is toward the inner structure of the unibody or toward the opposite end or side of the vehicle, Figure 20–17.

To provide some control on secondary damage and to provide a safer passenger compartment, a unibody vehicle is designed with *crush zones.* These crush zones are engineered to collapse in a predetermined fashion, Figure 20–18. The effects of the impact shock wave is reduced as it travels through and is dissipated by the body structure.

In other words, front impact shocks are absorbed by the front body and crush zones, Figure 20–19. Rear shocks are absorbed by the rear body. Side shocks will be absorbed by the rocker panel, roof side frame, center pillar, and door.

Impact damages on unibody vehicles can be described as:

Frontal unibody damage results from a head-on collision with another object or vehicle. The impact of a collision depends upon the vehicle's weight, speed, area of impact, and the source of impact. In the case of a minor impact, the bumper is pushed back, bending the front side members, bumper stay, front fender, radiator support, radiator upper support, and hood lock brace.

If the impact is further increased, the front fender will contact the front door. The hood hinge will bend up to the cowl top. The front side members may also buckle into the front suspension crossmember, causing it to bend, Figure 20–19. If the shock is great enough, the front fender apron and front body pillar (particularly front door hinge upper area) will be bent, which will cause the front door to drop down. In addition, the front side members will buckle. The front suspension member will bend. The dash panel

Figure 20–17 Note how roof has shifted sideways because its inertia tried to keep it from rapidly moving with impact. *(Babcox Publications)*

Figure 20–18 These are crush zones on unibody vehicle. They should be checked closely after collision.

Figure 20–19 With hard collision, frame rails can buckle and even separate or tear away from other parts.

and front floor pan may also bend to absorb the shock.

If a frontal impact is received at an angle, the attachment point of the front side member becomes a turning axis. Lateral as well as vertical bending occurs. Since the left and right front side members are connected together through the front crossmember, the shock from the impact is sent from the point of impact to the front side member of the opposite side of the vehicle.

Rear unibody damage occurs if the vehicle is moving backward and hits something or if hit by another vehicle from behind. When the impact is comparatively small, the rear bumper, the back panel, trunk lid, and floor pan will be deformed. Also, the quarter panels will bulge out.

If the impact is severe enough, the quarter panels will collapse to the base of the roof panel. On four door vehicles, the center body pillar might bend. Impact energy is absorbed by the deformation of the above parts and by the deformation of the kick-up of the rear side member.

Side unibody damage will cause the door, front section, center body pillar, and even the floor to deform. When the front fender or quarter panel receives a large perpendicular impact, the shock wave extends to the opposite side of the vehicle.

When the central area of the front fender receives an impact, the front wheel is pushed in. The shock wave extends from the front suspension crossmember to the front side member. If severe, the suspension parts are damaged and the front wheel alignment and wheelbase may be changed. The steering gear or rack can also be damaged by side impacts.

Top impacts can result from falling objects or from a rollover of the vehicle. This type of damage NOT only involves the roof panel but also the roof side rail, quarter panels, and possibly the windows might be damaged as well.

When a vehicle has rolled over and the body pillars and roof panels have been bent, the opposite ends of the pillars will be damaged as well. Depending on the manner in which the vehicle rolled over, the front or back sections of the body will be damaged, too. In such cases, the extent of the damage can be determined by the deformation around the windows and doors.

The typical *collision damage sequence* on a unibody structure happens like this:

1. In the first microseconds of impact, a shock wave attempts to shorten the structure. This causes a lateral or vertical bending in the central structure. Most of the forces that broadcast impact shock to remote areas occur at this instant. Since the structure is stiff and springy, it tends to snap back to its original shape—at least momentarily.

2. As the collision event continues, visible crushing occurs at the point of impact. Impact energy is absorbed in the deforming structure (helping protect passenger compartment). Remote areas might buckle, tear, or pull loose.

3. In a well-designed unibody structure, impact forces reaching the passenger compartment cause the side structure to bow out away from the passengers (never in) distorting side rails and door openings.

Widening is similar to side sway damage in BOF vehicles and is indicated by the width measurement being out of tolerance.

4. Even if the initial impact is dead center, secondary impact can introduce torsional loads that cause a general twisting of the structure. Unibody structural twisting, like twisting of a conventional vehicle frame, is usually the last collision event. It is indicated by combinations of height and width measurements being out of tolerance.

DIMENSIONAL REFERENCES

Two major dimensional references are indicated in all body dimension manuals: the datum plane and centerline.

A *datum line*, or *datum plane*, is an imaginary flat surface parallel to the underbody of the vehicle at some fixed distance from the underbody. It is the plane from which all vertical or *height dimensions* are taken by the vehicle manufacturer. It is also the plane that is used to measure the vehicle during repair. The datum is normally shown on dimension charts from the vehicle's side view.

The *center plane*, or *centerline*, divides the vehicle into two equal halves: the passenger side and the driver side. The centerline is shown on dimension charts in either the bottom or top views. It can sometimes be found on some vehicles in the form of body center marks. *Body center marks* are stamped into the sheet metal in both the upper and lower body areas of the vehicle. They can save time when taking measurements.

All width or *lateral dimensions* of symmetrical vehicles are measured from the center. That is, the measurement from the centerline to a specific point on the right side will be exactly the same as the measurement from the centerline to the same point on the left side. One side of the structure would be a perfect mirror image of the other. Most vehicles are built symmetrically. But if the vehicle is NOT symmetrical (asymmetrical), the self-centering gauges will NOT align and will NOT indicate a true center reference.

It is usually necessary to think of the vehicle as a rectangle divided into three zero plane sections. The *three zero plane sections* break the vehicle into three areas—front, center, and rear. The torque box location is used as the dividing lines. This three-section principle is a result of the vehicle's design and the way it reacts during a collision.

Symmetrical means that the dimensions on the right side of the vehicle are equal to the dimensions on the left side of the vehicle. If the vehicle is asymmetrical, these dimensions are NOT the same. In such a case, use gauges that can be adjusted to compensate for the asymmetry. See Figure 20–20.

VEHICLE MEASURING BASICS

In unibody construction, each section should be checked for diagonal squareness by comparing diagonal lengths. Length and width should also be compared. The center section should be used as a base when reading structural alignment. All measurements and alignment readings should be taken relative to the center section.

Start measuring in the center or middle section. If it is NOT square, then move to the undamaged end of the vehicle to find three correctly positioned reference points.

Keep in mind that to accurately measure a vehicle, you must start with at least three dimensions you

know are right. The way to do this is to check the squareness of the vehicle. If the vehicle is NOT symmetrical, refer to the dimension chart for correct measurements .

Remember! The terms "control point" and "reference point" have different meanings. The *control points* used in manufacturing are NOT necessarily the same as the reference points the collision repair technician uses to measure the vehicle. *Reference points* refer to the points, bolts, holes, and so on, used to give unibody dimensions in body specification manuals. The distance between reference points can be measured with either a tram bar or a tape measure, Figure 20–21.

A vehicle cannot be properly repaired unless all of the reference points are returned to pre-accident specifications. To achieve this, the collision repair technician or you must:

1. Measure accurately to analyze damage.

2. Measure often when pulling out damage.

3. Recheck all measurements after straightening.

Types of Measuring Equipment

Because of the importance of measuring during repairs, many kinds of special equipment have been

Figure 20–20 Body dimension manual will give measurements for reference points for specific make and model vehicle. If symmetrical, measurements on both sides are same. If unsymmetrical, measurements will be different on each side. *(Hein-Werner® Corporation)*

Measurement With a Tram Bar

Measuring Pin

A

Measurement With a Tape Measure

B

Figure 20–21 These are two basic methods of measuring a vehicle. A: Tram bar tips are inserted or touched on reference points. B: Tape measure can also be used to measure between points.

developed by manufacturers. Each provides the capability to measure very quickly and accurately. Although a number of styles of measuring equipment can be found in collision repair shops, most of it can be divided into three basic systems:

1. Gauge measuring systems
2. Universal measuring systems
3. Dedicated fixture systems

Gauge Measuring Systems

Gauge measuring systems use sliding metal rods or bars, and adjustable pointers with rules scales to measure body dimensions. The tape measure, tram bar, the self-centering gauge, and the strut tower gauge can be used separately or in conjunction with one another.

Tram bars are used for measurement; self-centering gauges check for misalignment. Supported by MacPherson strut tower domes, the strut tower gauge allows visual alignment of the critical reference points of unibody vehicles. The tram bar, self-centering gauge, and strut tower gauge are available as a unit or as separate vehicle diagnostic tools.

The tracking gauge is used to check alignment of the front and rear wheels. It is another popular measuring gauge. If the front and rear wheels are NOT in alignment, the vehicle will NOT handle properly.

Keeping Records

Since reference point measurements must be taken and written down several times in a repair operation, a method of tabulation must be devised. One way to accomplish this is to use a *data chart* or *tabulation chart.*

In the first column of the tabulation chart, write the location of what is being measured. Numbers or letters can be used. The second and third columns contain the manufacturer's specifications taken from the body dimension manual and actual distance as it exists on the damaged vehicle. The 1-2-3 are the readings taken at measurement step 1, measurement step 2, and so on. That is, as each pull is made, the measurements should be recorded, including those dimensions that have been corrected. This chart tells the collision repair technician at a glance how the job stands in restoring the vehicle to its pre-accident state.

NOTE! STRAIGHTENING OR PULLING WILL BE EXPLAINED IN DETAIL IN THE NEXT CHAPTER.

Using Tram Bars and Tapes

The *tram bar* is a measuring rod with two adjustable pointers attached to it, Figure 20–21. The pointers slide along the bar's length and are adjustable for height. Since the tram bar measures one dimension at a time, each must be recorded and cross-checked from two additional reference points. At least one must be a diagonal measurement.

The best areas to select for tram bar measurements are the attachment points for suspension and mechanical parts. These are critical to alignment. Throughout the pulling and straightening process, critical reference points must be measured (and recorded) repeatedly with the tram bar to monitor progress and to prevent overpulling.

The tram bar might have a scale superimposed on it. However, since almost all dimension charts list measurements in metric, use a steel tape with both English and metric scales to set up the tram bar. The tape can also be used to take quick measurements between reference points. Be sure the tape has been checked for accuracy before using it.

NOTE! MORE ACCURATE MEASUREMENTS CAN BE TAKEN IF THE FRONT END OF A TAPE MEASURE IS MACHINED AS IN FIGURE 20–22.

Pointed Tip **Round Tip**

After Machining

Figure 20–22 Grind down tip of tape measure like this. Smaller tip will make more accurate measurements in reference holes.

ITS TIP CAN THEN BE MORE FULLY INSERTED INTO THE REFERENCE POINT HOLE.

Reference point holes are frequently larger in diameter than the tram bar tip. To measure accurately with the tram bar when the holes are the same diameter, measure like edge to like edge. Study Figure 20–23.

When the holes are NOT the same size, they will usually be the same type of hole: round, square, or oblong. To find the center-to-center measurement, measure inside edge to inside edge, then outside edge to outside edge. Add the results of the two measurements and divide by 2.

For example, two round holes, one 12.5 mm in diameter, the other 38 mm in diameter, have an inside measurement of 762 mm and an outside measurement of 812 mm. The center-to-center dimension is (762 mm + 812 mm) divided by 2 = 787 mm. The 787 mm is the dimension for the tram bar. Center at the smallest hole and the other end should center at the larger hole. If NOT, there is damage to the unibody. Refer to Figure 20–24.

The term *point-to-point measurement* refers to the shortest distance between two points, as shown in Figure 20–25. The term *datum measurement* refers to the distance between two points when measured with a tram gauge, Figure 20–25.

A few body dimension manuals give the measurements based on the bar's length. Here, the bar of the tram becomes the datum plane beneath the vehicle. The pointers are set at the horizontal height dimensions specified on the dimension chart. It is important to always check the method used on the dimension chart because the two distances are NOT the same.

In using a tram bar for measuring, the vehicle dimensions are needed to accurately assess and correct the damage. If the vehicle dimensions are NOT available, use an undamaged vehicle of the same make, year, model, and body style as a source to obtain the correct factory dimensions. Frequently, if

Tram Bar

Edge of Hole   **Edge of Hole**

Tape Measure

Figure 20–23 Note various methods for measuring distance between reference points.

only one side of a vehicle has been damaged, it also is possible to take measurements on the undamaged side. Set the tram bar using the undamaged side. Then use it to measure the damaged side to make comparison measurements.

Upper Body Measurement

Upper body damage can also be determined by the use of a tram bar and a steel measuring tape. Their use is basically the same as when doing an underbody evaluation. Dimension charts have measurements for many upper body reference points.

Figure 20–24 Note how to measure holes of different sizes with tram gauge.

Figure 20–25 When specs are given, they can be point-to-point or datum measurements.

Front Body Measurement

When a damaged vehicle needs the hood and front side member replaced, you should take measurements during the repair. Even if only the front, right side of the vehicle body received the impact, the left side will usually be damaged also. Therefore, the extent of deformation must be checked before pulling.

Figure 20–26 shows the typical front body reference points. They should be measured and checked against the dimension chart for the specific vehicle.

When checking front end dimensions, measure the attachment points for suspension and mechanical parts. These are critical to proper alignment. Each dimension should be checked from two additional reference points with at least one reference point being a diagonal measurement.

Figure 20–26 Dimensions manual will give front end body reference points like these.

Note that the longer the dimension, the more accurate the measurement. A measurement from the lower cowl to the engine cradle is a better gauge than a measurement from a lower cowl to another lower cowl area. This is because the longer dimension takes in a larger area of the vehicle. The use of two or more measurements from each reference point assures greater accuracy. It also helps identify the extent and direction of any panel damage.

Body Side Panel Measurement

Body side structure damage can be evaluated by the fit and operation of the doors when opened and closed. Deformation around the door openings can cause an uneven gap and air or water leaks. Thus, accurate measurements must be taken. The tram bar is used to measure the body side panel. See Figure 20–27.

Figure 20–27 Note typical side reference points.

Diagonal line measurement compares reading across an opening or between four reference points to determine damage. Damage can be detected if the left-to-right symmetry of the body is used for measuring diagonal lines, as shown in Figure 20–28A. Use this measuring method if:

1. The data on the engine compartment and underbody are missing.

2. There is no data available in the body dimension chart.

3. The vehicle has been severely damaged in a rollover.

The diagonal line measurement method is NOT adequate when inspecting damage to both sides of the vehicle or in the case of twisting. This is because the left-to-right difference in the diagonal lines cannot be measured, Figure 20–28B.

If deformation is the same on the left and right, left to right difference will NOT be apparent. Refer to Figure 20–28C.

In Figure 20–29, the measurement and comparison of the left and right lengths between yz and YZ will give an even better indication of damage conditions. This method should be used in conjunction with the diagonal line measurement method. This method can be applied where there are parts that are symmetrical on the left and right sides.

Rear Body Measurement

Deformation of the rear body can be analyzed by the fit and action when the deck lid is opened and closed, Figure 20–30. Damage to this area can cause water leakage around the deck lid seal. Any wrinkle in the rear floor is usually due to buckling of the rear frame rail, a major problem. Thus, measure the rear body together with the underbody. In this way, the straightening work can be performed effectively.

Keep in mind that all reference points need to be checked from two or more reference points. Diagonal measurements are a good way to cross-check dimen-

Figure 20–29 Study this diagonal line measurement example.

sional reference points. Correct use of self-centering gauges will also reveal the kind of misalignment that would be shown by diagonal tram bar measurements.

Note the various measurement points in Figure 20–31. Refer to the body dimension manual to find where these points are located.

Self-centering Gauges

Self-centering gauges show alignment or misalignment by projecting points on the vehicle's structure into the technician's line of sight. See Figure 20–32.

Self-centering gauges are installed at various control areas on the bottom of the vehicle, Figure 20–33, page 380. They have two sliding horizontal bars that remain parallel as they move inward and outward. This action permits adjustment to any width for installation on various areas of the vehicle.

Self-centering gauges are used to establish the vehicle centerline and datum plane. Use the gauges in sets of four or more. Adjust and hang them at the locations indicated in the dimensional data manual to establish the datum plane. The body manual will also give information for adjusting them to hang on the

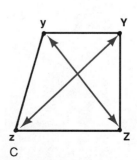

Figure 20–28 Study use of diagonal line measuring technique. A: Yz equals yZ, no warping. B: Yz is less than yZ, deflection to left. C: Yz is greater than yZ, deflection to right.

2 Door

772
(30.39)

772
(30.39)

772
(30.39)

668
(26.94)

655
(25.79)

888
(34.96)

V

W

X

Y

W

y

3 Door or 5 Door

3-door 1,024 (40.31)
5-door 1,019 (40.12)

3-door 1,008 (39.37)
5-door 943 (37.13)

3-door 1,224 (48.19)
5-door 1,178 (46.38)

3-door 993 (39.09)
5-door 935 (36.81)

978
(38.50)

3-door 1,220 (48.03)
5-door 1,174 (46.22)

V
X
X
W
v
x
w

V Point

X Point

Y, y Points

Symbol	Name	Hole. diam.
V	Back window upper frame center mark	2R (0.08)
W, w	Rear spring support hole – front	10 (0.39)
X	Upper back reinforcement center mark	2.5R (0.098)
Y, y	Rear floor pan bumper installation hole – front	40 (1.57)

V, v Points

Front
Outer

W, w Points

Front

Symbol	Name	Hole. diam.
V, v	Back door installation hole – outer	13 (0.51)
W, w	Rear floor pan bumper installation hole – front	40 (1.57)
X, x	Rear spring support hole – rear	10 (0.39)

Figure 20–30 Note rear body reference points for two body styles.

A

C

B

D

Figure 20–31 Here are several body reference point examples. *(Chief Automotive Systems, Inc.)* A: Checking location of upper corner of radiator support during replacement. B: Checking reference hole location on frame rail. C: Checking reference hole in engine cradle. D: Checking reference point on rear shock tower.

Scale

Center Pin

Scale Holder

Horizontal Bar

A

B

Figure 20–32 Self-centering gauge is used to check for major frame and unibody damage. A: Note parts of self-centering gauge. *(I-CAR)* B: Four self-centering gauges are often suspended under vehicle to form datum plane and center plane. *(Blackhawk Collision Repair, Inc., Subsidiary of Hein-Werner® Corporation)*

Front Floor Under Reinforcement Reference Hole

**If Repaired,
It Can Be Used**

**Unusable
(Damaged Hole)**

Figure 20–33 Do not hang gauges from damaged reference holes or points.

same plane under the vehicle. Scales are provided for adjusting the gauges to hang the correct distance down under the vehicle, Figure 20–34.

Begin by setting up the *base gauges* or the two gauges hung near the center off the vehicle. Usually, the torque box area is used. Generally, these will be gauges numbered two and three. Add other gauges as needed and use the base gauges for reference.

When inspecting for damage, first hang self-centering gauges from two places where there is no visible damage, then hang two more gauges where there is obvious damage. Then, sight the gauges hung at both the undamaged and damaged locations and check to see if the gauges are parallel to each other or if the centering pins are misaligned.

The gauges are also equipped with center pins or sights, which remain in the center of the gauge regardless of the width of the horizontal bars. This allows the technician to read centerline throughout the length of the vehicle.

When sighting gauges for parallel, always stand directly in the middle, scanning with both eyes. To ensure accuracy, readings should be made at the outer edge of the self-centering gauge, NOT in the middle. See Figure 20–35.

The further one stands from the gauges while reading, the more accurate the reading will be. Standing close changes the line of sight to the front gauges so drastically that an accurate reading is nearly impossible.

Self-centering gauges should always be set at the same height or plane. Different heights will change the angle of sight and give a false reading. Sighting from the end of the vehicle opposite the damage can make readings more accurate. With practice, you can

Figure 20–34 Scales on gauges should be set to match specifications in dimensions manual. Note how scale reading and part of tool must be added to adjust gauge properly. *(I-CAR)*

A

C

B

Figure 20–35 Note basic method of using self-aligning gauges. *(Chief Automotive Systems, Inc.)* A: After properly mounting self-centering gauges, sight down pins to see if vehicle is out of alignment. B: Pins on each gauge are in alignment indicating that frame or unibody is not damaged from collision. C: Pins and gauge rods are not in alignment indicating major frame or unibody damage has resulted.

improve the damage analysis with self-centering gauges.

The sighting of centerline pins must be done with one eye. Since the center section is the base for gauging, your line of sight must always project through the pins of the base gauges. Observing pins in other sections of the body will then reveal how much they are out of alignment.

NOTE! NEVER ATTACH SELF-CENTERING GAUGES TO ANY MOVABLE PARTS SUCH AS CONTROL ARMS OR SPRINGS.

Each self-centering gauge has two vertical scales—one on the left side, one on the right. These scales are adjusted vertically to assure that the horizontal bars accurately reflect true positions.

Once hung in specific locations, the gauges generally remain on the vehicle throughout the entire repair operation. This is true unless they interfere with straightening, anchoring, or with the tram bar.

Special centering gauges are available that can be used to check such items as body pillar damage.

The same system of alignment is employed when using gauges to check underbody damage. Some self-centering gauges can be adjusted for asymmetrical vehicles as well. Again, check the dimensional data for these asymmetrical vehicles. Follow directions provided with the gauges.

Using Datum Plane

To read for datum, all gauges must be on the same plane. After hanging all four gauges, read across the top to determine if datum is correct. If all four gauges are parallel, the vehicle is on datum. If they are NOT parallel, the vehicle is off datum. Refer back to Figure 20–35.

Since the datum line is an imaginary plane, datum heights can be raised or lowered to facilitate gauge readings. Just remember that if the datum height is changed at one gauge location, all the gauges must be adjusted an equal amount to maintain accuracy.

While datum readings are usually obtained from self-centering gauges, there are individual gauges

Upper Horizontal Bar

Pointer

Vertical Scales

Center Pin

Lower Horizontal Bar

A

Strut Tower Gauge

CL

Distance From
Centerline to
Tower Reference Point

CL

Distance From
Centerline to Ball Joint

B

Figure 20–36 Strut tower gauge is commonly used with modern unibody vehicles. It is used with other gauges. *(I-CAR)* A: Study parts of strut tower gauge. B: When installed, you can check alignment of top of strut towers and also lower parts. They should generally be equal distances from centerline.

available for measuring datum heights. These datum gauges are usually held in position by magnetic holders. Remember that the dimensions that allow the vehicle to be level with the road are measured from the datum plane.

Using Centerline

To check for centerline misalignment, use the four self-centering gauges hung on datum. To establish the true centerline, the center pin on the No. 2 gauge must be lined up with the center pin on the No. 3 gauge. Then the center pins of No. 1 and No. 4 can be read relative to the centerline of the base.

Frame or unibody damage will affect the centerline reading. If a vehicle has a diamond condition, a shortened rail or subrail, or an out-of-level condition, the centerline reading may be affected. Further inspection by gauging or measuring might be necessary.

Using Strut Tower Gauges

Supported by the shock-spring towers, the *strut tower gauge* allows visual alignment of the upper body area. It shows misalignment of the strut tower/upper body parts in relation to the vehicle's centerline plane and datum plane. See Figure 20–36.

The strut tower gauge features an upper and lower horizontal bar, each with a center pin. The upper bar is usually calibrated from the center out. Pointers are used to mount the gauge to the strut tower/upper body locations.

Using dimension charts, the strut tower gauge is adjusted to the correct dimensions. You must use the vertical scales that link the upper and lower horizontal bars to set the lower bar at the datum plane. With the lower bar set to align properly, the upper pointers should be located at reference points on the strut towers. If NOT, the strut towers are damaged and pushed out of alignment. This would tell you that straightening would be needed so that front suspension and wheels can be aligned properly. Look at Figure 20–37.

NOTE! THE STRUT TOWER GAUGE IS USED MOST OFTEN TO DETECT MISALIGNMENT OF STRUT TOWERS. HOWEVER, IT CAN ALSO BE USED TO DETECT MISALIGNMENT OF A RADIATOR CORE SUPPORT, COWL, QUARTER PANELS, AND SO ON.

Diagnosing Damage with Gauges

To correct collision damage, pull or push the damaged area in the opposite direction of impact. The

Figure 20–37 Note how strut tower gauge is used. *(Chief Automotive Systems, Inc.)* A: Strut tower gauge is adjusted and mounted using manual specifications. B: Pointers on strut tower gauge should touch exact reference point on strut towers. If not, the towers are bent out of alignment and must be straightened. C: Lower centering pin on strut tower gauge can also be used with other self-centering gauges to check for damage.

Twisting

Figure 20–38 If self-centering gauges are out of alignment as shown here, the frame or unibody is twisted.

repair must be made in the reverse sequence that it happened. Therefore, the damage must be measured in the reverse sequence.

When measuring damage, keep in mind that a vehicle is similar to a building. If the foundation is NOT square and level, the rest of the structure will be uneven also. The vehicle's foundation, which is the center section of the vehicle, is measured for twist and diamond first. These two measurements will tell the collision repair technician if the foundation is square and level. The remaining measurements use the foundation as a reference.

Twist Damage. The first damage condition to look for is twist. Twist is the last damage condition to occur to the vehicle. Therefore, it should be the first measured. Twist is a condition that exists throughout the entire vehicle.

Twist damage exists when one side of the vehicle is pushed low or high on one end (front or rear) and then moves in the opposite direction (low or high) on the other end. At the same time, the opposite side would have exactly the opposite damage.

To check for twist, sight down your properly hung self-centering gauges. Twist will show up when the gauges are not parallel. If a true twist exists, the gauges would read like those shown in Figure 20–38.

Mash Damage. *Mash damage* is present when any section or frame member of the vehicle is shorter than the factory specifications. It is measured with a tram bar.

When using a tram bar on a mash damaged vehicle, be sure to make the measurement called for in the dimension chart. The amount of mash is determined

Figure 20–39 Measuring mash damage on unibody vehicles: A: High front impact with secondary damage in the rear; B: right front corner impact; C: direct front impact; D: low front impact; E: high front impact; and F: high rear impact.

Figure 20–40 Side view of gauges shows sag. One gauge is lower than other in cowl area.

by subtracting the actual measurement from the specified measurement. See Figure 20–39.

Sag Damage. *Sag damage* is a condition where the area of the frame or unibody is lower than normal. Sag often occurs at the cowl area or at the front crossmember. The ends of the crossmember will be closer than normal and the center will be too low.

Again, your four self-center gauges are used to check for a sag condition. Sag is indicated when one gauge is lower than the others. Look at Figure 20–40.

Side Sway (Widening) Damage. *Side sway* is present when the front, center, or rear portion of the vehicle is out of lateral alignment. Use your four self-centering gauges to check for side sway.

If the centering pin on any gauge does NOT line up horizontally with the others, side sway damage is present. If they all line up, there is no side sway deformation.

A center hit on the vehicle causes a misalignment known as double side sway. While this results from a severe impact in the center section, it affects the entire vehicle. The dimension of both front and rear sections must be checked during the pulling of double side sway damage.

Universal Measuring Systems

Universal measuring systems have the ability to measure several reference points at the same time, making the job much easier and more accurate, Figure 20–41. However, universal systems still require a degree of skill and attention to detail to operate properly. But to get the proper readings, the equipment must be set using the manufacturer's specifications.

Universal measuring systems can be mechanical, laser, or a combination of the two.

With a universal measuring system, all the reference points can be checked by just moving around the vehicle. You can quickly determine where each reference point on the vehicle is in comparison to the measuring system.

If a reference point on the vehicle is NOT in the same position as the dimension chart says it should be, the reference point on the vehicle is wrong. When the system is set up properly, you can monitor the key points by simply looking at the pointers. If the pointers are out of position, then the vehicle is NOT dimensionally correct. Thus, that reference point is out of

Figure 20–41 Note major parts of universal measuring system. *(Chief Automotive Systems, Inc.)*

Figure 20–42 Measuring system shows major damage. While using pulling equipment to straighten damage, measurements of progress must be taken. *(Chief Automotive Systems, Inc.)*

position and must be brought back to pre-accident specifications. See Figure 20–42.

> *WARNING! The pointers can be damaged during pulling. Lower the pointers, if necessary, to clear the way for the pull. This will avoid damaging or misaligning the measuring system.*

While the important vehicle dimensions can be found in body dimension manuals, most universal measuring equipment manufacturers have specific dimension charts for their equipment. These charts, one for each vehicle model manufactured, serve as guides to use before and during the repair.

The dimension chart usually illustrates two views of the vehicle underbody. Some charts also give underhood and upper body dimensions. The latter is most important with the plastic paneled mill and drill pad dimensions.

Remember! Many equipment manufacturer's dimension charts are intended only for that specific piece of equipment. Because of this variation between systems, it would be difficult to explain how each manufacturer's system measures a vehicle. You will need to read the equipment owner's manual for these details.

Before beginning any universal measuring operations, be sure to:

1. Remove detachable damaged body parts, both mechanical and sheet metal body panels.
2. If the damage is severe, perform rough straightening to the center section or foundation of the vehicle.

3. If the mechanical parts are left in the vehicle and an overhang condition exists, this must be compensated for.

Mechanical Measuring Systems

A typical mechanical system, Figure 20–43, consists of:

1. A bridge(s) that runs the length of the vehicle from front to back.
2. Sliding arms that mount to the bridge. They can be moved from front to back on the bridge for length measurements. They can also be moved outward or inward, for width measurements.
3. Pointers that are mounted on the arms. They can be adjusted up or down for height measurements.
4. Specific fixtures for the make and model vehicle, Figure 20–44.

The pointer may accept special adapters to fit over a bolt head or into a reference point hole. The equipment manufacturer will provide instructions for this type of setup.

Mechanical measuring systems are designed and used according to guidelines found in the equipment manufacturer publications. They are written for each family of body styles. Mechanical systems look complicated, but are easy to use after reading their directions carefully.

Dedicated Bench and Fixture Measuring Systems

The *dedicated bench and fixture system* acts a "go-no-go" gauge. It is a completely different type of measuring method. Instead of taking actual measurements, dedicated fixtures are used to check body or frame alignment.

Figure 20–43 This is a typical mechanical measuring system.

Measuring Adapters

Scale

Height
Tube

Figure 20–44 Different adapters may be provided with measuring system. This will simplify measurements from different kinds of reference points. *(Car-O-Liner)*

The *dedicated bench* consists of a strong, flat work surface to which fixtures are attached, Figure 20–45.

Fixtures are thick metal parts that bolt between the vehicle and bench to check alignment. They are designed from the vehicle manufacturer's drawings. The fixtures physically check mountings or other key locations of the underbody.

If the fixtures fit the vehicle properly, the technician knows that the underbody and strut towers are in perfect alignment, Figure 20–46. All that is necessary is to straighten the vehicle until the reference points match the fixtures. No other underbody measurements are usually required.

The dedicated bench and fixture measuring system requires a specific set of fixtures for each family of body styles. If the collision repair shop does NOT own the required fixtures, they can be rented. The bench has built-in reference positions, and the fixtures are positioned to the specific references according to instructions supplied by the manufacturer. At least three fixtures must be positioned on the bench before the vehicle is mounted. Generally these are the torque-box fixtures. However, the damage to a specific vehicle will dictate which fixtures should be used.

Figure 20–47 shows four of the more common types of fixtures. They are:

1. *Bolt-on Fixtures*—used when attachment is required to steering or suspension mountings. The studs or bolts on the vehicle are used to attach the fixtures. Depending on the damage, the fixtures can either be bolted to the vehicle first and lined up with the bench during the repair. They can also be attached to the bench first and lined up with the vehicle during repair.

2. *Pin-type Fixtures*—used most often to mate with reference point holes in the underbody. They can also be used to mate with suspension mounting holes.

3. *Strut Fixtures*—used in the same manner as a pin-type fixture. A typical strut fixture consists of a bottom plate assembly as with the other fixtures, an adjustable shaft with a cross pin, and a bolt-on top plate.

4. *Bench Extensions*—included where the length of the vehicle requires that fixtures be positioned beyond the bench surface. The extensions are always used at the rear of the vehicle. Each extension is drilled with holes on top and on the bottom.

Most fixtures share a common attachment method to the transverse beams. The base plate for each fixture is drilled with holes and is marked with a part number and the location on the transverse beam. Stamped at the rear of each fixture base are the numbers that correspond to the numbers on the transverse beam.

Make sure these numbers are on the same side as the numbers on the transverse beam.

Once the vehicle is mounted on the bench, at least three fixtures should be set up on the undamaged area of the vehicle. Then, place as many fixtures as possible in the damaged area of the vehicle. The fixtures perform a number of functions:

1. They show where a reference point should be located.

2. They provide gauging of all the reference points at the same time. No measuring is required. If all the points line up, the steering, suspension, engine mounts, and so on are in alignment.

3. Once lined up with the fixtures, they can hold these parts in position while further straightening is done. This eliminates the "pull-measure, pull-measure" sequence required with universal measuring systems.

4. They allow accurate assembly of parts on the vehicle before actually welding those pieces together. A good example of this would be a

Figure 20–45 Dedicated bench uses thick frame work and fixtures to check unibody or frame alignment. *(Blackhawk Collision Repair, Inc., Subsidiary of Hein-Werner® Corporation)*

Figure 20–46 Dedicated fixtures are provided for each make of vehicle. They serve as go-no-go gauges.

lower rail and strut tower assembly on some unibody vehicles.

The sequence is as follows:

1. Position and hold the lower rail pieces on the fixtures.

2. Weld them together.

3. Position and hold the strut tower pieces on top of the rail.

4. Weld them in their correct position.

Laser Measuring Systems

The laser measuring system uses a strong beam of light, beam splitters, and targets, to measure vehicle

Bolt-on Fixture

Top Pin

Cross Pins

Fixture

Pin-Type Fixture

Bolt

Top Plate

Cross Pin

Fixture

MacPherson Strut Fixture

Fixture/Bench Attachment Holes

Bench Extension

Transverse Beam Attachment Holes

Stamped Part Number

Hole Numbers

Fixture Number Identification

Figure 20–47 Note various fixture types.

damage. It is extremely accurate when properly installed and used. See Figure 20–48.

The word *LASER* is an acronym for Light Amplification by Stimulated Emission Reaction. All laser measuring systems operate basically the same way. The laser unit is aimed at a target or measuring scale. The target or scale is either hung from or attached to

the vehicle. Some systems even use parts of the vehicle as targets. Look at Figure 20–49.

There are several types of systems available. However, all laser systems work either from the centerline or from the datum plane reference. See Figure 20–50.

Measurements are taken by observing the laser beam on the targets. Some targets are clear, allowing the laser beam to pass through. Several *clear targets* can be used with one laser light source.

Beam splitters, or *laser guides*, are capable of reflecting the laser beam to additional targets. Using combinations of transparent targets and beam splitters, it is possible to measure several dimensions on a vehicle at the same time using a single laser source.

Three-dimensional laser systems use up to three laser units to give length/width/height coordinates anywhere on the vehicle. They will check deck lid openings, cowls, door openings, hinges, pillars, and roof lines, Figure 20–51. With such a system, a single laser unit can be used to make measurements in conjunction with measuring devices such as a tape measure or calibrated bar. See Figure 20–52.

Laser measuring systems are made up of both optical and mechanical parts. For example, in the clear target system, the optical parts are:

1. Laser power unit, which emits a safe, low-powered laser beam
2. Beam splitters that project beams at a precise right angle so height, width, and length can be measured simultaneously
3. Laser guide that reflects the laser beam at exactly 90 degrees

Other items used with laser measuring devices include calibrated bars. They attach to the vehicle or

Strut Tower Accessory

Laser Beam

Laser Unit

Transparent Scale

Length Rail

Beam Splitter

Width Rail

Figure 20–48 Study basic parts of typical laser measuring system. Laser unit directs beam of light throughout system. Beam splitters and scales give readings quickly and accurately.

Figure 20–49 Laser light moves in straight line unless redirected by reflector or splitter. *(Kansas Jack, Division of Hein-Werner® Corporation)*

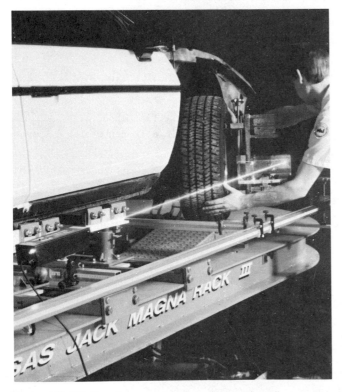

Figure 20–50 One laser can be used to make all measurements with some systems. *(Kansas Jack, Division of Hein-Werner® Corporation)*

Figure 20–51 A three-dimensional laser system allows length, width, and height measurements at one time. *(Kansas Jack, Division of Hein-Werner® Corporation)*

act as support devices for the laser unit itself. Scales are hung from reference points on the underside of the vehicle. The laser beam passes through the center of the scale on the target when the measuring point is in its correct position.

Some laser measuring systems permit the technician to monitor upper body dimensions. For instance,

pillar locations and window openings can be checked easily with a laser.

Some laser systems also offer an integral four-wheel alignment capability, Figure 20–53. Wheel alignment on the measuring system is beneficial. Suspension problems can be measured and corrected during frame or unibody repairs.

The accuracy of laser measurement systems depends on their proper installation. When a laser beam is projected through one target to another, the targets must be optically perfect. Otherwise, the laser beam will be deflected as it passes through the targets. The deflection will be magnified by the distance

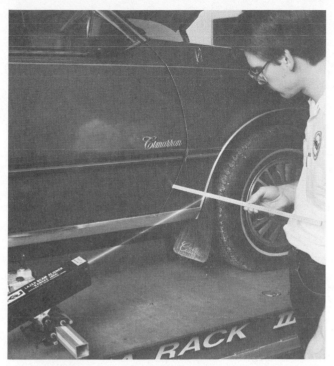

Figure 20–52 Laser unit can also be used in combination with other tools, like tape measure. *(Kansas Jack, Division of Hein-Werner® Corporation)*

Figure 20–53 Some laser measurement systems will also let you check and adjust wheel alignment, saving time. *(Kansas Jack, Division of Hein-Werner® Corporation)*

between the targets. This effect can result in serious error. Laser targets that become scratched or warped should be discarded.

When properly set up, the laser system can generally stay with the vehicle during the pulling and

straightening process, like the mechanical systems. However, if the laser or mounting bars are in danger of being damaged during the pull, they must be moved.

Laser measuring systems provide direct, instantaneous dimensional readings so that the reference points in both the damaged and undamaged areas of the vehicle can be monitored continually during the pulling and straightening operation.

Computerized Measuring Systems

Computerized measuring systems use data from the measuring system for fast entry and checking of vehicle dimensions. In one such system, Figure 20–54, measurements are made electronically and are displayed digitally on the laser guide.

With the hand unit connected, measurements appear immediately on the computer screen. The hand unit has storage capacity for data and specifications of up to four different vehicle models. The vehicle measurements can be quickly compared with specifications. Deviations are also displayed.

If the measurements and deviations need to be documented, the hand unit can be connected to a printer to provide a printout. Measurements are available either on disk or via modem from the manufacturer's main computer. All data and specifications can be stored in the shop's personal computer.

Figure 20–54 Some measuring systems will output data into a hand-held unit or directly into a computer. The computer-stored data for vehicle dimensions, estimating, and so on can then be used to streamline measurement, estimating, parts ordering, and other tasks. *(Car-O-Liner)*

More Information

Manufacturers of measuring systems constantly furnish updates and bulletins on their products. Be sure to read and study them because they will help to make the repair procedure easier.

Remember! The best measuring system in the world will NOT help if you do NOT take the time to learn how to use it correctly. Damage cannot be repaired if it cannot be found; and damage cannot be found without precise, careful measurements.

Summary

- There are two basic types of automotive construction: Body-over-frame (BOF) vehicles and unibody (or monocoque) vehicles.

- Vehicle damage is broken down into five categories: side sway, sag, mash, diamond, and twist.

- The three basic measuring equipment systems are: gauge, universal, and dedicated.

- Universal measuring systems have the ability to measure several reference points at the same time, making the job easier and more accurate. Universal measuring systems can be mechanical, laser, or a combination of the two.

- The laser measuring system uses a strong beam of light, beam splitters, and targets to measure vehicle damage. It is extremely accurate when properly installed and used.

Technical Terms

vehicle measurement	*gauge measuring systems*
measurement gauges	*tabulation chart*
reference points	*tram bar*
BOF	*point-to-point*
side sway damage	*measurement*
sag damage	*datum measurement*
mash damage	*diagonal line*
diamond damage	*measurement*
twist damage	*base gauges*
cone concept	*strut tower gauge*
primary damage	*universal measuring*
secondary damage	*systems*
widening	*dedicated bench*
datum plane	*fixtures*
centerline	*LASER*
body center marks	*beam splitters*
symmetrical	*computerized measuring*
asymmetrical	*systems*

Review Questions

1. On some unibody designs, which has a fixed (non-adjustable) value?
   a. Camber
   b. Caster
   c. Both a and b
   d. Neither a nor b

2. The _____ is a measuring rod with two adjustable pointers attached to it.

3. From what part of a unibody vehicle are all height dimensions taken?
   a. Datum plane
   b. Center plane
   c. Centerline
   d. Reference point

4. Explain the difference between control points and reference points.

5. All unibody measurements and alignment readings should be taken relative to what section?
   a. Front
   b. Rear
   c. Center
   d. Both a and b

6. What are body center marks?

7. The _____ _____, or _____, divides the vehicle into two equal halves: the passenger side and the driver side.

8. Define the term "datum plane" and explain how it is used.

9. When checking front end dimensions, Technician A measures from the lower cowl area to the front mount of the engine cradle. Technician B measures from one lower cowl area to another. Whose measurement will provide a better reading?
   a. Technician A
   b. Technician B
   c. Both A and B
   d. Neither A nor B

10. Describe the four events during a typical collision damage sequence on a unibody structure.

11. What are self-centering gauges used to establish?
    a. Datum plane
    b. Vehicle centerline
    c. Both a and b
    d. Neither a nor b

12. Technician A stands three feet (one meter) away from a self-centering gauge when taking a read-

ing, while Technician B stands six feet (two meters) away.

Who will get the more accurate reading?

a. Technician A

b. Technician B

c. Both A and B

d. Neither A nor B

13. List five safety rules to follow before starting a vehicle damage evaluation.

14. _____ _____ are special tools used to check specific frame and body points. They allow you to quickly measure the direction and extent of vehicle damage.

15. What is sag damage?

Activities

1. Obtain and study the operating manual for several types of measurement systems. Write a report or summary of unique methods for using each type of equipment.

2. Using a body dimensions manual, locate the data for one specific make and model vehicle. Note the locations of the reference points. Make a few practice measurements on this vehicle.

3. Visit body shops. Ask the owner if you can watch a technician measuring damage on an actual vehicle. Write a report on your visit.

CHAPTER 21

FRAME-UNIBODY STRAIGHTENING

Objectives

After studying this chapter, you should be able to:

- List the types of straightening equipment and explain their operation.

- Describe basic straightening and aligning techniques.

- Identify safety considerations for using alignment equipment.

- Plan and execute collision repair procedures.

- Identify signs of stress/deformation and make the necessary repairs.

- Determine if a repair or replacement can be done before, during, or after pulling.

Introduction

The major steps for repairing a heavily damaged vehicle are given in Figure 21–1. Study them!

Vehicles with major damage must often have their frame or body structures straightened. Vehicle straightening involves using high powered hydraulic equipment, mechanical clamps, chains, and a measuring system to bring the frame or body structure back to its original shape, Figure 21–2. At the same time, it might involve the replacement of welded panels that are severely damaged.

Body aligning or pulling is often thought to be a "rough and tough" physical operation. Actually, it is a relatively easy step-by-step task if proper equipment and methods are used. An important requirement when straightening is accuracy. For example, wheel alignment is directly affected by body-frame alignment; if not properly straightened, you or a mechanic will not be able to align the wheels of the vehicle.

Improper straightening techniques are costly and time consuming mistakes. Accurate vehicle alignment affects safety, repair time, repair quality, and the confidence of your customer. This chapter will summarize the most important methods for realigning a vehicle with major damage.

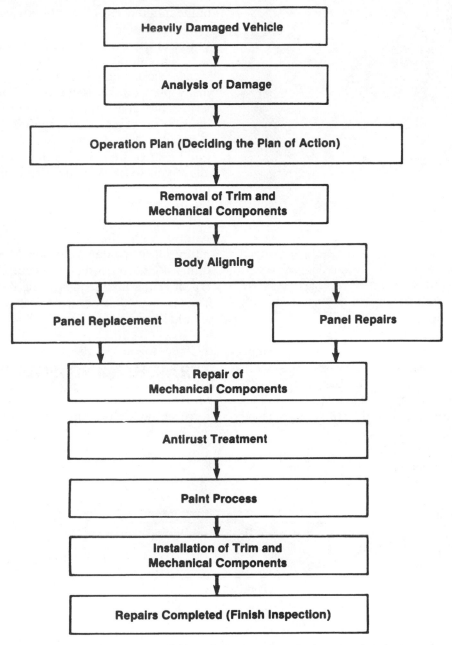

Figure 21–1 Study major steps for collision repair. Note that panel replacement is done after frame or unibody straightening.

ALIGNMENT BASICS

The term *pulling* refers to using alignment equipment to stretch the damaged metal back out to its original shape. The vehicle is secured and held stationary by the equipment. Then, clamps and chains are attached to the damaged area. When the hydraulic system is activated, the chains slowly pull out the damage. Measurements are made at body-frame reference points while pulling to return the vehicle to its original dimensions.

When realigning a vehicle, a pull force or *traction* should be applied in the opposite direction as the force of the impact. This is illustrated in Figure 21–3. When determining the direction of a pull, you must set the equipment to pull perpendicular to the damage.

The *single pull method* uses only one pulling chain and it works well with minor damage on one part. A small bend in a part can often be straightened with a single pull.

With major damage to several panels, a *multiple*

Figure 21-2 Straightening or aligning equipment is powerful enough to pull out even the worst collision damage. Knowledge of the equipment, vehicle structure, and common sense are needed to repair badly damaged vehicles. *(Car-O-Liner)*

pull method with several pulling directions and steps are needed, Figure 21–4. With major damage, body panels are often deformed into complex shapes with altered strengths in the damaged areas. To pull in only the opposite direction would not work because of the differences in the strength and recovery rates of each panel.

Use the method that works best for the given situation. Since applying force in only one place will not always work, you often have to exert pulling force on many places at the same time. For convenience, the term "direction opposite to input" will be used to describe the effective pulling direction.

To alter the direction while pulling, divide the pulling force into two or more directions. This will allow you to change the direction of the *composite force*, that is, the force of all pulls combined. Look at Figure 21–5.

The pulling and straightening process must remove both direct and indirect damage. It must return all of the damaged metal back to pre-accident dimensions. To do this, the equipment must reverse the direction and sequence the damage occurred in. The damage that occurred last during the collision should be pulled out first.

STRAIGHTENING EQUIPMENT

Straightening equipment is used to apply tremendous force to move the frame or body structure back into

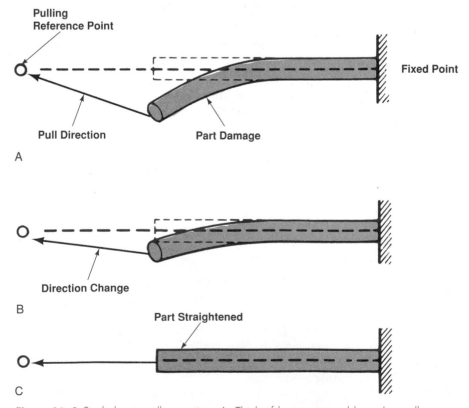

Figure 21-3 Study basic pulling action. A: Think of how you would need to pull on part to return it to original position. B: As you pull on part, angle of pull might change slightly. C: Part has been pulled back to its original shape.

Figure 21–4 Note how to find general pulling direction. A: Damage input came from right front. Damage was from directions Y and Z. B: Basically, apply straightening equipment force in direction opposite to input force. C: If metal pulls out at different rates, change pulling direction as needed.

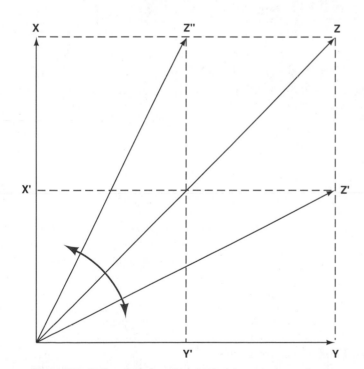

$$X + Y = Z$$
$$X + Y' = Z'$$
$$X' + Y + Z''$$

Figure 21–5 If pulling force is divided between two directions (X and Y), the composite or total force direction (Z) will change freely with adjustments to force in the two directions. This shows that using two chains to pull allows for better adjustment of pulling direction.

alignment. Straightening equipment includes anchoring equipment, pulling equipment, and other accessories. See Figure 21–6.

The *anchoring equipment* holds the vehicle stationary while pulling and measuring. Anchoring can be done by fastening the frame or unibody of the vehicle to anchors in the shop floor or to the straightening equipment rack or bench. The objective of the anchoring system is to hold the vehicle solidly in place while pulling forces are applied. It must also distribute pulling forces throughout the vehicle.

The *pulling equipment* uses hydraulic power to force the body structure or frame back into position. There are many different types of pulling equipment available. Regardless of their design or operating features, each system uses the same basic pulling theory and is used in a similar manner.

Hydraulic rams use oil pressure from a pump to produce a powerful linear motion. When you electrically activate the system, oil is forced into the ram cylinder. The ram is then pushed outward with tremendous force. This pulls on the chain attached to the vehicle to remove the damage. The rams can be mounted in or on the pulling towers, posts, or between the vehicle and anchoring system.

Pulling posts or towers are strong steel members used to hold the pulling chains and hydraulic rams. Depending upon equipment design, they can be positioned at whatever location is needed to make the pull. They push against the bench as the pull is made.

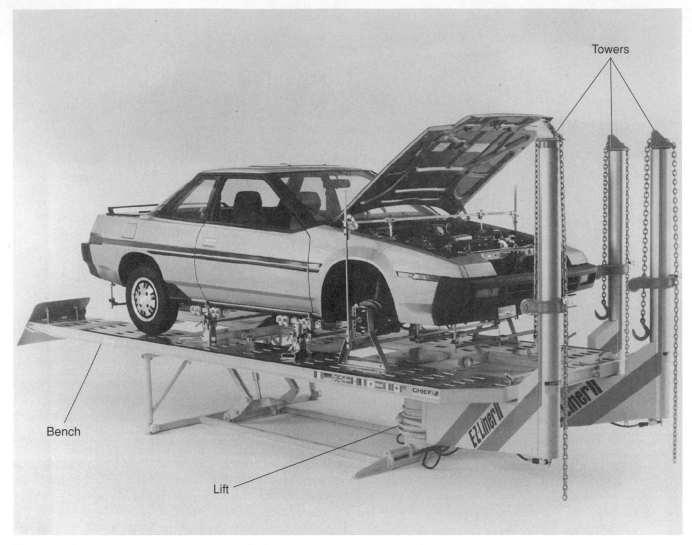

Towers

Bench

Lift

Figure 21–6 Although the specific instructions vary with equipment, the principles of frame or unibody straightening are the same. Note how large clamps are placed under unibody to keep vehicle from moving. Large towers or posts on front of equipment can then be used to pull out damage. Measurement equipment is needed to monitor pull and straightening process *(Chief Automotive Systems, Inc.)*

This eliminates the need for separate anchoring to keep the pulling equipment from sliding under the bench as the pull is made.

> ***Danger!*** *The amount of pulling pressure required to remove damage should not be too high. If the pulling equipment is straining during the pulling process, something is wrong. If this happens, stop pulling! Release tension, and re-evaluate the setup to find the problem. If too much pressure is applied, parts or equipment can be damaged and series injuries could result.*

You should be familiar with a variety of anchoring and pulling systems and their general operation.

In-Floor Straightening Systems

In-floor straightening systems have anchor pots or rails cemented or mounted in the shop floor. Some use *anchor pots* or small steel cups in various locations in the shop floor, Figure 21–7A. Others use a system of steel *anchor rails* in the floor so that an infinite number of pulling-holding locations can be used, Figure 21–7B. Both systems must be balanced both in direction and force of the pull. Look at Figure 21–8.

To provide the pulling force for straightening, the anchor pot system can use hydraulic rams and pulling posts or towers. The floor grid system generally uses hydraulic rams to provide the pulling force.

Figure 21–7 These systems are called in-floor systems because they anchor the vehicle to the shop floor. *(Blackhawk Collision Repair, Inc. Subsidiary of Hein-Werner Corporation.)* A: Anchor pot system uses small steel cups imbedded in shop floor for anchoring vehicle. B: Rail anchoring system uses steel beams in floor for holding vehicle secure while straightening.

Figure 21–8 Anchoring setup must balance holding power as needed for pulling direction and force.

Figure 21–9 Chain tighteners or shorteners are used to remove slack from anchoring chains.

An in-floor system is ideal for a small body shop. After the rams and the other power accessories have been neatly stored away, the area can be used for other body shop purposes. Also in-floor systems provide single or multiple pulls, and positive anchoring without sacrificing shop space.

Anchor clamps are bolted to specific points on the vehicle (unibody pinchwelds for example) to allow the attachment of anchor chains. They distribute pulling force to prevent metal tearing.

The vehicle is usually supported using *cross tube anchor clamps* which link both sides of the vehicle. The cross tube anchor clamps are placed over the cross tube and tightened securely. Chains are then attached to the cross tube anchor clamps.

Anchor chains are attached from the floor anchors to the clamps attached to the vehicle. The anchor chains and clamps must hold the vehicle securely while straightening. *Chain tighteners* or shorteners are used to take slack out of the anchor chains. See Figure 21–9.

Rack Straightening Systems

A *rack straightening system* is generally a drive-on system with a built-in anchoring and pulling mechanism. Most racks tilt hydraulically so that vehicles can either be driven on or pulled into position with a power winch.

A *power winch* normally uses an electric motor and steel cable to provide a means of pulling the damaged vehicle onto the rack. One is shown in Figure 21–10.

Rack straightening systems are generally stationary. They are capable of making multiple pulls. Pulling towers are generally attached to the rack. Depending on the system, there can be two or more

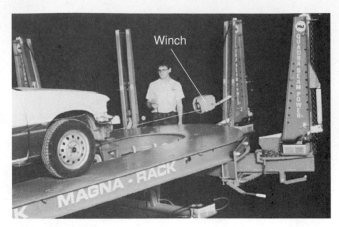

Figure 21-10 Most racks tilt hydraulically so that vehicle can be winched or driven into position. Note winch on this rack. *(Kansas Jack, Division of Hein-Werner® Corporation)*

Figure 21-11 Note basic pulling directions on this rack. *(Kansas Jack, Division of Hein-Werner® Corporation)* A: Hydraulic pulling towers and chains are positioned to force damage upward. B: Pulling towers and chains are positioned to pull downward.

towers. On some systems, the towers can be positioned 360 degrees around the rack. In other systems, the positioning is limited to the front and sides of the rack. See Figure 21–11.

Bench Straightening Systems

A *bench system* is generally a portable or stationary steel table for straightening severe vehicle damage. Some benches tilt. Others have drive-on ramps and the bench can be raised straight up or down as needed. Refer to Figure 21–12.

A *bench-rack system* is a hybrid machine that allows quick loading like a rack and other features of a bench. The table will often tilt like a rack for quick loading of the vehicle. It will also provide the accuracy and convenience of a bench once the vehicle is on the machine.

Straightening system accessories include the various chains, clamps, hooks, adapters, straps, and stands needed to mount various makes and models of vehicles. Some are shown in Figure 21–13.

A *bench computer* can sometimes be provided to assist you in the straightening-measuring process. Shown in Figure 21–14, it can be wired to a main PC (personal computer) for the transfer of data to and from the office. The computer might be used to retrieve body dimension specifications and also do other functions.

An *operating manual* and other publications are provided to give detailed information on using the exact type of straightening equipment properly. You must always refer to these materials when working. They give anchoring and pulling instructions, the accessories needed for each vehicle, and other essential information. See Figure 21–15.

Danger! It is beyond the scope of this text to detail the use of every type of body-frame alignment equipment. Always refer to the manufacturer's instructions when in doubt!

Portable Pullers

A *portable puller* is a hydraulic ram and post mounted on caster wheels. This type of pulling of equipment can be easily rolled around the vehicle to extract damage by means of chains and clamps. It is often used to repair or pull minor damage, Figure 21–16.

Being easily moveable, this equipment can easily set the traction direction to the damage input, Figure 21–17. Many units of this type will only pull in one direction.

1. Lift Jack Assembly
2. Movable Crossmember
3. Pump Action
4. Tower Pinning Holes
5. Tower Pin
6. Front Movable Crossmember
7. Auxiliary Ram Lines
8. Pump Lid
9. Tower Tie Bolt
10. Crossmember Lock

Figure 21–12 Study parts of bench system. *(Chief Automotive Systems, Inc.)*

Other Straightening Equipment

An *engine crane* can be formed on most racks or benches to raise and remove an engine. A bar is added to the post or tower to provide a vertical pulling action for engine removal. Look at Figure 21–18.

An *engine stand* is sometimes needed to hold a power plant after removal from the vehicle. It will hold the engine on small rollaround framework for convenience.

An *engine holder* can be used to support the engine-transmission assembly when the cradle must be unbolted or removed. It rests on the inner fenders and is adjustable in width. A chain(s) is/are used

between the holder and engine to keep it from falling down while working.

A *portable pulling-pushing arm* can be anchored next to the vehicle to remove damage, Figure 21–19. With a pulling/pushing arm, the unit can pivot completely around the end of the bench from the center position on the special flange. In the other positions, it can reach the end and one side of the bench. The unit can also be used anywhere along the side of the bench by hooking the inner clamp on the outer flange on the opposite side.

Portable hydraulic rams or *portable power units* are small piston and cylinder assemblies for removing minor damage. Shown in Figure 21–20, they are possi-

Figure 21–13 Note various accessories used during straightening. (Chief Automotive Systems, Inc.)

Figure 21–15 When using straightening or alignment equipment, always refer to manufacturer's instructions. (Car-O-Liner)

bly the most versatile of all body aligning tools. They can be used to push or pull in restricted areas. Portable power units can spread, clamp, pull, and stretch parts, Figure 21–21. In Figure 21–22, some actual repairs are being done.

MEASURE AS YOU PULL!

As discussed, *vehicle measurement* is done by using specialized tools and equipment to measure the location of reference points on the vehicle. These measurements are then compared to published dimensions

Figure 21–16 Portable puller on wheels allows easy movement around vehicle. It will make single pulls on minor damage quickly. Note how vehicle is anchored to cross tube and stands. (Used with permission of Nissan Motor Corporation)

Figure 21–14 Some alignment equipment uses small computer and keyboard to help speed alignment process. (Car-O-Liner)

Figure 21–17 With portable puller, you can easily set traction or pulling direction. (Used with permission of Nissan Motor Corporation)

Figure 21–18 This pulling tower has been set up to remove engine from vehicle. *(Kansas Jack, Division of Hein-Werner® Corporation.)*

Figure 21–19 Portable pulling-pushing arm anchors to floor. *(Blackhawk Collision Repair, Inc. Subsidiary of Hein-Werner® Corporation.)*

from an undamaged vehicle. After studying damage measurements, straightening equipment can then be used to pull the frame or body back into alignment. See Figure 21–23.

Always measure as you pull! This is critical to competent work. You must monitor how the vehicle is

Figure 21–20 Study parts of portable hydraulic ram system. *(Norco Industries, Inc.)* A: Hydraulic pump is heart of system. When handle is moved up and down, hydraulic pressure flows out hose to various attachments, like ram. B: When using pump, hose should must not face upward or air can enter system. C: Note various attachments for ram. D: Threaded connections and pins hold attachments on ram.

Figure 21–21 Study how portable ram can be used to push, spread, clamp, pull, and stretch damaged parts. *(Blackhawk Collision Repair, Inc., Subsidiary of Hein-Werner® Corporation.)*

reacting to the pulling operation. This will let you modify pulling directions and locations as needed.

The challenge faced by the collision repair industry is to find out which panels are out of place, and in which direction and how far they have moved. Only then can a proper plan be devised to bring the vehicle back to proper dimensions. You must accurately measure and monitor the entire vehicle while pulling. Refer to Figure 21–24.

For example, if you accidentally overpull parts, you may have to replace them. Since replacement was not initially required on the estimate, you may have to do this extra work free of charge. Both you and the shop would lose money and time. Remember! Always measure as you pull!

A vehicle cannot be properly repaired unless all of the reference points are returned to pre-accident dimensions. To achieve this, you must:

1. Measure accurately to analyze damage.

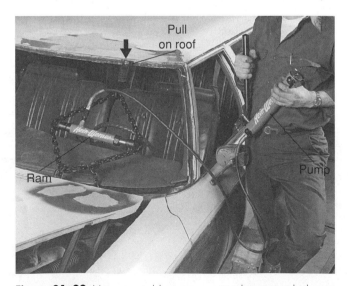

Figure 21–22 Here, portable power unit, chains, and clamps are being used to pull roof lip down so windshield fits properly. *(Hein-Werner® Corporation)*

Figure 21-23 Measurement is vital aspect of straightening. Measurements give you feedback about the progress of the pull. (*Chief Automotive Systems, Inc.*)

Figure 21-25 Measurement is done while pulling to check progress of straightening equipment. (*Chief Automotive Systems, Inc.*)

Figure 21-24 Measurement is done before pulling so you can develop a plan for removing damage. (*Chief Automotive Systems, Inc.*)

2. Measure often when pulling out damage, Figure 21-25.
3. Recheck all measurements after straightening.

PART REMOVAL

A general rule: Remove only the parts that prevent you from getting to the area of the vehicle being repaired. At one time, you had to remove the suspension and drive line completely from a unibody vehicle before putting it on the bench. With most of the current straightening systems, and such accessories as the engine holder, this is no longer necessary. Major straightening operations can be done with major mechanical parts intact.

Depending on the construction of the vehicle and the location and degree of damage, there will be cases where it will be more convenient to remove parts before proceeding with the repair. Carefully analyze the vehicle and the damage to determine what must be removed. It is sometimes best to remove parts before putting the vehicle on the bench. You might have better access to the fasteners.

Take the time to carefully study the locations of engine and transmission mounts, suspension mounts, and whether or not these parts themselves are damaged. See Figure 21-26.

PLANNING THE PULL

When planning the pulling process, the technician should determine the following:

1. The direction of the pulls
2. How to repair the damage in the reverse (first-in, last-out) sequence in which it occurred during the collision
3. Plan the pulling sequence with the pulls in the opposite direction from those that caused the damage
4. The correct attachment points of the pulling clamps
5. The number of pulls required to correct the damage
6. Which parts must be removed to make the pulls

Many times it may be best to draw out the repair plan prior to actually pulling the vehicle. This drawing should show OEM and actual dimensions, anchoring, and pulling locations.

The easiest way to determine where to pull from is to picture the damage being removed by pulling with "your bare hands." The pulling process will work in the exact same manner.

Figure 21-26 Before pulling, you frequently may have to remove some parts so you can properly repair damage. *(Chief Automotive Systems, Inc.)* A: Bumper and other parts over unibody are commonly removed before straightening. B: Technician is removing suspension system so straightening can be done effectively.

Before attempting any repair work, determine exactly the collision procedure that should be taken. A little extra time spent on such an analysis and operational plan can save hours of work.

As a general rule, vehicle straightening is needed whenever the damage involves the suspension, steering, or powertrain mounting points. This, of course, would include situations such as a side collision where the suspension parts and their mountings are not damaged directly, but because of deformation in the center section of the vehicle's structure, the whole body is out of alignment.

Determine whether a particular collision meets this rule either by eye, where there is obvious damage, or by making some general measurements with a tape measure or tram gauge. These would include diagonal measurements to check for diamond and length measurements to check for mash. Try to get as good an idea as possible of where the damage begins and ends. Use all the dimension data available,

including body/frame dimension books, vehicle manufacturer's manuals, or by checking against an undamaged vehicle.

STRAIGHTENING SAFETY

When using aligning equipment, inadequate attention to safety can result in part damage and serious injury.

1. Use the alignment equipment correctly according to the instruction manual.

2. Never allow unskilled or improperly trained personnel to operate aligning equipment.

3. Make sure the rocker panel pinchwelds and chassis clamp teeth are tight.

4. Always anchor the vehicle securely before making a pull. Check that the chassis clamps and anchor bolts are tightened.

5. Always use the size and grade (alloy) chain recommended for pulling and anchoring. Use only the chain supplied with the aligning equipment.

6. Drawing chains must be positively attached to the vehicle and/or anchoring locations so that they will not come off during the pulling operation. Avoid placing chains around sharp corners.

7. Before pulls are made, apply counter supports so you do not pull the vehicle off the bench or rack.

8. Never use a service jack for supporting the vehicle while working on or under it. Always use jack stands for supporting the vehicle.

9. A pull clamp can always slip and cause sheet metal tear. Prevent bodily harm and material damage by always using safety wires.

10. Never stand in line with a chain or clamp. Chain breakage, clamp slippage, or sheet metal tearing could cause injury or damage. Remember, it can be dangerous to work inside the vehicle when pulls are being made.

11. Cover pulling chains with a heavy blanket. If a chain breaks, this will keep the chain from being thrown across the shop.

Before doing any pulling work, protect the body and externally attached parts as follows:

1. Remove or cover interior parts (seats, instruments, carpet).

2. When welding, cover glass, seats, instrument panels, and carpet with a heat-resistant material.

3. Be careful not to scratch or damage parts that do not require painting. If the painted surface is scratched, be sure to repair that portion. Even a

small flaw in the painted surface might cause corrosion and an unhappy customer.

STRAIGHTENING BASICS

Body-over-frame vehicles can usually be straightened and realigned with a series of single-direction pulls. Overpulling or tearing metal was not a very big issue when body metal was thicker. However, this is seldom the case when repairing today's 24-gauge steel.

Remember that a unibody vehicle is designed to spread collision forces throughout the structure. Most unibody repairs demand multiple pulls, which sometimes means four or more pulling points and directions during a single straightening and alignment setup.

Remember! A single, hard pull in one direction on a unibody vehicle can tear the metal before it is straight. Due to the design of today's vehicles, there simply is not enough material available in any one place to transmit sufficient force to complete a repair. Again, as in the anchoring system, the pulling force must be distributed through several attaching points.

Multiple pulls should be used whenever possible, especially when making the initial pulls. This will spread the force of the pull over a larger area to minimize tearing. They will also allow the technician to pull on several areas, and at different angles, at one time. Multiple pulls often make the correction of indirect damage easier. They can be made using one or more pulling posts or towers, hydraulic rams, or adjustable pulling towers on racks or benches.

By first pulling a little, holding the pressure, then pulling on another area, allows damage to be removed in a more controlled manner.

When pulling, DO NOT:

1. Cut away any sheet metal that could possibly be used to attach pulling clamps. The damaged sheet metal is usually the best place to attach pulling clamps.
2. Attach a pull to any suspension or mechanical parts; use only the mounting points.

The most important points to remember when pulling are:

1. Reverse direction and sequence.
2. Use multiple pulls whenever possible.
3. Pull, measure, pull, measure.
4. Always think safety.

ANCHORING PROCEDURES

If there are four anchoring points used during pulling operations, the anchoring points must be able to withstand the total pulling force applied without damaging them. See Figure 21–27. Depending on the angle of the pull, the forces may not be distributed equally. The anchoring points nearest the pull may be loaded more than the others.

Multiple anchoring systems are available in many different designs. The anchoring systems are designed for use on different designs of equipment and type of vehicle to be anchored.

On body-over-frame vehicles, multiple anchoring is accomplished by using chains. The anchoring chains are attached to the frame in the four torque box areas. These are the strongest points on the frame. The other ends of the chain are attached to the bench, rack, floor grid, or anchor pots in the floor.

On most unibody vehicles, multiple anchoring is accomplished using four *pinchweld clamps*, Figure 21–28. The pinchweld clamps are attached to the body

Figure 21–27 When anchoring vehicle, remember that anchoring strength must be equal to or higher than pulling force that will be applied.

Figure 21–28 Unibody cars are anchored using pinchweld clamps. Four are normally used in center section of vehicle. (Car-O-Liner)

at the front and rear of the rocker panel pinchwelds. The bottom of the pinchweld clamps are fastened to the bench or rack, Figure 21–29.

Some floor grid or anchor pot systems use pinchweld clamps and cross tubes. The *cross tubes* pass through the pinchweld clamps and run from one side of the vehicle to the other. They are supported by four safety stands. One safety stand is positioned at each pinchweld clamp location. They are anchored to a floor grid or anchor pots using chains or a lock arm and wedges. This is also called *chainless anchoring.*

Figure 21–29 Pinchweld clamps must be securely tightened to lower underbody of vehicle. Bottom of clamps are fastened to bench. (Chief Automotive Systems, Inc.)

Some unibody vehicles do not have pinchwelds, or they are too weak to withstand pulling forces. These vehicles require the use of a different type of anchoring system that attaches to suspension or mechanical parts mounting locations. Many equipment manufacturers have special anchoring adapters available for these vehicles. If the equipment manufacturer does not have specific anchoring recommendations for the vehicle being repaired, a creative anchoring solution will be needed.

Sandwich clamps can be used to anchor the vehicle if they are installed in areas where there are double or triple layers of structural metal. If anchoring in this manner, always use caution and common sense when anchoring the vehicle. Monitor the anchoring locations closely.

Here are some common cautions and tips to be used when anchoring vehicles:

1. Do not wrap chains around suspension parts.
2. Always remove all slack from anchoring chains prior to pulling.
3. Always follow equipment manufacturer's pinchweld clamp tightening sequences.
4. Always remove all grease and undercoating from the pinchweld flanges and the clamp jaws before installing clamps.
5. Do not use chains that are not designed for pulling and anchoring equipment, for example, tow chains.
6. Make sure that fuel and brake lines will not be crushed by the pinchweld clamps.
7. Follow equipment manufacturer's recommendations for pinchweld clamp locations. Many times the clamp locations are provided on dimension charts so that the clamps do not obstruct the measuring system.

When pulling, make sure that the anchoring force is at least as great as the pulling force being applied. Also, make sure that the pulling force does not exceed the anchoring force. If the pulling force is greater than the anchoring force, anchoring points on the vehicle will be damaged. Monitor the pinchwelds during the entire pulling process. Make sure pinchwelds are not straining, buckling or distorting.

A frame type vehicle can be anchored by placing a suitable plug hook in the fixture holes located on the bottom of the frame rail. Blocking should be used to keep the hook in line with the frame rail. Make an identical hookup on both sides of the vehicle, Figure 21–30.

When anchoring the vehicle in preparation for pulling, lean toward "over anchoring" or "over clamping." An extra anchor point or two takes very little time and surely cannot hurt anything.

Anchoring Body-Over-Frame Vehicles

Figure 21–30 With body-over-frame vehicles, anchoring cannot be done with pinchweld clamps. Since full frame is thick and strong, chains are secured to frame for straightening. *(Blackhawk Collision Repair, Inc., Subsidiary of Hein-Werner® Corporation.)*

WHEEL CLAMPS

Wheel clamps are used to load the suspension with the wheel and tires removed with the vehicle on the rack or bench. They allow you to access parts behind the wheels and tires. They also provide more accurate measurement of body alignment because the suspension is not left hanging unsupported. See Figure 21–31.

After raising the suspension with a jack and removing the wheel, bolt the wheel stand over the lug studs, Figure 21–32. You can then lower the wheel stand onto the surface of the bench or rack.

When anchoring a vehicle, remember that the anchoring force must oppose the pulling force. A good example is a side-front pull illustrated in Figure 21–33.

Figure 21–31 Note use of pinchweld clamps and wheel stands. *(Chief Automotive Systems, Inc.)*

Figure 21–32 If you need to remove wheels and tires, wheel stands are needed to apply load to suspension system so measurements are more accurate. *(Chief Automotive Systems, Inc.)*

**Anchor Chains
Prevent Vehicle
Rotation**

Direction Of Pull

Figure 21-33 Note position of chains for anchoring a front, side pull. This will keep vehicle from rotating. *(Blackhawk Collision Repair, Inc., Subsidiary of Hein-Werner® Corporation.)*

Figure 21-34 Pulling clamps bolt to structure of car. Then, pulling chains can be attached to these clamps. *(Car-O-Liner)*

ATTACHING PULLING CHAINS

Pulling chains transfer pulling force from the straightening equipment to the damaged area on the vehicle. One end of the pulling chain is fastened to the hydraulic ram, post, or tower, and the other end to the pulling clamps or adapters.

Pulling clamps bolt around or onto the vehicle so a pulling chain can be attached to the vehicle, Figure 21-34. After determining where to pull from, the pulling clamps can be attached to any point that can withstand the force of the pull. Examples of where to attach the pulling clamps are:

1. Bumper energy absorber mounts and bolt holes, Figure 21-35
2. Steering, suspension, and mechanical mounting points
3. Damaged sheet metal
4. Weld-on tabs
5. Pinchweld flanges

Do not attach a pull to any suspension or mechanical parts; use only the mounting points.

Body-over-frame vehicles have frames that are ⅛–¼" (3–6 mm) thick. This thick metal can withstand single hard pulls without tearing.

On unibody vehicles the technician must use more care when pulling. Single hard pulls can tear the thin metal. To prevent tearing, multiple pulls should be used. If needed, use more than one clamp to assure that the metal does not tear, Figure 21-36.

Figure 21-35 Note clamps used for this multiple pull. Also note pulley used to produce down-pull. *(Chief Automotive Systems, Inc.)*

Set the pulling clamp so that the line extending along the path of the pulling force passes through the middle of the teeth of the clamp. If this is not done, rotational force will act on the clamp to pull it off, further damaging the section.

Nylon pull straps provide an additional means of making pulls when in difficult areas. They are sometimes used on double pull hook-ups, Figure 21-37.

When you are straightening a bend in a frame rail, make sure the clamp is attached to the correct portion of the rail, as shown in Figure 21-38. This will help stretch and pull out the damage. With this type of dam-

Figure 21–36 Additional clamps should be used when there is a chance that metal tearing will result. *(Blackhawk Collision Repair, Inc., Subsidiary of Hein-Werner® Corporation.)*

- **Pulling Surface A Is Effective.**
- **Pulling Surface B Has Little Effect.**

Damaged Area

Pulling Direction

Figure 21–38 When pulling bent box section, clamp on side of part that is bent. This will help stretch and straighten part better than clamping on other side of box section.

Figure 21–37 Nylon pull straps are handy when you cannot use normal clamping methods. *(Bee Line Co.)*

Straight Pull

Front Side Member

Clamp

Hook

Side Pull

Figure 21–39 When straightening a part, like this front rail, pulling from two directions is efficient method of straightening. Note pulling arm on one pulling chain.

age, you might use a second pulling chain from the side to help straighten the damage. See Figure 21–39.

A *welded-pull tab* can be used if you need to pull where there is no place to attach a clamp. Illustrated in Figure 21–40, weld a small piece of steel plate onto the vehicle unibody where needed. Then, you can bolt the pulling clamp onto the metal tab. After pulling, use an air-cutoff tool to carefully remove the weld without damaging the body.

Pulling adapters are special straightening equipment accessories that allow you to pull in difficult situations. They come in various shapes and sizes for specific tasks.

Strut pulling plates are designed to bolt onto the top of strut towers for pulling. Spacers and hardened

bolts are used to secure the strut pulling plate to the threaded holes in the strut tower. Then, the pulling chain can be attached to the plate. See Figure 21–41.

EXECUTING A PLANNED PULLING SEQUENCE

Mentioned earlier, the overall pulling sequences should be preplanned. However, determining the

Figure 21–40 When you need to pull and there is no place to attach clamps, weld small metal tabs onto body structure. Then, you can attach clamp and chain to metal tab.

proper attachment points and pulling directions should be fine tuned and evaluated as you work. By noting the amount of body displacement and its direction related to alignment reference points, you can adjust pulling direction and force as needed.

Figure 21–41 Special pulling adapters, like this strut tower adapter, are handy when making some pulls. Adapter bolts to top of shock tower from straightening it. Note how collar and roller and tower have been positioned for level, side pull. (*Chief Automotive Systems, Inc.*)

The progress toward alignment should be monitored with the measuring system during the pull. Since the body (sheet metal) has elasticity, the structure will partially return to its postdamaged condition even if the body is pulled back to the prescribed dimensions. Therefore, estimate the amount of return in advance and make allowance for it during the pulling operations.

The pull procedure or sequence simply consists of solving a variety of small problems rolled into one. Find your first problem, and begin working on it. Then, move to the next problem and so on.

Because of the power of the rams, the metal will begin moving as soon as the chain slack is taken up. There is no need to worry whether or not the ram has the capability to move the metal. This frees up the technician to concentrate on the straightening problem.

Simply make the pulls a little at a time, relieve the stress, take a measurement. When using a bench, check how close the fixtures are to their corresponding reference points on the body, and start the sequence again.

Normally, work from the center section outward. First, correct the length. Then, correct side sway damage. Finally, correct height.

Remember! Approach the straightening operation as though it was going to be done with your bare hands. Determine how the metal should be moved to mold it back into shape if the only tools available were your hands. How many areas could be moved at one time and in which directions? This is the key to effective pulling.

Due to the high-strength and heat-sensitive characteristics of the many unibody vehicles, do not attempt to make an alignment or straightening pull in one step. Instead, use a sequence that consists of a pull, hold the pull, more pull, hold, and so on. This will allow more time for working the metal, allow the metal more time to relax, and allow more time for checking the progress of alignment for clamping, repair or reattachment by welding, and so on.

That is, start the hydraulics moving, slowly and carefully. Watch the movement closely. Is it doing what it is supposed to do? If it is on the right track, keep on going. If not, determine why and make the angle or direction adjustment and try again.

PULLING DIRECTIONS

There are a number of setups for pulling and pushing in different directions. We will review the most common ones.

The pulling arrangement with the *vector system* is determined by a simple triangle. By changing the shape of the triangle formed by the pulling equipment and chains, you can alter pulling directions.

The setup shown in Figure 21–42 is used for pulling up and out. The ram, the base unit, and the chain form the triangle. As the ram is extended, one side of the triangle becomes longer. This causes the ram to swing to the right because the chain is locked to the ram. As it swings to its new position, the damaged vehicle is pulled upward and over. Tremendous forces can be exerted in a carefully planned direction using this principle.

Figure 21–43 shows a triangular arrangement that will provide more of a straight out pull. Note that the ram is placed at an angle to the right of true vertical. As force is applied, the ram will swing to the right pulling the damaged sections with it. When setting up a pull, make sure the ram is at the proper height. This can be controlled by adding the proper length of tubing onto the ram.

Remember! At no time should pulling continue if the chain between the ram and the anchor goes beyond perpendicular, Figure 21–43. If this occurs, chain overloading could result because of the added stress placed on the anchored end of the chain. To avoid this condition, be sure that the chain lock head is not placed behind the chain anchor.

As higher, longer pulls are needed, the vector system automatically trades power for motion, Figure 21–44. Some systems allow several feet (meters) of chain travel in one continuous pull. The system can easily pull up, out, or down.

In a typical pull setup at frame rail height, the power ram is set so that the angle between the ram and the pulling chain is equal to the angle between the ram and the anchor. With several tons (Kilograms) of force and a large amount of chain travel, you can easily make lower, tough, structure pulls.

For an out and down pull, less tubing is needed, Figure 21–45A. Another way to make a down pull is to attach a chain between the vehicle and floor anchors. By pulling on the chain bridge, the vehicle is forced down, Figure 21–45B.

A horizontal pull on a rail can be accomplished by placing the ram at about a 45-degree angle, Figure 21–45C.

Upward Pull

A

Outward Pull

B

Figure 21–42 Note how vector or angles of ram and chain alter pulling direction. *(Blackhawk Collision Repair, Inc., Subsidiary of Hein-Werner® Corporation.)* A: Upward pull is produced by this arrangement. B: Straight out pull is produced with this configuration.

Figure 21–43 When setting up equipment, do not allow angle of pull to go beyond 90 degrees or a strain can break pulling chain or other parts. *(Blackhawk Collision Repair, Inc., Subsidiary of Hein-Werner® Corporation.)*

Figure 21–44 Note how changing length of ram tube affects pulling direction. (Blackhawk Collision Repair, Inc., Subsidiary of Hein-Werner® Corporation.)

By adding tubing to the ram, a straight out pull on the cowl can be accomplished, Figure 21–45D.

To pull straight out at the roof line, use the ram with extension tubes as shown in Figure 21–45E.

Upward pulls are very easy to set up, Figure 21–45F. In most cases, the ram is in a vertical position. This pull setup will produce an upward and slightly outward pull.

The same type of setup can be used at roof height by adding extensions to the ram, Figure 21–45G.

Although pushing is not used to the extent it once was in collision damage repair, the capability to push is still important, Figure 21–45H. The vector system provides push capability from any angle around the vehicle by means of a simple triangular setup.

It is also possible to push from underneath the vehicle at whatever angle that is needed, Figure 21–46A. This push setup can be used to effectively remove sag at the cowl area, Figure 21–46B.

OVERPULLING

Overpulling is done by pulling the damage slightly beyond its original dimension. If done in a controlled way, the metal will flex back slightly when tension is released. The body-frame reference points will then line up properly. If done too much, overpulling might not be a correctable error. See Figure 21–47.

Overpulling damage results from failing to measure accurately and often. To prevent overpull damage on unibody vehicles, measure the progress when pulling the damaged area.

Remember, you can stretch a piece of string into a straight line, but there is no way to push it straight

back. On any damaged metal pulled or stretched beyond the critical control dimension, it is difficult to shrink or compress it back. In most instances, the only way the overpulled panel can be repaired is by replacement of body parts. This is a very time consuming, costly mistake.

When pulling damage, the metal will creep or spring back when the pulling tension is released. A slight overpull may be necessary to obtain the desired dimensions. Use the following pulling sequence when intentionally overpulling:

1. Pull the damage.
2. Stress relieve.
3. Release the pulling tension to allow the metal to creep back and become comfortable.
4. Measure.
5. Repeat as needed to obtain the desired dimensions.

The key is to pull and measure during the entire pulling process. Failure to do so can result in an area being overpulled. An overpull occurs to the point where the metal will not spring back.

> **WARNING!** *Never slot bolt holes to obtain alignment of the adjacent parts. This will only hide the problem, not correct it.*

Danger! *Because the force of the pull on a unibody is transmitted through the entire body structure, the technician must use extreme caution when pulling. This includes:*

1. Monitor the anchoring locations during the entire pulling operation.
2. Watch for weld seams that are splitting.
3. Listen for popping sounds. These can indicate welds breaking.
4. Clean the jaws of the clamps prior to installation.
5. Remove any grease or undercoating from the attachment points.
6. Make sure that wires, lines and hoses will not be damaged when pulling.
7. Never stand directly in front of or behind the pulling equipment.
8. Do not overload the pulling equipment. If this happens, release the tension and rethink the pull.
9. Use safety chains, blankets or tarps wrapped over pulling chains to minimize backlash if a chain or clamp lets loose.

A   **Down and Out Pull**

B   **Down Pull Using A Chain "Bridge"**

C   **Straight Pull**

D   **Add Extension Tubes For Higher Pulls**

E   **To Pull At Roof Line, Use Ram With Extension Tubes.**

F   **Up And Outward Pull**

Upward Roof Line Pull

Typical Push Set Up

G

H

Figure 21–45 Study single pull setups. *(Blackhawk Collision Repair, Inc., Subsidiary of Hein-Werner® Corporation.)*

Figure 21–46 Note two setups for pushing. (Blackhawk Collision Repair, Inc., Subsidiary of Hein-Werner® Corporation.) A: Ram is being used to push up and sideways on vehicle. B: With front of frame rails anchored, ram is being used to remove sag at cowl area.

Figure 21–47 Overpulling stretches parts beyond original dimensions. If done in controlled manner, it can speed repairs. If done too much, parts would have to be replaced.

10. Monitor the pressure gauge on the pulling equipment. Refer to manufacturer recommendations for maximum pressure allowed.

ALIGNING FRONT END DAMAGE

First, pull the side member on the replacement side in the direction opposite to the impact direction. Then, repair the fender apron and side member on the repair side. Also, repair the front fender apron and

side member installation areas on the replacement side.

There are many cases where the entire fender apron or side member on the repair side is deflected left or right only. Measure the diagonal dimensions A and B, as shown in Figure 21–48. Then, correct that distance while keeping an eye on the repair condition. The operation can be done efficiently if the fender apron upper reinforcement is pulled at the same time as the side member.

If there is severe bending damage to the side member on the repair side, separate the front crossmember and radiator upper support and repair them separately. Grip the inside face of the side member. While pulling it forward, pull the broken piece from the inside or push it from the outside. After repairing the bent portion, match up the dimensions to the standard diagonal dimensions.

To repair the other front fender apron and side member area, the main repairs are near the dash panel and the cowl panel. If the impact was severe, the damage will extend into the front body pillar (the door would fit poorly in this case). Simply gripping the front edge of the side member of the fender apron and pulling will not repair this major damage, Figure 21–49A. In this case, cut the fender apron and side member near the installation area, clamp near the major panel damage, and pull (keep an eye on the door fit conditions).

At the same time that the pillar is being pulled forward, pushing can be done from the interior side with a power ram, Figure 21–49B.

During front body aligning, confirm pulls by measuring the dimensions at reference holes. This is often done at the front floor reinforcement and rear of the front fender installation holes.

If the impact to the front side member structure is severe, there is a tendency for it to take the shape shown in Figure 21–50. The height of the standard measuring point might be distorted. Further, the front

Figure 21–48 As you pull out front damage, measure your progress.

Pulling The Damaged Portion Of The Cowl, Upper and Front Pillar

Pulling The Damaged Portion Of The Dash Panel

A

Pushing With a Portable Ram Power

Pulling The Front Body Pillar

B

Figure 21–49 With major front damage, you may have to cut away damaged parts so you can pull near cowl area. A: With fender apron cut off, attach clamps next to cowl and pull. B: Pulling at cowl and pushing from behind with portable power unit may be needed.

side member often has a reference point in the rear that has a tendency to be deflected upward when damaged. See Figure 21–51.

To correct lateral bending damage of the front, the clamping point receiving the greatest force is point B

Damage

Input

The Height Of The Reference Hole Drops

Figure 21–50 During this front collision, frame rail has been pushed back and down.

Damage

Input

Reference Point At Rear Of Member Is Deflected Upward

Figure 21–51 During this front collision, frame rail has been pushed back and up.

A

C

D

B

E

Traction Direction

Figure 21–52 Note setup and pull for correcting lateral damage. Blocking devices should be used to link side rails together.

in Figure 21–52, which must be clamped securely. If point C is not secured, point A cannot be pulled. A blocking device should be used at points D and E. Holding devices should also be placed across the underbody to help transmit pulling force to both sides of the vehicle.

REAR DAMAGE REPAIRS

Usually, the rear bumper is impacted during rear-end collisions. The impact force will usually propagate through the ends of the rear side members or nearby panels. The rear collision will also cause damage to the kick-up area. The wheelhousings may deform causing the entire quarter panel to move forward. If the impact is severe enough, it will have an effect on the roof, door panels, and center body pillar.

Attach clamps or hooks to the rear portion of the rear side member, rear floor pan, or quarter panel rear end portion, Figure 21–53. Pull while measuring the dimensions of each part of the underbody and door openings. As you pull, inspect panel fit and part clearances.

Figure 21-53 Pulling rear damage is not as complex in most instances because you do not have to deal with steering and engine. *(Kansas Jack, Division of Hein-Werner® Corporation)*

Figure 21-54 Here, portable unit is being used to pull badly damaged quarter to repair door opening. After pulling, quarter panel will be replaced. *(Wedge Clamp International, Inc.)*

Relieve the stress in the quarter panel by pulling on the side member only. If the wheelhousing or the roof side inner panel is clamped and pulled along with the rear side member, the clearances with the door panel can be corrected. See Figure 21-54.

With rear structure twist from a front impact, the rear lower preliminary pulling will restore some of the lower alignment points. Moving forward with subsequent pulls, the alignment and number of anchoring points will, of course, move right along with them.

After pulling, sections too damaged for repairs and requiring replacement can be cut away at this time.

SIDE DAMAGE ALIGNING

If there is a severe impact to the center of the rocker panel, the floor pan will deform. The entire body will take on a curved shape, like a "banana." To align this type of damage, use a method similar to straightening a piece of bent wire. The two ends of the body are pulled apart and the side that is caved in is pulled outward. This can often be fixed with three-way pulling, Figure 21-55.

Anchoring unitized body vehicles for side pulls can be very difficult due to the limited chain hook-up areas, Figure 21-56. When making a side pull on the end of a vehicle, the center section can be anchored by passing a chain around the pinchweld clamp and hooking to the edge of the bench. Tension/anchoring can be applied by attaching the pull chain to the pinchweld clamp.

The portable beam and knee can be used as a side anchor with either inside or outside contact, Figure 21-57. By attaching the pull chain to the portable beam and knee, it can be used as a pulling attachment.

It is advisable to make an end-to-end stretch pull when pulling outward on the center section of a vehicle. This is shown in Figure 21-58.

If pulling high on the body, tie the vehicle down on the opposite side, Figure 21-59.

CORRECTING SAG

Blocking under the low area and pulling down on the high end will correct sag. The vehicle must also be tied down to the straightening system at the opposite end.

Anchoring the high portion of the vehicle to the straightening system with chains and pushing up at the low spot will also remove the sag, Figure 21-60.

Figure 21-55 For inside damage, you may have to pull in three directions as shown. *(Used with permission of Nissan Motor Corporation)*

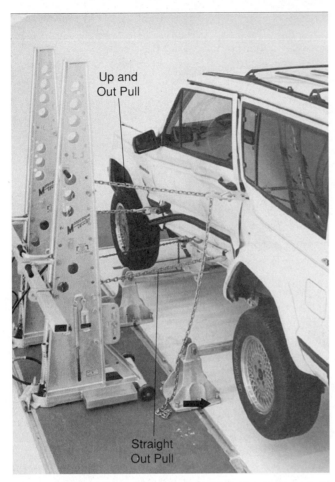

Figure 21–56 Multiple pulls are being used to correct side damage. *(Wedge Clamp International, Inc.)*

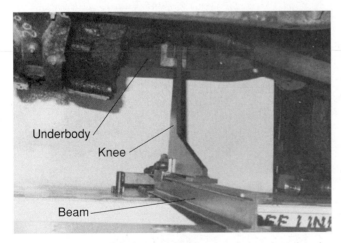

Figure 21–57 Portable beam and knee has been placed under vehicle to aid pulling. *(Bee Line Co.)*

Figure 21–58 Here, equipment is being used to make end-to-end stretch pull. *(Bee Line Co.)*

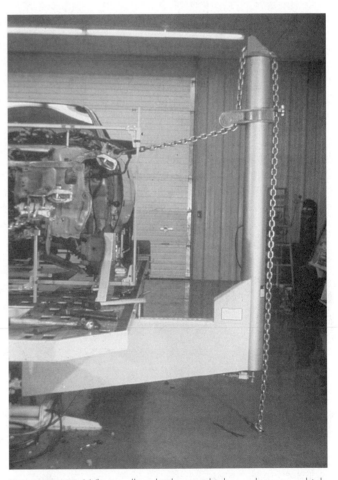

Figure 21–59 When pulling high on vehicle, make sure vehicle is anchored securely. *(Chief Automotive Systems, Inc.)*

When using the pulley and base for the downward pull, the tower pull chain must be in lowest position.

Sag can also occur at the front frame crossmember. The ends of the crossmember will be closer than normal and the center will be too low. This condition can be corrected by using three hydraulic rams and two chains. Look at Figure 21–61.

DIAMOND CORRECTION

To pull a diamond condition, place a pulling tower or ram on each end of the bench base on opposite sides.

A

B

Figure 21–60 Sag is common problem with front end impacts. *(Bee Line Co. and Chief Automotive Systems, Inc.)* A: Hydraulic jack has been placed under low spot on vehicle. B: By anchoring front section, jack will push up and remove sag out cowl area.

Figure 21–61 Note typical method for correcting crossmember sag. *(Blackhawk Collision Repair, Inc., Subsidiary of Hein-Werner® Corporation.)*

Adjust chain height and attach chains to vehicle as described for end pull corrections. Block or anchor one side of vehicle to prevent side movement. Activate the pull ram while measuring the results.

STRESS RELIEVING

Stress is defined in metallurgical books as the internal resistance a material offers to being deformed when subjected to a specific load (force). In the industry, *part stress* can be defined as the internal resistance a material offers to corrective techniques. This resistance or stress can be caused by:

1. Deformation
2. Overheating
3. Improper welding techniques

Indicators of stress include:

1. Misaligned door, hood, trunk, and roof openings, Figure 21–62
2. Dents and buckles in aprons and rails
3. Misaligned suspension and motor mounts
4. Damaged floor pans and rack and pinion mounts
5. Cracked paint and undercoating
6. Pulled or broken spot welds
7. Split seams and seam sealer

Stress relieve locked-up metal by hammering and/or heating while pulling, Figure 21–63. First, mark the creases or folds to make them more visible, Figure 21–64. Pull the damaged metal to tension, then loosen it up with hammering and heat if needed. Increase the tension and loosen it again. See Figure 21–65.

If some of the buckles are folded so tightly that they threaten to tear, it might be necessary to use a little heat. However, use heat carefully.

Only heat on the corners and double panels where there is sufficient strength. Use heat carefully and as a

Figure 21–62 These are signs of stress and deformation.

**Grain Begins To Relax And Return
To Its Original State Relieving Stress.**

Figure 21–63 Stress can be relieved with hammering and/or heat.

Figure 21–64 Mark creases so they are more visible before pulling. (Chief Automotive Systems, Inc.)

Figure 21–65 Technician is hammering on stress areas with pulling force applied. (Chief Automotive Systems, Inc.)

means of releasing locked-up metal. Do not use heat as a means to soften up an area. Although a heat torch is not recommended on HSS metals, it can sometimes be used with care. Refer to Figure 21–66.

If the damage requires the use of heat, follow the manufacturer's recommendations. Their instructions

Figure 21–66 Controlled heat can also be used to remove stress. (Chief Automotive Systems, Inc.)

will be written for the exact metal composition of the vehicle.

Never attempt to cool the heated area by using water or compressed air. Allow it to cool naturally. Rapid cooling can cause the metal to become hard and, in some cases, brittle.

The best way to monitor heat applications is with a *heat crayon, thermal melt stick,* or *themal paint.* Stroke or mark the cold piece with the crayon. When the stated temperature has been reached, the mark will liquefy. Heat crayons are quite precise and far more accurate than the common body shop technique of watching for specific color change.

STRESS CONCENTRATORS

Stress concentrators are designed into unibody vehicles to control and absorb collision forces, minimize structural damage, and increase occupant protection. They result in a localized concentration of stress as a load is applied. See Figure 21–67.

Do not remove designed stress concentrators. Follow the vehicle manufacturer's recommendations for straightening or replacement of parts that have designated stress concentrators.

A quality repair can be achieved only if function, durability, and appearance have been restored. When stress is not removed, the following possibilities can occur:

1. Fatigue caused by loading and unloading of suspension and steering part.

2. In the event of a second similar collision, less force is required to cause the same or greater damage. This could jeopardize the occupants of the vehicle.

3. The vehicle can dimensionally distort causing handling problems.

Stress Concentrators

Figure 21–67 *Stress concentrators are often designed into unibody structure.*

FINAL ALIGNMENT CHECKS

Once the repair is completed, including all straightening and welding operations, the alignment procedures are ready for a final check. If the vehicle was repaired without using fixtures, final measurements should be made and compared to the body/frame dimensions book.

Begin the final checks by slowly walking around the vehicle looking for obvious signs of misalignment. Large gaps between the roof lines and doors are a good sign that small amounts of damage are still present. If fixtures or jigs were used, go back and check all the fixture control points. Do they still line up true, without having to force or hammer the fixture?

Review the repair order or estimate to be sure everything was done. It is easier to make additional pulls now rather than waiting until more steps have been completed and then finding additional damage.

Among other items that should be carefully inspected are:

1. Check down low at the alignment between the door and rocker sill. This should be a straight and narrow gap.

2. Check the general alignment of all the upper body areas. Make sure everything looks as though nothing was ever out of alignment.

3. Open and close the doors and deck lid. Do they feel tight and secure when latched? Make sure they close smoothly and open easily.

Summary

- Vehicle straightening involves the use of high-powered hydraulic equipment, mechanical clamps, chains, and a measuring system to bring the frame back to its original shape.

- Straightening equipment includes anchoring equipment, pulling equipment, hydraulic rams, and pulling posts.

- Stress is the internal resistance a material offers to being deformed when subjected to a specific force. It can be caused by: deformation, overheating, or improper welding techniques.

- Indicators of stress include: misaligned doors; dents in aprons and rails; cracked paint and undercoating; and split seams and seam sealer.

- Once repairs are complete, it is time for a final alignment check. All measurements must be checked against factory specifications to ensure quality work.

Technical Terms

pulling	*engine holder*
single pull method	*portable power unit*
multiple pull method	*dedicated bench*
composite force	*fixtures*
straightening equipment	*pinchweld clamps*
anchoring equipment	*transport slots*
pulling equipment	*wheel clamps*
hydraulic rams	*pulling clamps*
pulling posts	*welded-pull tab*
anchor pots	*pulling adapters*
anchor rails	*strut pulling plate*
anchor clamps	*vector system*
rack straightening	*overpulling*
system	*overpulling damage*
power winch	*part stress*
bench system	*stress relieving*
bench computer	*heat crayon*
portable puller	*stress concentrators*
engine crane	

Review Questions

1. Which of the following is not an in-floor system?
   a. Anchor-pot system

b. Modular rail systems
c. Chainless anchoring system
d. None of the above

2. Technician A says that in-floor systems provide fast hookup and positive anchoring without sacrificing space. Technician B says that in-floor systems cannot perform multiple pulls.
Who is correct?
a. Technician A
b. Technician B
c. Both A and B
d. Neither A nor B

3. Technician A says that it is necessary to have at least four reference points on the undamaged part of the vehicle that can be used to set the vehicle up properly on the bench. Technician B says a straightening system should be used whenever the damage involves the suspension, steering, or powertrain mounting points.
Who is correct?
a. Technician A
b. Technician B
c. Both A and B
d. Neither A nor B

4. Generally, how should you apply pulling force to a damaged vehicle?

5. Portable hydraulic rams have the capability to:
a. Pull
b. Push
c. Spread
d. All of the above

6. Technician A always removes the suspension and driveline completely from a unibody vehicle before putting it on the bench. Technician B says that single-pull systems cannot be used on unibody vehicles.
Who is correct?
a. Technician A
b. Technician B
c. Both A and B
d. Neither A nor B

7. When anchoring a unibody vehicle in preparation for pulling, Technician A leans toward "over anchoring." Technician B sometimes temporarily welds a piece of steel to a section.
Who is correct?
a. Technician A
b. Technician B
c. Both A and B
d. Neither A nor B

8. Define the term "anchoring equipment."

9. Define the term "pulling equipment."

10. Why are anchor clamps used instead of hooks when pulling?

11. Technician A says that in most instances the only way the overpull panel can be repaired is by replacement. Technician B says heat can be used to correct an overpull.
Who is correct?
a. Technician A
b. Technician B
c. Both A and B
d. Neither A nor B

12. When should the repair or replacement of severely damaged sections that cannot be restored by the pulling operation take place?

13. Which of the following is true?
a. Cracked paint and undercoating is a sign of stress.
b. Most of the stress relieving will be "cold work."
c. The best way to monitor heat applications is with a heat crayon.
d. All of the above

14. How is a power winch used in a body shop.

15. When planning the pulling process, list six rules to remember.

16. List eleven basic safety rules for pulling out damage.

17. What are the four most important points to remember when pulling?

18. On most unibody vehicles, multiple anchoring is accomplished using four _____ _____.

19. _____ _____ _____ are designed to bolt onto the top of shock towers for pulling.

20. What are stress concentrators?

Activities

1. Visit a body shop. Observe an experienced technician using straightening equipment. Write a report on your visit.

2. Read the operating manuals for different types of straightening equipment. Compare their differences and similarities.

3. Inspect several badly damaged vehicles. Write a report on what repairs would have to be made.

OTHER OPERATIONS

CHAPTER 22

REPLACING STRUCTURAL PARTS, CORROSION PROTECTION

Objectives

After studying this chapter, you should be able to:

- List parts of the vehicle which are considered structural.

- List the steps necessary for replacing a part along factory seams.

- Describe how spot welds are separated.

- Explain how new body panels can be positioned on a vehicle body.

- List the steps for welding new body panels in place.

- Describe how to install foam panel fillers.

- Section rails, rocker panels, A- and B-pillars, floor pans, and trunk floors.

- Define corrosion and describe the common factors in rust formation.

- Identify the principal methods of corrosion protection.

- Choose the correct anti-corrosion materials and equipment.

- List common types of seam sealers and explain where each should be used.

- Explain why I-CAR recommends against front full body sectioning.

Introduction

Most accidents will involve at least some parts replacement. While many parts on a vehicle add to its structural integrity, some parts play a greater role. These parts are known as structural parts. *Structural parts* can be defined as those parts of the vehicle which:

1. Support the weight of the vehicle
2. Absorb collision energy
3. Absorb road shock

The illustration in Figure 22–1 shows parts which are generally considered to be structural. These parts include:

1. Radiator core support
2. Front rails
3. Strut towers
4. Rocker panels
5. A-pillar (hinge pillar)
6. B-pillar (center pillar)
7. Rear rails
8. Rear strut towers
9. Suspension cross-member

Restoring corrosion is also a vital aspect of collision repair. Failing to do so can result in major structural failure. Corrosion of structural parts can severely impair the handling and crash worthiness of the vehicle. This damage might NOT be evident until an accident, but then it will be too late.

NOTE! FOR COMPLETE COMPREHENSION OF THE INFORMATION IN THIS CHAPTER, YOU SHOULD HAVE ALREADY STUDIED CHAPTER 9, WELDING AND CUTTING.

Figure 22–1 Note typical structural parts of vehicle.

REPAIR OR REPLACE GUIDELINES

The decision to repair or replace a structural part will be based on the judgment and skill of the technician/appraiser. A simple rule is:

If the part is bent, repair it.
If the part is kinked, replace it.

Whenever possible and practical, the part should be repaired rather than replaced. See Figure 22–2.

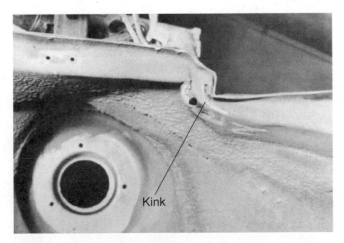

Figure 22–2 This badly kinked part would require replacement. It is too severely damaged for straightening.

TYPES OF STRUCTURAL REPLACEMENTS

Structural replacement can take one of two forms: replacement at factory seams and sectioning.

Replacement of panels along *factory seams* (end or edge of panel) should be done when practical and economical. The result is almost identical to factory production in both strength and appearance. Replacement of damaged parts along factory seams is common practice in collision repair. Parts should be replaced along factory seams whenever it is practical and possible.

Sectioning involves cutting the part in a location other than a factory seam. This might or might NOT be a factory-recommended practice. Special care must be taken. Sectioning a part should be analyzed to make sure it will NOT jeopardize structural integrity.

There are three general types of structural parts:

1. Closed sections, such as rocker panels, front rails, A-, and B-pillars
2. Hat channels, such as rear rails
3. Single layer, flat parts, such as floor pans and trunk floors

Most manufacturers have specific recommendations for parts replacement. Always follow the procedures described in the body repair manual.

When planning to section a structural part:

1. Check the body repair manual for model specific sectioning procedures.

2. If specific sectioning recommendations do NOT exist, follow the general guidelines presented here. Body repair manuals are available through various publishers and dealerships.

Keep in mind that the vehicle must be returned to pre-accident condition. Failure to restore pre-accident crushability may affect future air bag deployment, leading to liability exposure.

When choosing a sectioning location, look for a uniform area with enough clearance to perform welding operations.

You should not section in or near:

1. Suspension mounting locations

2. Structural part mounting locations

3. Dimensional reference holes

4. Compound shapes

5. Reinforcements (except as noted)

6. Compound structures

7. Collapse/crush zones

8. Engine or drivetrain mounting locations.

DETERMINING SPOT WELD POSITIONS

To start removal of a structural panel, you usually must first locate all factory spot welds. Remove the paint film, sealer, or other coatings covering the joint area to find the spot welds.

One way to do this is to scorch the paint film with a propane torch and remove it with a wire brush. Because propane has a cooler flame than oxyacetylene, it is the best choice for loosening the paint film. A coarse wire wheel or brush attached to a drill can be used to remove the paint, sealers, and other coatings.

Scrape off thick portions of undercoating or seam sealer before scorching the paint. Do NOT burn through the paint film so that the sheet metal panel begins to turn color. Heat the area enough only to soften the paint and then brush or scrape it off. It is NOT necessary to remove paint from areas where the spot welds are visible through the paint film.

In areas where the spot weld locations are NOT visible after the paint is removed, carefully drive a chisel between the panels. Doing so will cause an outline of the spot welds to appear.

SEPARATING SPOT WELDS

After the spot welds have been located, there are several methods of separating them. You can use a hole saw, compound drill bit, conventional drill bit, cutoff tool, or spot weld cutting tool. Regardless of which is used, be careful NOT to cut into the lower panel if it is to be used. Also be sure to cut out the spot welds without creating an excessively large hole.

If needed, center punch each spot weld before drilling. This will keep the bit from wandering. See Figure 22–3.

Make sure the bits are sharp, and use the same pressure on the drill as if you were drilling mild steel. The speed at which the bit turns should be slower

A

B

Figure 22–3 After removing paint hiding any spot welds, they can be easily seen and removed. *(Used with permission of Nissan Motor Corporation)* A: Center punching will help drill stay in center of spot welds. B: Use drill to cut out spot weld. Do not drill through lower panel if it is to be reused.

than for mild steel. This will keep the heat from affecting the metal.

Figure 22–4 shows how a cutoff tool can be used to remove spot welds.

After the spot welds have been removed, drive a chisel between the panels to separate them. Be careful NOT to cut or bend the undamaged panel. Look at Figure 22–5.

Remember! A chisel should never be used by itself to remove spot welds. This will create excessive damage to adjacent panels.

SEPARATING CONTINUOUS WELDS

In some vehicles, panels are joined by continuous MIG welding. Since the welding bead is long, use a grinding wheel or cutoff tool to cut through the weld. Be careful NOT to cut into or through the undamaged panels. Hold the cutoff tool at a 45-degree angle to the joint. After grinding through the weld, use an air chisel to separate the panels. Look at Figure 22–6.

Figure 22–4 Cutoff tool provides another way of removing spot welds holding panels. A: Carefully hold cutoff tool over spot weld to grind it away. B: Stop grinding when you have cut down to lower panel.

SEPARATING BRAZED AREAS

Brazing may be used at the ends of outer panels or at the joints of the roof and body pillars to improve finish quality. Depending upon the type of brazing, brazed joints can be removed with a torch or by cutting.

Figure 22–5 Only after removing spot welds can you use chisel to separate panels. *(Mustang Monthly Magazine)*

Figure 22–6 Cutoff tool is often used to separate panels joined by arc brazing. Carefully cut along weld bead. Do not cut into panel underneath.

To separate soft brazed areas, melt the brazing metal with a torch. Use moderate heat to protect the undamaged panels. In areas where arc brazing is used, the fusion temperature of the brazing metal is higher than with ordinary brazing. This type requires too much heat for melting with a torch. Areas that are arc brazed should be separated by grinding.

NOTE! ORDINARY BRAZING CAN BE DISTINGUISHED FROM ARC BRAZING BY THE COLOR OF THE BRAZING METAL. ORDINARY BRAZED AREAS ARE THE COLOR OF BRASS. ARC-BRAZED AREAS ARE A REDDISH COPPER COLOR.

PREPARING VEHICLE FOR NEW PANEL

Always refer to the appropriate body repair manual for the type and placement of welds. The manual will also give other details for the specific vehicle.

After removal of the damaged panels, prepare the vehicle for installation of the new panels:

1. Grind off the welding marks, Figure 22–7. Use a wire brush to remove dirt, rust, paint, sealers, and so on from the joint surfaces. Zinc coatings should NOT be removed.

2. Remove paint and undercoating from the backsides of the panel joining surfaces on parts that will be spot welded during installation.

3. Smooth the mating flanges with a hammer and dolly.

Figure 22–7 After removing damaged panel, carefully grind and smooth small beads left from spot welds. *(Mustang Monthly Magazine)*

4. Apply weld-through primer to areas where bare metal is exposed.

PREPARING REPLACEMENT PANEL

Since all new parts are coated with primer, it is important that this coating be removed from the flanges to allow the welding current to flow properly. Also, holes for plug welds must be drilled precisely.

To prepare a replacement panel for welding, follow these steps:

1. Use a disc sander to remove the paint from both sides of the spot weld area. Do NOT grind into the panel. Do NOT heat it too much. You do NOT want the panel to turn blue or warp.

> *WARNING! Whenever possible, grind so that sparks fly down and away. Always wear proper eye protection when grinding.*

2. Apply weld-through primer to the welding surfaces where the zinc coating was removed.

3. Drill holes for plug welding. Always refer to the body repair manual for the size of plug weld holes. Always be sure to duplicate the location and number of spot welds used at the factory.

4. Be sure all plug weld holes are of the proper diameter. If a recommended hole size is NOT given in the repair manual, drill $\frac{5}{16}$ inch (8 mm) holes.

5. If the new panel is sectioned to overlap any of the existing panels, rough cut the new panel to size using an air saw or a cut-off wheel. The edges should overlap the portion of the remaining panel by $\frac{3}{4}$ to 1 inch (19 to 25 mm).

Remember! If the overlap portion is too large, it will make positioning of the panel difficult. If the overlap is too small, structural integrity will suffer.

POSITIONING NEW PANELS

Aligning new panels is a very important step in repairing unibody vehicles. Improperly aligned panels will affect both the appearance and quality of the repaired vehicle.

Use a measuring system to determine the installation position. Remember that the fit of the new and old parts must be within specifications. Whether

Figure 22-8 If they are provided, align any marks on new panel with ones on vehicle. *(Used with permission of Nissan Motor Corporation)*

structural or cosmetic panels are being replaced, proper measurement and fit are critical.

Panel alignment marks can be provided to help position parts before welding. Some are shown in Figure 22–8.

Once you have the part in relative position, use locking pliers to hold it in place. Measure the position of the panel and adjust its location if needed. Refer to Figure 22–9.

Figure 22-9 Locking pliers are commonly used to hold panel in position. *(© American Honda Motor Co., Inc.)*

> *WARNING! All measurements must be accurate before welding body panels in position.*

Panel Positioning and Measurement

The vehicle must be properly positioned on the bench before the new panel can be correctly aligned. All straightening must be done before replacing panels. Otherwise, proper alignment of the new panels will be impossible.

As an example of a typical procedure for structural part replacement, we will describe the replacement of a front fender apron, front crossmember, and radiator core support.

1. Match the assembly reference marks on the installation areas of the front fender apron and the rail. Secure them with locking pliers. Parts that have no assembly reference marks should be positioned in the same location as the old parts.

2. Align the parts by measuring the length between reference points. Temporarily install the front crossmember by tack welding one spot. Make any length adjustments by light tapping. Use a hammer against a wood block to adjust the panel without damage, Figure 22–10A.

Figure 22–10 Carefully measure and position panel before welding. A: Use wood block and light blows to adjust panel as needed. B: Jack is sometimes handy for supporting panel. Use measuring system to check panel positioning. C: Measure lower diagonal and width dimensions. D: Note basic method for measuring fender apron dimensions. E: After inner part, apron in this example, is secured, install next component, radiator support. F: Measure each component's location before final welding.

3. Mark a positioning line at the end of the part that is NOT welded. Use locking pliers to hold the parts together. You can also drill small holes and fasten them together with sheet metal screws. Mark a line on the apron area but do NOT weld the panels together.

4. Use measuring system to match the height of the new parts to the parts on the opposite side of the vehicle, Figure 22–10C. Support the new parts with a hydraulic jack to make sure that the height does NOT change at all.

5. Measure the lower diagonal and width dimensions, Figure 22–10C. Support the parts with a hydraulic jack so that the height does NOT change. Then, adjust the rail as needed to obtain the correct dimensions. Confirm the height dimensions again.

6. Take care to position the front crossmember so that both the left and right ends are uniform.

7. Once the dimensions of the rail match the dimensions found on the dimension chart, secure the part in place. The suspension crossmember can also be installed with fixtures. Use a sufficient number of plug welds to fasten the joining area of the rail to the front crossmember.

8. Make sure that the apron's upper length has NOT changed. Confirm by checking for shifting of the marked line.

9. Measure the diagonal dimensions between the fender rear installation hole and the strut tower hole or fender front installation hole, Figure 22–10D.

10. Measure the width dimension of the strut tower and the front fender bolt hole and fasten them together. If the width dimension does NOT match the body dimension manual, make a small adjustment. Be careful of changes in diagonal dimensions. Temporarily install and fasten the radiator upper support and the radiator support, Figure 22–10E.

11. Measure the rail width dimensions. Set the measuring system to the proper measurement and adjust the apron as needed. Lightly fasten the support with locking pliers and tap it softly by hand to move it in place.

Figure 22–11 Follow all safety rules when welding a panel. *(Mustang Monthly Magazine)*

12. Measure the diagonal dimensions for the side supports, Figure 22–10F. Be sure these dimensions match.

13. Temporarily install the front fender and inspect it for proper fit with the door and hood. If the clearance is NOT correct, it might be because the fender apron or the rail height is NOT correct.

14. Measure as previously described, and verify the overall dimensions once more before welding.

WELDING NEW PANELS

When satisfied with the position and dimensions of the new panel, it can be permanently welded in place,

Figure 22–11. Under ideal circumstances, the general welding procedure for panels should be:

1. Apply weld-through primer to bare metal surfaces.

2. Clamp parts in place.

3. Tack weld parts in position.

4. Remeasure part positions.

5. Plug weld parts in final position.

6. Grind cosmetic weld surfaces.

Remember that it is very important to duplicate exactly the location and number of original factory spot welds.

SECTIONING

As mentioned, sectioning involves cutting and replacing panels at locations other than factory seams. When body parts need to be replaced, replacing them at factory seams is the logical first choice. However, this is impractical when many seams have to be separated in undamaged areas. In some repairs, sectioning of parts such as rails, pillars, and rocker panels may be required to make their repair economically feasible. See Figure 22–12.

Remember that sectioning requires precision, as well as strict adherence to recommended procedures. Always check the body repair manual for the manufacturer's procedure for the specific sectioning location.

As a collision repair technician, never forget that sectioning finally comes down to sound judgment. It

Figure 22–12 Note common sectioning areas on vehicle.

is the technician who must assure the quality of the repair through the proper application of tested and proven procedures.

Unibody parts to be sectioned involve these types of construction:

1. Closed sections, such as rocker panels and A- and B-pillars

2. Hat or open U-channels, such as rear rails

3. Single layer or flat parts, such as floor pans and trunk floors

With structural parts, it is best to treat them all like high-strength steel. Then you do NOT have to identify every piece of high-strength steel. Also, you can use a MIG welder on all repairs.

Using New Versus Recycled Assemblies

Recycled assemblies are undamaged parts from another damaged vehicle that are used for repairs. The use of recycled assemblies in collision repair makes sense for a number of reasons:

1. Fewer welds need to be made when using recycled assemblies compared to new, separate parts.

2. Less factory corrosion protection is disturbed.

3. More measuring is required when welding separate new parts and attaching them to the vehicle.

4. There is an abundance of recycled assemblies available in most areas.

Section Locations

When deciding where to section, look for an area with a uniform cross section. Check the body repair manuals and bulletins provided by the vehicle manufacturers. Much of this literature provides specific instructions on how and where to section.

Sectioning Joint Types

There are three basic types of sectioning joints. They are the:

1. Lap joint

2. Offset butt joint

3. Butt joint with insert

Lap

Offset Butt

Butt With Insert

Types Of Joints

Figure 22–13 These are the three basic types of joints used for sectioning. *(I-CAR)*

A - Pillars

B - Pillars

Rocker Panels

Rails

Figure 22–14 A butt joint with an insert produces a very strong repair.

One of these joints, or a combination of these joints, will be used for all sectioning procedures. The type of joint used for a specific repair will depend upon the location and design of the structural part. See Figure 22–13.

A butt joint with insert is used mainly on closed sections, such as rocker panels, A- and B-pillars, and rails. *Inserts* make it easy to fit and align the joints correctly. They also help make the welding process easier.

Another basic joint is an *offset butt joint* without an insert. This type is also known as a *staggered butt joint.* The staggered butt joint is used on A- and B-pillars and front rails.

The third type is a lap joint which is used on rear rails, floor pans, trunk floors, and B-pillars.

The configuration and makeup of the part being sectioned might call for a combination of joint types. Sectioning a B-pillar, for instance, might require the use of an offset cut with a butt joint in the outside piece and a lap joint in the inside piece. See Figure 22–14.

Using Lap Joints. Lap joints are used on floor pans, trunk floors, rear rails and other flat or hat channel shaped parts.

When welding lap joints:

1. Parts should be overlapped at least 1 inch (25 mm) if NOT otherwise specified. Refer to Figure 22–15.

2. Use plug welds in the overlap area. Weld from the top piece down.

3. Close the bottom edge with a continuous weld bead.

4. Seal lap joints in floor pans and trunk floors to prevent water and fumes from entering.

Using Offset Butt Joints. Offset butt joints are used for closed sections such as A- and B-pillars. They are used on B-pillars to avoid disturbing the D-ring anchor. Offset butt joints are also used where three or more pieces join in the construction of a part, making it difficult or impossible to use an insert.

Using Butt Joint with Insert. The butt joint with insert is used on closed sections such as: rocker panels, A-pillars, B-pillars, and front rails. Look at Figure 22–16.

The insert is made from a section of either the replacement or damaged part, Figure 22–17. The insert is used for these reasons:

Figure 22–15 Lap joints should overlap about an inch (25 mm). Use both plug and continuous welds to join parts. *(I-CAR)*

1. It provides a backing for the MIG butt weld.
2. It keeps burn-through to a minimum.
3. It ensures a completely closed joint.
4. It aligns the parts for the best possible fit.

An insert should be twice the width of the cross section. For example, if the widest dimension is 2 inches (50 mm), the insert should be 4 inches (100 mm) long.

NOTE! WHEN SECTIONING FRONT AND REAR RAILS, DO NOT PUT INSERTS IN COLLAPSE AREAS. STRENGTHENING THESE PARTS WILL CHANGE THE WAY COLLISION DAMAGE IS ABSORBED, POSSIBLY ENDANGERING THE PASSENGERS.

Sectioning—Butt Joint Method

Procedures for sectioning with butt joint with insert:

1. Length of insert is twice the width of the part at its widest point.

2. Cut insert pieces from either the damaged part or replacement panel. Use a section that closely matches contours.

3. Trim away flanges. Make lengthwise cuts in the insert.

4. Check fit of the individual pieces of the insert. There should be no gaps between the insert and the inside of the rail or pillar.

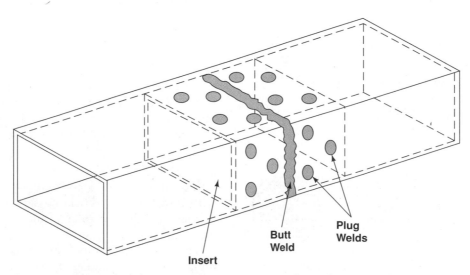

Figure 22–16 Note how butt joint with an insert is typically made. *(I-CAR)*

Figure 22–17 Insert can be made by cutting off excess material from new or old part. *(Used with permission of Nissan Motor Corporation)*

5. Drill ⁵⁄₁₆ inch (8 mm) plug weld holes so that heat affect zones from the butt weld and plug welds don't overlap.

6. Remove burrs from all panels.

7. Remove all paint, undercoating, and seam sealers. Do NOT remove galvanizing.

8. Apply weld-through primer.

9. Make test welds.

10. Fit the insert and secure in place.

11. Butt the pieces up leaving a gap the thickness of the panels being welded.

12. Check measurements and fit.

13. Tack weld and measure again.

14. Complete and dress all welds. Make sure the joint is completely closed and the weld has penetrated the insert.

15. Prep for corrosion protection and top coats.

The most common joints used to section front and rear rails are butt joint with insert and the lap joint. The butt joint with insert is used most often on front rails. Lap joints are commonly used on rear hat channel rails.

There is an additional combination lap joint/offset butt joint procedure that is used on front rails. This procedure should only be used when tested repair procedures are available for the specific vehicle being repaired.

Making Cut Templates. Parts must be measured and marked prior to making cuts. This can be easily done by making a cutting template:

1. Decide where to section.

2. Cut damaged section off the vehicle.

3. Apply a sturdy, wide tape to remaining section.

4. Use a razor to cut the tape around various reference holes and the cut line.

4. Remove the tape.

5. Align holes cut in the tape to identical holes on the replacement part.

6. Apply tape template to replacement panel.

7. Cut along the tape template cut line.

Heavy paper and masking tape can also be used to create a template.

Sectioning Front Rails—Insert Method

Front rail sectioning using butt joint with insert:

1. Decide where to section.

2. Measure and mark the cuts on both parts.

3. Make straight cuts along cut lines.

WARNING! *Don't throw any parts away until the repair is done.*

---

4. Make and fit insert to rail sections.
5. Drill ⁵⁄₁₆ inch (8 mm) plug weld holes so that heat affect zones from the butt weld and plug welds don't overlap.
6. Remove burrs from all panels.
7. Remove all paint, undercoating, and seam sealers. Do NOT remove galvanizing.
8. Apply weld-through primer.
9. Make test welds.
10. Fit the insert and secure in place.
11. Butt the pieces up leaving a gap or the thickness of the panels being welded.
12. Check measurements and fit.
13. Tack weld and measure again.
14. Complete and dress all welds. Make sure the joint is completely closed and that the weld has penetrated the insert.
15. Prep for corrosion protection and top coats.

Sectioning Rails—Combined Joint Method

Rails are also sectioned using combined lap and offset butt joints.

1. Remove engine, transmission, and cradle as a unit.
2. Locate and drill factory spot welds that attach upper rail to the cowl at the base of the windshield.
3. Remove paint, undercoating, and seam sealers from the spot weld areas.
4. Remove the two spot welds that hold the upper rail to the rear outer flange of the strut tower. These spot welds can be accessed through the hole at the rear of the upper rail.
5. Remove spot welds that attach the strut tower to the rail extension panel at the base of the strut tower.
6. Remove paint, undercoating, and seam sealers from inside the engine compartment.
7. Remove sound deadening material from the wheelhouse.
8. Prepare to section the rail in front of the strut tower center point. Because of the inner reinforcement, this area is ideal for sectioning. See Figure 22–18.
9. Make a staggered cut on the inner and outer lower rail. An electric reciprocating saw with a laminated blade makes the best cuts.
10. Before cutting, remove the two spot welds that attach the reinforcement to the inside of the lower rail. One is on the wheelhouse side of the rail. The other is on the bottom of the rail. Refer to Figure 22–19.
11. Cut the engine side of the rail about 12 inches (305 mm) from the cowl. This is near the end of the inner reinforcement.

Caution: Do Not Cut
Inner Reinforcement!

Approximately 12" (305 mm) On Driver
Side 14" (356 mm) On Passenger Side

Cut Line - Continuous Edge Weld
Overlap: 1/16" (1.5 mm) To 1/4" (6 mm) Max

Figure 22–18 Since sectioning of front frame rails is critical to integrity of vehicle, use great care. This is a typical example on unibody vehicle. However, always refer to manufacturer's recommendations. Do not cut inner reinforcements. *(Used by permission from Tech-Cor, Inc.)*

Engine Side
Cut Line

Wheelhouse
Side Cut Line

Approximately
3-5" (76-127 mm)

Allow For Overlap at Cut Lines
1/16-1/4" (1.5-6 mm)

Figure 22–19 Note how offset cut is used to section front rails. *(Used by permission from Tech-Cor, Inc.)*

12. Cut the wheelhouse side of the rail 3–5 inches (76–127 mm) behind the engine side cut.

13. Use a staggered butt joint for sectioning the rail. The parts should overlap $\frac{1}{16}$–$\frac{1}{4}$ inch (1.5–6 mm) to aid in alignment and welding. To prepare for the overlap, cut the corners of the original part $\frac{1}{4}$ inch (6 mm).

14. Position the replacement part OVER the original part. This will allow the corrosion protection treatments inside the rail to better penetrate the joint. Any part of the cuts exposed after fitting must be welded shut.

15. Separate the opposite side lower rail extension from the lower rail. First, drill the spot welds that attach the radiator core support and apron extension panel.

16. Next, carefully fold up the apron extension panel to expose the other spot welds that attach the rail extension to the rail. This should loosen the damaged part so it can be removed.

17. Prepare the used assembly. Remove the spot welds and make the lower rail offset cut the same as on the damaged parts. Be sure to inspect, measure, and if necessary, straighten the used assembly.

NOTE! WHEN CUTTING THE REPLACEMENT RAIL, REMEMBER TO ADD $\frac{1}{16}$–$\frac{1}{4}$ INCH (1.5–6 MM) TO THE LENGTH MEASUREMENT ON THE REPLACEMENT RAIL FOR THE OVERLAP.

18. Align the replacement assembly and secure in place. Measure to make sure parts are dimensionally correct.

19. Weld the assembly into position using I-CAR's MIG welding guidelines.

20. Clean the welds carefully to reduce the chance of corrosion.

21. Apply corrosion protection.

This example was for sectioning the driver side rail. Although the dimensions will be different, the passenger side can also be completed the same way.

Be sure to work with the locations of welds and reinforcements, NOT just the dimensions. Measurements given here are approximate. Locations of reinforcements can vary by model year.

Be sure NOT to confuse this procedure with front full body sectioning. This procedure is NOT front full body sectioning. Section closed sections using a butt joint with insert or offset butt joint. In this procedure, the joint is offset, with the inner and outer rails cut at different points. This produces a staggered butt joint. A slight overlap $\frac{1}{16}$–$\frac{1}{4}$ inch (1.5–6 mm) is used to ensure a tight fit for welding purposes. This eliminates the need for inserts.

Areas with inner reinforcements should NOT be sectioned. Cutting in the area of reinforcements can create problems. In the example described here, the rail is carefully cut around the reinforcement. The reinforcement adds a backup. This results in a joint with the best possible features:

1. An offset
2. Tight fit due to the overlap
3. Reinforcement as a bridge between the two parts

Test results indicate that this type of repair performs the same as the original part during a collision.

Sectioning Hat Channels—Rear Rails

Most rear rails are hat channels attached to the trunk floor. To section hat channel rear rails:

1. Decide where to section. Stay forward of all collapse zones.
2. Measure and mark the cuts on both parts.
3. Remove spot welds attaching rail to the floor pan. Drill from the trunk side.
4. Make straight cuts along cut lines.
5. Drill two to three $5/16$ inch (8 mm) plug weld holes in the overlap area.
6. Remove burrs from all panels.
7. Remove all paint, undercoating, and seam sealers from the floor pan. Do NOT remove galvanizing.
8. Apply weld-through primer.
9. Make test welds.
10. Fit the replacement panel, overlapping the original by 1 inch (25 mm) and secure in place.
11. Check measurements and fit.
12. Tack weld and measure again.
13. Plug weld the overlap area. Alternate sides to minimize heat build-up.
14. Plug weld through the trunk floor into the rail flanges.
15. Weld along the lap joint.
16. Dress all welds.
17. Prep for corrosion protection and top coats.

A "window" is cut into the outer rail to access a weld site on the reinforcement. A butt joint with insert repair is made to the rail reinforcement.

The more complicated the structure, the more challenging the repair procedure. Manufacturers are using multiple part designs more often to increase the rigidity of the passenger compartment. This is of increased importance with convertibles.

Sectioning Rocker Panels

When sectioning rocker panels, the two joints most commonly used are butt joint with insert or a lap joint. In some cases, only the outer panel is replaced or the rocker may be replaced with or without the B-pillar attached. If the B-pillar is attached, then a B-pillar section will have to be made at the same time.

Use a butt weld with insert when installing a recycled rocker panel with B-pillar attached, or when installing a recycled quarter panel. If working on a three-piece design, remove the outer panel first.

Basic guidelines for replacing rocker panels are:

1. Carefully plan the repair before making the first cut.
2. When cutting rocker panels, or other structural parts, use a reciprocating saw to get an accurate cut and to reduce the heat affect zone.
3. Use inserts whenever possible.
4. Be sure to completely weld all seams.
5. Use plug welds to secure any inserts used.

To remove and replace the outer rocker panel:

1. Cut around the pillar bases, leaving an overlap area. Stay about 2 inches (51 mm) from the pillars to avoid any reinforcements.
2. Cut outer panel ends. Keep in mind that you will overlap those areas when replacing the rocker panel.
3. Cut or drill out the spot welds along the pinch-weld seams. Separate panels.
4. Cut replacement panel to allow for a 1 inch (25 mm) overlap of the pillar bases and panel ends, Figure 22–20.
5. Drill $5/16$ inch (8 mm) plug weld holes so that heat affect zones from the butt weld and plug welds don't overlap. Plug welds along the pinchweld should be made following manufacturer's recommendations. If recommendations are NOT available, duplicate the number and location of the original welds. Plug welds also have to be made in the overlap areas.
6. Remove burrs from all panels.
7. Remove all paint, undercoating, and seam sealers. Do NOT remove galvanizing.
8. Apply weld-through primer.
9. Make test welds.
10. Check measurements and fit.
11. Tack weld and measure again.
12. Complete and dress all welds. Make sure the joints are completely closed.
13. Prep for corrosion protection and top coats.

Figure 22–20 Note typical cut and weld locations for replacing a rocker panel.

Sectioning Rocker Panels—Insert Method

To section a rocker panel using a butt joint with insert:

1. Plan the cut to be near the middle of the door opening.
2. Cut straight across the rocker panel.
3. Make an insert from either the damaged or replacement part.
4. Check the insert for fit, Figure 22–21.
5. Cut the replacement part to fit.
6. Drill ⁵⁄₁₆ inch (8 mm) plug weld holes on both the vehicle and replacement parts. Stagger holes to avoid overlapping heat affect zones.
7. Remove burrs from all panels.
8. Remove all paint, undercoating, and seam sealers. Do NOT remove galvanizing.
9. Apply weld-through primer.
10. Make a test weld.
11. Fit the insert and secure in place.
12. Butt the pieces up leaving a gap about the thickness of the panels being welded.
13. Check measurements and fit.
14. Tack weld and measure again.
15. Complete and dress all welds. Make sure the joint is completely closed and that the butt weld has penetrated the insert.
16. Complete other necessary sectioning or welding procedures.
17. Prep for corrosion protection and top coats.

Sectioning Multi-Part Rocker Panels

The *multiple part rocker* assembly is made up of several pieces of sheet metal with internal reinforcements. Reinforcements make it more difficult to use inserts. It is also more important to plan the exact order the work will be done. This will ensure that all the welding will be done in the right sequence. Also, the various rocker parts will be cut so as to provide maximum reinforcement to one another.

1. Plan cut in middle of door.
2. Cutting points for various parts of rocker assembly should be planned so panels overlap, providing continuity for one another.

Figure 22–21 Insert can be made and used with rocker panel replacement. *(I-CAR)*

3. If more than just the outer rocker is being replaced, you will have to separate the rocker assembly into its individual parts.

4. Work from the inside out, starting with the inner rocker or main floor side member. Then, attach the flat reinforcement, the channel reinforcement, and finally the outer rocker. Check the fit at various points to make sure all is correct.

5. Cut a piece of the rocker to form an insert, providing backing for the weld.

6. Be sure to weld all butt and lap joints completely closed. Weld in segments to minimize heat distortion. Use weld-through primer. •

7. Finish inside of all cavities and outside weld joints with 2-part epoxy primer. Apply anti-corrosion compound to enclosed areas.

NOTE! YOU MAY HAVE TO TREAT SOME OF THE CAVITIES BEFORE FINAL ASSEMBLY IN ORDER TO BE ABLE TO REACH ALL AREAS.

Sectioning A-Pillars

A-pillars use either two or multiple piece construction. They can be sectioned using butt joint with insert or an offset butt joint.

A butt joint with insert or an offset butt joint can be used on two-piece A-pillars. On multiple piece A-pillars, the design of the part will guide repair planning. There is often an inner reinforcement at the upper and lower ends, so an offset butt joint may be the only choice. Reinforcement locations vary, so refer to a body repair manual to properly plan the repair. Use an insert if the design of a multiple piece pillar allows.

Sectioning A-Pillars—Insert Method

Sectioning an A-pillar is similar to sectioning other closed sections. To section an A-pillar using a butt joint with insert:

1. Plan the cut in the middle of the pillar. Stay clear of channel areas for motorized seat belt systems.

2. Use a jig to help locate and guide the cut.

3. Remove damaged part.

4. Cut the replacement part to fit.

5. Make and fit insert to A-pillar sections.

6. Drill ⁵⁄₁₆ inch (8 mm) plug weld holes so that heat affect zones from the butt weld and plug welds don't overlap.

7. Remove burrs from all panels.

8. Remove all paint, undercoating, and seam sealers. Do NOT remove galvanizing.

9. Apply weld-through primer.

10. Make test welds.

11. Fit the insert and secure in place.

12. Butt the pieces up leaving a gap about the thickness of the panels being welded.

13. Check measurements and fit.

14. Tack weld and measure again.

15. Complete and dress all welds. Make sure the joint is completely closed and that the weld has penetrated the insert.

16. Prep for corrosion protection and top coats.

Sectioning A-Pillars—Butt Joint Method

A-pillars can also be sectioned using an offset butt joint. To section an A-pillar using the offset butt joint:

1. Choose cut locations that are between spot welds.

2. Using a jig to guide and locate the cuts, cut through one side of the A-pillar. Cut through the flange but NOT into the flange on the other side.

3. Make a second cut on the opposite side 2–4 inches (50–100 mm) from the first cut. Cut through the flange but NOT into the flange on the other side.

4. Drill out the spot welds.

5. Cut the replacement part to fit, Figure 22–22.

6. Drill ⁵⁄₁₆ inch (8 mm) plug weld holes so that heat affect zones from the butt weld and plug welds don't overlap.

7. Remove burrs from all panels.

8. Remove all paint, undercoating, and seam sealers. Do NOT remove galvanizing.

9. Apply weld-through primer.

10. Make test welds.

A-A Cross Section

A

Approx. 0.079" (2 mm)

Notch

Cutting Jig

Inner Front Pillar

Cutting Jig

Outer Front Pillar

B

Figure 22–22 Sectioning A-pillars is similar to sectioning other parts. Check manufacturer recommendations for exact procedures. *(Used with permission of Nissan Motor Corporation)* A: Note typical location of area to be cut and of spot welds that must be removed to replace an A-pillar. B: Cutting jig can be made and placed over part to help you make a straight cut through pillar.

Outer Cut Point

Inner Cut Point

5/16" (8 mm) Plug
Weld Holes

A

Butt Weld

Cut Piece
Of New Part

Main Floor
Side Member

Reinforcements

30-40 mm

B

Figure 22–23 Note how pillar and part have been cut. Plug welds and continuous butt joint weld will secure pillar properly. *(Used with permission of Nissan Motor Corporation)*

11. Check measurements and fit.

12. Tack weld and measure again.

13. Complete and dress all welds. Make sure the joint is completely closed.

14. Prep for corrosion protection and top coats.

Replacing Foam Fillers

Some manufacturers place foam inside of panels. *Foam fillers* are used to add rigidity and strength to structural parts. They also reduce noise and vibrations. Cutting and welding will damage the foam. Replacing the foam fillers must be part of the repair procedure.

Some vehicle manufacturers are using urethane foam in A- and B-pillars, and other locations. The manufacturer may or may NOT consider the foam filler to be structural. The use and location of foam fillers are different from vehicle to vehicle. Follow manufacturer's recommendations for replacing or sectioning foam-filled panels.

Some OEM replacement parts come with the foam already in the part. When the parts come without foam filler, or foam filler needs to be replaced, a product designed specifically for this application must be used to fill the panel.

> *WARNING! Single part urethane foams made for home use CANNOT be used for replacing automotive foam fillers.*

Cutting and welding will damage the foam. Replacing the foam fillers must be part of the repair procedure. When sectioning foam-filled A-pillars, the foam filler is removed in the repair area. It is then replaced after all welding is completed. See Figures 22–23 and 22–24.

Some manufacturers have specific recommendations for the type of replacement foam filler needed. The repair usually calls for a foam filler that, when cured, doesn't change in volume due to differences in temperature and humidity. There may also be specific requirements for foam density given in ounces per cubic inch (grams per cubic centimeter).

Sectioning B-Pillars

B-pillars can be sectioned using butt joint with insert or an offset butt and lap joint combination. The B-pillar sectioning procedure can be complicated by:

A

B

C

Figure 22–24 Study basic steps for replacing part filled with foam. *(Used with permission of Nissan Motor Corporation)* A: After cutting off damaged part, use chisel and hammer to remove foam from area to be welded. B: Fit replacement part with cut on vehicle. C: After welding, inject recommended type of foam into panel.

1. Seat belt D-rings and anchors
2. Reinforcements built in at the rocker panel and roof
3. Motorized seat belt track and mounting points
4. Seat belt retractors and tensioners

When sectioning B-pillars on vehicles equipped with explosive belt tensioners, disconnect and remove the seat belt mechanism. Other restraint systems may require the removal of motors, tracks, cables, and belts.

Care should be taken when reinstalling restraint system parts. Check the service manual for installation procedures. Installation sequence and proper torque can affect the operation of restraint systems.

B-pillars should be sectioned using the butt joint with insert whenever the design of the B-pillar allows it.

Sectioning B-Pillars—Insert Method

To section two-piece B-pillars using the butt joint with insert:

1. Cut below the D-ring anchor point, away from motorized seat belt system tracks. See Figure 22–25.
2. Make a three-sided insert from the damaged or replacement part. A three-sided insert is used because the D-ring reinforcement prevents the use of a full insert.
3. Cut panels so that the replacement panel overlaps inside of the existing part by 3½ inches (90 mm) and the outer panels are butted together.
4. Drill ⁵⁄₁₆ inch (8 mm) plug weld holes so that heat affect zones from the butt, lap, and plug welds don't overlap.
5. Remove burrs from all panels.
6. Remove all paint, undercoating, and seam sealers. Do NOT remove galvanizing.
7. Apply weld-through primer.
8. Make test welds.
9. Fit the insert and secure in place.
10. Butt the pieces up, leaving a gap of about the thickness of the panels being welded.
11. Check measurements and fit.
12. Tack weld and measure again.
13. Lap weld the upper edge and complete the plug and butt welds. Dress all welds. Make sure the joints are completely closed.
14. Prep for corrosion protection and top coats.

Figure 22–25 B-pillars are normally sectioned using butt joint with an insert. *(I-CAR)*

D - Ring Anchor

MIG Plug Welds

5/16' (8 mm) Plug Weld Holes

Sectioning B-Pillars—Combination Joint Method

B-pillars with complex designs are sectioned using the offset butt and lap joint. To section B-pillars using the offset butt and lap joint, Figure 22–26:

1. Cut the outer panel above the D-ring mount being careful NOT to cut into the inner panel.
2. Cut the inner panel below the D-ring reinforcement.
3. Cut out spot welds along the pinchweld and separate the pieces.
4. Cut the replacement inner panel to overlap the existing inner panel by approximately 3½ inches (90 mm).
5. Cut the replacement outer panel to butt against the existing outer panel.
6. Drill ⁵⁄₁₆ inch (8 mm) plug weld holes along pinchweld flanges. Stagger the holes (new inner to new outer) so that heat affect zones don't overlap.

Figure 22–26 B-pillars with complex designs are sectioned using the offset butt and lap joint. *(I-CAR)*

7. Remove burrs from all panels.

8. Remove all paint, undercoating, and seam sealers. Do NOT remove galvanizing.

9. Apply weld-through primer.

10. Make test welds.

11. Check measurements and fit.

12. Tack weld and measure again.

13. Lap weld the upper edge of the new inner panel. Complete the plug and butt welds. Dress all welds. Make sure the joints are completely closed.

14. Prep for corrosion protection and top coats.

Sectioning Floors

Floor pans and trunk floors are sectioned using lap joints. It is critical to completely seal the joints following the sectioning procedure to keep moisture and exhaust gases out of the passenger compartment. Do NOT cut through any reinforcements or critical areas, such as seat belt anchoring points.

When sectioning floor pans and trunk floors, the rear section always overlaps the front section, Figure 22–27. This allows road splash to stream past the bottom edge of the joint and NOT strike the joint head on.

Figure 22-27 Floors are normally sectioned using lap joints. The back part should be placed on top of front part to help keep out road debris and water. *(I-CAR)*

To section floor pans:

1. Make cuts in areas free of reinforcements, seat, or seat belt anchoring points.
2. Cut the replacement panel to overlap the existing panel by at least 1 inch (25 mm).
3. Drill 5/16 inch (8 mm) plug weld holes.
4. Remove burrs from all panels.
5. Remove all paint, undercoating, and seam sealers. Do NOT remove galvanizing.
6. Apply weld-through primer.
7. Make test welds.
8. Check measurements and fit.
9. Tack weld and measure again.
10. Weld the plug welds from the top down.
11. Weld a continuous bead along the bottom lap joints.

12. Dress welds and prime.
13. Apply caulk to top side joints and primer and seam sealers to under side joints.
14. Prep for corrosion protection and top coats.

Sectioning Trunk Floors

The procedure for sectioning trunk floors is the same as that for sectioning floor pans, with some variations:

1. There is generally a suspension crossmember under the trunk floor near the rear suspension. Whenever possible, section the trunk floor above the crossmember rear flange.
2. Plug weld the trunk floor lap joint to the crossmember, welding the plug welds from the top. See Figure 22-28. The bottom, continuous lap weld is NOT needed because of the strength added by the crossmember.
3. On vehicles that have no crossmember, the lower edge must have a continuous lap weld.
4. In either case, caulk the top side joint, apply a primer and seam sealer to the under side joint. Top coat as necessary.

Full Body Sectioning

One of the most drastic repairs that can be performed is full body sectioning. *Full body sectioning* is replacing the entire rear section of a collision damaged vehicle with the rear section of a salvage vehicle. It may be more economical than trying to rebuild the damaged vehicle using new parts. Full body sectioning requires the highest quality workmanship possible.

Figure 22-28 Note common method for installing trunk floor. *(I-CAR)*

Jigs are often used to help locate and guide the cut when sectioning. They are used on any sectioning procedure where an offset butt joint is used. Precise cuts are essential when sectioning.

Full body sectioning procedures require sectioning the two A-pillars, two rocker panels and the floor pan. When this procedure is properly performed, sectioned vehicles have been shown to be as strong and serviceable as an undamaged vehicle. Refer to Figure 22–29.

Full body sectioning is complicated by anti-lock brake systems. The replacement vehicle must be so equipped, or the ABS system parts must be retrofitted.

Location and function of body computers may change, even within the same production year of a given vehicle. Check the locations of these computers on both the damaged vehicle and the salvage section.

I-CAR recommends that full body sectioning be done as a rear-body section only. I-CAR does NOT recommend front full body sectioning at other locations for the following reasons:

1. VIN would NOT match registration and title.
2. Matching mileage, condition, and accessories would be difficult.
3. Powertrain warranty could be affected.

When performing a full body sectioning, complete disclosure must be made to the vehicle owner. A conference between the owner, insurance appraiser, and repairer is suggested. Then, all parties will be aware of exactly what will be done to repair the vehicle.

Replacing Adhesives

Some vehicle manufacturers use structural adhesives along certain weld seams. These two-part epoxy adhesives are sometimes called *weld-bond adhesives* because spot welds are placed through the adhesive.

Weld-bond adhesives are used to add strength and rigidity to the vehicle body. They also improve corrosion protection in weld seams. Adhesives also help control noise and vibrations.

Parts most commonly weld-bonded are:

1. A- and B-pillars
2. Rocker panels
3. Roof panels
4. Rear quarter panels

If adhesives are disturbed by repairs, they must be replaced. Follow recommendations in the body repair manual.

Some manufacturers use *structural adhesives* in place of welds. One example is around the wheel openings and sail panel reinforcement. This is a different type of adhesive than the weld-bond adhesive. Check the body repair manual for information on the use of structural adhesives.

CORROSION

Corrosion is a chemical reaction, called *oxidation* or *rust,* formed when three ingredients are present:

Full Body Sectioning

Figure 22–29 Full body sectioning involves, literally, cutting vehicle in half. A vehicle with front damage and another with rear damage are used to produce one repaired vehicle. This is a major operation. *(I-CAR)*

Figure 22–30 Corrosion is due to moisture, road salt, acid rain, and pollutants which act on body structure.

1. Oxygen
2. Exposed metal
3. Moisture, Figure 22–30

Oxidation occurs in two steps:

1. Stable metal and oxygen atoms break down into positively and negatively charged particles called ions. See Figure 22–31.
2. These ions are unstable, and combine with each other to form metal oxides, which are more stable.

A necessary ingredient for oxidation to occur is an electrolyte.

1. Electrolyte is moisture.
2. Moisture is the only part of the oxidation process that repair shops can do anything about.
3. Moisture is controlled by applying coatings to the metal surface to act as a moisture barrier.

Full Rustout

Figure 22–31 Corrosion or rust can be minor or major. This is an example of major corrosion damage which would require part replacement.

4. Coatings do break down with weather exposure.
5. The best coating systems are those that last the longest.
6. Coatings only slow down the process of corrosion. Stopping it permanently is a difficult challenge.

Corrosion Protection

Even with all of the care taken to protect vehicles, corrosion protection breakdown still occurs. The breakdown falls into three general categories:

1. Paint film failure
2. Collision damage
3. Repair process

During a collision, the protective coatings on a vehicle are damaged, Figure 22–32. This occurs NOT just in the areas of direct impact, but also in the indirect damage zones. Seams pull apart, caulking breaks loose, and paint chips and flakes. Locating the damage and restoring the protection to all affected areas remains a key challenge for the collision repair technician.

Even touching a bare metal surface with bare hands adds corrosion causing agents. Make sure bare hands do NOT contact bare metal that has been cleaned for refinishing.

When dealing with the zinc coating on a galvanized body structure, there are two important things to remember:

1. If at all possible, do NOT remove it.
2. If it must be removed, replace it. See Figure 22–33.

To be effective, the coating must be applied to clean surface. The coating must also be tight and unbroken.

When performing collision repairs:

1. Preserve the original coating as much as possible.
2. Use conversion coatings to create a zinc phosphate coating on the steel surface.
3. Use weld-through primers on bare metal in weld areas.

The collision repair shop's interest in rust is twofold. First, the technician must be able to repair rust damage. Second, the technician must be able to provide treatment that will prevent rusting from recurring.

When restoring corrosion protection:

1. Use a complete system.
2. Do NOT mix different manufacturers' products.
3. Follow manufacturer's instructions.
4. Do NOT skip steps.

Both Sides Rust-Proofing Steel

One Side Rust-Proofing Steel (Back Side Only)

Figure 22–32 Note corrosion protection for different panels. *(Copyright Mazda Motor of America, Inc. Used by permission)*

Corrosion Protection Safety

As with other materials used in collision repair, the use of corrosion protection materials requires that you follow safety rules. The most basic rules are:

1. Epoxy systems can create skin irritation, so wear gloves and avoid skin contact.

2. If skin contact has occurred, wash hands with soap and hot water. Then apply a skin cream.

3. If adhesive accidentally contacts the eyes, wash immediately with clean water for 15 minutes. Then consult a physician.

4. Spot welding in weld-bond joints can generate gases that can be harmful if inhaled. Be sure to work in a well-ventilated area and wear a respirator.

Anti-Corrosion Materials

Anti-corrosion materials can be divided into four broad categories:

1. *Anti-corrosion compounds* are either wax- or petroleum-based anti-corrosion compounds resistant to chipping and abrasion. They can undercoat,

Figure 22–33 Note how corrosion attacks galvanized and non-galvanized parts. (Volkswagen Of America)

deaden sound, and completely seal the surface. They should be applied to the underbody and inside body panels so that they can penetrate into joints and body crevices to form a pliable, protective film. See Figures 22–34 and 22–35.

2. *Seam sealers* prevent the penetration of water, mud, and fumes into panel joints. They serve the important role of preventing rust from forming between adjoining surfaces.

3. *Weld-through primers* are used between the two pieces of base metal at a weld joint.

4. *Rust Converters* change ferrous (red) iron oxide to ferric (black/blue) iron oxide. Rust converters also contain some type of latex emulsion which seals the surface after the conversion is complete. These prod-

ucts offer an interesting alternative for areas that cannot be completely cleaned.

NOTE! SOME MANUFACTURERS DO NOT RECOMMEND THE USE OF RUST CONVERTERS.

Applying Corrosion Protection Materials

Care is needed when applying anti-corrosion compounds. Keep the material away from parts that conduct heat, electrical parts, labels and identification numbers, moving parts. Avoid applying corrosion protection materials to:

Figure 22–34 Always replace corrosion protection materials when doing body work. Note access holes so you can apply anti-corrosion materials to inside of panels. *(Used with permission of Nissan Motor Corporation)*

1. Seat belt retractors and passive restraint guide rails
2. Hidden headlamp assemblies
3. Power window motors and cables
4. Exhaust system
5. Engine and accessories
6. Air filter
7. Air lift shock absorbers
8. Transmission parts
9. Shift linkages
10. Speedometer cables
11. Brake parts
12. Locks, key cylinders, and door latches
13. Power antennas
14. Theft prevention labels
15. Driveshaft

Typical enclosed and exposed interior and exterior panels are shown in Figure 22–36. The corrosion

Figure 22-35 Make sure you use spray wand to replace corrosion material inside panels, especially around welded joints. *(I-CAR)*

E = Enclosed
EI = Exposed Interior
EE = Exposed Exterior

Figure 22-36 Study enclosed, exposed interior, and exposed exterior parts. *(Courtesy of Chrysler Corporation)*

Figure 22–37 Seam sealers must be applied in a continuous bead along edges of panels. *(Used with permission of Nissan Motor Corporation)*

protection process for exposed joints and seams can be summed up as follows:

1. Thoroughly clean the joint or seam.
2. Apply primers and seam sealers, Figure 22–37.
3. Apply final primer coat(s).
4. Apply a topcoat.

In general, anti-corrosion procedures for exposed exterior underbody surfaces are as follows:

1. Clean with a wax and grease remover. If needed, remove any loose sound deadening material. They can create moisture pockets for corrosion.

2. Prime with self-etch primer. You can also treat with metal conditioner and conversion coating, and prime with 2-part epoxy primer.

3. Apply top coat and sealer to primed areas or apply anti-corrosion compound with a self-etch.

Summary

- Structural parts are those parts of a vehicle which: support the weight of the vehicle; absorb collision energy; and absorb road shock.

- A simple rule regarding repairing versus replacement is:

    If the part is bent, repair it.
    If the part is kinked, replace it.

- Sectioning involves cutting and replacing panels at locations other than at factory seams. Sectioning of parts such as rails, pillars, and rocker panels may be required to make their repair economically feasible.

- Full body sectioning is replacing the entire rear section of a collision damaged vehicle with the rear section of a salvage vehicle. It may be more economical than trying to rebuild damaged vehicle with new parts.

- Corrosion breakdown falls into three general categories: paint film failure; collision damage; and the repair process.

Technical Terms

structural parts
factory seams
sectioning
panel alignment marks
recycled assemblies
inserts
offset butt joint
multiple part rocker
foam fillers

full body sectioning
weld-bond adhesives
structural adhesives
oxidation
anti-corrosion
 compounds
seam sealers
weld-through primers

Review Questions

1. List three functions of structural parts.

2. If the part is bent, _____ it. If the part is kinked, _____ it.

3. When should you replace panels along factory seams?

4. What is sectioning?

5. You should not section in or near these eight areas.

6. How do you start removal of a structural panel?

7. List five tools that can be used to remove spot welds.

8. A chisel should never be used by itself to remove spot welds. True or false?

9. All straightening must be done before replacing panels. True or false?

10. List the six general steps for welding panels.

11. Why should you use recycled assemblies whenever possible? Give four reasons.

12. These are three basic types of sectioning joints.
    a. Lap joint
    b. Offset butt joint
    c. Butt joint with insert
    d. All of the above
    e. None of the above

13. When cutting panels, Technican A uses a template. Technician B uses a jig.
    Who is correct?
    a. Technician A
    b. Technician B
    c. Both Technicians
    d. Neither Technician

14. _____ _____ are used to add rigidity and strength to structural parts.

15. Avoid applying corrosion protection materials to these 15 areas or parts.

Activities

1. Inspect a badly damaged vehicle. List the structural parts that would require replacement.

2. On the same vehicle, summarize the procedures for structural part replacement.

3. Visit a body shop. Ask the owner to allow you to watch a technician replacing a structural part.

CHAPTER 23

INTERIOR AND TOP REPAIRS

Objectives

After studying this chapter, you should be able to:

- Identify the major parts of a vehicle's interior.

- Remove and replace seats.

- Summarize how to replace seat covers.

- Replace carpeting.

- Service an instrument cluster, and other dash parts.

- Remove and replace a vinyl roof.

- Explain how to replace headliners.

Introduction

During a serious collision, interior parts can be damaged, Figure 23–1. The vehicle's dashboard, steering wheel, and other parts can all be damaged. This would include dash panels, headliners, seats, and related parts. For this reason, you should be familiar with procedures for replacing interior parts. This chapter will also review the servicing of vinyl tops.

NOTE! CHAPTER 13 DESCRIBES THE SERVICE OF DOORS, WINDOW GLASS, AND ALSO EXPLAINS HOW TO FIX AIR AND WATER LEAKS. CHAPTER 27 EXPLAINS THE OPERATION AND REPAIR OF PASSIVE AND ACTIVE RESTRAINT SYSTEMS. OTHER CHAPTERS ALSO GIVE INFORMATION RELATING TO INTERIOR REPAIRS; SO REFER TO THE INDEX AS NEEDED.

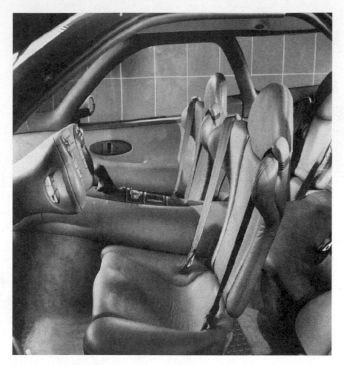

Figure 23-1 Interior parts can be damaged in a collision. Therefore, you should have basic knowledge of how to replace interior parts. *(Courtesy of General Motors Corporation)*

SEAT SERVICE

Seats are often damaged during a collision. They can be damaged by the inertia of its occupant, by side impact intrusion into the passenger compartment, or stained by blood. You might also have to remove seats for carpet replacement or floor panel repairs.

A *bucket seat* is a single seat for one person. A *bench seat* is a longer seat for several people. Both require similar methods during service.

Figure 23-2 Note major parts of a typical bucket seat. *(© American Honda Motor Co., Inc.)*

Seat Removal

Four bolts normally secure the seat to the floor. To remove the front seat hold-down bolts, slide the seat fully backward. This will allow easier access to the front bolts. Then, slide the seat forward to remove the two rear hold-down bolts.

After disconnecting any wiring and other parts attached to the seat, carefully lift it out of the vehicle.

A rear bench seat is often held in position by screws or spring loaded clips. The screws are normally at the front, bottom of the seat. When removed, the seat can be pushed back and lifted up and out.

With spring clips, use your hands to force the seat down and back. This will free the hidden clips and allow you to lift the bench seat out.

Seat Parts

Figure 23–2 shows the parts of a typical front seat:

1. *Seat cushion*—bottom section of seat which includes cover, padding, and frame.
2. *Seat back*—rear assembly that includes cover, padding, and metal frame.
3. *Headrest*—padded frame that fits into top of seat back.

4. *Headrest guide*—sleeve that accepts headrest post and mounts in seat back.
5. *Recliner adjuster*—hinge mechanism that allows adjustment of seat back to different angles.
6. *Seat track*—mechanical slide mechanism that allows seat to be adjusted forward or rearward.

Seat Cover Service

The seat cover is a cloth, vinyl, or leather cover over the seat assembly. The cover may require replacement when damaged. You must disassemble the seat to replace the covers. See Figures 23–3A and B.

Hog rings and clips normally stretch and hold the seat cover over the seat frame and padding. They are located on the bottom of the seat cushion or rear of the seat back. Remove them and you can lift off the seat cover, Figure 23–3C. The new cover can then be installed in reverse order of removal. Refer to Figure 23–3D.

NOTE! WHEN SERVICING SEATS, REFER TO THE MANUFACTURER'S MANUAL FOR DETAILS. PROCEDURES VARY.

A

B

Figure 23–3 These are basic steps for replacing seat upholstery. This is sometimes done by a shop specializing in upholstery work. (Courtesy of Ford Motor Company) A: Disassemble seat cushion and seat back. B: Remove cover over back of seat. It may be held by screws or snap-in clips.

Hog Rings Used To Secure The Seat Cushion Insert Pad And Trim Cover Assembly To The Cushion Frame Assembly

Cushion Insert Trim Cover

Seat Cushion Outer Trim Cover (1 Required Each Side)

Hog Rings Used To Secure The Seat Cushion Insert Trim Cover After Installing The Outer Trim Cover To The Cushion Frame Assembly

84

82

C

D

82 **Cover**

84 **Pad**

Figure 23–3 con't C: Hog rings and clips hold seat cover to seat frame. Removal of rings and clips will free cover. D: Remove old seat cover and install new one. Make sure cover is fitted properly and stretched tight when installing hog rings and clips.

Skid Strips

Rear Floor Carpet

Wheelhouse Cover

Cargo Floor

Carpet

Front Floor Carpet

Tailgate Carpet

Retainer

Skid Strip

Trim Panel

Figure 23–4 Carpeting often comes in several sections. You may not have to replace complete carpet set. Note covers and skid strips that help secure carpeting. *(Courtesy of Chrysler Corporation)*

CARPETING SERVICE

Carpeting can be stained or torn during a collision. If it cannot be cleaned with a strong carpet cleaner or if torn, the carpeting must be replaced. The major parts of *interior carpeting* are shown in Figure 23–4.

To replace carpeting, you must remove the seats, seat belt anchors, trim pieces, and any other parts mounted over the carpeting. This might include the console, any electronic control units, and wiring harness bolted down to the carpet. Screws and clips hold these parts and the carpet down into place. See Figure 23–5.

After removal, the new carpet is installed in the reverse order of removal. Make sure the new carpet is stretched out smooth and properly centered before installing any fasteners. An adhesive may be required between the carpet and floor in some locations. Refer to the service manual if in doubt.

Figure 23–5 Note parts that must be removed to replace carpeting in this vehicle. (© American Honda Motor Co., Inc.)

HEADLINER SERVICE

A *headliner* is a cloth or vinyl cover over the inside of the roof in the passenger compartment. It can be torn or damaged during a collision. Some thick cloth or vinyl covered foam headliners are bonded directly to the roof panel. Others are thin vinyl suspended by metal rods and bonded around the edges of the roof.

To service a headliner, first remove all of the trim pieces around the edges of the roof. Various screws and clips secure the trim pieces. Refer to Figure 23–6. You may also have to remove the sun visors, grab handles, and other parts for headliner service, Figure 23–7.

When installing a foam-backed headliner, be careful not to overbend and kink it. Center it in position. Then, install it in reverse order of removal. Again, refer to the service manual if in doubt.

Figure 23–8 summarizes how to install a vinyl headliner mounted on metal rods.

INSTRUMENT PANEL SERVICE

The *instrument panel* bolts in the front of the passenger compartment on the firewall or cowl. It contains the instrument clusters, radio, glove box, vents, vinyl or leather-covered pad, and other parts.

When parts of the instrument panel are damaged in a collision, they must be removed and replaced. An exploded view of a typical instrument panel is shown in Figure 23–9. Study the relationship of the parts.

Many instrument panel parts can be replaced without unbolting the dash pad. Then instrument cluster, vents, and many trim pieces can be removed and replaced with the main part of the dash intact. Vents often snap into place. A thin screwdriver can often be used to release and remove most vents.

Some of the screws and bolts that secure instrument panel parts can be difficult to find and remove. Some are along the bottom of the dash. Others are on the sides. A few fasteners can be inside openings in the instrument panel. You will have to remove parts to access these fasteners. See Figure 23–10, page 466.

Figure 23–6 These are typical parts that must be removed to replace a headliner. *(Courtesy of Chrysler Corporation)* A: Remove roof side trim. B: Remove front pillar trim. C: Remove rear pillar trim. D: Remove upper quarter trim.

Figure 23–7 This is a thick foam type headliner. Note parts that must be serviced to replace headliner. Also note how headliner is held secure by trim pieces. (© American Honda Motor Co., Inc.)

INSTRUMENT CLUSTER SERVICE

An *instrument cluster* contains the speedometer, gauges, indicating lights, and similar parts. It may require service when damaged in a collision or when parts are not working.

To service an instrument cluster, first disconnect the battery. This will prevent the chance of an electrical fire if wires short to ground.

Remove the instrument panel cover. Several screws secure it. Next, remove the screws that hold the cluster to the dash. Pull the cluster out far enough to disconnect the wires and speedometer cable. Then lift the cluster out. Bulbs can be replaced from the rear of the cluster.

To replace gauges or the speedometer, you must disassemble the cluster. To disassemble the instrument cluster, remove the small screws that hold the plastic lens plate over the housing.

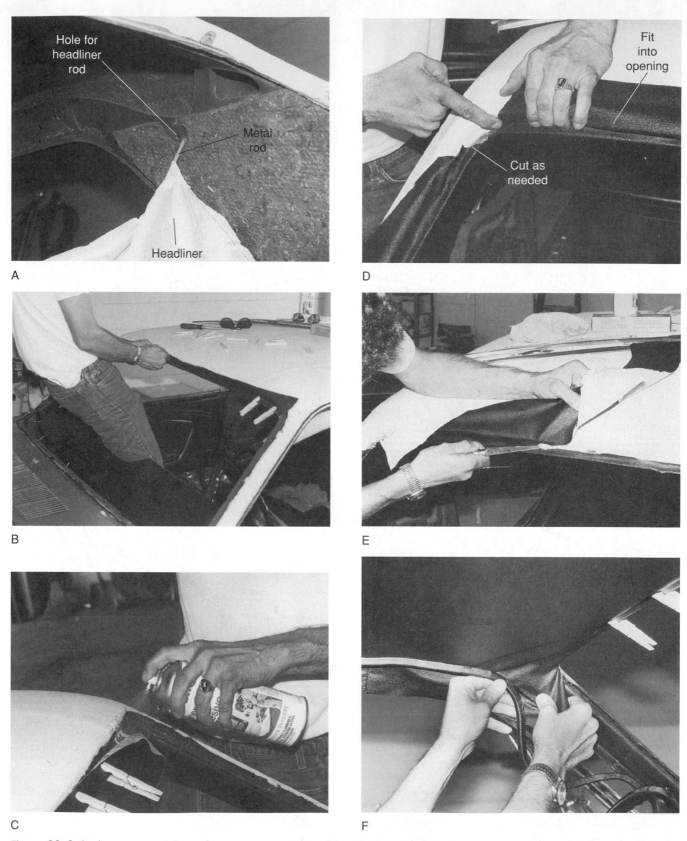

A

Hole for
headliner
rod

Metal
rod

Headliner

B

C

D

Fit
into
opening

Cut as
needed

E

F

Figure 23–8 Study major steps for replacing conventional vinyl headliner with adhesive. *(Mustang Monthly Magazine)* A: Install the metal bows into the new headliner. Fit the ends of the bows into the holes in the body. B: Stretch the headliner over the lip on the roof panel. Secure it with clothes pins or clamps. Make sure it is centered and fitted properly. C: Apply the recommended adhesive to the body lip wherever the headliner wraps around the lip. D: Work the headliner down into its groove around the body to allow the adhesive to secure the headliner. E: Cut off excess material as needed. F: Install trim pieces that also help secure headliner.

Figure 23–9 Study major parts of instrument panel. *(Courtesy of Chrysler Corporation)*

Ref. No.	Description
1	Lap Heater Duct
2	Lap Heater Duct
3	Hood Release Cable Bracket
4	Demister Grille
5	Demister Grille
6	Glove Box
7	Meter Cover
8	Meter Case
9	Combination Meter Pad
10	Combination Meter Case
11	Center Panel
12	Recirculation/Fresh Air Changeover Control Wire Connection
13	Mode Selection Control Wire
14	Water Valve Control Wire Connection
15	Center Reinforcement
16	Horn Pad
17	Steering Wheel
18	Fuse Box Cover
19	Fuse Box Assembly
20	Instrument Panel

WARNING! Keep your fingers off the inside of the instrument lens. Finger prints on the inside of the lens can collect dust that cannot be wiped off after you reinstall the cluster.

WARNING! Make sure the speedometer reading of the new or replacement unit is the same as the old one. You are breaking a federal law if you alter a speedometer reading. Check local laws for rules pertaining to reporting speedometer service.

With the lens removed, you can then replace gauges and speedometer head. Screws on the rear of the cluster normally hold each unit in place. Again, keep fingerprints off the faces of the gauges and speedometer. They will show up easily after installation.

Install the instrument cluster parts in reverse order of removal. Remember to connect all wires and the

Figure 23–10 Bolts and screws that hold instrument panel can be hard to find. Service manual will give fastener locations. *(Subaru of America and Fuji Industries, Ltd.)*

speedometer cable, if used, to the cluster. Check the operation of all dash lights and gauges after installation.

VINYL ROOF SERVICE

Roof panels are sometimes covered with a vinyl coated fabric. Full vinyl roofs and landau roofs can be repaired or completely replaced. Replacement procedures vary depending on the roof design, attachment method, and trim molding design. Most vinyl covers are glued directly to the roof panel. Others are padded with foam rubber. Vinyl covers are adhered to the roof panels with adhesive. A number of mechanical fasteners are also used to secure the vinyl cover to the edges of the roof.

Some replacement covers come with a preapplied adhesive backing. Others require that you apply an adhesive to install vinyl top. Foam rubber pads are applied following the basic procedure described for vinyl top installation.

Types of Vinyl Top Repairs

Vinyl top repairs fall into three categories. One is complete replacement of the vinyl material. This can be necessary due to direct damage to the roof or due to weathering of the material. If not properly maintained, the vinyl material will discolor, blister, and peel.

Partial removal of a vinyl roof is sometimes necessary to repair damage to the rear quarter panel or windshield A-pillar. Minor repairs—such as cuts and abrasions—can also be made with a patching compound or rebonded with a soldering iron. Refer to the

material's instructions for using vinyl repair materials. Procedures vary.

Vinyl Top—Replacement

When a vinyl top has been damaged beyond repair, replace the vinyl following this procedure.

1. Unpack the new cover and spread it out to remove the wrinkles.

2. Remove the trim moldings that cover the edges of the vinyl material.

3. If necessary, remove the blind quarter inner trim to gain access to the ornament retaining nuts. Some vehicles also require removal of interior garnish molding to gain access to weatherstrip retaining screws. Be very careful when removing drive nails. Avoid stretching the holes so that the nails can be reinstalled in the same holes.

4. Clean excess cement and sealer from the roof edges and the windshield and back light. If necessary, use a heat gun to soften the cement and ease removal.

5. Using the heat gun, soften the edges of the material so that it can be pulled from the roof. Use a pair of pliers to grasp the vinyl edge and peel the cover from the roof. If necessary, use the heat gun to soften the cement.

6. Carefully observe how the vinyl is fitted to the roof panel. The new cover must be installed identically.

7. After the vinyl has been removed, remove the old cement from the roof, using an adhesive remover. The roof must be smooth and level before applying the new vinyl fabric. If lumps of adhesive remain intact, the new top will be lumpy.

8. Mask around the roof to avoid getting cement on the glass and the paint area. Masking is especially important if using a spray adhesive.

9. Lay the new roofing material over the roof. Verify that it fits properly.

10. Remove the fabric and use chalk to mark the centerline of the roof. Measure carefully so that the line is accurate. Then, fold the fabric in half and mark the centerline on the cloth side of the vinyl.

11. Place the vinyl on the roof and align the centerlines. Fold one-half of the vinyl back to the centerline.

12. Apply a vinyl roof cement to one-half of the fabric, Figure 23–11. Do not apply adhesive to areas that cover the upper quarter panel, roof sides, or the area around the door, windshield, and rear windows.

13. Starting at the centerline, also apply vinyl roof cement to the exposed half of the roof top. Be sure to carefully follow the adhesive manufacturer's instructions. Some adhesives must be brushed or rolled on. Others are designed to be sprayed on. However applied, the adhesive must be applied evenly. There should be no skips, voids, globs, or pools of adhesive.

14. Allow for the manufacturer's suggested tack time. Then, carefully roll the vinyl over the cement. Smooth out any wrinkles or air bubbles. Be careful to keep the vinyl aligned with the roof. A stiff plastic squeegee can be used to work out

air bubbles. To work out wrinkles, use a heat gun to soften the vinyl and adhesive. Hold the gun 1 to 2 inches (25 to 50 mm) from the vinyl. Rotate the gun in a circular motion. Apply pressure with the squeegee to smooth the wrinkles out.

15. Apply adhesive to the remaining half of the roof and cover as described earlier. Smooth the cover over the roof and stretch out all wrinkles.

16. Apply adhesive to the body and underside of the cover in the area below the rear window (if applicable). Position the cover and remove any wrinkles.

17. Apply adhesive to the roof sides and door openings and to the underside of the cover. Make angle cuts at the corners as necessary. Then, stretch the cover and cement in place. Pull the material taut, using vinyl roof cover pliers.

18. On vehicles with frenched backlights, carefully apply adhesive to this area. Be sure to use a spatula type tool to fold the roof cover back under the rear window opening panel.

19. Trim the roof cover at the windshield and rear window openings. Leave ½ inch (13 mm) of material at the openings for cover attachment in the window opening recess. See Figure 23–12.

20. Apply adhesive to the rear window opening and the underside of the roof cover. Make angle cuts as necessary at the corners and cement the material in the rear window opening recess. Trim the cover around the molding retainer weld studs.

Figure 23–11 Spread adhesive evenly onto roof so lumps will not form under vinyl. *(3M Adhesives, Coatings and Sealers Division)*

Figure 23–12 Work vinyl top down into recessed lip around body. Make sure top does not have bubbles or wrinkles, then install trim. *(Courtesy of Ford Motor Company)*

21. Apply adhesive to the windshield opening and the underside of the roof cover. Make angle cuts as necessary at the corners and cement the material in the windshield opening recess. Trim the cover around the molding retainer weld studs.

22. At each roof rear quarter, locate and punch two holes for the roof side ornament on models so equipped. Install each side ornament with the studs entering the punched holes.

23. From inside the vehicle, install the retaining nuts on the studs and apply a silicone sealant around the nuts.

24. Reinstall interior trim panels, garnish moldings, weatherstrips, and exterior moldings.

25. Clean the glass, moldings, top, and surrounding area.

Vinyl Top—Partial Removal

If partial removal of the vinyl roof is necessary, follow this procedure. Remove trim from the affected area and pull the vinyl material up. Peel it away from the area, following techniques discussed earlier.

Place shop rags in the fold of the material to prevent it from creasing. If the repair area requires welding or heat shrinking, make sure that the material is pulled far enough away so that it will not be damaged by the heat.

After the area has been repaired and refinished, apply cement to the area and smooth the vinyl back into place. Pull it tight and work out any wrinkles. Clean up excess cement, and reapply the trim.

After the repair has cured for several days, wrinkles can appear in the vinyl. Use an electric household iron pressed over a damp cloth to soften the material and remove the wrinkles. A heat gun and a stiff squeegee can also be used. If the wrinkles cannot be removed with one of these methods, pull the fabric up and reglue the area.

Summary

- The typical parts of a front seat include: seat cushion, seat back, headrest, headrest guide, recliner adjuster, and seat track.

- To replace carpeting, you must remove the seats, seat belt anchors, trim pieces, and any other parts mounted over the carpeting. This might include the console, any electronic control units, and wiring harness bolted down to the carpet.

- Vinyl top repairs fall into three categories: complete replacement, partial removal, and minor repairs.

Technical Terms

bucket seat

bench seat

dash assembly

headliner

headrest

headrest guide

hog rings

instrument panel

recliner adjuster

seat cushion

seat back

seat track

Review Questions

1. How do you remove a front bucket seat?

2. List and explain the six basic parts of a front bucket seat.

3. These are used to stretch and hold the seat covers on the seat.
   a. Hog rings
   b. Screws
   c. Bolts
   d. Adhesive

4. To replace carpeting, you must typically remove which parts?

5. A _____ is a cloth or vinyl cover over the inside of the roof in the passenger compartment.

6. List the typical parts of an instrument panel.

7. A vehicle needs to have its instrument cluster lens replaced. Technician A says to keep fingers off the inside of the instrument lens. Technician B says to disconnect wires and the speedometer cable before pulling the cluster too far out of the dash. Who is correct?
   a. Technician A
   b. Technician B
   c. Both Technicians
   d. Neither Technician

8. In your own words, how do you replace a vinyl roof?

Activities

1. Inspect several older vehicles. List any damage or deterioration to the interior. Make a damage report.

2. Look how a convertible top is serviced in a repair manual. Write a summary report of how the top is replaced.

CHAPTER 24

MECHANICAL REPAIRS

Objectives

After studying this chapter, you should be able to:

- Explain the basics of front, rear, and computer-controlled suspension systems.

- Describe the design and operation of parallelogram, rack-and-pinion, power, and four-wheel steering systems.

- Define the elements of proper wheel alignment, including caster, camber, toe, thrust line, steering axis inclination, and turning radius.

- Differentiate between drivetrain and suspension problems and those caused by a bad CV-joint.

- Understand how various brake systems work, and describe the procedures for manual and pressure bleeding.

- Perform key cooling and air-conditioning system repairs and maintenance.

- Inspect an exhaust system, and describe the guidelines for working on an emission control system.

Introduction

After a collision, it is often necessary to remove mechanical parts. This would include suspension, steering, drivetrain, and engine parts, Figure 24–1. Today, a collision repair technician should be able to service these assemblies. Some areas require collision repair technicians to be certified to perform mechanical repairs.

Figure 24–1 After a collision, a technician will often have to remove and replace mechanical parts. This would include engine, drivetrain, suspension, and steering parts. (*Courtesy of General Motors Corporation*)

WARNING! When diagnosing and repairing mechanical parts, always refer to the service manual for the specific vehicle. Never attempt to work with mechanical components without the aid of a service manual. It will give the detailed procedures and specifications for doing competent work. Refer to Figure 24–2.

NOTE! SINCE MANY MECHANICAL SYSTEMS ARE ELECTRONICALLY OR COMPUTER CONTROLLED, REFER TO CHAPTER 26. THIS CHAPTER COVERS THESE SUBJECTS.

Figure 24–2 Upon frontal impact, damage to radiator and front of engine is common. (*Audi of America*)

POWERTRAIN

The *powertrain* is all of the parts that produce and transfer power to the drive wheels. This includes the engine, transmission or transaxle, drive axle, and other related parts.

Engine

The *engine* provides energy to move the vehicle and power all accessories, Figure 24–3. Most cars and trucks use gasoline engines while a few use diesel engines. The basic parts of a typical internal combustion, piston engine include:

Block—the foundation of the engine; all the other engine parts are either housed in or attached to the block. A *cylinder* is a round hole bored (machined) in the block that guides piston movement.

Piston—transfers the energy of *combustion* (burning of air-fuel mixture) to the connecting rod. *Rings* are circular seals installed around the top sides of the piston. They keep combustion pressure and oil from leaking between the piston and cylinder wall (cylinder surface). A *connecting rod* is a link that attaches the piston to the crankshaft.

Crankshaft—changes reciprocating (up and down) motion of the piston and rod into more useful rotary (spinning) motion. Power to turn the driving wheel comes from the rear of the crank and accessories are driven off the front.

Cylinder head—covers and seals the top of the cylinder. It contains valves, rocker arms, and sometimes, the camshaft. The *combustion chamber* is a small enclosed area between the top of the piston and bottom of the cylinder head. The burning of the air-fuel mixture occurs in the combustion chamber.

Valves—flow control devices which open to allow air-fuel mixture into and exhaust out of the combustion chamber. *Valve springs* hold the valves closed when they do NOT need to be open. They also return the valve train parts to the at-rest position.

Camshaft—controls the operation of valves. It can be located in the block or the cylinder head. A *lifter* is a cylindrical part that rides on the camshaft lobes and transfers motion to the push rods. The *push rods* are hollow tubes that transfer motion from the lifters to rocker arms. The *rocker arms* are levers that transfer camshaft action from the push rods to the valves.

Flywheel—a heavy metal disc used to help keep the crankshaft turning smoothly. It also connects engine power to the transmission. A larger gear on the outside of the flywheel engages the starting motor when cranking the engine for starting.

Figure 24–3 Study basic parts of engine. Intake valve allows air and fuel to enter combustion chamber. When mixture burns, it forces piston and rod down. This spins crankshaft to produce usable power for drivetrain. *(Courtesy of General Motors Corporation)*

ENGINE SUPPORT SYSTEMS

Various *engine support systems* are powered by the engine to protect the engine from damage and to power accessory systems.

Lubrication System

The *lubrication system* forces oil to high friction points in the engine. This keeps the moving parts from quickly wearing and failing.

The *oil pump* forces motor oil through passages inside the engine. It can be driven by the crankshaft or by a gear on the camshaft. Oil *galleries* are the passages through the block, heads, and other parts for oil flow through the engine. An *oil pickup* is a tube with a filter screen for drawing oil out of the pan and into the pump. A *pressure relief valve* limits the maximum amount of oil pressure.

The *oil pan* holds an extra supply of motor oil. Also called the *sump*, it bolts to the bottom of the engine block. An *oil drain plug* is provided in the oil pan for draining and changing the engine oil. The *oil filter* traps debris and prevents it from circulating through the engine oil galleries.

Lubrication System Service. In a collision, the oil filter, oil pan, and related parts are sometimes damaged. They are made of thin metal and can be crushed and ruptured easily.

When starting an engine before or after repairs, check the oil level with the *oil dipstick*, Figure 24–4. Also, always look under the vehicle for oil leakage. If you find an oil leak, shut the engine off immediately. Find and fix the source of the oil leak.

Cooling System

A *cooling system* maintains the correct engine operating temperature. It is often damaged in a collision and must be restored to its pre-accident condition. Shown in Figure 24–5, the basic parts of a cooling system are:

Antifreeze is used to prevent freeze-up in cold weather and to lubricate moving parts. Antifreeze also prevents engine overheating. A *coolant recovery system* stores an extra supply of coolant for the system.

The *radiator* transfers coolant heat to the outside air. The radiator *pressure cap* prevents the coolant from boiling. A *radiator fan* draws outside air through the radiator to remove heat.

The *water pump* circulates coolant through the inside of the engine, hoses, and radiator. The *water jackets* are passages in the engine for coolant. The

thermostat regulates coolant flow and system operating temperature.

A *heater system* uses coolant heat and a heater core (small radiator under dash) to warm the passenger compartment. The **automatic transmission cooler** uses the radiator to reduce transmission fluid temperature.

Cooling System Service. Cooling system problems normally result in engine overheating. In collision repair, problems may be due to a crushed water pump, bent drive pulleys, thermostat housing, or large leak. Always inspect closely for these problems and proper coolant level before starting the engine.

Antifreeze should be NOT be reused. Antifreeze contains additives, lubricants, and rust inhibitors which break down over time. Antifreeze should be replaced with a 50/50 mixture of antifreeze and water. Always follow antifreeze manufacturer's recommendations. Some warranties will NOT be honored if the antifreeze recommended by the manufacturer is NOT installed.

An *antifreeze tester*, commonly called a *hydrometer*, is used to determine the freeze-up protection of the coolant mixture. Pull a sample of the vehicle's coolant solution into the tester. Then, read the lowest temperature the coolant will withstand without freezing.

Cooling fans are either belt driven or electric. Their operation is critical for proper cooling of both the cooling and air conditioning systems.

When inspecting belt driven fans, inspect the belts for cracks, tears, glazing, and proper tension. Check the fan blades for cracks and the fan clutch for leaks.

When inspecting electric fans, check electrical connections for corrosion and reconnection following repairs. Look for cut, pinched, or burned wires. Make sure the fan comes on when the engine reaches normal operating temperature and when the A/C is turned on.

Radiator caps should be inspected for calcium deposits which could prevent the cap from operating. They are rated to maintain different pressures and should be replaced according to pressure recommended by the manufacturer.

A *radiator cap pressure test* is done using a cooling system pressure tester, as illustrated in Figure 24–6. The tester gauge should stop increasing its pressure reading when the cap rating is reached.

The *radiator cap pressure rating* is stamped on the cap. If the cooling system is disassembled during repair or parts are replaced, a pressure test should be performed.

A *cooling system leak test* is performed by installing the tester on the radiator neck. Pump the tester handle until its gauge equals the cap pressure

Engine Oil Dipstick

See Selecting Engine Oil For Recommended Type

Figure 24–4 Dipstick should show engine oil even with full mark. *(Courtesy of Chrysler Corporation)*

rating. A loss of pressure or coolant means there is a leak, Figure 24–6.

When mounted on the front or side of the engine, the thermostat housing can also be damaged during a collision.

Exhaust System

The *exhaust system* collects and discharges exhaust gases caused by the combustion of the air/fuel mixture within the engine. It also quiets the noise of the running engine.

The *header pipe* is steel tubing that carries exhaust gases from the engine's exhaust manifold to the catalytic converter. The *catalytic converter* is a thermal reactor for burning and chemically changing exhaust byproducts into harmless gases. The *intermediate pipe* is tubing that is sometimes used between the header pipe and catalytic converter or muffler.

A *muffler* is a metal chamber for dampening pressure pulsations to reduce exhaust noise. The *tailpipe* is a tube that carries exhaust gas from the muffler to rear of the vehicle.

Exhaust System Service. The exhaust system can also be damaged during a collision, requiring partial replacement. Its parts may also need removal during major collision repairs.

Danger! *When inspecting or working on the exhaust system, remember that its parts get very hot when the engine is running. Contact with them could cause a severe burn.*

Figure 24–5 Study basic parts of cooling system and trace flow. *(Used with permission of Nissan Motor Corporation)*

Figure 24–6 Cooling system pressure tester is commonly used to check condition of system. *(Courtesy of Chrysler Corporation)* A: With tester mounted on radiator, pump in cap rated pressure. Then, check for leakage. System should hold pressure. B: Mount cap on tester and pump handle. Cap should release pressure at its rating. Cap pressure rating is printed on cap.

Because of constant changes in recommended catalytic converter servicing and installation requirements, check with the vehicle manufacturer for the latest data regarding replacement.

To check the exhaust system's condition, grab the tailpipe (when cool). Try to move it up and down and side to side. There should be only slight movement in any direction.

To check further, start the engine (never in a closed shop). Stuff a rag in the tailpipe and feel around every joint for leaks. If one is found, try tightening the clamp. If this does not stop the leak, it must be repaired.

If needed, raise the vehicle. Check the clamps and hangers that fasten the exhaust system to the underbody. Also, jab at all rusted areas in the system with an old screwdriver. If the blade sinks through the metal at any point, that part is badly rusted. You can also tap on parts with a hammer or mallet. A ringing sound indicates that the metal is good. A badly corroded part gives out a dull thud, from thinned metal. If loud, there is usually a large leak or an internally rusted muffler.

Remember! There is only one way to repair faulty exhaust system parts; replace them. It might not be necessary to take off all exhaust system parts. You can usually separate each part and replace them individually.

Fuel System

The vehicle's *fuel system* must carefully feed the correct amount of fuel into the engine. If too much or too little fuel is admitted, the engine will NOT run efficiently.

A *carburetor fuel system* uses air flowing into the engine to pull the correct amount of gasoline from the carburetor. *Carburetors* which are mechanical fuel-air mixing devices, have been phased out and replaced by gasoline injection systems.

A *gasoline injection system* has sensors and a computer to control electrically operated fuel valves, called *fuel injectors.* The injectors are located in the intake manifold. When the intake valve opens, the fuel is sprayed into the intake port and pulled into the combustion chamber by air flow.

A *diesel injection system* uses a high pressure, mechanical pump to force fuel directly into the engine's combustion chambers. No spark plugs are needed. The pistons squeeze the intake air which gets heated enough to start the fuel burning.

A *fuel tank* is a container that stores fuel. The *fuel pump* is a mechanical or electric part for forcing fuel to engine. *Fuel lines* are tubing and hoses that route fuel from tank to engine. A *fuel filter* is used for straining out debris in the fuel. The *fuel pressure regulator* is a part that controls the amount of fuel pressure at the fuel injectors.

> ■ *Danger! Before disconnecting any part of a fuel system, you may have to relieve fuel pressure. Many fuel injection systems retain pressure, even when the engine is not running.*

DRIVETRAIN

The *drivetrain* uses engine power to turn the drive wheels. It includes everything after the engine—the clutch, transmission, drive shaft, drive axles. Drivetrain designs vary. Some cars use a *manual transmission* (hand shifted). Others use an *automatic transmission* (shifts gear automatically using internal oil pressure).

The *transmission* is an assembly with series of gears for increasing torque to the drive wheels so the car can accelerate properly. It provides high power for acceleration in lower gears and good gas mileage in higher gears. With an automatic transmission, a *torque converter* (fluid coupling) is used in place of a clutch.

A *transaxle* is a transmission and differential combined into a single housing or case. Both automatic and manual transaxles are available.

Figure 24–7 Study parts of tripod CV-joint. It is sometimes used in inboard joint. *(Illustration Courtesy of Perfect Circle-Dana Corp.)*

A *clutch* is a device used to couple and uncouple engine power to a manual transmission or transaxle. It uses a friction disc, pressure plate, flywheel face, and release bearing for activation.

Front-wheel drive vehicles use a transaxle to transfer engine torque to the front drive wheels. *Constant velocity axles* or *CV-axles* transfer torque from the transaxle to the wheel hubs. They can be found on rear-wheel drive (RWD), four-wheel drive (4WD), all-wheel drive (AWD) vehicles, and front-wheel drive (FWD) vehicles. Refer to Figures 24–7 and 8.

Front-engine, *rear-wheel drive* vehicles use a conventional transmission, drive shaft, and rear axle assembly to transfer power to the rear drive wheels. Look at Figure 24–9.

A *drive shaft* is a long tube that transfers power from the transmission to rear axle assembly. It has *universal joints* at both ends that allows flexibility of the suspension while maintaining driving force.

The *rear axle assembly* is the housing which contains the ring gear, pinion gear, differential assembly, and axles. Rear suspension springs attach to the housing.

A *differential assembly* is a unit within the drive axle assembly. It uses gears to allow different amounts of torque (turning force) to be applied to each drive wheel while the vehicle is making a turn.

Figure 24–8 Study parts of ball and cage or Rzeppa CV-joint. It is used on outboard, and sometimes inboard joint. *(Illustration Courtesy of Perfect Circle-Dana Corp.)*

Figure 24–9 Note parts of front engine, rear-wheel drive vehicle. (Audi of America)

Drivetrain Service

Begin drivetrain inspection by checking the condition of the CV-joint boots. Splits, cracks, tears, punctures, or thin spots require replacement. If the boot appears rotted, this indicates improper greasing or excessive heat. Squeeze-test all boots. If any air escapes, replace the boot. Also replace any boots that are missing.

Keep in mind that any discoloring of the housing at the bearing grooves is normal. All CV-joints are heat treated.

If the inner boot appears to be collapsed or deformed, venting it (allowing air to enter) might solve the problem. Place a round-tipped rod between the boot and drive shaft. This equalizes the outside and inside air and allows the boot to return to its normal shape.

Make sure that all boot clamps are tight. Missing or loose clamps should be replaced. If the boot appears loose, slide it back and inspect the grease inside for possible contamination.

A milky or foamy appearance indicates water contamination. A gritty feeling when rubbed between the fingers indicates dirt. In either case, repack the joint with new grease.

On front-wheel drive transaxles with equal length half shafts, inspect the intermediate shaft U-joint, bearing, and support bracket for looseness by rocking the wheel back and forth and watching for any movement.

Various drivetrain and suspension problems can be confused with symptoms produced by a bad CV-joint. The following list of symptoms should help guide the technician to a proper diagnosis:

A vibration that increases with speed is rarely due to CV-joint problems or FWD half shaft imbalance. An out-of-balance tire or wheel, an out-of-round tire or bent rim are the more likely causes. It is possible that a bent half shaft as a result of collision or towing damage could cause a vibration, as could a missing damper weight.

A drive shaft should be checked for signs of contact against the chassis or rubbing. Rubbing can be a symptom of a weak or broken spring or engine mount, or chassis misalignment.

It may be required to remove the drivetrain to make structural repairs. Because modern unibody

Figure 24–10 Label wires and hoses as they are disconnected during service of mechanical-electrical assemblies to avoid later confusion.

Figure 24–11 Angle gauge can be used to check alignment of drive shaft. If not aligned, vibration and U-joint wear can result. *(Courtesy of Chrysler Corporation)*

vehicles tend to have very crowded engine compartments, removal of the drivetrain allows ready access to structural panels.

When servicing parts of a drivetrain in collision repair, always refer to the service manual. It will give the instructions and specs needed to do proper repairs.

Label all wires, hoses, and other parts to help with reassembly, Figure 24–10. This will save time and prevent confusion later.

Sometimes, only engine and transmission removal are needed during collision repair. This might be needed for major frame or unibody straightening or structural part replacement.

When removing a drive shaft, mark its alignment in the rear axle assembly. Some shafts are factory balanced on the vehicle. If you change its orientation, vibration can result.

Proper drive shaft angles must also be maintained to prevent vibration and chatter of the drive shaft and CV-joints. An angle gauge may be needed to check for drive shaft alignment, Figure 24–11.

BRAKE SYSTEM

The *brake system* uses hydraulic pressure to slow or stop wheel rotation with brake pedal application.

The *brake pedal* transfers the driver's foot pressure into the master cylinder. The *master cylinder* develops *hydraulic pressure* (oil pressure) for the system.

Brake lines and *hoses* carry fluid out to the wheel cylinders. The *wheel cylinders* use hydraulic pressure to push the brake pads or shoes outward.

The *brake pads* or *shoes* have friction lining for rubbing on the brake rotor or drum. The *brake rotors* or *drums* provide heavy metal friction surfaces bolted between the hub and wheel. A *caliper* holds the piston(s), and brake pads on disc brakes. Refer to Figures 24–12 and 13.

The *parking* or *emergency brake* uses a steel cable to physically apply the brake shoes or pads.

Power brakes is a standard hydraulic brake system with a vacuum, hydraulic, or electric assist. A booster unit is added to help apply the master cylinder and brakes.

Figure 24–12 Caliper mounts over disc on disc brakes. When fluid pressure enters caliper, piston is pushed outward. This applies brake pads to spinning rotor or disc to slow or stop vehicle.

Figure 24–13 Drum mounts over brake shoes and wheel cylinders on drum brakes. Wheel cylinders push out on shoes to apply brakes.

Brake System Service

When applicable, inspect brake system for:

1. Kinked or bent brake lines
2. Cut hoses
3. Damaged rotors or drums
4. Backing plate interfering with drum
5. Damage to caliper or mounting area
6. Damage to master cylinder or booster
7. Dash lamp operation if equipped with ABS

Brake lines are seamless steel, reinforced flexible rubber, or nylon. They use two types of flared ends, ISO flare or double flare. Brake lines must be replaced with same material as used by the factory. Brake lines should be replaced if kinked or severely bent.

When servicing brake lines:

1. Do NOT use copper, aluminum, or rubber hoses.
2. Do NOT repair nylon brake lines.
3. Do NOT use compression fittings.
4. Route in the same locations as the factory.
5. Reinstall all supporting clamps and springs that were removed during repair.

Brake fluid absorbs moisture. Its container should NOT be left open to atmosphere. Make sure to use the proper type of brake fluid. Vehicles can require DOT 3, 4, or 5. Check the master cylinder label or markings for type used.

Do NOT reuse fluid drained from system. It may contain contaminants that will damage the system.

Brake system bleeding is done to remove air from the brake fluid. To do this:

1. Clean bleeder screw.
2. Attach drain hose to bleeder screw and submerge other end in a clear jar partially filled with brake fluid.
3. Bleed one wheel at a time.
4. Start with the wheel closest to, or farthest from, the master cylinder (follow manufacturer's recommendations).
5. Have helper pump brake pedal several times, then hold with moderate pressure.
6. Slowly open bleeder screw.
7. Allow fluid/air to flow through, then close bleeder screw.
8. Repeat as needed until fluid runs clear without air.
9. Repeat at all wheels, following manufacturer's recommended order, making sure that master cylinder doesn't run dry.
10. Refill master cylinder.

Anti-Lock Brake System Service

Anti-lock brakes service is similar to conventional brakes. However, electronic parts are added to operate the system. Most ABS brakes have self-diagnosis. The computer will output a trouble code if an electrical-electronic malfunction develops. You can refer to charts in the service manual to see what each number code means. This will tell which part might be at fault.

For example, if a trouble code indicates a problem with one of the wheel speed sensors, make sure it is adjusted properly and undamaged. You may also need to test the sensor and its wiring. See Figure 24–14.

NOTE! FOR MORE INFORMATION ON ANTI-SKID BRAKE SYSTEM SERVICE AND TROUBLE CODES, REFER TO CHAPTER 26.

WARNING! When installing the wheels back onto a vehicle, torque the lug nuts to specs. Use a crisscross pattern as shown in Figure 24–15. The service manual will give lug nut torque values.

STEERING SYSTEMS

The *steering system* transfers steering wheel motion through gears and linkage rods to swivel the front wheels. When you turn the *steering wheel,* a *steering*

Figure 24–14 When servicing anti-lock brakes, refer to service manual for details. Some systems have specs for clearance between tone wheel and wheel speed sensor. Use brass feeler gauge when adjusting clearance. *(Courtesy of Chrysler Corporation)*

Figure 24–15 To avoid warpage of brake drum, rotor, hub, and wheel, torque lug nuts to specs in crisscross pattern. *(Courtesy of Chrysler Corporation)*

shaft extends down through the *steering column* and rotates the steering gearbox. The *steering gearbox,* either a worm or rack and pinion type, changes the wheel rotation into side movement for turning the wheels. A series of *linkage rods* connect the steering gearbox with the steering knuckles.

Parallelogram Steering

Parallelogram steering uses two tie-rod assemblies connected to the steering arms to support a long center link, Figure 24–16. The *center link* holds the tie-rods in position. An *idler arm* supports the center link on one end. The other end of the center link is attached to the *pitman arm* on the gearbox.

The arrangement forms a parallelogram shape (each end moves equal and parallel to the other end).

On some systems, a *steering damper* is attached to the frame and the steering linkage to help absorb road shocks and wheel shimmy.

Rack-and-Pinion Steering

Rack-and-pinion steering uses a simplified steering system that weighs less and takes up less space than parallelogram steering. For these reasons, it is used on most unibody vehicles. Refer to Figure 24–17.

The rack-and-pinion steering unit takes the place of the idler arm, pitman arm, center link, and gearbox used in parallelogram systems. It consists of a *pinion gear* at the end of the steering shaft, which meshes with a toothed shaft (a bar with a row of teeth cut into one edge) known as the *rack.* When the steering wheel is turned, the pinion rotates in a circle and moves the rack sideways—left or right—to turn the wheels.

Two inner *tie-rod ends* are threaded onto the end of the rack and are covered by rubber bellows boots. These *boots* protect the rack from contamination by dirt, salt, and other road particles. The inner tie-rods are threaded onto the outer tie-rod ends, which connect to the steering arms.

Four-Wheel Steering

Four-wheel steering systems swivel all four tires when cornering. They can be mechanical, hydraulic, or electro-hydraulic in design. Refer to Figure 24–18.

Figure 24–16 Study parts of parallelogram steering. This is an older design.

Figure 24–17 Note parts of more common rack-and-pinion steering. *(Courtesy of Ford Motor Company)*

The front wheels provide most of the steering ability. The rear wheels swivel at less of an angle to improve handling. Rear wheel steering operation is determined by one or more of the following:

1. Vehicle speed
2. Steering wheel travel
3. Speed at which the steering wheel is turned
4. Direction of vehicle travel

Four-wheel steering systems have been around for years. Because these systems are going to be even more common in the future, the collision repair industry will have to adapt to them. See Figure 24–19.

When driving, the vehicle's tires are subject to the forces of grip, momentum, and steering input. These forces compete with each other during steering maneuvers. With front-wheel steering, the rear of the vehicle is always trying to catch up to the directional changes of the front wheels. This causes the vehicle to sway or yaw. As a normal part of operating a vehicle, the driver learns to adjust to these forces without thinking about them.

The idea behind four-wheel steering is that a vehicle requires less driver input for any steering maneuver. As with two-wheel steering, grip holds the four wheels on the road. However, when the driver turns the wheel slightly, all four wheels react to the steering input, causing slip angles to form at all four wheels. The entire vehicle moves in one direction rather than the rear half attempting to catch up to the front half. The vehicle responds more quickly to steering input because rear wheel lag is eliminated.

Since each system is unique in its construction and repair needs, the service manual for the vehicle must be followed for proper diagnosis, repair, and alignment of a four-wheel steering system.

Power Steering

The power steering unit is designed to reduce the amount of effort required to turn the steering wheel. It also reduces driver fatigue on long drives and makes it easier to steer the vehicle at slow speeds, particularly during parking.

Power steering can be broken down into two design arrangements: conventional and electronically controlled. In the conventional arrangement, hydraulic power is used to assist the driver. An engine drive *power steering pump* forces pressurized oil through the system.

Power steering hoses carry the oil to and from the pump. A *hydraulic piston* on the steering linkage or in the gearbox helps turn the wheels. *Hydraulic valves* control power assist.

With a *computer assisted steering* system, *sensors* provide feedback for the computer. The *computer* or electronic control unit can then precisely control power assist as variables change. Mechanical steering is still provided with an electrical failure.

With *electronically controlled power steering,* the conventional power steering parts are replaced with electronic controls and an electric motor. The electric motor is mounted in the rack assembly. A DC motor armature with a hollow shaft is used to allow passage of the rack through it. The outboard housing and rack are designed so that the rotary motion of the armature can be transferred to linear movement of the rack.

NOTE! FOR MORE INFORMATION ON ELECTRONIC AND COMPUTER SYSTEMS, REFER TO CHAPTER 26.

Figure 24–18 Note basics of four-wheel steering. Turning steering wheel operates front wheels normally. However, fluid is also sent to rear control valve which controls steering of rear wheels. Rear wheels turn just slightly. *(Courtesy of Mitsubishi Motor Sales of America, Inc.)*

Collapsible Steering Columns

Collapsible steering columns crush under force to absorb impact. This reduces injuries to driver. Steering column collapse is managed in two parts, upper and lower. The lower section of the column is linked to two or more universal joints. It uses universal joints that allow section to fold.

The upper section of the steering column uses collapsible steel mesh or shaft and tube. The shaft is locked to the tube and designed to give under pressure. The shaft can be locked to tube using plastic inserts, or steel balls in a plastic retainer.

Collapsible columns need to be measured following a collision. This measurement is compared to dimensions given in the service manual. If the steering column is shorter than the specification given in the service manual, replace the steering column assembly. Never try to repair it.

Caution! When working on a collapsible steering column, do not hammer on or bump column parts. With the column removed from the mounts, it is extremely susceptible to impact damage. See Figure 24–20.

A slight impact on the column end can collapse the steering shaft or loosen the plastic inserts that maintain column rigidity. When removing the steering wheel, use a puller. Do not hammer or pound on any components during removal.

NOTE! AIR BAGS ARE EXPLAINED IN CHAPTER 27, RESTRAINT SYSTEMS.

Steering System Service

To check a rack-and-pinion system, begin by raising the vehicle and taking the weight off the front suspension. Visually inspect the steering system for physical damage. Check the boots for leaks, inspect the tie-rods. Examine the mounting points for any distortion. Inspect the tie-rod ends. Grab the tie-rod near the tire and try pushing it up and down. Any looseness indicates damage or wear.

Check the inner tie-rod socket by squeezing the bellows until the socket can be felt. With your other hand, push and pull on the tire. Looseness in the socket indicates damage, or wear. With both hands, try to swivel a tire right and left while watching for play. If excessive movement is noted, wear or damage is likely. Observe the rack-and-pinion at the same time. Any movement might indicate a problem.

Remember that rack-and-pinion units must be mounted on a level plane. Misalignment of the rack-and-pinion will cause changes in the steering geometry during jounce/rebound. This condition cannot be corrected by changing the length of the tie-rods.

Here are some steering service tips that should be kept in mind:

1. Torque all steering system fasteners to specs with a torque wrench. Refer to the manual for an exact value.

Figure 24–19 This is a mechanical four-wheel steering system. (Copyright Mazda Motor of America, Inc. Used by permission)

2. Always install new cotter pins. Never reuse old cotter pins. If one were to fall out, a fatal accident could result.

3. Never try to straighten any steering system parts. Always replace bent or damaged parts.

4. Protect a power steering system from dirt and moisture at all times. If the system must be open, be sure to plug or tie off all openings with plastic.

5. Always replace the fluid lost with the recommended type.

6. Check power steering hose routing when reassembling the system. Always route and hang hoses identical to the factory installation. Avoid

contact with other parts. Watch for rubbing against moving parts.

7. Use proper tools when servicing a steering system. If you do not use the right tool, parts can be damaged.

SUSPENSION SYSTEMS

The *suspension system* allows the tires and wheels to move up and down with road surface irregularities. Its major parts include the following, Figure 24–21.

Control arms mount on the frame to swivel up and down. *Ball joints* on the out end of the control arms allow the steering knuckles to swivel and turn. The *steering knuckles* hold the wheel bearings and wheels. The hubs mount on the wheel bearings to hold the wheels or rims. The *wheels* hold the tires. *Springs* support the weight of the car and allow suspension flexing. *Shock absorbers* are dampening devices that absorb spring oscillations (bouncing) to smooth the vehicles ride quality. They may be gas, oil, or air filled type.

In unibody construction, the body provides the critical mountain positions for the suspension and steering. For instance, the inner fender skirts in conventional body-over-frame construction prevent dirt and road splash from entering the engine compartment. In unibody construction, they are called strut towers and fender aprons and have additional task of providing the upper mounting controls for the strut suspension system.

Figure 24–20 Wheel puller is needed to remove steering wheel. Never hammer on steering column or damage could result. (Copyright Mazda Motor of America, Inc. Used by permission)

MacPherson Strut

Stabilizer Bar

Coil Spring

Control Arm

Strut Rod

Steering Knuckle

Figure 24–21 *Study major parts of strut suspension. (Courtesy of Ford Motor Company)*

Front Suspension

There are two main types of unibody front suspension systems: the short/long arm (SLA) independent and the strut. The strut, as shown in Figure 24–21, is by far the most commonly used, but independent front systems are making a comeback. The main reason for the return of the modified short/long arm suspension is that it allows a lower hood profile, thus offering improved aerodynamics.

The upper (short) and lower (long) control arms on the traditional independent front suspension function primarily as locators, fixing the position of the system and its components relative to the vehicle. They are attached to the frame with *bushings* that permit the wheel assemblies to move up and down separately in response to irregularities in the road surface. The outer ends are connected to the wheel assembly with ball joints inserted through each arm into the steering knuckle.

Strut suspension is dramatically different in appearance from the traditional independent front suspension. The MacPherson strut assembly typically includes the spring, upper suspension locator, and shock absorber. It is mounted vertically between the top arm of the steering knuckle and the inner fender panel. Although there are several strut systems in use, all variations operate in basically the same manner.

Many unibody vehicles have lower control arms attached directly to the front rails. Others have lower control arms attached to suspension subframes or crossmembers that are bolted directly to the front rails.

The suspension system mounting locations in the unibody structural panels must be able to withstand the load transferred by vertical movement. In the case of strut suspensions, the vertical load is transferred directly from the upper strut mount to the top panel.

Rear Suspension

There are three principal types of rear suspensions: live axle, semi-independent or dead axle, and independent. The introduction of independent rear suspensions was brought about by concerns for improved traction and ride and prompted the introduction of independent front suspensions. If the wheels can move separately on the road and energy forces can be maintained, traction and ride will be improved.

Other Suspension Systems

Twin I-beam suspension is a combination of a solid axle and independent suspension. Two large I-beams form the lower control arms. See Figure 24–22.

Trailing arm rear suspension systems provide little, if any, independent movement of the rear wheels. They are commonly used on front drive vehicles, Figure 24–23. Also, called a *dead axle*, a solid rear axle holds the two wheel assemblies.

Air spring suspension uses air springs to support the vehicle load. The air springs replace or supplement the conventional spring suspension. It provides for automatic front and rear load leveling. It will increase and decrease air pressure in the spring to raise, lower, or level vehicle as needed.

Air spring suspension parts include a computer, air springs, air compressor, height sensors, and air lines, Figure 24–24. The sensors send signals to the computer about the ride height and attitude of the vehicle. The computer can then react to road condition and driving conditions. It sends out control signals to the compressor and valves to increase or decrease pressure in each air spring as needed.

Suspension System Service

Always inspect the suspension system for signs of damage from the collision. Damaged or worn suspension parts should be replaced. When worn or damaged, these parts can upset the settings of the entire suspension, steering, and drive line systems.

Loose, worn, or broken attaching parts will allow the rear wheels to shift. This will cause premature tire wear as well as short U-joint life. A metallic jingling sound when driving over small bumps or unusual tracking indicate the need for service.

Caution! The manufacturer has designed certain suspension, steering, and alignment features into the unibody vehicle. Do not try to straighten or

Figure 24–22 Twin I-beam suspension can be found on some trucks. *(Courtesy of Ford Motor Company)*

Figure 24–23 Trailing arm suspension, or dead axle, is sometimes found at rear of front-wheel drive vehicles. *(Courtesy of Chrysler Corporation)*

bend any of the pieces that make up the suspension system.

When servicing suspension system parts, refer to the service manual for details. It will give procedures and specifications for the exact part. Always use a torque wrench to tighten suspension system fasteners to specs.

AIR CONDITIONING SYSTEMS

An *air conditioning system* is designed to cool the passenger compartment. System designs vary. For example, some air conditioning systems use an accumulator while others use a receiver-drier. Look at Figure 24–25.

Figure 24–24 Air spring suspension uses synthetic rubber bags instead of coil springs. This provides smoother ride and easy way to allow computer to adjust suspension system. *(Courtesy of Ford Motor Company)*

Figure 24–25 Study difference between two common air conditioning systems. *(Courtesy of Mitchell International, Inc.)*

Receiver-driers and *accumulators* serve the same basic purposes. They use a desiccant bag to remove moisture from the system. Their difference is the location. The accumulator is between the evaporator and compressor. The receiver-drier is between the condenser and expansion device. They act as storage tanks.

Air conditioning systems are divided into two sides, high and low, Figure 24–26. The dividing points are the compressor and the expansion device.

The *A/C high-side* contains high pressure/high temperature refrigerant. Its hoses feel hot to the touch.

High-side hoses are generally smaller in diameter than the low-side.

The *A/C low-side* contains low pressure/low temperature refrigerant. Its hoses feel cold to the touch. Low-side hoses are generally larger in diameter than the high-side.

Air Conditioning System Service

Discharging air conditioning systems removes refrigerant from the system and must always be done

Figure 24–26 High-side includes condenser, receiver-drier, output side of compressor, and connecting lines. Low-side includes evaporator, expansion valve outlet, and inlet side of compressor. Evaporator mounts under dash of vehicle. *(Courtesy of Mitchell International, Inc.)*

before parts are removed. Some compressors use a special back seating service valve that allows the compressor to be removed without completely discharging the system.

When removing refrigerant from the system, remember to use a recovery system, Figure 24–27.

A *recovery system* will capture the used refrigerant and keep it from contaminating the atmosphere. Most will also filter the refrigerant for reuse. Since equip-

ment varies, refer to the user's manual for detailed procedures.

Manufacturer's receiver-drier and accumulator replacement recommendations vary. Generally, if the system has been open for several days, the receiver-drier should be replaced.

Evacuating an air conditioning system is done to remove air and moisture from the system. It must be done anytime air has entered the system. Evacuating

Figure 24-27 Recovery machine is needed to capture used refrigerant which can then be recycled, thus protecting the atmosphere.

is done by vacuum lowering the boiling point of the moisture, converting it to vapor (steam) and removing it.

Before *charging* (filling) the system with refrigerant, determine the amount and type of refrigerant used. This information is found in the service manual, on the label on the radiator support or compressor. Do NOT mix different types of refrigerants. Charging can be done with a gauge set or with a charging station, Figure 24-28.

Purging uses refrigerant to push air and dirt out of the hoses. It prevents air and other contaminants from being pushed into the A/C system. Always purge the gauge hoses before charging.

Refrigerant oil lubricates moving parts in the A/C system. Use only refrigerant oil. Do NOT use any other type of oil. Make sure to use the type recommended for the system being serviced. For example, some oils are designed only to be used with specific types of refrigerant. Using a different type can result in damage to the compressor and seals and other parts.

General rules are to add the amount of oil that was removed during discharge. There are adapters available to use refrigerant pressure to add oil during recharging.

Too much oil can cause reduced cooling. The oil takes up space normally used by the refrigerant. It can also damage the compressor and seals. Too little oil can cause poor lubrication of the system, premature compressor wear, and poor system performance.

An open can of refrigerant oil can collect dirt and moisture. Adding contaminated refrigerant oil to the system can cause corrosion, which can result in the failure of the compressor and other parts.

There are several ways to find refrigerant leaks:

1. Electronic leak detector
2. Refrigerant cans with dye

Figure 24-28 Charging or filling of A/C system can be done with gauge set or charging station. Correct amount of refrigerant must be metered into system. *(Courtesy of General Motors Corporation)*

3. Soap and water solution in spray bottle

A sight glass is used to check the amount of refrigerant in system. It is located on receiver-drier or in-line. When viewing the sight glass:

1. Clear = completely full or completely empty
2. Oil streaks = no refrigerant
3. Foam or constant bubbles = low refrigerant charge
4. Clouded = desiccant being circulated through system

Electronic leak detectors are battery-operated instruments that use an audio sound to alert to the presence of gas leak. They are designed to detect different types of gases.

When checking for refrigerant leaks, always check along the bottom of the hoses, fitting, seals, and other possible leakage points. This is because the refrigerant is heavier than air and is easier to detect below these parts.

Due to their possible depleting effect on the ozone layer, chlorofluorocarbon (CFC) and hydrochlorofluorocarbon (HCFC) are being phased out. This includes R-12 and other refrigerants used in air conditioning and refrigeration systems.

Environmental agencies call for a gradual phase out of most ozone-depleting substances. They state that R-12 systems can be serviced using recovered and recycled refrigerant. After filtering, this R-12 can then be used again in another vehicle. This reuse is designed to extend the supply of refrigerant.

R-134a is the present replacement for R-12. It is less harmful to the ozone layer. New vehicles are being designed to run on this new refrigerant. The compressor and other parts are designed to be used with R-134a.

> *WARNING! R-134a is NOT compatible with R-12. Also, R-134a oils are NOT compatible with R-12 oils. This requires separate service equipment. To avoid a mistake, R-134a uses metric quick-connect service ports. The high-side port is larger, so the same charging hoses cannot be used.*

Mixing of R-12 and R-134a, even in trace amounts, can be fatal to a system. This mistake can cause damage to seals, bearings, compressor reed valves and pistons. Mixing refrigerants can also cause desiccants used in R-12 systems to break down and form harmful acids when used with R-134a.

Refrigerant Handling Tips

Although most A/C repairs and service work is done in specialty air-conditioning shops, there are a number of pointers that the collision repair technician must keep in mind.

Danger! *Wear hand and face protection when working on an air conditioning system. When refrigerant escapes from the system or the supply tank, it can cause severe frost bite burns.*

Most A/C failures are caused by moisture entering the system. Moisture interacting with refrigerant causes sludge and hydrochloric acid to form. This will attack the delicate parts of the compressor. The resulting acid will also eat away at the aluminum components of the evaporator and condenser.

The release of R-12 into the atmosphere is prohibited by current environmental regulations. Never vent the refrigerant into open air. Use a recovery/recycling machine.

When removing or opening up the A/C unit, seal all openings. These can be synthetic rubber, tight fitting caps, plugs, or plastic wraps. Use sturdy rubber bands or wire ties to hold plastic wraps in place securely.

If an A/C system has been open to the atmosphere more than a few hours, do the following:

1. Change the oil.
2. Flush each component separately with nitrogen gas before charging.
3. Replace the receiver-drier or accumulator.
4. During evacuation, hold the system at high vacuum for a minimum of 30 minutes to pull out air and moisture.
5. Recharge without leaking refrigerant.

EMISSION CONTROL SYSTEMS

Emission control systems are used to prevent potentially toxic chemicals from entering the atmosphere. The most common of these are the exhaust gas recirculation (EGR), catalytic converter, air injection, and positive crankcase ventilation (PCV) systems. See Figure 24–29.

The *exhaust gas recirculation* (EGR) valve opens to allow engine vacuum to siphon exhaust into the intake manifold. The EGR valve consists of a poppet and a vacuum actuated diaphragm. When ported vacuum is applied to the diaphragm, it lifts the poppet off its seat. Intake vacuum then siphons exhaust into the engine. The exhaust entering the combustion chambers lowers peak combustion temperatures. This reduces oxides of nitrogen pollution.

Figure 24-29 Emission control system helps prevent toxic chemicals from entering earth's atmosphere. Study this diagram which shows several emission control systems. *(Used by permission of Nissan Motor Corporation)*

EGR and canister control solenoid valve

EGR temperature sensor (For California model)

ECM (ECCS control module)

Battery

Radiator fan relay

Fuel tank

Fuel pump

Mass air flow sensor (Hot film type)

Throttle position sensor

IAC valve-air regulator

IAC valve-AAC valve

IAC valve-FICD solenoid valve

From air conditioning

Fuel pressure regulator

Spark plug

Carbon canister

Injector

Engine coolant temperature sensor

Oxygen sensor

Knock sensor

Three-way catalytic converter

EGR valve

EGR control-BPT valve

PCV valve

Ignition switch

IG

ST

Air conditioning switch

Power steering pressure switch

Power transistor

Crankshaft position sensor built into distributor

Ignition coil

Neutral position switch (M/T) Inhibitor switch (A/T)

Transaxle

Vehicle speed sensor

Muffler

⬜ : Intake air flow

⬛ : Exhaust gas flow

491

The *catalytic converter,* mounted in the exhaust system, plays a major role in emission control. The catalytic converter works as a gas reactor. Its catalytic function is to speed up the heat-producing chemical reaction between the exhaust gas to reduce air pollutants in the exhaust.

The *fuel evaporative system* pulls fumes from the gas tank and other fuel system parts into a charcoal canister. The *charcoal canister* absorbs and stores vaporized fuel. When the engine is started, these vapors are drawn into the engine and burned. This prevents this source of pollution from entering our atmosphere.

The *Positive Crankcase Ventilation System,* abbreviated PCV, channels engine crankcase blowby gases into engine intake manifold. They are then drawn into the engine and burned. This prevents crankcase fumes from entering the atmosphere.

Emission Control System Service

Many times emission control systems are damaged in a collision. They must be serviced as part of the repair. The Clean Air Act, which is a Federal Law, makes the collision repair technician responsible for the emission control system. The law requires technicians to restore emission control system to their original design. It also prescribes penalties for shops and technicians who alter emission control systems or fail to restore them to proper working condition.

The following guidelines must be strictly adhered to when working on emission control systems:

1. Damaged parts must be replaced with good parts. Eliminating damaged parts to avoid replacing them is against the law.

2. Using parts that prevent proper operation of the emission control system is also against the law.

3. Proper repairs to the emission control system must be made to manufacturer's specifications.

4. All replacement parts for emission control systems must satisfy the original design requirements of the manufacturer.

Summary

- The powertrain is all of the parts that produce and transfer power to the drive wheels. This includes the engine, transmission or transaxle, drive axle, and other related parts.
- The four vehicle steering systems are parallelogram, rack-and-pinion, power, and four-wheel.
- The suspension system allows the tires and wheels to move up and down with road surface irregularities. The types of suspension systems are front, rear, and computer-controlled.
- Refrigerant leaks in an air conditioning system may be found by using: electronic leak detector; refrigerant cans with dye; or soap and water solution in spray bottle.
- Emission control systems are used to prevent potentially toxic chemicals from entering the atmosphere. The most common are the exhaust gas recirculation (EGR), catalytic converter, air injection, and positive crankcase ventilation (PCV) systems.

Technical Terms

powertrain	*center link*
engine	*idler arm*
block	*pitman arm*
cylinder head	*rack-and-pinion steering*
flywheel	*rack*
oil pan	*tie-rod end*
oil filter	*boots*
oil drain plug	*power steering pump*
oil dipstick	*collapsible steering*
antifreeze	*column*
radiator pressure cap	*suspension system*
water pump	*control arms*
thermostat	*ball joints*
antifreeze tester	*shock absorber*
radiator cap pressure test	*air spring suspension*
cooling system leak test	*twin I-beam*
exhaust system	*A/C low-side*
drivetrain	*discharging*
transmission	*recovery system*
transaxle	*evacuating*
CV-axle	*charging*
drive shaft	*purging*
differential	*electronic leak detector*
brake system	*R-12*
master cylinder	*R-134a*
wheel cylinders	*EGR*
caliper	*catalytic converter*
brake system	*fuel evaporative system*
bleeding steering system	*PCV*
parallelogram steering	

Review Questions

1. This would NOT be part of an engine.
   a. Block
   b. Control arm
   c. Connecting rod
   d. Cylinder head

2. Technician A says that antifreeze contains additives, lubricants, and rust inhibitors which break down over time. Technician B says that antifreeze should be replaced with a 50/50 mixture of antifreeze and water.
   Who is correct?
   a. Technician A
   b. Technician B
   c. Both Technicians
   d. Neither Technician

3. An _____ _____, commonly called a _____, is needed to determine the freeze-up protection of the coolant mixture.

4. How do you test a cooling system for leakage?

5. Parallelogram steering is an older system being phased out by rack-and-pinion steering. True or false?

6. Upon examining a collapsed steering column, Technician A decides to attempt a repair of the collapsed portion. Technician B says the collapsed portion must be replaced.
   Who is correct?
   a. Technician A
   b. Technician B
   c. Both A and B
   d. Neither A nor B

7. List seven steering service tips.

8. These mount on the out end of the control arms to allow the steering knuckles to swivel and turn.
   a. Bushings
   b. Coil springs
   c. Shocks
   d. Ball joints

9. Do not try to straighten or bend any of the pieces that make up the suspension system. True or false?

10. Explain the difference between the A/C high- and low-sides.

11. Why must you use a refrigerant recovery system?

12. Why should you evacuate an air conditioning system?

13. What are three ways of finding refrigerant leaks?

14. Which emission control subsystem is responsible for channeling blowby gases into the fuel intake area?
    a. Engine control
    b. Positive crankcase ventilation
    c. Evaporative
    d. Exhaust gas recirculation

15. What is the engine's temperature control?
    a. Thermostat
    b. Radiator cap
    c. Cooling fan
    d. Coolant

16. When checking for refrigerant leaks, always check along the _____ of the hoses, fitting, seals, and other possible leakage points.

17. This is a replacement for R-12.
    a. R-13a
    b. X-29a
    c. SRC-123a
    d. R-134a

18. Why must you wear hand and face protection when working on an air conditioning system?

19. List four guidelines for working on emission control systems.

20. When evacuating an A/C system that has been open to the atmosphere for an extended period, Technician A holds the system at high vacuum for 30 minutes. Technician B replaced the receiver-drier.
    Who is correct?
    a. Technician A
    b. Technician B
    c. Both A and B
    d. Neither A nor B

Activities

1. Inspect a vehicle with collision damage. Use the methods in this chapter to find mechanical damage. Make a report of your findings.

2. Refer to manufacturer service manuals. Read about the troubleshooting and repair of mechanical systems.

CHAPTER 25

WHEEL ALIGNMENT

Objectives

After studying this chapter, you should be able to:

- Define the term "wheel alignment."

- Inspect tires, steering, and suspension systems before alignment.

- Check and adjust caster, camber, and toe.

- Describe toe-out on turns, steering axis inclination, and tracking.

- Summarize alignment equipment variations.

Introduction

In collision repair, *wheel alignment* involves positioning the vehicle's tires so that they roll properly over the road surface. Wheel alignment is essential to safety, handling, fuel economy, and tire life. See Figure 25–1.

Following a collision, a vehicle would require an alignment if:

1. There is damage to any steering and suspension parts.

2. There is damage to any steering or suspension mounting locations.

3. There was engine cradle damage or a position change.

4. Suspension or steering parts were removed for access to body parts.

Remember! Wheel alignment is done to fine tune body-frame adjustments. The job of the collision repair technician is to make sure that everything can be "fine tuned" and the wheels can be aligned properly.

Figure 25–1 Wheel alignment involves final adjustment of the steering and suspension systems to make the wheel roll properly over road surface. If structural body repairs were made properly, this is a relatively simple task using modern equipment. *(Hunter Engineering Company)*

WHEEL ALIGNMENT BASICS

Improper wheel alignment will cause rapid tire wear and poor handling. Basic wheel alignment angles include:

1. Caster
2. Camber
3. Toe
4. Thrust line (tracking)
5. Steering axis inclination
6. Turning radius
7. Included angle

Caster

Caster is the angle of the steering axis of a wheel from true vertical, as viewed from the side of the vehicle, Figure 25–2. It is a directional stability adjustment. Caster is measured in degrees.

Caster has little effect on tire wear. Caster affects where the tires touch the road compared to an imaginary centerline drawn through the spindle support. Caster is the first angle adjusted during an alignment.

Positive caster tilts the tops of the steering knuckles toward the rear of the vehicle, Figure 25–3. It aids in keeping the vehicle's wheels traveling in a straight line. The wheels resist turning and tend to return to the straight-ahead position.

Negative caster is just the opposite, Figure 25–3. It tilts the tops of the steering knuckles toward the front

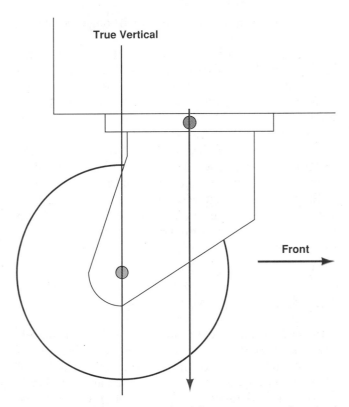

Figure 25–2 Caster is the angle of the steering axis of a wheel from true vertical when viewed from the side. It is a directional stability adjustment. *(I-CAR)*

of the vehicle. Negative caster makes the wheels easier to turn. However, it produces less directional stability. The wheels tend to follow imperfections in the road surface.

Caster is designed to provide steering stability. The caster angle for each wheel should be almost equal. Unequal caster angles will cause the vehicle to steer toward the side with less caster. Too much negative caster can cause the vehicle to have "sensitive" steering at high speeds. The vehicle might

Figure 25–3 Note difference between positive and negative caster. *(Ammco Tools)*

wander as a result of too much negative caster. Look at Figure 25–4.

Several factors can adversely affect caster. The most common problem is worn or loose strut rod bushings and control arm bushings. Caster adjustments are not provided on some strut suspension systems. Where they are provided, they can be made at the top or bottom mount of a strut suspension.

Caster is measured in degrees from true vertical. Specifications for caster are given in degrees positive or negative. Typically, more positive caster is used with power steering. More negative caster is used with manual steering to reduce steering effort. Also, a vehicle pulls to the side with the least amount of caster, Figure 25–5.

Camber

Camber is the angle represented by the tilt of the wheels inward or outward from vehicle centerline when viewed from the front of the vehicle. It assures that all of the tire tread contacts the road surface. Camber is measured in degrees. It is usually the second angle adjusted during a wheel alignment. Refer to Figure 25–6.

Left Turn, Spindle Moves Down

Right Turn, Spindle Moves Up

Figure 25–4 With positive caster, note how spindle moves down with left turn and then up with right turn. *(Hunter Engineering Company)*

Figure 25–5 Vehicle will pull to side with least caster. This can be used to counteract road crown that produces steering wheel pull. *(I-CAR)*

Camber is usually set equally for each wheel. Equal camber means each wheel is tilted outward or inward the same amount.

Positive camber has the top of the wheel tilted out, when viewed from the front. The outer edge of the tire tread contacts the road.

Negative camber has the top of the wheel tilted inward when viewed from the front. The inner tire tread contacts the road surface more. Note how camber changes when turning, Figure 25–7.

Camber is controlled by the control arms and their pivots. It is affected by worn or loose ball joints, control arm bushings, and wheel bearings. Anything that changes chassis height will also affect camber.

Camber is adjustable on most vehicles. Some manufacturers prefer to include a camber adjustment at the spindle assembly. Camber adjustments are also provided on some strut suspension systems at the top mounting position of the strut. Remember that camber adjustment also changes SAI or the included angle.

Figure 25-6 Camber is tilt of wheel in or out from centerline when viewed from the front of vehicle. *(I-CAR)*

Figure 25-7 Camber changes in turns. Therefore, its adjustment affects cornering stability. *(Hunter Engineering Company)*

Very little adjustment will be required if the strut tower and lower control arm positions are in their proper place. If you find serious camber error and suspension mounts have not been damaged, it is an indication of bent suspension parts. In this case, diagnostic angle and dimensional checks should be made to the suspension parts. Damaged parts must be replaced.

Toe

Toe is the difference in the distance between the front and rear of the left- and right-hand wheels. Toe can be measured in inches or millimeters or degrees, depending upon the equipment used.

Toe adjustment is critical to tire wear. If properly adjusted, toe makes the wheels roll in the same direction. If toe is NOT correct, the misaligned wheels will scuff or drag the tires sideways, causing rapid tire wear.

Remember! *Excessive toe* (in or out) will cause a SAWTOOTH EDGE on the tire tread from dragging the tire sideways.

Toe-in results when the front of the wheels are set closer than the rear. The wheels point in at the front. *Toe-out* is the just the opposite. It has the front of the wheels farther apart than at the rear. The wheels point out at the front.

Toe is a very critical tire wearing angle. Wheels that do not track straight ahead have to drag as they travel forward.

Rear-wheel drive vehicles are often adjusted to have toe-in at the front wheels. Toe-in is needed to compensate for tire rolling resistance, play in the steering system, and suspension system action. The tires tend to toe-out while driving. By setting the wheels for a small toe-in of about 1/16 inch (1.5 mm), the tires will roll straight ahead over the road surface.

Front-wheel drive vehicles need to have their front wheels set for a slight toe-out. The front wheels pull and propel the vehicle. As a result, they are forced forward by drivetrain torque. This tries to make the wheels point inward while driving. Front-wheel drive toe-out of 1/16 inch (1.5 mm) is typical.

Steering Axis Inclination

Steering axis inclination (SAI) is the angle between true vertical and a line through the upper and lower pivot points, as viewed from the front. Look at Figure 25–8.

Figure 25–8 Steering axis inclination (SAI) is a diagnostic angle used to indicate structural misalignment. *(I-CAR)*

On collision damaged vehicles, SAI can help in diagnosing misalignment of a vehicle structure. For example, SAI can be used with structural measurements to diagnose:

1. Strut tower misalignment
2. Shifted engine cradle or crossmember
3. Control arm mounting location damage
4. Misaligned frame or body structure

SAI will generally indicate a damaged structure, but may also indicate parts damage. For example, if a lower control arm is bent, the lower ball joint location will be changed. The angle between the steering axis and true vertical will also change.

SAI is an engineering angle designed to project the weight of the vehicle to the road surface for stability. SAI also helps the steering system return to straight-ahead after a turn. SAI should be checked because it can help locate other problems. Incorrect SAI generally indicates structural misalignment. See the chart in Figure 25–9.

If the vehicle has 0 (zero) SAI, the upper and lower ball joints (or strut pivot points) would be located directly over one another. Problems associated with this simple relationship include tire scrub in turns, lack of control, and increased effort during turn recovery.

If the SAI is tilted, a triangle is formed between ball joints and spindle. An arc is then formed when turning. There is a high point at straight-ahead position and a drop downward when turning to each side. This motion travels through the control arms to the springs and finally to the weight of the vehicle. The forces generated in a turn are actually trying to lift the vehicle. The effect of SAI offsets the lifting forces and helps to pull the tires back to straight-ahead when the turn is finished.

When the SAI angle includes the camber angle, the sum of the two is called the *included angle*. Problems that occur with this built-in angle can be due to a bent spindle, a bent upper or lower control arm or strut, or a badly worn or damaged ball joint. These damaged components must be replaced before doing the alignment. Doing an alignment without checking all the angles can result in error.

Turning Radius

Turning radius, called *toe-out on turns,* is the different amount each wheel moves during a turn. It is built into the steering geometry. Turning radius is designed to allow the inside wheel to turn a few degrees more than the outside wheel during a turn. This makes the inside wheel turn in a smaller circle. Refer to Figure 25–10.

SAI DIAGNOSTIC REFERENCE CHART				
Suspension System	SAI	Camber	Included Angle	Probable Cause
Short/	Correct	Less	Less	Bent Knuckle
Long Arm	Less	Greater	Correct	Bent Lower Control Arm
Suspension	Greater	Less	Corrrect	Bent Upper Control Arm
System	Less	Greater	Greater	Bent Knuckle
MacPherson	Correct	Less	Less	Bent Knuckle and/or Bent Strut
Strut	Correct	Greater	Greater	Bent Knuckle and/or Bent Strut
Suspension	Less	Greater	Correct	Bent Control Arm or Strut Tower (out at top)
	Greater	Less	Correct	Strut Tower (in at top)
	Greater	Greater	Greater	Strut Tower (in at top) and spindle and/or Bent Strut
	Less	Greater	Greater	Bent Control Arm or Strut Tower (out at top) Plus Bent Knuckle and/or Bent Strut
	Less	Less	Less	Strut Tower (out at top) and Knuckle and/or Strut Bent or Bent Control Arm
Twin I	Correct	Greater	Greater	Bent Knuckle
Beam	Greater	Less	Correct	Bent "I" Beam
Suspension	Less	Greater	Correct	Bent "I" Beam
	Less	Greater	Greater	Bent Knuckle

Figure 25–9 Chart shows which parts might cause SAI, camber, and included angle problems.

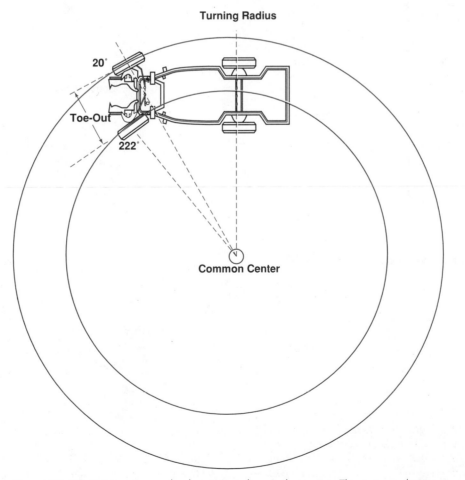

Figure 25–10 In turns, inner wheel must turn sharper than outer. This is termed toe-out on turns or turning radius. *(Hunter Engineering Company)*

As an example, during a left turn the left wheel will turn approximately 20 degrees while the right wheel will turn approximately 18 degrees. A bent steering arm will affect turning radius. See Figure 25–11.

Thrust Line (Tracking)

Tracking is the parallel alignment of the rear wheels, the vehicle centerline, and the front wheels. If a vehicle is tracking properly, its rear wheels will follow the

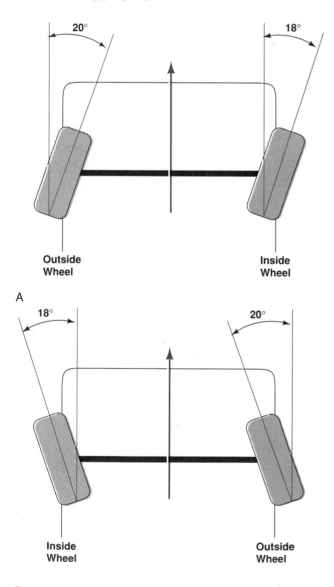

Figure 25–11 To check or read turning radius, wheels are mounted on turning radius gauges that read in degrees. Refer to the service manual for exact specifications for the vehicle. If toe-out on turns is not correct, replace bent or damaged parts. *(I-CAR)* A: Turn steering wheel until left wheel reads 20 degrees. Then read other gauge. It should be about two degrees less. B: Turn steering wheel other way until right degree wheel reads 20 degrees. Then, other wheel should read about 18 degrees.

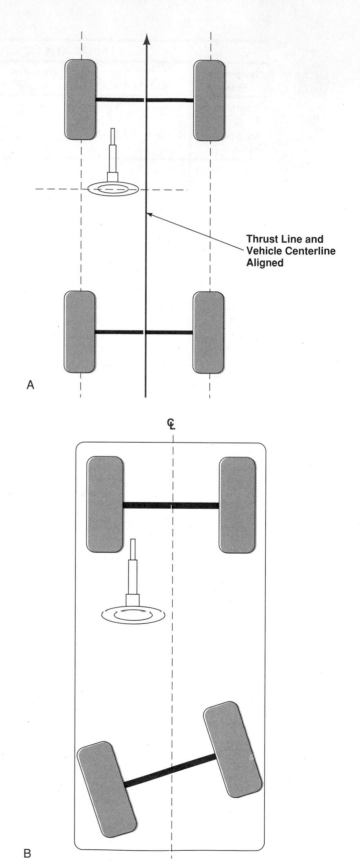

Figure 25–12 Tracking checks whether rear and front wheel are following each other. *(Hunter Engineering Company)* A: Proper tracking has rear wheels following in tracks of front wheels. B: Improper tracking has rear wheels turned so they do not follow front, nicknamed "dog tracking."

centerline of the vehicle when moving straight ahead. Tracking problems require the driver to turn the steering wheel to have the vehicle travel in a straight line. Refer to Figure 25–12.

To check tracking, wet an area of roadway, drive the vehicle through it. Then, continue driving out of the water, enough to make measurable tracks. The rear-wheel tracks should be an equal distance from the front-wheel tracks on both sides. Incorrect tracking is often caused by worn springs, offset rear axle, or rear toe problems.

You must make sure the vehicle runs straight down the road. The rear tires must track (follow) directly behind the front tires when the steering wheel is straight. The geometric centerline of the vehicle should parallel the road direction. This will be the case when rear toe or the rear axle is parallel to the vehicle's geometric centerline in the straight-ahead position.

NOTE! OFFSET AXLES RESULTING FROM A COLLISION WILL NOT BE IN LINE WITH THE CENTERLINE. YOU CAN SET TOE CORRECTLY BUT ALIGNMENT WILL BE INCORRECT IF THE AXLE HAS BEEN PUSHED FORWARD OR REARWARD DURING THE COLLISION.

Thrust Angle

Thrust angle is the angle between the thrust line and vehicle centerline, Figure 25–13. It should be zero if it aligns with the vehicle centerline.

With most manufacturers, a *positive (+) thrust angle* results if the thrust line projects to the RIGHT of the vehicle centerline as seen from the top of the vehicle. A *negative (–) thrust angle* results if the thrust line projects to the LEFT of the vehicle centerline as seen from the top of the vehicle, Figure 25–14.

Some wheel alignment equipment manufacturers consider the thrust angle as positive if the thrust line projects to the left and negative if the thrust line projects to the right of the vehicle centerline as seen from the top of the vehicle. Make sure you understand how the terms are used.

If a vehicle has a thrust angle reading of 0–.3°, the vehicle will generally not have a tracking problem.

If rear toe is not parallel to the vehicle centerline, a "thrust" direction to the left or right will be created. The vehicle will tend to travel in the direction of the thrust line, rather than straight ahead.

To correct this problem, begin by setting individual rear toe equal in reference to the geometric centerline. Four-wheel alignment machines check individual toe on each wheel. Once the rear wheels are in alignment with the geometric centerline, set the individual front toe in reference to the thrust angle. This assures that

Figure 25–13 Tracking problems require the driver to turn the steering wheel to have the vehicle travel in a straight line. This alters thrust line of vehicle. *(Hunter Engineering Company)*

the steering wheel will be straight ahead for straight-ahead travel.

If you set the front toe to the vehicle geometric centerline, ignoring the rear toe angle, a cocked steering wheel can result.

Remember! Collision damage causing rear axle setback or offset will adversely affect tracking. The rear axle, as with four-wheel steering, affects vehicle direction. Make sure the axles are in the correct position during an alignment. Modern four-wheel alignment equipment will automatically check axle positions and alignment.

Included Angle

Included angle is the sum of both camber and SAI angles. It is calculated by adding positive camber to the SAI angle. Include angle is calculated by subtracting negative camber from the SAI angle. It should generally be within ½° from side to side, Figure 25–15.

Figure 25–14 Study difference between positive and negative thrust angles. *(Hunter Engineering Company)*

As an example, if camber is 2° positive and SAI is 12°, the included angle is 14°. If camber is 2° negative and SAI is 12°, the included angle is 10°.

On collision damaged vehicles, the included angle can help in diagnosing damaged parts between the upper and lower pivot points.

Wheelbase

Wheelbase is the measurement between the center of the front and rear wheel hubs. During collision repairs, individual wheelbase can be used as a diagnostic measurement. See Figure 25–16.

Wheelbase is measured to determine the forward and rearward position of each wheel. It is measured

from identical known good points on the body structure or frame. Wheelbase measurements can be used to identify caster or axle positioning problems at each wheel.

Wheelbase is generally acceptable if the difference is within ⅛″ (3 mm) from side to side.

Different individual wheelbases from side to side:

1. Are generally created by frame or chassis misalignment following a collision;

2. May be caused by the movement of an engine cradle;

3. Will change caster by moving the lower ball joint or pivot point forward or rearward in relation to the upper pivot point; and

4. May be designed in by the vehicle maker on some vehicles.

Figure 25–15 Included angle is the sum of both camber and SAI angles. It is calculated by adding positive camber to the SAI angle. *(I-CAR)*

Figure 25–16 During wheel alignment, you may have to check wheelbase to find reason for improper wheel alignment. Set-back of one or more wheels may have resulted from collision. *(Courtesy of Mitchell International, Inc.)*

Set-Back

Set-back is when one front wheel is moved back. It creates an unequal wheelbase between the left and right sides of a vehicle. Set-back may be caused by an impact to a front wheel assembly that moves a lower control arm, engine cradle, or radius rod backwards. It may be designed into some suspension systems.

Set-back should be set the same from side to side unless designed into the suspension system. Specifications are generally not listed in a spec manual, but if designed into the suspension system, can be identified by wheelbase specifications that are listed different from side-to-side.

Excessive set-back may cause a vehicle to pull to the side where set-back exists. Pulling may also occur during braking.

PRE-ALIGNMENT CHECKS

Before making adjustments, conduct the following pre-alignment checks:

1. VISUALLY INSPECT everything visible with the vehicle sitting on the shop floor, steering wheel effort, play in steering, and power steering fluid. This also includes checking for uneven tire wear and mismatched tire sizes or types. Look for normal wear as well as the results of collision damage. Look for towing damage as well.

Reading tires involves inspecting tire tread wear and diagnosing the cause. Improper camber and toe show up as specific tread patterns.

2. MEASURE RIDE HEIGHT. Each of the front and rear wheels must carry the same amount of weight. The vehicle is designed to ride at a specific

Front

Rear

Figure 25–17 *Curb height or ride height can affect wheel alignment. Vehicle should be at curb weight when measuring. Measure from specified points on vehicle to level shop floor. If not correct, springs may have weakened or suspension parts may have been damaged. (FMC Automotive Equipment Division)*

height, sometimes referred to as *ride* or curb *height*, Figure 25–17. Ride height specs are published in the service manuals and some alignment spec books.

Ride height is measured from the shop floor to specific points on the vehicle. Ride height should be correct before performing a wheel alignment. Various conditions that affect ride height and alignment include the following:

Vehicle load affects weight on the front suspension and affects alignment angles. Heavy load in trunk takes weight off front suspension and changes caster and camber angles. Coil and leaf springs should be checked and replaced if broken or sagged beyond tolerance. Torsion bars should be checked and adjusted if ride height is incorrect. Spring mounting locations, air spring suspensions, system faults, and shock absorbers can also affect ride height.

If the vehicle leans to one side or seems to be lower on one side than on the other, something is wrong. To isolate the problem, place a jack in the center of the main crossmember in the front of the vehicle. Raise the front of the vehicle, and look at the rear of the vehicle. If the rear looks level, then the problem is in the front suspension, on the side of the vehicle that shows the lean. If the rear is not level, then the problem is with the low side of the rear suspension.

3. INSPECT THE UNDERSIDE of the vehicle for problems. With the vehicle raised, inspect all steering components such as control arm bushings, upper strut mounts, pitman arm, idler arm, center link, tie-rod ends, ball joints (if equipped) for looseness, popping sounds, binding, and broken boots. Damaged parts must be repaired before adjusting alignment angles.

4. ROAD TEST the vehicle. Begin the alignment with a road test. While driving the vehicle, check to see that the steering wheel is straight. Feel for vibration in the steering wheel as well as in the floor or seats. Notice any pulling or abnormal handling problems, such as hard steering, tire squeal while cornering, or mechanical pops or clunks. This helps find problems that must be corrected before proceeding with the alignment.

Make sure the steering wheel is properly centered during your road test. If not, you will have to adjust the tie-rod ends to center it with the wheel straight ahead.

DIAGNOSTIC CHECKS

The analysis of ride and handling complaints involves the consideration of diagnostic angles. Suspension system parts must be considered as moving parts in vehicle operation; diagnostic checks evaluate the parts as they move.

When a vehicle has a steering problem, the first diagnostic check should be a visual inspection of the entire vehicle for anything obvious; bent wheels, misalignment of the cradle, and so on. If there is nothing obviously wrong with the vehicle, make a series of diagnostic checks without disassembling the vehicle.

One of the most useful checks that can be made with a minimum of equipment is a jounce-rebound check. Look at Figure 25–18.

Jounce is the motion caused by a wheel going over a bump and compressing the spring. During jounce the wheel moves up toward the chassis. Jounce can be simulated by sitting on the bumper and pushing down on the vehicle. The vehicle should jounce equally on both sides.

Rebound is the motion caused by a wheel going into a dip or returning from a jounce and extending the spring. During rebound, the wheel moves down away from the chassis. Rebound can be simulated by

Figure 25–18 Note difference between jounce and rebound. *(Hunter Engineering Company)*

lifting up on the bumper. The vehicle should lift equally on both sides.

A *jounce-rebound check* will determine if there is misalignment in the rack-and-pinion gear. For a quick check, unlock the steering wheel and see if it moves during jounce and/or rebound. For a more careful check, use a pointer and a piece of chalk. Use the chalk to make a reference mark on the tire tread and place the pointer on the same line as the chalk mark.

Jounce and rebound the suspension system a few times while someone watches the chalk mark and the pointer. If the mark on the wheel moves unequally in and out on both sides of the vehicle, chances are there

is a steering arm or gear out of alignment. If the mark does not move or moves equally in and out on both sides of the vehicle, the steering arm and gear are probably all right.

The next diagnostic check is for turning radius. This check evaluates the proper relationship of the two front wheels as they are turned through a steering arc. To measure turning radius, one wheel is turned on a turn plate or protractor a given amount; the amount of rotation of the opposite wheel is measured with a similar turn plate or protractor. The process is then repeated with the opposite wheel. The results are compared right to left to determine if the two front wheels are rotating through the same arc.

On a typical turning radius check, the left front wheel is turned out 20 degrees and the right wheel rotation is measured. The readings will usually not match with the right wheel. The right wheel should turn in the same amount or about 2 degrees less. The difference accounts for the turning radius difference between the inside and outside wheels during cornering.

The process is repeated with the right wheel. It is turned 20 degrees out. The movement of the left wheel is measured on the protractor or turn plate. The left wheel should turn in the same amount or about 2 degrees less.

By design, a vehicle might use a different turning radius from one side to the other. If in doubt, refer to the manufacturer's specifications. If these measurements do not repeat within 2 degrees, damage to the steering arms or gear is indicated. Turning radius measurements are especially useful in determining whether an improper toe condition is caused by poor wheel alignment or damaged suspension components.

NOTE! RADIAL TIRES CAUSE PROBLEMS WHEN THEY HAVE DEFECTIVE BELTS, UNUSUAL WEAR PATTERNS, UNEVEN AIR PRESSURE, OR ARE MISMATCHED. THESE TIRE PROBLEMS CAN CAUSE THE TECHNICIAN TO MISDIAGNOSE STEERING AND ALIGNMENT PROBLEMS.

Bent wheels are common after a collision. Sometimes, wheel damage can be so small it is difficult to detect visually. A dial indicator can be used to measure actual wheel runout, Figure 25–19.

Loose tie-rod ends are another common problem. They can wear quickly and cause play in the steering. Never try to align wheels if there are loose, worn tie-rod ends, Figure 25–20.

Remember! Before making any adjustment affecting caster, camber, or toe-in, the following checks should be made first:

**Front and Rear Wheel
Axial Runout**

Standard:
Aluminum Wheel: 0 - 0.3 mm (0 - 0.01 in)

**Front and Rear Wheel
Radial Runout**

Standard:
Aluminum Wheel: 0 - 0.3 mm (0 - 0.01 in)

Figure 25–19 Bent wheels are common problem in collision repair. Dial indicator will let you accurately check axial and radial runout of wheels. (© American Honda Motor Co., Inc.)

1. Make sure the vehicle is sitting on a level surface (side to side and front to rear).

2. Rotate the tires if needed. Check the tires for similar tread design, depth, and construction.

3. Make sure all tires are inflated to recommended pressure.

4. Inspect for worn or bent parts and replace. Much of this should be checked during body/frame correction.

5. Check and adjust wheel bearings if necessary. Spin tires. Check for looseness or unusual noises.

6. Check for unbalanced loading (proper chassis height). This should be checked after body/frame correction. Remove objects from trunk and passenger compartment.

7. Check for loose ball joints, tie-rod ends, steering relay rods, control arms, and stabilizer bar attachments.

8. Check for runout of wheels and tires.

9. Check for defective shock absorbers.

10. Check the condition and type of equipment being used. Follow the manufacturer's instructions for using the equipment.

WHEEL ALIGNMENT PROCEDURES

After a thorough inspection and replacement of any damaged parts, wheel alignment adjustment is next. The main purpose of wheel alignment is to allow the wheels to roll without scuffing, dragging, or slipping on the road.

Figure 25–20 Always check tie-rod ends for wear before adjusting wheel alignment. Play in joint must be within specs. (Saab Cars USA, Inc.)

The adjustment order—caster, camber, toe—is recommended regardless of the make of vehicle or its type of suspension. Methods of adjustment vary. Refer to the manufacturer's service manual for details.

A typical alignment procedure for a wheel alignment is as follows:

1. Obtain manufacturer's specifications for the vehicle's wheel alignment checks and adjustments. Specs will vary depending upon the design of the vehicle.

2. Mount the alignment equipment on the vehicle, following the owner's manual directions. Equipment designs and operating procedures vary. Therefore, you must refer to the materials published by the equipment maker for proper use. See Figure 25–21.

3. Check steering and axis inclination.

4. Check and adjust camber. If the equipment shows camber to be within specs, no adjustment is necessary. If not within specs, you must change camber the right amount and direction. In Figure 25–22, note typical methods of adjusting camber.

5. Check and adjust caster. If the car tends to pull to one side or if equipment readings are off, change caster. Again, refer to Figure 25–22 for adjustment methods.

6. Check turning radius. Replace parts if needed.

7. Check and adjust toe LAST. Refer to Figure 25–23.

Toe is the last adjustment made in an alignment. It is made at the tie-rods. Toe adjustments on a rack-and-pinion unit must be made evenly

Figure 25–21 Alignment equipment basically uses turning radius gauge (degree wheel) and caster-camber gauge (level) to measure alignment angles. Tires are centered on top of turning radius gauges. Wheel adapter holds caster-camber gauge. *(Hunter Engineering Company)*

Figure 25–22 Study various ways of adjusting caster, camber, SAI, and included angle. *(Illustrations Courtesy of Perfect Circle-Dana Corp.)* A: Shims are often provided for upper-lower control arm suspension systems. Different thickness shims in front and rear changes caster. Inserting same size shims only changes camber, SAI, and included angle. B: Turning eccentric cam bolt will pivot control arm in and out for SAI, included angle, and camber-caster adjustment. C: Shortening or lengthening strut rod will pivot outer end of lower control arm to alter caster. D: Cam bolts on lower end of strut will pivot steering knuckle as needed for camber, SAI, and included angle adjustment. E: Many strut suspensions have slotted holes for adjustment of caster, camber, SAI, and included angle. If not slotted, aftermarket kits are available to allow for adjustment.

Figure 25–22 (Continued) F: Different thickness shims can be placed between rear knuckle and strut to adjust alignment.

on both sides of the rack-and-pinion gear. If they are not made evenly, the rack assembly will be off-center in the gear. This can cause a pull due to the steering wheel being off-center. This pull condition is especially common with power-assisted

rack-and-pinion gears. The steering assembly must be centered before these adjustments are made.

8. Document your readings and adjustment values.

ALIGNMENT EQUIPMENT VARIATIONS

Note that most modern wheel alignment equipment are computer controlled, Figure 25–24. They will actually guide you through the alignment process, giving step-by-step instructions. Some equipment will even warn you if any alignment angle is not acceptable. This greatly simplifies the wheel alignment process.

Today most vehicles use a four-wheel alignment. Approximately 80 percent of today's vehicles require front- and rear-wheel alignment. This is due to the growing number of vehicles with independent rear suspensions. Collision repair of any magnitude usually requires at least a four-wheel alignment check.

ROAD TEST AFTER ALIGNMENT

After making your wheel alignment adjustments, road test the vehicle. Make sure the vehicle does not pull to one side of the road, vibrate, or exhibit other troubles.

See Figures 25–25 and 26. They are troubleshooting charts for the steering and suspension systems.

Figure 25–23 Toe is adjusted by shortening or lengthening tie-rod ends. If steering wheel is centered, change length of right and left sides equally. This will keep steering wheel centered. If steering wheel is not centered, change tie-rods differently to center wheel. (Courtesy of Ford Motor Company)

Figure 25–24 Today's computerized alignment equipment will guide you through alignment procedure. This unit uses arrows and scales to show readings of alignment angles all at once. It also lets you know which readings are within specs and which are not. (Hunter Engineering Company)

SUSPENSION PROBLEM DIAGNOSIS

Check	Problem					
	Noise	Instability	Pulls to One Side	Excessive Steering Play	Hard Steering	Shimmy
Tires/Wheels	Road or tire noise	Low or uneven air pressure; radials mixed with belted bias ply tires	Low or uneven air pressure; mismatched tire sizes	Low or uneven air pressure	Low or uneven air pressure	Wheel out of balance or uneven tire wear or overworn tires; radials mixed with belted bias ply tires
Shock Dampers (Struts/ Absorbers)	Loose or worn mounts or bushings	Loose or worn mounts or bushings; worn or damaged struts or shock absorbers	Loose or worn mounts or bushings	—	Loose or worn mounts or bushings on strut assemblies	Worn or damaged struts or shock absorbers
Strut Rods	Loose or worn mounts or bushings	Loose or worn mounts or bushings	Loose or worn mounts or bushings	—	—	Loose or worn mounts or bushings
Springs	Worn or damaged	Worn or damaged	Worn or damaged, especially rear	—	Worn or damaged	—
Control Arms	Steering knuckle control arm stop; worn or damaged mounts or bushings	Worn or damaged mounts or bushings	Worn or damaged mounts or bushings	—	Worn or damaged mounts or bushings	Worn or damaged mounts or bushings
Steering System	Component wear or damage	Component wear or damage	Component wear or damage	Component wear or damage	Component wear or damage	Component wear or damage
Alignment	—	Front and rear, especially caster	Front, camber and caster	Front	Front, especially caster	Front, especially caster
Wheel Bearings	On turns or speed changes: front-wheel bearings	Loose or worn (front and rear)	Loose or worn (front and rear)	Loose or worn (front)	—	Loose or worn (front and rear)
Brake System	—	—	On braking	—	On braking	—
Other	Clunk on speed changes: trans-axle; click on turns: CV joints; ball joint lubrication				Ball joint lubrication	Loose or worn friction ball joints

Figure 25–25 Study chart that shows suspension system problems that can affect alignment.

STEERING PROBLEM DIAGNOSIS

Check	Problem					
	Noise	Instability	Pull to One Side	Excessive Steering Play	Hard Steering	Shimmy
Tires/Wheels	Road or tire noise	Low or uneven tire pressure; radial tire lead	Low or uneven tire pressure; radial tire lead	Low or uneven tire pressure	Low or uneven tire pressure	Unbalanced wheel; uneven tire wear; over-worn tires
Tie-Rods	Squeal in turns: worn ends	—	Incorrect toe: tie-rod length	Worn ends	Worn ends	Worn ends
Mounts or Bushings	Parallelogram steering: steering gear mounting bolts, linkage connections; rack-and-pinion steering: rack mounts	Idler arm bushing	—	Parallelogram steering: steering gear mounting bolts, linkage connections; rack-and-pinion steering: rack mounts	Parallelogram steering: steering gear mounting bolts, linkage connections; rack-and-pinion steering: rack mounts	Parallelogram steering: steering gear mounting bolts, linkage connections; rack-and-pinion steering: rack mounts
Steering Linkage Components	Bent or damaged steering rack	Incorrect center link or rack height	Incorrect center link or rack height	Worn idler arm, center link, or pitman arm studs; worn or damaged rack	Idler arm binding	Worn idler arm, center link, or pitman arm studs
Steering Gear	Improper yoke adjustment on rack-and-pinion steering	—	—	Improper yoke adjustment on rack-and-pinion steering; worn steering gear or incorrect gear adjustment on parallelogram steering; loose or worn steering shaft coupling	Parallelogram steering: low steering gear lubricant, incorrect adjustment; rack-and-pinion: bent rack, improper yoke adjustment	—
Power Steering	—	—	—	—	Fluid leaks; loose, worn, or glazed steering belt; weak pump; low fluid level	—
Alignment	—	—	Unequal caster or camber	—	Excessive positive caster, excessive scrub radius (incorrect camber and/or SAI)	Incorrect caster

Figure 25–26 Study chart for diagnosing steering system problems.

Summary

- Wheel alignment involves positioning the vehicle's tires so that they roll properly over the road surface. Wheel alignment is essential to safety, handling, fuel economy, and tire life.

- Caster is the angle of the steering axis of a wheel from true vertical, as viewed from the side of the vehicle. It is a directional stability adjustment.

- Camber is the angle represented by the tilt of the wheels inward or outward when viewed from the front of the vehicle. It assures that all of the tire tread contacts the road surface. It is usually the second angle adjusted during a wheel alignment.

- Toe is the difference in the distance between the front and rear of the left- and right-hand wheels. It is critical to tire wear.

Technical Terms

wheel alignment   *thrust angle*
caster   *wheelbase*
camber   *set-back*
toe   *reading tires*
steering axis inclination   *curb height*
included angle   *jounce*
turning radius   *rebound*
tracking

Review Questions

1. List four reasons a vehicle would require an alignment after doing collision repair.

2. Give six basic wheel alignment angles.

3. _____ _____ tilts the tops of the steering knuckles toward the rear of the vehicle, when viewed from the side of the vehicle.

4. _____ _____ has the top of the wheel tilted out, when viewed from the front. The outer edge of the _____ _____ contacts the road.

5. Camber is adjustable on most vehicles. True or false?

6. Explain the importance of proper toe adjustment.

7. Technician A says that rear-wheel drive vehicles are often adjusted to have toe-in at the front wheels. Technician B says that front-wheel drive vehicles need to have their front wheels set for a slight toe-out.
   Who is correct?
   a. Technician A
   b. Technician B
   c. Both Technicians
   d. Neither Technician

8. SAI can be used with structural measurements to diagnose:
   a. Strut tower misalignment
   b. Control arm mounting location damage
   c. Misaligned frame or body structure
   d. All of the above
   e. None of the above

9. Define the term "tracking."

10. This is the measurement between the center of the front and rear wheel hubs.
    a. Scrub
    b. Tracking
    c. Toe
    d. Wheelbase

11. How and why do you read tires?

12. How do you measure vehicle ride height?

13. In your own words, how do you inspect the underside of a vehicle before a wheel alignment?

14. Summarize the eight major steps for a wheel alignment.

Activities

1. Visibly inspect the alignment and tire wear on several cars. Try to find one with obvious misalignment. Write a report of your findings.

2. Refer to the operating manual for alignment equipment. Read through the specific procedures for the alignment equipment. Summarize any unique procedure and prepare to discuss it with the class.

CHAPTER 26

ELECTRICAL REPAIRS

Objectives

After studying this chapter, you should be able to:

- Define the terms voltage, current, and resistance.

- Use various kinds of electrical test instruments.

- Find electrical problems.

- Explain the operation of automotive electrical-electronic systems.

- Describe the operation of computer systems.

- Use a vehicle's self-diagnosis capabilities.

- Use scanners to find electrical-electronic problems.

Introduction

Electrical systems, such as the ignition, charging, starting, lighting, and computer systems, perform needed functions for a vehicle. It is almost impossible to work on any section of a vehicle without handling some type of electrical part.

Electrical system repair is an essential aspect of repairing a collision-damaged vehicle. Electrical repairs are becoming more common due to the increased use of computer-controlled systems. These repairs can be made complicated by the many computer circuits running throughout the body structure.

This chapter will summarize the operation and repair of electrical-electronic systems.

NOTE! IN THIS TEXT, THE TERM "ELECTRICAL" REFERS TO NON-SOLID STATE COMPONENTS, LIKE RELAYS, SOLENOIDS, CIRCUIT BREAKERS. "ELECTRONIC" REFERS TO SOLID STATE COMPONENTS, LIKE DIODES, TRANSISTORS, AND COMPUTERS.

ELECTRICAL TERMINOLOGY

Various vehicle systems are controlled by a series of electrical controls and devices. To understand electricity, you must become familiar with three electrical terms: current, voltage, and resistance. See Figure 26–1.

Current is the movement of electricity (electrons) through a wire or circuit. It is measured in amperes or amps using an ammeter. The common electrical symbol for current is "A" or "I."

Voltage is the pressure that pushes the electricity through the wire or circuit. The *power source* generates the voltage which causes current flow. Voltage is measured in volts using a voltmeter. The symbol for voltage is "E" or "V." Refer to Figure 26–2.

Resistance is a restriction or obstacle to current flow. It tries to stop the current caused by the applied voltage. Circuit or part resistance is measured in ohms using an ohmmeter. The symbol for resistance is R or Ω.

A *conductor* carries current to the parts of a circuit. *"Hot wires"* connect the battery positive to the components of each circuit. *Insulation* stops current flow and keeps the current in the metal wire conductor. The body structure provides the *ground* conductor back to the battery negative cable.

Electric Circuits

An *electric circuit* contains a power source, conductors, and a load. Some resistance is designed into a circuit in the form of a load. The *load* is the part of a circuit that converts electrical energy into another form of energy (light, movement, heat, etc.), Figure 26–2. Other parts are added to this

simple circuit to protect it from damage and to do more tasks.

A *series circuit* has only one conductor path or leg for current through the circuit. Current must flow through the wires and components one after the other. If any part of the circuit is *opened* (disconnected), all of the series circuit stops working.

A *parallel circuit* has two or more legs or paths for current. Current can flow through either leg independently. One path can be *closed* (electrically connected) and the other opened, and the closed path will still operate.

A *series-parallel circuit* has both series and parallel branches in it. It has characteristics of both circuit types. All the circuit in a vehicle can be classified and tested using the rules of these three circuits.

Ohm's Law

Ohm's Law is a math formula for calculating an unknown electrical value (amps, volts, or ohms) when two values are known. If you know two values, you can mathematically calculate the third unknown value.

For instance, if you know that a circuit has 12.6 volts and 2 amps, what is the circuit resistance? Plug your two known values into Ohm's Law and you can find out (12.6 divided by 2 equals 6.3 amps). Look at Figure 26–3.

Magnetism

Magnetism involves the study of how electric fields act upon ferrous (iron containing) objects. Many electrical-electronic parts utilize magnetism.

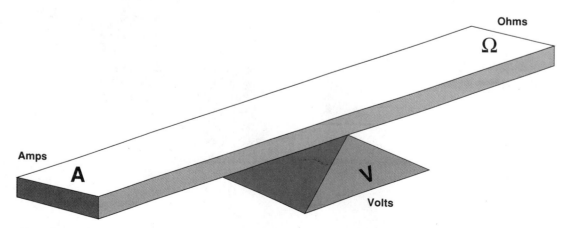

Figure 26–1 There is a relationship between three basic values of electricity. Volts is pressure that powers circuit. Ohms is needed to control amps. A change in one value affects others. *(I-CAR)*

Figure 26–2 Note comparison of electric and hydraulic circuits. Both use same principles. *(I-CAR)* A: Electric circuit has battery as power source, switch to control current, and light bulb as load. B: Hydraulic circuit has reservoir, valve, and hydraulic motor as basic parts.

A *flux* or *magnetic field* is present around permanent magnets and current carrying wires. This invisible energy is commonly used to move metal parts. An *electromagnet* is a set of *windings* (wires wrapped around) an iron core. When current flows through the windings, a powerful magnetic field is produced. Electric motors, solenoids, relays and other parts use this principle.

DIAGNOSTIC EQUIPMENT

Locating an electrical fault is NOT possible without using *diagnostic tools* (meters, test lights, jumper wires, etc.). Keep in mind that today's delicate electronic systems can be damaged if the wrong methods and equipment are used.

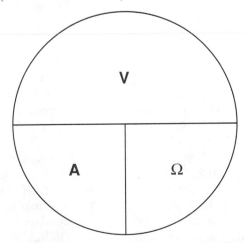

Voltage = Current × Resistance

Current = Voltage ÷ Resistance

Resistance = Voltage ÷ Current

Figure 26–3 Ohm's Law is simple formula for calculating electrical values in circuit. *(I-CAR)*

Digital Volt-Ohm Meter   **Analog Volt-Ohm Meter**   **Test Light**

Figure 26–4 These are basic electrical testing tools. Each has its advantages and disadvantages. *(Courtesy of Chrysler Corporation)*

Multimeters

A *multimeter* is a voltmeter, ohmmeter, and ammeter combined into one case. Also called a *VOM* (Volt-Ohm-Ammeter), it can be used to measure actual electrical values for comparison to known good values. Refer to Figure 26–4.

The *digital multimeter (DVOM)* has a number readout for the test value. This type is recommended by auto manufacturers because it will NOT damage delicate electronic components. A high impedance (10 mega-ohm input) DVOM is recommended to avoid damaging sensitive components. Digital readouts give the precise measurement needed for proper diagnosis. DVOMs are used in conjunction with the vehicle's service manual.

An *analog multimeter (AVOM)* has a pointer needle that moves across the face of a scale when making electrical measurements. Use of an AVOM can damage sensitive electronic components. They should

only be used when testing all electrical, NOT electronic, circuits. They help show a fluctuating or changing reading, like from an intermittent (changing) problem.

Test Light, Jumper Wires

An externally powered *test light* is often used to determine if there is current flowing through the circuit. One lead of the test lamp is connected to a good ground. The other lead connects to a point in the circuit. If the lamp lights, current is present at that point. Look at Figure 26–5.

Whenever a technician has an electrical system problem that does NOT directly concern the computer, a test light is handy.

Connect the light to the voltage source and to ground. If the test light does NOT glow, there is an open circuit somewhere. If the light is on, but the part does NOT work, the part is probably bad.

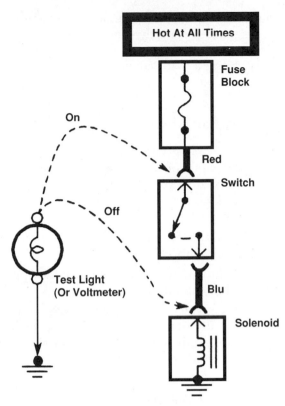

Figure 26–5 Test light provides fast way of probing for voltage. Make sure you are using a high impedance type when testing computer circuits. *(Courtesy of General Motors Corporation)*

> *WARNING! Test lights should NOT be used randomly, only when specified in the service manual procedures. They are NOT to be used on solid state circuits. They can damage electronic parts if their impedance (internal resistance) is too low.*

Jumper wires are used to temporarily bypass circuits or components for testing. They consist of a length of wire with an alligator clip at each end. They can be used to test circuit breakers, relays, lights, and other components, Figure 26–6.

Using Multimeters

When measuring resistance, always disconnect the circuit from the power source. The multimeter must never be connected to a circuit in which current is flowing. Doing so can damage the meter.

Use the service manual to determine the normal resistance of the part being checked. For example, a computer system sensor may have a normal resis-

Figure 26–6 Jumper wires can be used to bypass resistive components or to connect power directly to parts to check their operation.

tance reading of 45-55 ohms. You would select the "200" range on the multimeter. This is because the resistance reading of 44-55 ohms will be 200 ohms or less.

Always refer to the multimeter owner's manual before using the multimeter for diagnostic purposes. You must make sure that you understand how to use the multimeter before performing diagnostics. All multimeters are fairly similar, but there can be differences between makes.

To measure resistance:

1. Connect the multimeter test leads to opposite ends of the circuit or wire being tested.
2. Set the range selector switch on the highest range position. Turn the multimeter on.
3. Reduce the range setting until the meter shows a reading near the middle of its scale. Some DVOMs have an *auto ranging* function that adjusts the settings automatically.

Checking Continuity

A circuit remains closed and operational when it has *continuity* or a continuous conductor path. Typically, the service manual will ask for a continuity check of a wire or part. The continuity check is done to see if the electrical circuit has a complete path without any opens.

1. Connect the multimeter test leads to the opposite ends of the wire or part being tested.
2. Set the range selector switch on the highest resistance range position.
3. Read the meter. An *infinite reading* (maximum resistance) shows an open. A zero reading shows continuity.

Measuring Voltage

The multimeter allows you to select either alternating current voltage (ACV) or direct current voltage (DCV). The ACV is selected when measuring alternating current voltage. *AC current* is the type of current that is found in your home wiring.

DCV is selected when measuring direct current voltage. *DC current* is what is normally measured in the automobile. Some signals from sensors, however, can be AC or alternating.

When using the multimeter to measure voltage, the selection of the range scale is very important. If the voltage reading will be 12-14 volts, select the 20 V range on the multimeter. This range is selected because the voltage reading will be less than 20 volts.

Measuring Current

Current or amperage is sometimes measured to check the consumption of power by a load. For example, current draw is often measured when checking the condition of a starting motor.

Modern ammeters have an *inductive pickup* that slips over the wire or cable to measure current. With older ammeters, the circuit had to be disconnected and the meter connected in series to measure current.

A high current draw indicates a low resistance, like from a dragging or partially shorted motor. A low current draw means there is a high resistance in the circuit, like from a bad connection or dirty motor brushes.

Checking for Shorts

Many times adjoining wires within a wiring harness get pinched together or severed in a collision. A multimeter check will detect a severed wire.

When checking for a short between two adjoining wires in a harness:

1. Set the multimeter range selector switch the same as for a continuity check.

2. Connect the multimeter test leads to the opposite ends of the adjoining wires.

3. Because the wires are insulated, there should be a reading of almost infinity on the multimeter. If the multimeter reads zero the wires are shorted to ground or another ground wire.

WIRING DIAGRAMS

To determine and isolate electrical problems, it is often necessary to trace through the electrical circuit using a *wiring diagram*, Figure 26–7.

Figure 26–7 Wiring diagram is like a "road map" of circuit being tested. It shows how wires lead to different locations or parts in circuit. It also gives color codes, abbreviations, and other information for troubleshooting. *(Courtesy of General Motors Corporation)*

Abbreviations are used on wiring diagrams so that more information can be given. The service manual will have a chart explaining each abbreviation, number, and symbol on the diagram. The abbreviations for one auto maker are in Figure 26–8.

Electrical symbols are graphic representations of electrical-electronic components. Symbol charts can be found at the front of the wiring diagram section of the service manual. One is given in Figure 26–9.

The symbol used to identify a part is either a universal symbol or an auto manufacturer's symbol. Since manufacturers use different symbol designs for some parts, follow the symbol chart for the specific wiring diagram being used.

Most wires on wiring diagrams will be identified by their insulation color. *Wire color coding* allows you to find a specific wire in a harness or in a connector, Figure 26–10. The color code abbreviation chart can also be found at the front of the wiring diagram section of the service manual. Remember, different auto makers use different color coding abbreviations on their wiring diagrams.

Many wiring diagrams found in the service manuals also have circuits numbered. *Circuit numbering* is used to specify exactly which part of the circuit the service manual is referring to.

Remember! A wiring diagram is more like a "book" than a "picture." You can't understand a wiring

ABBREVIATIONS

Abbreviation	Meaning of Abbreviation	Abbreviation	Meaning of Abbreviation
A	Ampere (S)	ICM	Ignition control module
ABS	Anti-lock brake system	IG	Ignition
ASM	Assembly	kW	kilowatt
AC	Alternating current	LH	Left hand
A/C	Air conditioning	M/T	Manual transmission
ACC	Accessories	OD	Over drive
A/T	Automatic transmission	OPT	Option
C/B	Circuit breaker	RH	Right hand
CSD	Cold start device	RR	Rear
EI	Electronic ignition	RWAL	Rear wheel anti-lock brake system
EBCM	Electronic brake control module	ST	Start
ECGI	Electronic control gasoline injection	STD	Standard
ECM	Engine control module	SW	Switch
EGR	Exhaust gas recirculation	SWB	Short wheel base
EFE	Early fuel evaporation	TCM	Transmission control module
4A/T	4-speed automatic transmission	3A/T	3-speed automatic transmission
4X4	Four-wheel drive	V	Volt
FL	Fusible link	VSV	Vacuum switching valve
FRT	Front	W	Watt (S)
H/L	Headlight	WOT	Wide open throttle

Figure 26–8 Service manual will give chart such as this one explaining abbreviations. *(Reprinted with permission by American Isuzu Motors Inc.)*

Legend Of Symbols Used On Wiring Diagrams

Positive	Closed Contact	Armature And Brushes
Negative	Closed Switch	Connector
Ground	Open Switch	Male Connector
Fuse	Closed Ganged Switch	Female Connector
Gang Fuses With Buss Bar	Open Ganged Switch	Wire Continues Elsewhere
Circuit Breaker	Two Pole Single Throw Switch	Wire Goes To One Of Two Circiuts
Capacitor	Pressure Switch	Splice
Ohms	Solenoid Switch	Splice Identification
Resistor	Mercury Switch	Thermal Element
Variable Resistor	Diode Or Rectifier	Timer
Series Resistor	By - Directional Zener Diode	Multiple Connector
Coil	Motor	Wiring With Optional Wiring Without
Step Up Coil		"Y" Windings
Open Contact		Digital Readout
Single Filament Lamp	Thermistor	Fuel Injector
Dual Filament Lamp	Gauge	Denotes Wire Goes Through Bulkhead Disconnect
L.E.D. - Light Emitting Diode	Sensor	Denotes Wire Goes Through Steering Column Connector
Denotes Wire Goes Through Instrument Panel Connector	Denotes Wire Goes Through Grommet To Engine Compartment	Denotes Wire Goes Through Grommet
		Heated Grid Elements

Figure 26–9 Study typical symbols used on wiring diagrams. (Courtesy of Chrysler Corporation)

diagram just by glancing at it. Like a book, you must read the diagram carefully all the way through for a complete understanding.

A *wiring harness* has several wires enclosed in a protective covering. A vehicle has several wiring harnesses, usually named after its location in the vehicle. The service manual will give illustrations with code numbers for locating parts and connections, Figure 26–11.

The service manual may also give a *part location diagram* for finding electrical parts (harnesses, sensors, switches, computers, etc.). One is given in Figure 26–12.

Wht/Blk

WHT.....White	ORN.....Orange
YEL......Yellow	PNK.....Pink
BLK......Black	BRN.....Brown
BLU......Blue	GRY.....Gray
GRN.....Green	PUR.....Purple
RED......Red	LT BLU.....Light Blue
	LT GRN.....Light Green

Figure 26-10 Wire color codes are abbreviated on wiring diagrams. Study common abbreviations. (© American Honda Motor Co., Inc.)

Body Ground

Figure 26-11 Wire harness illustrations will give location of connectors, grounds, and so on. Charts in manual will explain numbers and letters denoting harness configuration. (Used with permission of Nissan Motor Corporation)

COMPUTER HARNESS

C1	Engine control module (ECM) *
C2	DLC diagnostic connector
C3	"Check Engine" Malfunction indicator lamp
C5	ECM harness ground
C6	Fuse panel
C8	ECM main relay
C9	Fuel pump fuse 15A
C10	Injector resistor
C11	Oxygen 10A heater fuse
C12	30A ECM main fusible link

ECM CONTROLLED COMPONENTS

1	Fuel injector
2	Idle air control
3	Fuel pump relay
6	Ignition control module ignition control
6a	Ignition coils
7	Knock sensor Module under charcoal canister
12	Exhaust Gas Recirculation (EGR) VSV
13	Air conditioning relay
14	Evaporate emission canister purge VSV
15	Induction air control plate system VSV

ECM INFORMATION SENSORS

A	Manifold Absolute Pressure
B	Heated oxygen sensor
C	Throttle position sensor
D	Engine coolant temperature
F	Vehicle speed sensor
H	Crank angle sensor
J	Knock sensor (under intake assembly)
K	Power steering pressure switch (in-line)
L	Intake air temperature

⬡ **EGR VALVE**

★ **CHASSIS GROUNDS**

EMISSION COMPONENTS (NOT ECM CONTROLLED)

N1	Crankcase vent valve (PCV)
N2	Exhaust gas recirculation valve back pressure transducer
N3	Spark plugs
N4	Fuel rail test fitting (for fuel pressure test)
N15	Fuel vapor canister

* The ECM is located behind the console in the lower dash.

Figure 26–12 Parts location diagrams show where sensors, and other parts are located on vehicle. *(Reprinted with permission by American Isuzu Motors Inc.)*

**SPST Switch
(Single Pole Single Throw)
Lights**

**Multiple Pole
Multiple Throw Switch
Door Ajar Light**

**Multiple Pole
Multiple Throw Switch
Power Window Wipers**

**Typical Mercury Switch
Deck Lid**

**SPDT Switch (Single
Pole Double Throw)
Door Lock / Unlock**

**Coolant Temperature
Switch**

Figure 26-13 Note various types of switches. *(Courtesy of Chrysler Corporation)*

ELECTRIC COMPONENTS

A *switch* is used to turn a circuit on or off manually (by hand). When the switch is CLOSED (on), the circuit is complete (fully connected) and will operate. Various types can be found in today's vehicles, Figure 26–13. A bad switch will often be open in both the closed and open positions.

An *inertia switch* is designed to shut the electric fuel pump off after a collision. Shown in Figure 26–14, they must be reset for the engine to restart after a collision. A button on the side of the inertia switch must be pressed to reclose the fuel pump circuit.

A *solenoid* is an electromagnet with a movable core or plunger. When energized, the plunger is pulled into the magnetic field to produce motion. Solenoids are used in many applications: door locks, engine idle speed, emission control systems, etc. See Figure 26–15. A bad solenoid can develop winding opens, shorts, or a high resistance problems.

A *relay* is a remote control switch. A small switch can be used to energize the relay. The relay coil then acts upon a movable arm to close the relay contacts. This allows a small switch to control high current going to a load. A relay is commonly used with electric motors since they draw heavy current, Figure 26–16. The service manual will often give relay locations for the specific make and model vehicle, Figure 26–17.

A bad relay will often have burned points that prevent current flow to the load. They can also develop coil opens and shorts that keep the points from closing.

**Front Of
Vehicle**

**Hinge
Support**

**Inertia
Switch**

**Left Inner
Wheel House**

Figure 26-14 Inertia switch is often found in trunk. Button on side of switch must be pressed to reset switch so fuel pump will operate. *(Courtesy of Ford Motor Company)*

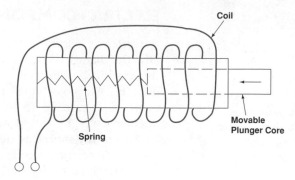

Figure 26-15 Solenoid is the winding wrapped around a movable core. Current flow produces magnetic field that pulls core into winding. *(I-CAR)*

Figure 26-16 Relay is coil mounted next to contact points. Small current through coil attracts and closes points. Then, large load current flows through contacts. *(Courtesy of Mitsubishi Motor Sales of America, Inc.)*

Compressor Clutch Relay
Wire Colors: WHT, YEL/BLK, RED and BLU/RED

Condenser Fan Timer Relay
Wire Colors: WHT/GRN, GRN, BLU/YEL and BLU/RED

Igniter Unit

Std Model:
Radiator Fan Relay
L and LS:
ALS Motor Relay

Dimmer Relay

Lighting Relay

Radiator Fan Relay
(L and LB)

Under-Hood Relay Box

Under-Hood Relay Box

Power Window Relay

ALB fail Safe Relay
(L and LS Only)
(PNK Connector)

ALB Fail Safe Relay
(L and LS Only)
(YEL Connector)

Condenser Fan Relay   Radiator Fan Timer Relay

Figure 26–17 Service manual will give illustrations showing locations of relays. (© American Honda Motor Co., Inc.)

Motors use permanent and electromagnets to convert electrical energy into a rotation motion for doing work. Some examples are the electric starting motor for the engine and stepper motors for computer control of parts, Figure 26–18.

Faulty motors can have worn bushings, brushes which decrease efficiency. They can also have winding shorts and opens that prevent motor operation.

**Permanent
Magnet Armature**

**Field
Windings**

**To
Computer**

**Flat On Pintle Valve
Shaft Keeps Shaft
From Turning**

Figure 26–18 Motor uses rotating armature inside stationary magnetic fields, converting electrical energy into rotating motion. *(I-CAR)*

CIRCUIT PROTECTION DEVICES

Circuit protection devices prevent excess current from burning wires and components. With an overload or short, too much current tries to flow. Without a fuse or breaker, the wiring in the circuit would heat up. The insulation would melt and a fire could result.

FUSES

Fuses burn in half with excess current to protect a circuit from further damage. They are normally wired between the power source and the rest of the circuit. There are three types of fuses in automotive use: cartridge, blade, and ceramic. Refer to Figure 26–19.

from the fuse panel and look at the element through the transparent plastic housing. Look for internal breaks and discoloration.

The *ceramic fuse* is used on many European imports. The core is a ceramic insulator with a conductive metal strip along one side. To check this fuse, look for a break in the contact strip on the outside of the fuse.

All fuse types can be checked with a circuit tester or multimeter. A *blown fuse* will have infinite resistance.

Fuse ratings are the current at which the fuse will blow. Fuse ratings are often printed on the fuse. Always replace a fuse with one of the same amp rating. If NOT, part damage can result from excess current flow.

A *fuse box* holds the various circuit fuses, breakers, and flasher units for the turn and emergency lights. It is often under the instrument panel, behind a panel in the foot well, or in the engine compartment.

Caution! Never permanently bypass a fuse or circuit breaker with a jumper wire. Do it only for test purposes.

Figure 26–19 Fuses protect circuits from over-current damage. *(Courtesy of General Motors Corporation)*

The *cartridge fuse* is found on most older domestic vehicles and a few imports. It is composed of a strip of metal enclosed in a glass or transparent plastic tube. To check the fuse, look for a break in the internal wire or metal strip. Discoloration of the glass cover or glue bubbling around the metal end caps is an indication of overheating.

Late-model domestic vehicles and many imports use **blade** or **spade fuses.** To check the fuse, pull it

FUSE LINKS

Fuse links or *fusible links* are smaller diameter wire spliced into the larger circuit wiring for over-current protection. Fuse links are normally found in the engine compartment near the battery. They are often installed in the positive battery lead that powers the ignition switch and other circuits that are live with the key off. Look at Figure 26–20.

Figure 26–20 Fuse links are often located in engine compartment right after battery. They have small wire that will burn to protect circuit from shorts. *(Courtesy of Chrysler Corporation)*

Fuse link wire is covered with a special insulation that bubbles when it overheats. This indicates that the fuse link has melted. If the insulation appears good, pull lightly on the wire. If the fuse link stretches, the wire has burned in half. When it is hard to determine if the fuse link is burned out, perform a continuity check.

Caution! Do NOT mistake a resistor wire for a fuse link. The resistor wire is generally longer and is clearly marked "Resistor—do NOT cut or splice."

When replacing fuse links, first cut the protected wire where it is connected to the fuse link. Then, solder a new fuse link of the same rating in place. Since the insulation on manufacturers' fuse links is flameproof, never fabricate a fuse link from ordinary wire because the insulation may NOT be flameproof.

A number of new electrical systems use maxi-fuses in place of traditional fuse links. Maxi-fuses look and operate like two-prong blade fuses, except they are much larger and can handle more current. Maxi-fuses are located in their own underhood fuse block.

Maxi-fuses are easier to inspect and replace than fuse links. To check a maxi-fuse, look at the fuse element through the transparent colored plastic side

housing. If there is a break in the element, the maxi-fuse has blown. To replace it, pull it from its fuse box or panel. Always replace a blown maxi-fuse with a new one having the same ampere rating.

CIRCUIT BREAKERS

Circuit breakers heat up, and open with excess current to protect the circuit, Figure 26–21. They do NOT suffer internal damage like a fuse. Many circuits are protected by circuit breakers. They can be fuse panel mounted or in-line. Like fuses, they are rated in amperes.

Each circuit breaker conducts current through an arm made of two types of metal bonded together (known as a *bimetal arm*). If the arm starts to carry too much current, it heats up. As one metal expands farther than the other, the arm bends, opening the contacts and breaking the current flow.

In the *cycling breaker,* the bimetal arm will begin to cool once the current to it is stopped. Once it returns to its original shape, the contacts close and power is restored. If the current is still too high, this cycle of breaking the circuit will be repeated.

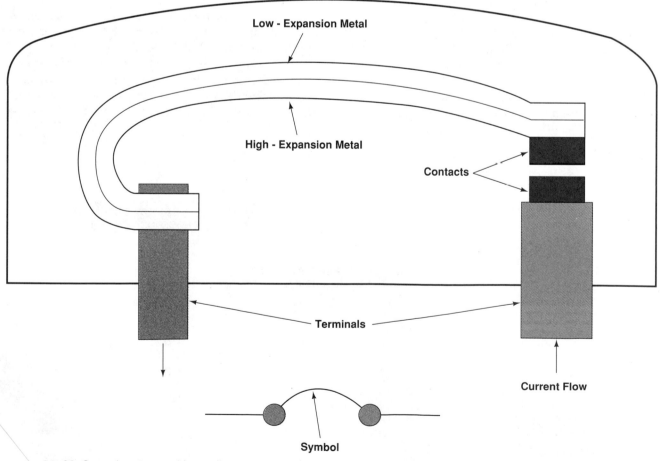

26–21 Circuit breaker used bimetal arm to open circuit with too much current.

Cycling circuit breakers are generally used in circuits that are prone to occasional overloads. These include power windows, in which a jammed or sticking window can overwork the motor. In this situation, a circuit breaker prevents the motor from burning out.

Noncycling breakers open and must be manually reset to close the circuit. In automotive work, two types of noncycling circuit breakers are used. One is reset by removing the power from the circuit. The other type is reset by depressing a reset button.

WARNING! When replacing fuses and circuit breakers, install one with the same amp rating. A higher rated unit could cause an electrical fire.

ELECTRICAL-ELECTRONIC SYSTEMS

The modern vehicle has numerous electrical-electronic systems, each designed to do a specific task. Some of these include:

Ignition System

The *ignition system* produces an electric arc in a gasoline engine to cause the fuel to burn. It must fire the spark plugs at the right time. The resulting combustion pressure forces the pistons down to spin the crankshaft. See Figure 26–22.

The *ignition coil* is a step-up transformer that produces high voltage (30,000 volts or more) needed to make current jump the spark plug gap. A switching device is either contact points or an electronic circuit that causes the ignition coil to discharge its electrical energy. Either a distributor or the computer controls the operations of the ignition coil.

Spark plug wires are high tension wires that carry coil voltage to each spark plug. The *spark plugs* use ignition coil high voltage to ignite the fuel mixture in the engine's combustion chambers.

Electronic Fuel Injection

Electronic fuel injection uses solenoid type injectors (fuel valves) and computer control to meter gasoline into the engine. An in-tank electric pump pulls fuel out of the gas tank. A second, in-line fuel pump then pushes fuel up to the engine.

A *pressure regulator* on the *fuel rail* (large fuel log or line at engine) limits maximum system pressure.

Starting and Charging Systems

The *starting system* has a large electric motor that turns engine flywheel. This spins or "cranks" the crankshaft until the engine starts and runs on its own power. See Figure 26–23.

The *ignition switch* in the steering column is used to connect battery voltage to a starter solenoid or relay. Other ignition switch terminals are connected to other electrical circuits. A *starter solenoid,* when energized, connects the battery and starting motor.

The *starting motor* is a large DC motor for rotating the engine flywheel. It normally bolts to the rear, lower, side of an engine. A few are mounted inside the engine, under the intake manifold. The *flywheel ring gear* meshes with the starter-mounted gear while cranking.

The *charging system* recharges the battery and supplies electrical energy when the engine is running, Figure 26–24. An alternator or belt driven DC generator produces this electricity.

A *voltage regulator,* usually mounted on the alternator, controls alternator output. *Charging system voltage* is typically 13 to 15 volts.

To quickly check the condition of a charging system, connect a voltmeter across the battery. With the engine off, you will read battery voltage. It should be above 12.5 volts. If not, the battery needs charging or is defective. When you start the engine with all electrical accessories ON (lights, radio, etc.), the voltage must stay above battery voltage. If NOT, there is something wrong with the charging system.

Engine No-Start Problem. Remember! If an engine cranks but fails to start, check for "spark" and "fuel." Both are needed for an engine to operate. See Figure 26–25.

To **CHECK FOR SPARK,** pull off one of the spark plug wires. Install an old spark plug into the wire and lay the spark plug on engine ground. When you crank the engine, a bright spark should jump across the spark plug gap. If not, something is wrong with the ignition system (blown fuse, damaged wires, crushed components, etc.).

If you have spark, **CHECK FOR FUEL.** This can often be done by installing a pressure gauge on the engine's fuel rail. A special test fitting is usually provided for a pressure gauge. With the engine cranking or the key on, the gauge should read within specs. If not, something is keeping the electric fuel pump(s) from working normally. Check for a clogged fuel filter, blow pump fuse, or wiring problem.

With older carbureted engines, you can look inside the carburetor to check for fuel. With the engine and air cleaner off, move the throttle opened and closed.

Figure 26–22 Note basic parts of an ignition system. Modern systems use computer to control coil instead of distributor. (© American Honda Motor Co., Inc.)

Figure 26–23 Study typical starting system. Trace wires from battery, through ignition switch, relay, solenoid, and motor. *(Reprinted with permission by American Isuzu Motors Inc.)*

Figure 26–24 Study charging system circuit. *(Courtesy of Chrysler Corporation)*

Figure 26–25 Read through typical troubleshooting chart.

This should make fuel squirt into the carburetor and engine. If not, something is preventing normal fuel flow from the tank to the engine.

ELECTRICAL PROBLEMS

Common electrical problems in a collision-damaged vehicle generally result from impact damage to wires and electrical-electronic components. These problems can be classified as opens, shorts, grounds, and abnormal resistance values.

An *open circuit* is an unwanted break in an electrical circuit. With an open circuit, current flow ceases and the circuit is dead. This effect can occur in a wire or in an electrical part, such as a light bulb filament.

A *short circuit* is an unwanted wire-to-wire connection in an electrical circuit, Figure 26–26. A short occurs when the insulation is worn between two adja-

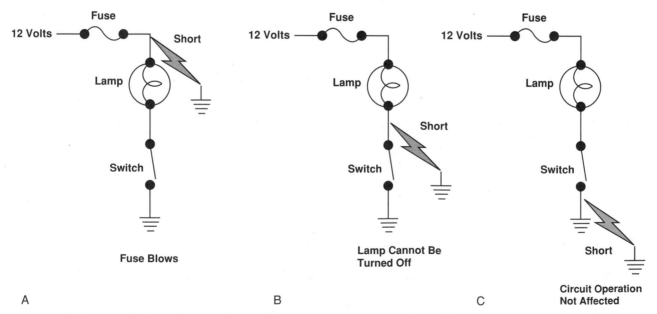

Figure 26–26 Location of short will have different effects on circuit. (I-CAR) A: Short at this location would blow fuse. B: Short here would bypass switch and bulb would always glow, even with switch open. C: Short at ground would not affect circuit.

cent wires and each wire contacts each other. Shorts often occur when wires are damaged or pinched due to collision damage.

A short can also result to ground, termed a *grounded circuit.* A grounded circuit condition occurs when the insulation on a wire is worn and the metal in the wire touches the metal of the vehicle body or frame.

When this occurs, the current is allowed to flow directly to ground without flowing to the electrical parts in the circuit. In other words, the current takes the *path of least resistance.* A low resistance or short to ground will blow the fuse or trip the circuit breaker for that circuit.

Bad grounds prevent current from returning to the battery. They are the most common cause of electrical system problems. If just the ground for one part is faulty, it will only affect the one circuit. If a major ground is faulty, many circuits will fail all at once. A major ground is one that connects the battery to the engine block or body. Sometimes a short is intermittent—it shorts momentarily when the vehicle bounces heavily or jars. A flickering dash light is an example of this.

An *abnormal resistance* is due to a bad connection or partial short. When tested, the circuit or component will show a value that is NOT within specs. For example, a high resistance in a light circuit will make the bulbs burn dimly. This is because the abnormally high circuit resistance is NOT allowing enough current to flow through the bulbs.

Diagnostic Charts

Diagnostic charts give possible causes for electrical problems and symptoms. They are important tools for collision repair technicians and insurance appraisers. A general electrical diagnostic chart is in Figure 26–27.

Most auto manufacturers use some type of diagnostic flow chart to aid technicians in the repair of electrical/electronically controlled systems. Diagnostic flow charts provide a systematic approach to troubleshooting and repair. They are found in service manuals and are given by vehicle make and model.

During the diagnosis, start at the top of the chart and follow the sequence down. The chart will point to the next area to move to after each check is performed. Work through the entire chart, step-by-step. Perform the repairs or parts replacements as indicated.

BATTERIES

A *battery* stores electrical energy chemically. It provides current for the starting system. It also provides current to all other electrical systems when the engine is NOT running.

Because of the potential electrical problems caused by a collision, always disconnect both battery cables right away. This will prevent the chance of an "electrical fire" while working.

When removing or disconnecting the battery, the ignition must be off to prevent voltage spikes. *Voltage spikes* are voltage surges that can destroy many microcircuits in today's electronic systems.

It is a good idea to remove the battery completely from the vehicle before doing any collision repair work. Once the battery has been placed on a bench, it should be checked for a cracked case and similar damage. In many cases with frontal collisions, the battery will have to be replaced.

A charge indicator which shows battery state of charge is often built into the top of the battery. It shows different colors to indicate battery condition.

A voltmeter or a specialized *battery tester* will also check battery condition (specific gravity or voltage). A good, fully charged battery will show 12.5 to 12.6 *open circuit volts* (nothing turned on). See Figure 26–28.

Charging a Battery

The procedure for charging a battery with a battery charger is as follows:

1. Disconnect the negative battery cable.
2. Check the battery casing for damage.
3. Check the water level and add water if necessary.
4. Loosen the vent caps, if the battery is so equipped.
5. Attach the charger clamps to the battery. Connect the red cable to the battery positive. Connect the black cable to negative.
6. Set the charger to the recommended settings.
7. Turn on the charger.
8. When charging is completed, turn off the charger.
9. Remove the charger clamps, negative first.
10. Replace the vent caps (if applicable).
11. Attach the negative battery cable.

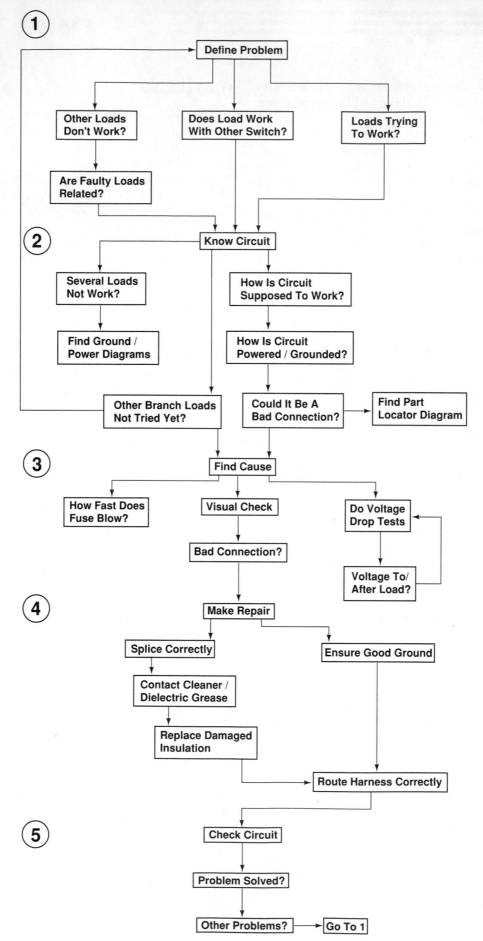

Figure 26–27 Read through chart showing basic troubleshooting method. *(I-CAR)*

Figure 26–28 Accurate voltmeter will check state-of-charge of battery. Fully charged battery should have 12.6 volts.

When charging is completed:

1. Turn off charger.

2. Remove charger clamps.

3. Replace vent caps.

4. Attach negative battery cable.

Jump Starting

Although it is a common practice in some collision repair shops, avoid jump starting whenever possible. The discharged battery can explode. This is true of both the vehicle being started and the vehicle providing the jump.

Jumper cables are used to connect two batteries together when one is "dead" (discharged). Connect the jumpers positive to positive and negative to negative. Connect the last jumper to a negative ground away from the battery. This will prevent any spark near the battery, Figure 26–29.

Special care is also necessary when charging or jump starting to avoid damaging computer circuits. Make sure everything is turned off and do not connect the jumper cables backwards.

When jump starting cannot be avoided, use the following procedure:

1. Inspect the battery casing for damage.

2. Position the two vehicles so the jumper cables will reach. Make sure the vehicles are NOT touching.

3. On the vehicle to be started, turn off all switches and lamps.

4. Connect one end of the jumper cable to the positive terminal of the discharged battery.

Figure 26–29 Jumper cables must be connected carefully to prevent sparks or part damage. Connect positive to positive and negative to negative in proper sequence. Note how last connection is away from battery on any good engine ground. *(Volkswagen of America)*

5. Connect the other end of the jumper cable to the positive terminal of the booster battery.

6. Connect one end of the other cable to the negative terminal of the booster battery.

7. Connect the other end to an engine bolt head, A compressor, alternator mounting bracket, or other ground. Do NOT connect it to the negative battery terminal of the discharged battery.

8. Make sure that the jumper cables are NOT in the way of moving engine parts.

9. Start the engine in the vehicle with the booster battery. Let it run a minute, then start the other vehicle.

10. Leave all switches off. Reduce engine speed to idle on both vehicles to prevent damage to the electrical system.

11. Disconnect all cables in reverse order, starting with the ground connection on the vehicle with the discharged battery.

Before reinstalling the battery after body work, clean its terminals. Use a battery post tool to remove a thin layer of oxidized metal from the terminals and battery cable ends. This will reduce resistance at the battery connections.

When installing a battery, make sure the ignition is off. Reconnect the positive battery cable and then the negative battery cable.

Battery Safety

■ *Danger! Batteries produce hydrogen gas when discharging or being charged. This gas, if ignited, can make a battery explode! Acid and battery parts can fly into the shop. Charge only in a well-ventilated area.*

1. Keep batteries away from welding operations, open flames, sparks, or other heat sources.
2. Do NOT charge batteries with cracked cases.
3. Do NOT smoke near batteries.
4. Batteries will charge faster if they are warm.
5. Do NOT charge a frozen battery.

Electrolyte in the battery is a mixture of water and sulfuric acid. When handling batteries, keep in mind that the electrolyte contains powerful sulfuric acid.

Wear eye protection whenever handling or charging the battery. Do NOT tilt the battery when carrying it. Be careful NOT to let electrolyte get on clothing, skin, or painted surfaces.

If the battery acid does spill, neutralize with baking soda. Immediately wash the skin or eyes with water and seek medical attention.

LIGHTING AND OTHER ELECTRIC CIRCUITS

The *lighting system* feeds electricity to light bulbs throughout the vehicle. A few are the headlight, turn light, stop light, backup light, emergency flasher, and interior light circuits.

Automotive lighting systems have become increasingly more sophisticated. Headlights and tail lights have grown into multiple-light systems. Indicator lights on the instrument panel commonly warn of failure or improper operation of the charging system, seat belts, brake system, parking brakes, door latches, computer systems, and other items.

When lights fail to function, check the bulb first. If the bulb is good, trace for an open feeding current to the dead bulb.

Other electrical circuits (horn, power windows, etc.) use the same principles just discussed. If needed, refer to the service manual for diagrams of each circuit. Circuit designs vary from vehicle to vehicle.

REPAIRING WIRING AND CONNECTIONS

Some damaged wiring can be repaired if correct procedures are followed, Figure 26–30. Be sure to follow the manufacturer's recommendations for wire repair.

When servicing electrical wiring, remember the following rules:

1. Never tug on the connectors. Use the special tools designed to separate the connectors. This will minimize the possibility of having electrical problems caused by intermittent contact.
2. Route wiring in the same location as the OEM.
3. Protect the electrical connectors from moisture and corrosion by using dielectric grease.
4. Use the same size and type of wiring for repairs. This is especially critical with sensor circuits that are affected by the slightest resistance change.
5. Air bag systems require specific repair procedures and materials.

SOLDER REPAIR

Soldering uses moderate heat and solder to join wires or other parts. All copper wire joints should be soldered, if possible.

A pencil type soldering iron is recommended for this procedure rather than a soldering gun, Figure 26–31. This is because guns have heavy coils that can create induced current in nearby components and damage them.

Be sure to use *rosin-core solder,* NOT acid-core, when soldering electrical connections. Acid fluxes create corrosion and can damage electronic components. In addition, dielectric grease is frequently used to protect connections from corrosion. When using this product, which has no acid content, follow the manufacturer's instructions and be sure NOT to cut into the moisture-sealed connector joints with test equipment probes.

Use the following procedure to make a solder connection:

1. Remove all traces of dirt and corrosion.
2. Strip the insulation back about ½ inch (13 mm) on each wire.
3. Wind the wires tightly together.
4. Heat the wire joint, NOT the solder. Touch the solder to the joint. Allow it to flow into the joint. Do NOT use too much solder.
5. Allow the joint to cool.
6. Gently pull on both ends of the wire to make sure the repair is secure.

Figure 26–30 Note use of connector to splice wire. A: Slide heat shrink tube over wire. B: Crimp connector down over wire ends. C: Solder connector to wires to assure good electrical connection. D: Use heat gun to shrink plastic tube around repair.

When soldering under a restricted area, under the instrument panel for example, hold the soldering iron above the joint. The solder will flow down toward the heat source and joint.

A *shrink tube* can also be used over the joint to further protect the connection from corrosion. When heated, the tube shrinks in size and provides a coating over the repair much like the original insulation.

Liquid electrical tape can also be applied over the joint with a brush. This will help make the electrical connection waterproof.

Electrical tape is made of flexible, thin plastic. It can be used around wire splices when the connection will NOT be exposed to moisture.

Using Splice Sleeves

Splice sleeves are compressed down over wires to connect them. Some manufacturers use aluminum in their wiring harnesses. Since aluminum cannot be sol-

Figure 26–31 Soldering gun should be used to join wires and prevent problems later.

dered, splice sleeves are good for this task. Avoid using splice sleeves when you can solder wires together. They can loosen with prolonged vibration.

To install a splice sleeve, proceed as follows:

1. Remove all traces of dirt and corrosion.

2. Strip the insulation back about ⅜ inch (9 mm) on each wire.

3. Match the splice sleeve to the wire diameter.

4. Insert the wire into the splice sleeve until the wire meets the stop in the center of the sleeve.

5. Select the proper sized jaw on the crimp tool for the splice sleeve being used.

6. Crimp both ends of the splice sleeve.

7. Heat the splice sleeve with a heat gun until the sealer oozes out of the ends.

8. Allow to cool.

9. Gently pull on both ends of the wire to make sure the repair is secure.

ELECTRICAL CONNECTOR SERVICE

An automotive electrical connector includes two plastic, snap-together fittings. They allow several wires to connect together securely. Various connector designs are used on vehicle and each requires a different method for disconnection.

If needed, inspect electrical connectors when trying to find opens. They can be torn apart or damaged in the collision, Figure 26–32. Figure 26–33 shows several ways to disconnect connectors.

COMPUTER SYSTEMS

Almost all vehicle systems are now controlled by computer. This would include the fuel, ignition, charging, suspension and brake, climate control, and other systems.

As shown in Figure 26–34, a basic *computer system* consists of:

1. Sensors (input devices)

Figure 26–32 Inspect connectors for these problems. They can be damaged during collision.

Figure 26–33 There are various methods for unlocking connectors. Refer to service manual if in doubt.

2. Actuators (output devices)

3. Computer (electronic control unit)

The *sensors* are devices that convert a condition (temperature, pressure, part movement, etc.) into an electrical signal. They send electrical input signals back to the computer, Figure 26–35. Once the computer analyzes the sensor data, it produces a preprogrammed output that is sent to system actuators.

Actuators are devices (solenoids or servo motors for example) that moves when responding to electrical signals from the computer. In this way, a computer system can REACT to sensor inputs and then ACT upon these conditions by operating the motors or solenoids. Refer to Figure 26–36.

The *computer* is a complex electronic circuit that produces a known electrical output after analyzing electrical inputs. Today's vehicles can have one or

Figure 26–34 Study basic computer system circuit. (I-CAR)

Figure 26–35 Numerous sensors provide inputs for computer.

Figure 26–36 Relays, solenoids, and motors provide outputs for computer system.

more computers that monitor and control the operation of electrical systems.

Self-Diagnostics

Computer self-diagnostics means the computer system can detect its own problems. Most electronic systems have built-in, self-diagnostic capabilities. Examples would be ABS braking systems and air bag systems.

If problem exists, the computer will turn on a warning light in the instrument panel. This would tell you to use self-diagnostics to find the source of the trouble. The computer performs a self-check each time the ignition key is turned to the ON position.

The self-check makes sure that all of the bulbs, fuses, sensors, and electronic control modules are working. If the self-check finds a problem, it might store a *fault code* (code representing specific circuit or part with a problem) for later servicing. A fault code is recorded into the computer's memory whenever the system malfunctions.

An *assembly line diagnostic link* (ALDL) connector is provided for reading fault or trouble codes. This connector can be located in the passenger or engine compartment.

To read computer fault codes, plug a *scan tool* into the ALDL connector. The scan tool will then convert the computer number code into an explanation of the problem. The code numbers are then displayed on the tester's display screen. This is the best way to find electrical problems on modern vehicles.

Since fault codes vary from model to model, the service manual and scanner owner's manual must be consulted.

Before reading fault codes, do a visual check to make sure the problem is NOT a result of wear, loose connections, or faulty vacuum hoses. Inspect the air cleaner and throttle body or fuel injection system. Do

NOT forget the PCV system and hoses and make sure the vapor canister is NOT flooded. Look at the wiring harnesses and connectors and the charging and alternator system; the connectors are especially important. The low level electrical signals in today's electronic circuits cannot tolerate the increased resistance caused by corrosion in connector contacts.

If you do not have a scan tool, you can use *computer self-diagnosis* to find circuit problems. By jumping across specific terminals on the ALDL connector or turning the ignition key on and off as directed, the computer will flash a Morris type code indicating the problem. You can note these flashes and compare them to manual details to find the problem.

The computer itself is a highly reliable electronic device, Figure 26–37. Trouble is more often caused by damaged wiring, connections, or sensors. The computer is one of the last parts to suspect with computer system malfunctions.

Computers can be found in just about any location on the vehicle. These include:

1. Under the dash
2. Under the seats
3. Under the hood
4. Behind kick panels
5. In the trunk

A *PROM* is a programmable read-only memory chip mounted in the computer. If you have to replace a computer, you must install the PROM from the old computer into the new one. This will assure that the computer is programmed for the equipment on the vehicle being serviced.

Disconnecting the battery can erase stored electrical/electronic system fault codes on some vehicles. Sometimes you can pull and reinstall the computer fuse to erase fault codes. Always refer to the service manual for specific information about computer system service.

PROTECTING ELECTRONIC SYSTEMS

The last thing a technician wants to do when a vehicle comes into the shop for collision repair is create problems. This is especially true when it comes to electrical systems and electronic components. There are proper ways to protect automotive electrical systems and electronic components during storage and repair.

1. Disconnect the battery cables (negative cable first) before doing any kind of welding. To avoid the possibility of explosion, completely remove the battery when welding under the hood or on the front end. Also, make sure the ground connection is clean and tight. Position the ground clamp as close as possible to the work area to avoid current seeking its own ground.

2. Whenever disconnecting or removing the battery on a computer-controlled vehicle, remember that the memory for radio station selection, seat position,

Figure 26–37 Computers can be located in various locations in vehicle.

climate control setting, and any other "driver programmable" options are erased. When delivering the vehicle, advise the customer that he or she must reprogram these settings. Or better yet, record them before beginning and reprogram them yourself before delivery.

3. Static electricity can cause problems. Avoid it by grounding yourself before handling new displays. One way is to touch a good ground with one hand before handling the display with the other hand. Another way is to use a grounding strap that attaches to the wrist and then to the vehicle.

4. Avoid touching bare metal contacts. Oils from the skin can cause corrosion and poor contacts.

5. Be careful about the placement of welding cables. Keep the electrical path as short as possible by placing the ground clamp near the point of welding. Also, do NOT let the welding cables run close to electronic displays or computers.

6. Take care when handling electronic displays and gauges. Never press on the gauge face because this could damage it.

7. If a fault code indicates a problem with the oxygen sensor, extra caution is required. The oxygen sensor wire carries a very low voltage and must be isolated from other wires. If NOT, nearby wires could add more induced voltage. This gives false data to the computer and can result in a driveability problem. Some manufacturers use a foam sleeve around the oxygen sensor wire to keep it separate and insulated from other wires.

8. The sensor wires that connect to the computer should never be rerouted. The resulting problem might be impossible to find. When replacing sensor wiring, always check the service manual and follow the routing instructions.

9. Remove any computer that could be affected by welding, hammering, grinding, sanding, or metal straightening. Be sure to protect the removed computer by wrapping it in a plastic bag to shield it from moisture and dust.

10. Be careful NOT to damage wiring when welding, hammering, or grinding.

11. Be careful NOT to damage connectors and terminals when removing electronic components. Some may require special tools to remove them.

12. Always route wiring in the same place it was originally. If NOT, electronic crossover from the current-carrying wires can affect the sensing and control circuits. Reuse or replace all electrical shielding for the same reason.

Summary

- Current is the movement of electricity (electrons) through a wire or circuit. It is measured in amps.
- Voltage is the pressure that pushes the electricity through the wire or circuit. It is measured in volts.
- Resistance is a restriction or obstacle to current flow. It is measured in ohms.
- Some diagnostic equipment used in finding electrical faults includes the multimeter, test light, and jumper wires.
- The modern vehicle has numerous electrical-electronic systems, including the ignition, starting, and charging systems.
- Computer self-diagnostics means the computer system can detect its own problems. Most electronic systems have built-in, self-diagnostic capabilities.

Technical Terms

electrical system	wiring harness
current	inertia switch
voltage	solenoid
resistance	relay
conductor	motors
insulation	fuse
ground	fuse ratings
load	fuse box
series circuit	fuse link
parallel circuit	circuit breaker
open	ignition system
closed	starting system
Ohm's Law	charging system
magnetic field	diagnostic chart
electromagnet	battery
windings	jumper cables
multimeter	soldering
digital multimeter	sensors
analog multimeter	actuators
test light	computer
jumper wires	computer self-
continuity	diagnostics
AC current	fault code
inductive pickup	assembly line diagnostic
wiring diagram	link
electrical symbols	scan tool
wire color coding	PROM

Review Questions

1. Define the terms "current," "voltage," and "resistance."

2. A _____ _____ has only one conductor path or leg for current through the circuit.

3. A _____ _____ has two or more legs or paths for current.

4. If a circuit has 12.6 volts applied and 4.2 ohms, how much current would flow through the circuit.

5. What is a multimeter?

6. A lighting circuit has an intermittent problem. The bulbs go on and off. Technician A says to use a DVOM to find the trouble. Technician B says to use an AVOM.
   Who is correct?
   a. Technician A
   b. Technician B
   c. Both Technicians
   d. Neither Technician

7. Why should you not use test lights on electronic circuits?

8. Explain the difference between AC and DC.

9. The service manual may also give a _____ _____ _____ for finding electrical components (harnesses, sensors, switches, computers, etc.).

10. A vehicle has been in a collision and will not start. Technician A says to try resetting the inertia switch. Technician B says to first prime the engine with gasoline.
    Who is correct?
    a. Technician A
    b. Technician B
    c. Both Technicians
    d. Neither Technician

11. How does a fuse operate?

12. With the engine running, how much voltage should be across the battery terminals?
    a. 12 to 15 volts
    b. 18 volts
    c. 12.6 volts
    d. 13 to 15 volts

13. If an engine cranks but fails to start, what should you do?

14. How do you use jumper wires?

15. Be sure to use _____ _____, NOT _____, when soldering electrical connections. Acid fluxes create corrosion and can damage electronic components.

16. In your own words, explain the basic parts and operation of a computer system.

17. How do you use a scan tool?

18. Computers can be located:
    a. Under the dash
    b. Under the seats
    c. Under the hood
    d. Behind kick panels
    e. All of the above
    f. None of the above

Activities

1. Read the operating manual for a multimeter. Write a report on its use and safety rules.

2. Use a voltmeter to check the action of a charging system. How much voltage is the system producing across the battery? Discuss your findings with the class.

CHAPTER 27

RESTRAINT SYSTEM REPAIRS

Objectives

After studying this chapter, you should be able to:

- Explain the difference between an active and passive restraint system.

- Describe the parts that make up a seat belt system and their functions.

- Learn how to service seat belts.

- Become familiar with the different types of child car seats.

- Identify and become familiar with the operation, diagnosis, and repair of air bag systems.

Introduction

A *restraint system* is designed to help hold people in their seats and prevent them from being injured during a collision. All new vehicles come equipped with some form of restraint system. See Figure 27–1.

This chapter will summarize the operation and repair of seat belt and air bag systems. This is important because these systems can be damaged or deployed during a collision. Since they are crucial to safety, you must know how to service a restraint system properly.

The installation of air bags will be required on all cars and light trucks in the near future. This increase will require the collision repair technician/adjuster to become familiar with their operation, diagnosis, and repair.

Figure 27–1 Restraint systems are now common. As a collision repair technician, you must know service rules for seat belt and air bag systems. (© American Honda Motor Co., Inc.)

ACTIVE AND PASSIVE RESTRAINTS

An *active restraint system* is one that the occupants must make an effort to use. For example, in most vehicles the seat belts must be fastened for crash protection. Conventional, manually-operated seat belts would be classified as an active restraint system.

A *passive restraint system* is one that operates automatically. No action is required to make it functional. Two types are automatic seat belts and air bags.

SEAT BELT SYSTEMS

Seat belts are strong nylon straps with special ends attached for securing people in their seats. *Lap belts* are the seat belts that extend across a person's lap. *Shoulder belts* extend over a person's chest and shoulder, Figure 27–2. A *seat belt buckle mechanism* allows you to put the seat belt on and take it off.

Seat belt anchors allow the one end of the belts to be bolted to the body structure. Look at Figure 27–3. A *belt retractor* is used to remove slack from the belts so they fit snugly. Various mechanisms are used in belt retractors. One is shown in Figure 27–4, page 549.

A *seat belt reminder system* uses sensors and a warning system to remind the driver to fasten his or her seat belt. On active systems, the driver's side front seat belt uses a 4- to 8-second fasten seat belt

reminder light and sound signal. This is designed to remind you if the lap and shoulder belts are NOT fastened when the ignition is turned ON. If the driver's seat belt is NOT buckled, the reminder light and sound signal will automatically shut off after a few seconds.

On the passive system, the belt warning light will glow for a few seconds. An audible signal will sound if the driver's lap and shoulder belt is NOT buckled. The system will also signal if the ignition is on and the driver's door is open or if a system failure occurs.

The active belt system consists of a single continuous length of webbing. The webbing is routed from the anchor (at the rocker panel), through a self-locking latch plate (at the buckle), around the guide assembly (at the top of the center pillar), and into a single retractor in the lower area of the center pillar.

The passive system for coupes and late model sedans differs from the active in that two retractors are used. One is provided for the seat belt and a second for the shoulder belt. Both retractors are located behind the front door trim panels.

Seat Belt Service

When servicing or replacing lap and shoulder belts, remember:

Rear Limit Switch & Shoulder Belt Buckle Switch

Guide Rail Assembly

Automatic Belt Drive Motor

Front Limit Switch

Belt Anchor

Lap Belt

Shoulder Belt Assembly

Belt Retractor

Lap Belt Buckle And Switch (Driver's Side Only)

: N•m (kg-m, ft-lb)

Control Module

Automatic Seat Belt And ELR Control Modules

● **Control Modules Are Located Under The Center Of Instrument Panel**

Figure 27–2 Note major parts of seat belts. *(Used with permission of Nissan Motor Corporation)*

Figure 27–3 Always check action of seat belt retractors after a collision. They must operate normally. *(Reprinted with permission by American Isuzu Motors Inc.)*

1. Do NOT intermix types of seat belts on front or rear seats.

2. Keep sharp edges and damaging objects away from belts.

3. Avoid bending or damaging any portion of the belt buckle or latch plate.

4. Do NOT attempt repairs on lap or shoulder belt retractor mechanisms or lap belt retractor covers. Replace with new replacement parts.

5. Tighten all seat and shoulder belt anchor bolts as specified in the service manual. Use a torque wrench.

A visual and functional inspection of the belts themselves is very important to assure maximum protection for vehicle occupants. The following inspection checklist provides a typical, detailed seat belt inspection.

1. Check for twisted webbing due to improper alignment when connecting the buckle.

2. Fully extend the webbing from the retractor. Inspect the webbing and replace with a new assembly if the following conditions are noted.

In situations where the manufacturers do NOT have specific recommendations, perform a visual inspection of the system. Check seat belt webbing for:

1. Twists

2. Cuts or damage

3. Broken or pulled threads

4. Cut loops

5. Color fading or stains

Any of these defects may cause the seat belt webbing to be weakened and possibly fail during a collision.

To inspect seat belt buckles, do the following:

1. Insert the tongue of the seat belt into the buckle until a click is heard. Pull back on the webbing quickly to assure that the buckle is latched properly.

2. Replace the seat belt assembly if the buckle will NOT latch.

3. Depress the button on the buckle to release the belt. The belt should release with normal finger pressure.

Figure 27–4 This seat belt tensioner works with air bag system. It fires gas charge to help pull seat belts tight around person. It must be replaced after collision. *(Illustration provided courtesy of Mercedes Benz-North America, Inc.)*

4. Replace the seat belt assembly if the buckle cover is cracked, the push button is loose. Also replace the unit if the pressure required to release the buckle is too great.

To inspect a belt retractor assembly, remember to:

1. Grasp the seat belt webbing. While pulling from the retractor, give the belt a fast jerk. The belt should lock up.

2. Drive the vehicle in an open area away from other vehicles. Drive at about 5 to 15 mph (8 to 24 km/h). Quickly apply the foot brake. The belt should lock up.

3. If the retractor does NOT lock up under these conditions, remove and replace the seat belt assembly.

To inspect seat belt anchors, you should check the seat belt anchorage for signs of movement or deformation. Replace if necessary. Position the replacement anchor exactly the same as in the original installation.

> *WARNING! Do NOT bleach or dye the belt webbing. This could weaken the belt fabric. If needed, clean with a mild soap solution and water.*

CHILD SEATS

A *child seat* is a small, supplemental seat designed to protect small children from collision injuries. There are three types of child car seats: rear facing, forward facing, and a combination. The car seat is often secured with a lap and shoulder seat belt (using a locking clip provided by the car seat manufacturer) or just a lap belt. An intregal child seat is built into the rear seat by the vehicle manufacturer.

No one can be sure a child car seat will prevent injury in an accident. However, the proper use of the car seat should reduce the risk.

Danger! Aftermarket child seats may NOT be suitable for use in the front seat with an air bag system. Some seats locate the child too close to the air bag. Injury to the child could result from bag deployment. Warn your customers of this danger!

AIR BAG SYSTEMS

An *air bag system* automatically deploys a large nylon bag during frontal collisions, Figure 27–5. One or more air bags can be used. The *driver-side air bag* deploys from the steering wheel center pad. The *passenger-side air bag* deploys from behind a small door in the right side of the dash.

The air bag system will only deploy during frontal impacts. Air bags may NOT deploy in side or rear impacts, or in rollover situations. The angle of the collision determines whether the air bag will deploy. A frontal impact must occur within about 30 degrees of the vehicle's centerline for the air bag to activate.

While the location and design of the air bag system varies from manufacturer to manufacturer, all air bag systems have similar parts, Figure 27–6. These include:

1. Air bag module—inflator mechanism and nylon bag that expand to protect driver or passenger during collision.

2. Air bag system sensors—inertia sensors that signal computer of collision.

3. Control unit—computer that operates system and detects faults.

Figure 27–5 With frontal impact, air bag deploys to protect driver. Seat belts should be used even with air bag.

4. Wiring harness—wiring and connectors that link system parts.
5. Dash indicator lamp—dash bulb that warns of system problem.

Danger! *The air bag system is designed to be used with seat belts.*

Air Bag Module

The *air bag module* is composed of the nylon bag and an igniter-inflator mechanism enclosed in a metal-plastic housing. All air bag module components are packaged in a single container mounted in the center of the steering wheel pad or dash, Figure 27–7. This entire assembly must be serviced as one unit when repair of the air bag system is required.

The *air bag* is a strong nylon bag attached to the metal frame of the module. Vent holes in the bag allow for rapid deflation after deployment.

Figure 27–6 Study major parts of air bag system.

Figure 27–7 Driver air bag module mounts in steering wheel. Note parts.

Figure 27–8 Study parts of inflator module. Squib spark fires igniter. Igniter makes gas generating pellets burn, causing gas expansion into air bag.

The *air bag igniter* produces a small spark when an electrical signal is sent from the control unit. When the electrical current is applied, the igniter produces an electric arc across two small pins. This spark ignites an igniter charge. This charge rapidly burns and causes the gas generating pellets to burn and produce rapid gas expansion. See Figure 27–8.

Once ignited, the *propellant charge* is progressive burning sodium azide, which converts to nitrogen gas as it burns. Heat causes the chemicals in the unit to produce a large amount of nitrogen gas. The nitrogen gas then fills the air bag in a fraction of a second. As the air bag inflates, the steering wheel cover is forced to split open allowing full inflation.

The driver is then protected by the gas-filled bag instead of being restrained by the seat belts alone. In addition, there is some facial protection against flying objects.

Almost as soon as the bag is filled, the gas is cooled and vented. This deflates the bag right after the collision energy is absorbed. Vents allow rapid deflation. This prevents the driver or passenger from being

Figure 27–9 Passenger side air bag works in same way but is under small door in dash. *(I-CAR)*

Figure 27–10 This inertia sensor uses metal ball held by magnet. Collision force throws ball forward and into contacts. This signals computer of collision. *(I-CAR)*

pinned into the vehicle and also allows normal vision right after deployment.

Passenger-side air bags are very similar in design to the driver's unit. The actual capacity of gas required to inflate the bag is much greater. The bag must span the extra distance between the occupant and the dashboard at the passenger seating location. See Figure 27–9.

Another part relating to an air bag is the knee diverter. A *knee diverter* cushions the driver's knees from impact and helps prevent the driver from sliding under the air bag during a collision. It is located underneath the steering column and behind the steering column trim.

Air Bag Sensors

Two or more sensors are used in air bag systems, impact sensors and arming sensors.

Impact sensors are the first sensors to detect a collision because they are mounted at the front of the vehicle. Impact sensors are usually located in the engine compartment, while the safing sensor is usually located in the passenger compartment.

The *safing* or *arming sensor* ensures that the particular collision is severe enough to require that the air bag be deployed.

Both impact and arming sensors are inertia sensors. *Inertia sensors* detect a rapid deceleration to produce an electrical signal. Some air bag sensors use a small

metal ball held in place by a permanent magnet, Figure 27–10. The sensor ball is thrown forward by the inertia of the collision. It then touches two electrical terminals that closes the sensor circuit to the computer.

Another air bag sensor design uses a weight attached to a coil spring. During impact, the weight is thrown forward. This overcomes spring tension, to close the sensor contact. This also closes the circuit to signal the computer of a possible collision. Both the impact sensor and a safing sensor must close at the same time for air bag inflation. They work together to provide a fail-safe system to prevent accidental air bag deployment. When both an impact sensor and a safing sensor close, the diagnostic control module sends a signal to the igniter, which starts a chemical reaction to inflate the bag.

It is important to remember that the tandem action of at least one main sensor and a safing sensor will activate the system.

Air Bag Controller

The *air bag controller* analyzes inputs from the sensor to determine if bag deployment is needed. If at least one impact sensor and the arm sensor are closed, it sends current to the air bag module. This fires the air bag. The electronic control unit also provides failure data and trouble codes for use in servicing various aspects of most systems.

Air Bag System Servicing

Before servicing a vehicle equipped with an air bag, the system must be *disarmed* (all sources of electricity for igniter disconnected). Procedures for disarming the air bag system vary.

Manufacturers may specify removal of the system fuse or disconnection of the module. Always refer to the service manual for exact procedures for disarming the system. This will help prevent electrical system damage and accidental deployment of the new air bag. Always disconnect the negative battery cable.

> *WARNING! Air bag systems may be equipped with an* **energy reserve module** *that allows the air bag to deploy in the event of a power failure. It must be removed from the system or allowed to discharge for a period of time ranging from a few seconds to 30 minutes after disconnecting the battery.*

Danger! Even with the battery disconnected, the reserve module can fire the air bag. If you are working near the bag, serious injury could result.

After deployment, use a shop vacuum to clean the passenger compartment. Residual powder, which is an eye and skin irritant can be present. Vacuum the dash, vents, seats, carpet and other surfaces contaminated with this powder. See Figure 27–11.

Air bag system parts replacement after a deployment will vary. Check for specific manufacturer recommendations on parts replacement. Most recommend replacement of all sensors and sometimes the electronic control unit.

When replacing air bag system sensors, double-check that the system is disarmed before removing any sensor. The service manual will give sensor locations. Make sure you have the correct replacement sensor. During installation, check that the *sensor arrow* (directional arrow stamped on sensor) is facing forward. If a sensor is installed backwards, the air bag will NOT deploy during the next accident.

To remove the deployed air bag, remove the small screws from the rear of the steering wheel. You can then lift out the module and disconnect its wires. Wear safety glasses and a respirator while removing the deployed bag. This will protect you from the residual powder.

Inspect all parts for damage. Parts that have visible damage should be replaced. This would include the steering wheel, steering column, and related parts. Damage to the electrical wiring may also require wiring harness replacement.

Obtain the correct replacement parts from the manufacturer. Also refer to the service manual for exact procedures. System designs vary.

Danger! When carrying a live (undeployed) air bag module, be sure the bag and trim cover are pointed away from your body. This will help reduce the chances of serious injury if the bag accidentally inflates. When laying a module down on a work surface, make sure the bag and trim cover are face up to minimize a "launch effect" of the module if the bag suddenly inflates.

Do NOT carry any system parts by the wire harness or pigtails. Follow manufacturer's policies if any part is dropped or shows visible signs of damage. Follow manufacturer's policies for replacing parts following a deployment.

Do NOT attempt to repair any parts unless specified by the manufacturer. Do NOT apply any electrical power to any part unless specified by the manufacturer.

The air bag module must be replaced following a deployment. Often the coil or *clock spring*, which is the electrical connection between the steering column and the air bag module, will also have to be replaced. Look at Figure 27–12.

Remember! There is no need to fear working with air bag equipped vehicles, but they must be treated with respect. Common sense can go a long way when working on these systems. By following some simple rules, air bags can be safely serviced.

1. Always have the service manual on hand when working with an air bag equipped vehicle.

2. When servicing a vehicle that has an undeployed air bag, follow the manufacturer's instructions for disarming the system. You should also have the system disarmed when installing a new air bag.

3. Wear rubber gloves and eye protection when servicing the air bag following a deployment. In case of skin or eye irritation, wash thoroughly with water and seek medical attention.

4. Disarm the air bag system prior to performing any welding operations.

5. Keep arms out of the steering wheel spokes when working on an air bag. It can shatter bones if accidentally deployed. Also keep your head to one side of the bag during installation.

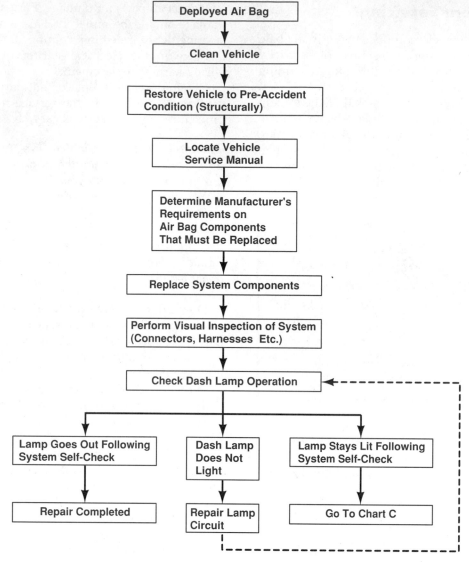

Figure 27–11 Study chart showing major steps for air bag system service. *(I-CAR)*

6. Follow the manufacturer's guidelines on force drying paint on vehicles equipped with an air bag.

7. Air bag disposal procedures vary depending on if the air bag has been deployed or NOT.

8. If the air bag module is defective or the vehicle is to be scrapped, the air bag should be manually deployed using the procedures described in the service manual. Do NOT dispose of an undeployed air bag.

9. On air bag modules that cannot be manually deployed, the disposal procedure is to ship it back to the manufacturer using the packaging that the replacement module came in. By using the replacement part's packaging, all of the needed warning labels are already on the package.

The air bag system performs a self-check every time the ignition is turned to the ON position. During the self-check the air bag dash lamp indicator will light steady or blink. When the self-check is completed, the lamp should go OFF. If the lamp stays lit, there is a system fault present.

Make sure a final sweep is made for codes or accident information using the approved scan tool. Carefully recheck the wire and harness routing before releasing the car.

A final inspection of the job should include checking to make sure the sensors are firmly fastened to their mounting fixtures, with the arrows on them

Horn Contact Tower

Lower Steering Column Connector

Steering Wheel Inflator Module Connector

Underside View

Figure 27-12 Clock spring may require replacement after air bag deployment. Refer to service manual directions. *(Courtesy of Chrysler Corporation)*

facing forward. Be certain all the fuses are correctly rated and replaced.

Summary

- An active restraint system is one that the occupants must make an effort to use, such as manually-operated seat belts. A passive restraint system operates automatically, such as automatic seat belts and air bags.

- A child seat may be rear facing, front facing, or a combination. It is often secured with a lap and shoulder seat belt.

- Most air bag systems have these components: air bag module, air bag system sensors, control unit, wiring harness, and dash indicator lamp.

Technical Terms

restraint system	*air bag module*
active restraint	*arming sensor*
passive restraint	*impact sensor*
lap belts	*air bag controller*
shoulder belts	*disarmed*
belt anchors	*energy reserve module*
air bag system	*clock spring*

Review Questions

1. An active restraint system is one that the occupants must make an effort to use. True or false?

2. Seat belt _____ allow the one end of the belts to be bolted to the body structure.

3. How does a seat belt reminder system operate?

4. What five things must you check when inspecting seat belt webbing?

5. Aftermarket child seats are always suitable for use in the front seat with an air bag system. True or false?

6. List and explain the five major parts of an air bag system.

7. The _____ _____ _____ is composed of the nylon bag and an igniter-inflator mechanism enclosed in a metal-plastic housing.

8. How does gas cause an air bag to inflate?

9. Explain the operation of air bag system sensors.

10. Before servicing a vehicle equipped with an air bag, the system must be _____. Even with the battery disconnected, the _____ _____ can fire the air bag.

11. How do you handle a live air bag module?

12. List 9 rules for working with air bag systems.

Activities

1. Inspect a vehicle's restraint systems. List the types of restraints installed in the vehicle. Does it have shoulder harnesses and air bag(s)? List your findings.

2. Refer to a repair manual for a specific make and model vehicle. Summarize the procedures for service after air bag deployment.

ESTIMATING ENTREPRENEURSHIP

CHAPTER 28

ESTIMATING REPAIR COSTS

Objectives

After studying this chapter, you should be able to:

- Explain how damage repair estimates are determined.

- Identify and explain the most common abbreviations used in crash estimating guides.

- Describe the methods of determining the repairability of a damaged vehicle.

- Explain the difference between flat-rate labor time and overlap labor time when making a cost estimation.

- Make a rough estimate of the time required to refinish a given collision repair job.

- Explain the difference between direct and indirect damage and locate both types.

- Apply a systematic approach to damage analysis.

- Perform steering and suspension quick checks.

- Identify the key operating features of manual and computerized estimating systems.

- Compare manual and computerized estimating.

- Explain how electronic photos and a computer can streamline the estimating process.

Introduction

An *estimate*, also called a *damage report* or *appraisal*, calculates the cost of parts, materials and labor for repairing a collision-damaged vehicle. Developed by the estimator, it is a written or printed summary of the repairs needed. The estimate is used by the customer, insurance company, shop management, and technician. See Figure 28–1.

Estimates must be accurately written. Repair costs are a major consideration for both the owner and the collision repair shop. Insurance companies generally require at least two written estimates from two separate shops. Usually, the shop that submits the lowest estimate gets the work. Therefore, the profit margins for a collision repair shop depend heavily on the accuracy of estimates. Insurance companies can also write their own estimates.

This chapter will help you understand how both manual and electronic estimates are prepared.

Figure 28–1 Estimating collision repair costs can be a challenge. You must evaluate many variables to analyze what must be done to repair vehicle. *(Used by permission from Tech-Cor Inc.)*

DAMAGE ANALYSIS

For an estimate to clearly establish a true cost of repairs, a thorough damage analysis must be performed on the wrecked vehicle. *Damage analysis* involves locating all damage using a systematic series of inspections, measurements, and tests. This allows repairs to be done right the first time and it also prevents cost overruns. Look at Figure 28–2.

Before starting damage analysis, you should:

1. If possible, discuss the collision with the owner or driver of the vehicle to obtain information which may help during damage analysis.

2. Identify the vehicle completely. Include VIN number, year, make, model, engine, and optional equipment, Figure 28–3.

3. List mileage.

4. Identify and note pre-collision damage.

5. Check wheels and tires, including spare. Damaged wheels may provide clues about the collision.

6. Confirm the point of impact and analyze how the damage has traveled.

Figure 28–2 Besides obvious damage, there is often hidden damage under body structure that must be found. *(Used by permission from Tech-Cor Inc.)*

DIRECT AND INDIRECT DAMAGE

One of the reasons unibody vehicles are a challenge to repair is because of the way the body reacts to colli-

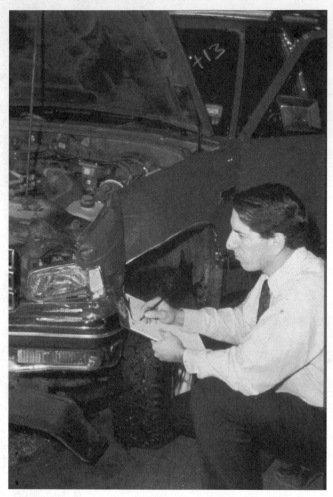

Figure 28–3 Estimator must have thorough knowledge of vehicle construction and body shop methods to develop accurate estimate of repair costs. *(Used by permission from Tech-Cor Inc.)*

sion forces. There are two types of damage which must be identified. They are direct (primary) damage and indirect (secondary) damage.

Direct damage occurs in the area of immediate impact as a direct result of the vehicle striking an object. Direct damage is usually easy to locate and analyze. Refer to Figure 28–4.

Indirect damage is caused by the shock of collision forces traveling through the body and inertial forces acting upon the rest of the unibody. Indirect damage can be more difficult to completely identify and analyze. It may be found anywhere on the vehicle, Figure 28–5.

Before doing anything else, take time to carefully perform an overall visual inspection and try to determine the direction of impact and the areas of indirect damage.

VEHICLE INSPECTION

When doing a visual inspection, the direction of impact will affect the parts damaged. If the vehicle was hit in the front, side, or rear, you will know to check specific areas and parts for damage. See Figure 28–6.

You should use a damage analysis checklist to make sure nothing is overlooked, Figure 28–7.

Inspect the entire vehicle for damage, looking for:

1. Alignment of doors, Figure 28–8.
2. Alignment of the hood and deck lid.
3. Gaps between panels.

Figure 28–4 Direct or primary damage occurs at point of impact. Indirect or secondary damage occurs elsewhere as forces travel through body structure. *(Used with permission of Nissan Motor Corporation)*

Figure 28–5 Note indirect damage at rear of vehicle that was in frontal collision. *(Used by permission from Tech-Cor Inc.)*

4. How the doors, hood, and deck lid open and close, Figure 28–9.
5. Ripples in roof, fenders, or quarter panels away from direct impact.
6. Cracked or stressed paint.
7. Cracked seam sealers.
8. Cracked or broken glass.
9. Smooth operation of windows.
10. Damage to interior (instrument panel, seats, seat belts, etc.), deployed air bag, stained carpet, and other problems, Figure 28–10.
11. Indications of previous damage.
12. Remove parts if needed to analyze hidden damage, Figure 28–11.
13. If frontal collision, inspect part in engine compartment for damage.
14. Check under the vehicle for fluid leaks which are signs of mechanical damage.

You should also:

1. Note angle of impact(s).
2. Mark areas of direct damage.
3. Note indicators of indirect damage.
4. Note areas of pre-existing damage.

Always raise a badly damaged vehicle off the floor so that a good visual inspection can be made of all underbody and drivetrain parts. In some unibody vehicles, it might even be necessary to remove the drivetrain and suspension parts to make a thorough damage inspection.

In other words, the estimator must give the entire vehicle a thorough inspection—top to bottom and front to rear—and take nothing for granted. If something is missed on the original estimate, it often becomes difficult to reopen it for further negotiations later. On the other hand, some estimates do include

A

B

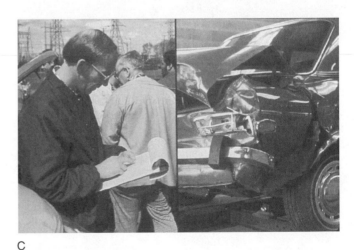

C

Figure 28–6 When doing an estimate, direction of impact will tell you much about resulting damage. A: Frontal impact will often damage bumper, grille, hood, fenders, aprons, frame rails, radiator, and sometimes engine parts. *(Used by permission from Tech-Cor Inc.)* B: Side impact will often damage door, quarter panel, pillars, roof, and rocker panel. C: Rear impact will often damage rear bumper, back panel, valance, tail lights, trunk floor, quarter panels, wheelhouse, and rear rails. *(Used by permission from Tech-Cor Inc.)*

DAMAGE ANALYSIS CHECKLIST

1. ❑ **STRUCTURAL MEMBERS**
   - ❑ Front Rails
   - ❑ Upper Rails
   - ❑ Tie bars, Upper and Lower (Core Support)
   - ❑ Crossmembers
   - ❑ Side Panels
   - ❑ Apron Assembly
   - ❑ Cowl Panel
   - ❑ A-Pillars
   - ❑ B-Pillars
   - ❑ Rocker Panel
   - ❑ Floor Pan
   - ❑ Rear Rails
   - ❑ Rear Crossmembers
   - ❑ Rear Floor Pan
2. ❑ **FRONT BUMPER**
   - ❑ Front Cover
   - ❑ Reinforcement
   - ❑ Energy Absorber
   - ❑ Molding
   - ❑ Valance
3. ❑ **GRILLE**
   - ❑ Grille
   - ❑ Emblem
   - ❑ Support
4. ❑ **FRONT LAMP**
   - ❑ Lamps
   - ❑ Assemblies
   - ❑ Trim/Door/Moldings
5. ❑ **COOLING SYSTEM**
   - ❑ Radiator
   - ❑ Recovery Tank
   - ❑ Fan
   - ❑ Fan Motor
   - ❑ Shroud
   - ❑ Hoses
   - ❑ Pump/Pulley/Belt
6. ❑ **ENGINE**
   - ❑ Crankshaft Pulley
   - ❑ Engine Mounts
   - ❑ Mount Brackets
   - ❑ Transmission Mounts
   - ❑ Oil Pan
   - ❑ Pumps (Fuel, Water, Power Steering)
   - ❑ Valve Cover(s)

   Exhaust
   - ❑ Catalytic Converter
   - ❑ Exhaust Manifold(s)
   - ❑ Pipe
   - ❑ Muffler

Alternator
   - ❑ Assembly and Mounts
   - ❑ Pulley/Belt

Electrical
   - ❑ Main Computer Module
   - ❑ Ignition Coil
   - ❑ Distributor Cap
   - ❑ Wires

Emission System
   - ❑ Air Pump
   - ❑ Vapor Canister

Air Conditioner
   - ❑ Condenser
   - ❑ Compressor
   - ❑ Pulley/Belt
   - ❑ Drier
   - ❑ Evaporator Core
   - ❑ Blower Motor
   - ❑ A/C Lines/Hoses

7. ❑ **HOOD**
   - ❑ Panel
   - ❑ Hinges
   - ❑ Latch
   - ❑ Latch Release
   - ❑ Moldings/Trim
8. ❑ **FRONT FENDER**
   - ❑ Fender
   - ❑ Wheelhouse
   - ❑ Moldings/Trim
   - ❑ Side Marker Lamps
9. ❑ **WHEELS/TIRES**
   - ❑ Wheel Covers
   - ❑ Wheel
   - ❑ Tires
   - ❑ Spare Tire
10. ❑ **FRONT SUSPENSION**
    - ❑ ABS Dash Indicator Lamp Brakes-Rotors/Calipers/Drums
    - ❑ Bearing/Hub Assemblies
    - ❑ Splash Shields
    - ❑ Brake Lines
    - ❑ Strut/Shock Assemblies
    - ❑ Strut Mounts
    - ❑ Springs
    - ❑ Control Arms & Strut Rods
11. ❑ **FRONT DRIVE AXLE**
    - ❑ Shaft Assembly
    - ❑ Axle Shaft
    - ❑ CV (Constant Velocity) Joints
    - ❑ Boots

Figure 28–7 A damage analysis checklist is handy during visual inspection. Read through checklist. *(I-CAR)*

hidden damage clause that permits added charges to the original estimate if hidden damages are discovered later.

Taking photographs of the vehicle to keep with the documentation is also a good idea. Photos can be use-ful if there are any questions about a repair. Videotaping the vehicle before and after repairs can also be helpful.

Discussed shortly, modern computerized estimating systems can utilize electronic photos and digitize

Figure 28–8 When inspecting damage, look for gaps between panels away from point of impact. This can help you find indirect damage. *(I-CAR)*

Figure 28–9 Note damage on this vehicle.

Figure 28–11 Sometimes, it is necessary to remove parts to find all damage. *(Used by permission from Tech-Cor Inc.)*

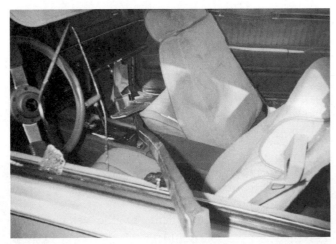

Figure 28–10 Interior damage can vary from light to major. Check for deployed air bag, damaged instrument panel, seats, seat belts, carpet, and other parts that could add to repair costs.

video footage for finalizing the estimate when at the office computer.

INTERIOR INSPECTION

The interior of the vehicle must also be inspected. Check for damage caused by collision forces, unrestrained passengers or cargo. Inspect glass and mirrors. Check door handles and door locks for proper operation. Refer again to Figure 28–10.

Inspect alignment of glove box door. Misalignment may indicate instrument panel damage. Check interior controls for proper operation. Also inspect the console and shift lever.

Check seats and the restraint system for damage. Check seat belt buckles, webbing, and anchoring points. Check for deployed air bags and operation of motorized seat belts.

DAMAGE QUICK CHECKS

Damage quick checks can be done to analyze problems with the body structure, steering, and suspension systems. They can assist in determining if further steering system or suspension measurements are necessary, namely:

1. Centering the steering wheel
2. Jounce/rebound steering gear check
3. Strut rotation check
4. Run-out check
5. Strut position check

A *steering wheel center check* involves making sure the steering wheel has not been moved off center to do part damage. It is done by doing the following:

1. Turn the steering wheel all of the way through its travel, lock to lock.
2. Count the number of turns from one lock position to the other.
3. Divide this number by two, and turn the steering wheel back that distance. The steering wheel should now be centered. Mark the center top of the steering wheel with a piece of tape.
4. Check the position of the steering wheel.
5. Check the position of the front tires, Figure 28–12A.

To analyze the steering wheel position:

1. If the steering wheel looks centered and the front tires point straight ahead, steering gear, steering column, and steering arms are probably NOT damaged.
2. If the steering wheel is more than slightly off center and the tires are straight, steering gear damage is possible.
3. If the steering wheel is centered and the tires are NOT pointed straight ahead, steering arm damage is possible.

The *jounce/rebound steering gear check* involves pushing down on the front or rear of the vehicle to load the suspension, and then allowing the vehicle to bounce back up. This check can help to identify damage to the steering gear, column, or tie rods.

1. Locate the top center of the steering wheel rim.
2. Mark the center top of the steering wheel with a piece of tape.
3. At the front of the vehicle, perform several jounce/rebound sequences while observing the steering wheel.

If the steering wheel rotates back and forth during the jounce/rebound sequences, then steering system damage is possible, Figure 28–12B. This check can

indicate damage to the rack-and-pinion which can cause bump steer.

To do a *strut rotation check* to find damage:

1. Loosen strut shaft upper lock nut ½ to 1 full turn.
2. Rotate the strut shaft with a wrench.
3. While rotating strut shaft, use the fender lip as a reference and look for any noticeable change in camber. Movement can indicate a bent strut shaft.
4. When completed, re-tighten the lock nut.

If damage is suspected, inspect the strut carefully for signs of impact, bent housing or other obvious damage. This check will NOT work with struts that don't have an accessible strut shaft.

To do a *strut position check* to analyze damage:

1. Turn the wheels until they are pointed straight ahead.
2. Measure between the tire and strut.
3. Compare to the distance on the other side, Figure 28–13.
4. If a difference is noted, then look for a bent or damaged strut, bent wheel, damaged drum or rotor, or damaged steering knuckle.

A *wheel run-out check* will show if there is damage to a rotating part of a wheel assembly. To do this:

1. Remove any trim rings, wheel covers, and so on.
2. Raise the wheel assembly off the ground.
3. Using a safety stand or other steady rest, lay a pointer (screwdriver, pen or pencil, etc.) to within ⅛″ (3 mm) of the first step of the wheel (where the tire bead is seated).
4. Spin the wheel and watch the distance between the wheel and the pointer. Look at Figure 28–14.
5. If more than a visible variance exists, remove that wheel, replace with a known good wheel, and repeat the check.
6. If the variance is still present, then a rotating part of the wheel assembly is damaged.
7. When spinning the tire, listen for noise which might indicate wheel bearing damage.

DIMENSION MANUALS

When analyzing damage for making an estimate, you may need to use unibody-frame measuring equipment to determine the extent of the damage. See Figure 28–15.

After taking measurements on the vehicle, compare them to the body dimension manual. The manual will give illustrations of known good distances from specific body-frame points. By comparing your

A

B

Figure 28–12 Note two quick checks to find steering and suspension damage. *(I-CAR)* A: Center steering wheel between full right and left positions. Then, check to see if tires are facing straight ahead. If either is not facing straight ahead, damage is indicated. B: While someone rotates steering wheel one way and then the other, watch front of body. If it rises and falls slightly, mechanical damage is indicated.

Figure 28–13 Measure between each tire and strut. Different measurements indicate damage. *(Chief Automotive Systems, Inc.)*

Figure 28–14 With tire off ground, spin tire. If tire wobbles, wheel is bent. Dial indicator is needed for more accurate measurements of run-out. *(I-CAR)*

measurements to these known good measurement, you can determine the extent and direction of damage, Figure 28–16.

Severe collisions from any direction often cause the frame or unitized body to distort. At one time the estimator could check this damage with the naked eye and would be fairly close in giving an estimate. But with the unibody, the "eyeballing" technique is sometimes NOT enough to detect misalignment. It is far better to use measuring gauges or devices to check for misalignment. Unless the estimator is thoroughly skilled in the use of such tools, it is wise to consult with an experienced technician to determine the time necessary to get the vehicle back into proper alignment.

Refer to Chapter 20 for more information on this subject.

Figure 28–15 When in doubt about extent of structural damage, use measuring system. It will accurately show damage. (Wedge Clamp International, Inc.)

COLLISION ESTIMATING GUIDES

Collision estimating guides help with filling out the estimate, Figure 28–17. Whether in manual or electronic form, estimating guides contain:

1. Illustrated parts breakdowns
2. Part names and numbers
3. Flat rate times
4. Part prices
5. Other miscellaneous information

Crash estimating guides can be used as a reference for pricing parts. However, never use them to determine the absolute price. Usually, these guides will list the name of the part, the year of the vehicle it will fit, its part number, the estimated time required to replace, and the current price. The current prices are the factory-suggested list prices. Parts that have been discontinued are usually listed. The price that appears in the guide is the last available one.

Each collision estimating guide will have procedure ("P") pages. These procedure pages provide important information such as:

1. Arrangement of material
2. Explanation of symbols used
3. Definitions of terms used
4. How to read and use the parts illustrations
5. Procedure explanations, including which operations are included and which are NOT
6. How discontinued parts information is displayed
7. How interchangeable part information is displayed
8. Additions to labor times
9. Labor times for overlap items

Figure 28–16 Dimension drawings will give measurement points and specifications to help analyze damage. (Courtesy of Mitchell International, Inc.)

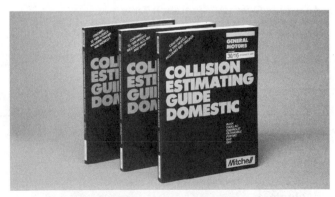

Figure 28–17 Collision estimating guides give information to help calculate cost of repairs. Part names, part costs, labor times, and labor rates are given. (Courtesy of Mitchell International, Inc.)

10. How to identify structural operations
11. How to identify mechanical operations

DAMAGE REPORT TERMINOLOGY

Anyone working with collision estimating guides must be familiar with the terms and abbreviations used, Figure 28–18. A few abbreviation examples are:

R & I—to remove and install. *R & R* means to remove and replace.

Overhaul—to remove an assembly from the vehicle, disassemble, clean, inspect, replace parts as needed, reassemble, install, and adjust (except wheel and suspension alignment).

D & R—to disconnect and reconnect. Disconnect, unplug, or unbolt the assembly at the point it is attached to the subject part.

Included operations—are those that can be performed individually, but are also part of another operation.

Overlap—occurs when replacement of one part duplicates some labor operation required to replace an adjacent part.

Refer to the procedure pages to identify all terms used.

PART COSTS

When should you repair or replace body parts? This question must be answered almost daily in collision repair shops. Actually, the decision often is a judgment call.

To help you decide whether to repair or replace panels, remember this statement.

If it is bent, repair it!
If it is kinked, replace it!

From earlier chapters, a part is kinked if bent over 90 degrees. A bend would be damage less than 90 degrees.

There are several other factors to consider: type of surface, location of damage, and extent of damage. The following are some useful guidelines:

1. If the damage is in a flat surface, it will straighten more easily than a sharp fold or buckle

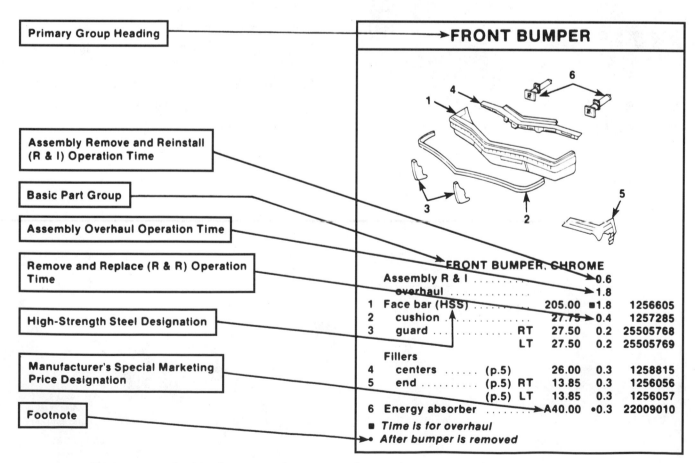

Figure 28–18 This is an example of an illustration and its meanings from crash estimating guide.

along a corner. Kinks along sharply formed edges almost always require replacement.

2. If the damage is located near the end of a rail, with the crush zone unaffected, replacement is NOT as critical as when the damage is in the crush zone or further into the rail. A kink in the crush zone calls for replacement.

3. If the damage is located near engine or steering mounting areas, repeated stress loading can create fatigue failure. Kinks at these mounting points require replacement rather than repair.

4. Tightly folded metal that is "locked" due to severe work hardening requires replacement.

Part costs are also affected by whether the parts are new or recycled. New parts might require more time to install than good recycled parts. They will usually cost more too.

Recycled parts will already have corrosion protection and sound deadening, where new parts might not. However, recycled parts might have minor damage that must be repaired. All of this must be considered when writing the estimate. As can be seen, there are many variables that can affect the repair/replace decision.

WRITING ESTIMATES

An estimate or *damage report* must include basic information about the vehicle. A *manually written estimate* is done long hand by filling in information on a printed form, Figure 28–19. An *electronic* or *computer written estimate* is done using a personal computer and printer. You should understand how both are done.

A damage report or estimate includes:

1. Customer information, including name, address, and phone.

2. Vehicle information—year, make, model, body type, license number, odometer reading, VIN, paint code, and trim colors.

3. Options—remote mirrors, power windows, power door locks, anti-lock brakes (ABS), air conditioning, and so on.

4. Date the vehicle was received and promised completion date.

5. It may be helpful to make sketches of the damaged areas of the vehicle. Many damage report forms provide a place to do this. With computer estimating systems, electronic photos or videos can also be helpful.

6. List whether new or recycled parts will be used during the repair.

7. Summarize cost of parts and labor, Figure 28–20.

At least three copies of the written estimate should be made. One is kept by the shop, one is given to the insurance company, and the other is given to the customer. An estimate is a *firm bid* for a given period of time—usually for 30 days. The reason for a given time period is obvious: part prices change and damaged parts can deteriorate.

The estimate is also considered the authorization to complete the repair work as listed, but ONLY when it is agreed upon and signed by the owner or by the owner and insurance company appraiser. The estimate explains the legal conditions under which the repair work is accepted by the collision repair shop. It protects the shop against the possibility of undetected damage that might be revealed later as repairs progress.

Many insurance policies contain a *deductible clause* which means that the owner is responsible for the first given amount of the estimate (usually $100 to $500). The remaining cost is paid by the insurance company. In such cases, both the customer and insurance company should authorize the estimate.

Another important function of the estimate is that it serves as a basis for writing the work order or operational plan. It is usually prepared from the damage appraisal of the estimator (using the written estimate) and a visual inspection by the shop supervisor and/or a technician.

The *work order* outlines the procedures that should be taken to put the vehicle back in top condition. It is also a valuable tool to both the estimator and the shop foreman, since it lists the actual times necessary to do the job.

Following are additional factors to be considered when writing an estimate. Such added time is usually negotiated between the estimator and the insurance company or customer.

1. Time for the setup of the vehicle on a frame machine and damage diagnosis

2. Time for pushing, pulling, cutting, and so on to remove collision-damaged parts

3. Time to straighten or align related parts

4. Time to remove undercoating, tar, grease, and similar materials

5. Time to repair rust or corrosion damage to adjacent parts

6. Time for the free-up of rusted or frozen parts

7. Time for drilling for ornamentation or mounting holes

8. Time for filling or plugging unneeded holes in new parts

9. Time to repair damaged replacement parts prior to installation

B&J
Collision Estimating Services

ESTIMATE OF REPAIRS
No 002128

SHEET NO. __1__ OF __1__ SHEETS

NAME KAREN Miller	ADDRESS 1143 RAILROAD ST. CRESSONA, PA. 17929	PHONE HOME 395-2719 BUS. 623-7347 DATE 12-17-95

YEAR 1994	MAKE Ford	MODEL P.V.	LICENSE NO. MAE 917	MILEAGE 14864	SERIAL/V.I. NO. 1FTDF15YSGNA69994

INSURANCE COMPANY Amerisure	TYPE OF INSURANCE COL	ADJUSTER	PHONE	CAR LOCATED AT mf6. 4/95

PARTS NECESSARY AND ESTIMATE OF LABOR REQUIRED	PAINT COST ESTIMATE	PARTS COST ESTIMATE	LABOR COST ESTIMATE
① FRONT FACE BAR Chrome No gds or Pads		205 82	.5
① " STONE deflecTOR	1 0	40 50	.5
① LefT HEADLAMP dooR (with aRgeNT GRill)		52 32	2
① " " Shield		3 20	
① " fRONT fendeR	3 1	133 00	1 6
① " " " APRON		60 47	1 0
② Wheels 15" 55.60 ea.		111 20	6
② Stems and Balance		2 50	5
② HUB CAPS		43 46	—
RePAiR RadiaToR SuppoRT		—	2 0
ALign FRONT End		—	1 5
① LefT dooR trim Panel		73 40	
STRiPe LefT FRONT fendeR		15 00	.5
LABOR 23.0 HRS @ 23.00		575 00	
(NoTe May Be FRONT SuSPeNSion dAmAge)			
PAINT MAT.		89 10	
UNdeRCOAT		15 00	
TOTALS		1,419 .97	

INSURED PAYS $_____ INS. CO. PAYS $_____ R.O. NO._____	GRAND TOTAL	1,419.97
INS. CHECK PAYABLE TO_____	TOWING & STORAGE	

The above is an estimate, based on our inspection, and does not cover additional parts or labor which may be required after the work has been opened up. Occasionally, after work has started, worn, broken or damaged parts are discovered which are not evident on first inspection. Quotations on parts and labor are current and subject to change. Not responsible for any delays caused by unavailability of parts or delays in parts shipment by supplier or transporter.

ESTIMATOR _____

	TAX	85.20

AUTHORIZATION FOR REPAIRS. You are hereby authorized to make the above specified repairs to the car described herein.

SIGNED X_____   DATE _____ 19

TOTAL OF ESTIMATE	$ 1,505.17

Figure 28–19 Here is an example of a handwritten estimate. Read through it carefully.

TIME/DOLLAR CONVERSION TABLE

Dollar Per Hour Rates

Time	.50	$1.00	$10.00	$15.00	$20.00	$25.00	$30.00	$35.00	$40.00	$45.00	$50.00
0.6	.30	.60	6.00	9.00	12.00	15.00	18.00	21.00	24.00	27.00	30.00
0.7	.35	.70	7.00	10.50	14.00	17.50	21.00	24.50	28.00	31.50	35.00
0.8	.40	.80	8.00	12.00	16.00	20.00	24.00	28.00	32.00	36.00	40.00
0.9	.45	.90	9.00	13.50	18.00	22.50	27.00	31.50	36.00	40.50	45.00
1.0	.50	1.00	10.00	15.00	20.00	25.00	30.00	35.00	40.00	45.00	50.00
1.1	.55	1.10	11.00	16.50	22.00	27.50	33.00	38.50	44.00	49.50	55.00
1.2	.60	1.20	12.00	18.00	24.00	30.00	36.00	42.00	48.00	54.00	60.00
1.3	.65	1.30	13.00	19.50	26.00	32.50	39.00	45.50	52.00	58.50	65.00
1.4	.70	1.40	14.00	21.00	28.00	35.00	42.00	49.00	56.00	63.00	70.00
1.5	.75	1.50	15.00	22.50	30.00	37.50	45.00	52.50	64.00	67.50	75.00
1.6	.80	1.60	16.00	24.00	32.00	40.00	48.00	56.00	64.00	72.00	85.00
1.7	.85	1.70	17.00	25.50	34.00	42.50	51.00	59.50	68.00	76.50	85.00
1.8	.90	1.80	18.00	27.00	36.00	45.00	54.00	63.00	72.00	81.00	90.00
1.9	.95	1.90	19.00	28.50	38.00	47.50	57.00	66.50	76.00	85.50	95.00
2.0	1.00	2.00	20.00	30.00	40.00	50.00	60.00	70.00	80.00	90.00	100.00
2.1	1.05	2.10	21.00	31.50	42.00	52.50	63.00	73.50	84.00	94.50	105.00
2.2	1.10	2.20	22.00	33.00	44.00	55.00	66.00	77.00	88.00	99.00	110.00
2.3	1.15	2.30	23.00	34.50	46.00	57.50	69.00	80.50	92.00	103.50	115.00
2.4	1.20	2.40	24.00	36.00	48.00	60.00	72.00	84.00	96.00	108.00	120.00
2.5	1.25	2.50	25.00	37.50	50.00	62.50	75.00	87.50	100.00	112.50	125.00

Figure 28–20 Chart can be used to convert time from estimating guide into actual labor charge per hour.

10. Time to check suspension and steering alignment/toe-in

11. Time for removal of shattered glass

12. Time to rebuild, recondition, and install aftermarket parts, NOT including refinishing time

13. Time for application of sound-deadening material, undercoating, caulking, and painting of the inner areas

14. Time to restore corrosion protection.

15. Time to R & I main computer module when necessary in repair operations

16. Time to R & I wheel or hub cap locks

17. Time to replace accessories such as trailer hitches, sun roofs, and fender flares

ESTIMATING SEQUENCE

When estimating any type of damage, a logical sequence must be followed. Before making a written estimate, the estimator should visually inspect the entire vehicle, paying special attention to damaged subassemblies and parts that are mounted to (or part of) a damaged part.

The estimator must consider the same points as the technician does before making any decision on repair work. Most estimators start from the outside of the vehicle and work inward, listing everything on paper—by vehicle section—that is bent, broken, crushed, or missing.

For example, if the front grille and some of the related parts are damaged, list the needed repairs or replacements as follows:

1. Front Grille .... Replace
2. Opening Panel .... Straighten and replace
3. Deflector (or Valance ...Replace Panel)
4. Headlight Door ....Replace
5. Grille Opening Panel ....Refinish

Notice that the parts are listed in a definite sequence according to factory disassembly operations or exploded views as provided in service manuals or crash estimating guides.

FLAT RATE OPERATIONS

The *flat rate* is a preset amount of time and money charged for a specific repair operation. As a rule of thumb, repair costs should never exceed replacement costs. If repairs and straightening will NOT produce a quality job, then the estimate should list the required new parts. Sheet metal parts usually offer the most opportunities for repair and straightening. As a result, sheet metal repair, replacement, and panel refinishing generally account for the largest number of estimate dollars.

To reduce parts costs, many insurance appraisers and some customers might want to use recycled parts. Recycled parts are removed from wrecked vehicles by *recyclers* (salvage yards). There is always a chance that such parts have been previously damaged and repaired. For this reason, it is important to carefully inspect all recycled parts before they are installed to be sure that they are in usable condition.

Each damaged vehicle poses different problems that must be solved to arrive at a final decision concerning repair versus replacement. The most difficult questions arise when a vehicle is involved in a major collision.

If the frame rails received extensive damage, for instance, the estimator might want to consider listing their replacement rather than the more costly job of installing a complete new frame assembly. Another option is to list the replacement of a front side rail section or a complete front frame section. These solutions might be more practical (from a time and cost approach) than making repairs with frame straightening equipment.

On the other hand, estimating damage to the body shell is often a much more difficult job. Knowing what would be needed to restore the body shell to its original dimensions and configuration requires a good deal of experience. If body shell distortion is suspected, it can be checked by careful measurement prior to listing any necessary repair of straightening procedures. Generally, a clue to minor body distortion (twist, sag, side sway) is if any cracking of stationary glass is noted, yet there is no visible sign of a direct impact with any object.

LABOR COSTS

The procedure pages of crash estimating guides usually provide an explanation of what the labor time does and does NOT include. For example, replacing a panel or fender includes removing, installing, and aligning. It does NOT include the installation of molding or antennas, refinishing, pin striping, or application of decals. Also NOT considered are rusted or inaccessible bolts, undercoating, and alignment or straightening of damaged adjacent parts.

The labor time reported in crash estimating guides is to be used as a guide only. The times are principally based on data reported by vehicle manufacturers or manual publishers who have arrived at them by repeated performance of each operation under normal shop conditions. An explanation is listed in the guide of the established requirements for the average technician, working under average conditions and following the procedures outlined in the service manuals.

The times reported apply only to standard models listed in identification sections of the crash estimating guide. They do NOT apply to vehicles with equipment other than that supplied by the vehicle manufacturer as standard or regular production options. If other equipment is used, the time might have to be adjusted higher.

All labor times given in crash estimating guides include the time necessary to insure proper fit of the new part. The times are based on new, undamaged parts installed as an individual operation. Additional time has NOT been added to compensate for collision damage to the vehicle. Removal and replacement of exchanged or used parts are also NOT considered. If additional aligning or repairs must be made, such factors should be considered when making an estimate.

When jobs overlap, reductions in the labor times must be considered. This occurs when replacement of one part duplicates some labor operations required to replace an adjacent part. For example, when replacing a quarter panel and rear body panel on the same vehicle, the area where the two parts join is considered overlap. Where a labor overlap condition exists, less time is required to replace adjoining parts collectively than is required when they are replaced individually.

Another labor cost reduction is noted as included operations. These are jobs that can be performed individually but are also part of another operation.

As an example, when replacing a door, the suggested time would include the replacement of all parts attached to the door, except for the ornamentation. It would be impossible to replace the door without transferring these parts. Consequently, the time involved in transferring them would be included operations and should be disregarded because the times for the individual items are already included in the door replacement time.

REFINISHING TIME

Making a correct estimate of the amount of time required to refinish panels, doors, hoods, and so forth is a vital part of an estimator's job. Although the wide range of materials and conditions sometimes makes it difficult to arrive at a precise refinishing cost, there are a number of generally approved concepts that will help an estimator arrive at a fair judgment of the amount of materials that will be needed for the job.

Flat rate manuals list a labor time plus a materials allowance (in dollars) for many different refinishing operations. Independently published crash estimating guides list the labor times, but NOT the dollar value of the materials required.

In most crash estimating guides on the market today, the time required for refinishing is shown in the parentheses adjacent to the part name. The refinishing time generally includes:

1. Cleaning/light sanding
2. Making adjacent panels
3. Priming/scuff sanding
4. Final sanding/cleaning
5. Mixing paint/filling spray equipment
6. Applying color coat
7. Removing masking
8. Buffing or compounding (if required)
9. Cleaning equipment

Refinishing time generally does NOT include:

1. Cost of paints or materials
2. Matching and/or tinting
3. Grinding, filling, and smoothing welded seams
4. Blending into adjacent panels
5. Removal of protective coatings
6. Custom painting
7. Undercoating
8. Anti-corrosion materials
9. Sound-deadening
10. Refinishing underside of hood or deck lids
11. Covering entire vehicle prior to refinishing
12. Additional time to produce custom, non-OEM finishes

The refinishing times given in most estimates are for one color on new replacement parts—outer surfaces only. Additions to refinishing times are usually made for the following operations:

1. Refinishing underside of hood
2. Refinishing underside of trunk lid
3. Edging new part
4. Two-tone operations
5. Stone chip (protective material)
6. Clear coat (basecoat/clearcoat) after deduction for overlap

TOTAL LABOR COSTS

Once all the repairs and labor times have been entered on the estimate form, refer to the estimating guide's time/dollar conversion table. It is used to con-

vert labor time into dollars to fit local labor or operating rates per hour.

When establishing labor rates, the shop overhead (including such items as rent, management and supervision, supplies, and depreciation on equipment) must be determined. Then the actual labor cost of all employees and the profit required to keep the business operating must be added to the shop overhead to obtain a dollar rate for repairs. This rate is usually figured on an hourly basis. Keep in mind that labor times shown in crash estimating guides are listed in tenths of an hour.

TOTALING THE ESTIMATE

Once all the columns of the estimating form—parts, labor, and refinishing cost—are filled out, they can be added together for a subtotal. To this figure, add any extra charges such as wrecker and towing fee, storage fee, and state and local taxes. These figures, added to the subtotal, will give the grand total of the estimate.

While more and more large collision repair shops are doing repair jobs such as wheel alignment, rust-proofing, and tire placement, smaller operations still "farm-out" or "sublet" these jobs to specialty shops.

When the work is done, the specialty shop bills the collision repair shop for the work. Generally, this is done at a rate less than the normal retail labor cost. In this way, the collision repair shop can charge the normal retail cost and still make a small profit.

Shops that sublet work usually have a "sublet" column on the estimate where the retail labor cost is marked. This figure is added to the rest to obtain the grand total of the estimate.

If the customer wants extra work performed (damage that occurred prior to collision), this should be noted as *customer-requested,* or C/R, repairs. As a general rule, the insurance company will NOT pay for customer-requested repairs. Often a separate estimate must be made in such cases.

COMPUTERIZED ESTIMATING

Computerized estimating systems using a *PC* (personal computer) may provide more accurate and consistent damage reports. The use of computers makes dealing with thousands of parts on hundreds of vehicles more manageable. See Figure 28–21.

Computerized estimating systems store the collision estimating guide information in a computer. This eliminates a lot of time in looking up parts and labor times, and manually entering and totaling them on a

Figure 28–21 Computer estimating is much more efficient than trying to figure repair costs long hand. *(Courtesy of Mitchell International, Inc.)*

Figure 28–22 This laptop computer can be taken out to vehicle during damage analysis. It can also be used in office to finalize damage report. *(Courtesy of Mitchell International, Inc.)*

form. The computer prepares a damage report, while still allowing the possibility of a manual override when necessary. Look at Figure 28–22.

Computers are revolutionizing the art of estimating by making enormous amounts of data readily accessible. There are basically two types of computer estimating systems: dial-up systems and resident or in-shop systems.

The *dial-up estimating system* relies on data stored in a mainframe computer at a remote location. The data in the mainframe is usually accessed via a telephone *modem* (device for sending and receiving computer data over phone lines). The shop may be charged a fee whenever data from the mainframe is accessed.

An *in-shop estimating system* has all of the data needed at the shop office, usually on CD-ROMs. They do NOT require a fee for each estimate. Modern computer estimating systems store electronic database containing up-to-date part prices and labor times that can be retrieved from the shop's computer system.

With the use of these sophisticated programs, estimators can now use the stored data to make virtually error-free estimates rapidly at a very low cost.

Data Wand, Bar Codes

When at the vehicle gathering data about the damage, many computerized systems use a data wand. A *data wand* is a small hand-held electronic data gathering tool, often with a keypad and read head for bar codes. It is used to gather and store data for later downloading into the office's personal computer. See Figure 28–23.

First, you can use the data wand keyboard to input the vehicle VIN, make, model, and other information. By pressing the keys on the data wand this information will be stored on its internal memory.

Bar codes are a series of lines that represent other data, like a damaged part, Figure 28–24. The data wand can be moved over a bar code printed in a spe-

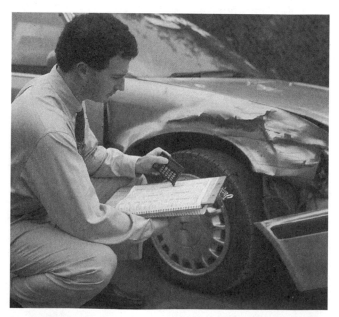

Figure 28–23 Some computer estimating systems have a data wand. Key pad allows you to input vehicle information —VIN, make, model, year, etc. It can also be used in conjunction with booklet that contains bar codes for each section and part of vehicle. By running wand over bar code corresponding to parts, data wand will store information in electronic memory. *(Courtesy of Mitchell International, Inc.)*

Figure 28–24 Note how bar code guide has information that can be used with data wand. *(Courtesy of Mitchell International, Inc.)*

cial collision estimating guide. For example, if a fender is damaged, run the wand over the bar code for that part. The unit will then store the data electronically for later use when in the office.

Computer Database

Once information has been gathered at the vehicle, the estimator will take this data into the office. The damage data is then *downloaded* (entered) into the personal computer, Figure 28–25. This allows the operator to use the speed and convenience of a computer and estimating program to make up the estimate. An *estimating program* is software (computer instructions) that will automatically help find parts needed, labor rates, and calculate total for the repairs. The estimating program is often on computer *floppy discs* (removable magnetic discs of data) or on a compact disc (optical data on disc).

Figure 28–25 Estimating program is designed for helping estimator quickly and accurately calculate repair costs. Data wand can download information for manipulation by personal computer. *(Courtesy of Mitchell International, Inc.)*

Figure 28–27 Here is computer display of exploded view of fender assembly. Estimator can quickly see all parts and select which ones require replacement or repair. *(Courtesy of Mitchell International, Inc.)*

Figure 28–26 Computer estimating systems often have database of dimension manual for faster retrieval of specifications. *(Courtesy of Mitchell International, Inc.)*

To use the program, you must load the data into the PC's memory. This will then let you pull up images from an electronic dimension manual, Figure 28–26. Modern systems will retrieve exploded views of assemblies in electronic form, Figure 28–27.

Many programs automatically deduct for overlap. The program notes operations as "Incl." if they are part of a larger operation. The program may also identify judgment times.

The estimating program can access a huge database (computer file) of information. The computer *database* includes part numbers, part illustrations,

labor times, labor rates and other data for filling out the estimate. Quick searches can be done to move through this database quickly and efficiently.

The most common and modern way of storing an estimating database is the CD-ROM. One *CD-ROM* or compact disc can hold all of the crash estimating guides, dimension manuals, as well as other information for every make and model vehicle. The compact disc database contains the same basic information that is in the collision estimating guide. See Figure 28–28.

Labor time information for a given operation is taken from the same sources as in the collision estimating guides. A portable hand-held computer is used with a light wand to scan parts and labor operations from a reference book. This information is then fed into a personal computer for making calculations.

A CD-ROM drive is wired to the office computer. The PC can then operate the drive and access this huge amount of data. CD-ROM data can be pulled into the PC's memory for manipulation.

Advanced computer estimating systems will even allow you to input photos of the wrecked vehicle into the computer, Figure 28–29.

An *electronic camera* can be used to take photos of the vehicle's damage and store them as digital data. The camera can be connected to the computer to download these *digital images* (pictures stored as computer data) into memory or onto the computer's internal hard drive.

The estimator can look at these photos on the computer screen or monitor while finalizing the estimate.

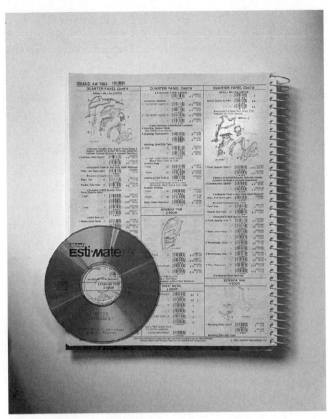

Figure 28–28 CD-ROM provides a vast database for computer estimating system. One CD-ROM can hold a whole set of books in electronic form. *(Courtesy of Mitchell International, Inc.)*

Figure 28–29 This advanced computer estimating system will let you download pictures taken with electronic camera or a video camera. Estimator can refer to these images when working on estimate. *(Courtesy of Mitchell International, Inc.)*

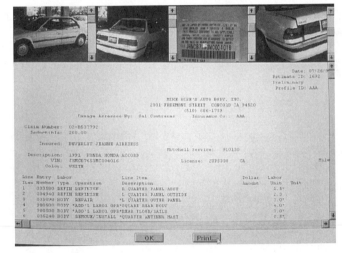

Figure 28–30 Pictures of damaged vehicle can be pulled up and reexamined. They can also be sent to insurance adjuster so he or she can view vehicle damage without leaving office. *(Courtesy of Mitchell International, Inc.)*

The electronic images can also be sent to the insurance adjuster so he or she can evaluate the vehicle's damage. See Figure 28–30.

A *printer* can be used to make a hard copy (printed images on paper) for the customer, insurance adjusters, and shop personnel. You can quickly print vehicle dimension drawings, part views, or the estimate. Look at Figure 28–31.

When working with any estimating system, either manual or computer, those working with the damage report must understand:

1. Where vehicle options are listed, so these can be double-checked for accuracy.
2. Which labor rates are shown for a given operation and how to identify them.
3. What times and amounts are judgment items, and how these were generated.
4. Which times and amounts have been overridden.
5. Which times are included, and which are not.

Only by understanding all of these can a judgment be made on whether the damage report is accurate. Each system will produce a unique look.

FRONT CLIPS

In some situations, such as a severely damaged front end, an estimator might want to consider the purchase and installation of a used front end assembly. In the body repair trade this is referred to as a *"front clip."* This assembly generally includes the front bumper and supports, grilles and baffles, and radiator and its supporting members, the hood and its hinges (or hood torsion bars), the front fenders and skirts, all front lights, the wiring, and all other related parts.

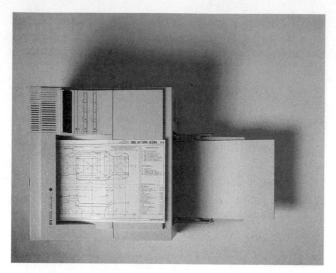

Figure 28-31 Once computer estimate is done, it can be printed out on laser printer. At least three copies should be made. (Courtesy of Mitchell International, Inc.)

Often, this method of making collision repairs to the front end will decrease the total time the vehicle is in the shop.

SECTIONING

Another operation that may be flat-rated in the crash estimating guides is sectioning. *Sectioning* involves cutting off the damaged part and welding on a new one. Often times it is less expensive and time consuming to section a damaged panel and weld part of a new panel in place than to replace the entire panel. As discussed earlier, rails and other parts may be sectioned. Sectioning disturbs less OEM corrosion protection and spot welds. In some cases, it is the best repair procedure to choose. However, the crash estimating guides do NOT always provide flat rate time for sectioning.

TOTAL LOSS

A *total loss* occurs when the cost of the repairs exceeds the value of the vehicle. The insurance company or customer would normally NOT want the vehicle repaired. Instead, the insurance company will write a check to cover the cost of a replacement vehicle. An equivalent year, make and model vehicle is then purchased by the customer.

The insurance company usually determines if a vehicle is a total loss. The company will evaluate the estimate and market prices for comparable vehicles when making this decision. Older vehicles are written up as a total loss more than late model vehicles. This is because of their low replacement cost.

The totaled vehicle will usually be auctioned or sold to a salvage yard or recycler. The recycler will then disassemble the vehicle and sell its parts for a profit.

Summary

- An estimate, also called a damage report or appraisal, calculates the cost of parts, materials, and labor for repairing a collision-damaged vehicle.

- Direct damage occurs in the immediate area of the collision. Indirect damage is caused by the shock of collision forces traveling through the body and inertial forces acting upon the rest of the unibody.

- Refer to literature such as dimension manuals and collision estimation guides to aid in the estimation process.

- Estimates may be manually written, or electronically (computer) written. Computerized estimating uses a personal computer, printer, and may use a data wand for storing and gathering data.

Technical Terms

estimate	*deductible clause*
damage analysis	*work order*
direct damage	*flat rate*
indirect damage	*PC*
steering wheel center	*dial-up estimating*
check	*system*
jounce/rebound steering	*in-shop estimating*
gear check	*system*
strut rotation check	*data wand*
strut position check	*bar codes*
wheel run-out check	*download*
collision estimating	*estimating program*
guide	*floppy disc*
R & I	*database*
R & R	*CD-ROM*
overhaul	*electronic camera*
D & R	*electronic image*
included operations	*printer*
overlap	*front clip*
manually written	*sectioning*
estimate	*total loss*
computer written	
estimate	

Review Questions

1. How many copies of the written estimate should be made?
   a. One
   b. Two
   c. Three
   d. Four

2. An _____, also called a _____ _____, or _____, calculates the cost of parts, materials and labor for fixing the collision-damaged vehicle.

3. Before starting damage analysis, list six things you should do.

4. When inspecting a collision-damaged unibody vehicle, Technician A looks for damage only near the area of impact. Technician B looks for damage both in the area of impact and some distance away.
   Who is correct?
   a. Technician A
   b. Technician B
   c. Both A and B
   d. Neither A nor B

5. What is the smallest increment in which labor times are listed in crash estimating guides?
   a. Hours
   b. Half hours
   c. Quarter hours
   d. Tenths of an hour

6. Explain the difference between direct and indirect damage.

7. When you inspect the entire vehicle for damage, what 14 problems must you look for?

8. How do you analyze the center position of a steering wheel?

9. This check will find a bent wheel.
   a. Strut rotation check
   b. Strut position check
   c. Run-out check
   d. Overrun check

10. List five things included in collision estimating guides.

11. _____ _____ are those that can be performed individually, but are also part of another operation.

12. _____ occurs when replacement of one part duplicates some labor operation required to replace an adjacent part.

13. Give the statement or rule for determining whether to repair or replace a part.

14. A damage report or estimate includes these seven items.

15. How do you use a data wand with a computerized estimating system?

16. The most common and modern way of storing an estimating database is the:
    a. CD-ROM
    b. floppy disc
    c. Magnetic tape
    d. None of the above

Activities

1. Manually write an estimate on a vehicle with minor damage. Use manuals to find the cost of parts and labor. Calculate the total repair costs for the damage.

2. Visit a shop with a computerized estimating system. Ask the shop owner if you can observe the system in use.

CHAPTER 29

ENTREPRENEURSHIP, JOB SUCCESS

Objectives

After studying this chapter, you should be able to:

- Describe desirable traits of collision repair technicians.

- Summarize job responsibilities of industry personnel.

- Define the term "entrepreneur."

- Advance into other automotive related professions.

Introduction

According to economic predictions, there will be a strong demand for collision repair technicians in the future.

Our nation is now, and always will be, a "nation on wheels." You have selected an excellent area of study—collision repair technology. With this knowledge base, you should be able to earn a good living for as long as there are cars and trucks on the road.

Job openings are common as people move up into other positions and retire. Always read newspapers to stay aware of job openings. Some may pay better or offer better *benefits* (insurance, vacation time, holiday pay, etc.) than your present job.

COLLISION REPAIR TECHNICIAN

A *collision repair technician* is a highly skilled professional capable of doing a wide variety of tasks. This person must have a working knowledge of mechanics, electronics, measurement, welding, cutting, straightening, painting, and so on.

Collision repair technicians earn good money. There is also a constant demand for well-trained body people. After finishing your training and gaining practical experience, you should be proud of becoming a collision repair technician.

Specialized technicians concentrate their study in one area. Some shops have specialized paint technicians, sheet metal technicians, masking technicians, frame rack technicians, and so on. This allows each person to be more efficient at their own skill area; more vehicles are repaired and greater profit is made.

RELATED PROFESSIONS

Related professions are jobs that require an understanding of auto body repair, Figure 29–1. There are many related professions that you can advance into after gaining a working knowledge of body repair. By understanding the body repair and furthering your education, you may be able to get a job with:

1. Insurance company—adjuster, agent.
2. Materials manufacturer—paint, filler, or other company.
3. Parts suppliers—new, used, and remanufactured parts companies.
4. Auto manufacturer—factory representative, designer, engineer, Figures 29–2 and 3.
5. Instructor—teach collision repair classes.

ENTREPRENEURSHIP

An *entrepreneur* is a person who starts his or her own business. This business might be a body shop, materials supply house, parts warehouse, or similar endeavor. You might want to consider being an entrepreneur someday.

If you start your own business: you would need to understand bookkeeping, payroll, state and local laws controlling the industry.

After mastering the knowledge needed to do collision repair work, you will become more marketable. These skills of a body technician can help when applying for other jobs or starting a business.

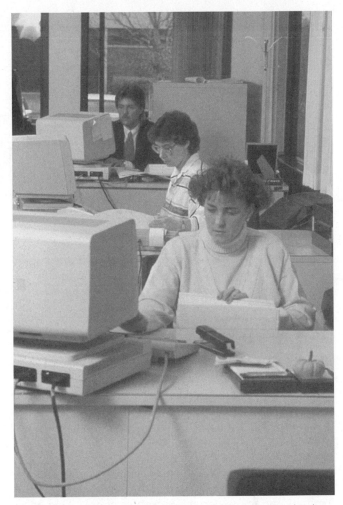

Figure 29–1 If you understand auto body repair technology and terminology, it may help you get a job in a related profession, such as this insurance adjuster position. *(Used by permission from Tech-Cor Inc.)*

Figure 29–2 If you prove yourself as a dependable collision repair shop worker, it will help you advance into other positions. This is a vehicle assembly plant with numerous types of job offerings. *(Courtesy of Chrysler Corporation)*

Figure 29–3 Here, workers are hand sculpting a vehicle body. This will help them study design characteristics and make final parts for body. *(Courtesy of General Motors Corporation)*

COOPERATIVE TRAINING PROGRAMS

Some schools offer *cooperative education programs* which allow you to have a job and get school credit at the same time. If available, you could be hired to work and train in a real body shop. Some "co-op" programs pay a small wage while you learn.

During cooperative training, you might be a helper technician. You would work under and be further trained by an experienced professional. This is an excellent way of gaining practical, hands-on experience. And remember, experience is the best teacher.

If you are still in school, check with your instructor and guidance counselor about cooperative education programs in your area.

KEEP LEARNING!

Try to learn something job-related every day. Always learn from your mistakes. Read technical magazines and other publications. While working, try to think of more efficient ways of working. Consider new tools and techniques. This attitude will help you become more productive.

USE A SYSTEMATIC APPROACH

Develop a more *systematic approach* for doing your job. A systematic approach involves organizing and using a logical sequence of steps to accomplish a task or job. A systematic approach will result in your selecting more efficient ways of working.

Ask yourself these kinds of questions:

1. Did I take all needed tools to the vehicle?
2. Is there a better tool for a specific task?
3. Have I been reading the manufacturer's instructions (paints, plastic filler, equipment, and so on)?
4. Is my body in the right position to protect myself and feel comfortable?

WORK TRAITS

Work traits are those things, aside from skills, that make you a good or bad employee. Work traits often determine whether you keep a good job or get fired. The most important work traits are:

1. *Reliability* means being at work on time, being at work every day, and doing the job right. This is the most important job trait. Without it, you will have a difficult time keeping a job.

For example, if you always miss work, you will affect everyone in the shop. If the vehicle has been promised on Friday and you are NOT there, either someone else has to do your work, or, the vehicle may NOT get done on time. Then the customer will be unhappy and will never return to your shop again. If this continues, the "word of mouth" will ruin the reputation of the shop and profits will decline.

2. *Social skills* are important so that other workers and customers like you. Many times you will need the help of another worker to complete a difficult, two-person task. If you are not liked by others, you will find many tasks almost impossible.

A good body shop will have a "team of workers" that help each other succeed and prosper. They will exchange information, help each other with small tasks, and enjoy working together. You spend much of your life on the job; so why NOT enjoy it?

3. *Productivity* is a measure of how much work you get done. A highly productive technician will turn out a large amount of work. This will result in higher pay for the technician and more profits for the shop.

You want to balance productivity and quality. If you try to cut corners and get too much done too quickly, quality will often suffer. You must use proper work habits, common sense, and hard work to be productive.

4. *Professionalism* is a broad trait the includes everything from being able to follow orders to pride in workmanship. A professional does everything "by the book." He or she never cuts corners (for instance, leaving out the hard-to-reach bolt) trying to get the repair finished. Always think, dress, and act like a professional.

A professional:

1. Is customer oriented
2. Is up-to-date on vehicle developments
3. Keeps up with advancements in the repair industry
4. Pays attention to detail
5. Ensures that his/her work is up-to-specs
6. Participates in trade associations

Summary

- A collision repair technician is a highly skilled professional capable of a wide variety of tasks. This person must have a working knowledge of mechanics, electronics, measurement, welding, cutting, straightening, painting and so on.

- Specialized technicians concentrate their study in one area such as painting, sheet metal, or masking. This allows a person to be more efficient in their chosen skill; more vehicles are repaired and greater profit is made.

- An entrepreneur is a person who starts his or her own business. This business may be a body shop, materials supply house, parts warehouse, or similar endeavor.

- Work traits are those things other than skills, that rate you as an employee. The most important work traits are: reliability, social skills, productivity, and professionalism.

Technical Terms

benefits
related professions
entrepreneur
cooperative education
programs
systematic approach

work traits
reliability
social skills
productivity
professionalism

Review Questions

1. According to economic predictions, there will be a strong demand for collision repair technicians in the future. True or false?

2. What are job benefits?

3. What are five areas of employment related to collision repair technology?

4. An _____ is a person who starts his or her own business.

5. Some schools offer this type of program which allows you to have a job and get school credit at the same time.
   a. Work release
   b. Work-Ed
   c. Cooperative education
   d. Continuing education

6. In your own words, describe the need for reliability, social skills, productivity, and professionalism when on the job.

Activities

1. Visit a small collision repair related business—parts house, parts supply store, body shop, and so on. Ask the owner how he or she started the business. Write and give a class report.

2. Visit the library and obtain published materials on starting your own business. Create a wall display describing what it takes to start a business.

GLOSSARY

A/C Low Side   One side of the air conditioning system. It contains low pressure/low temperature refrigerant.

Abrasive Blasting   The process of using air pressure, a blasting gun, and an abrasive to remove old paint.

AC Current   The electrical current found in home wiring.

Accelerator   A fast evaporating thinner or reducer for speeding the drying time.

Accidents   Unplanned events that hurt people, break tools, damage vehicles, or have other adverse effects on the business and its employees.

Acetylene Pressure   Pressure leaving acetylene pressure regulator of oxyacetylene welding outfit. Typically ranges from 1 to 12 psi (kPa).

Acid Core Solder   Used for doing non-electrical repairs, as on radiators.

Acorn Nut   A nut closed on one end for appearance and to keep water and debris off the threads.

Acrylic Resin Adhesive   A two-part somewhat flexible adhesive (liquid and powder) used on small surface areas. It is waterproof and not affected by gasoline or water.

Active Gas   A type of shielding gas that combines with the weld to contribute to weld quality.

Active Restraint System   A restraint system where the occupants must make an effort to use it, i.e., fastening the seat belt.

Adhesion Bonding   Uses oxyacetylene to melt a filler metal onto the work piece for joining.

Adhesive-Bonded Door Skin   A door skin that is bonded, not welded, to the door frame.

Adhesive Bonded Parts   Metal or plastic parts that are held together by the use of a high strength epoxy or special glue.

Adhesive Release Agent   A chemical that dissolves most types of adhesives.

Adhesive Remover   A chemical used to clean off the remaining vinyl glue after removal of a stripe or decal.

Aftermarket Repair Manuals   Books published by publishing companies rather than the manufacturer. They are not as detailed but can give enough information needed for most repairs.

Agitator Paint Cup   A small air motor in the spray gun moves a mixing paddle up and down keeping the metallic flakes mixed and evenly distributed in the cup.

Air Bag Module   An assembly composed of the nylon bag and an igniter-inflator mechanism enclosed in a metal-plastic housing.

Air Bag Controller   This analyzes inputs from the sensor to determine if bag deployment is needed.

Air Conditioning Gauges   Used to measure operating pressures in a vehicle's air conditioning system.

Air Conversion Unit   Acts as in-line regulators to convert high pressure main line air pressure to low pressure, high volume air. They use existing shop air from the compressor.

Air Couplings   These allow you to quickly install and remove air hoses and air tools.

Air Cutoff Tool   A tool that uses a small abrasive wheel to rapidly cut or grind metal.

Air Dams   A part that improves aerodynamics by restricting air passing under the vehicle body, thus reducing turbulence and resistance to airflow.

Air Drills   Uses shop air pressure to spin a drill bit.

Air File   A long, thin air sander for working large flat surfaces on panels.

Air Filter Drain Valve   Allows you to remove trapped water and oil from the filter.

Air Hammer   Uses back and forth hammer blows to drive a cutter or driver into the work piece.

Air Hose Leak Test   A method used to find body leaks. Place a soapy water solution on possible leakage points and use low pressure air on the inside of the vehicle. Bubbles will form wherever there is a leak.

Air Hoses Sizes   Given as inside diameters of passage through hose.

Air Line Filter-Drier   Used in the air line to remove moisture and debris from the air flowing through the air lines. It is designed to trap and hold water and oil that passes out of the compressor air pump.

Air Nibbler   A tool used like tin snips to cut sheet metal. It has an air-powered snipping blade that moves up and down.

Air Polisher   Used to smooth and shine painted surfaces by spinning a soft buffing pad.

Air Ratchet   A wrench, like the hand wrench, it has a special ability to work in hard-to-reach places.

Air Replacement System   Exhausts the air from spray booths continuously during the spraying process.

Air Saw   It uses a reciprocating (back and forth) action to move a hacksaw type of blade for cutting parts.

Air Spring Suspension   A type of suspension that uses air springs to support the vehicle load.

Air Tool Lubrication   A few drops of special air tool oil, lightweight motor oil, or a mixture of oil and automatic transmission fluid should be used on all air tools.

Air Vent Hole   It allows atmospheric pressure to enter the cup of the spray gun.

Air-Supplied Respirator   A half-mask, full face piece, hood, or helmet, to which clean, breathable air is supplied through a hose from a separate air source. It provides protection from isocyanate paint vapors and mists, as well as from hazardous solvent vapors.

Airless Plastic Welding Uses an electric heating element to melt a small _ inch diameter rod with no external air supply.

Aligning Punch A long and tapered tool used to align body panels and other parts.

Alignment Rack Used to measure and adjust the steering and suspension of a vehicle after repairs.. Also known as Front End Rack.

All-Wheel Drive Two differentials are used to power all four drive wheels.

Allen Wrench A hex, hexagon, or six-sided wrench. It will install or remove set screws.

Analog Multimeter (AVOM) A multimeter with a pointer needle that moves across the face of a scale when making electrical measurements.

Anchor Clamps A device bolted to specific points on the vehicle to allow the attachment of anchor chains. They distribute pulling force to prevent metal tearing.

Anchor Pots Small steel cups imbedded in shop floor for anchoring vehicle when pulling out major damage.

Anchor Rails Steel beams in floor for holding vehicle secure while straightening.

Anchoring Equipment It holds the vehicle stationary while pulling and measuring.

Angle Measurement Divides a circle into 360 or more parts called degrees.

Anti-Chip Coating Also called gravel guard, chip guard, or vinyl coating, it is a rubberized material used along a vehicle's lower panels.

Anti-Corrosion Compounds Water or petroleum-based compounds resistant to chipping and abrasion. They can undercoat, deaden sound, and completely seal the surface.

Anti-Lacerative Glass Glass with one or more additional layers of plastic affixed to the inside of the glass. It gives added protection against shattering and cuts during impact.

Antifreeze A liquid used to prevent freeze-up in cold weather and to lubricate moving parts. It also prevents engine overheating.

Application Stroke A side-to-side movement of the spray gun to distribute the paint mist properly on the vehicle.

Arm Sets A resistance spot welding part that holds welding tips and conducts current to tips.

Arming Sensor A sensor that ensures that the particular collision is severe enough to require that the air bag be deployed.

ASE Tests Multiple-choice questions pertaining to the service and repair of a vehicle.

Assembly Line Diagnostic Link (ALDL) A connector provided for reading fault or trouble codes. It can be located in the passenger or engine compartment.

Automatic Transmission A transmission that shifts through gears automatically using a hydraulic system.

AWS American Welding Society.

Backing Strip Also referred to as an insert, it is made of the same metal as the base metal and can be placed behind the weld. It helps proper fit-up and supports the weld.

Ball Joints A part of the suspension system, they are located on the outer end of the control arms allowing the steering knuckles to swivel and turn.

Ball Peen Hammer A flat face hammer for general striking and a round peen end for shaping sheet metal, rivet heads, or other objects.

Banding Coat The depositing of enough paint on edges or corners of surfaces.

Bar Codes A series of lines that represent other data.

Bare Metal Treatment A process that prepares the metal for primer.

Base Gauges First two body gauges hung near the center of the vehicle, usually at torque box area when measuring major damage.

Base Material The material to be welded, usually metal or plastic.

Basecoat Patch A small area on the vehicle's surface without clearcoat that enables the painter to check for color match with tri-coat colors.

Battery A device that stores electrical energy chemically. It provides current for the starting system and current to all other electrical systems when the engine is not running.

Battery Charger Converts 120 volts AC into 13 to 15 volts DC for recharging drained batteries.

Bay A work area for one vehicle. Also termed a repair stall.

Beam Splitters Also referred to as laser guides, they are capable of reflecting the laser beam to additional targets.

Bench Computer Assists in the straightening-measuring process.

Bench Grinder A stationary, electric grinder mounted on a work bench or pedestal stand. It is used to sharpen chisels, punches, and to shape other tool tips.

Bench Seat A longer seat for several people.

Bench System Generally a portable or stationary steel table for straightening severe vehicle damage.

Benefits An employment term referring to insurance, vacation time, holiday pay, etc.

Bent A term that describes a part where the change in the shape of the part between the damaged and undamaged areas is smooth and continuous, or straightening the part by pulling restores its shape to pre-accident condition without areas of permanent deformation.

Blasters Air powered tools for forcing sand, plastic beads, or another material onto surfaces for paint removal.

Bleeder Spray Gun It allows air to pass through the gun at all times, even when the trigger is not pulled back. It does not have an air control valve. The trigger only controls fluid needle movement.

Block Sanding A simple back and forth scrubbing action with the sandpaper mounted on a rubber blocking tool.

Body Center Marks Locations stamped into sheet metal in both upper and lower body areas of vehicle. They can save time when taking measurements to determine extent and direction of major.

Body Clips Specially shaped retainers for holding trim and other body pieces requiring little strength. The clip often fits into the back of the trim piece and through the body panel.

Body File A type of file that has very large, open teeth for cutting plastic body filler. They often have a separate blade that fits into a handle.

Body Jack Also known as porta-powers, they can be used with frame/panel straighteners or by themselves. It produces a powerful pushing action.

Body Nut A flange on the nut that helps distribute the clamping force of the thin body panel or trim piece to prevent warpage.

Body Repair Manual A guide that gives information about the body, i.e., the plastic types used on the vehicle.

Body Shop Office An office containing business equipment and where paper work is handled.

Body Shop Tools Specialized tools designed for working with body parts.

BOF Body-over-frame vehicle construction.

Bolt A metal shaft with a head on one end and threads on the other.

Bolt Diameter Sometimes termed bolt size, it is measured around the outside of the threads.

Bolt Grade Markings Lines or numbers on the top of the head to identify bolt hardness and strength.

Bolt Head Size It is the distance measured across the flats of the bolt head.

Bolt Head The part of a bolt that is used to torque or tighten the bolt.

Bolt Length Measures the length of the bolt from the end of the threads to the bottom of the bolt head.

Bolt Strength Indicates the amount of torque or tightening force that should be applied.

Bolt Thread Pitch It is a measurement of thread coarseness.

Bolt Torque A measurement of the turning force applied when installing a fastener.

Bookkeeper A person who performs the accounting duties, i.e., invoices, checks, bills, banking, taxes.

Boots They protect the rack in the rack-and-pinion steering unit from contamination by dirt, salt, and other road particles.

Box End Wrench A wrench with closed ends that surround the bolt or nut head.

Brake System It uses hydraulic pressure to slow or stop wheel rotation with brake pedal application.

Brake System Bleeding A process that removes air from the brake fluid.

Breaker Bar Also called a flex handle, it provides the most powerful way of turning bolts and nuts.

Bucket Seat A single seat for one person.

Bump Caps Protective head gear worn when working beneath the hood or under the vehicle.

Bumper Shock Absorbers A part used to absorb some of the impact of a collision and reduce damage.

Bumpers A part designed to withstand minor impact without damage.

Bumping Hammer A hammer used to bump out large dents.

Burn Mark A mark on the back of a weld that indicates a good weld penetration.

Burn Test A test which involves using a flame and the resulting smoke to determine the type of plastic. It is no longer recommended.

Burn-Through This results from penetrating too much into the lower base metal which burns a hole through the back side of the metal.

Burnback In MIG welding this occurs when the electrode wire melting rate is faster than the wire speed.

C-Clamp A screw attached to a curved frame. It will hold objects on a work surface or drill press while working.

Cabinet Blaster A stationary enclosure equipped with a sand or bead blast tool.

Cable Hood Release Consists of hood release handle, hood release cable, hood latch and hood striker.

Cap Protective head gear to keep hair safe and clean when sanding, grinding, and doing similar jobs.

Cap Screw A term that describes a high strength bolt.

Capillary Attraction In brazing, it is the natural flow of the filler material into the joint.

Captive Spray Gun System Individual guns that are set up and used for applying each different type of material.

Carbon Monoxide (CO) An odorless, invisible gas that comes from vehicle exhaust.

Carburizing Flame Also called a reducing flame, it is obtained by mixing slightly more acetylene than oxygen.

Card Masking Involves using a simple masking pattern to produce a custom paint effect.

Cartridge Filter Respirators A rubber face piece that conforms to the face and forms an airtight seal. Used to protect against vapors and spray mists of nonactivated enamels, lacquers, and other nonisocyanate materials.

Cartridge Gun A device used to apply adhesive or sealer to body panels.

CD-ROM A compact disc that stores information.

Center Link It supports the tie-rods in position in parallelogram steering.

Center Orifice Located on the spray gun air cap at the fluid nozzle. It creates a vacuum for the discharge of the paint.

Center Punch A pointed tool used to start a drilled hole or mark parts. The indentation will keep a drill bit from wandering out of place.

Center Section Also called midsection, it typically includes the body parts that form the passenger compartment.

Certified Crash Tests A test performed using a real vehicle and sensor-equipped dummies that show how much impact the people would suffer during a collision.

Chain Wrench A wrench used to grasp and turn round objects. It is used to remove stuck or damaged engine oil filters or to adjust exhaust systems.

Channel Lock Pliers Pliers that have several settings for grasping different size objects; also known as rib joint pliers.

Charging A term used to describe filling the air conditioning system with refrigerant.

Charging Station A machine for automatically recharging an air conditioning system with refrigerant.

Charging System It recharges the battery and supplies electrical energy when the engine is running.

Chisel A tool used for some cutting operations such as shearing off rivet heads or separating sheet metal parts.

Chuck Movable jaws that close down and hold the drill bit.

Circular Sander It spins its pad and sandpaper around and around in a circular motion.

Classroom An area provided for lectures, demonstrations and meetings of shop personnel.

Clock Spring The electrical connection between the steering column and the air bag module.

Closed A term that refers to an electrically-connected electrical circuit.

Closed Coat A type of grit on sandpaper and discs, the resin completely covers the grit. This bonds the grit to the paper or disc more securely.

Cold Weather Solvent Designed to speed solvent evaporation, so the paint flows and dries in a reasonable amount of time.

Collapsible Steering Columns They crush under force to absorb impact, thus reducing injuries.

Collision Estimating Guide A manual or computer software program that gives information to help calculate the cost of repairs.

Collision Estimating Manuals Guides that give information for calculating the cost of repairs.

Collision Repair Auto body repair, restoring a damaged vehicle back to its original condition, structurally and cosmetically.

Collision Repair Technician A highly skilled professional who repairs damage from an accident.

Color Blindness A physical condition that makes it difficult for a person's eyes to see colors accurately.

Color Coded Plastic welding rods are identified by color.

Color Corrected Lights Used in the spray booth to make color show up properly.

Color Directory A publication containing color chips and other paint-related information for most makes and models of vehicles.

Color Matching Manuals Guides that contain information needed for finishing panels, so that the repair has the same appearance as the old finish.

Color Matching The steps needed to make the new finish match the existing finish on the vehicle.

Color Spectrum By passing light through a prism, light is broken down into its separate colors. White light contains all colors or the full spectrum.

Color Tree A guide used to locate colors three dimensionally when matching colors.

Colorcoat See topcoat.

Combination Wrench A wrench with an open end and a box end.

Combustibles Substances capable of igniting and burning such as paints, thinners, reducers, gasoline, dirty rags.

Compact Car The smallest body classification, also known as economy car. It normally uses a small 4-cylinder engine, is very lightweight, and gets the highest gas mileage.

Component A part, refers to the smallest units on a vehicle.

Composite Force The force of all pulls combined.

Composite Plastics Also called "hybrids," they are blends of different plastics and other ingredients designed to achieve specific performance characteristics.

Compressive Strength The property of a material to resist being crushed.

Compressor Drain Valve Located on the bottom of the compressor storage tank, it allows you to drain out water.

Compressor Oil Plugs Provided for filling and changing air pump oil on a compressor.

Compressor Pressure Valve It prevents too much pressure from entering the compressor tank.

Computer A complex electronic circuit that produces a known electrical output after analyzing electrical inputs.

Computer Estimating Preparing an estimate via computer. This streamlines the process by automating the written estimate.

Computer Self-Diagnostics The computer can detect its own problems.

Computer Written Estimate A damage report that is completed by using a personal computer and printer.

Computerized Measuring Systems A system that uses data from the measuring system for fast entry and checking of vehicle dimensions.

Computerized Paint Matching Systems Software that uses data from the spectrophotometer to help in how to match the paint color.

Conductor It carries current to the parts of a circuit.

Cone Concept As the force of impact penetrates the unibody vehicle, it folds and collapses, and the impact is absorbed by an ever-increasing area of the unibody. Visualize the point of impact as a cone.

Continuity A continuous conductor path.

Continuous Weld A single weld bead along a joint.

Control Arms A part of the suspension system, it mounts on the frame to swivel up and down.

Cooling System Leak Test A test performed by installing the tester on the radiator neck. A loss of pressure or coolant means there is a leak.

Cooperative Education Programs A curriculum offered by a school that allows you to have a job and get school credits at the same time.

Cosmetic Filler Typically a two-part epoxy or polyester filler used to cover up minor imperfections on reinforced plastics.

Cotter Pin A pin that helps prevent bolts and nuts from loosening or it fits through pin to hold parts together. They are also used as stops and holders on shafts and rods.

Cowl The body parts at the rear of the front section, right in front of the windshield.

Cream Hardeners Used to cure body fillers.

Crescent Wrench Also referred to as an adjustable wrench, it has movable jaws to fit different head sizes.

CRI Color Rendering Index, it is the index for measuring how close a lamp in indoor lighting is to actual daylight.

Curb Height Also called ride height, each of the front and rear wheels must carry the same amount of weight, thus allowing the vehicle to ride at a specific height.

Current Adjuster A circuit relay that is activated by a series coil in the charging circuit.

Current The movement of electricity (electrons) through a wire or circuit.

Custom Body Panels Aftermarket parts that alter the appearance of the vehicle.

Custom Masks Involves drawing a design on thin posterboard, then cutting it out, taping it onto the vehicle and spray painting it for a custom pattern in the paint.

Custom Painting Using multiple colors, metal flake paints, multi-layer masking, and special spraying techniques to produce a personalized look.

Custom-Mixed Colors Paint colors that are mixed to order at the paint supply distributor.

Cutting Torch A torch with three valves; two valves for adjusting gas flow and a third valve for oxygen. The heat of the flame, combined with the blast of oxygen, will rapidly cut thick steel.

CV-Axle Constant Velocity Axle, they transfer torque from the transaxle to the wheel hubs.

Cyanoacrylates One-part, fast curing adhesives used to help repair rigid and flexible plastics. Also referred to as CAs.

Cylinder Head Covers and seals the top of the cylinder.

Damage Analysis Involves locating all damage, using a systematic series of inspections, measurements, and tests.

Damage Appraisal See Estimating.

Data Wand A small hand-held electronic data-gathering tool, often with a keypad and read head for bar codes.

Database A computer file. An estimating database would include part numbers, part illustrations, labor times, labor rates, and other data for filling out the estimate.

Dead Blow Hammer A hammer that has a metal face filled with lead shot (balls) to prevent rebounding. It will NOT bound back up after striking.

Decimal A number value that divides the inch into parts. It is used when precision is important.

Decimal Conversion Chart It allows you to quickly change from fractions, to decimals, to millimeters.

Dedicated Bench A strong, flat work surface to which fixtures are attached.

Deformation Refers to the new, undesired bent shape the metal takes after an impact or collision.

Dent Puller A slide hammer with a threaded tip, a hood tip, or a suction cup.

Destructive Testing A test that forces the weld apart to measure weld strength. Force is applied until the metal or weld breaks.

Diagnosis Charts Charts that give logical steps for finding the source of problems.

Diagonal Cutting Pliers Pliers that have cutting jaws that will clip off wires flush with a surface; they are also known as side cut pliers.

Dial-Up Estimating System A system that relies on data stored in a mainframe computer at a remote location. The data is usually accessed via a telephone modem.

Die A tool used for cutting threads on the outside of bolts or studs.

Differential Assembly A unit within the drive axle assembly. It uses gears to allow different amounts of torque to be applied to each drive while the vehicle is making a turn.

Digital Images Pictures stored as computer data.

Digital Multimeter (DVOM) A multimeter that gives a digital readout for the test value.

Dinging Hammer A hammer used for final shaping.

Disarmed All sources of electricity for air bag igniter are disconnected.

Disc Adhesive A product used to apply nonstick sandpaper to the backing pad of a sander.

Disc Adhesive A special non-hardening glue that comes in a tube. It can be placed on the pad to adhere the paper to the sander.

Disc-Type Grinder The most commonly used portable air grinder. It is operated like the single-action disc sander.

Discharging The removal of refrigerant from the air conditioning system.

Dollies Also referred to as dolly blocks. Used like a small, portable anvil; generally used on the backside of a panel being struck with a hammer.

Door Alignment Tool A tool used to slightly bend and adjust sprung doors and hatches.

Door Frame The main steel frame of the door.

Door Glass Channel It serves as a guide for the glass to move up and down. It is a U-shaped channel lined with a low friction material.

Door Glass It must allow good visibility out of the door.

Door Intrusion Beam A part that is welded or bolted to the metal support brackets on the door frame to increase door strength.

Door Latch It engages the door striker on the vehicle body to hold the door closed.

Door Lock Assemblies It usually consists of the outside door handle, linkage rods, the door lock mechanism, and the door latch.

Door Regulator A gear and arm mechanism for moving the glass.

Door Skin The outer panel over the door frame. It can be made of steel, aluminum, fiberglass, or plastic.

Door Striker Wrench A special socket designed to fit over or inside door striker posts. It will allow you to turn and loosen the post for adjustment or placement.

Door Striker It holds the door closed.

Door Trim Panel An attractive cover over the inner door frame.

Double Masking Using two layers of masking paper to prevent bleed-through or finish-dulling from solvents.

Dowel Pin Small rod or pin that helps hold or align parts.

Downdraft Spray Booth Forces air from the ceiling down through exhaust vents in the floor.

Download A computer term meaning to enter data.

Draw-Down Bar A machine bar that evenly distributes 1 mil of unreduced paint to a card or sheet of plastic. It is used to check how much hiding the paint will provide.

Drills Used to make accurately sized holes in metal and plastic parts. Both air and electric drills are available.

Drive Shaft A long tube that transfers power from the transmission to rear axle assembly.

Dry Metallic Paint Spray The aluminum flakes are trapped at various angles near the surface of the paint film making the paint appear lighter and more silver.

Dry Sanding A term describing sanding done with coarser non-waterproof sandpaper, without using water.

Dry Sandpaper Designed to be used without water.

Dual Action Sander A sander that moves in two directions at the same time. It produces a much smoother surface finish.

Duct Tape A thick tape with a plastic body. It is sometimes used to protect parts from damage when grinding, sanding, or blasting.

Dulled Finish This occurs where the spray pattern overlaps an already sprayed but dry area when painting.

Dust Coat A light, dry coating that is similar to a mist coat.

Dust Respirator A filter that fits over your nose and mouth to block small airborne particles while sanding or grinding.

Dustless Sanding System A system designed to draw airborne dust into a storage container, much like a vacuum cleaner, by using a blower or air pump.

Duty Cycle The number of times the welder can safely operate at a given amperage level continuously over 10 minutes.

Earmuffs Provides protection to your eardrums from damaging noise levels in the metalworking areas.

Earplugs Provides protection to your eardrums from damaging noise levels in the metalworking areas.

Edge Masking Taping over panel edges and body lines prior to machine buffing or polishing to protect the paint from burn-through.

EGR Exhaust Gas Recirculation. It is a valve that opens to allow engine vacuum to siphon exhaust into the intake manifold.

Elastic Deformation The ability of metal to stretch and return to its original shape.

Electric Adhesive Cutter A device that plugs into 120 volts to produce a vibrating action to assist in cutting the adhesive around glass.

Electrical Fires Results when excess current causes wiring to overheat, melt and burn.

Electrical Repairs Repairing electrical components such as wiring, sensors.

Electrical Symbols Graphic representations of electrical-electronic components.

Electrical Systems Anything powered by the battery, i.e. ignition, lights, radio, heat, air conditioning.

Electrode Tips A resistance spot welding part that allows current flow through spot weld.

Electromagnet A set of windings.

Electronic Camera A camera used to take photos of the vehicle's damage and store them as digital data.

Electronic Leak Detector A device that uses a signal generator tool and signal detector to find body leaks.

Electrostatic Spray Gun Electrically charges the paint particles at the gun to attract them to the vehicle body.

Emblem Adhesive Designed to hold hard plastic and metal parts. It is also referred to as plastic adhesive.

Emergency Telephone Numbers A list of telephone numbers clearly posted next to the shop's telephone including a doctor, hospital, fire and police.

Encapsulated Glass See modular glass.

Energy Reserve Module It allows the air bag to deploy in the event of a power failure.

Engine A machine that provides energy to move the vehicle and power all accessories.

Engine Crane A device that can be formed on most racks or benches to raise and remove an engine.

Engine Holder A device used to support the engine-transmission assembly when the cradle must be unbolted or removed.

English Measuring System Fractions and decimals are used for giving number values.

English-Metric Conversion Chart It allows you to convert from English to metric or from metric to English values.

EPA (Environmental Protection Agency) A government agency responsible for environmental protection.

Epoxy Primer A two-part primer that cures fast and hard.

Estimate Also called a damage report or appraisal, it calculates the cost of parts, materials and labor for repairing a collision-damaged vehicle.

Estimating Program Software that will automatically help find parts needed, labor rates, and calculate total for the repairs.

Exhaust System It collects and discharges exhaust gases caused by the combustion of the air/fuel mixture within the engine.

Explosions Air pressure waves that result from extremely rapid burning.

Extensions A part that fits between the socket and its drive handle. They allow you to reach in and install the socket when surrounded by obstructions.

Factory Packaged Colors Ready mixed paints.

Factory Seams The end or edge of panels.

Fastened Parts Parts held together with various fasteners (bolts, nuts, clips, etc.); fenders, hood, and grill.

Fault Code A code representing a specific circuit or part with a problem.

Fender Cover Material placed over the vehicle body to protect the paint from chips and scratches while working.

Fender Washer A washer with a very large outside diameter for the size hole. They provide better holding power on thin metal and plastic parts.

Fiber-Reinforced Plastics (FPR) Plastic panels reinforced with fiber.

Fiberglass Body Filler A plastic filler with fiberglass material added. It is used for rust repair or where strength is important.

Fiberglass Cloth Made by weaving the fiberglass strands into a stitched pattern.

Fiberglass Mat A series of long fiberglass strands irregularly distributed to form a patch. It is used to strengthen and form a shape for the resin liquid.

Fiberglass Resin Another form of plastic body repair material. It is a thick resin liquid.

File A category of hand tools used to remove burrs, sharp edges, and to do other smoothing tasks.

Filler Filing Using a coarse "cheese grater" or body file to rough shape the semi-hard filler. You will knock off the high spots and rough edges.

Filler Material Material from a wire or rod that is added to the weld joint.

Filler Mixing Board A clean, nonporous surface for mixing filler and hardener.

Filler Oversanding A condition that results when the filled in area is below the desired level, which makes it necessary to apply more filler.

Filler Undersanding A condition that results when the filled area is higher or thicker than the surrounding panel.

Filler-Over-Catalyzation A condition caused by using too much hardener for the amount of filler.

Filler-Under-Catalyzation A condition caused by not using enough hardener in the filler.

Fillet Weld A weld joining two surfaces with their edges or faces at about right angles to each other. It may be a lap joint or T-joint.

Final Detailing Term used to describe the location and correction of any defection that may cause customer complaints. The steps are sanding and filing; compounding; machine glazing; and hand glazing.

Fine Line Masking Tape A very thin, smooth surface plastic masking tape. Also termed flush masking tape.

Finishing Area An area where the body is painted. Also known as the Paint Booth Area.

Finishing Hammer A hammer used to achieve the final sheet metal contour.

Fire Extinguisher An instrument designed to quickly smother a fire. There are several types available for putting out different kinds of fires.

Fire Rapid oxidation of flammable material producing high temperatures.

Firewall The panel dividing the front section and center, passenger compartment section. Sometimes termed dash panel or front bulkhead.

First Aid Kit This includes many medical items such as sterile gauze, bandages, scissors, bandaids, and antiseptics that are needed to treat minor shop injuries.

Fisheye Eliminator A paint additive that helps smooth the paint when small craters or holes in the paint film are a problem.

Fit Test A test performed prior to using a respirator. It checks for respirator air leaks, making both negative and positive pressure checks.

Flat Rate A preset amount of time and money charged for a specific repair operation.

Flat Washer A washer used to increase the clamping surface area. They prevent the smaller bolt head from pulling through the sheet metal or plastic.

Flat Welding The pieces are parallel with the bench or shop floor.

Flattener An agent added to paint to lower gloss or shine.

Flex Agent An additive that allows primers and paints to flex or bend without cracking.

Flop Also termed flip-flop, it refers to a change in color hue when viewing from head-on and then from the side.

Floppy Discs Removable magnetic discs of data used with a computer.

Flow Meter A device that measures the movement of air, gas, or a liquid past a given point.

Fluid Control Knob A part of the spray gun; it changes the distance the fluid needle moves away from its seat in the nozzle when the trigger is pulled. This controls paint flow.

Fluid Control Valve On a spray gun, it can be turned to adjust the amount of paint or other material emitted.

Fluid Needle A part of the spray gun; it open or shuts off the flow of paint.

Fluid Needle Valve It seats in the fluid tip on a spray gun to prevent flow or can be pulled back to allow flow.

Fluid Nozzle A part of the spray gun; it forms an internal seat for the fluid needle.

Fluorescent Light Artificial light that has more violets and reds than daylight.

Fluorine Clearcoat Used to improve resistance to UV radiation; protect from weathering, chalking, oxidation, and industrial fallout; improve luster of the finish; and reduce required maintenance, such as waxing and polishing.

Foam Fillers Foam that is placed inside of panels to add rigidity and strength to structural parts. They also reduce noise and vibration.

Forced Drying Curing fresh paint by using special heat lamps or other equipment to speed the process.

Four-Wheel Drive A system that uses a transfer case to send power to two differentials and all wheels. The transfer can be engaged and disengaged to select two- or four-wheel drive.

Fraction A number value that divides the inch into parts, It is used when precision is not critical.

Frame Horn The very front of the frame rails where the bumper attaches.

Frame Rack Accessories The many chains, special tools, and other parts needed to perform the many different frame straightening operations.

Frame Rails The long steel members that extend along the sides of the vehicle.

Framed Doors A type of door design, it surrounds the sides and top of the door glass with a metal frame, helping keep the window glass aligned.

Front End Rack Used to measure and adjust the steering and suspension of a vehicle after repairs. Also known as Alignment Rack.

Front Fender Aprons The inner panels that surround the wheels and tires to keep out road debris.

Front Fenders Part that extends from the front doors to the front bumper. They cover the front suspension and inner aprons.

Front Section Also called nose section, it includes everything between the front bumper and the firewall.

Fuel Evaporative System It pulls fumes from the gas tank and other fuel system parts into a charcoal canister.

Full Body Sectioning Replacing the entire rear section of a collision-damaged vehicle with the rear section of a salvage vehicle.

Full Cutout Method A method of windshield replacement used when the original adhesive is defective or requires complete removal.

Full Wet Coat A heavy, glossy coat applied over the tack coat. It makes the paint lay down smooth and shiny.

Full-Face Shield Full face protection used when there is danger from flying particles, as when grinding.

Full-Size Car The largest body classification. It is large, heavy, and often uses a high performance V-8 engine.

Funnel Instruments used when pouring fluid from a container into a small opening.

Fuse A circuit protection device.

Fuse Box This holds the various circuit fuses, breakers, and flasher units.

Fuse Link Smaller diameter wire spliced into the larger circuit wiring for over-current protection.

Fuse Rating The current at which the fuse will blow.

Fusion Welding Joining different pieces of metal together by melting and fusing them into each other.

Gas Flow Rate A measurement of how fast gas flows over the weld puddle in MIG welding.

Gasoline A highly flammable petroleum or crude oil-based liquid that vaporizes and burns rapidly.

Gauge Measuring Systems A method that uses sliding metal rods or bars, and adjustable pointers with rules scaled to measure body dimensions.

Get Ready A thorough clean-up before returning the vehicle to the customer.

Glazing Putty A material made for filling small holes or sand scratches.

Goggles Eye protection suitable when handling chemicals.

Graduated Pail Used to measure liquid materials when mixing.

Grain Structure In a piece of steel, it determines how much it can be bent or shaped.

Gravity Feed Spray Guns The cup is mounted on top of the spray gun head so the material flows down without external air pressure.

Grease Gun A device used to lubricate high friction points on a vehicle's steering and suspension systems.

Grinders Used for fast removal of material. They are often used to smooth metal joints after welding and to remove paint and primer.

Grinding Discs Round, very coarse abrasives used for initial removal of paint, plastic, and metal (weld joints).

Grit Number System Denotes how coarse or fine the abrasive is.

Grit Sizes A term that refers to the coarseness of sandpaper.

Ground Electrical path back to the battery negative cable through wires, cables or body structure.

Gun Angle Consists of two different angles; the angle of the gun to the work place, and the angle of direction of travel.

Gun Arching Uneven film thickness, paint runs, excessive overspray, dry spray and orange peel caused by not moving the spray gun parallel with the surface.

Gun Body The part of the spray gun that holds the parts that meter air and liquid. It also holds the spray pattern adjustment valve, fluid control valve, air cap, fluid tip, trigger, and related parts.

Gun Heeling Uneven film thickness, excessive overspray, dry spray and orange peel caused by allowing the spray gun to tilt.

Hacksaw A tool sometimes used to cut metal parts.

Halo Effect An unwanted shiny ring or halo that appears around a pearl or mica paint repair. It is caused by the paint being wetter in the middle and drier near the outer edges of the repair.

Hammer-Off-Dolly A method used to straighten metal just before the final stage of straightening.

Hammer-On-Dolly A method used to stretch metal and to smooth small, shallow dents and bulges.

Hand Blaster A small, portable tool for blasting parts and panels on the vehicle.

Hand Cleaner Used to wash hands.

Hand Compound Compound designed to be applied by hand on a rag or cloth.

Hand Compounds An oil based rubbing compound that provides lubrication; best on small or blended areas.

Hand Glazes Used for final smoothing and shining of the paint.

Hand Tools General tools such as wrenches, screwdrivers, pliers and other common tools.

Handscraper A hand tool that will easily remove gaskets and softened paint (paint stripping chemical used). They are used on flat surfaces.

Hard Brazing Brazing with materials that melt at temperatures above 900_F (486_C).

Hardtop A body design that does not have a center pillar to support the roof, but must be reinforced to provide extra strength. It is available in 2- and 4-door versions.

Hardtop Doors A type of door design, the glass extends up out of the door without a frame around it. The glass itself must seal against the weatherstripping in the door opening.

Hatchback A body design that has a large third door at the back. This design is commonly found on small compact cars, allowing for more rear storage space.

Head-On View Compares the test panel to the vehicle straight on, or perpendicular.

Headlight Aimers Equipment used to adjust the direction of the vehicle headlights.

Headlight Aiming Screw A screw with a special plastic adapter mounted on it. The adapter fits into the headlight assembly.

Headrest Guide The sleeve that accepts the headrest post and mounts in seat back.

Headrest The padded frame that fits into the top of the seat back.

Heat Crayons Used to determine the temperature of the aluminum or other metal being heated. They will melt at a specific temperature and warn you to prevent overheating.

Heat Setting Determines the length of the arc when MIG welding. Also called voltage.

Heat Sink Compound A paste that can be applied to parts during welding to absorb heat and prevent warpage.

Helicoil® Also referred to as a thread insert, it can be used to repair badly damaged internal threads.

Helper An apprentice type worker that learns by helping experienced technicians.

High Efficiency Spray Gun Designed to reduce VOC emissions by only using 10 psi air pressure at the gun head. Also called HVLP for high volume, low pressure or LVLP for low volume, low pressure.

High Spot Also called a bump, it is an area that sticks up higher than the surrounding surface.

High-Solids Paint The non-liquid contents of paint needed to reduce air pollution or emissions when painting.

High-Strength Steel (HSS) Sheet metal that is stronger than low-carbon or mild steel because of heat treatment.

Hinged Parts Parts that swing up and open such as doors, hoods, and decklids.

Hog Rings A device that stretches and holds the seat cover over the seat frame and padding.

Hood The hinged panel for accessing the engine compartment (front-engine vehicle) or trunk area (rear-engine vehicle).

Hood Adjustments Adjustments made at the hinges, at the adjustable stops, and at the hood latch.

Hood Hinge Spring Tool A hooked tool that should be used to stretch the spring off and on.

Hood Hinge Spacers A part that helps adjust the hood.

Hood Hinges A part that allows the hood to open and close while staying in alignment.

Hood Latch Mechanism This keeps the hood closed and releases the hood when activated.

Hood Latch Adjustment This controls how well the hood striker engages the latch mechanism.

Hood Latch Part of the cable hood release, it has metal arms that grasp and hold the hood striker.

Hood Release Cable Part of the cable hood release, it is a steel cable that slides inside a plastic housing. One end fastens to the release handle and the other to the hood latch.

Hood Release Handle Part of the cable hood release, it can be pulled to slide a cable running out to the hood latch.

Hood Stop Adjustment A device that controls the height of the front of the hood.

Hood Striker Part of the cable hood release, it bolts to the hood and engages the hood latch when closed.

Horizontal Welding The pieces are turned side-ways. Gravity tends to pull the puddle into the bottom piece.

Hose Clamp A clamp used to hold radiator hoses, heater hoses and other hoses onto their fittings.

Hot Air Plastic Welding Uses a tool with an electric heating element to produce hot air which blows through a nozzle and onto the plastic.

Hot Weather Solvent A reducer or thinner. It is designed to slow solvent evaporation to prevent problems.

HVLP See High Efficiency Spray Gun

Hydraulic (oil-filled) Equipment operated by oil under pressure.

Hydraulic Jacks A device used to raise the vehicle.

I-CAR See Inter-Industry Conference on Auto Collision Repair.

Idler Arm It supports the center link on one end in parallelogram steering.

Ignition System This produces an electric arc in a gasoline engine to cause the fuel to burn. It must fire the spark plugs at the right time. The resulting combustion pressure forces the pistons down to spin the crankshaft.

Impact Driver A screwdriver that is hit with a hammer to rotate tight or stuck screws. The body of the driver can be rotated to change directions for installing or removing.

Impact Sensors The first sensors to detect a collision because they are mounted at the front of the vehicle.

Improper Coverage A term that means the paint film thickness is not uniform or too thin. It is caused by not triggering exactly over the edge of the panel or from improper spray overlap.

Improper Spray Overlap A term that means you are not covering half of the previous pass with the next pass.

In-Line Oiler An attachment that will automatically meter oil into air lines for air tools.

In-Shop Estimating System A system that has all of the data needed at the shop office, usually on CD-ROMs.

Incandescent Light Artificial light that has more yellow, oranges and reds than daylight.

Included Angle The sum of the SAI angle and the camber angle.

Included Operations A repair that can be performed individually, but is also part of another repair.

Incorrect Gun Stroke Speed A term that means you are moving the gun too slowly or quickly.

Indirect Damage Damage caused by the shock of collision forces traveling through the body and inertial forces acting upon the rest of the unibody.

Inductive Pickup A device that slips over the wire or cable to measure current.

Inert Gas A type of shielding gas which protects the weld, but does not combine with the weld.

Inertia Switch Designed to shut the electric fuel pump off after a collision.

Infrared Drying Equipment Uses special bulbs to generate infrared light for fast drying of paint materials.

Inner Wheelhousings Surround the rear wheels.

Inserts Metal backing sometimes installed in weld repairs of closed sections, such as rocker panels, R- and B-pillars and rails.

Inside Calipers A tool designed for measuring inside parts. They are accurate to about 1/64 in.

Instrument Panel The assembly that includes the soft dash pad, instrument cluster, radio, heater and AC controls, vents and similar parts. Also known as dash assembly.

Insulation It stops current flow and keeps the current in the metal wire conductor.

Integral Unit is built as one-piece instead of two or more.

Inter-Industry Conference on Auto Collision Repair An advanced training organization dedicated to promoting high quality practices in the collision repair industry.

Intermediate Car The medium body classification. It can use 4, 6, or 8 cylinder engine, has average weight, and physical dimensions.

Intermix System A full set of paint pigments and solvents that can be mixed at the body shop.

ISO Codes "International Symbols" is a way of identifying an unknown plastic. The code is molded into the plastic part.

Jam Nut A thin nut used to help hold larger, conventional nuts in place.

Joint Fit-Up Refers to holding work pieces tightly together, in alignment, to prepare for welding. It is critical to the replacement of body parts.

Jounce/Rebound Steering Gear Check A test that involves pushing down on the front or rear of the vehicle to load the suspension, and then allowing the vehicle to bounce back up. It is used to identify damage to the steering gear, column, or tie rods.

Jumper Cables Cables used to connect two batteries together when one is discharged.

Jumper Wires A device used to temporarily bypass circuits or components for testing.

Jumpsuit The proper clothing to wear in the paint spraying area.

Key A device used by equipment manufacturers to retain parts in alignment.

Key Used to tighten the chuck on the drill.

Kick Panels The small panels between the front pillars and rocker panels.

Kinked A term that describes a part that has a sharp bend or a small radius, usually more than 90 degrees, or after straightening, there is a visible crack or tear in the metal, or there is permanent deformation that cannot be straightened to its pre-accident shape without the use of excessive heat.

Kneading Hardener Squeezing the tube of hardener back and forth with your fingers to mix the material.

Lace Painting Involves spraying through lace fabric to produce a custom pattern in the paint.

Ladder Frame A frame that has long frame rails with a series of straight crossmembers formed in several locations.

Laminated Plate Glass Two thin sheets of glass with a layer of clear plastic between them. It is used for windshields.

Lap Belts Seat belts that extend across a person's lap.

Lap Joint A weld made on overlapping surfaces.

Leak Detector A tool for finding refrigerant leaks in lines, hoses and other parts of an air conditioning system.

Leather Shoes To prevent falls and foot injuries, thick leather shoes with nonslip soles should be worn.

Left-Hand Threads Nuts and bolts that must be turned counterclockwise to tighten.

Let-Down Panel A test panel painted with a tri-coat finish to help you find the correct amount of coats needed to achieve a color match with vehicle being painted.

Lid Shock Absorbers Usually a spring-loaded, gas-filled unit that holds the lid open and causes it to close more slowly.

Lid Torsion Rods Spring steel rods used to help lift the weight of the lid.

Lifetime Tool Guarantee A tool that will be replaced or repaired if it ever fails or breaks.

Lift Safety Catch A device on a hydraulic jack. When engaged it ensures that the lift cannot lower while working underneath the vehicle.

Light Body Filler A filler formulated for easy sanding and fast repairs. It is used as a very thin top coat of filler for final leveling.

Light Temperature A rating of lighting in "Kelvin." For painting, a lamp rating or temperature of 6000-7000 Kelvin is recommended.

Line Wrench Also referred to as tubing or flare nut, it has a small split in its jaw to fit over lines and tubing.

Linear Measurements Straight line measurements of distance. Commonly used when evaluating major structural damage after a collision.

Lint-Free Coveralls The proper clothing to wear in the paint spraying area.

Liquid Masking Material A masking system that seals off the entire vehicle to protect undamaged panels and parts from paint overspray.

Lock Cylinders A tumbler mechanism that engages the key so that you can turn the key and disengage the latch.

Locksmith Tool Also termed "slim jim," it is used to open locked doors on cars and trucks.

Long Spray Distance A spray gun distance that causes a greater percentage of the thinner to evaporate, resulting in orange peel or dry spray.

Long-Hair Fiberglass Filler A fiberglass filler with long strands of fiberglass for even more strength.

Low Impedance Refers to low resistance in meters used to test modern electronic circuits.

Low Spot Also called a dent, it is an area that is recessed below the surrounding surface.

Lumen Rating The measurement of a lamp's brightness.

LVLP See High Efficiency Spray Gun

Machine Compound A compound formulated to be applied with an electric or air polisher.

Machine Compounds A rubbing compound that is water based to disperse the abrasive while using a power buffer.

Machine Grinding A process used to remove old finish from small flat areas and gently curved areas.

Machine Screw A screw that is threaded its full length and is relatively weak.

MAG Metal Active Gas, describes the welding process when the primary gas of the shielding gas is active.

Magnetic Field Also known as flux, it is an invisible energy present around permanent magnets and current carrying wires.

Magnetic Guide Strip Used to help guide the pin striping tool for making straight or slightly curved pin stripes.

Major Repairs Refers to the replacement of large body sections and frame straightening.

Manometer An instrument that indicates when the intake filters in a spray booth are overloaded.

Manual Estimating Preparing a written estimate using crash estimating books and collision damage manuals.

Manual Transmission A transmission that must be hand shifted through each forward gear.

Manually Written Estimate A damage report that is completed in long hand by filling in information on a printed form.

Manufacturer's Instructions Very detailed procedures for the specific product.

Manufacturer's Specifications Measurements given by a manufacturer for proper repair of their vehicles.

Manufacturer's Warnings Procedures given by the manufacturer for the safe use of their product.

Marble Effect A custom paint job made by forcing crumpled plastic against a freshly painted stripe or area.

Masking Coating Also called masking liquid, it is usually a water-based sprayable material for keeping overspray off body parts.

Masking Cover A specially shaped cloth or plastic cover for masking specific parts.

Masking Machine A machine designed to feed out masking paper while applying masking tape to one edge of the paper.

Masking Paper A special paper designed to be used to cover body parts not to be painted.

Masking Paper Dispenser A device that automatically applies tape to one edge of the masking paper as the paper is pulled out.

Masking Plastic Used just like masking paper to cover and protect parts from overspray.

Masking Tape An adhesive used to hold masking paper or plastic into position. It is a high tack, easy-to-tear tape.

Master Cylinder It develops hydraulic pressure for the brake system.

Measurement Gauges Special tools used to check specific frame and body points. They allow you to quickly measure the direction and extent of vehicle damage.

Measurements Number values that help control processes in collision repair.

Measuring System A special machine used to gauge and check the amount of frame and body damage. It compares known good measurements with those on the vehicle being repaired.

Mechanical Repairs Repairing mechanical components such as water pump, radiator, etc.

Mechanical Systems Chassis parts of an automobile such as steering, braking, and suspension systems.

Melt-Flow Plastic Welding The most commonly used airless welding method. It can be utilized for both single-sided and two-sided repairs.

Metallic Paint Paint with large reflective pigment flakes added.

Metalworking Area An area where parts are removed, repaired and installed.

Micrometer A device that is used to measure mechanical parts when high precision is important.

MIG Contact Tip Also call tube, it transfers current to the welding wire as the wire travels through.

MIG Nozzle It protects the contact tip and directs the shielding gas flow.

MIG Welding Gun Also called a torch, it delivers wire, current, and shielding gas to the weld site.

MIG-MAG The welding process, when nearly equal active and inert combinations of shielding gases are used.

Mil Gauge Used to measure the thickness of the paint on the vehicle.

Mild Steel Also called low-carbon steel, it is a sheet metal that has a low level of carbon and is relatively soft and easy to work.

Mini Van A smaller version of the box shaped van.

Minor Repairs Repairs requiring minimum time and effort, i.e. small dents, scratches.

Mixing Board The surface used for mixing the filler and its hardener.

Mixing By Parts For a specific volume of paint or other material, a specific amount of another material must be added.

Mixing Chart A guide that converts a percentage into how many parts of each material must be mixed.

Modular Glass Also known as encapsulated glass, it has a plastic trim molding attached to its edge to fit the contours of the vehicle more closely.

Molded Core A curved body repair part made by applying plastic repair material over a part and then removing the cured material.

Molding Tool A tool used to separate adhesive held molding or trim.

Motors A machine that uses permanent and electromagnets to convert electrical energy into a rotation motion for doing work.

MRD A mid-engine, rear-wheel drive vehicle. The engine is located right behind the front seat or centrally located.

Multi-Stage Finishes A type of glamour finish.

Multiple Part Rocker An assembly of several pieces of sheet metal with internal reinforcements.

Multiple Pull Method A method used on major damage, it involves several pulling directions, and steps are needed.

National Institute for Automotive Service Excellence (ASE) Offers a voluntary certification program that is recommended by the major vehicle manufacturers in the United States.

Needle Nose Pliers Pliers that have long, thin jaws for reaching in and grasping small parts.

Negative Pressure Test Part of the Fit Test. Performed by placing the palms of both hands over the cartridges and inhaling. A good fit is evident if the face piece collapses onto your face.

Neutral Flame Also referred to as a standard flame, it is produced by mixing acetylene and oxygen in a 1 to 1 ratio.

New Part Primer Coat Replacement panels that are primed by the manufacturer or part supplier to protect the metal against corrosion.

Non-Bleeder Spray Gun It releases air only when the trigger is pulled back. They have an air control valve. The trigger controls both fluid needle movements and the air control valve.

Nut A fastener that uses internal (inside) threads and an odd shaped head that often fits a wrench. When tightened onto a bolt, a strong clamping force holds the parts together.

OEM Finish Factory paint jobs.

Office Manager The person who oversees various aspects of the business, i.e., letters, estimates.

Offset Butt Joint A basic joint without an insert. It is also known as a staggered butt joint.

Oil Dipstick A device used to check the oil level.

Oil Drain Plug It is located in the oil pan for draining and changing the engine oil.

Oil Filter It traps debris and prevents it from circulating through the engine oil galleries.

Oil Pan It holds an extra supply of motor oil. Also known as the sump, it bolts to the bottom of the engine block.

½ Inch Impact An impact wrench with a ½-inch size drive head. It is shaped like a pistol with a hand grip hanging down. It is frequently used to service wheel lug nuts.

One-Part Putty Spot putty applied directly out of tube or container. It takes longer to harden than two-part and can shrink more easily.

Open Coat A type of grit on sandpaper and discs, the resin that bonds the grit to the paper only touches the bottom of the grit.

Open End Wrench A wrench with three-sided jaws on both ends.

Opened A term that refers to a disconnected electrical circuit.

Orifice A hole in the bottom of the viscosity cup.

Outside Calipers A tool that will make rough external measurements.

Overall Refinishing Painting the whole vehicle.

Overhead Welding The piece is turned upside down.

Overlap Strokes The process of making each spray gun coat cover about half of the previous coat of paint.

Overlay Dry Method A method of installing stripes or decals that does not involve the use of soapy water. All surfaces are clean and dry.

Overlay Wet Method A method of installing stripes or decals that involves using soapy water to help simplify the application of larger decals and striping.

Overmasked A term that means the painter must touch up the part of the vehicle that should have been painted.

Overpulling Damage Results from failing to measure accurately and often when pulling on unibody vehicles.

Overspray Leak The term that describes the results of not sealing the masking paper or plastic and getting overspray on unwanted surfaces.

Oxidizing Flame It is obtained by mixing slightly more oxygen than acetylene.

Oxygen Pressure Pressure leaving oxygen pressure regulator of oxyacetylene welding outfit. Typically ranges from 5 to 100 psi (kPa).

Pad Cleaning Tool A metal star wheel and handle that will clean dried polishing compound out of the pad.

Paint A term that generally refers to the visible topcoat.

Paint Adhesion Check A test to see if the old paint is adhering properly.

Paint Binder The ingredient in a paint that holds the pigment particles together.

Paint Blending Tapering the new paint gradually into the old paint.

Paint Booth Area An area where the body is painted. Also known as the Finishing Area.

Paint Drying Room A dust-free room that speeds up drying, produces a cleaner job, and increases the volume of refinishing work.

Paint Film Breakdown A term for checking, cracking, or blistering of paint.

Paint Formula The percentage of each ingredient that is needed to match an OEM color.

Paint Mixing Stick Used to help mix paints, solvents, catalysts, and other additives right before spraying.

Paint Mixing Instructions Directions on how to mix the paint; usually given on the paint can label.

Paint Mixing Blending the paint and thinner or reducer to the correct thickness or viscosity.

Paint Mixing Room A safe, clean, well-lit area for a painter to store, mix, and reduce paint materials.

Paint Overlap The area where one vertical painted area overlaps the new area being painted.

Paint Prep Area An area where the vehicle is readied for painting or refinishing.

Paint Preparation Preparing the vehicle for spraying or refinishing.

Paint Reference Charts Found in service manuals, they give comparable paints manufactured by different companies.

Paint Runs Excess paint thickness flows down when spraying.

Paint Scuffing A term used to describe roughing the paint for better paint adhesion.

Paint Sealer An innercoat between the topcoat and the primer or old finish to prevent bleeding.

Paint Selection Determining the right paint for the job, so that the new paint matches the old and to assure long life.

Paint Settling A term that describes when the paint sits idle and pigments, metallic flakes, or mica particles settle to the bottom.

Paint Solvent The liquid solution that carries the pigment and binder so it can be sprayed.

Paint Stirring Stick Wooden sticks for mixing the contents after being poured into the spray gun cup or container.

Paint Stripper A powerful chemical that dissolves paint for fast removal of an old finish.

Paint Surface Chips A result of mechanical impact damage to the paint film: door dings, damage from road debris, etc.

Paint Surface Protrusion A particle of paint or other debris sticking out of the paint film after refinishing.

Paint System All materials (primers, catalysts, paints) are compatible and manufactured by the same company.

Paint Thickness Measurement of distance between surface of paint and body of vehicle. Viscosity of paint; affected by reduction or thinning.

Paint Viscosity A term that refers to the paint's thickness or ability to resist flow.

Painted Flames A custom painting technique often used on "hot rods" or older street rods.

Painter Prep Area A shop area that provides a clean area for a painter to dress, a clean storage for painting suits, and a place to clean and store personal safety equipment.

Painter's Stretch Hood Protective head gear for the paint booth.

Painting Environment The suitable conditions for painting, i.e., cleanliness, temperature/humidity, light, and compressed air/pressure.

Paintless Dent Removal A method of using picks to remove small dents without having to repaint the panel.

Pan A floor related component, i.e. front floor pan.

Panel Alignment Marks Marks that can be provided on new parts to help position them for welding.

Panel Cutters A tool that will precisely cut sheet metal, leaving a clean, straight edge that can be easily welded.

Panel Replacement Removing and installing a new panel or body part.

Panel Straightening Bending or shaping the panel back to its original position, using hand tools and equipment.

Part Gap Also known as clearance, it is the distance measured between two adjacent parts, hood-to-fender gap for example.

Partial Cutout Method Refers to using some of the original adhesive during windshield replacement.

Partial Frame A frame that is a cross between a solid frame and a unibody.

Particle Respirator See Dust Respirator.

Parts Manager A person in charge of ordering, receiving and distributing parts.

Passive Restraint System A restraint system that operates automatically, i.e., automatic seat belts and air bags.

Pattern Control Knob A part of the spray gun; when closed, the spray pattern is round. As the knob is opened, the spray becomes more oblong in shape.

PC See Personal Computer.

PCV Positive Crankcase Ventilation System. It channels engine crankcase blowby gases into the engine intake manifold.

Pearl Paint Paint with medium size reflective pigment particles, such as mica, that give it luster or shine that tends to change color with the viewing angle.

Percentage Reduction Materials must be added in certain proportions or parts.

Perimeter Frame A frame that has the frame rail near the outside or perimeter of the vehicle.

Personal Computer Also referred to as a PC, it is used to keep track of business transactions, complete damage reports, and performs electrical tests on vehicles.

Phillips Screwdriver A hand tool that has two crossing blades for a star-shaped screw head.

Physical Injury A general category that includes cuts, broken bones, strained backs and similar injuries.

Piano Wire Fine steel wire that can be used to cut the adhesive around glass.

Pick A tool used to reach into confined spaces for removing tiny dents or dings.

Picking Hammer A hammer with a pointed end used to raise small dents from the inside, and a flat end for hammer-and-dolly work to remove high spots and ripples.

Pin A device used by equipment manufacturers to retain parts in alignment.

Pin Punch It has a straight shank for use after a starting punch. It will push a shaft completely out of a hole.

Pin Striping Brushes Brushes with very long soft horse hairs that are used to apply paint in a small, controlled area.

Pin Striping Tool A serrated roller to deposit a painted pin stripe.

Pinchweld Clamps Attached to the body at the front and rear of the rocker panel pinchwelds; four are normally used.

Pipe Wrench A type of adjustable wrench for holding and turning round objects. It has sharp jaw teeth that dig into and grasp the part.

Pitch Spacing between resistance spot welds.

Pitman Arm It supports the center link on one end in parallelogram steering.

Plastic Flame Treating A torch flame is used to oxidize and chemically prepare the plastic for adhesion.

Plastic Gloves Used to protect hands from the harmful effects of corrosive liquids, undercoats, and finishes.

Plastic Hammer A hammer used for making light blows where parts can be easily damaged.

Plastic Memory A term that refers to plastic that wants to keep or return to its original molded shape.

Plastic Speed Welding A type of welding that uses a specially designed tip to produce a more uniform weld and at a high rate of speed.

Plastic Stitch-Tamp Welding A type of welding used primarily on hard plastics, like ABS and nylon, to insure a good base/rod mix.

Plastic Welder A tool used to heat and melt plastic for repairing or joining plastic parts.

Plastic Welding Uses heat and sometimes a plastic filler rod to join or repair plastic parts.

Plastics Refers to a wide range of materials synthetically compounded from crude oil, coal, natural gas, and other natural substances.

Pliers A hand tool used for working with wires, clips and pins. They will grasp and hold parts, like your fingers.

Plotting Color The process of identifying paint color in a graphic way based on value, hue, and chroma.

Pneumatic Windshield Cutter A device that uses shop air pressure and a vibrating action to help cut the adhesive around glass.

Pocket Scale A pocket size ruler.

Point-To-Point Measurement A term that refers to the shortest distance between two points.

Polishing Using very fine compound to bring the paint surface up to full gloss.

Polishing Compound Also called machine glaze, it is a fine grit compound designed for machine applications.

Polishing Pad A cotton or synthetic cloth cover that fits over the polisher's backing plate.

Polyester Putty Finishing filler.

Pop Rivets A fastener used to hold two pieces of sheet metal together.

Portable Power Units Small piston and cylinder assemblies for removing minor damage.

Portable Puller A hydraulic ram and post mounted on caster wheels.

Positive Pressure Test Part of the Fit Test. Performed by covering up the exhalation valve and exhaling. A proper fit is evident if the face piece billows out without air escaping from the mask.

Post-Painting Operations Things done after painting such as removing masking tape, reinstalling parts, cleaning the vehicle.

Power Tools Tools that use air pressure or electrical energy to aid repairs.

Powering Steering Pump It forces pressurized oil through the power steering system.

Premixed Paint Paint that is ready to spray.

Prep Solvent A fast drying solvent often used to clean a vehicle. It removes wax, oil, grease, and other debris that could contaminate and ruin the paint job.

Pressure Gauge A device that reads in pounds per square inch or kilograms per square centimeter.

Pressure Multiplier It usually applies welder arm pressure.

Pressure Tank Spray Gun Similar to the pressurized pot, except it uses a much larger storage container for paint materials.

Pressurized Pot Also referred to as a pressure cup spray gun, it uses air pressure inside the paint cup or tank to force the material out of the gun.

Primer-Filler A very thick form of primer-surfacer. It is sometimes used when a very pitted or rough surface must be a filled and smoothed quickly.

Printer A machine used with a computer to make a hard copy (printed images on paper).

Productivity A measure of how much work you get done.

Professional Refers to the attitude, work quality and image that a business and its workers project to customers.

Professionalism A broad trait that includes everything from being able to follow orders to pride in workmanship.

Progression Shop An assembly line type of organization with specialists in each area of repair.

Proportional Numbers Denotes the amount of each material needed.

Pull Rod A tool that has a handle and curved end for light pulling of dents.

Pull Welding You aim or angle the gun back toward the weld puddle.

Pulling Adaptors Special straightening equipment accessories that allow you to pull in difficult situations.

Pulling Clamps They bolt around or onto the vehicle, so a pulling chain can be attached to the vehicle.

Pulling Equipment It uses hydraulic power to force the body structure or frame back into position.

Pulling Posts Also known as towers, they are strong steel members used to hold the pulling chains and hydraulic rams.

Push Welding You aim or angle the gun ahead of the weld puddle.

Push-In Clip Usually made of plastic, they are used to hold body panels.

R12 An ozone depleting refrigerant that is being phased out of use.

R134a A refrigerant. It is the present replacement for R12.

Rack A toothed shaft that is part of the rack-and-pinion steering unit.

Rack Straightening System Generally a drive-on system with a built-in anchoring and pulling mechanism.

Radiator Cap Pressure Test A test done using a cooling system pressure tester. The tester gauge should stop increasing its pressure reading when the cap rating is reached.

Radiator Core Support The framework around the front of the body structure for holding the cooling system radiator and related parts.

Radiator Pressure Cap Prevents the coolant from boiling.

Ratchet A common type of socket drive handle with a small lever that can be moved for either loosening or tightening bolts and nuts.

Reading Tires Involves inspecting tire tread wear and diagnosing the cause.

Rear Bulkhead Panel A panel that separates the passenger compartment from the rear trunk area.

Rear Section Also known as tail section or rear clip, it consists of the rear quarter panels, trunk or rear floor pan, rear frame rails, trunk or deck lid, rear bumper, and related parts.

Rear Shelf A thin panel behind the rear seat and in front of the back glass. It often has openings for rear stereo speakers. Also known as package tray.

Rear Spoiler A part that mounts in the trunk lid to alter the airstream at the rear of the body to increase body down force. This helps rear wheel traction at highway speeds.

Recliner Adjuster A hinge mechanism that allows adjustment of the seat back to different angles.

Recovery Station A machine used to capture the old, used refrigerant so that it does not enter and pollute the atmosphere.

Recovery System It captures the used refrigerant from the air conditioning system and keeps it from contaminating the atmosphere.

Recycled Assemblies Undamaged parts from another damaged vehicle that are used for repairs.

Refinishing Materials A general term referring to the products used to repaint the vehicle.

Related Professions Any job or work that has something in common with a specific category of work.

Reliability A quality meaning dependable.

Repair Stall A work area for one vehicle. Also termed a bay.

Resistance A restriction or obstacle to current flow.

Restraint System Designed to help hold people in their seats and prevent them from being injured during a collision.

Retarder A slow evaporating thinner or reducer used to retard or slow drying.

Reveal Moldings Used to cover the adhesive, they are held in place by adhesive grooves in the body, or by clips.

Reverse Masking A masking method that requires you to fold the masking paper back and over the masking tape.

Reverse Polarity Also called "DC Reverse," it is when the electrode is positive and the workpiece is negative.

Ribbon Sealer Sealer that comes in strip form and is applied by hand.

Right-Hand Threads Nuts and bolts that must be turned clockwise to tighten.

Rocker Panels Also known as door sills, they are strong beams that fit at the bottom of the door openings.

Roof Panel A large multi-piece panel that fits over the passenger compartment.

Rosin Core Solder A type of solder designed for doing electrical repairs.

RRIM Reinforced Reaction Injection Molded, a two-part polyurethane composite plastic. Part A is the isocyanate. Part B contains the reinforced fibers, resins, and a catalyst. The parts are mixed and injected into a mold.

Rubber Body Insulators Used between the frame and body to reduce noise and vibration.

Rubber Gloves Used to protect hands from the harmful effects of corrosive liquids, undercoats, and finishes.

Rubber Mallet A solid rubber head that is fairly heavy. It is often used to gently bump sheet metal without damaging the painted finish.

Rubberized Undercoat A synthetic-based rubber material applied as a corrosion or rust preventive layer.

RWD A front engine, rear-wheel drive vehicle. The engine is in the front and the drive axle is in the rear.

Safety Using proper work habits to prevent personal injury and property damage.

Safety Glasses Eye protection suitable for minor danger.

Safety Program A written shop policy designed to protect the health and welfare of personnel and customers.

Safety Signs Provided to give information that helps to improve shop safety, such as fire exits, fire extinguisher locations, dangerous or flammable chemicals and other information.

Sand Scratches This is a result of final sanding with too coarse a sandpaper, or not allowing materials (usually primer-surfacer or spot putty) to dry fully before painting.

Sander Pad A soft mounting surface for the sand paper.

Sanding Discs Round sandpaper normally used on an air-powered orbital sander.

Sanding Sheets Sandpaper in square sheets that can be cut to fit sanding blocks.

Sandpaper A heavy paper coated with an abrasive grit. It is the most commonly used abrasive in auto body repair.

Scale The most basic tool for linear measurement, it is also referred to as a ruler.

Scan Tool A device used to read and convert computer fault codes.

Scanner Cartridge Installed into the scanner for the specific make and model car or truck being tested. It holds the information needed for that vehicle.

Scanner A device used to diagnose or troubleshoot vehicle computer system and wiring problems

Screw A fastener often used to hold nonstructural parts on the vehicle.

Screw-on Slide Hammer Removes deeper dents and creases.

Scuff Pads Tough synthetic pads used to clean and lightly scratch the surface of paints so the new paint will stick.

Sealers Used to prevent water and air leaks between parts. They are flexible, which prevents cracking.

Seam Sealers These prevent the penetration of water, mud, and fumes into panel joints. They also prevent rust from forming between adjoining surfaces.

Seat Back The rear assembly that includes cover, padding, and metal frame.

Seat Belt Anchors A device that allows one end of the seat belt to be bolted to the body structure.

Seat Cushion The bottom section of a seat which includes cover, padding, and frame.

Seat Track The mechanical slide mechanism that allows the seat to be adjusted forward or rearward.

Sedan A body design with a center pillar that supports the roof. They come in 2- and 4-door versions.

Self-Darkening Filter Lenses A welding filter lens that instantly turns dark when the arc is struck.

Self-Defrosting Glass It has a conducting grid or invisible layer that carries electric current to heat the glass.

Self-Etching Primer A primer that has acid in it to treat bare metal so the primer will adhere properly.

Self-Locking Nut A nut that produces a friction or force fit when threaded onto a bolt or stud.

Self-Stick Sandpaper Sandpaper with adhesive applied to it during manufacturing.

Self-Tapping Screw A screw that has a pointed tip to help cut new threads in parts.

Service Manual Abbreviations Represents technical terms or words and saves space in the service manual.

Service Ports Small test fittings in the air conditioning system to which the air conditioning gauges are connected.

Set Screw A screw that frequently has an internal drive head for an Allen wrench. It is used to hold parts onto shafts.

Shading Coats A progressive application of paint on the boundary of spot repair areas so that a color difference is not noticeable. Also referred to as blend coats.

Shakeproof Lock Washer Washers with teeth or bent lugs that grip both the work and the nut. They are also referred to as teeth lock washers.

Shear Strength A measure of how well a material can withstand forces acting to cut or slice it apart.

Sheet Metal Screw A screw that has pointed or tapered tips. They thread into sheet metal for light holding tasks.

Sheet Metal Gauge Instrument used to measure body or repair panel thickness or gauge size (a number system that denotes the thickness of sheet metal).

Sheet Molded Compounds (SMC) Fiber-reinforced composite plastic panels.

Shielding Gas It protects the weld from the atmosphere and prevents oxidation of the base metal.

Shock Absorbers Dampening devices that absorb spring oscillations (bouncing) to smooth the vehicle's ride quality. It is a part of the suspension system.

Shop Air Lines Thick steel pipes that feed out from the tank to several locations in the body shop.

Shop Layout The general organization or arrangement of work areas.

Shop Owner A person who is concerned with and understands all phases of work performed in the shop.

Shop Supervisor A person who oversees personnel and day-to-day shop operations.

Short Spray Distance A spray gun distance that causes the high velocity mist to ripple the wet film.

Shoulder Belts Seat belts that extend over a person's chest and shoulder.

Shrinking Hammer A finishing hammer with a serrated or cross-grooved face. They are used to shrink spots that have been stretched by excessive hammering.

Shrinking Metal Removes strain or tension on damaged, stretched sheet metal.

Side Draft Spray Booth Moves air sideways over the car or truck. An air inlet in one wall pushes fresh air into the booth. A vent on the opposite wall removes the booth air.

Side Orifice Located on the spray gun air cap, it determines the spray pattern by means of air pressure.

Side-Tone View Compares the test panel to the vehicle on a 45–60 degree angle.

Single Pull Method A method that uses only one pulling chain; it works well with minor damage on one part.

Single-Sided Plastic Welds A type of weld used when the part cannot be removed from the vehicle.

Siphon Spray Gun It uses air flow through the gun head to form a suction that pulls paint into the air stream.

Skin Hem Folded door edge.

Skip Welding It produces a continuous weld by making short welds at different locations to prevent overheating.

Sliding Calipers A tool that measures inside, outside, and depth dimensions with high accuracy.

Slip-Joint Pliers Also known as combination pliers, they will adjust for two sizes.

Slotted Nut Also known as a castellated nut, it is grooved on top, so that a safety wire or cotter pin can be installed into a hole in the bolt.

Smoke Gun A device used to find air leaks around doors and windows.

Snap Ring A non-threaded fastener that installs into a groove machined into a part. They are used to hold parts on shafts.

Snap Ring Pliers Pliers that have tiny tips for fitting into clips or snap rings. Both external and internal types are available.

Snap-Fit Parts Parts that use clips or interference fit to hold together.

Social Skills The ability to get along with co-workers and customers.

Socket Drive Size The size of the square opening for the drive handle.

Socket Wrench Cylinder-shaped, box end wrench for rapid turning of bolts and nuts.

Soft Brazing Brazing with materials that melt at temperatures below 900°F (468°C).

Soldering A process using moderate heat and solder to join wires or other parts.

Soldering Gun A tool used to heat and melt solder for making electrical repairs.

Sonotrode In ultrasonic welding it is the equivalent of an electrode.

Sound Deadening Material Insulation materials that prevent engine and road noise from entering the passenger compartment.

Sound-Deafening Pads Often bonded to the inside surface of truck cavities and doors to reduce noise, vibration, and harshness. It is made of plastic or asphalt-based material.

Spark Lighter A device that produces a spark and ignites an oxy-acetylene torch.

Specialty Shop Repair facility that only works on one part or system of a vehicle.

Speed Handle A tool that can be rotated to quickly remove or install loose bolts and nuts.

Spider Webbing A technique accomplished by forcing paint through the air brush in a very thin, fibrous type spray.

Split Lock Washer   A washer used under nuts to prevent loosening by vibration. The ends of these spring-hardened washers dig into both the nut and the work to prevent rotation.

Spoiled Hardener   Hardener that remains thin and watery after thoroughly kneading it.

Spoons   An instrument used to pry out damage, struck with a hammer to drive out damage, and as a dolly in hard-to-reach areas.

Spot Weld Drill   A specially designed drill for removing spot-welded body panels.

Spot Weld Timer   Adjusts the time that the current passes through the joint.

Spout   A device designed to install into a can for handy pouring.

Spray Booth   Designed to provide a clean, safe, well-lit enclosure for painting.

Spray Gun Air Cap   Works with the air valve to control the spray pattern of the paint. It screws over the front of the gun head.

Spray Gun Angle   A term that refers to whether the gun is tilted up or down or sideways.

Spray Gun Cap   It often fits onto the bottom of the spray gun body to hold the material to be sprayed.

Spray Gun Distance   The distance from the gun tip to the surface being painted.

Spray Gun Lubrication   Placing a small amount of oil on packing and high friction points.

Spray Gun Speed   A term that refers to how fast the gun is moved sideways while painting.

Spray Gun Triggering   Involves stopping the paint spray before you stop moving the gun sideways.

Spray Gun Washer   Enclosed equipment that automatically cleans a spray gun.

Spray Pattern   The shape of the atomized spray from the spray gun when it hits the body.

Spray Pattern Test   A process to check the operation of the spray gun on a piece of paper.

Spray-Out Panel   A test panel that checks the paint color and also shows the effects of the painter's technique.

Spraying   The physical application of paint using a spray gun.

Spreader   A tool used to apply filler to low spots in body panels.

Spring Compressor   A tool used to remove and install the small spring used on some door hinges.

Spring Hammering   A method of bumping damage with a hammer and a dinging spoon.

Spring Hangers   These are sometimes formed on the frame to hold the suspension system springs.

Spring Hose Clamp   A clamp made of spring steel with barbs on each end. Squeezing the ends opens and expands the clamp.

Spring Scale   A device that measures pulling force.

Spring-Back   The tendency for metal to return to its original shape deformation.

Squeeze-Type Resistance Spot Welding   A type of welding that uses electric current through the base metal to form a small, round weld between the base metals.

Standard Screwdriver   A hand tool that has a tip with a single flat blade for fitting into the slot in the screw.

Starting Punch   Also known as a drift punch, it has a fully tapered shank and will drive pins, shafts and rods partially out of holes.

Starting System   A large electric motor that turns the engine flywheel. This spins or "cranks" the crankshaft until the engine starts and runs on its own power.

Station Wagon   A body design that extends the roof straight back to the rear of the body. A rear hatch or window and tailgate open to allow access to the large storage area.

Stationary Parts   Parts that are permanently welded or adhesive bonded into place like the floor, roof, and quarter panels.

Steering System   It transfers steering wheel motion through gears and linkage rods to swivel the front wheels.

Steering Wheel Center Check   A test that involves making sure the steering wheel has not been moved off center to do part damage.

Step-Down Gun   Internally restricts the inlet pressure of 40–100 psi to 10 psi at the air cap. They do NOT require the use of a turbine or air conversion unit. They use existing shop air from the compressor.

Stick Arc Welding   Also known as shielded arc welding, it uses a welding rod coated with a flux for fusion welding.

Stitch Welding   A continuous weld in one location, but with short pauses to prevent overheating.

Straight Polarity   Also called "DC straight" it is when the electrode is negative.

Straightening Equipment   Anchoring equipment, pulling equipment, and other accessories used to apply tremendous force to move the frame or body structure back into alignment.

Straightening System   A hydraulic machine for pulling a badly damaged frame or unibody structure back into proper alignment. Also termed a frame rack.

Stress Relieve   Freeing locked-up metal by hammering and/or heating while pulling.

Stressed Hull Structure   A concept where all force applied is not concentrated in one place, but is dispersed over the surface.

Stretched Metal   Metal that has been forced thinner in thickness and larger in surface area by impact.

Structural Adhesive   An adhesive used to bond parts together, in place of welds.

Structural Filler   Used to fill the larger gaps in the panel structure while maintaining strength. It adds to the structural rigidity of the part.

Structural Parts   Those parts of a vehicle which support the weight of the vehicle, absorb collision energy, and absorb road shock.

Strut Position Check   A test to check the position of the struts, thus determining if there is any damage.

Strut Pulling Plates   A device designed to bolt onto the top of shock towers for pulling.

Strut Rotation Check   A test to see if the strut is damaged.

Strut Tower Gauge   Allows visual alignment of the upper body area. It shows misalignment of the strut tower/upper body parts in relation to the vehicle's centerline plane and datum plane.

Stubby Screwdriver   A screwdriver with a very short shank for use in tight or restricted areas.

Stud Spot Welder   It joins pull rods on the surface of a panel so that you do not have to drill holes. It is the best way to pull dents.

Suction Cup Tool   A large synthetic rubber cup for sticking onto parts. They are often used to hold window glass when holding or moving the glass, or also to pop out large surface area dents in panels.

Sunlight   The standard by which other light sources are measured. It contains the entire visible spectrum of light.

Support Members   Used in high stress areas and often bolted to the bottom of the unibody to hold the engine, transmission and suspension in alignment, and to reduce body flex.

Surface Evaluation   A close inspection of the old paint to determine its condition.

Surface High Spot   An area that shows up when sanding quickly cuts through the guide coat.

Surface Inspection   Examining the old body surface condition before preparing it for new paint.

Surface Low Spot   An area that shows up when sanding will not remove the guide coat.

Surface Roughness   A measurement of paint film or other surface smoothness in a limited area.

Surface Temperature Thermometer   A thermometer used to measure the surface of the vehicle and the material to be used on the vehicle.

Surface Thermometer   When using a paint drying room, it measures panel temperatures to prevent overheating damage.

Surface Waviness   A measurement of an area's general levelness or trueness.

Suspension System   It allows the tires and wheels to move up and down with road surface irregularities.

Swirl Marks   Round or curved lines in the paint caused by buffing.

Systemic Approach   An organized and logical sequence of steps to accomplish a task or job.

Tabulation Chart   A chart used to log reference point measurements during a repair.

Tack Cloth A rag with coating that holds dust and debris.

Tack Coat Also known as mist coat, it is a very light, mist coat applied to the surface first. It allows the application of heavier wet coats without sagging or runs.

Tack Weld A weld used to temporarily hold two pieces in place before doing the permanent weld.

Tack-Rag A cloth used to remove any loose dust and other debris on vehicle surfaces.

Tailgate A door that allows access to the rear of a station wagon.

Tape Rule Also known as tape measure, it will extend out for making very long measurements.

Taper Pin A pin with a larger diameter on one end than on the other. It is used to locate and position matching parts or to secure small pulleys and gears to shafts.

Tempered Glass A single piece of heat-treated glass that shatters into small pieces when broken. It is used for side and rear glass.

Tensile Strength The property of a material that resists forces applied to pull it apart.

Test Light An instrument used to determine if there is current flowing through the circuit.

Thermometer A device used to measure temperature.

Thermosetting Plastics A type of plastic that undergoes a chemical change by the action of heating, a catalyst, or ultraviolet light. They are hardened into a permanent shape that cannot be altered by reapplying heat or catalysts.

Thermostat Regulates coolant flow and system operating temperature.

Thread Pitch Gauge A device that measures bolt thread pitch.

Three Body Sections For simplicity and to help communication in the auto body repair, a vehicle is divided into front, center, and rear sections.

⅜ Drive Impact An impact wrench with a smaller size drive head.

Three-Way Tailgate On most unibody station wagons, it is the rear gate that can be operated as a tailgate with the glass fully down, or as a door with the glass up or down.

Thrust Angle The angle between the thrust line and vehicle centerline.

Tie-Rod Ends There are two that thread onto the end of the rack and are covered by rubber bellows boots in the rack-and-pinion steering unit.

Tin Snips The most common metal cutting tool.

Tinted Glass It contains a shaded vinyl material to filter out most of the sun's glare. Both laminated and tempered glass can be tinted.

Tinting Altering the paint color slightly to better match the new finish with the old finish.

Tire Changer A machine for quickly dismounting and mounting tires on and off wheels.

Tire Pressure Gauge An instrument that will accurately measure tire air pressure.

Tool and Equipment Storage Room An area for safely keeping specialized tools and equipment.

Tool Box A place to store and protect tools.

Tool Holders Refers to clip racks, pouches, or trays that help you organize small tools.

Torch Shrinking Uses the heat of an oxyacetylene torch to release tension in the panel.

Torque Boxes The structural parts of the frame designed to allow some twisting to absorb road shock and collision impact.

Torque Pattern A tightening sequence that assures that parts are clamped down evenly by several bolts or nuts.

Torque Specifications Tightening values for the specific bolt or nut.

Torque Wrench A tool used to measure tightening or twisting force.

Torsional Strength The property of a material that withstands a twisting force.

Touch-Up Spray Gun A very small gun, ideal for painting small repair areas.

Tram Gauge A special body dimension measuring tool. It determines the direction and amount of body misalignment damage.

Transfer Efficiency The percentage of paint a spray gun is capable of depositing on the surface.

Transmission An assembly with a series of gears for increasing torque to the drive wheels so the car can accelerate properly.

Travel Speed When welding, it is the speed you move the gun across the joint.

Tread Depth Gauge An instrument that will quickly measure tire wear.

Trim Pad Tool A tool designed to reach behind interior panels to pop out and remove clips.

Trim Screw A screw that has a washer attached to it. It improves the appearance and helps keep the trim from shifting.

Trunk Floor Panel A stamped steel part that forms the bottom of the rear storage compartment.

Turbine Spray System The unit produces its own pressure and does NOT use shop air.

Twin I-Beam Suspension A combination of a solid axle and independent suspension. Two large I-beams form the lower control arms.

Two-Part Adhesive Systems An adhesive that consists of a base resin and a hardener (catalyst). When mixed together they form an acceptable alternative to welding for many plastic repairs.

Two-Part Putty Spot putty that comes with its own hardener for rapid curing.

Two-Sided Plastic Weld The strongest type of weld because you weld both sides of the part.

Two-Stage Paints Consists of two distinct layers of paint: basecoat and clearcoat.

UL (Underwriters Laboratories) Nonprofit organization that operates laboratories to investigate materials, devices, products, equipment and construction methods to define any hazards that may affect life and property.

Undermasked A term describing an area that must be cleaned with solvent or polishing compound to remove overspray.

Unibody A type of construction where body parts are welded and bolted together to from an integral frame. Lighter, thinner, high-strength steel alloys or aluminum alloy is used.

USC The abbreviation for United States Customary, which is the system used to measure bolt head size.

Utility Knife A hand tool with a retractable blade used for cutting or trimming.

Vacuum Gauge A device that reads vacuum, negative pressure or "suction." It reads in inches of mercury or kilograms per square centimeter.

Vacuum Suction Cup A tool that uses a remote power source (separate vacuum pump or air compressor airflow) to produce negative pressure (vacuum) in the cup. It is used to pull out larger, deeper dents than a suction cup.

Variance Chips Several samples of color used to help match paint color variations.

Vehicle Construction How the vehicle was manufactured, there are many variations.

Vehicle Dimension Manual A guide that gives body and frame measurements from undamaged vehicles.

Vehicle Left-Side This is the steering wheel side on vehicles built for American roads.

Vehicle Preparation The final steps prior to painting, including cleaning, sanding, stripping, masking, priming, and other related tasks.

Ventilated Has openings for air circulation.

Vertical Welding The pieces are turned upright. Gravity tends to pull the puddle down the joint.

Vinyl A soft, flexible, thin plastic material often applied over a foam filler.

Vinyl Adhesive An adhesive designed to bond a vinyl top to the vehicle body.

Vinyl Decals A more complex and decorative pressure-sensitive material than tape stripes.

Vinyl Overlay Remover A chemical that dissolves plastic vinyl to aid its removal.

Vinyl Prep A chemical solution that opens the pores of the vinyl material, preparing it for color and/or clearcoating.

Vinyl Tape A tough, durable, decorative, striping material adhered to the vehicle's finish. It has a pressure-sensitive backing that bonds securely to the finish

Viscosity Cup   A devise used to measure the thickness or fluidity of the mixed materials, usually paint. It is a small stainless steel cup attached to a handle.

Viscosity Cup Seconds   Number of seconds paint should take to flow out of viscosity cup if thinned or reduced properly.

Vise   A device used to secure or hold parts during hammering, cutting, drilling and pressing operations. It normally bolts onto a workbench.

Vise Caps   Soft lead, wood, or plastic vise jaw covers that will protect a part from marring.

Vise Grip Pliers   Also known as locking pliers, they have jaws that lock into position on parts. The jaws can be adjusted to different widths.

Visual Weld Inspection   The most practical method of inspection on a repaired vehicle because the weld is not taken apart. It involves looking at the weld for flaws, proper size and proper shape.

VOC Tracking Systems   A computerized system that helps monitor and record materials used in order to abide by environmental regulations.

Voltage   The pressure that pushes the electricity through the wire or circuit.

Wash Primer   A type of sprayable surface treatment that eliminates the need for a conversion coating.

Wash-Up   A thorough cleaning of the vehicle before repairs begin.

Washer   A device used under bolts, nuts, and other parts. They prevent damage to the surfaces of parts and provide better holding power.

Water Hose Test   A method used to find body leaks, water is sprayed onto the possible leakage areas, while someone watches for leaks inside the vehicle.

Water Pump   It circulates coolant through the inside of the engine, hoses, and radiator.

Waterbase Paint   Paint that uses water to carry the pigment.

Weatherstrip Adhesive   An adhesive designed to hold rubber seals and similar parts in place.

Weatherstripping   A rubber seal that prevents leakage at the joint between the movable part (lid, hatch, door) and the body.

Weld-Bond Adhesives   A two-part epoxy structural adhesive placed along certain weld seams. Spot welds are placed through the adhesive.

Weld Cracks   Cracks on the top or inside the weld bead.

Weld Distortion   Uneven weld bead.

Weld Legs   The width and height of the weld bead.

Weld Overlap   Excess weld metal mounted on top and either side of weld bead.

Weld Penetration   Indicated by the height of the exposed surface of the weld on the back side. It is needed to assure maximum weld strength.

Weld Porosity   Holes in the weld.

Weld Spatter   Drops of electrode on and around weld bead.

Weld Throat   This refers to the depth of the triangular cross section of the weld.

Weld-Through Primer   A primer used to add zinc anticorrosion protection to weld zones.

Weld Undercut   A groove melted along either side of the weld and left unfilled.

Welded Door Skin   Spot welds hold the skin onto its frame.

Welded Parts   Metal or plastic parts that are permanently joined by melting the material, so that it flows together and bonds when cooled.

Welded-Pull Tab   A small piece of steel plate welded onto the unibody. It is used if you need to pull where there is no place to attach a clamp.

Welder Amperage Rating   It gives the maximum current flow through the weld joint. The thickness of the metal being welded determines the amperage needed.

Weldface   The exposed surface of the weld on the side where you welded.

Welding Filter Lens   Sometimes called filter plate, it is a shaded glass welding helmet insert for protecting your eyes from ultraviolet burns.

Weldroot   The part of the joint where the wire electrode is directed.

Wet Edge   The area just painted that is still wet when starting to paint a new adjoining area.

Wet Metallic Paint Spray   The aluminum flakes have sufficient time to settle in the wet paint, making the color appear darker and less silver.

Wet Sandpaper   Sandpaper that can be used with water for flushing away sanding debris that would otherwise clog fine grits.

Wheel Alignment Machine   A machine used to measure wheel alignment angles so they can be adjusted.

Wheel Clamps   Wheel clamps are used to load and hold suspension with wheels and tires removed with vehicle on the rack or bench.

Wheel Cylinders   It uses hydraulic pressure to push the brake pads or shoes outward.

Wheel Puller   A device used to remove steering wheels, engine pulleys, and similar pressed-on parts.

Wheel Run-Out Check   A test that will show if there is damage to a rotating part of a wheel assembly.

White Light   A mixture of various colors of light.

Windings   Wires wrapped around an iron core.

Window Antenna Wire   A wire for radio reception, placed either between the layers of laminated glass (windshield), or printed on the surface of the glass (rear window).

Window Regulator   A gear mechanism that allows you to raise and lower the door glass.

Windshield Gasket   A rubber molding shaped to fit the windshield, body and trim.

Windshield Knife   A hand tool designed to cut through the sealant used on some windshields. It has a sharp cutter blade and two handles.

Wire Color Coding   The wire insulation is colored for easy identification.

Wire Speed   In welding, it is how fast the rollers feed the wire into the weld puddle.

Wire Stick-Out   The distance between the end of the gun's contact tip and the metal being welded.

Wiring Diagram   A drawing of an electrical circuit used to determine and isolate problems.

Wiring Harness   Several wires are enclosed in a protective covering.

Woodruff Key   A key used to prevent hand wheels, gears, cams, and pulleys from turning on their shaft.

Work Hardening   The limit of plastic deformation that causes the metal to become hard where it has been bent.

Work Life   The time when it is still possible to disturb the adhesive and have the adhesive set up for a good bond.

Work Order   It outlines the procedures that should be taken to put the vehicle back in top condition.

Work Traits   Qualities, aside from skills, that make you a good or bad employee, i.e., reliability, productivity, professionalism.

Worm Hose Clamp   A clamp that uses a screw that engages a slotted band. Turning the screw reduces or enlarges clamp diameter.

Wrench Size   The distance across the wrench jaws.

X-Frame   A frame that has two long members crossing over in the middle of the frame rails. Also called a back-bone frame.

Yield Point   The amount of force that a piece of metal can resist without tearing or breaking.

Yield Stress   The amount of strain needed to permanently deform a test specimen of sheet metal.

Zone Concept   It divides the horizontal surfaces of the vehicle into zones defined by character lines and moldings. It requires refinishing of an entire zone or zones with basecoat, mica intermediate coats, and clearcoats.

ABBREVIATIONS USED BY COLLISION REPAIR TECHNICIANS AND ESTIMATORS

The estimator and collision repair technician must be able to communicate verbally as well as in writing. Both in estimates and work procedure reports most estimators use abbreviations. Generally, these abbreviations are the same as those used in crash estimating guides. Some abbreviations are even used verbally. For example, three of the most commonly used abbreviations in a body shop are:

- **R&I: Remove and Reinstall.** The item is removed as an assembly, set aside, and later reinstalled and aligned for a proper fit. This is generally done to gain access to another part. For example, R&I bumper would mean that the bumper assembly would have to be removed to install a new fender or quarter panel.
- **R&R: Remove and Replace.** Remove the old parts, transfer necessary items to new part, replace, and align.
- **O/H: Overhaul.** Remove an assembly from the vehicle, disassemble, clean, inspect, replace parts as needed, then reassemble, install and adjust (except wheel and suspension alignment).

In addition to these abbreviations, the following terms are those accepted by most estimating guides, shop manuals, and estimators. They are the ones used in most written forms.

A	Manufacturer has no list price for the part.
ABS	Anti-lock Brake System
A/C	Air Conditioner
ACRS	Air Cushion Restraint System
adj	adjuster or adjustable
A/F	Air Fuel Ratio
AIR	Air Injector Reactor
alt	alternator
alum	aluminum
amp	ampere
approx.	approximately
assy	assembly
A/T	Automatic Transaxle
AT	Automatic Transmission
auth	authority
auto	automatic
aux	auxiliary
B+	Battery Voltage
bat.	battery
bbl	barrel
bk	back
blwr	blower
bmpr	bumper
brg	bearing
brk	brake
brkt	bracket
Bro	Brougham
btry	battery
btwn	between

B-U	Back-Up
bush	bushing
Calif	California
chnl	channel
c/mbr	cross member
cntr	center
col	column
comp	compressor
compt	compartment
conn.	connector
cond	conditioning or conditioner
cont	control
conv	converter or convertible
cor	corner
cov	cover
Cpe	Coupe
C/R	Customer Requested
crossmbr	cross member
c/shaft	crankshaft
ctl	control
Ctry	Country
Cust	Custom
CV	Constant Velocity
cyl	cylinder
D	Discontinued part
d	drilling operational time
da	dash
dbl	double

def	deflector		ID	Inside Diameter
dehyd	dehydrator		ign	ignition
desc	description		in	inch
dia	diameter		incl	includes
diag	diagonal		INJ	Injection
dist	distributor		in-lb	inch-pounds
div	division		inr	inner
Dlxe	DeLuxe		inst	instrument
DP	Dash Pot		inter	intermediate
dr	door		IP	Instrument Control Panels
ea	each		L	Left
ECU	Electronic Control Unit		LED	Light Emitting Diode
EFI	Electronic Fuel Injection		LF	Left Front
EGR	Exhaust Gas Recirculation		LH	Left Hand
elec	electric		lic	license
emiss	emission		lp	lamp
eng	engine		LR	Left Rear
EP	Exhaust Purging		LS	Left Side
equip	equipment		lwr	lower
evap	evaporator			
exc	except		max	maximum
exh	exhaust		mdl	model
extn	extension		mldg	molding
			MT	Manual Transmission
FED	Federal (All States Except Calif.)		mtd	mounted
flr	floor		mtg	mounting
Fndr	Fender		muff	muffler
Fr & Rr	Front & Rear			
frm	from		NAGS	National Auto Glass Specification
fr or rr	front or rear		neg	negative
ft	foot			
ft-lb	foot-pounds		OD	Outside Diameter
FWD	Front Wheel Drive		OD, O/D	Overdrive
			OEM	Original Equipment Manufacturer
gal	gallon		opng	opening
gen	generator		orna	ornament
GND	Ground		O/S	Oversize
grds	guards		otr	outer
grv	groove			
			p	paint operational time
harn	harness		pass	passenger
H'back	Hatchback		PCV	Positive Crankcase Ventilation
hd	heavy duty		pkg	package
HDC	Heavy Duty Cooling		plr	pillar
hdr	header		pnl	panel
HEI	High Energy Ignition		pos	positive
Hi Per	High Performance		PS	Power Steering
horiz	horizontal		psi	pounds per square inch
H.P.	High Performance		pt	pint
hp	horsepower		Pwr	Power
hsg	housing			
HSLA	High Strength Alloy Steel		qtr	quarter
HSS	High Strength Steel			
HT	Hard Top		R	Right
H'Top	Hard Top		rad	radiator
hyd	hydraulic		R-L	Right or Left
Hydra	Hydramatic		rec	receiver

refl	reflector	TE	Thermactor Emission
reg	regulator	tel	telescope
reinf	reinforcement	trans	transmission
reson	resonator	TWC	Three-Way Catalyst
RH	Right-Hand		
Sed	Sedan	U/D	Underdrive
ser	serial or series	upr	upper
shld	shield	U/S	Undersize
sidembr	side member		
sig	single		
SIR	Supplemental Inflatable Restraint	vent	ventilator
spd	speed	vert	vertical
spec	special	vib	vibration
SRS	Supplemental Restraint System	VIR	Valve-In-Receiver
Sta	Station		
stab	stabilizer		
stat	stationary	w/	with
Std	Standard	w/b	wheel base
stl	steel	WB	Wheelbase
strg	steering	WD	Wheel Drive
Sub	Suburban	Wgn	Wagon
sup	super	w'house	wheelhouse
supt	support	whl	wheel
surr	surround	whlse	wheelhouse
susp	suspension	wndo	window
SW	Station Wagon	w/o	without
		wo/	without
tach	tachometer	wshd	windshield
t & t	tilt & telescope or tilt & travel	w'strip	weatherstrip

APPENDIX B

MEASUREMENT EQUIVALENTS

CONVERSION FACTORS		
Multiply	**By**	**To obtain**
Length		
Millimeters (mm)	0.03937	Inches
	0.1	Centimeters (cm)
Kilometers (km)	0.6214	Miles
	3281	Feet
Inches	25.4	Millimeters (mm)
Miles	1.6093	Kilometers (km)
Area		
Inches^2	645.16	Millimeters^2 (mm^2)
	6.452	Centimeters^2 (cm^2)
Feet^2	0.0929	Meters^2 (m^2)
	144	Inches^2
Volume		
Centimeters^3 (cc)	0.06102	Inches^3
	0.001	Liters (L)
Liters (L)	61.024	Inches^3
	0.2642	Gallons
	1.0567	Quarts
Inches^3	16.387	Centimeters^3 (cc)
Feet^3	1728	Inches^3
	7.48	Gallons
	28.32	Liters (L)
Fluid ounces (oz)	29.57	Milliliters (mL)
Mass		
Gram (g)	0.03527	Ounce
Kilograms (kg)	2.2046	Pounds
	35.274	Ounces
Force		
Ounce	0.278	Newton (N)
Pound	4.448	Newton (N)
Kilogram	9.807	Newton (N)
Torque		
Foot-pounds	1.3558	Newton-meters (Nm)
	0.1383	Kilogram/meter (kg/m)
Inch-pounds	0.11298	Newton-meters (Nm)
	0.0833	Foot-pounds

CONVERSION FACTORS (CONTINUED)

Multiply	By	To obtain
Torque		
Kilogram-meters (Kg/m)	7.23	Foot-pounds
	9.80665	Newton-meters (Nm)
Pressure		
Atmospheres	14.7	Pounds/square inch (psi)
	29.92	Inches of mercury (In. Hg)
Inches of mercury (In. Hg)	0.49116	Pounds/square inch (psi)
	13.1	Inches of water
	3.377	Kilopascals (kPa)
Bars	100	Kilopascals (kPa)
	14.5	Pounds/square inch (psi)
Kilogram/cu² (Kg/cm²)	14.22	Pounds/square inch (psi)
	98.07	Kilopascals (kPa)
Kilopascals (kPa)	0.145	Pounds/square inch (psi)
	0.2961	Inches of mercury (In. Hg)
Pascal	1	Newton/square meter (N/m²)
Fuel Performance		
Miles/gallon	0.4251	Kilometers/liter (km/L)
Velocity		
Miles/hours	1.467	Feet/second
	88	Feet/minute
	1.6093	Kilometers/hour (km/h)
Kilometers/hour	0.27778	Meters/second (m/s)

TORQUE CONVERSIONS
(FOOT-POUNDS, NEWTON-METERS, METER-KILOGRAMS)

ft/lb	0	1	2	3	4	5	6	7	8	9
0	0	1.35	2.70	4.05	5.40	6.75	8.10	9.45	10.8	12.1
10	13.5	14.9	16.2	17.6	18.9	20.3	21.6	22.9	24.3	25.6
20	27.0	28.3	29.7	31.0	32.5	33.7	35.1	36.4	37.8	39.1
30	40.5	41.8	43.2	44.5	45.9	47.2	48.6	49.9	51.3	52.6
40	54.0	55.3	56.7	58.0	59.4	60.7	62.1	63.4	64.8	66.1
50	67.5	68.8	70.2	71.5	72.9	74.2	75.6	76.9	78.3	79.6
60	81.0	82.3	83.7	85.0	86.4	87.7	89.1	90.4	91.8	93.1
70	94.5	95.8	97.2	98.5	99.9	101	102	103	105	106
80	108	109	110	112	113	114	116	117	118	120
90	121	122	124	125	126	128	129	130	132	133
100	135	136	137	139	140	141	143	144	145	147
110	148	149	151	152	153	155	156	157	159	160
120	162	163	164	166	167	168	170	171	172	174
130	175	176	178	179	180	182	183	184	186	187

Note: The following formulas can be used:

$$\text{ft-lb} \times 1.35 = \text{Nm}$$
$$\text{ft-lb} + 7.23 = \text{mkg}$$

For meter-kilograms within 5%, divide Newton-meters by 10 (move the decimal point one place left).
For greater accuracy, divide by 9.81.

DECIMAL AND METRIC EQUIVALENTS

Fractions	Decimal (in.)	Metric (mm)	Fractions	Decimal (in.)	Metric (mm)
1/64	.015625	.397	33/64	.515625	13.097
1/32	.03125	.794	17/32	.53125	13.494
3/64	.046875	1.191	35/64	.546875	13.891
1/16	.0625	1.588	9/16	.5625	14.288
5/64	.078125	1.984	37/64	.578125	14.684
3/32	.09375	2.381	19/32	.59375	15.081
7/64	.109375	2.778	39/64	.609375	15.478
1/8	.125	3.175	5/8	.625	15.875
9/64	.140625	3.572	41/64	.640625	16.272
5/32	.15625	3.969	21/32	.65625	16.669
11/64	.171875	4.366	43/64	.671875	17.066
3/16	.1875	4.763	11/16	.6875	17.463
13/64	.203125	5.159	45/64	.703125	17.859
7/32	.21875	5.556	23/32	.71875	18.256
15/64	.234275	5.953	47/64	.734375	18.653
1/4	.250	6.35	3/4	.750	19.05
17/64	.265625	6.747	49/64	.765625	19.447
9/32	.28125	7.144	25/32	.78125	19.844
19/64	.296875	7.54	51/64	.796875	20.241
5/16	.3125	7.938	13/16	.8125	20.638
21/64	.328125	8.334	53/64	.828125	21.034
11/32	.34375	8.731	27/32	.84375	21.431
23/64	.359375	9.128	55/64	.859375	21.828
3/8	.375	9.525	7/8	.875	22.225
25/64	.390625	9.922	57/64	.890625	22.622
13/32	.40625	10.319	29/32	.90625	23.019
27/64	.421875	10.716	59/64	.921875	23.416
7/16	.4375	11.113	15/16	.9375	23.813
29/64	.453125	11.509	61/64	.953125	24.209
15/32	.46875	11.906	31/32	.96875	24.606
31/64	.484375	12.303	63/64	.984375	25.003
1/2	.500	12.7	1	1.00	25.4

TAP AND DRILL
BIT DATA

DECIMAL EQUIVALENTS AND TAP DRILL SIZES			DECIMAL EQUIVALENTS AND TAP DRILL SIZES		
Drill Size	Decimal	Tap Size	Drill Size	Decimal	Tap Size
1/64	.0156		27	.1440	
1/32	.0312		26	.1470	
60	.0400		25	.1495	10–24
59	.0410		24	.1520	
58	.0420		23	.1540	
57	.0430		5/32	.1562	
56	.0465		22	.1570	10–30
3/64	.0469	0–80	21	.1590	10–32
55	.0520		20	.1610	
54	.0550	1–56	19	.1660	
53	.0595	1–64, 72	18	.1695	
1/16	.0625		11/64	.1719	
52	.0635		17	.1730	
51	.0670		16	.1770	12–24
50	.0700	2–56, 64	15	.1800	
49	.0730		14	.1820	12–28
48	.0760		13	.1850	12–32
5/64	.0781		3/16	.1875	
47	.0785	3–48	12	.1890	
46	.0810		11	.1910	
45	.0820	3–56, 4–32	10	.1935	
44	.0860	4–36	9	.1960	
43	.0890	4–40	8	.1990	
42	.0935	4–48	7	.2010	1/4–20
3/32	.0937		13/64	.2031	
41	.0960		6	.2040	
40	.0980		5	.2055	
39	.0995		4	.2090	
38	.1015	5–40	3	.2130	1/4–28
37	.1040	5–44	7/32	.2187	
36	.1065	6–32	2	.2210	
7/64	.1093		1	.2280	
35	.1100		A	.2340	
34	.1110	6–36	15/64	.2344	
33	.1130	6–40	B	.2380	
32	.1160		C	.2420	
31	.1200		D	.2460	
1/8	.1250		E, 1/4	.2500	
30	.1285		F	.2570	5/16–18
29	.1360	8–32, 36	G	.2610	
28	.1405	8–40	17/64	.2656	
9/64	.1406		H	.2660	

DECIMAL EQUIVALENTS AND TAP DRILL SIZES		
Drill Size	Decimal	Tap Size
I	.2720	5/16-24
J	.2770	
K	.2810	
9/32	.2812	
L	.2900	
M	.2950	
19/64	.2968	
N	.3020	
5/16	.3125	3/8-16
O	.3160	
P	.3230	
21/64	.3281	
Q	.3320	3/8-24
R	.3390	
11/32	.3437	
S	.3480	
T	.3580	
23/64	.3594	
U	.3680	7/16-14
3/8	.3750	
V	.3770	
W	.3860	
25/64	.3906	7/16-20
X	.3970	
Y	.4040	
13/32	.4062	
Z	.4130	
27/64	.4219	1/2-13
7/16	.4375	
29/64	.4531	1/2-20
15/32	.4687	
31/64	.4844	9/16-12
1/2	.5000	

DECIMAL EQUIVALENTS AND TAP DRILL SIZES		
Drill Size	Decimal	Tap Size
33/64	.5156	9/16-18
17/32	.5312	5/8-11
35/64	.5469	
9/16	.5625	
37/64	.5781	5/8-18
19/32	.5937	11/16-11
39/64	.6094	
5/8	.6250	11/16-16
41/64	.6406	
21/32	.6562	3/4-10
43/64	.6719	
11/16	.6875	3/4-16
45/64	.7031	
23/32	.7187	
47/64	.7344	
3/4	.7500	
49/64	.7656	7/8-9
25/32	.7812	
51/64	.7969	
13/16	.8125	7/8-14
53-64	.8281	
27/32	.8437	
55/54	.8594	
7/8	.8750	1-8
57/64	.8906	
29/32	.9062	
59/64	.9219	
15/16	.9375	1-12, 14
61-64	.9531	
31/32	.9687	
63/64	.9844	
1	1.000	

PIPE THREAD SIZES			
Thread	Drill	Thread	Drill
1/8-27	R	1 1/2-11 1/2	1 47/64
1/4-18	7/16	2-11 1/2	2 7/32
3/8-18	37/64	2 1/2-8	2 5/8
1/2-14	23/32	3-8	3 1/4
3/4-14	59/64	3 1/2-8	3 3/4
1-11 1/2	1 5/32	4-8	4 1/4
1 1/4-11 1/2	1 1/2		

METRIC TAP DRILL SIZES		
Diameter and Pitch	Metric Drill	Inch Drill
5 × .80	4.20	11/64
6 × 1.00	5.00	13/64
7 × 1.00	6.00	15/64
8 × 1.25	6.75	17/64
10 × 1.50	8.50	11/32
12 × 1.75	10.25	13/32

Note: Nominal outside diameter minus the pitch equals the tap drill size for 75% thread contact area.

DECIMAL EQUIVALENTS OF NUMBER SIZE DRILLS

No.	Size of Drill (Inches)	No.	Size of Drill (Inches)	No.	Size of Drill (Inches)	No.	Size of Drill (Inches)
1	.2280	21	.1590	41	.0960	61	.0390
2	.2210	22	.1570	42	.0935	62	.0380
3	.2130	23	.1540	43	.0890	63	.0370
4	.2090	24	.1520	44	.0860	64	.0360
5	.2055	25	.1495	45	.0820	65	.0350
6	.2040	26	.1470	46	.0810	66	.0330
7	.2010	27	.1440	47	.0785	67	.0320
8	.1990	28	.1405	48	.0760	68	.0310
9	.1960	29	.1360	49	.0730	69	.0292
10	.1935	30	.1285	50	.0700	70	.0280
11	.1910	31	.1200	51	.0670	71	.0260
12	.1890	32	.1160	52	.0635	72	.0250
13	.1850	33	.1130	53	.0595	73	.0240
14	.1820	34	.1110	54	.0550	74	.0225
15	.1800	35	.1100	55	.0520	75	.0210
16	.1770	36	.1065	56	.0465	76	.0200
17	.1730	37	.1040	57	.0430	77	.0180
18	.1695	38	.1015	58	.0420	78	.0160
19	.1660	39	.0995	59	.0410	79	.0145
20	.1610	40	.0980	60	.0400	80	.0135

DECIMAL EQUIVALENTS OF LETTER SIZE DRILLS

Letter	Size of Drill (Inches)	Letter	Size of Drill (Inches)
A	.234	N	.302
B	.238	O	.316
C	.242	P	.323
D	.246	Q	.332
E	.250	R	.339
F	.257	S	.348
G	.261	T	.358
H	.266	U	.368
I	.272	V	.377
J	.277	W	.386
K	.281	X	.397
L	.290	Y	.404
M	.295	Z	.413

HELICOIL TAP DRILL SIZES

Inches		Metric	
Thread	Tap Drill Size	Thread	Tap Drill Size
1/4–20	17/64	5 × 0.8	13/64
5/16–18	21/64	6 × 1.0	1/4
3/8–16	25/64	7 × 1.0	9/32
7/16–14	29/64	8 × 1.25	21/64
1/2–13	17/32	10 × 1.50	13/32
		12 × 1.75	31/64

APPENDIX D

REFERENCE TABLES

DRY TORQUE RECOMMENDATIONS

Diameter	Grade 5		Grade 6		Grade 8	
	Coarse	Fine	Coarse	Fine	Coarse	Fine
1/4	108[a]	120[a]	132[a]	156[a]	17	19
5/16	17	20	23	25	34	37
3/8	31	35	40	45	60	68
7/16	50	55	64	72	96	108
1/2	75	85	98	110	145	165
9/16	110	120	140	160	210	235
5/8	150	170	195	220	290	330

[a]Any torque less than 15-lb is given in in-lb.

LUBRICATED TORQUE RECOMMENDATIONS
(REDUCED 33 PERCENT)

Diameter	Grade 5		Grade 6		Grade 8	
	Coarse	Fine	Coarse	Fine	Coarse	Fine
1/4	72[a]	80[a]	88[a]	104[a]	136[a]	152[a]
5/16	135[a]	160[a]	15	17	22	25
3/8	21	23	26	30	40	45
7/16	33	37	43	48	64	72
1/2	50	57	65	73	96	110
9/16	73	80	93	107	140	157
5/8	100	113	130	147	193	220

[a]Any torque less than 15-lb is given in in-lb.

METRIC DRY TORQUE RECOMMENDATIONS

Diameter (mm)	Pitch	Grade 8.8	Grade 12.9
6	1.00	84[a]	132[a]
7	1.00	132[a]	20
8	1.25	18	29
8	1.00	20	32
10	1.50	33	58
10	1.25	35	61
10	1.00	38	64
12	1.75	59	100
12	1.50	65	110

[a]Any torque less than 15 ft-lb is given in in.-lb.

METRIC
LUBRICATED TORQUE RECOMMENDATIONS
(REDUCED 33 PERCENT)

Diameter (mm)	Pitch	Grade 8.8	Grade 12.9
6	1.00	56[a]	88[a]
7	1.00	88[a]	160[a]
8	1.25	144[a]	19
8	1.00	160[a]	21
10	1.50	22	39
10	1.25	23	41
10	1.00	25	43
12	1.75	39	67
12	1.50	43	73

[a]Any torque less than 15 ft-lb is given in in.-lb.

TORQUE
VALUES

The following charts give the standard torque values for bolts, nuts, and taperlock studs of SAE Grade 5 or better quality.

GENERAL TIGHTENING TORQUE FOR BOLTS, NUTS, AND TAPERLOCK STUDS			
Thread Diameter		Standard Torque	
Inches	Millimeters	ft.-lb.	N·m*
Standard Thread		Use these torques for bolts and nuts with standard threads (conversions are approximate).	
1/4	6.35	9 ± 3	12 ± 4
5/16	7.94	18 ± 5	25 ± 7
3/8	9.53	32 ± 5	45 ± 7
7/16	11.11	50 ± 10	70 ± 15
1/2	12.70	75 ± 10	100 ± 15
9/16	14.29	110 ± 15	150 ± 20
5/8	15.88	150 ± 20	200 ± 25
3/4	19.05	265 ± 35	360 ± 50
7/8	22.23	420 ± 60	570 ± 80
1	25.40	640 ± 80	875 ± 100
1-1/8	28.58	800 ± 100	1100 ± 150
1-1/4	31.75	1000 ± 120	1350 ± 175
1-3/8	34.93	1200 ± 150	1600 ± 200
1-1/2	38.10	1500 ± 200	2000 ± 275
		Use these torques for bolts and nuts on hydraulic valve bodies.	
5/16	7.94	13 ± 2	20 ± 3
3/8	9.53	24 ± 2	35 ± 3
7/16	11.11	39 ± 2	50 ± 2
1/2	12.70	60 ± 3	80 ± 4
5/8	15.88	118 ± 4	160 ± 6

GENERAL TIGHTENING TORQUE FOR BOLTS, NUTS, AND TAPERLOCK STUDS (CONTINUED)

Thread Diameter		Standard Torque	
Inches	Millimeters	ft.-lb.	N·m*
Taperlock Stud		Use these torques for studs with taperlock threads.	
1/4	6.35	5 ± 2	7 ± 3
5/16	7.94	10 ± 3	15 ± 5
3/8	9.53	20 ± 3	30 ± 5
7/16	11.11	30 ± 5	40 ± 10
1/2	12.70	40 ± 5	55 ± 10
9/16	14.29	60 ± 10	80 ± 15
5/8	15.88	75 ± 10	100 ± 15
3/4	19.05	110 ± 15	150 ± 20
7/8	22.23	170 ± 20	230 ± 30
1	25.40	260 ± 30	350 ± 40
1-1/8	28.58	320 ± 30	400 ± 40
1-1/4	31.75	400 ± 40	550 ± 50
1-3/8	34.93	480 ± 40	650 ± 50
1-1/2	38.10	550 ± 50	750 ± 70

*1 Newton-meter (N·m) is approximately the same as 0.1 mkg.

The torques shown in the charts that follow are to be used on the part of 37° flared, 45° flared and inverted flared fittings (when used with steel tubing), O-ring plugs, and O-ring fittings.

TORQUE FOR FLARED AND O-RING FITTINGS

Inverted 45° Flared   **37° Flared**

Tube Size (O.D.)	mm	3.18	4.78	6.35	7.92	9.52
	in.	.125	.188	.250	.312	.375
THREAD SIZE (in.)		5/16	3/8	7/16	1/2	9/16 5/8
TORQUE N·m		5 ± 1	11 ± 1	16 ± 2	20 ± 2	25 ± 3
TORQUE lb.-in.		45 ± 10	100 ± 10	145 ± 20	175 ± 20	225 ± 25

TORQUE FOR FLARED AND O-RING FITTINGS

		45° Flared		O-Ring Fitting—Plug			Swivel Nuts		
Tube Size (O.D.)	mm	12.70	15.88	19.05	22.22	25.40	31.75	38.10	50.80
	in.	.500	.625	.750	.875	1.000	1.250	1.500	2.000
THREAD SIZE (in.)		3/4	7/8	11/16	1-3/16 1-1/4	1-5/16	1-5/8	1-7/8	2-1/2
TORQUE N·m		50 ± 5	75 ± 5	100 ± 5	120 ± 5	135 ± 10	180 ± 10	225 ± 10	320 ± 15
TORQUE lb.-ft.		35 ± 4	55 ± 4	75 ± 4	90 ± 4	100 ± 7	135 ± 7	165 ± 7	235 ± 10

INDEX

Page numbers followed by *f* refer to figures, by *t* to tables.